MW00647451

My Fellow Servants

Essays on the History of the Priesthood

My Fellow Servants

Essays on the History of the Priesthood

William G. Hartley

BYU Studies
Provo, Utah

Copyright © 2010 Brigham Young University. All rights reserved.

Front cover image: detail of *The Sacred Susquehanna* by Glen Hopkinson; back cover: *The Sacred Susquehanna* by Glen Hopkinson. Visit glenhopkinson.com.

Cover design: Catharine Verhaaren Gruver

Some images courtesy of the Church Archives, The Church of Jesus Christ of Latter-day Saints, Salt Lake City. Some images courtesy of L. Tom Perry Special Collection, Harold B. Lee Library, Brigham Young University, Provo, Utah. Images from the Library of Congress are in the public domain.

All articles are reprinted by permission. Original publication data appears at the end of each article before any endnotes.

Opinions expressed in this publication are the opinions of the author and his views should not necessarily be attributed to The Church of Jesus Christ of Latter-day Saints, Brigham Young University, or BYU Studies.

No part of this book may be reprinted or reproduced or utilized in any form or by any electronic, digital, mechanical or other means, now known or hereafter invented, including photocopying and recording or in an information storage or retrieval system, without permission in writing from the publisher. To contact BYU Studies, write to 1063 JFSB, Brigham Young University, Provo, Utah 84602-6720, or visit http://byustudies.byu.edu.

Library of Congress Cataloging-in-Publication Data

Hartley, William G.
  My fellow servants : essays on the history of the priesthood / William G. Hartley.

  p. cm.
  Includes index.
  ISBN 978-0-8425-2767-5 (paper back : alk. paper)

1. Priesthood—Church of Jesus Christ of Latter-day Saints—History. 2. Priesthood—Mormon Church—History. 3. Church of Jesus Christ of Latter-day Saints—History. 4. Mormon Church—History. I. Title.
  BX8659.H37 2010
  262'.149332--dc22
              2010027691

Printed in the United States of America

10 9 8 7 6 5 4 3 2 1

Contents

Illustrations

Introduction

THE PRIESTHOOD IS FUNDAMENTAL to the operations and organization of
The Church of Jesus Christ of Latter-day Saints at every level. Every ward
and every stake is led by the priesthood. This book is a collection of essays
that represent my lifetime of research on the history of the restored priesthood. The chapters have been gathered from many publications, some of
which were fairly obscure, so most of the information presented here will
be new to the vast majority of readers.

The topic of priesthood is important to every Church member. Some
are priesthood holders, some are married to such, and some are raising
young members of the priesthood. In branches, wards, and stakes, all members interact regularly with priesthood leaders. Understanding the historical origins of priesthood policies and operations gives all people useful
perspectives and insights into why things are done the way they are in the
order of the Church. God works in various ways (not all of them mysterious) his wonders to perform, and looking closely at those efforts brings
awareness of what God wants accomplished and how.

While other historians are experts on certain Church presidents or
broad historical periods, I have concentrated my research career on how
the Church has functioned decade by decade at grass-roots levels. My
interest has been in the operations of the Church's local units and programs.

Because the Church has been guided by revelation, these ward operations, priesthood assignments, and quorum structures have seen significant alterations and redirections since the Church was first organized.

INTRODUCTION AND ESTABLISHMENT

Joseph Smith started the Church in 1830 but did not establish it all at once. The organization developed line upon line. For example, it did not have stakes until 1834, so what were local Church operations like before there were stakes? The first wards were organized in Nauvoo, so how were local operations conducted before there were wards and ward bishops? Nauvoo's nearly eleven thousand Saints attended church meetings on Sundays not in church buildings (chapels) but in private homes or outdoors in groves. In the mid-nineteenth century, people used the terms *stake* and *branch* interchangeably, such that some branches, for example, had high councils. We find that some Utah wards during the 1850s had a bishop and a president. Under President Brigham Young's direction, Melchizedek Priesthood men, not boys, filled the Aaronic Priesthood ranks by serving as *acting* deacons, *acting* teachers, and *acting* priests. Only after 1877 did Church leaders expect boys to receive at least one lesser priesthood ordination before becoming elders, and only after 1908 did boys, as a rule, advance through all three Aaronic Priesthood ranks before adulthood. The sixth Article of Faith says that we believe in the office of pastor, and in the 1850s and 1860s pastors were an important leadership position in the Church in the British Isles. Between the two world wars, in some locations women prepared the sacrament tables by baking the bread and laundering, starching, and ironing the tablecloths. During World War II, a Salt Lake City bishop enlisted Beehive girls to collect fast offerings because he lacked deacons. Thousands of men once received ordination, not as elders, but as seventies when they were called on stake missions. When I was young, we attended stake conferences quarterly, at which the sacrament was administered during the Sunday afternoon session. Not very long ago, Church leadership included Assistants to the Twelve, and more recently Regional Representatives served throughout the world.

Early in the Utah pioneer period the first meetinghouses of log or adobe were so small that only a small percentage of a ward's members attended sacrament meetings. For more than two decades, pioneer wards had no Relief Society, Primary, or Mutuals, and the Sunday School was only for children, not adults. By the 1880s, many wards had a meetinghouse, an amusement hall, a Relief Society building, a granary, and a bishop's tithing office. In time, the first three buildings became consolidated under one roof housing a chapel, amusement hall, and Relief Society room. Soon after 1900, most members rejoiced when individual glass sacrament cups replaced the common goblet that was passed down a row from which everyone took turns sipping. From the 1890s until the 1940s, not silence but vocal solos and musical numbers accompanied the passing of the sacrament.

Such past practices, since replaced, show that leaders in the restored Church regularly adapt operations to various circumstances. Articles in this volume examine most of the interesting developments just mentioned; they present Church history from an administrative perspective, particularly regarding how directives at the top actually became implemented, or not, at the ward, quorum, and member level.

For Church members and leaders, a guiding principle needs to be made clear. As explained in a revelation given to Church President John Taylor on April 14, 1883, that announced revisions in Seventies work, the Lord can, in essence, redeploy his troops as he sees fit:

> Thus saith the Lord unto the First Presidency, unto the Twelve, unto the Seventies and unto all my holy Priesthood, let not your hearts be troubled, neither be ye concerned about the management and organization of my Church and Priesthood and the accomplishment of my work. Fear me and observe my laws and I will reveal unto you, from time to time, through the channels that I have appointed, everything that shall be necessary for the future development and perfection of my Church, for the adjustment and rolling forth of my kingdom, and for the building up and the establishment of my Zion. For ye are my Priesthood and I am your God. Even so. Amen.[1]

A similar expression of priesthood adaptability came when the First Council of Seventy objected to seventies quorum presidents being taken into bishoprics without the First Council's permission. Wasn't it wrong not to consult with the First Council, they asked? President John Taylor and counselor George Q. Cannon answered that it was discourteous but not wrong, and then admonished, "It is not wise to have cast iron rules by which to fetter the Priesthood. The Priesthood is a living, intelligent principle, and must necessarily have freedom to act as circumstances may dictate or require."[2] In

1926, Elder Rudger Clawson, as the President of the Quorum of the Twelve, dealt with a question about how bound the Church should be to revelations given in an early era. Previous revelations, he said, "must be construed with reference to the whole text of our law and the principles which control our government. In such a construction it will not be difficult to reconcile present practice or such further policies which may be adopted with the letter and spirit of the texts [of the revelations]." Further, he said,

> The doing of the work of the Lord must always be of chief concern. The whole organization of the Church is, in the last analysis, a facility, an agency for that high purpose. So that, while we do not desire to be understood to make an effort to minimize the value and importance of adhering to the general directions given in the revelations for the organization and maintenance of the quorums, we do express the firm conviction that these scriptural directions are, as hereinbefore stated, subject to the interpretation of the inspired servants of the Lord who preside over the Church, whose interpretations will always be made with reference to the needs of the Church and the progress of the work.[3]

Based on this, we should actually expect adaptations to continue to be introduced as new administrative needs and circumstances arise.

EARLY PRIESTHOOD STUDIES

Soon after Leonard Arrington became the Church Historian in 1972, he hired me and a half dozen other historians to form the History Division in the Church Historical Department. In our first meetings, we explored what research area each should focus on. Those knowledgeable in specific arenas, such as Dean C. Jessee with expertise about Joseph Smith, were assigned to pursue those subjects. One night Leonard said he awoke feeling impressed that I should tackle priesthood history. "Bill," he said, "why don't you write histories, maybe forty pages each, of the deacons, the teachers, and the priests?" That assignment launched my priesthood-related research.

I found only three books in 1972 that dealt with Church government. Eight years earlier, Lee A. Palmer had published *Aaronic Priesthood through the Centuries*, which briefly highlighted several priesthood turning points since 1829, giving me some research starting points. A standard source by then out of date was Elder John A. Widtsoe's *Priesthood and Church Government*, first published in 1939, which explained Church operations then current but not how those came to be, historically. Helpful for understanding Church operations at the turn of the twentieth century was Joseph B. Keeler's small 1904 handbook, *The Lesser Priesthood and Notes on Church Government*. Beyond those, I identified a handful of theses and dissertations that tackled Church governance historically and read a few dated, celebratory histories about the Sunday School and the Young Men's Mutual Improvement Association (YMMIA). I found there existed a dearth of serious studies of past organizational and priesthood developments. My research from then on constantly probed major developments in the past not recognized as such and hence not studied or written about.

In 1973 a Melchizedek Priesthood Committee of the Twelve created a Research Task Committee to research and report about various Church operations and practices and how they came to be. In May of that year, I was called to serve on that task committee, whose responsibility was "bringing together the basic research necessary to give an historical understanding and perspective of priesthood roles, callings, duties and other similar priesthood and Church government information."[4] That calling required my release from ward or stake callings for two years, and I spent many Sundays in the Church Archives researching priesthood issues. Our task committee received a list of fundamental questions to research as soon as possible. For example, What is a quorum? What is a stake? Can all Melchizedek Priesthood holders attend the same quorum? Do bishopric counselors need to be high priests? What is the work of the elders quorums? What has been the relationship between the Presiding Bishop and Aaronic Priesthood quorums? In response we submitted a series of research reports. So by career and by Church-service assignment, I became immersed in studying the Church's organizational development.

Our History Division, after seven years, was transferred to Brigham Young University and became the Joseph Fielding Smith Institute for Latter-day Saint History, where, for the next quarter century, we continued to carry out our First Presidency–assigned mission to write responsible history about the Church. I kept studying Church offices, programs, and operations until my retirement from the university in 2009.

I retired before finishing several studies I had started, among them a history of ward teaching, a study of tithing operations while William B. Preston was Presiding Bishop, and an examination of local Church administration between 1877 and 1908 that I call "When Stakes Were in Full Flower." Many more such studies are needed; hopefully, other scholars will tackle these one day—scholars who, like me, find such topics the opposite of boring.

OVERVIEW OF CHAPTERS IN THIS VOLUME

Part One contains two essays focusing on priesthood restoration. Chapter 1 shows that *restore* means not only to bestow but also to implement. Similar to a tree, priesthood at first was a sprout, then a seedling; it eventually developed a trunk, branches, leaves, and blossoms, all of which are explored here. Joseph Smith was both a priesthood restorer and priesthood bearer. Chapter 2 tracks what baptized members were expected to do before the Church was formally organized.

Part Two provides five essays dealing with the Aaronic Priesthood. Chapter 3 documents when, why, and how the offices of deacon, teacher, and priest, filled by men in the nineteenth century, shifted from men to boys gradually, and sometimes informally, in response to practical needs. Chapter 4 explains why in the nineteenth century high priests, seventies, and elders filled the Aaronic Priesthood offices, serving as *acting* deacons, *acting* teachers, and *acting* priests, and how quorums then were stake, not ward, entities. Chapter 5 gives a history of how the work of the office of bishop adapted and altered over time to accommodate changing Church needs, including what bishops did before wards existed, and how bishops received, stored, and disbursed tithing in kind. As the next chapter shows, Newel K. Whitney's successor as Presiding Bishop, Edward Hunter, assumed an office barely developed, and during the next thirty-three years he firmly carved the Presiding Bishopric's niche into the Church's General Authority hierarchy. One of Bishop Hunter's major contributions, the subject of chapter 7, was revamping the tithing system between 1852 and 1855 by making ward bishoprics, not the Presiding Bishopric, responsible to receive tithes and make individual tithing settlements with the saints.

Part Three contains five chapters dealing with Melchizedek Priesthood operations. Biographies of Brigham Young devote much attention to the move west, colonizing, emigration, missionary outreach, economics, Indian relations, politics, and theology, but rarely assess him carefully as a leader of the priesthood or explore in detail how stakes, wards, and quorums—the Church's fundamental organizational units—functioned during his administration. Chapter 8 fills that gap while identifying twelve historically important contributions he made to the shape and development of priesthood operation in the Church. Starting in 1852 and continuing into the 1860s, pastors filled a leadership layer between mission president and conference president in the British Mission. Chapter 9 defines, explains, and illustrates the office and calling of a pastor in that mission between 1852 and 1855 when the office was introduced, implemented, and defined.

Just before he died in August 1877, President Brigham Young engineered a thorough and massive priesthood reorganization, which chapter 10 explains and evaluates. This reorganization involved every stake, 241 wards, hundreds of quorums, and more than a thousand leadership positions. His detailed instructions for that reorganization provided the Church's first comprehensive handbook of instructions regarding priesthood and Church government.

During most of the nineteenth century, men called on missions were ordained as nongeneral authority seventies, belonging ever after to a specific quorum of seventies, even if they moved from where their original quorum was located. Chapter 11 concentrates on two uncanonized revelations to President John Taylor in the 1880s that led to a Churchwide restructuring and revitalizing of the seventies' work. Chapter 12 shows that organized and systematic priesthood work as we know it today actually dates from the period between 1908 and 1922, when a specially called General Priesthood Committee instituted a Churchwide priesthood reform and reorganization movement under President Joseph F. Smith. The energetic program established ordination ages for boys to be deacons, teachers, and priests and gave them boy-level duties to perform; ward priesthood meetings replaced letting quorums meet separately at different times during the week; a new ward teaching program standardized, boosted, and monitored monthly home visits; and for the first time the Church published lesson manuals for the quorums.

In the book's fourth and final part, eight chapters examine the Church's organizational and administrative history broadly. Chapter 13 provides an overview and synthesis of specific developments that previous chapters have discussed. Chapters 14 contains examples and an overview history of baptisms and baptizing since 1829, and chapter 15 shows how Saints have observed the Sabbath Day, including types of sacrament, fast, and conference meetings and sacrament customs since 1830, such as the use of the common cup. Chapter 16 demonstrates how the terms *stake* and *branch* were used interchangeably during the Joseph Smith and early Brigham Young periods and how the terminology for Church units became specific only over time. Chapter 17 treats the pivotal Nauvoo years when Church leaders introduced wards as an administrative unit (so fundamental and encompassing now) primarily for tithing and assisting the poor; this was at a time when a stake had but one quorum each of deacons, teachers, priests, and elders. Chapter 18 gives readers an overview of Mormon wagon and handcart emigration, showing how Church leaders and members consistently tried to honor covenants made in Nauvoo to assist the poor to emigrate, culminating in the 1860s in a brilliant "down and back" system of sending Utah wagons and teams, loaned in return for tithing credits, to retrieve emigrants waiting to cross the plains. Chapter 19 answers the question of what it meant in the pioneer era to be "active in the church," before auxiliaries existed, when wards had few jobs to be filled, Utah had no temples, and meetinghouses were too small for all in the ward to attend sacrament meeting. A final chapter contains the dramatic story of Dutch members at the end of World War II overcoming their bitterness toward Germany when a wise mission president convinced them to grow welfare potatoes and send barrels of herring to starving German Saints.

These previously published chapters have undergone only minimal editing, mostly for consistency within this volume. Whenever possible, the editors tried to include the original illustrations; however, some of those images were no longer available so many additional ones have been added.

ACKNOWLEDGMENTS

I am very pleased that this volume contains, under one cover, many of my efforts to understand the Church's organizational past. I am in debt to colleagues and institutions that made it possible for me to research and publish this array of priesthood and administrative studies. Thank you Church History Division and colleagues from the Joseph Fielding Smith Institute for Latter-day Saint History, particularly Leonard J. Arrington, Davis Bitton, James B. Allen, Dean C. Jessee, Maureen Ursenbach Beecher, Ronald K. Esplin, Richard L. Jensen, Gordon Irving, Ronald W. Walker, Dean L. May, Glen M. Leonard, Bruce D. Blumell, D. Michael Quinn, Carol Cornwall

Madsen, Jill Mulvay Derr, and Gene A. Sessions. Valued, specific encouragement for my priesthood studies came from Larry C. Porter, Steve F. Gilliland, Gregory A. Prince, Ronald O. Barney, Richard Nietzel Holzapfel, and David J. Whittaker. Stanley B. Kimball was my Mormon Trail guru, and my interviews with Symen Stam and Cornelius Zappey gave me the heart of the Dutch potato story. Likewise, well-meant thanks go to many journal, magazine, and book editors and publishers, outside peer reviewers, photo archivists, research assistants, and, in that awful era before computers, History Division and Smith Institute typists, particularly Debbie Liljenquist (Biggs) and Marilyn R. Parks. Research repositories I heavily used were the Church Historical Department library and archives, Church Family History Library, and BYU's Lee Library and L. Tom Perry Special Collections.

David J. Whittaker, who proposed this essay collection, deserves many thanks. And the BYU Studies staff, particularly editor in chief John W. Welch and senior executive editor Heather M. Seferovich, guided this book through production from start to finish. Editing interns Holly A. Mueller, Elizabeth Pew, Kimberly Webb Reid, and Chris Rosenquist along with production editors Catharine Verhaaren Gruver and Marny K. Parkin, who also indexed this volume, performed valuable services.

A final thanks goes to my own personal priesthood "fellow servants"—quorum advisors, presidencies, and quorum members who helped me on my wonderful journey as a deacon, teacher, priest, elder, high priest, and bishop.

NOTES

1. "Revelation Given through John Taylor," James R. Clark, ed., *Messages of the First Presidency of the Church of Jesus Christ of Latter-day Saints, 1833–1964*, comp. James R. Clark, 6 vols. (Salt Lake City, Utah: Bookcraft, 1965), 2:354.

2. First Council of Seventy Minutes, December 15, 1886, Church History Library, The Church of Jesus Christ of Latter-day Saints, Salt Lake City.

3. Rudger Clawson to President Heber J. Grant, Extracts of Council of the Twelve Minutes and First Council of the Seventy, 1888–1941, December 9, 1926, microfilm, Church History Library.

4. Melchizedek Priesthood Committee of the Twelve to the author, May 9, 1973, filed in the author's loose-leaf 1973 diary.

Priesthood Restoration

1

"Upon You My Fellow Servants"
Restoration of the Priesthood

IF ASKED WHEN AND HOW THE PRIESTHOOD was restored, most Church members would answer, "In 1829, John the Baptist and Peter, James, and John gave Joseph Smith and Oliver Cowdery the Aaronic and the Melchizedek priesthoods." Such a simple answer, however, is but a part of the story, the beginning segment of Joseph Smith's receiving authority and implementing it. For priesthood to be restored, it must not only be bestowed but also implemented—put into effect.[1]

Priesthood, which encompasses powers, keys, ordinances, offices, duties, organizations, and attitudes, did not come to Joseph Smith in full bloom. Like a tree, priesthood restoration unfolded from seed to shoot, to trunk, to branches, to leaves, to blossoms. Moroni promised priesthood would be restored. From that announcement (the seed) until 1843, when Joseph first exercised the highest temple sealing powers (the blossom), priesthood progressively unfolded.

Joseph Smith did not record all he experienced or was taught about priesthood, so our picture of priesthood restoration is incomplete. In 1835 he lamented that gaps in his and others' records meant that "we cannot bear record to the Church and to the world, of the great and glorious manifestations which have been made to us with that degree of power and authority we otherwise could."[2] Unlike the details he recorded about John the

Baptist's visit, Joseph mentioned visits from Peter, James, and John, Adam, Elijah, Elias, Moses, and other messengers but gave few details of what they said or how they gave him keys and authority. Joseph received a revelation about the seventy that he did not put into writing.[3]

PRELIMINARIES TO PRIESTHOOD

In 1823, when Joseph Smith was seventeen, Moroni planted the priesthood seed in Joseph's heart by instructing him not only about plates but also about priesthood. Quoting Malachi, Moroni four times said the Lord would reveal "the Priesthood, by the hand of Elijah the prophet" (D&C 2:1). Moroni said nothing of John the Baptist or Peter, James, and John, only that Elijah would reveal priesthood to someone, someday.

While Joseph Smith was translating the plates, priesthood seed found roots. Joseph encountered many Nephite references to priesthood, which made him ponder what priesthood was. The Book of Mormon was his first primer on priesthood and how it functioned in ancient times. He learned that even the people of Limhi, who desired baptism, could not receive it, because "there was none in the land that had authority from God." Lacking authority, "they did not ... form themselves into a church" (Mosiah 21:33–34). Alma, their contemporary who was hiding in the wilderness, however, received "authority from the Almighty God" by which he began baptizing (Mosiah 18:13).

Joseph Smith no doubt paid keen attention to the Nephite account of church operations at Zarahemla. Alma, Joseph learned, was a "high priest" and "founder of their church," and "none received authority to preach or to teach except it were by him from God" (Mosiah 23:16–17). In time, Alma established churches throughout the land of Zarahemla and ordained priests and teachers "over every church" (Mosiah 25:19). A priest preached "according as it was delivered to him by the mouth of Alma" (Mosiah 25:21).

Among the Nephites there was a priestly "order of God" or "holy order of God." Alma the Younger "ordained priests and elders, by laying on his hands according to the order of God, to preside and watch over the church" (Alma 6:1). Alma referred to "the order after which I am called" (Alma 5:49) and explained in detail the "high priesthood being after the order of his Son," which made men "high priests forever" (Alma 13:7, 9). Melchizedek, Alma taught, was "a high priest after this same order" (Alma 13:14). Alma and his co-workers "preached after the holy order of God by which they were called" (Alma 43:2). Further, Joseph Smith learned that Ammon was a "high priest" in Jershon (see Alma 30:19–20) and that Helaman and "high priests" guided the church (Alma 46:38).

If the young translator grew curious about the high priest's office and consulted his Bible, he would have found one reference to Jesus Christ being a high priest after the order of Melchizedek (see Heb. 5:10) and one reference in the Psalms to "the order of Melchizedek" (Ps. 110:4). But such references produce questions, not answers. What does "the order of Melchizedek" refer to? Why would Jesus be a high priest in that order? What connection did Jesus' being a high priest after the order of Melchizedek have with the Book of Mormon's "order of the Son of God"? In Genesis,

Beginning in his youth and continuing into adulthood, Joseph Smith Jr. received many revelations concerning Christ's church and his priesthood. Library of Congress.

Joseph found that Melchizedek was a contemporary of Abraham, a king of Salem, and a "priest of the most high God" who blessed Abraham and received tithes from him. Genesis is silent about any order of priests that Melchizedek headed (see Gen. 14:18–20).

While translating, Joseph Smith learned that Nephi, son of Helaman, taught that "there were many before the days of Abraham who were called by the order of God; yea, even after the order of his Son" (Hel. 8:18). This same Nephi, much like Moses, who parted the sea, possessed power from God to smite the earth, split a temple, level a mountain, and have God smite people (see Hel. 10:6–10). This Nephi received from God "power, that whatsoever ye shall seal on earth shall be sealed in heaven; and whatsoever ye shall loose on earth shall be loosed in heaven" (Hel. 10:7). Probably the translator recognized that this power Nephi received was the same binding and loosening power that Jesus gave his apostle Peter (see Matt. 16:18–19).

By the time Joseph Smith finished translating the plates, they had taught him that baptisms must be performed only by proper authority, God must give that authority, there exists "an order" of priesthood, and the churches had high priests, priests, and teachers. He knew that before Abraham's time there existed "an order of God," that Moses and other prophets received great power over the elements, and that Nephite prophets had power to seal on earth, an act which heaven would honor.

From Jesus' ministry in the Americas, Joseph Smith learned that Jesus chose twelve disciples to lead his church, gave men power to baptize (see 3 Ne. 11:21), to ordain others, to administer the sacrament (see 3 Ne.18:5), to bestow the Holy Ghost (see 3 Ne. 18:37), to form churches (see 4 Ne. 1:1), and to choose replacements for the Twelve (see 4 Ne. 1:14). Joseph found that Jesus' twelve disciples had authority to bestow the Holy Ghost and to ordain priests and teachers, and that elders and priests could administer the sacrament (see Moro. 2–6).

It needs to be stressed that Joseph Smith, during the priesthood restoration process, firmly believed in the Book of Mormon and revered its teachings about priesthood. He did not treat them casually or lightly.

RESTORATION OF THE AARONIC PRIESTHOOD

When Joseph Smith told others what the translations said, believers asked what they should do. He inquired of the Lord, who said that believers who were "called to the work" should thrust in their sickles and study (D&C 4:3).[4] At first the believers needed no particular priesthood authority to preach repentance and to convert people to gospel principles explained in the forthcoming Book of Mormon.

While translating material relating to baptism—probably in 3 Nephi—Joseph Smith and Oliver Cowdery needed and sought divine advice. "Our souls were drawn out in mighty prayer," Oliver said, "to know how we might obtain the blessings of baptism and of the Holy Spirit, according to the order of God" (the Book of Mormon phrase) "and we diligently sought for the right of the fathers and the authority of the holy priesthood, and the power to administer in the same." The two "repaired to the woods" and there "called upon the name of the Lord."[5]

Joseph said they went into the woods "to pray and inquire of the Lord respecting baptism for the remission of sins, that we found mentioned in the translation of the plates."[6] According to Oliver, they "called upon him in a fervent manner," after which they heard "the voice of the Redeemer," which "spake peace to us."[7] Joseph's version says that while they were praying and calling on the Lord, "a messenger from heaven descended in a cloud of light."[8] Oliver's description said "the veil was parted." He said "our eyes beheld—our ears heard." The angel came as in the "blaze of day, above the glitter of the May sunbeam" then shining.[9]

Joseph and Oliver's experience of seeing, hearing, feeling, and being physically touched by a celestial being overwhelmed their senses and emotionally shook them to the core. They heard the angel's voice, "I am thy fellow-servant." This soft answer dispelled their fears. Said Oliver: "We listened, we gazed, we admired! 'Twas the voice of the angel from glory— 'twas a message from the Most High, and as we heard we rejoiced." While hearing the voice, Oliver said, the messenger's "love enkindled upon our souls" and wrapped them "in a vision of the Almighty!" He added: "Where was room for doubt? Nowhere; uncertainty had fled."[10]

Continuing, Oliver struggled to verbalize what they had experienced: "The angel of God came down clothed with glory and delivered the anxiously looked for message, and the keys of the Gospel of repentance. What joy! what wonder! what amazement!"[11]

Oliver, in the earliest recorded account of the Aaronic Priesthood restoration, written in 1833, said that Joseph "was ordained by the angel John unto the lesser or Aaronic priesthood, in company with myself . . ., after which we repaired to the water, even to the Susquehannah River and were baptized, he first ministering unto me and after—I to him."[12]

The men bowed themselves down, filled with surprise and wonder. According to Oliver they "received under his hand the Holy Priesthood" and heard these words: "Upon you my fellow servants, in the name of Messiah, I confer this Priesthood and this authority, which remain upon earth, that the sons of Levi may yet offer an offering unto the Lord in righteousness!"[13]

Surprisingly, Joseph's early accounts do not contain the terms *Aaronic* or *lesser priesthood*.[14] Not until about ten years later, when he wrote what is now section 13 of the Doctrine and Covenants,[15] did Joseph make clear that John the Baptist bestowed the Aaronic Priesthood: "Upon you my fellow servants, in the name of Messiah I confer the Priesthood of Aaron, which holds the keys of the ministering of angels, and of the gospel of repentance, and of baptism by immersion for the remission of sins; and this shall never

This picture by George Washington Crocheron depicts the events of May 15, 1829, when Joseph Smith Jr. and Oliver Cowdery received the Aaronic Priesthood from John the Baptist. Library of Congress.

be taken again from the earth, until the sons of Levi do offer again an offering unto the Lord in righteousness."

Oliver wrote of "the majestic beauty and glory that surrounded us." He said that each sentence John uttered carried with it "joy, peace, and wisdom" and was delivered "by the power of the Holy Ghost. You will believe me when I say, that earth, nor men, with the eloquence of time, cannot begin to clothe language in as interesting and sublime a manner as this holy personage." Oliver felt this encounter with an angel was "past description" and an "expression of the Savior's goodness."[16]

The angel instructed Joseph and Oliver to baptize each other—Joseph baptized Oliver first, then Oliver baptized Joseph. Then Joseph reordained Oliver, and Oliver, Joseph. "Immediately on our coming up out of the water after we had been baptized, we experienced great and glorious blessings from our Heavenly Father. No sooner had I baptized Oliver Cowdery, than the Holy Ghost fell upon him, and he stood up and prophesied many things which should shortly come to pass. And again, so soon as I had been baptized by him, I also had the spirit of prophecy, when standing up, I prophesied concerning the rise of this Church, and this generation of the children of men. We were filled with the Holy Ghost, and rejoiced in the God of our salvation."[17]

Possessing power and authority to baptize, Joseph and Oliver baptized several people. By the time three months had passed, Samuel and Hyrum Smith and David, John, and Peter Whitmer Jr. had been baptized. What would be part of the main trunk of the priesthood tree was now in place.

RESTORATION OF MELCHIZEDEK PRIESTHOOD

Joseph and Oliver became eager to receive authority to bestow the Holy
Ghost, as promised them by John the Baptist. "We had for some time made
this matter a subject of humble prayer," Joseph said, and while staying at
the home of Peter Whitmer Sr. they "engaged in solemn and fervent prayer"
to obtain that blessing. In response, "the word of the Lord came unto us
in the chamber, commanding us that I should ordain Oliver Cowdery to
be an Elder in the Church," that Oliver should ordain Joseph to the same
office, and that then they should ordain others. But, they were told, they
should defer the ordination.[18] Apparently, shortly after this revelation, Peter,
James, and John visited them and restored the Melchizedek Priesthood. But
the exact date of their visit "has always been a puzzle in Mormon history,"
because early records fail to mention the event.[19] A positive circumstantial
case can be made that Peter, James, and John must have appeared in late
May or early June 1829—soon after the visit of John the Baptist.[20]

In Doctrine and Covenants 27:12 the Lord discusses "Peter, and James,
and John, whom I have sent unto you, by whom I have ordained you and
confirmed you to be apostles, and especial witnesses of my name, and bear
the keys of your ministry."[21] This verse, which was added after 1833 to the
record of the revelation, indicates that Joseph and Oliver received authority
to be apostolic special witnesses—the term *Melchizedek Priesthood* is absent.

Oliver Cowdery, late in 1833, said that after the visit of John the Baptist,
"we received the high and holy priesthood" but gave no details.[22] Joseph,
writing in 1842, rejoiced that he heard "the voice of Peter, James, and John
in the wilderness" near the Susquehanna River, "declaring themselves as
possessing the keys of the kingdom, and of the dispensation of the fulness
of times!" (D&C 128:20).

Through hindsight and better knowledge of the Melchizedek Priesthood obtained after 1835, Joseph and Oliver's later writings linked Peter,
James, and John with bestowing upon them the Melchizedek Priesthood.
Joseph Smith's 1838 history indicates that the visit of John the Baptist had
been directed by Peter, James, and John, "who held the keys of the Priesthood of Melchizedek, which Priesthood, he said, would in due time be
conferred on us."[23] Joseph, in July 1839, asked: "How have we come at the
Priesthood in the last days?" and then answered: "It came down, down, in
regular succession. Peter, James, and John had it given to them and they

gave it to others."[24] Oliver Cowdery in 1849 told a few Saints that "Peter, James, and John, holding the keys of the Melchizedek Priesthood," ordained men to that priesthood.[25]

Joseph and Oliver's ordinations made each of them "an apostle of Jesus Christ" and "an elder" (D&C 20:2–3). Joseph Smith, as Apostle and First Elder, now was caretaker for a priesthood whose main trunk already supported small branches. Brigham Young later explained that Joseph Smith had first to be an Apostle in order to organize and build the kingdom of God. "The keys of the eternal Priesthood, which is after the order of the Son of God, are comprehended by being an Apostle. All the Priesthood, all the keys, all the gifts, all the endowments and everything preparatory to entering into the presence of the Father and the Son, are in, composed of ... [are] incorporated within the circumference of, the Apostleship."[26]

ORGANIZING A CHURCH

Joseph and Oliver knew during 1829 that they would organize a church. Revelations that year told of "the rising up and the coming forth of my church" (D&C 5:14) and "the foundation of my church" (D&C 18:4). In 1829, Cowdery drafted a version of what became in 1830 the first manual for Church government—now Doctrine and Covenants 20. Called "Articles of the Church of Christ," it was a revelation to Oliver, who is "called with the same calling as Paul," to "baptize those who repent." The revelation explained the method of baptism, the words to use when ordaining priests and teachers, and the sacrament prayer. The document was signed, "Behold I am Oliver I am an Apostle of Jesus Christ."[27]

During 1829, Joseph and Oliver baptized and ordained others to the priesthood. David Whitmer, in old age, said that by August 1829, six elders had been ordained, the other four being himself, Samuel and Hyrum Smith, and Peter Whitmer. David said that "we preached, baptized, and confirmed members into the Church of Christ" during the next eight months. He added, "We were an humble happy people."[28]

Preaching, converting, baptizing, ordaining, holding meetings of believers—these activities show that an informal church was in operation in 1829. Then, Whitmer said, in part because "the world had been telling us that we were not a regularly organized church, and had no right to officiate in the ordinance of marriage, hold church property, etc.," a more formal, legal entity needed to be formed.[29] Sometime early in spring 1830, Joseph Smith told his friend Joseph Knight Sr. that "there must be a church formed."[30] Joseph received a revelation giving the exact date for this formal organizing to occur.[31]

On April 6 more than fifty people met at the Whitmer house in Fayette to formally create the Church of Christ.[32] By vote, Joseph Smith was sustained as First Elder and Oliver as Second Elder, and they ordained each other as such. Joseph and Oliver blessed bread and wine and administered the sacrament. Then they laid hands on various members and bestowed the Holy Ghost. Joseph and Oliver ordained a few men to the priesthood. Father Joseph Knight reported that "Joseph gave them instructions how to Bild up the Church."[33]

David Whitmer was one of the first members of the Church to be ordained an elder. Courtesy Perry Special Collections.

This meeting followed the blueprint given to Joseph Smith in Father Whitmer's chamber in June 1829, which outlined that at a future meeting of the baptized, the group must vote to sustain Joseph and Oliver to be ordained as First and Second Elders in the Church of Jesus Christ, vote to sustain Joseph and Oliver as their spiritual teachers, partake of the sacrament, allow Joseph and Oliver to ordain each other and then ordain others, and then confer the gift of the Holy Ghost upon those baptized (see D&C 18).

At the meeting, a revelation was received that said Joseph should be called and recognized by the Church as "a seer, a translator, a prophet, an apostle of Jesus Christ, an elder" (D&C 21:1).

A revelation that month said that prior baptisms in other churches were not valid and that "although a man should be baptized an hundred times it availeth him nothing" (D&C 22:2).[34]

At the first conference of the Church, on June 9, 1830, the members received and canonized the Church government manual that stemmed from Oliver Cowdery's 1829 "Articles and Covenants" (D&C 20).[35] It was read at succeeding conferences and carried about by elders on missionary journeys and preaching assignments to be read to the believers.[36]

Regarding priesthood, the articles stipulated that Joseph Smith was called of God and "ordained an apostle of Jesus Christ, to be the first elder of this church" (D&C 20:2). Oliver was second elder, and "an apostle is an elder" authorized to baptize, administer the sacrament, bestow the Holy Ghost, teach, expound, and conduct meetings under the guidance of the Holy Ghost (see D&C 20:38–45). Taking the revelation literally, Joseph and Oliver tried to perform their duties, and they did baptize, administer the sacrament, bestow the Holy Ghost, teach, and conduct meetings. They not only received authority but used it diligently.

The articles gave specific duties to each of four priesthood offices—main branches—of elder, priest, teacher, and deacon. Taken together, the four offices had responsibility to perform ordinances, conduct meetings, and visit members to see that all did their duty (see D&C 20:38–59). Various churches, or branches, would be guided and coordinated at quarterly conferences of the elders (see D&C 20:62–65).[37]

This revelation on Church organization built upon the Book of Mormon pattern, with the addition of deacons. The offices had a graded order from least (deacon) to highest (elder), with the First and Second Elders as the top officers, all unpaid.[38]

During the conference, new officers were ordained: Samuel H. Smith, an elder, by Oliver Cowdery; Joseph Smith Sr., Hyrum Smith, and Martin Harris as priests; and Hiram Page and Christian Whitmer as teachers. The conference gave licenses to the seven elders present and to three priests and two teachers to preach and teach.

By 1830 the priesthood tree had a sturdy trunk with several branches. Authority had been restored, that is, bestowed and shared. Joseph and early members called it "authority," but not Melchizedek or Aaronic Priesthood or even priesthood.[39] Priesthood bearers proselyted, baptized, confirmed, administered the sacrament, ordained, and conducted meetings as "they

[were] directed and guided by the Holy Spirit," and managed the Church (D&C 46:2). By February 1831, elders were blessing the sick through the laying on of hands (see D&C 42:43–48).[40]

Nevertheless, priesthood restoration was not complete. Still lacking were several branches, leaves, and blossoms: offices, understanding of greater and lesser priesthoods, the sealing keys, the priesthood temple ordinances, and the discovery of how priesthood offices should intermesh into a workable whole.

HIGHER AND LESSER PRIESTHOODS

During the next five years, Church relocations and growth and new revelations caused the single priesthood trunk to fork into clearly defined Aaronic and Melchizedek main branches, each properly budded. Many converts, like Solomon Humphrey, "got baptized and ordained an elder" and preached.[41] Increasing numbers of priesthood officers required that men be grouped into quorums, their duties clearly differentiated by office, and units governed and coordinated.

Quarterly elders conferences supervised ordaining and preaching assignments. In December 1831 the Lord said converts were to "be ordained and sent forth to preach"—all men (and selected older boys)[42] were to receive ordination to an office (D&C 36:5). But in February 1831, the Lord instructed that no one was to preach or build up the Church "except he be ordained by some one who has authority, and it is known to the church that he has authority and has been regularly ordained by the heads of the church" (D&C 42:11). Two years later, Joseph Smith taught that "there has been too much haste" in ordaining men to the priesthood, and some had not "magnified their calling at all."[43]

A new office, a vital new limb of the priesthood tree, appeared on February 4, 1831, when Joseph Smith received a revelation calling Edward Partridge to be "ordained a bishop unto the church," an office not foreshadowed in the available Nephite records (D&C 41:9). Two months earlier, the office was anticipated, however, when the Lord asked that men be appointed by the voice of the Church "to look to the poor and the needy" and to "govern the affairs of the property of this church" (D&C 38:35–36). The bishop was to be assisted by elders as his counselors (see D&C 42:72).[44]

By year's end, Newel K. Whitney became the second bishop. He served Ohio Saints, and Partridge served those in Missouri.

Both bishops received the duty "to keep the Lord's storehouse," manage consecrated properties, receive funds, keep elders' accounts, pay Church expenses, and care for the poor (see D&C 72:8–19). Bishops were not considered Aaronic Priesthood officers until later. For a few months "bishops and elders," by revelation, governed local affairs.[45] An August 1831 revelation said that elders in Missouri should be governed by conferences and that the bishop should direct the conference (see D&C 58:58–61).

By late 1831 the first deacons were ordained.[46]

In 1831, Joseph introduced another new office—a shoot that quickly became a branch of the trunk—high priest. No identifiable revelation announced or explained it, although high priests in the Book of Mormon led the church before Christ's visit to the Americas. On June 3, 1831, Joseph Smith directed that more than twenty men, including himself, be ordained to the "high priesthood."[47] Not until 1835 was this called "Melchizedek Priesthood"; rather, contemporaries used its Book of Mormon name, the "high priesthood of the holy order of God" (Alma 13:6).

This new calling produced a priesthood trunk divided into "higher" and "lesser" branches. Only high priests received this higher priesthood; elders, priests, teachers, and deacons held the lower priesthood.[48] Because the high priests were the highest officers in the Church, the high priests' president was the presiding officer in the Church. Joseph Smith, who had led the Church as its First Elder, now led because he was the President of the High Priesthood. Within a year, he called counselors to assist him—the first First Presidency, in current terms.[49] As usual, Joseph took his duties seriously and labored diligently to preside over the expanding priesthood.

On February 16, 1832, as part of the vision of the three degrees of glory, Joseph Smith and Sidney Rigdon were shown that among those who would receive God's fullest rewards in the hereafter were "priests of the Most High, after the order of Melchizedek"—the earliest reference in revelations to a Melchizedek Priesthood (D&C 76:57).

During September 1832, Joseph received a major revelation concerning priesthood (see D&C 84). It told of the temple to be reared at Kirtland—implying a priesthood tie to temples yet to come. The revelation traced the "Holy Priesthood" (D&C 84:6) back from Moses through Noah to Adam, told of a priesthood placed upon Aaron and his seed, and said the "Holy

Priesthood" was the "greater priesthood" (D&C 84:25–26). Anciently, God had removed the Holy Priesthood from Israel, but "the lesser priesthood continued" (D&C 84:26). This lesser priesthood held keys of the preparatory gospel of repentance and baptism and "the law of carnal commandments" that passed down from Aaron to John the Baptist (D&C 84:27).

The priesthood revelation explained that the "offices of elder and bishop are necessary appendages belonging unto the high priesthood" and that the "offices of teacher and deacon are necessary appendages belonging to the lesser priesthood" (D&C 84:29–30). Holders of both priesthoods one day would offer sacrifices in a temple to be built. The Lord covenanted with those who received both priesthoods and magnified their callings that they would receive "all that my Father hath" (D&C 84:38). In the revelation, the Lord compared the priesthood to the human body, which needs head and feet and "every member" so that "the system may be kept perfect" (D&C 84:110). He instructed high priests to "take with [them] those who are ordained unto the lesser priesthood" as assistants (D&C 84:107). "Let every man stand in his own office, and labor in his own calling" (D&C 84:109). The high priests, elders, and priests "should travel" as proselyters (D&C 84:110). Deacons and teachers should be standing ministers locally.

High priest councils governed Church operations in Missouri and Ohio until 1834, when stakes were created.[50] The creation of the first stake high council—"the standing council" at Kirtland—occurred on February 17, 1834 (D&C 102:1, 3). The First Presidency served as council presidency, much like a stake presidency today.[51] Missouri received a twelve-man "council of high priests"[52] and a presidency of Zion (the Second Presidency) on July 3, 1834. By early 1835, high councils were considered stake entities (see D&C 107:36).

More main branches sprang forth on the priesthood tree. Joseph Smith bestowed the first patriarchal blessing, on December 18, 1833, upon his father and mother, two brothers, and Oliver Cowdery. Then Joseph's father was ordained to the Patriarchal Priesthood and given the keys of blessings.[53]

Then, commanded by God and shown in vision and by the Holy Spirit what to do, Joseph conducted a special priesthood conference on February 14, 1835, where the Three Witnesses selected Twelve Apostles.[54] Two weeks later, Joseph explained the calling of the Twelve:

They are the Twelve Apostles, who are called to the office of traveling high council, who are to preside over all the churches of the
Saints among the Gentiles, where there is no presidency established,
and they are to travel and preach among the Gentiles, until the Lord
shall command them to go to the Jews. They are to hold the keys of
this ministry to unlock the door of the kingdom of heaven into all
nations and to preach the Gospel to every creature. This is the power,
authority and virtue of their Apostleship.[55]

Two weeks later, a quorum of Seventy was called into being, perhaps
bearing some relationship to the seventy elders Moses called or to seventy
missionaries the Savior ordained.[56] "The Seventies," Joseph Smith taught,
"are to constitute traveling quorums, to go into all the earth, whithersoever
the Twelve Apostles shall call them." He and his counselors ordained the
number who were present.[57] By December 1836, two more quorums of seventy had been formed. Questions arose concerning which priesthood office
had the higher authority, high priests or seventies? Joseph instructed that
high priests could not be ordained as seventies, but the controversy lasted
for decades.[58]

A month after the Apostles and the Seventy were called, Joseph Smith
received another key priesthood revelation which, like a manual of instructions, clearly explained Melchizedek and Aaronic Priesthood offices, duties,
and interrelationships (see D&C 107). It provided the first details about
structuring Aaronic Priesthood work.

"There are, in the church, two priesthoods," the revelation begins. The
first is Melchizedek and "all other authorities or offices in the church are
appendages to this priesthood.... The office of an elder comes under the
priesthood of Melchizedek" (D&C 107:1, 5, 7). High priests administer in
spiritual things and can officiate in the office of elder, priest, teacher, or
deacon. The Aaronic Priesthood is a lesser priesthood that has power in
administering "in outward ordinances" (D&C 107:20). A high priest can
serve as bishop.

The revelation taught that the Church's three Presiding High Priests are
the "quorum of the Presidency" of the Church. The Twelve Apostles are a
traveling high council directed by the Church Presidency. The seventy are
to travel into the world to preach. Stake high councils govern within their
stake. The Twelve have a duty to ordain patriarchs (evangelical ministers[59])

and "to ordain and set in order all the other officers of the church" (D&C 107:58). Groups of ninety-six elders, forty-eight priests, twenty-four teachers, and twelve deacons are each to have their own presidencies, and the priests' president is a bishop. Literal descendants of Aaron can be bishops and serve without counselors. "The bishopric is the presidency" of the Aaronic Priesthood (D&C 107:15). The Seventy have a seven-man presidency. The high priests have a Presiding High Priest, who "is to preside over the whole church, and to be like unto Moses" (D&C 107:91). Church court systems are outlined. The revelation concludes with a call for all officers to learn and do their own duties.

In fall 1835 the Church published the first edition of the Doctrine and Covenants. Unlike the Book of Commandments of 1833, this 1835 collection featured the priesthood revelations first. It opened with the Articles and Covenants (D&C 20), the newly received priesthood revelation (D&C 107), and the 1832 priesthood revelation (D&C 84).

ELIJAH AND SEALING AUTHORITY

Even though all the priesthood offices had been revealed and their duties and organizations explained, the priesthood restoration process still lacked the promised visit of Elijah and the connection to temples. Moroni had promised Joseph Smith that Elijah would come to reveal "the priesthood" (D&C 2:1). Sidney Rigdon had been told by revelation that his labors had been preparing the way for Elijah, "which should come" (D&C 35:4). The Prophet pushed the completion of the Kirtland Temple because the Lord in 1833 had commanded him that "you should build a house, in the which house I design to endow those whom I have chosen with power from on high" (D&C 95:8).[60]

Designed according to revelation, the temple's lower auditorium had elevated pulpits on the east end for Melchizedek Priesthood presidencies and on the west for Aaronic Priesthood presidencies.[61] For the first time in this dispensation, priesthood and temple were firmly intertwined. On March 27, 1836, Joseph Smith dedicated the temple, and during subsequent days the priesthood quorums and their leaders received the ordinance of washing of feet, anointings, and the beginnings of temple endowments.

On April 3, 1836, the Prophet and Sidney Rigdon bowed in solemn prayer in the temple and beheld several remarkable visions about which

As part of the First Presidency of the Church during the dedication of the Kirtland Temple in 1836, Sidney Rigdon witnessed spiritual visions and manifestations. Courtesy Church Archives.

they recorded neither details nor emotional reactions (see D&C 110). The Lord appeared and accepted the temple. Moses appeared and committed the keys of the gathering of Israel. Elias committed to them keys of the dispensation of the gospel of Abraham. Then came the visit promised by Malachi and reiterated by Moroni in 1823. Elijah "stood before us," Joseph said, and bestowed the keys for turning hearts of fathers to children and children to fathers—the sealing powers (D&C 110:13–15).

But Joseph, now possessing great priesthood keys and powers, did not implement the higher priesthood ordinances made possible by the sealing powers until the Nauvoo Temple was under construction. Early in 1841 the Lord instructed his prophet that when the Nauvoo Temple was built, he would show Joseph "all things" pertaining to "the priesthood thereof" (D&C 124:42). Rooms should be prepared in the temple for all the grades and offices of the priesthood. Joseph Smith started using the sealing powers on behalf of deceased people in 1842 by authorizing baptisms for the dead. Even as workmen built the temple, the Lord promised that "I am about to restore many things to the earth, pertaining to the priesthood" (D&C 127:8).

In 1842, after giving the Twelve responsibility for leadership at home as well as abroad, Joseph Smith introduced them and other leaders to the full temple endowment by personally "instructing them in the principles and order of the Priesthood, attending to washings, anointings, endowments and the communication of keys pertaining to the Aaronic Priesthood, and so on to the highest order of the Melchisedek Priesthood."[62]

During his final five years, Joseph Smith, after serious meditations in Liberty Jail, did more teaching than ever before. As prophet-teacher, he taught in depth about the priesthood. By letter from Liberty Jail, he explained crucial priesthood principles of success and failure (see D&C 121:34–46). Men might receive the priesthood, he said, but lose it by caring too much about worldly matters, seeking honor and power, covering their sins, and exercising authority through compulsion or unrighteous dominion. Priesthood bearers lacked power or influence unless they practiced persuasion, long-suffering, gentleness, meekness, and genuine love. Men must learn "this one lesson," he emphasized, that the priesthood must connect with the powers of heaven "and that the powers of heaven cannot be controlled nor handled only upon the principles of righteousness" (D&C 121:35–36). Unrighteousness causes the Spirit to withdraw, which in turn causes the priesthood power to withdraw.

In Nauvoo, Joseph Smith preached several vital discourses to explain priesthood. In September 1842 he told of various beings from Adam forward who had declared their dispensations to him and given him keys and "the power of the priesthood" (D&C 128:20–21). In mid-1843 he taught that a man receives the fullness of the priesthood by keeping the commandments and obeying all the ordinances of the temple.[63]

In October 1843 the prophet-teacher explained that there are three "grand orders" of priesthood, Melchizedek, Patriarchal, and Levitical. Regarding the Patriarchal order he said: "Go to and finish the temple, and God will fill it with power, and you will then receive more knowledge, concerning this priesthood."[64]

A year before his death, Joseph Smith recorded the capstone revelation of the priesthood restoration sequence. On July 12, 1843, he dictated the celestial marriage revelation, wherein the Lord said he would "give unto thee the law of my Holy Priesthood, as was ordained by me and my Father before the world was" (D&C 132:28). He conferred upon Joseph "the keys of the power of this priesthood" so that whatsoever Joseph sealed or loosed on earth would be sealed or loosed in heaven and be eternally valid, including marriages (D&C 132:46–48, 59). Joseph taught the Twelve that only one man on the earth at a time—the President of the Church—could hold the keys of the sealing power, and sealings had to be performed by him or "by his dictation."[65]

Three months before his death, Joseph delivered his last priesthood sermon, and emphasized the importance of Elijah and the sealing authority. In it he asked: "What is this office and work of Elijah? It is one of the greatest and most important subjects that God has revealed." He taught that "the spirit, power, and calling of Elijah is, that ye have power to hold the key of the revelations, ordinances, oracles, powers and endowments of the fulness of the Melchizedek Priesthood," and have power to turn hearts of children on earth to deceased fathers. It is by the Spirit of Elijah, he said, "that we redeem our Dead" and "connect ourselves with our fathers which are in heaven, and seal up our dead to come forth in the first resurrection." By the power of Elijah we "seal those who dwell on earth to those who dwell in heaven." He added that "the power of Elijah is sufficient to make our calling and election sure."[66]

The Prophet introduced complete temple endowments to selected confidants, who became part of what was called the Holy Order. Men received endowments first, but, as charter members of the Nauvoo Female Relief Society were told by Bishop Whitney, in Joseph's presence, "without the female all things cannot be restor'd to the earth—it takes all to restore the Priesthood."[67] The final step of priesthood restoration came during 1843, when Emma Smith became the first woman to obtain temple endowments, and she and Joseph received the highest temple rites.[68] On September 28 the Prophet introduced the "fullness of priesthood ordinances" to a few dozen trusted believers. This group, or Holy Order, was kept small, he explained, to restrict the knowledge of the ordinances until the temple was completed and members could receive them in a properly dedicated edifice.[69]

With the granting of temple endowments, sealings of spouses for eternity, and granting the fullness of the priesthood, Elijah's part of the priesthood restoration work was fully implemented. The priesthood tree stood complete with trunk, branches, and leaves and was bearing good fruit. Twenty years after Moroni's first visit, through the Prophet Joseph Smith, "the fullness of priesthood" was operational on earth and available to tried, tested, and worthy Latter-day Saints. Joseph had faithfully restored and nurtured the mighty priesthood tree to mature size, shape, beauty, and usefulness.

Joseph Smith was both priesthood restorer and priesthood bearer. He received and honored the Aaronic Priesthood. He received and honored the Melchizedek Priesthood. Like all other priesthood holders, he received powers and duties and had to learn how to exercise and magnify them. His history is peppered with incidents when, as priesthood bearer, he taught, visited and cared for members, administered the sacrament, presided, anointed and blessed the sick, dedicated sites, bestowed and radiated the Holy Ghost, gave blessings, ordained, blessed children, and baptized.

For Joseph, priesthood was restored not only to the Church but to him as well. He received, honored, exercised, and cherished the power and authority God had granted him, and he felt great joy when others did the same—all of whom traced their priesthood lineage back to and through him.

This article was originally published in The Prophet Joseph: Essays on the Life and Mission of Joseph Smith, *ed. Larry C. Porter and Susan Easton Black (Salt Lake City: Deseret Book, 1988), 49–72.*

NOTES

1. Basic priesthood history is outlined in John A. Widtsoe, *Priesthood and Church Government,* rev. ed. (Salt Lake City: Deseret Book, 1965); Joseph B. Keeler, *The Lesser Priesthood and Notes on Church Government* (Salt Lake City: Deseret News, 1904); D. Michael Quinn, "The Evolution of the Presiding Quorums of the LDS Church," *Journal of Mormon History* 1 (1974): 21–38; and Lee A. Palmer, *Aaronic Priesthood through the Centuries* (Salt Lake City: Deseret Book, 1964).

2. Joseph Smith Jr., *History of The Church of Jesus Christ of Latter-day Saints,* ed. B. H. Roberts, 2d ed., rev., 7 vols. (Salt Lake City: The Church of Jesus Christ of Latter-day Saints, 1932–51), 2:198–99 (hereafter cited as *History of the Church*).

3. *History of the Church,* 2:202.

4. References in Doctrine and Covenants 5 to Martin Harris's waiting to be ordained were added a few years later.

5. Joseph Smith Sr., Patriarchal Blessing Book 1, December 18, 1833, 8–9, L. Tom Perry Special Collections, Harold B. Lee Library, Brigham Young University, Provo, Utah.

6. *History of the Church,* 1:39.

7. *History of the Church,* 1:43n.

8. *History of the Church,* 1:39.

9. *History of the Church,* 1:43n.

10. *History of the Church,* 1:43n.

11. *History of the Church,* 1:43n.

12. *History of the Church,* 1:43n.

13. *History of the Church,* 1:43n.

14. Doctrine and Covenants 27:8 notes John's bestowing the Aaronic Priesthood on Joseph and Oliver, but the reference was added to the revelation years later. See Robert

John Woodford, "The Historical Development of the Doctrine and Covenants," 3 vols. (PhD diss., Brigham Young University, 1974), 1:394.

15. Doctrine and Covenants 13 was written by Joseph Smith for his history about ten years after the appearance of John the Baptist. Section 13 was first printed in the Doctrine and Covenants in 1876. Woodford, "Historical Development," 1:233.

16. *Messenger and Advocate* 1 (October 1834): 16.

17. *History of the Church,* 1:42.

18. *History of the Church,* 1:60–61.

19. Richard L. Bushman, *Joseph Smith and the Beginnings of Mormonism* (Chicago: University of Illinois Press, 1984), 240n55.

20. Larry C. Porter, "Dating the Melchizedek Priesthood," *Ensign* 9 (June 1979): 5–10. Others see evidence pointing to a later restoration date: see Bushman, *Joseph Smith and the Beginnings of Mormonism,* 162–63, 240–41; and Lyndon Cook, "Joseph Smith and the High Priesthood," address to *Sunstone* Symposium, August 26–29, 1987.

21. Woodford, "Historical Development," 1:394. See Book of Commandments (1833), section 28; 1835 Doctrine and Covenants, section 50.

22. Joseph Smith Sr., Patriarchal Blessing Book 1, December 18, 1833, 8–9.

23. *History of the Church,* 1:40.

24. *History of the Church,* 3:387.

25. *History of the Church,* 1:42n.

26. Brigham Young, in *Journal of Discourses,* 26 vols. (Liverpool: Latter-day Saints' Book Depot, 1855–86), 1:134–35.

27. Woodford, "Historical Development," 1:293.

28. David Whitmer, *An Address to All Believers in Christ* (Richmond, MO: By the author, 1887; reprint, Concord, CA: Pacific Publishing, 1959), 32.

29. Whitmer, *Address to All Believers in Christ,* 33.

30. Hartley, *"They Are My Friends": A History of the Joseph Knight Family, 1825–1850* (Provo, UT: Grandin Book, 1986), 207, 208.

31. *History of the Church,* 1:64–65.

32. Joseph Smith in writing to John Wentworth on March 1, 1842, said that the Church was first organized "in the town of Manchester." See Dean C. Jessee, *The Personal Writings of Joseph Smith* (Salt Lake City: Deseret Book, 1984), 216.

33. Jessee, *Personal Writings of Joseph Smith,* 143–48.

34. Bushman, *Joseph Smith and the Beginnings of Mormonism,* 153.

35. Donald Q. Cannon and Lyndon W. Cook, eds., *The Far West Record: Minutes of The Church of Jesus Christ of Latter-day Saints, 1830–1844* (Salt Lake City: Deseret Book, 1983), 1.

36. Woodford, "Historical Development," 1:292–93.

37. Doctrine and Covenants 20:66–67, which mentions bishops, high councilors, and high priests, was not part of the original revelation.

38. Bushman, *Joseph Smith and the Beginnings of Mormonism,* 147–48.

39. Cook, *Sunstone* address; Bushman, *Joseph Smith and the Beginnings of Mormonism,* 240.

40. In July 1830 Joseph was told he had power to heal the sick (D&C 24:13), and in December he and Sidney Rigdon were told that those who asked in faith could "heal the sick" and disabled (D&C 35:9).

41. Larry C. Porter, "A Study of the Origins of The Church of Jesus Christ of Latter-day Saints in the States of New York and Pennsylvania, 1816–1831" (PhD diss., Brigham Young University, 1971; Provo, UT: BYU Studies and Joseph Fielding Smith Institute for Latter-day Saint History, 2000), 265.

42. Robert L. Marrott, "History and Functions of the Aaronic Priesthood and the Offices of Priest, Teacher, and Deacon in the Church of Jesus Christ of Latter-day Saints, 1829 to 1844" (master's thesis, Brigham Young University, 1970).

43. Joseph Smith, *Teachings of the Prophet Joseph Smith*, sel. Joseph Fielding Smith (Salt Lake City: Deseret Book, 1976), 42.

44. The reference in Doctrine and Covenants 42:71 to high priests assisting the bishop was added later. It is not in the 1833 Book of Commandments version (44:54), 95.

45. See Book of Commandments 44:56; 49:23; 51:6. The latter reads "bishop and elders" but was later changed in Doctrine and Covenants 48:6 to read "presidency and the bishop."

46. The first deacons of record were Titus Billings, Serenes Burnett, and John Burk, who attended an October 25, 1831, conference. Cannon and Cook, *Far West Record*, 19; *History of the Church*, 1:219. Revelations in January and February 1831 list elders, priests, and teachers but not deacons, indicating that no deacons were then functioning. Doctrine and Covenants 38:40; 42:12, 70.

47. Cannon and Cook, *Far West Record*, 7. Joseph Smith in retrospect said that "the authority of the Melchizedek Priesthood was manifested and conferred for the first time upon several of the Elders." *History of the Church*, 1:175–76.

48. For a good analysis of high priesthood versus Melchizedek Priesthood problems, see Lyndon W. Cook, *The Revelations of the Prophet Joseph Smith* (Provo, UT: Seventies Mission Bookstore, 1981), 136–37n6.

49. Quinn, "Evolution of the Presiding Quorums," 25.

50. James B. Allen and Glen M. Leonard, *The Story of the Latter-day Saints* (Salt Lake City: Deseret Book, 1976), 78–79.

51. *History of the Church*, 2:29.

52. Cannon and Cook, *Far West Record*, 70.

53. Quinn, "Evolution of the Presiding Quorums," 26; Smith, *Teachings of the Prophet*, 39; *History of the Church*, 3:381.

54. *History of the Church*, 2:182–200.

55. Kirtland Council Minute Book, February 27, 1835, 88, quoted in Quinn, "Evolution of the Presiding Quorums," 27–28.

56. Numbers 11:16, 17, 24, 25; Luke 10.

57. *History of the Church*, 2:202.

58. James N. Baumgarten, "The Role and Function of the Seventies in LDS Church History" (master's thesis, Brigham Young University, 1960).

59. "An Evangelist is a Patriarch, even the oldest man of the blood of Joseph or of the seed of Abraham. Wherever the Church of Christ is established in the earth, there should be a Patriarch for the benefit of the posterity of the Saints, as it was with Jacob in giving his patriarchal blessing unto his sons, etc." *History of the Church*, 3:381.

60. See also Doctrine and Covenants 38:32.

61. On the east were seats for the Melchizedek Presiding Council (First Presidency), Presiding Melchizedek High Priesthood (the Twelve, or the Kirtland High Council),

the Melchizedek High Priesthood (high priests quorum), and the Presiding Elder
Melchizedek (elders quorum) and on similar west pulpits for the Bishop Presiding
Aaronic (Bishop), Presiding Aaronic Priest (Priests), Presiding Teacher Aaronic
(Teachers), and Presiding Deacon Aaronic (Deacons). See Milton V. Backman Jr., *The
Heavens Resound* (Salt Lake City: Deseret Book, 1983), 160.

62. *History of the Church,* 5:2.
63. Smith, *Teachings of the Prophet,* 308.
64. Smith, *Teachings of the Prophet,* 323; see also note 59 above.
65. Quorum of the Twelve Apostles to William Smith, August 10, 1845, Brigham Young
    Papers, Church History Library, The Church of Jesus Christ of Latter-day Saints, Salt
    Lake City.
66. Smith, *Teachings of the Prophet,* 337–38.
67. Carol Cornwall Madsen, "Mormon Women and the Temple: Toward a New Under-
    standing," in *Sisters in Spirit: Mormon Women in Historical and Cultural Perspective,* ed.
    Maureen Ursenbach Beecher and Lavina Fielding Anderson (Urbana: University of
    Illinois Press, 1987), 85.
68. It appears that Joseph Smith and Emma were sealed in eternal marriage on May 28,
    1843. (By then, at least, the Prophet was sealing eternal marriages.) Andrew F. Ehat,
    "Joseph Smith's Introduction of Temple Ordinances and the 1844 Mormon Succession
    Question" (master's thesis, Brigham Young University, 1982), 61–63, 263–65.
69. Madsen, "Mormon Women and the Temple," 85.

2   Every Member *Was* a Missionary

THEY WENT WITHOUT PURSE OR SCRIPT, and they operated without missionary prep classes, discussion outlines, handbooks, mission leaders, visual aids, or brochures. Yet the Church's very first convert-missionaries, armed with strong testimonies, Bible expertise, perhaps a Book of Mormon or two, and firsthand contact with Joseph Smith, managed by the end of 1830 to bring the Church, as the Lord promised, "out of the wilderness" (D&C 33:5).

Missionary work began even before the Church was organized. The first recorded, divine command to spread the gospel came in 1823 when Moroni instructed young Joseph to tell his father what he, Moroni, had taught the youth the night before. The two Josephs talked, and father believed son. During the next years, Joseph shared many of his heavenly lessons with his family, and they trusted his truthfulness.

At that point no public ministry was possible because young Joseph had neither authority nor full understanding. Until the gold plates were obtained, translated, and published, and until a formal Church was established, to what could he convert people? The six years following Moroni's first visit was a time for preparation, not preaching; a time for learning, not converting.

But while Joseph prepared, a rumor with her ten thousand tongues became the first missionary of the Restoration. Stories about Joseph and the gold plates were "noised abroad" quickly in the Palmyra area. If some local folk dug up the Hill Cumorah seeking other gold, most waited for further gossip about the mysterious Smiths. By divine design, more than by coincidence, many truth seekers passed through Palmyra to become religiously disturbed by the gold plates stories they heard. Proselyting would not wait, and like cracks in a dam about to burst, people interrupted Joseph's translation labors to hear about his heavenly visitations.

Joseph was the first missionary, although not in the sense of traveling far and wide to preach. At first only his family and a few friends were trusted with these sacred truths.

The Joseph Knight family, for whom Joseph worked near Colesville, New York, were among the first few he told. Joseph Knight Jr. recalled that in November 1826 Joseph "made known to my father and I, that he had seen a vision, that a personage had appeared to him and told him where there was a gold book of ancient date buried, and if he followed the directions of the Angel he could get it. We were told it in secret; I being the youngest son, my two elder brothers did not believe in such things; my father and I believed what he told us."[1]

While Joseph struggled to translate, his father visited him at Harmony in February 1829. By revelation the Lord taught Joseph Smith Sr. a theme repeated in numerous revelations: "The field is white already to harvest" (D&C 4:4). But the time for harvesting was not yet. Joseph's older brother Hyrum three months later was similarly told about the great harvest but warned to "wait a little longer, until you shall have my word, my rock, my church, and my gospel" (D&C 11:16).

Like Joseph, his family conversed about his doings cautiously. Young Oliver Cowdery, temporarily boarding with the Smiths in Manchester, learned from them about Joseph's mission. He wanted to doubt. He discussed the matter with his friend David Whitmer, then visiting Palmyra. Troubled, Oliver prayed about Joseph's claims one night "and the Lord manifested to him that they were true."[2] He soon sought out Joseph at Harmony, Pennsylvania, but stopped along the way at the Whitmers to tell David what he was doing. Following long discussions with Joseph, Oliver agreed to serve as his scribe while Joseph translated the Book of Mormon. Oliver later wrote letters to David—including recent lines from the translation—testifying of the work.

Both Joseph and Oliver eagerly awaited completion of the translation and wondered about the Lord's plan for them. When John the Baptist bestowed upon them the authority to baptize, on May 15, 1829 (D&C 13), a major new missionary step was taken, for now the entire world needed to be given the chance to receive proper baptism. Such a crusade still had to wait for the translating to be done, but henceforth visitors, such as Joseph's brother Samuel a few days later, not only received teachings but also baptism.

John Whitmer, converted by the testimonies of Oliver Cowdery and Joseph Smith Jr., allowed Joseph to work on translating the Book of Mormon while boarding free of charge at the Whitmer home in Fayette, New York. Courtesy Church Archives.

The Whitmers, convinced by Oliver's letters, invited Joseph and Oliver to their home at Fayette, where free board and room and transcribing help were provided, and interested investigators came to hear the gospel. At the Whitmers', the translation work was finished by August 1829. By that time, Hyrum Smith and three Whitmer brothers, David, John, and Peter, had requested and received baptism. Christian Whitmer copied some Book of Mormon teachings from Joseph's manuscript, and then his three baptized brothers used the copy to preach to nearby neighbors and relatives from August 1829 to April 1830. Perhaps the Whitmers thereby caused Joseph more interruptions, because during his Fayette stay he received "numerous inquirers." He and Oliver and the Whitmers "continued to bear testimony and give information as far as we had opportunity."[3]

Once the Book of Mormon printing project started, public interest in Joseph Smith increased. "There begins to be a great call for our books in this country," wrote Joseph from Harmony to Oliver, who was in Palmyra supervising the printing. "The minds of the people are very much excited when they find that there is a copyright obtained and there is really [a] book about to be printed." The E. B. Grandin print shop in Palmyra became a stopping place for the "curious and the serious." Local residents enjoyed informing visitors about this unusual excitement in their tiny town. And like a magnet, the printing project attracted earnest seekers of truth.[4]

One was Thomas B. Marsh of Boston, who visited nearby Lyonstown, New York. The lady of the house where he lodged asked if he knew about the "gold book." This being news to him, he asked so many questions she sent him to Palmyra. At Grandin's shop, Martin Harris talked with him, arranged for him to take proof sheets of the first sixteen pages of the Book of Mormon, and then escorted Thomas to the Smith home at Manchester. There, Oliver Cowdery spent part of two days telling him about Joseph's work. Thomas returned to Massachusetts "highly pleased with the information I had obtained concerning the new found book." He displayed the sixteen pages, shared his impressions, and converted his family. Later, when he learned that the Church was organized, he moved his family to Palmyra, and in September 1830 he was baptized and immediately called on a mission (D&C 31). Within five years Thomas Marsh became one of the first Twelve Apostles called in this dispensation.[5]

A few months after Thomas's 1829 visit, Solomon Chamberlain felt called by the Spirit to debark from his westbound canal boat and go to Palmyra. The family he lodged with talked of the "gold Bible," and the news shook him: "There was a power like electricity went from the top of my head to the end of my toes." He immediately cut across the fields for half a mile to reach the Smith home.

There he shared with the Smiths his own religious experiences. At age nineteen he had a vision of hell and another of three heavens. He fervently sought salvation, and prayer brought release. Another vision showed him "there was no people on the earth that was right," but that God shortly would raise up a church after the apostolic order. "If you are a visionary house," he pleaded, "I wish you would make known some of your discoveries for I think I can bear them." They did and he did. He felt instant testimony. He, too, obtained page proofs from Grandin's shop—sixty-four pages—which he took with him as he resumed his journey to Canada.

He then became an unbaptized missionary of Mormonism, preaching the Book of Mormon to many listeners on his seven-hundred- to eight-hundred-mile trip. He found no one who had heard of the "gold Bible," so he exhorted all to receive it when it was published.

He sold copies of the book as soon as it came off the press. He preached to groups of Methodists, including gatherings of ministers, who "utterly rejected me and the Book of Mormon." One leader condemned him by saying: "If it was of God, do you think he would send such a little upstart as you are round with it?" One group Solomon addressed included the brothers Brigham and Phineas Young. At a Baptist meeting a large group "received the work, but there was no one to baptize them." As soon as the Church was organized, Solomon went to Fayette, where Joseph baptized him. Solomon then established a branch of the Church in Lyons.[6]

In March 1830 the Book of Mormon was printed, and on April 6 the Church was formally organized. Both events produced a new, stepped-up phase in missionary work. Baptisms increased rapidly. On April 6 Joseph could not contain his extreme joy at seeing his own father accept baptism, along with many others. Succeeding Sundays saw more baptisms take place, and at least one local minister, Reverend Diedrich Willers of the Fayette German Reformed Church, became alarmed. On June 18—the Church was barely two months old—he penned a warning letter to minister colleagues in Pennsylvania. In it he summarized and criticized the Book of Mormon, which seemed to him to be the key to Mormon conversions. The book's effects, he noted, "already extend upon members of various Christian persuasions." He personally knew the converts named Whitmer because they once had belonged to his congregation. "For the past several Sundays many people of both sexes have been immersed by them, and so many during the week that their numbers in the region hereabouts may amount to at least 100 persons."[7] His estimate, which may be fairly accurate, indicates that vigorous missionary work had begun at last. No longer would proselyting depend upon visitors coming to inquire, although that trend continued, but now ordained priesthood holders were sent forth specifically to preach and baptize.

If Samuel H. Smith was told in April 1830 that he was "not as yet called to preach before the world" (D&C 23:4), that situation soon changed. Ordained an elder on June 9, he took summer trips into neighboring counties, alone or with his parents, to sell the Book of Mormon. His efforts seemed fruitless until he later learned that one copy he left with a Methodist minister had helped to convert Reverend John P. Greene and his wife, her brothers Phineas and Brigham Young, Fanny Young Murray, and the latter's daughter—who was married to Heber C. Kimball.

Phineas Young read the book twice, felt a conviction that it was true, preached it to his congregation, and then departed on a scheduled preaching trip among Canadian Methodists, at the invitation of his brother Joseph. On the way, he and Joseph Young stopped at Lyons to see their old friend Solomon Chamberlain. Now a Mormon convert, Solomon preached for two hours to the Youngs, and by the time Phineas reached Canada he felt he no longer could preach Methodism. So he talked instead of the Book of Mormon—another example of proselyting by an unbaptized convert.[8] He circulated his copy of the book among family members, including his brother Brigham. Subsequent missionary contacts brought the Youngs, Kimballs, and Greenes into the Church.

Joseph Smith Sr., a newly ordained priest, likewise used that summer to thrust his sickle into ripe fields—in this case by taking his fourteen-year-old son Don Carlos and traveling to St. Lawrence County to preach to his father's family. Asael Smith rejoiced over his son's message, and Asael's son John—brother of Joseph Sr.—converted, as did John's son George A. Smith, who later, as one of the Twelve, recalled the missionaries' visit:

> I had never seen them before, and I felt astonished at their sayings. Uncle Joseph and Don Carlos were anxious to get to Stockholm to see grandfather. Accordingly they started, and my father went to carry them. I and my mother spent the whole of Saturday, all day and Sunday night in reading the Book of Mormon.[9]

The father and son missionary team, while at Stockholm, also converted an elderly Baptist exhorter, Solomon Humphrey, who then journeyed to meet Joseph and was baptized.

This was a day of religious hunger, of Bible experts, of itinerant preachers. And when these types linked up with Mormonism, they became good missionaries. It was not unusual then "for a man to hear Mormonism preached one day, be baptized the next, be ordained an elder on the following day, and the day after that be out preaching Mormonism."[10] Parley P. Pratt's conversion was such a case.

Parley P. Pratt, a New Yorker lately of Ohio and a recent convert to Sidney Rigdon's brand of Campbellism, knew nothing of the "gold Bible." But as he journeyed east by canal, the Spirit prompted him to send his wife on ahead so he could stop to preach near Palmyra. A Baptist deacon told him about the Book of Mormon and let him read it. The book struck home so forcefully that he sought out the Smiths. Joseph was absent, but Hyrum taught Parley his first lessons about Mormonism. Parley then journeyed to Fayette and met Joseph. On September 1, 1830, Oliver Cowdery baptized, confirmed, and ordained Parley an elder, and Parley then preached to many local gatherings and baptized several. He rejoined his wife and relatives and converted his nineteen-year-old brother, Orson.[11]

Along with specific mission calls in late 1830 to men like Thomas Marsh, Ezra Thayer, Northrop Sweet, and Orson Pratt, Joseph by revelation called Oliver Cowdery to head up a special mission to the Lamanites (D&C 31, D&C 33, D&C 34). From 1823 to 1830 Joseph's foremost mission had been to prepare himself and to make the Book of Mormon available to the world. In July 1828 the Lord instructed him that the primary reason the plates had been preserved was so "the Lamanites might come to the knowledge of their fathers, and that they might know the promises of the Lord, and that they may believe the gospel and rely upon the merits of Jesus Christ" (D&C 3:20). Therefore, Oliver (D&C 28), Peter Whitmer Jr. (D&C 30), and then Parley P. Pratt and Ziba Peterson (D&C 32) were called in October 1830 to go to Missouri as special missionaries to the Lamanite nations.

Their knapsacks and satchels loaded with copies of the Book of Mormon, the quartet headed west. After a stop at the Cattaragus Indian reservation in western New York, they made a second proselyting stop at the door of Parley's former pastor, Reverend Sidney Rigdon, at Mentor, Ohio. Sidney listened, let them preach to his congregation, and two weeks later became a Latter-day Saint. His conversion was considered the most effective advertising received by the Church since its inception, and it triggered a chain reaction that resulted in 130 baptisms before the missionaries departed and hundreds of others later as the new Ohio converts themselves turned into missionaries.[12] On the Missouri frontier, however, government agents refused to allow Indian tribes to listen to the missionaries.

While the Lamanite missionaries worked in the west, new converts Sidney Rigdon and Edward Partridge traveled east in December, met Joseph Smith, and added their labors to the New York missionary work. Sidney, probably the most culturally eloquent speaker the young Church had, drew crowds in many important towns before he and Joseph journeyed to Kirtland in January.

Because of the work of these first missionaries, and others whom records do not identify, the six-month-old Church by December 1830 had about 190 members in New York and hundreds more in the Kirtland area. The white field was being harvested, and the Church stepped unhesitatingly into the role it has never since relinquished, that of a missionary Church committed to preaching the gospel to every nation, tongue, and people. While missionary methods have changed many times during the past 150 years, the basic reason for proselyting remains unchanged since the Lord first issued it in June 1829 for the benefit of the very first converts:

> Remember the worth of souls is great in the sight of God;
>
> For, behold the Lord your Redeemer suffered death in the flesh; wherefore he suffered the pain of all men, that all men might repent and come unto him.
>
> And he hath risen again from the dead, that he might bring all men unto him, on conditions of repentance.
>
> And how great is his joy in the soul that repenteth!
>
> Wherefore, you are called to cry repentance unto this people.
>
> And if it so be that you should labor all your days in crying repentance unto this people, and bring, save it be one soul unto me, how great shall be your joy with him in the kingdom of my Father!
>
> And now, if your joy will be great with one soul that you have brought unto me in the kingdom of my Father, how great will be your joy if you should bring many souls unto me! (D&C 18:10–16).

This article was originally published in Ensign 8 *(September 1978): 21–28.*

NOTES

1. Larry C. Porter, "A Study of the Origins of The Church of Jesus Christ of Latter-day Saints in the States of New York and Pennsylvania, 1816–1831" (PhD diss., Brigham Young University, 1971; Provo, UT: BYU Studies and Joseph Fielding Smith Institute for Latter-day Saint History, 2000), 184.

2. Joseph Smith Jr., *History of The Church of Jesus Christ of Latter-day Saints,* ed. B. H. Roberts, 2d ed., rev., 7 vols. (Salt Lake City: Deseret Book, 1971), 1:35 (hereafter cited as *History of the Church*).

3. S. George Ellsworth, "A History of Mormon Missions in the United States and Canada, 1830–1869" (PhD diss., University of California at Berkeley, 1941), 63–64; *History of the Church*, 1:51.

4. Richard Lloyd Anderson, "Gold Plates and Printer's Ink," *Ensign* 6 (September 1976): 75.

5. "History of Thos. Baldwin Marsh," *Deseret News*, March 24, 1858, 18.

6. "A Short Sketch of the Life of Solomon Chamberlain," photocopy of typescript, Church History Library, The Church of Jesus Christ of Latter-day Saints, Salt Lake City.

7. D. Michael Quinn, trans. and ed., "The First Months of Mormonism: A Contemporary View by Rev. Diedrich Willers," *New York History* 54 (1973): 331.

8. Ivan J. Barrett, *Joseph Smith and the Restoration* (Provo, UT: Brigham Young University Press, 1973), 144–45.

9. George A. Smith, in *Journal of Discourses*, 26 vols. (Liverpool: Latter-day Saints' Book Depot, 1855–86), 5:103.

10. Ellsworth, "A History of Mormon Missions," 38.

11. Parley P. Pratt, *Autobiography of Parley Parker Pratt* (Salt Lake City: Deseret Book, 1964), 36–46.

12. Porter, "Study of the Origins of the Church," 281–84; Journal History of the Church, October 1830, Church History Library, microfilm copy in Harold B. Lee Library, Brigham Young University, Provo, Utah.

Aaronic Priesthood

3 From Men to Boys
LDS Aaronic Priesthood Offices, 1829–1996

During Fast Sunday in a typical contemporary LDS ward, male deacons, ages twelve and thirteen, fan out through the ward's population, distributing and collecting blue fast-offering envelopes. At the chapel, ordained male teachers, ages fourteen and fifteen, put white or clear sacrament cups into thirty-six-holed trays, place them with empty bread trays and slices of unbroken bread on the sacrament table, and cover all with a fine white cloth. During the sacrament meeting, other teachers are posted at chapel doors as ushers, though they escort no one to seats. Priests, ages sixteen, seventeen, and eighteen, break the bread and then bless the bread and the water, reading the prayer from a printed card. Deacons carry first the bread trays, then the water trays, among the congregation according to a predetermined order. After the meeting, the teachers clear off the sacrament table, clean the trays, and put trays and tablecloths away. During the next four weeks, many of those same teachers and priests accompany adult men to the homes of members as junior companion home teachers.[1]

In the LDS Church today, teenage boys are ordained to the Aaronic Priesthood offices of deacon, teacher, and priest according to their ages. Adults holding these offices are either newly active after "stopping out" in one of these stages during adolescence or are newly baptized members. In contrast, nineteenth-century presiding authorities called adult males to the Aaronic Priesthood, allowing these offices to only a small number of youths.

This rare photograph of a sacrament meeting in the tabernacle in Ephraim, Utah, in the early 1870s shows three mature men officiating at the sacrament table. Courtesy Church Archives.

To document when, why, and how the three Aaronic Priesthood offices shifted from men to boys, gradually and sometimes informally, requires a detailed and somewhat complex analysis.[2] Bishops, although Aaronic Priesthood officers, are not included since they preside by Melchizedek Priesthood authority.

General Authorities directed the transformation; but none cited publicly (and available records do not record) any specific revelation or divine inspiration that prompted or confirmed the changes. Rather, the policy evolved gradually, punctuated by sudden spurts, in response to practical needs. Elder Bruce R. McConkie acknowledged that youths now receive priesthood because of "needs of the present day ministry," a practice that has been "confirmed by the inspiration of the Spirit" to those holding "the keys of the kingdom."[3] Still, the transitions were not always smooth nor free from ambiguities for leaders and members.

Without understanding these shifts in Aaronic Priesthood work, LDS leaders and historians cannot accurately interpret many early Church records, teachings, and events.[4] Historical awareness of priesthood offices and quorums is vital to understanding the role of the LDS male throughout history; priesthood callings and quorum membership have been men's primary participatory involvement and connection with Mormonism. Although all Mormon women currently "belong" to Relief Society, and all members belong, at various points, to Primary, Young Men's or Young Women's Mutual Improvement Association (MIA), Scouts (if male), or Sunday School classes, such involvements are not comparable to "holding" the priesthood. Priesthood is something the recipient has. It is a permanent and lifelong possession that exists even when the bearer lives where there are no wards or other Church units. Women do not "have" or "hold" the Relief Society.

To assess what it has meant to be a Mormon male in the sweep of LDS history and how the religion has defined and redefined masculinity will require examination of more than priesthood involvement. What participation and expectations, for instance, are or have been built into Primary, MIA, Religion Class, Scouting, and Sunday School, seminary, Institute, and missions over the years? This paper explores, but is not the definitive treatment of, the Aaronic Priesthood or its relation to and management by General Authorities, stake leaders, or Melchizedek Priesthood quorums. Nor does space allow us to explore deeply the gender and masculinity issues these priesthood developments reflect or influence.[5] Rather, I focus on the historical development of the offices of deacon, teacher, and priest as they have related to male maturity levels, and on how and why such functions have been altered and adapted over time.

The transformation of Aaronic Priesthood occurred in six stages, identifiable in hindsight but probably not fully understood by their participants.

1. 1829–46. Adult males were called to Aaronic Priesthood offices as Church needs required.

2. 1847–77. Men holding the Melchizedek Priesthood became "acting" deacons, teachers, and priests. Their primary work was that assigned by revelation to priests and teachers: to teach the Saints righteous principles in their homes and to administer the sacrament.

3. 1877–1908. Every youth between twelve and twenty was expected to receive at least one Aaronic Priesthood office, usually that of deacon, but Melchizedek Priesthood holders continued to "act" as home teachers[6] and to administer the sacrament.

4. 1908–22. Aaronic Priesthood work was redesigned for youth with offices linked to age, with routine advancement of the worthy and

active, with new duties designed for youth, including handling the sacrament, and with teachers and priests involved in ward teaching.

5. 1920s–50s. These new age-linked Aaronic Priesthood functions became firmly institutionalized.

6. 1960s–90s. As part of the Priesthood Correlation program, ward teaching became home teaching, a Melchizedek Priesthood quorum responsibility, with Aaronic Priesthood males assisting as junior companions.

Accompanying these six periods of priesthood realignment were five interrelated developments that influenced the transfer of Aaronic Priesthood offices from men to youths.

1. Introduction of the temple endowment for missionaries or bridegrooms where proximity to a temple permitted; since the endowment required ordination to the Melchizedek Priesthood, these men were unavailable for Aaronic Priesthood offices.

2. Concerns for young men unprepared for missions and other adult responsibilities in the Church.

3. Tracking all teenage boys through all three Aaronic Priesthood offices instead of selectively using some in only one or two offices.

4. Redefining priesthood family visits and watchcare as Melchizedek rather than Aaronic Priesthood responsibilities.

5. Providing youthful deacons, teachers, and priests with useful priesthood assignments fitted to their ability levels—tasks that in many cases require no priesthood authority to perform.

1829–46: AARONIC PRIESTHOOD FOR MATURE MALES

In May 1829, John the Baptist bestowed the Aaronic Priesthood on Joseph Smith and Oliver Cowdery, then both in their early twenties.[7] Compared to the Melchizedek or higher priesthood, this was the lesser priesthood. An 1830 revelation (D&C 20) assigns several weighty duties to priests, teachers, and deacons. Granted the "keys of the ministering of angels," Aaronic Priesthood bearers are to preach, teach, expound, exhort, baptize, and administer the sacrament; to visit members in their homes and exhort them to pray vocally and secretly and to fulfill family duties; to ordain other officers; and to conduct meetings whenever higher officers are absent.

Ordained teachers are to watch over the Church constantly; strengthen members; eliminate iniquity, hard feelings, lying, backbiting, and evil speaking; ensure that the Church holds regular meetings; and assure that members perform their duties. Ordained deacons are to assist the teachers, but no specific assignments are spelled out. Only mature persons can adequately perform most of these responsibilities; and Mormonism's first generation clearly recognized that mature males should take on the duties of being "standing ministers unto the church" (D&C 84:111).

Martin Harris became one of the Three Witnesses to the Book of Mormon and was a close friend of Joseph Smith Jr. Harris served in a variety of Church callings, such as deacon, missionary, and high councilor. Courtesy Church Archives.

The earliest mention of ordained deacons is in the *Painesville Telegraph* on October 25, 1831. The first priests were fifty-nine-year-old Joseph Smith Sr., forty-seven-year-old Martin Harris, and two thirty-year-olds, Hyrum Smith and Newell Knight. Among the first teachers were forty-nine-year-old Hezekiah Peck, thirty-two-year-old Christian Whitmer, thirty-year-old Hiram Page, and twenty-year-old William Smith. Titus Billings, one of the first deacons, was thirty-eight. During the Church's first decade, Aaronic Priesthood offices were conferred on a few selected youths including William F. Cahoon, ordained a priest at seventeen, Don Carlos Smith, ordained to "the priesthood at 14," and Erastus and James Snow, teachers at fifteen and seventeen respectively.[8] Such cases are few.

William F. Cahoon's youthful experience as a teacher visiting the Joseph Smith family is fairly well known, although some retellings place it in Nauvoo instead of in Kirtland, where it occurred about 1831. Cahoon, born in 1813, visited the Smiths as an eighteen-year-old priest:

Being young, only about seventeen years [eighteen] of age, I felt my weakness in visiting the Prophet and his family in the capacity of teacher. I almost felt like shrinking from duty. Finally I went to his door and knocked, and in a minute the Prophet came to the door. I stood there trembling, and said to him, "Brother Joseph, I have come to visit you in the capacity of a teacher, if it is convenient for you."

He said, "Brother William, come right in, I am glad to see you; sit down in that chair there and I will go and call my family in." They soon came in and took seats. He then said, "Brother William, I submit myself and family into your hands," and then took his seat.

"Now Brother William," said he, "ask all the questions you feel like."

By this time all my fears and trembling had ceased, and I said, "Brother Joseph, are you trying to live your religion?"

He answered, "Yes."

I then said, "Do you pray in your family?"

He said "yes."

"Do you teach your family the principles of the gospel?"

He replied, "Yes, I am trying to do it."

"Do you ask a blessing on your food?"

He answered, "Yes."

"Are you trying to live in peace and harmony with all your family?" He said that he was.

I then turned to Sister Emma, his wife, and said, "Sister Emma, are you trying to live your religion? Do you teach your children to obey their parents? Do you try to teach them to pray?" To all these questions she answered, "Yes, I am trying to do so."

I then turned to Joseph and said, "I am now through with my questions as a teacher; and now if you have any instructions to give, I shall be happy to receive them."

He said, "God bless you, Brother William; and if you are humble and faithful, you shall have power to settle all difficulties that may come before you in the capacity of a teacher."

I then left my parting blessing upon him and his family, as a teacher, and took my departure.[9]

Kirtland and Missouri Stakes, 1834–38

The Church's first two stakes, at Kirtland and in Missouri, had elders, high priests, and, after 1835, seventies—men holding what became termed the Melchizedek Priesthood.[10] But priests, teachers, and deacons handled congregational matters. (Wards did not exist until the Nauvoo period.[11]) In the mid-1830s, Joseph Smith sent word to Church officers in Missouri that "the Teachers and Deacons are the standing ministers of the Church, and in the absence of other officers, they will have great things required at their hands. They must strengthen the members; persuade such as are out of the way, to repent and meekly urge and persuade everyone to forgive each other all their trespasses, offences and sins."[12]

In 1834 and 1835, the Missouri teachers quorum tackled a variety of tasks that required adult abilities: two labored with a brother having a tobacco problem, one worked with a couple having domestic difficulties, two tried to settle a dispute about steers, one labored with a person "for lying and extortion," and one took a deacon along to "settle a quarrel" among three "housewives."[13]

In 1838 the Missouri stake's priesthood passed a resolution that "the teachers, assisted by the deacons, be considered the standing ministry to preside each over his respective branch." A contemporary analogy said elders "quarried the stone" and sent it to Zion, where Aaronic Priesthood bearers "polished" it. In February 1838 the Missouri high council recommended that each neighborhood "choose for themselves a teacher, who is skilled in the work of God, faithful in his ministry, full of the Holy Ghost, and a friend to Joseph Smith … to take the watch-care over them and preside, … who shall be assisted by the other teachers and deacons in the branch."[14]

Adult deacons assisted the priests and teachers and took care of places of worship, a traditional responsibility for deacons in Christian churches.[15] For example, Henry Norman, an LDS deacon in England, probably in the 1850s, "had not only to seat the people in the house, but Make the wine for the sacrament, from the grape, & had my house licensed for preaching."[16]

Outside stake jurisdictions, priests and teachers presided in some branches. When missionaries converted clusters of people, they usually ordained one or more to conduct local religious affairs. In April 1840 England had thirty-five elders, fifty-five priests, thirty-seven teachers, and ten deacons. In both stakes and missions, Church staffing needs determined how many priests, teachers, or deacons were ordained.[17] Stakes sometimes called presidencies for Aaronic Priesthood quorums; but except for Missouri's teachers quorum, before 1839 no full quorums of forty-eight priests, twenty-four teachers, and twelve deacons existed as described scripturally (D&C 107).

Plans drawn in 1833 for temples in Missouri and Kirtland reserved four rows for the presidencies of the "Aaronic Priesthood," meaning a bishopric, and of the priests, teachers, and deacons quorums.[18] Such honors were certainly intended for men, not boys.

Aaronic Priesthood Matters at Nauvoo, 1839–46

In Nauvoo, stake (but not ward) Aaronic Priesthood quorums were organized and reorganized between 1841 and 1846.[19] Priests and teachers sporadically made home visits. From January to June 1845, the priests, teachers, and some deacons met at least monthly to coordinate such visits. The twenty-one priests averaged twenty-nine in age, although four were teenagers between seventeen and nineteen. Two-thirds were newly ordained; their average age at ordination was twenty-eight, eight were English, and the average length of time in the Church was four years. None had held higher office.

In short, Aaronic Priesthood practices in Nauvoo differed little from 1830s practices in Kirtland and Missouri: adults and selected older teens received Melchizedek and Aaronic Priesthood offices according to Church staffing needs. This pattern endured in general outline for the founders of the Reorganized Church of Jesus Christ of Latter Day Saints, organized in 1860 among Joseph Smith's followers who disaffiliated from the Twelve.

But two seeds were planted at Nauvoo that influenced future Aaronic Priesthood functioning in the LDS Church: the introduction of the temple endowment, for which Melchizedek Priesthood was a prerequisite, and the development of wards. Within forty years, these local units would eliminate stake Aaronic Priesthood quorums and make numerical quotas irrelevant except for deacons. At Nauvoo, Church officials created wards as local governing units headed by a bishop. In Utah, each new settlement area was considered a potential stake and was given a stake/branch/settlement president. Next, each settlement received one bishop, then more as growth caused the creation of additional wards. A high council, then a patriarch, completed the stake's organization. Because wards were the local unit of governance after the 1840s, priests and teachers did not preside except in missions or in emergencies.

1846–77: MELCHIZEDEK PRIESTHOOD HOLDERS FILL AARONIC PRIESTHOOD OFFICES

During the Saints' exodus from Nauvoo, Aaronic Priesthood quorums dissolved. At Winter Quarters, the Twelve created twenty-two wards and assigned a bishop for each, continuing the Nauvoo model. In camps and on the trail west, here and there leaders called men temporarily to serve as acting teachers to handle the needs of the moment. Salt Lake Stake was created on October 3, 1847, nine weeks after the Saints' arrival in Salt Lake Valley. On February 14, 1849, nineteen wards were created for Great Salt Lake City. Simultaneously, Presiding Bishop Newel K. Whitney started organizing stake-wide quorums for priests, teachers, and deacons for the already ordained.[20]

Wards, Bishops, and a Corps of Teachers

By the early 1850s, wards were considered the main local unit and bishops were the chief local officers, a norm that has continued to the present,[21] yet most revelations relating to priesthood were given prior to this time. As a result, general or Presiding Bishops were designated as the presidency of the Aaronic Priesthood (D&C 107:87–88; 68:16–17). During the Brigham Young period, Presiding Bishop Newel K. Whitney and his successor, Edward Hunter, exercised that presidency primarily by directing bishops in ward meetings, tithing, ward properties, and charity.

Ward bishops called men and some youths to enter the stake-level deacons, teachers, and priests quorums, but their duties were carried out in the wards. Bishops Whitney and Hunter held regular biweekly bishops meetings to coordinate public works, tithes, resources, immigration and immigrants, the needy, and the Aaronic Priesthood.

During the pioneer era, home visits assumed a more standard form. The bishop assigned men to do priests' and teachers' duties: to visit ward members, check on spiritual well-being, canvass for contributions, settle disputes, and help the needy. Some teachers heard charges of wrongdoing and decided guilt or innocence; but bishops handled most of these cases. The teachers quorum, in other words, was usually viewed as a ready source of manpower for such responsibilities as administering the sacrament, helping the needy, or, most urgently, conducting the home visits. (Visits varied from weekly to quarterly—or were simply sporadic.) Stake quorum leaders and the Presiding Bishopric periodically spearheaded drives to "fill up the quorums."[22] The primary goal was to supply necessary workers, not to see that all worthy males held priesthood office.

Endowments and Recruiting among the Aaronic Priesthood

It was generally the order to confer the lesser priesthood on those who had not received the higher priesthood. The number of those eligible thus was not large because, by the 1850s, the Church required missionaries from Utah and men marrying in the temple or Endowment House to be Melchizedek Priesthood holders.

The endowment was selectively introduced by 1843 in Nauvoo, made widely available to worthy men and women in 1845–46, and performed on a massive scale just before the exodus.[23] When the Endowment House was completed in Salt Lake City in May 1855, the First Presidency strongly encouraged Saints to keep the house busy.[24] For example, in May 1856, Dry Creek (Lehi), American Fork, Pleasant Grove, and Provo were assigned to send twenty people each for endowments and Springville to send forty. In issuing these quotas, Heber C. Kimball, Endowment House director and counselor in the First Presidency, encouraged bishops to send "many of the young and sprightly persons, who are strict to obey their parents."[25]

Records of the Kaysville elders quorum for 1865 show that thirty-six of its first members were ordained elders as teenagers, most in the Endowment House. Fourteen-year-old Ephraim P. Ellison, for example, was endowed on March 24, 1865.[26] A sampling of Endowment House and St. George Temple endowment records for the 1870s shows that the average age for male endowments was twenty-two, that the most popular age was twenty-three, and that several were endowed at fourteen.[27] Thus, the endowment made it nearly impossible to find capable and active men in wards near temples who did not already hold Melchizedek Priesthood. "We have many times tried to fill up these quorums by those who have not received Melchizedek Priesthood," Presiding Bishop Edward Hunter complained, "but [they] have been almost immediately called out to receive their endowment, leaving vacancies."[28]

In reaction, beginning in the 1860s, some leaders worried that the endowment was being bestowed too freely. Thirteen years before the first Utah temple opened at St. George in 1877, Brigham Young commented that perhaps men should "receive the [endowment] ordinances pertaining to the Aaronic order of the Priesthood" before missions but "do something that will prove whether you will honor that Priesthood before you receive" the Melchizedek Priesthood.[29] Had splitting the endowment been implemented, Aaronic Priesthood quorums could then have included returned missionaries. However, it was apparently more a warning to be worthy than a serious proposal.

Another source of depletion was invitations from Melchizedek Priesthood quorums to join their units. No permission for ordination was required from bishops, stake presidents, or the quorums to which the men already belonged, and the higher status made such ordinations desirable. This recruiting also drained Aaronic Priesthood quorums.[30] Higher quorums also recruited the unordained, since Aaronic Priesthood was not a prerequisite.[31]

Edward Hunter as Presiding Bishop (and hence Aaronic Priesthood president) criticized "lesser priesthood men rushing to be ordained High Priests or Seventies." Brigham Young and his counselors echoed in 1877: "It has been a difficult thing to keep young men in the elders quorum or in any of the quorums of the lesser priesthood."[32] However, with no policy against it, future Apostles Francis M. Lyman and Rudger Clawson were ordained elders at sixteen, and Clarence Merrill was ordained a seventy in 1857 at the same age.[33] In short, Melchizedek Priesthood quorums absorbed capable LDS adult manpower like a sponge, leaving few to receive Aaronic Priesthood ordinations.

Early Solution: Acting Priests, Teachers, and Deacons

In 1849 as the Salt Lake wards were organized, Brigham Young articulated three principles of Aaronic Priesthood work to then-Presiding Bishop Newel K. Whitney. These principles shaped Aaronic Priesthood duties for the next three decades and beyond. First, priesthood home visits and watchcare were the Aaronic Priesthood's primary duty. Second, choose "the best High Priests, the most substantial men" to be acting teachers, he instructed, so that wards could be "perfectly visited." Melchizedek Priesthood includes and encompasses the Aaronic Priesthood, so Melchizedek Priesthood bearers have inherent authority to perform all Aaronic Priesthood duties, ordinances, and functions (D&C 107:10–12). Third, they should "take young men with them, that they might also have experience in teaching," thereby implementing the apprenticeship system already suggested (D&C 84:106–7).[34] No age guidelines were included.

Because those holding the Melchizedek Priesthood can act in all the offices of the Aaronic Priesthood if called upon, bishops and stake Aaronic Priesthood quorum presidencies called and set them apart as *acting* priests, teachers, and deacons.[35] As early as 1852, Whitney was telling bishops, "If there be no members of the lesser priesthood in the Wards to act as teachers, take High Priests or Seventies or any other wise man."[36] Similarly, First Presidency counselor Jedediah M. Grant told Fort Ephraim Saints that "it is a good plan for the Bishop to have plenty of Lesser priesthood, that is, the High Priests & Seventies ordained [set apart] to act in the office of teacher & visit at least every family once a week."[37] Here and there, some bishops ordained a few mature youths as teachers so that ordained teachers and priests served with acting teachers and priests.

Whitney's successor, Edward Hunter, often preached, "Select the best men for teachers" to his bishops.[38] Acting teachers or acting priests consequently became ward officers, second in importance only to bishoprics in terms of practical ward work, and were sustained as ward officers. Most bishops met regularly with their quorum of acting teachers to hear reports about members and to transmit announcements, policy changes, and appeals for labor or contributions. "There was more depending upon the lesser priesthood than the High Priests or Seventies or Elders," Bishop Hunter said.[39] He called the lesser priesthood the "regulars," not the reserves.[40] They were "the laborers," the "acting priesthood," the doers in the wards. "The greatest engine in the Church is the teachers," President Jedediah M. Grant asserted. "It was very seldom we were called to exercise the Higher Priesthood," another leader observed.[41] Ordained teachers and priests, Bishop Hunter taught, were the Lord's authorized "watchmen to guard against all manner of iniquity" ranging from intoxication to Sabbath breaking and parental neglect.

Throughout Brigham Young's presidency, Melchizedek Priesthood men handled almost all Aaronic Priesthood work in Utah, doing double duty by "acting in both priesthoods."[42] One elderly man was a seventy who served as an acting teacher in two wards, an acting priest in one, and in the presidency of the stake's deacons quorum.[43] Another man, an elder, was both an acting deacon and acting teacher.[44] Bishop Hunter often exhorted priesthood men to "magnify both priesthoods," and Apostle Matthias Cowley's statement, "I was an elder before I was a deacon," was easily understood during the pioneer period.[45]

Each ward's corps of acting teachers or block teachers was small, sometimes but a dozen men. In Salt Lake City's Thirteenth Ward, home to many General Authorities, "the bishopric and block teachers, about twenty men, shouldered the ward's leadership and performed its labors."[46]

The most important duty of acting teachers was home visits. A survey of minutes during the pioneer era shows that these teachers visited eight to twenty families monthly, quarterly, or randomly. Because many wards assigned two men per block, by the 1850s, the appellation of block teachers developed.

By ordination and revelation, priests and teachers were peacemakers. "There was a power to settle difficulties vouchsafed to the lesser priesthood," Bishop Hunter taught, "that no other officer or member of the Kingdom can accomplish." Courts could decide cases, but only priests and teachers could reconcile the embittered parties: "The order of the church is to call in the labors of the teachers & if they cannot reconcile the parties it cannot be done," he taught.[47] In many wards, the teachers not only monitored the members' behavior but heard charges of sinful behavior, investigated allegations, and determined whether repentance was satisfactory or whether disfellowshipment or excommunication should be imposed. In Manti, "the right way was to bring a case first before the teachers meeting."[48] A Kanab bishop in the 1870s instructed that "it was the teachers' right to investigate a case and decide upon it, & if it did not give satisfaction, they had the right to appeal."[49]

Acting teachers not only performed the revealed duties of priests and teachers (home visits, watchcare, and dispute resolution), but also collected fast offerings,[50] assisted the poor, and administered the sacrament. In addition to ward sacrament meetings, a general valleywide sacrament meeting was held Sunday afternoons at the tabernacle from 1849 until 1894.[51] During the 1850s, Bishop Hunter assigned wards to bring the bread, have water ready, and then administer the sacrament. Ward bishops delegated acting teachers to handle these jobs, since they, and not ordained priests, were already assigned this task in local wards.[52]

In short, Melchizedek Priesthood holders acting in Aaronic Priesthood offices during Brigham Young's presidency were a trusted and hardworking ward elite. But what was the impact of this policy on young men and boys?

Slight Use of Young Men and Boys, 1849–73

Ward and stake records for the early 1850s indicate that a small number of "young men" and "boys" continued to receive priesthood callings while the system of acting officials was growing up. In 1852 a Brother Fielding asked at a bishops' meeting, "Should we ordain young men and boys who are wild?" Apostle Erastus Snow "presumed Bishop Hunter would be guided by the spirit, and the ordination may make them the best of men."[53] Perhaps the youngest boys ever given LDS priesthood were George J. Hunt, ordained a priest at age nine in 1861, and Solomon W. Harris, baptized and ordained a deacon at age eight.[54] It was not unusual for men in their twenties to be called "boys," especially if they were single.[55] "Ordain our boys to the lesser priesthood," bishops heard in 1852, "that they may commence in the harness," while 1854 minutes recorded approval of "the youth being ordained to the lesser priesthood; they were now doing quite a good work." One ward reported that "the principle portion of the young men had been ordained to the lesser priesthood."[56]

In the nineteenth century, "there was no sequence of events that marked the progress of boys from childhood to manhood," historian Anthony Rotundo reported, "and there were no key ages at which all youngsters reached important milestones." "The ... transition from boyhood to manhood began in a boy's teens and lasted until his twenties or even thirties." When it had any name at all, this period "was called youth."[57]

However, by the mid-1850s, Church leaders expressed caution about ordaining unmarried men. In October 1856 general conference, President Young expressed disapproval of ordaining inexperienced "young men" as deacons:

> When you have got your Bishop, he needs assistants, and he ordains Counsellors, Priests, Teachers, and Deacons, and calls them to help him; and he wishes men of his own heart and hand to do this. Says he, "I dare not even call a man to be a Deacon, to assist me in my

calling, unless he has a family." It is not the business of an ignorant young man, of no experience in family matters, to inquire into
the circumstances of families, and know the wants of every person.
Some may want medicine and nourishment, and be looked after,
and it is not the business of boys to do this, but select a man who
has got a family to be a Deacon.[58]

Even allowing for Young's typical hyperbole, overstated to make a point,
he was apparently not denouncing younger apprentices but rather insisting that senior teachers and priests be mature and capable. What Aaronic
Priesthood ordinations Young's sons received, if any, are not known, but at
least ten of his seventeen sons who survived childhood received Melchizedek Priesthood ordinations and endowments between the ages of eleven
and seventeen, on average at 16.9 years.[59] Apostle Wilford Woodruff, when
called to a mission in 1849, ordained nine-year-old Wilford Jr. a priest "so
he could act in his father's absence to administer the Lord's supper to the
family." He reordained this son at age thirteen, for an unknown reason. At
sixteen, young Wilford was ordained to the Melchizedek Priesthood and
endowed.[60]

Priesthood as Part of Youth Improvement Efforts

Eliza R. Snow admitted that "no thought was bestowed upon [the] spiritual
culture" of Zion's first generation of children until parents realized that "the
spirit of the world had crept in among our young people." As a result, children "often manifested but little regard for religious exercises," and "young
men generally sent on a mission were extremely ignorant of the first principles of the Gospel."[61] Children's shortcomings stemmed in part from the
fact that most adults and almost all youth did not regularly attend sacrament
meetings, in good part because of tiny chapels. Sunday Schools flourished for
children in the 1870s, but the smallness of meetinghouses meant they were
not expected to attend sacrament meetings.[62] Salt Lake City's Ninth Ward
reported in 1870 that only 31 of its 181 families regularly attended Sunday services and that 97 (50 percent) were "perfectly indifferent."[63] Hardly churched
and often barely schooled, many young people had limited religious experience and understanding. And unquestionably, some behaved badly.

Forty-four percent of Utah's population by 1880 were fourteen or
under—and Zion had its share of misbehavers.[64] Complaints from Salt Lake

City, Provo, and St. George included generalizations ("the growth of wickedness among our young people,"[65] "rowdyism is rampant") and specifics: "crowds of uncouth boys loitering around the stores halloing in the streets, and breaking horses on the Sabbath"; country boys with "uncouth and ill manners in refusing one half the road on meeting teams"; boys' "efforts to destroy the benches and dirty all they could with their feet, using pencils on the walls and nails on the rails of the bannisters"; roughs harassing a mentally handicapped Swiss boy and "strip[ping] off his clothes"; swearing (a leader told some deacons to stop saying "by hell"); youths coming home at all hours of the night "intoxicated and using the vilest language"; deacons going outside to smoke as soon as their meeting was dismissed, and boys considering that "when they can smoke a pipe or cigar, or chew tobacco it is a sign of manliness," or drinking whiskey for the same reason, "a gang" spitting "tobacco juice on the floor" at lectures and choir practices, forming gangs ("Provo roughs and Salt Lake roughs"); and boys throwing stones to break windows or "each others heads."[66] Noting such misbehaviors, leaders, who valued these youth, felt the Church could do more to help them.[67]

The auxiliary organizations were created to prevent boys and girls from growing up unindoctrinated, untrained, and unappreciative of their religion—Sunday Schools in the 1860s, Mutual Improvement Associations for young women in 1869 and for young men in 1875, and children's Primaries in 1878.[68] Leaders also began a modest effort to call boys into priesthood activities during the mid-1870s. Salt Lake Stake President Angus M. Cannon wanted bishops "to draw the young men into positions in the Priesthood and thus an excellent experience, and, at the same time, preserve them from evil associations." He reported a "marked improvement" in his own sons after they were ordained.[69] Priesthood service, proponents argued, like involvement in the auxiliaries, would help keep boys from evil practices while inculcating skills to qualify them for adult church service.

However, a primary reason for ordaining the youth was that adult men were reluctant to serve in the Aaronic Priesthood offices. Brigham Young instructed Edward Hunter in fall 1873 that each stake should have "a full quorum of Priests, Teachers, and Deacons properly organized."[70] A few months later, Hunter lamented that "he had tried to have the quorums of the lesser priesthood filled up for over 15 years past" but that the goal was "not quite accomplished yet."[71] "Nobody wanted to be a Deacon" and some declined to "condescend" to be ordained to these lesser offices.[72] "It is a difficult task," one bishop lamented, "to find a sufficient quantity of efficient teachers. I have thought of calling upon some of the boys."[73] "It is very hard to get the older men to act as Teachers," another noted, "but the young men come forward and are willing to take their parts and therefore we have to appoint young men where older ones should be."[74] A third recruited boys as deacons but wanted "a man selected as President of the Chorum the same to have general charge of this meeting House."[75]

Some bishops, naturally, resisted the new trend. Samuel G. Ladd, president of Salt Lake Stake's priests quorum, asked bishops to fill his quorum with "good responsible men and not boys." Priests, he said, should be "experienced men."[76] Similarly, Ephraim's bishop, Canute Peterson, told his ward priesthood holders in 1874: "We might think that these quorums should be filled with young men, but the Kingdom of God had increased and there was evils and iniquities in the church, and it is the duty of the lesser priesthood to look after these things, and for this reason men of experience was called."[77]

Despite reluctance, however, the reversal of a twenty-five year trend had begun, and bishops handpicked young men to be ordained deacons in the ward or at stake deacons meetings. In 1874, "many of our young men were being ordained to the offices of the Lesser Priesthood" in Provo.[78] A small number of "boys" or "young brethren" in Salt Lake City began attending deacons meetings with the older, acting deacons.[79] Most of these young deacons were fourteen or older, although James Leach, president of Salt Lake Stake's deacons quorum and acting bishop of Salt Lake Second Ward, enthusiastically suggested: "Boys from 10 years of age and upwards should come and be ordained deacons; they can assist to clean up the house."[80] Two years later, he reported that in Salt Lake Valley some hundred "boys" recently had been ordained as deacons.[81]

In the mid-1870s, deacons prepared meetinghouses for meetings; ushered; hauled food, fuel, and goods to the needy; and helped with the sacrament—tasks not beyond a youth's ability to handle. At monthly meetings of the Salt Lake Stake deacons quorum, the young newly ordained deacons received much seasoned advice: clean the meetinghouse; dust the seats; polish the stove; carry in coal; light the fires; have the sacrament trays, table, and clothes clean and neat; usher people to their seats; help keep order during church services; and even clean the "back-houses"—apparently the outhouses.[82]

But young, ordained deacons did not replace acting deacons. In 1877, the year Brigham Young died, Elder Matthias Cowley queried, "If we were all to stay away (from Aaronic Priesthood quorum meetings) because we are Elders or Seventies, where would the teachers and deacons quorums be?"[83] In Salt Lake Stake "the teachers quorum was made up mostly of elders who owed their allegiance to the Higher Quorums," while its priests quorum "was mostly made up of men having higher ordinations."[84] In mid-year, the First Presidency matter-of-factly noted that "when deacons, teachers and priests have been wanted it has generally been the case that seventies and high priests have had to be taken to act in those offices."[85] Although Brigham Young died in August, he and his counselors had already taken the position that all boys needed at least some priesthood experience.

1877–1908: ALL BOYS TO RECEIVE SOME PRIESTHOOD

The Priesthood Reorganization of 1877

Five months before Brigham Young's death in August 1877, he dedicated the Church's first fully functioning temple (St. George) in April. The temple connected the Church's priesthood operations with the heavenly priesthood, and that connection inspired the First Presidency and Twelve to thoroughly restructure and revitalize Utah's stakes, wards, and quorums. In the three decades of Church growth in Utah, a number of makeshift arrangements had developed—Apostles serving as stake presidents, unordained bishops, nonfunctioning quorums, too-large stakes, aging local leaders, and too few wards.

On July 11, 1877, the First Presidency issued a momentous circular letter that became the Church government handbook of its day.[86] None of the Aaronic Priesthood policies were new: home visits were an Aaronic Priesthood responsibility, qualified adults should do it, and young men should assist. High priests, seventies, and elders, when called upon by bishops, "should be willing to act in the offices of the lesser priesthood until priests, teachers, and deacons of the necessary experience are found." Other instructions to the bishops reiterated that "all … grievances and disputes" should be "settled by the Lesser Priesthood." Consequently, the policy continued to be to call "good faithful men" who are "exemplary in their moral conduct to act as teachers."[87]

The 1877 epistle clearly assumed that Aaronic Priesthood holders would be adults when it warned that "if teachers, priests and bishops, or other officers, suffer iniquity to exist in the church ... without taking action against it, they become partakers of other men's sins and they are unworthy of their positions." In dependent branches too small to be wards, "the bishop, to whose ward it belongs, should appoint a priest to preside, if there is one; if there is not, a teacher can be appointed" or a high priest or seventy could "act for the time being in the capacity of a priest."[88]

What *was* new for the Aaronic Priesthood, however, was the First Presidency's restructuring of quorum affiliation by ward instead of by stake. In organizing quorums of forty-eight priests, twenty-four teachers, and twelve deacons, the First Presidency circular said, "If there should not be a sufficient number for a quorum in one Ward, then they should be taken from others contiguous to it and most convenient for communication and meetings." Stake Aaronic Priesthood quorums ceased to exist.[89]

But perhaps the most far-reaching new policy was this: "It would be excellent training for the young men if they had the opportunity of acting in the offices of the lesser priesthood" as an apprentice "companion" to an "experienced priest or teacher." Not only would they thereby obtain "very valuable experience" but they "would be likely to place a higher value upon" Melchizedek Priesthood in the future. This policy affirmed the idea then current that *every* boy should receive *some* priesthood office.

Alexander McRae, bishop of a Salt Lake City ward, had told a general deacons meeting that "all boys in this church should learn the duties of a deacon," while a stake priests quorum officer believed that "it is the right of every boy born in the priesthood as a legal heir to have a portion as soon as he is able to magnify it."[90]

Increased Ordination of Youths

Within a year, hundreds received the Aaronic Priesthood, usually becoming deacons, and the practice of ordaining boys became well established. A Cache Valley bishop in late 1877 felt pleased that "a source of strength had been opened up through the organization of the Aaronic Priesthood, the young men acquitting themselves creditably."[91] But ordination was not linked to any particular age. In Hooper and West Weber Wards, leaders ordained "all the boys above fourteen years."[92] "The duties of a deacon are so easy," a Tooele leader noted in 1881, "that a boy of 12 or 14 years can do the duties."[93] Nineteenth Ward in Salt Lake City, during the 1870s and 1880s, ordained boys as young as nine and as old as nineteen.[94] In 1887, Apostle Francis M. Lyman told *Contributor* readers that "all our young men of fifteen years and upward receive some degree of the Priesthood."[95] In 1888 when Grantsville Ward organized its Aaronic Priesthood, it ordained eighteen priests ages fifteen to twenty.[96] In 1896, Salt Lake Sixth Ward ordained four deacons who were twelve, thirteen, fourteen, and sixteen.[97]

But some bishops, adhering to quorum maximums in the Doctrine and Covenants, allowed only twelve deacons at a time, and many adolescent boys reached adulthood during the 1880s and 1890s without Aaronic Priesthood callings.[98] For example, Anson B. Call was ordained an elder in 1884 without ever holding an Aaronic Priesthood office because his brother, the bishop of their Bountiful ward, "did not know that they could have more than one quorum in a ward at a time." Call felt "very badly when I was not chosen as one of the twelve for the Deacons." In contrast, Tooele Ward in 1883 had six deacons quorums so that all the local boys could be ordained.[99]

Tooele leaders also believed that "it was just as necessary for the young men to be ordained Deacons, Teachers, and Priests, as it is for school children to study in the 1st, 2nd, and 3rd, readers, for we must start at the lower round of the ladder and work up step by step."[100] Such stepwise advancement through the ranks was not universally implemented. James E. Talmage was ordained a deacon, a teacher, and an elder, but not a priest.[101]

Deacons' Callings and Duties

Because the revelation assigned no specific duties to deacons, bishops assigned young deacons ordained after 1877 a wide variety of tasks. In 1879 the Salt Lake City Sixth Ward deacons were collecting fast offerings, supervised by the acting teachers.[102] Deacons cut firewood for the poor, delivered food, and continued to act as meetinghouse custodians. Henry W. Hawley, a deacon during the 1880s, complained that too much work was involved in cleaning and heating the meetinghouse, so he resigned not just from the assignment but from being a deacon![103] In 1896, Apostle Joseph F. Smith observed: "It is in our day very necessary at times to select wise, judicious, experienced and sober men to fill the office of deacon," meaning in part men capable of maintaining the larger chapels.[104] Many wards, however, began hiring custodians during the 1890s, and the practice was widespread after 1900.

During the 1870s and 1880s, a few wards started letting deacons pass the sacrament. In 1873 in Kanab Ward, the acting teachers blessed the sacrament and the deacons "pass[ed] it to the people." When a ward member objected, citing the Doctrine and Covenants requirement that priests "administer" the sacrament, Bishop Levi Stewart told him that Brigham Young said passing the sacrament was not administering it, so it would be "perfectly right" for deacons to pass the sacrament.[105] St. George deacons in 1877, and Fourteenth Ward deacons in Salt Lake City in 1883 were passing the sacrament.[106] At the general bishops' meetings in 1883, in response to a question about whether deacons had the right to "carry around the sacrament," Bishop William L. N. Allen advised the group that the stake high council had recently decided yes.[107] In 1886, Kanab Stake leaders allowed deacons to pass the sacrament vessels but only if they were "sedate, responsible persons."[108]

Churchwide, however, few deacons or priests administered the sacrament. Elders acting as priests, rather than the ordained priests, administered the sacrament in most wards because people believed that young men could not give proper dignity to the ordinance.[109]

Young Teachers and Priests

Although youthful deacons became fairly common, young teachers and priests did not. Teachers quorums continued to be filled primarily by adults, although some missions called on youths to make up manpower shortages.[110] An 1881 report from Payson, Utah, noted that "aged men were selected to act as Priests, and the best men they could get for Teachers." Such priest-teacher pairs "usually visited the ward."[111] In 1902, Apostle Rudger Clawson noted that ordained teachers were youths between fourteen to twenty—"not … quite qualified to go out and teach the families of the Saints" unaccompanied by older men; however, he noted, some wards had called priests as companions to the ward teachers.[112] LeGrand Richards, later Presiding Bishop, was a youthful ward teacher in Tooele, Utah, just after the turn of the century. He and his senior companion prayed before making their visits, both gave messages in the homes, and they offered to pray before leaving. One woman told him they were the first ward teachers who offered to pray with her and her children since she came to Zion.[113]

Priests, teachers, and deacons continued to be considered ward officers, sustained in ward conferences, through the early twentieth century.[114]

The natural confusion between ordained and acting teachers resulted in an official explanation in the *Improvement Era* in 1902:

> There are in every ward a number of brethren selected to be acting teachers, under the direction of the Bishopric. These are usually men holding the Melchizedek Priesthood, but called to act in the lesser or Aaronic Priesthood for visiting and teaching purposes. They are appointed as aids to the Bishop, and he or one of his counselors presides at their meetings.
>
> The teachers' quorum ... is another body entirely. It consists of twenty-four ordained teachers presided over by three of their own number. They do not hold the higher or Melchizedek Priesthood. They act in the capacity of teachers in the ward to which they belong when called to do so under the direction of the Bishopric.
>
> But the two bodies of teachers should not be confounded. The acting teachers selected by the bishopric as their aids do not form a quorum at all. They have no fixed number, or distinct ordination as teachers.[115]

Lowry Nelson was a junior ward teacher about 1906 in rural Ferron, Utah. "On horseback," they visited "families living on farms outside the village," usually monthly to find out if anyone was in need or ill. In these pre-telephone days, "a monthly checkup served a purpose."[116]

1908–22: DESIGNING A YOUTH-LEVEL PRIESTHOOD

For three decades after the 1877 reorganization, Aaronic Priesthood work was characterized by the dual recognition that it was a good thing to introduce boys early to quorum activity but that most of the ward's real work required adult men's involvement. Presiding Bishop William B. Preston succeeded Edward Hunter in 1884 but gave virtually no new instructions regarding Aaronic Priesthood work and stopped holding the general bishops meetings. They had become unnecessary because the monthly stake priesthood meetings implemented by the 1877 reorganization gave bishops regular contact with stake presidents through whom General Authorities funneled most instructions for the wards.[117]

Charles W. Nibley, who succeeded Preston in 1907, strongly advocated youthful ordination and systematic Aaronic Priesthood work as important training for future Melchizedek Priesthood holders. He was a key promoter of such during his bishopric service to 1925.

Two factors influenced a reappraisal of Aaronic Priesthood work: missionary demographics and a greater interest in youth that was sweeping the nation as part of the Progressive Movement. During most of the nineteenth century, Mormon missionaries were typically married men. In 1886–90, 18 percent of missionaries were single; however, by 1895–1900, the figure was 51 percent.[118] A major reason was economic: a growing number of married men were salaried employees with larger mortgages. Sunday Schools and the Young Men's Mutual Improvement Association (YMMIA), but not priesthood quorums, provided training in public speaking and gospel study. In 1912, Nibley argued that better training of priests would silence "the present complaint which we sometimes hear that young boys are sent upon missions who are not prepared, and even, sometimes, not worthy of the authority of the higher priesthood."[119]

Second, throughout America, "Progressivism" generated a climate of concern for the mental and moral health of youth, for preventing juvenile delinquency, and for providing recreational facilities and opportunities. Coupled with a second emphasis of Progressivism on reforming government, schools, and business, the time was ripe for upgrading and reorganizing Aaronic Priesthood work. Efficiency experts armed with scientific studies and psychological insights were showing organizations how they could more effectively budget, manage, monitor reports, communicate, and produce measurable results. In the spirit of the times, Church auxiliaries were adopting new teaching methods and activity programs that appealed to the youth and to adults, age-grouping their classes, and providing centralized direction.[120]

Recognizing that priesthood quorum work "had been neglected," that "a great many young men" were not involved, and that Sunday Schools and Mutuals "had been actually doing the work that the quorums should do," such as teaching and developing speaking skills, General Authorities decided in 1908 to try to upgrade priesthood work throughout the Church.[121]

In early 1908 a General Priesthood Committee on Outlines was called to generate lesson manuals for local priesthood quorums and to evaluate ward-level priesthood activity.[122] Rather than producing a manual or two and disbanding, the committee found itself involved in a broad range of priesthood policy matters and remained active until 1922. At first the committee consisted of two Apostles and the Presiding Bishopric but grew to nearly twenty, including members of the Sunday School, YMMIA, and Religion Class general boards. President Joseph F. Smith had requested at April 1908 general conference that boys be given "something to do that will make them interested in the work of the Lord." Responding with enthusiasm and creativity, the committee proposed the major reforms known as the "Priesthood Movement."[123]

Elements of Priesthood Reform

A major development was the committee's recommendation that each boy move systematically through the Aaronic Priesthood callings. They suggested fixed age groupings: deacons should be ordained at twelve, teachers at fifteen, priests at eighteen, and elders at twenty-one.[124] These groupings let the committee write age-specific lessons and gave quorums a social function.

Second, the General Priesthood Committee, struggling with the assignment of producing lesson materials for teachers, dealt with the problem that ordained (young) teachers were seldom assigned to be acting teachers.[125] The debate was a stimulating one. Committee member B. H. Roberts argued that ordained teachers and priests bore the scriptural responsibility for home visits and that others should not do it. Another member, Joseph B. Keeler, who was also president of Utah Stake, disagreed, asserting that

TABLE 1.

Changes in Age of Ordination, 1908–70

Year	Deacon	Teacher	Priest	Elder
1908	12	15	18	21
1925	12	15	17	20
1934	12	15	17	19
1953	12	15	17	20
1954	12	14	16	20
1960	12	14	16	19
1970	12	14	16	18

"until teachers and priests are qualified to do this work, it will be necessary to call in the elders, seventies, and high priests to do the teaching." Roberts responded: "When will the quorums ever do the work required of them if they are put aside and others appointed for their work?" Keeler answered that "even the brightest of young men lack experience and it would always be necessary to have older men go with them to assist them in this work."[126]

The committee's solution was to rename these visits "ward teaching" and to redefine the program according to two principles: (1) elders have a scriptural obligation to "watch over the church" much like Aaronic Priesthood mandates (D&C 20:42), and (2) ward teaching was a bishop-supervised task independent of a specific office. By 1912 the committee created and implemented a standardized, structured churchwide ward teaching system and published a series of monthly messages in the Church's magazine for adults, the *Improvement Era*.[127] One message explained: "Ward teaching is a calling, just as missionary work abroad is a calling," and "no quorum is solely responsible for it."[128]

Apostle David O. McKay explained the new ward teaching program at general conference in October 1912. His twelve suggestions became a blueprint for at least the next three decades. Most dealt with stake and ward supervision and reports. He acknowledged the Church's traditional practice by observing, "Ward teaching requires the most experienced men in the ward. High priests, seventies and elders should look upon it as one of the most important duties of their calling." However, he added, this ideal "does not prevent younger men, who hold the Aaronic Priesthood, from being employed also." Another suggestion, reaffirming the apprenticeship principle, was that "every young man holding the office of priest" should be "properly trained" by working with an older and experienced man.[129]

This new program worked well; percentages rose steadily during the next decade, from 31 percent in 1912 to 54 percent in 1914 and 64 percent in 1920. At an Aaronic Priesthood convention held in Salt Lake City on October 2, 1921, Salt Lake Stake reported that, of its 718 ward teachers, 280 priests and teachers had done ward teaching the month before.[130]

New Duties for Aaronic Priesthood Bearers

The October 1911 general conference heard a report that the deacons were in fair condition but that teachers and priests quorum were not functioning:

"The local authorities generally fail to grasp the dignity and importance of the calling of the teacher and priest, and the boys cannot help but feel, as far as quorum work is concerned, that the organization has broken down and that they are being held on a kind of waiting list until they are old enough to be ordained elders."[131] The report continued with revealing Churchwide statistics: "There are 9,300 Teachers, 20,255 Deacons. In sixty-seven wards not one ordained Teacher and in twenty-one not one Priest. In slightly over one-third of the wards there is only one-half of a quorum of teachers, and in only fifty wards is there half of a priests quorum or more.... We have failed to live up to the Lord's plan."

The committee saw that one solution would be new assignments geared to the age abilities of boys. About a year later, Bishop Nibley sent a circular letter to bishops outlining numerous tasks the priests could do.[132] The reaction was enthusiastic. By fall 1913, some 500 out of 715 wards had priests classes, and 258 wards had quorums of at least twenty-five priests.[133]

To similarly invigorate teachers quorums, a 1913 *Improvement Era* article urged the bishops to make teachers "active and useful" and provided a list of suggested activities.[134] A master list of youthful tasks in 1916 summarized what deacons, teachers, and priests were already doing in various wards:

> *Deacons:* Collect fast offerings, carry messages for bishops, pass sacrament, prepare fuel for widows and elderly, care for the poor, pass out notices, pump organ at meetings, maintain church property, care for church cemeteries, keep order in meetinghouses, maintain meetinghouse grounds, assist in primary work, assist in Religion class work, usher, do Boy Scout work, attend the doors at meetings, distribute special notices.
>
> *Teachers:* Assist in ward teaching, assist with sacrament, instruct Boy Scouts, take charge of meetings occasionally, speak and sing at meetings, collect ward funds, assist in renovating meetinghouses, cut wood for poor, sing in choir, be clerks in branches, serve as officers in the auxiliaries, notify priesthood quorums of meetings.
>
> *Priests:* Administer the sacrament, pass the sacrament, assist in ward teaching, be Sunday School officers or teachers, be Mutual officers or teachers, baptize, be ward choristers, carry messages for bishopric, hold cottage meetings [preaching the gospel in homes], assist the elders, do missionary work in the ward, read scriptures

The deacons of Richmond Ward in Utah in 1915 show that efforts to recruit more young men to priesthood ranks were largely successful in this area. Improvement Era 18 *(July 1915): 838.*

at ward meetings, supervise fast offering collecting, help bishop care for tithes, help bishop with wayward boys, take part in meetings, haul gravel and make cement walks around meetinghouses, help with teams to level public squares, help supervise ward amusements.[135]

A relative few of these activities were scripturally assigned: priests and teachers assisting with ward teaching, priests administering the sacrament, and priests baptizing. However, most of the other jobs on the long list are tasks that can be done by anyone in a ward, male or female, assigned to do them. (See "Assignments Not Requiring Priesthood Authority" below).

Although most of the pieces of the priesthood movement were in place by 1916, the General Priesthood Committee continued to add refinements and encouragement for another five years before it was released, the First Presidency deciding that the next adjustments would be made by "existing quorums" and auxiliary leaders.[136]

One young man who advanced through Aaronic Priesthood ranks during this period was Harold B. Lee, later Church President. His ordinations show that the announced ordination ages of twelve, fifteen, eighteen, and twenty were only recommendations: Lee became a deacon just before he turned eleven, a teacher the month before he turned fourteen, a priest two months before he became sixteen, and an elder four months before age nineteen.[137]

In mission areas, because of the lack of temples, adult men were sometimes ordained to only the Aaronic Priesthood. The 1878 and 1891 statistical reports for Europe show that close to 20 percent of LDS men held some priesthood office, roughly the same figure as in U.S. stakes. But in the United States, about 25 percent of all priesthood holders had Aaronic Priesthood, compared to 40–44 percent in Europe. In 1891, European priests outnumbered deacons by about two to one, the reverse of the stakes' 1:2 ratio. Melchizedek Priesthood bearers outnumbered Aaronic Priesthood bearers 3:1 in the stakes but only 3:2 in Europe. The Australia Mission had a policy from 1896 to 1928 that men did not receive the Melchizedek Priesthood until they had immigrated to Zion and were ready to make temple covenants. Branch officers presided by Aaronic Priesthood authority. When local members protested, demanding the Melchizedek Priesthood for branch leaders, the mission replaced them with missionaries. British Saints learned of the general priesthood reforms in 1908; but in early 1909, when European Mission President Charles W. Penrose discussed the duties of priests, teachers, and deacons, he obviously assumed that men held those offices. However, by the year's end, he instructed that Church ward teaching regulations be carried out among Saints "everywhere," provided that Melchizedek Priesthood holders "may be called to officiate in the duties" of the lesser priesthood, "and they can take with them either priests, teachers, or deacons if necessary or expedient."[138]

1920s–50s: INSTITUTIONALIZING THE YOUTH PRIESTHOOD

The next three decades were a time of implementation as old ways gave way slowly to the new. It took a generation of labor for the priesthood reforms to be widely accepted and in reasonable working order.

Leader Reluctance

A major obstacle was the reservations some leaders had about giving youth serious priesthood labors. In pre-1920s statements, President Joseph F.

Smith criticized "a disposition in the church to hurry boys in the priesthood" or to advance those who were not performing in the offices they held.[139] E. H. Anderson of the General Priesthood Committee advocated ordination no earlier than fifteen because "boys were too young at the age of twelve."[140] Bishop Nibley proposed that young men serve missions as priests, rather than as elders or seventies; a successful mission would prove competency and worthiness for Melchizedek Priesthood and the temple endowment. Nothing came of his idea; endowment as a prerequisite for preaching to the world and the need for Melchizedek Priesthood to confirm and to bless the sick were well accepted.[141]

President Joseph F. Smith wanted Aaronic Priesthood callings to become a training ground for young men as they prepared for greater responsibilities in the Melchizedek Priesthood. Courtesy Perry Special Collections.

In many wards, members accustomed to seeing dignified older men handle the sacrament felt uncomfortable when boys took over. In 1909 and 1910, after the reforms had begun, one committeeman canvassed many wards to discover that older men still most frequently administered the sacrament. A second reported widespread reluctance to let priests bless the sacrament, and an *Improvement Era* article on sacrament procedures talked about the *elder* passing the sacrament.[142] Salt Lake City's Thirty-third Ward found a compromise and assigned Joseph W. Damron Jr., in his late sixties, to "preside" at the sacrament table during the 1920s to "add dignity and sacredness to the sacrament service" as administered by two young priests.[143]

There was similar reluctance to let boys be ward teachers. In one of his last public addresses in 1919, President Joseph F. Smith referred to the home visits of acting priests and teachers.[144] In 1921 the Presiding Bishopric reported that boys were not being advanced beyond deacons in some wards because they "are not qualified to do the work" (home visiting) required by revelation.[145]

In 1922, Presiding Bishop Charles W. Nibley and his counselors spearheaded a "new effort" with "hearty" support from the First Presidency and Twelve to invigorate the "neglected" Aaronic Priesthood. The new program consisted of "advancement ... for faithful service." Before each ordination, boys were "given examinations" by bishops to determine their diligence. The ordained teacher "should be assigned districts in the ward where he will accompany and assist the visiting [ward] teachers" while priests "may be called upon to administer the sacrament." Bishops were urged to use teachers and priests as "youthful ward teachers." Hugh Cannon, president of Liberty Stake (Salt Lake City), early in the 1920s reported accompanying two boys not older than fourteen on home visits in the Third Ward. The boys gave prayers, led songs, and stuck strictly to the purpose of the visits, thus demonstrating to Cannon "what the Lord had in mind when he placed the responsibility upon the ordained teachers." In 1927, Cannon visited six families with a young and inexperienced priest who, after his initial nervousness, took part in the home presentations and reported that he enjoyed it.[146]

Reluctance to depend on young teachers was, however, based on simple realities; and in some ways, the best evidence came during the late 1920s and early 1930s when some local leaders tried to apply the revelations literally. "In many parts of the Church ordained teachers and priests are being encouraged to become ward teachers," the *Improvement Era* reported in 1932.[147] Two years later, it described how in Cache Stake, "members of the Melchizedek Priesthood quorums are called to assist only when there are no available teachers or priests," and encouraged similar efforts as scripturally correct.[148]

The Presiding Bishopric instructed, "We may think that [a teacher] cannot do much by way of [ward] teaching. He can at least learn how to teach."[149] David A. Smith, counselor in the Presiding Bishopric, urged that ordained teachers be assigned to ward teach active families.[150] However, in 1940, the Presiding Bishopric recognized that pairing boys as ward teachers was not very effective and that "people will feel better about it if an older and more experienced brother takes the lead."[151] The practice of calling "acting teachers" diminished and died during the 1940s, replaced by the successful boy-adult "ward teacher" team, even though the terminology lingered throughout the 1930s.[152]

The Aaronic Priesthood Correlation Plan

On June 4, 1925, Sylvester Q. Cannon became the Presiding Bishop. His efforts in behalf of the Aaronic Priesthood reinforced auxiliary changes and peaking concerns about youthful inactivity and reluctance to serve. Surveys in 1931 showed "large numbers of boys" inactive in priesthood quorums, Sunday Schools, or YMMIA.[153] Apostle Richard R. Lyman admitted that same year that "the boy problem … is tremendously difficult."[154] Proposed as early as 1928 was a plan designed to increase boys' Church activity through better coordination between auxiliaries and quorums.[155] This Aaronic Priesthood Correlation Plan coordinated the YLMIA, YMMIA, Scouting program, Sunday School, and seminary at general, stake, and ward committees with representation from all five groups.[156] Announced in connection with April 1931 general conference, this plan, the *Improvement Era* subsequently explained in enthusiastic terms, "marshalls a large proportion of the man-power of the Church behind a program of training for young men of the Church. It has been called 'the most important movement in connection with the Aaronic Priesthood since it was restored to the earth.'"[157] The plan urged that boys fill quotas of assignments each year, with the result that quorums began keeping more detailed records.[158]

Bishop LeGrand Richards Energizes Aaronic Priesthood

This plan was the predecessor of LeGrand Richards's thorough revitalization of Aaronic Priesthood work during the fourteen years (1938–52) he was Presiding Bishop. During his tenure, Aaronic Priesthood work focused enthusiastically on boys' activity and achievement. "The most important problem of the Church today is the training of members of the Aaronic Priesthood," the Presiding Bishopric pronounced in 1938. "What the leadership of the Melchizedek Priesthood will be in the future is determined by the training and development of the members of the Aaronic Priesthood today."[159] The Presiding Bishopric created an elaborate achievement program in which boy priesthood holders and their quorums earned awards based on activity, worthiness, and priesthood assignments filled.[160] They promoted Aaronic Priesthood outings, better ways to collect fast offerings, sensible sacrament systems, ward committees to keep boy and girl programs fired up, and efficient reporting systems for monitoring church attendance, ward teaching, and fast offering collection.

For five years they sent stake and ward priesthood workers a newsletter called *Progress of the Church,* which contained instructions about all facets of Aaronic Priesthood work, motivating examples of quorum successes, and statistical charts comparing wards' and stakes' activity patterns. At stake conferences, they trained ward Aaronic Priesthood leaders; during general conferences, they trained bishops. Elder Milton R. Hunter praised "the work that has been done under the direction of the Presiding Bishopric of the Church with the boys of the Aaronic Priesthood," calling it an "outstanding achievement."[161] So successful was the Presiding Bishopric's program for boys that they were put in charge of the girls' activity program from 1942 to 1950 and similarly pumped new life into it.[162]

During the 1940s and 1950s, the Church employed several new lesson manuals, activity programs, award systems, and leadership innovations to keep boys involved.[163] From this foundation, wards and stakes have continued to operate quorums for specific age groups and keep boys busy with clearly defined priesthood duties that have changed little since then.

1960s–90s: PRIESTHOOD CORRELATION

During the 1960s, Priesthood Correlation produced major restructurings of the Church's priesthood operations.[164] These changes impacted Aaronic Priesthood work in ways not relevant to this paper, except that the Presiding Bishopric's leadership responsibilities for the Church's Aaronic Priesthood youth were transferred to the Young Men's general presidency.

Ward teaching was reorganized as "home teaching" and defined as "much more" than ward teaching. In the new program, which went into operation in 1964, Melchizedek Priesthood quorum leaders, rather than bishops, became responsible for calling, receiving reports from, and supervising the home teachers. Every Melchizedek Priesthood bearer "has this responsibility imposed upon him as an incident to his accepting the priesthood."[165] Home teachers, unlike ward teachers, were assigned by quorums, not by bishoprics.

Marion G. Romney of the First Presidency explained the evolution from acting teacher to home teacher: "By some it has been thought that some of the directions in the revelations referred only to ordained teachers. It would seem, however, that the responsibility has been placed upon every bearer of the Melchizedek Priesthood, and the priests as well as the teachers." It is the elders' calling to "watch over the Church," while priests and teachers help them.[166]

"ADULT AARONICS" AFTER 1908

Although the age-linked quorum advancements solved many problems, they created a persistent problem when boys, who stopped out because of inactivity, tried to catch up. Deacons, not advanced because of inactivity, did not want to return to a quorum of much younger and smaller boys. Adult men who were still deacons, teachers, or priests were obvious misfits. In 1911, President Joseph F. Smith urged bishops not "to mix up the old men, with bad habits, with the young boys."[167] In 1917, the General Priesthood Committee recommended that adult Aaronic Priesthood bearers be grouped separately and have their own presiding officers, but little came of it.[168] In 1930, local leaders were instructed to have adult Aaronic Priesthood members meet with the elders quorums.[169]

However, in 1932 a Salt Lake ward started separate adult Aaronic Priesthood classes, and the idea spread. The separate Aaronic Priesthood program for adults recommended in 1917 was formally introduced and promoted churchwide during the 1930s.[170] In subsequent years, the terminology has changed to Senior Aaronics, Aaronic Priesthood Over Twenty-one, Aaronic Priesthood Adults, Adult Members of the Aaronic Priesthood, and, most recently, Prospective Elders. For decades, special reactivation programs have periodically been implemented for them. Since the 1970s, these men have attended elders quorums and have been encouraged to take reactivation lessons and temple preparedness classes.[171]

ASSIGNMENTS NOT REQUIRING PRIESTHOOD AUTHORITY

Since 1908, Church leaders have identified and assigned Aaronic Priesthood youths a variety of "useful things to do." Some assignments, like blessing the

sacrament, baptizing, and helping with ward teaching, are scripturally man-
dated. However, many assignments now associated with deacons, teachers,
and priests require no priesthood authority. Examples are ushering, playing
the piano in church, or carrying messages.

Even passing sacrament trays among the congregation requires no
priesthood authority. With or without priesthood, men, women, and children one by one pass the sacrament tray or cups to the next person down the
row. Recognizing this reality, President Heber J. Grant wrote to a mission
president in 1928 that there was "no rule in the Church" that only priesthood
bearers could carry the sacrament to the congregation after it was blessed.
While it was "custom" for priesthood men or boys to pass around the bread
and water, he said, "it would in no wise invalidate the ordinance" if some
"worthy young brethren lacking priesthood performed it in the absence of
ordained boys" and he had "no objection" if it were done.[172]

Women and custodians usually prepared the sacrament table, so it did
not appear on a list of priesthood duties until 1933.[173] Metal sacrament trays
needed to be polished, and fine white linen or lace tablecloths needed to be
laundered, starched, and pressed, traditionally the work of women. Women
also baked the sacrament bread in many wards. Kate Coreless of Salt Lake
City's Fourth Ward took care of the sacrament table for a quarter century
after 1906. She crocheted the cloth, polished the silver trays, baked and
sliced the bread, and set the sacrament table.[174]

As late as 1943, the Presiding Bishopric publicized for bishops the example of young women in one ward who "take care of washing and sterilizing
the sacrament sets after each service."[175] Annette Steeneck Huntington
recalled that during the 1930s in Emigration Stake, the "young girls in MIA
... filled the water cups in the kitchen and placed the bread on the trays. We
then prepared the Sacrament table with the cloth and trays on it. It was a
wonderful privilege I shall always remember."[176] When paper cups replaced
glass cups in sacrament trays during the 1940s,[177] "dishwashing" ceased and
so did female involvement with sacrament vessels. Although women still
launder and press the linen, beginning in 1950, the Presiding Bishopric
assigned teachers to prepare the sacrament table, specifically requesting
that this task not be delegated to LDS girls or their mothers. However, in
1955, the Presiding Bishopric told Church members that young women
"where desired" could be assigned care of the table linens and trays following meetings.[178]

Although deacons have been assigned by bishops to collect fast offerings since the mid-nineteenth century, no priesthood ordination is necessary. A 1943 Aaronic Priesthood handbook recommended but did not
require "that the gathering of fast offerings be assigned to the Deacons."[179]
When Bishop Oscar M. Oleson of Salt Lake's Twenty-fourth Ward lacked
deacons during World War II, he asked Beehive girls to canvass half of the
ward. "During the past two years they did not once fail to cover their entire
district," he reported. The *Church News* ran a laudatory article and group
photograph of the girls, adding, "Now with an increase of boys in the deacon's quorum the girls are, rather reluctantly, turning this job back to the
priesthood."[180]

Since the 1950s, fast offering collection gradually became an official duty
assigned to deacons. However, because a number of duties now assigned to
deacons, teachers, and priests do not require ordination, leaders have the
option at any time to add new assignments for each office to fill or to transfer or share existing ones with other groups.

ASSESSMENT OF THE TRANSFORMATION

During the past hundred and sixty years, the Church has pragmatically
adapted its priesthood offices to meet changing needs.[181] Practical experience suggests that 1830 instructions about deacon, teacher, and priest duties,
including quorum sizes, were intended to serve the new Church in its early
years. Modification was required as the Church developed stakes, wards,
bishops, myriads of Melchizedek Priesthood quorums, and thousands of
born-in-the-Church sons to train for adult service.

When did the Aaronic Priesthood become a boys' priesthood? A
simplistic answer is: during the period between 1877 and 1908. However,
both the question and the answer are misleading. If the question is about
offices, the answer is correct, but wrong if it is about *function.* Functionally,
the most important labor of the lesser priesthood labor has always been its
home visits, performed primarily by men who were either ordained or acting teachers and priests. Church practice in 1877, as articulated by Apostle
John Taylor, was that "Seventies, High Priests, etc. who were called to act as
teachers, but were not ordained to this office, they already having all necessary authority, would remain for the present, but would be changed as
soon as arrangements could be made and exclusive teachers would fill that

quorum."[182] The hope of finding enough "exclusive teachers" was surrendered by 1912. When ward teaching was introduced during the 1912 reforms, the primary responsibility for home visits was transferred, with scriptural justification, to Melchizedek Priesthood bearers, where it has remained ever since, although boy priests and teachers participate as junior companions.

More than a century ago, LDS boys were ordained to "learn how" to be deacons, teachers, and priests by working with experienced men. Today, the apprenticeship principle still operates.[183] That is, boys become apprentice deacons, teachers, and priests at ages twelve, fourteen, and sixteen. If they could reach their twenties and thirties without receiving Melchizedek Priesthood, then, as mature adults with years of priesthood experience behind them, they could capably execute all of the more demanding aspects of the work assigned them in Doctrine and Covenants 20. Instead, youths tackle those duties as apprentices and by adulthood receive the Melchizedek Priesthood and added (but not replacement) responsibilities.

After 1908, but particularly since the 1930s, the Aaronic Priesthood has been fully operational as a training, teaching, and service arm in which boys receive at least six years of training in speaking, home teaching, quorum brotherhood, instruction about priesthood theory and gospel teachings, service, loyalty to Church leadership, handling the sacrament, baptizing, ushering, home teaching, and collecting fast offerings. Bringing youths into priesthood service has benefited both them and local church operations. Bishop Hunter's era was characterized by hard-to-fill Aaronic Priesthood quorums when few youths received priesthood; in contrast, virtually every ward today has quorums to which almost all active teenage boys belong. Thousands of Aaronic Priesthood quorums, multitudes of junior home teachers, routine weekly administrations of the sacrament, and regular monthly collections of fast offerings are surface indicators that the Aaronic Priesthood program is working rather well.

But what are the surface indicators *not* measuring? How effective have the Aaronic Priesthood operations proven to be for the Church and for priesthood bearers themselves? How well has the preparatory, apprenticeship principle worked in practice? Is the priesthood accomplishing what generations of leaders have pushed hard to have it do? This paper has identified the changing course of Aaronic Priesthood history since 1829 and provided only overview assessments of cause and effect. However, in-depth evaluations of effectiveness of the various Aaronic Priesthood programs require further study. If and when such thorough assessments are made, my historical overviews suggest several basic research questions.

For example, have the massive numbers of quorum meetings, ordinations, the calling and training of leaders, assignments executed, lesson manuals, handbooks, and activity programs produced the expected numbers of well-trained, firmly converted adult priesthood bearers? What are the retention realities? How many deacons, for example, become priests, elders, missionaries, and church-active adults? If significant dropout patterns are occurring, what priesthood program revisions are needed? Are present age-groupings, drawn from U.S. school grades, still the best clusterings for the United States and the myriad of cultures around the world? How involved are eighteen- to twenty-one-year-olds in elders quorums? Would such young men benefit more from raising the deacon age to fourteen, teachers to sixteen, and priests to eighteen? As gender concerns increase, what are the gains and drawbacks for young men and young women caused by assigning priesthood bearers tasks (preparing and passing the sacrament, collecting fast offerings, and ushering) that require no priesthood authority but from which women are excluded because they lack priesthood? Do elders who have gone through Aaronic Priesthood programs show markedly superior gospel knowledge and presentation skills to those of sister missionaries who have no priesthood training? Or are seminaries and institutes preparing youths better for missionary service than priesthood quorums do? Does a larger percentage of priesthood-trained male returned missionaries stay active in the Church compared to female returned missionaries? How well is home teaching being done churchwide? Does the apprenticeship under senior companions produce effective home teachers when junior companions become adults? Are young men receiving meaningful apprenticeship training in terms of the revealed responsibilities to preach, teach, expound, exhort, settle disagreements, teach prayer, and challenge iniquity among members? Further study is needed to assess these matters meaningfully.

Because General Authorities have restructured Aaronic Priesthood work every twenty to thirty years (1849, 1877, 1908, 1928, and the 1960s) to meet changing realities and as inspiration dictates, we can expect further adjustments. International growth, new social demands, and new generations of young people no doubt will cause additional pragmatic reshapings of priesthood practices to better bless both the Church and those ordained to Aaronic Priesthood offices.

This article was originally published in Journal of Mormon History 22 *(Spring 1996): 80–136, and received a Mormon History Association "Best Article Award."*

NOTES

1. In addition to these duties, deacons may also carry messages for the bishops during meetings; priests may perform baptisms and help ordain teachers and deacons. Since 1986, women have been ordained to priesthood offices in the RLDS (now Community of Christ) faith but never in the Utah-based church; all references to priesthood holders in this article therefore refer to males.

2. Joseph Fielding Smith's superficial discussion uses a few nineteenth-century examples that illustrate the shift without explaining it in his *Answers to Gospel Questions,* 5 vols. (Salt Lake City: Deseret Book, 1958), 2:8–14. Fundamental but dated overviews of the Aaronic Priesthood since 1829 are Lee A. Palmer, *Aaronic Priesthood through the Centuries* (Salt Lake City: Deseret Book, 1964); Joseph B. Keeler, *The Lesser Priesthood and Notes on Church Government* (Salt Lake City: Deseret News Press, 1904); and John A. Widtsoe, *Priesthood and Church Government,* rev. ed. (Salt Lake City: Deseret Book, 1965).

3. Bruce R. McConkie, *Mormon Doctrine,* 2d ed. (Salt Lake City: Bookcraft, 1966), 183.

4. See also William G. Hartley, "Ordained and Acting Teachers in the Lesser Priesthood, 1851–1883," *BYU Studies* 16, no. 3 (1976): 375–98; "The Priesthood Reorganization of 1877: Brigham Young's Last Achievement," *BYU Studies* 20, no. 1 (1979): 3–36; and "The Priesthood Reform Movement: 1908–1922," *BYU Studies* 13, no. 2 (1973): 137–56.

5. A good introduction to male gender development in this country is E. Anthony Rotundo, *American Manhood: Transformations in Masculinity from the Revolution to the Modern Era* (New York: Basic Books, 1993).

6. "Home teacher" is the contemporary term used for paired male representatives of the bishop who visit ward members in their homes. Earlier names are "block teacher" and "ward teacher," each explained below.

7. See Smith's account in Joseph Smith Jr., *History of The Church of Jesus Christ of Latter-day Saints,* ed. B. H. Roberts, 7 vols. (Salt Lake City: Deseret Book, 1976): 1:39–42; Cowdery's account is in *Messenger and Advocate* 1 (October 1, 1834): 15. LDS Doctrine and Covenants section 13 contains a revelation related to this ordination. See also Doctrine and Covenants 20, 68, 84, and 107.

8. Gregory A. Prince, *Power from on High: Development of Mormon Priesthood* (Salt Lake City: Signature Books, 1995), 26. Three deacons were ordained before this date. Palmer, *Aaronic Priesthood through the Ages,* 373, 387; Andrew Jenson, *Latter-day Saint Biographical Encyclopedia: A Compilation of Biographical Sketches of Prominent Men and Women in The Church of Jesus Christ of Latter-day Saints,* 4 vols. (Salt Lake City: Andrew Jenson History, 1901–36; reprint, Salt Lake City: Western Epics, 1971), 1:103, 795; William G. Hartley, "Snow on Fire," *New Era* 14 (January 1984): 38–41 (Erastus Snow as a teenager); *History of the Church,* 4:393.

9. "Recollections of the Prophet Joseph Smith: Elder William Farrington Cahoon," *Juvenile Instructor* 27 (August 15, 1892): 492–93. William was born November 7, 1813, baptized on October 10, 1830, ordained a priest by Oliver Cowdery on October 28, 1831, and spent the next year visiting the churches around Kirtland, exhorting the Saints to faithfulness and obedience. He visited the Smiths between October 28, 1831, and November 19, 1832. William Farrington Cahoon, Autobiography, microfilm of holograph, Church History Library, The Church of Jesus Christ of Latter-day Saints, Salt Lake City; see also Jenson, *LDS Biographical Encyclopedia,* 1:687.

10. Fundamental to understanding priesthood developments during the 1830s is understanding what "high priesthood," "higher priesthood," and "Melchizedek Priesthood" meant to contemporaries. See Robert J. Woodford, "The Historical Development of the Doctrine and Covenants," 3 vols. (PhD diss., Brigham Young University, 1974); Gregory A. Prince, *Power from on High: The Development of Mormon Priesthood* (Salt Lake City: Signature Books, 1995); Richard L. Bushman, *Joseph Smith and the Beginnings of Mormonism* (Urbana: University of Illinois Press, 1984); William G. Hartley, "'Upon You My Fellow Servants': Restoration of the Priesthood," in *The Prophet Joseph: Essays on the Life and Mission of Joseph Smith,* edited by Susan Easton Black and Larry C. Porter (Salt Lake City: Deseret Book, 1988): 49–72; D. Michael Quinn, *The Mormon Hierarchy: Origins of Power* (Salt Lake City: Signature Books, 1994), chaps. 1 and 2; Larry C. Porter, "The Restoration of the Priesthood," *Religious Studies Center Newsletter* 9 (May 1995): 1–12; and James N. Baumgarten, "The Role and Function of the Seventies in Latter-day Saint Church History" (master's thesis, Brigham Young University, 1960).

11. William G. Hartley, "Nauvoo Stake, Priesthood Quorums, and the Church's First Wards," *BYU Studies* 32, nos. 1–2 (1991): 57–80.

12. Joseph Smith, Oliver Cowdery, William W. Phelps, and John Whitmer to John M. Burk [and officers and members in Liberty, Missouri], Journal History of the Church, June 1, 1835, 3, Church History Library, microfilm copy in Harold B. Lee Library, Brigham Young University, Provo, Utah.

13. Minutes of Teachers Quorum at Kirtland, Ohio; Far West, Missouri; Nauvoo, Illinois, December 25, 1834, and January 31, February 28, March 29, and May 30, 1835, Church History Library.

14. Donald Q. Cannon and Lyndon W. Cook, eds., *Far West Record: Minutes of the Church of Jesus Christ of Latter-day Saints, 1830–1844* (Salt Lake City: Deseret Book, 1983), February 24 and July 6, 1838.

15. According to William Smith, *Smith's Bible Dictionary* (Old Tappan, NJ: Fleming H. Revell, 1975): 139, it is commonly believed that deacons in first-century Christianity prepared the rooms in which disciples met.

16. Salt Lake Stake Deacons Quorum Minutes, 1873–77, May 26, 1877, Church History Library (hereafter cited as Salt Lake Deacons Minutes).

17. Robert L. Marrott, "History and Functions of the Aaronic Priesthood and the Offices of Priest, Teacher, and Deacon in the Church of Jesus Christ of Latter-day Saints, 1829–1844" (master's thesis, Brigham Young University, 1970); Heber C. Kimball, "From England," *Times and Seasons* 1 (June 1840): 120–21; Roger Launius, "A Survey of Priesthood Ordinations, 1830–1844," *Restoration Trail Forum* 9 (May 1983): 3–4, 6.

18. Lauritz G. Petersen, "The Kirtland Temple," *BYU Studies* 12, no. 4 (1972): 400–9.

19. "Report of the First Presidency," *Times and Seasons* 2 (April 15, 1841): 385; *History of the Church*, 4:312, 5:169; Nauvoo Aaronic Priesthood Minutes and Biographical Sketches, January 13, 1844, to June 15, 1845, microfilm, Church History Library.

20. B. H. Roberts, *A Comprehensive History of The Church of Jesus Christ of Latter-day Saints, Century One*, 6 vols. (Provo, UT: Corporation of the President, The Church of Jesus Christ of Latter-day Saints, 1965), 3:302–3; Brigham Young Manuscript History, February 16, 1849, Church History Library.

21. "The ward is the ultimate unit of the Church," asserted John A. Widtsoe, LDS Apostle and administrative expert, in his *Progress of the Church of Jesus Christ of Latter-day Saints* (Salt Lake City: Deseret Book, 1941), 149.

22. Hartley, "Ordained and Acting Teachers," and Hartley, "Edward Hunter, Pioneer Presiding Bishop," in *Supporting Saints*, ed. Donald Cannon and David Whittaker (Salt Lake City: Bookcraft, 1985), 275–304. Main sources for the Brigham Young period, all at the Church History Library, are the Bishops Meetings with the Presiding Bishopric, Minutes, 4 vols., 1849–84 (hereafter cited as Bishops Minutes); Salt Lake Stake Deacons Minutes; and Presiding Bishop's Office, Aaronic Priesthood Meeting Minutes, 1857–77 (hereafter cited as General Aaronic Minutes).

23. On December 10, 1845, in Nauvoo, the full endowment was administered. By February 7, 1846, more than 5,600 tithe-paying adults received their endowments. An estimated 15,000 to 20,000 Saints, including children, lived in and around Nauvoo. Thus one-third to one-fourth of all Mormons and perhaps 80 to 90 percent of LDS adults were endowed. James B. Allen and Glen M. Leonard, *The Story of the Latter-day Saints*, 2d ed. (Salt Lake City: Deseret Book, 1992), 224.

24. Andrew Jenson, "Endowment House," *Encyclopedic History of the Church of Jesus Christ of Latter-day Saints* (Salt Lake City: Deseret News Publishing, 1941), 230.

25. Heber C. Kimball, Letter to the Bishops of Utah, May 19, 1856, Journal History.

26. Kaysville Elders Quorum Minutes, 1865, microfilm, Church History Library; Ephraim P. Ellison, Daybook, May 5, 1929, photocopy in author's possession.

27. Endowment House Record, Endowments, 1870–72, 1878–79, and St. George Temple, Endowments, 1877–78, both on microfilm, Family History Library, The Church of Jesus Christ of Latter-day Saints, Salt Lake City.

28. Bishop Edward Hunter, Letter to Elder Orson Hyde, General Tithing Store Letterbooks, October 17, 1873, Church History Library.

29. Brigham Young, in *Journal of Discourses*, 26 vols. (Liverpool: Latter-day Saints' Book Depot, 1855–86), 10:309, June 11, 1864. George Q. Cannon, who served as a counselor to Brigham Young and was still in the First Presidency, made the same proposal in a sermon at Provo, Utah, on January 14, 1894; George Q. Cannon, "Blessings Not Appreciated," *Deseret Weekly*, March 10, 1894, 349.

30. Seventies then were Melchizedek Priesthood officers, seventy to a quorum, directed by the seven-man First Council of the Seventy. Thirty-three quorums were organized in Nauvoo, and eventually there were hundreds. Most nineteenth-century missionaries were ordained seventies, then joined a seventies quorum when they returned home. Naturally, moving about fragmented these quorums and they were reorganized as stake entities beginning in 1883. The First Quorum of the Seventy, reconstituted in 1976,

consisted of General Authorities and replaced the Assistants to the Twelve. A Second Quorum, also of General Authorities but called for five-year terms, was instituted in 1989. Neither quorum has seventy members. Stake seventies quorums were phased out in October 1986. For histories of stake-level quorums, see Baumgarten, "Role and Function of the Seventies," and S. Dilworth Young, "The Seventies: A Historical Perspective," *Ensign* 6 (July 1976): 14–21.

31. In 1838 the Kirtland elders quorum heard but disregarded an objection to ordaining three "because of their not passing through the Lesser Priesthood." (A fourth candidate was disallowed, not because of priesthood status but for unchristian conduct.) Lyndon W. Cook and Milton V. Backman Jr., eds., *Kirtland Elders' Quorum Record 1836–41* (Provo, UT: Grandin Book, 1985), 46–47.

32. Bishops Minutes, January 17, 1854; Circular of the First Presidency, July 11, 1877, in *Messages of the First Presidency of The Church of Jesus Christ of Latter-day Saints, 1833–1964,* comp. James R. Clark, 6 vols. (Salt Lake City: Bookcraft, 1965–75), 2:286.

33. David S. Hoopes and LeRoy Hoopes, *The Making of a Mormon Apostle: The Story of Rudger Clawson* (New York: Madison Books, 1990), 42; Joseph B. Keeler, *First Steps in Church Government* (Salt Lake City: Deseret News Press, 1906), vii–viii; "Clarance Merrill, Pioneer," in *Our Pioneer Heritage,* comp. Kate B. Carter, 20 vols. (Salt Lake City: Daughters of Utah Pioneers, 1958–77), 9:319–29.

34. Journal History, February 16, 1849.

35. Bishops Minutes, December 7, 1882. Bishop Adam Spiers labeled it a "provision made" to allow the higher priesthood to officiate in the lesser; see Salt Lake City Tenth Ward, Ward Teachers Report Meeting, 1874–80, November 6, 1874, Church History Library.

36. Bishops Minutes, November 30, 1851.

37. Meeting at Fort Ephraim, May 13, 1855, in Minutes of Meetings, Miscellaneous Conference Minutes, typescript, Church History Library.

38. Bishops Minutes, September 6, 1866; August 18, 1870; and April 20, 1880.

39. General Aaronic Minutes, January 7, 1860.

40. Bishops Minutes, July 29, 1877.

41. Meeting at Fort Ephraim, May 13, 1855; General Aaronic Minutes, March 6, 1875.

42. Bishops Minutes, May 26, 1861.

43. John Picknell, Salt Lake Deacons Minutes, December 14, 1875. When he died in 1878, he was considered "an old citizen of Utah." "Passing," Journal History, July 7, 1878.

44. Salt Lake Deacons Minutes, January 27, 1877.

45. General Aaronic Minutes, January 5, 1861; Salt Lake Deacons Minutes, May 26, 1877.

46. Ronald W. Walker, "'Going to Meeting' in Salt Lake City's Thirteenth Ward, 1849–1881: A Microanalysis," in *New Views of Mormon History: A Collection of Essays in Honor of Leonard J. Arrington,* ed. Davis Bitton and Maureen Ursenbach Beecher (Salt Lake City: University of Utah Press, 1987), 150.

47. General Aaronic Minutes, June 2, 1877; and April 6, 1867; Bishops Minutes, April 6, 1867; and June 2, 1877; see also minutes for May 28, 1868; and January 4, 1873.

48. Sanpete Stake, Aaronic Priesthood Minute Book, 1873–77, January 26, 1875, Church History Library. Also see the New Orleans Branch Minutes, 1849–50 entries, Church History Library.

49. Kanab Ward Teachers Report Minutes, 1872–81, May 6, 1877, Church History Library.

50. Salt Lake City Eighth Ward Historical Record Book B, 1856–75, January 7, 1857, Church History Library.

51. Tabernacle Sunday services continued into the mid-twentieth century, but the last time the sacrament was regularly administered was April 1, 1894. Clerk's commentary, Journal History, April 1, 1894, and "At the Tabernacle," Journal History, April 16, 1894, records that Charles W. Penrose, in the tabernacle service that day, announced that henceforth the sacrament would be provided only in ward sacrament meetings. The Journal History also records that, beginning on July 1, 1932, the six stakes in the Salt Lake Valley began to conduct the afternoon Tabernacle services in turn; on March 25, 1938, this duty was assigned to the Temple Square Mission.

52. Bishops Minutes, February 11, 1852; November 10, 1859; and July 30, 1863; Salt Lake City Sixth Ward Record Book, 1869–80, entries for 1877–78, Church History Library. Adam Speirs, acting bishop of Salt Lake City Tenth Ward, assigned his acting teachers to carry out the assignment at the tabernacle and sent his ward's ordained (not acting) deacons to go in the morning to supply the water. Salt Lake City Tenth Ward, Ward Teachers Report Meeting, 1874–80, May 22, 1874.

53. Bishops Minutes, January 31, 1854.

54. Smithfield (Utah) Ward, Record of Members, Church History Library.

55. Salt Lake Stake Deacons Minutes refers to younger deacons as "boys," "young brethren," "little boys," and "the young." The February 4, 1877, entry quotes a Brother Andrews as stating that "the boys as well as myself belong to the Elders' quorum." Mormon Battalion veterans were called the "Mormon Battalion boys," regardless of age, just as, two hundred years earlier, Ethan Allen had led his Green Mountain "boys" against Fort Ticonderoga. The custom of referring to groups of mature men as boys (as in "a night out with the boys") and groups of mature women as girls ("going to lunch with the girls") persisted until the Civil Rights and women's liberation movements of the 1960s and 1970s drew attention to some demeaning aspects of this cultural custom.

56. Bishops Minutes, January 31, 1854.

57. Rotundo, *American Manhood*, 53, 56. Nineteenth-century children moved through dependency, semidependency (longer than adolescence), and independence. These stages were marked by experiences and abilities, not age. See Joseph F. Kett, *Rite of Passage: Adolescence in America, 1790 to the Present* (New York: Basic Books, 1977); and Elliott West, *Growing Up with the Country: Childhood on the Far Western Frontier* (Albuquerque: University of New Mexico Press, 1989).

58. Brigham Young, in *Journal of Discourses*, 2:89, October 6, 1854.

59. These sons, with endowment year and age in parentheses, are Joseph Angell (1852, 17), John Willard (1855, 11), Brigham Heber (1862, 16), Oscar Brigham (1862, 16), Ernest Irving (1868, 17), Willard (1868, 16), Hyrum Smith (1868, 17), Arte de Christa (1869, 14), Joseph Don Carlos (1869, 14), and Feramorz Little (1874, 15). Young family groups sheets, Family History Library, The Church of Jesus Christ of Latter-day Saints, Salt Lake City; Journal History, December 28, 1868. Brigham Young ordained John Willard an Apostle on November 22, 1855, according to Dean C. Jessee, *Letters of Brigham Young to His Sons* (Salt Lake City: Deseret Book, 1974), 92, the date at which he was endowed, according to family group records, or on February 4, 1864, according to Lynn M. Hilton, *The Story of Salt Lake Stake* (Salt Lake City: Salt Lake Printing Co., 1972), 117.

60. Thomas G. Alexander, *Things in Heaven and Earth: The Life and Times of Wilford Wood-ruff, a Mormon Prophet* (Salt Lake City: Signature Books, 1991), 178.

61. Eliza R. Snow, as quoted in L. D. Alder, "R.S. Reports," *Woman's Exponent* 6 (Febru-ary 15, 1878): 138; "Sunday School Meeting at Logan City," *Juvenile Instructor* 7 (Sep-tember 28, 1872): 155; "Mutual Improvement," *Contributor* 1 (October 1879): 13; Sunday School Board Minutes, July 1, 1872, Church History Library.

62. An 1877 First Presidency message encouraged the attendance of children at sacrament meetings "where there are Meeting Houses sufficiently spacious to admit of children." Circular of the First Presidency, July 11, 1877, in Clark, *Messages of the First Presidency*, 2:289.

63. Bishops Minutes, September 1, 1870.

64. Davis Bitton, "Zion's Rowdies: Growing up on the Mormon Frontier," *Utah Historical Quarterly* 50 (Spring 1982): 182–95. The 1880 census statement is on p. 184.

65. Bishops Minutes, June 28, 1877.

66. "Sunday School Meeting at Logan City," 155; Salt Lake Deacons Minutes, April 14, 1874; Bishops Minutes, December 20, 1860; and January 15, 1874; St. George Stake Lesser Priesthood Minutes, January 27, 1877, Church History Library; Salt Lake Stake Deacons Quorum Minutes, March 7, April 13, and September 14, 1875; Kanab Ward Teachers Report Minutes, 1872–81, February 16, 1873, Church History Library; Provo Bishops Meetings, August 17, 1869; June 7, 1870; and February 28, 1871, Church History Library; General Aaronic Minutes, February 5, 1876; and November 2, 1867.

67. Examples of girls' misbehavior include complaints that they missed meetings, "retailed scandal," drank tea, liked new dances, read forbidden novels, wouldn't carry out class assignments, and dated Gentiles. Salt Lake City Seventeenth Ward Young Ladies Cooperative Retrenchment Society Minutes, 1870s, Church History Library; St. George Stake Lesser Priesthood Minutes, February 6, 1879.

68. See the following entries from *Encyclopedia of Mormonism*, ed. Daniel H. Ludlow, 4 vols. (New York: Macmillan, 1992): Naomi M. Shumway, "Primary," 3:1146; B. Lloyd Poel-man, "Sunday School," 3:1424–27; Charles E. Mitchner and Mark E. Hurst, "Young Men," 4:1613–14; Elaine Anderson Cannon, "Young Women," 4:1616–17. See also *Jubi-lee History of Latter-day Saints Sunday Schools, 1849–99* (Salt Lake City: Deseret Sunday School Union, 1900); Susa Young Gates, *History of the Young Ladies' Mutual Improve-ment Association* (Salt Lake City: YLMIA General Board, 1911); Clarissa A. Beesley, "The Young Women's Mutual Improvement Association," *Improvement Era* 38 (April 1935): 243, 264–65, 271; and Carol Cornwall Madsen and Susan Staker Oman, *Sisters and Little Saints: One Hundred Years of Primary* (Salt Lake City: Deseret Book, 1979).

69. Salt Lake Stake Historical Record, November 3, 1877, Church History Library.

70. Edward Hunter, Letter to Joseph A. Young, September 18, 1873, General Tithing Store Letterbooks, 1872–75, Church History Library; Bishops Minutes, January 13, 1874. Although quorums were stake entities, deacons, teachers, and priests acted in wards under the bishop's directions.

71. Bishops Minutes, January 15, 1874.

72. General Aaronic Minutes, February 3, 1877; and September 4, 1875; Salt Lake Stake, High Priests Quorum Minutes, July 28, 1877.

73. Salt Lake Deacons Minutes, January 27, 1875.

74. Salt Lake Deacons Minutes, January 27, 1877; General Aaronic Minutes, November 6, 1875.

75. Salt Lake City Tenth Ward, Teachers Report Meeting, 1874–80, August 28, 1874.

76. General Aaronic Minutes, January 2, 1875; and January 1, 1876.

77. Sanpete Stake, Aaronic Priesthood Minute Book, 1873–77, February 2, 1874, Church History Library.

78. General Aaronic Minutes, February 6, 1875.

79. Salt Lake Deacons Minutes, March 10 and June 9, 1874.

80. Salt Lake Deacons Minutes, August 5, 1873; and March 10, 1874.

81. Bishops Minutes, August 10, 1876.

82. One ward, complaining of the "difficulty of getting deacons to officiate in their callings … had to hire men" as custodians. General Aaronic Minutes, September 2, 1865. For a time, Salt Lake Thirteenth Ward deacons were "not in active service" as a family living in the meetinghouse cleaned it. Bishops Minutes, December 22, 1881.

83. Salt Lake Deacons Minutes, May 26, 1877.

84. General Aaronic Minutes, May 6 and July 1, 1876.

85. Circular of the First Presidency [Brigham Young, John Willard Young, and George Q. Cannon], July 11, 1877, in Clark, *Messages of the First Presidency*, 2:283.

86. Hartley, "Priesthood Reorganization of 1877"; Circular of First Presidency, July 11, 1877, in Clark, *Messages of the First Presidency*, 2:283–95.

87. Presiding Bishopric, Form Letter to New Bishops, copied into Bishops Minutes, July 10, 1877; Bishops Minutes, December 21, 1882.

88. When Tooele Stake was reorganized in 1877, two new dependent branches, each presided over by a priest who was obviously an adult, were created. Tooele Stake Historical Record and Manuscript History, 1887, Church History Library.

89. Sanpete Stake's Aaronic Priesthood Minute Book ends in 1877 as do the General Aaronic Minutes and Salt Lake Deacons Minutes.

90. Salt Lake Deacons Minutes, January 27, 1877.

91. Bishop Robert Daines of Hyde Park Ward in "Minutes of the Quarterly Conference of the Cache Valley Stake of Zion," Journal History, November 4, 1877.

92. Weber Stake, Hooper and West Weber Wards, Minutes, September 23, 1877, Church History Library.

93. Tooele Lesser Priesthood Book 2, February 25, 1881, Church History Library.

94. Palmer, *Aaronic Priesthood through the Ages*, 392.

95. Francis M. Lyman, "Comments of the Day," *Contributor* 8 (July 1887): 356.

96. Grantsville Lesser Priesthood Record, 1874–88, October 23, 1888, Church History Library.

97. Salt Lake City Nineteenth Ward, Lesser Priesthood Minutes, 1880–1906, October 16, 1896, Church History Library.

98. Keeler, *First Steps in Church Government*, i.

99. "Life Story of Anson B. Call," 1954, typescript copy, 1, photocopy in my possession; Tooele Lesser Priesthood Book 2, February 5, 1883.

100. Tooele Lesser Priesthood Book 2, January 28, 1884. Tooele Stake President Francis M. Lyman also used the ladder analogy. Tooele Lesser Priesthood Book 2, March 9, 1878.

101. *Priesthood Restoration Commemoration* (Salt Lake City: The Church of Jesus Christ of Latter-day Saints, 1977), 10.
102. Salt Lake City Sixth Ward Council Meeting Minutes, February 3, 1879; and August 24, 1896, Church History Library.
103. Henry W. Hawley, *The Life Story of Henry W. Hawley* (n.p., n.d.), 17; copy in Church History Library; General Aaronic Minutes, February 5, 1870. Payson Utah Priests Quorum Minute Book, 1876–85, November 1876, Church History Library, reports assignments to deacons to gather firewood and buy lantern oil for meetings. Salt Lake City Sixth Ward, Record Book October 1869 to April 1880, March 9, 1877, Church History Library, reports that the deacons cleaned, lit, and warmed the building.
104. Joseph F. Smith, "Important Questions Answered," *Contributor* 17 (May 1896): 472.
105. Kanab Ward Teachers Minutes, December 15, 1873; and January 14, 1874.
106. Southern Utah Mission, St. George Stake 1869–86, Lesser Priesthood Record Book A, February 24, 1877, Church History Library; Salt Lake City Fourteenth Ward, First Quorum of Deacons Minutes, 1878–1908, Church History Library, see 1883 and 1884 meetings.
107. Bishops Minutes, December 6, 1883.
108. Kanab Stake Historical Record, December 8, 1886, Church History Library.
109. "The Duties of a Priest," *Juvenile Instructor* 32 (November 15, 1897): 690.
110. Gary L. Phelps, "Home Teaching: Attempts by the Latter-day Saints to Establish an Effective Program during the Nineteenth Century" (master's thesis, Brigham Young University, 1975), 95; "Teachers and Their Duties," *Millennial Star* 42 (March 1880): 136.
111. Bishops Minutes, November 26, 1881.
112. Rudger Clawson, in *Seventy-third Semi-annual Conference of The Church of Jesus Christ of Latter-day Saints* (Salt Lake City: Church of Jesus Christ of Latter-day Saints, 1902), 50.
113. Lucile C. Tate, *LeGrand Richards, Beloved Apostle* (Salt Lake City: Bookcraft, 1982), 22.
114. Logan Fourth Ward, Cache Stake, Historical Record, December 13, 1896, Church History Library; see Salt Lake City Sixth Ward, Council Meeting Minutes, December 30, 1880. Union Ward in Salt Lake County had twenty-four acting teachers for nine hundred members; they were sustained immediately after the bishopric in ward conferences. Gordon Irving, "Patterns of Religious Participation in Union Ward, 1877–1920 (Case Study: Sacrament Meeting Participation, 1910)," 1985, typescript, 10, photocopy in author's possession.
115. "Three Questions Answered," editorial, *Deseret News*, November 20, 1902; copy in Journal History.
116. Lowry Nelson, *In the Direction of His Dreams: Memoirs* (New York: Philosophical Library, 1985), 116.
117. The Presiding Bishopric merits more studies but its records are not open to researchers. Available studies include Orson F. Whitney's sketches of Presiding Bishops Edward Partridge, Newel K. Whitney, Edward Hunter, and William B. Preston in "The Aaronic Priesthood," *Contributor* 6 (October/September 1884 to September 1885); Donald Gene Pace, "The LDS Presiding Bishopric, 1851–1888: An Administrative Study" (master's thesis, Brigham Young University, 1978); D. Brent Collette, "In Search of Zion: A Description of Early Mormon Millennial Utopianism as Revealed through the

Life of Edward Partridge" (master's thesis, Brigham Young University, 1977); Larry N. Poulsen, "The Life and Contributions of Newell Kimball Whitney" (master's thesis, Brigham Young University, 1966); Tate, *LeGrand Richards*; and Hartley, "Edward Hunter, Pioneer Presiding Bishop."

118. William E. Hughes, "A Profile of the Missionaries of The Church of Jesus Christ of Latter-day Saints, 1849–1900" (master's thesis, Brigham Young University, 1986), 56, 161.

119. See General Priesthood Committee on Outlines, Minutes, 1908–22, August 6, 1912, Church History Library (hereafter cited as General Priesthood Committee). Only four months earlier, B. H. Roberts of the First Council of the Seventy urged a reversal of "the custom of sending mainly young men into the mission field" and advocated that "at least sufficient older men be in the field to add dignity to the work." General Priesthood Committee, April 2, 1912.

120. Thomas G. Alexander deals with both the "priesthood movement" and "administrative modernization" during this period in his *Mormonism in Transition: A History of the Latter-day Saints, 1890–1930* (Urbana: University of Illinois Press, 1986), 93–115. See also James B. Allen and Glen M. Leonard, *Story of the Latter-day Saints*, 2d ed. (Salt Lake City: Deseret Book, 1992), 461–67.

121. General Priesthood Committee, June 16 and 23, 1908.

122. Hartley, "Priesthood Reform Movement." The name was changed in late 1909 to the First Presidency and Twelve's Standing Committee on Priesthood Work and, after 1915, the General Committee on Courses of Study for the Priesthood. For simplicity, I call all three the General Priesthood Committee.

123. Joseph F. Smith, "Opening Address," in *Seventy-eighth Annual Conference of The Church of Jesus Christ of Latter-day Saints* (Salt Lake City: The Church of Jesus Christ of Latter-day Saints, 1908), 6; General Priesthood Committee, October 15, 1908; May 16 and December 9, 1910; and November 7, 1911.

124. General Priesthood Committee, June 5, 1908.

125. "Report of the Committee on Priesthood Outlines," *Improvement Era* 16 (May 1913): 735.

126. General Priesthood Committee, July 7, 1908; and May 9, 1909.

127. Hartley, "Ordained and Acting Teachers," 395–98; Rex A. Andersen, "A Documentary History of the Lord's Way of Watching Over the Church by the Priesthood through the Ages" (master's thesis, Brigham Young University, 1974).

128. "Ward Teaching," *Improvement Era* 16 (November 1912): 79–80.

129. "Ward Teaching," 79–83. In a major conference address on the same topic four years later, McKay stressed: "There is no more important work in the Church [than ward teaching]." His talk circulated in pamphlet form for years. David O. McKay, in *Eighty-seventh Semi-annual Conference of The Church of Jesus Christ of Latter-day Saints* (Salt Lake City: The Church of Jesus Christ of Latter-day Saints, 1916), 57–61; reprinted as McKay, "Ward Teaching—an Important Calling," *Improvement Era* 55 (May 1952): 356.

130. Presiding Bishop's Office, Annual Reports, 1915, 1920, Church History Library; *Minutes of the Aaronic Priesthood Convention Held in the Assembly Hall, Friday, October 2, 1921* (n.p., n.d.), Church History Library. Vernon L. Israelsen, "Changes in the Numbers and the Priesthood Affiliation of the Men Used as Ward Teachers in the Church of Jesus

Christ of Latter-day Saints, 1920 to 1935" (master's thesis, BYU, 1937), 25, described it as a "substantial increase."

131. "Address to the Priesthood," *Improvement Era* 15 (May 1912): 657.

132. General Priesthood Committee, August 6, 1912, cited in "Report of the Committee on Priesthood Outlines," 734.

133. General Priesthood Committee, September 2, 1913; "Report of the Committee on Priesthood Outlines," 734–39; H. H. Blood, "The Ordained Teacher," *Improvement Era* 16 (April 1913): 647–48.

134. Blood, "Ordained Teacher," 642–48. Other suggestions followed in "Ward Teaching and Class Efficiency," *Improvement Era* 17 (November 1914): 36–37.

135. General Priesthood Committee, June 1, 1916; "Practical Duties for Members of the Lesser Priesthood," *Improvement Era* 19 (July 1916): 845.

136. General Priesthood Committee, December 8 and 13, 1922.

137. Brent L. Goates, *Harold B. Lee: Prophet and Seer* (Salt Lake City: Bookcraft, 1985), 45.

138. "Statistical Report of the European Mission to Dec. 31, 1878," *Millennial Star* 41 (February 17, 1879): 110–11; "Statistical Report of the European Mission, for the Year Ending December 31, 1891," *Millennial Star* 54 (February 8, 1892): 86–87; 1878 membership statistical chart for stakes in Hartley, "Priesthood Reorganization of 1877," 27; Marjorie Newton, *Southern Cross Saints: The Mormons in Australia* (Laie, HI: Institute for Polynesian Studies, 1991), 180–84; "Minutes of the Newcastle Conference," *Millennial Star* 71 (March 24, 1909): 179–80; "Profitable Work for the Priesthood," *Millennial Star* 71 (December 16, 1909): 792–93.

139. General Priesthood Committee, December 12, 1911.

140. General Priesthood Committee, April 2, 1912.

141. General Priesthood Committee, August 6, 1912.

142. General Priesthood Committee, December 10, 1909; "The Holy Sacrament," *Improvement Era* 13 (April 1910): 570–71.

143. Joseph Warren Damron Jr., Journal, 1891–1945, vol. 8 (life summary section), Church History Library. Damron was born in 1866.

144. Joseph F. Smith, in *Eighty-ninth Annual Conference of The Church of Jesus Christ of Latter-day Saints* (Salt Lake City: The Church of Jesus Christ of Latter-day Saints, 1919), 144.

145. Presiding Bishopric, Circular Letter, November 1921, Church History Library.

146. See *Improvement Era*: "Greater Activity Urged in the Priesthood Quorums," 25 (December 1921): 174; "The Aaronic Priesthood to Receive Special Attention," 175; "The Aaronic Priesthood: Preparation, Ordination, and the Training of Young Men," (January 1922): 268–72 and (February 1922): 366–69; "Youthful Ward Teachers," 28 (June 1925): 785–86; "Aaronic Priesthood Standards," 29 (December 1925): 203; "A Message from the Presiding Bishopric," 28 (March 1926): 506–7; and "Ward Teaching," 32 (June 1929): 692–93.

147. "An Ordained Teacher Functions in His Calling," *Improvement Era* 35 (March 1932): 302.

148. "Melchizedek Priesthood Ward Teaching," *Improvement Era* 37 (June 1934): 364 and (April 1934): 229; "Ward Teaching by Aaronic Priesthood," *Improvement Era* 37 (January 1934): 43.

149. "The Aaronic Priesthood Correlation Plan in Operation," *Improvement Era* 35 (April 1932): 356.
150. David A. Smith, "Ward Teaching by Ordained Teachers," *Improvement Era* 37 (January 1934): 42.
151. "Ward Teaching," *Improvement Era* 43 (December 1940): 748.
152. According to the *Priesthood Manual: A Handbook for the Quorums of the Melchizedek Priesthood* (Salt Lake City: Deseret Book, 1933), 17: "In many wards there are not enough men to fill up the quorums of the Lesser Priesthood, and members of the High Priesthood are frequently found officiating as teachers." John A. Widtsoe, *Priesthood and Church Government in The Church of Jesus Christ of Latter-day Saints* (Salt Lake City: Deseret Book, 1939): 170 (unchanged in the 1954 revised edition, p. 170) stated: "There are a number of men selected in every ward to be acting Teachers. . . . These usually hold the office of either Elder, Seventy or High Priest." In the mid-1930s, Apostle Joseph Fielding Smith, recognized as the Church's doctrinal expert, wrote to a master's candidate: "I know of no work more important than that which has been assigned to the Ward Teacher and Ward Priest. . . . We have throughout the Church quite generally combined these two offices and placed the responsibilities of the Teachers and Priests upon the brethren we call Ward Teachers." Joseph Fielding Smith to Vernon I. Israelsen, July 14, 1935, in Israelsen, "Changes in the Numbers," 22–23.
153. "Church-wide Correlation Campaign in Youth Activity Starts on Oct. 22," *Church News,* published by *Deseret News,* October 17, 1931, 1.
154. "Church-wide Plan Announced for Correlation of Work among Youth," *Church News,* April 18, 1931, 6, 8.
155. Jerry "J" Rose, "The Correlation Program of The Church of Jesus Christ of Latter-day Saints during the Twentieth Century" (master's thesis, Brigham Young University, 1973), chap. 4, "Aaronic Priesthood Correlation."
156. Richard O. Cowan, "The Priesthood-Auxiliary Movement, 1928–1938," *BYU Studies* 19, no. 1 (1978): 114.
157. "Aaronic Priesthood Correlation Plan," *Improvement Era* 35 (February 1932): 232–33; Minutes of the Aaronic Priesthood Convention, April 4, 1931, 3, Church History Library.
158. "The New Priesthood Movement," *Improvement Era* 34 (June 1931): 479; "New Credit Plan Offered Boys in Priesthood Work," *Church News,* October 17, 1931, 3; "Assignments for Ordained Teachers," *Improvement Era* 36 (December 1933): 868; "Aaronic Priesthood Three-Point Campaign to Start January 1," *Improvement Era* 37 (November 1934): 679.
159. Presiding Bishopric, "Training of Youth Most Important," *Progress of the Church* 1 (July 1938): 1.
160. "Aaronic Priesthood Extension Plan Expands Correlation Plan," *Progress of the Church* 1 (September 1938): 1.
161. Milton R. Hunter, "Unparalleled Growth Marks All Phases of Church Endeavor," *Church News,* December 12, 1951, 13.
162. Tate, *LeGrand Richards,* 210; Cannon, "Young Women," 4:1618; *Deseret News 1985 Church Almanac* (Salt Lake City: Deseret News, 1984), 93, 96; "Bishop Richards Returns Girls' Program to MIA," *Church News,* June 25, 1950, 6. The Presiding Bishopric's monthly

Progress of the Church newsletter ceased in August 1943 and was replaced by a Presiding Bishopric page in the *Church News*.

163. For one example of the awards program, much refined from earlier ones, see "New Aaronic Priesthood Award Program Nearing the End of the First Year," *Improvement Era* 55 (October 1952): 756–57.

164. Allen and Leonard, *Story of the Latter-day Saints*, 596–98; Andersen, "Documentary History of the Lord's Way of Watching Over the Church"; Rose, "Correlation Program of the Church"; and explanatory talks by Elders Harold B. Lee, Gordon B. Hinckley, Richard L. Evans, and Marion G. Romney in *One Hundred Thirty-second Semi-annual Conference of The Church of Jesus Christ of Latter-day Saints* (Salt Lake City: The Church of Jesus Christ of Latter-day Saints, 1962), 71–83.

165. Marion G. Romney, "What Is Home Teaching?" talk delivered at Mission Presidents Seminar, Salt Lake City, June 1968, Church History Library.

166. Marion G. Romney, in *One Hundred Thirty-second Annual Conference of The Church of Jesus Christ of Latter-day Saints* (Salt Lake City: The Church of Jesus Christ of Latter-day Saints, 1962), 78–79.

167. General Priesthood Committee, December 12, 1911.

168. General Priesthood Committee, April 5 and November 1, 1917.

169. "Older Inactive Men Bearing the Aaronic Priesthood," *Improvement Era* 33 (October 1930): 817. See also "Work with Older, Inactive Members of the Aaronic Priesthood," *Improvement Era* 34 (July 1931): 546.

170. "Fifty Years Ago, Adult Aaronic Program Started," *Church News*, September 18, 1982, 10, 14; *Deseret News 1985 Church Almanac*, 93.

171. "Designation 'Adult Aaronic Priesthood' Changed," *Progress of the Church* 5 (September 1942): 36; The Church of Jesus Christ of Latter-day Saints, *General Handbook of Instructions* (Salt Lake City: The Church of Jesus Christ of Latter-day Saints, 1985), section 2, 4.

172. Heber J. Grant, Letter to Henry H. Rolapp, June 28, 1928, Heber J. Grant Letterbook, microfilm, Church History Library.

173. "Assignments for Ordained Teachers," *Improvement Era* 36 (December 1933): 868. Lists in 1908, 1925, and 1930 did not include sacrament preparation; see "Aaronic Priesthood Suggestions," *Improvement Era* 33 (March 1930): 349; "Assignments for Ordained Teachers," *Improvement Era* 36 (December 1933): 868; "Method of Administering the Sacrament," *Improvement Era* 26 (August 1923): 938, describes how a custodian prepared the table and filled the cups immediately before the service.

174. William G. Hartley, *Kindred Saints: The Mormon Immigrant Heritage of Alvin and Kathryne Christenson* (Salt Lake City: Eden Hill, 1982), 183.

175. "Youth in the Sacrament Meeting," *Progress of the Church* 6 (May 1943): 19.

176. Lucile G. Williams, comp., *Historical Highlights of the Twenty-first and North Twenty-first Wards, Emigration Stake* (Salt Lake City: n.p., 1971), 220.

177. The Presiding Bishopric urged: "Wards using glass cups are requested not to replace broken cups with glass, but instead to order the paper cups. It is our desire that as rapidly as possible paper cups shall be in use in all wards." "Paper Cups for Sacrament Service," *Progress of the Church* 3 (August 1940): 13.

178. "Teachers to Prepare Sacrament Table," *Church News,* April 2, 1950, 11; "Teachers Not to Assist Priests at Sacrament Table," *Improvement Era* 53 (December 1950): 1038; Presiding Bishopric, "Suggestions for Aaronic Priesthood Bearers Officiating in the Sacrament Service," *Improvement Era* 58 (June 1955): 466.

179. *Aaronic Priesthood Handbook* (Salt Lake City: Presiding Bishopric, July 1, 1943), 63.

180. "Girls 'Pinch-Hit' for Deacons," *Church News,* April 21, 1945, 5. Relief Society visiting teachers regularly collected items and money for charitable purposes from 1842 until 1944. "Collections by Relief Society Teachers Discontinued," *Church News,* August 19, 1944, 3.

181. Redeployments of priesthood offices and functions include the reduced role of the Presiding Patriarch, the home-or-abroad work of the Quorum of the Twelve, the temporary "office" of Assistant to the Twelve, the use of ordained seventies in missionary work, the changing tasks performed by the First Council of the Seventy and the First and Second Quorums of the Seventy, the temporary use of traveling Presiding Bishops, the introduction of administrative offices between the general and the stake levels (regional representatives, area presidents, and now area authorities), shortened terms of service for stake presidents and ward bishops, and the assignment of many duties to high councils besides disciplinary councils.

182. Salt Lake City Sixth Ward, Council Meeting Minutes, June 12, 1877, Church History Library.

183. "Aaronic Priesthood Messages," *Improvement Era* 32 (October 1929): 1041; "Training of Young Men Insures Effective Ward Teaching Corps," *Church News,* November 25, 1961, 10.

4 Ordained and Acting Teachers in the Lesser Priesthood, 1851–1883

If today's Latter-day Saint expects that Aaronic Priesthood work a century ago was basically the same as it is today, he or she will be surprised and confused when he or she examines records of the lesser priesthood in the Church's first decades in Utah. Those fading documents, often rich in detail, produce as many hard questions about priesthood operations as they do ready answers. In the records, for example, are references to deacons with temple endowments, and teachers quorums composed of adults, not boys. We read of bishops preventing priests from the local stake priests quorum from working in their wards, and of a set of deacons, teachers, and priests presidencies sustained at general conferences as "General Authorities." Teachers quorums served as courts to try recalcitrant individuals for their Church memberships. There are also frequent statements that the lesser priesthood quorums have more importance in gathered Zion than do the Melchizedek quorums.

It is important to analyze such references and attempt to describe Aaronic Priesthood work of a century ago for two reasons. First, only by knowing how the lesser priesthood operated during that period can we fully understand that era's priesthood matters involving elders, seventies, high priests, bishops, wards, stakes, temple ordinances, and judicial procedures. Second, today's priesthood practices, both Melchizedek and Aaronic,

are deeply rooted in the Church of
the nineteenth century and are best
understood when compared with Aaronic work as institutionalized during
that period.

One important key to understanding modern Aaronic Priesthood
operations is the paradox which leaders a century ago identified, wrestled
with, and finally circumvented. The
paradox stemmed from their fixed
belief that the revelations required
Aaronic Priesthood bearers, especially teachers and priests, to be spiritual adults capable of teaching gospel
principles, rooting out iniquity, and
settling disputes. But how could the
Church fill its Aaronic quorums with
such capable men when at the same

*Called to be the acting Presiding Bishop
in 1850, Edward Hunter worked with local
stake and ward authorities to implement
an effective program for ward teachers.
Courtesy Church Archives.*

time they qualified for and received the Melchizedek Priesthood? It could
not. So alternative methods for staffing the lesser quorums had to be
developed.

No time period more clearly demonstrates the problem than the years
when Edward Hunter presided over the lesser priesthood as Presiding
Bishop of the Church, 1851–83 (basically the period of Brigham Young's
presidency). Because ordained teachers were then the most important of
the lesser priesthood quorums, this paper examines the nineteenth-century
Aaronic Priesthood in terms of the ordained teachers' role in the Church,
both in theory and practice, especially during the Bishop Hunter era.[1]

EARLY LESSER PRIESTHOOD QUORUMS FILLED BY ADULTS

Theoretically, "the Melchizedek priesthood comprehends the Aaronic," but
the Church traditionally has treated "these two priesthoods" as separate
entities.[2] Melchizedek Priesthood bearers—the elders, seventies, and high
priests—are by revelation assigned higher spiritual responsibilities and
blessings of the Church. They are to preside as leaders, to "watch over the

Church," and serve proselyting missions, and they are eligible to receive full temple endowments, be married for the eternities, and know "the mysteries of the kingdom."[3]

Although the Aaronic Priesthood is termed a lesser, preparatory priesthood, it has awesome significance for the Church. It administers the two sacred ordinances directly relating to the Savior's atonement: baptism, to remove sin; and the sacrament, symbolizing the Savior's broken flesh and shed blood. To Aaronic males are vouchsafed the keys of the ministering of angels. Also, by revelation as recorded in Doctrine and Covenants 20, the Aaronic Priesthood is assigned important watchman work. Priests are instructed to "visit the house of each member, exhorting them to pray vocally and in secret and attend to all family duties." Teachers similarly are commanded to

> watch over the church always, and be with and strengthen them; And see that there is no iniquity in the church, neither hardness with each other, neither lying, backbiting, nor evil speaking; And see that the Church meet together often, and also see that all the members do their duty. (D&C 20:54–55)[4]

Earlier in this revelation a similar admonition to "watch over the Church" is given to elders—meaning all Melchizedek Priesthood bearers. But for nearly a century, Church leaders stressed that lesser priesthood teachers and priests, *not the Melchizedek men*, had the major responsibility for ward teaching. This interpretation of Section 20 is primarily responsible, as we shall see, for the Aaronic Priesthood paradox.

Early Church leaders tried to fill the lesser quorums with the most capable adults and young men available in the Ohio, Missouri, and Illinois gathering centers and in the mission branches. Such ordained brethren, particularly priests and teachers, served as local ministers presiding over branches, collecting and dispersing Church funds, dealing with membership discipline problems, and making pastoral visits to the homes of members.[5]

But manpower problems developed. Repeatedly the ranks of the lesser priesthood thinned out, due in large part to the active recruiting practices of Melchizedek Priesthood quorums seeking to keep their own units fully manned. By standards of the higher quorum, the faithful, lesser priesthood men were qualified to receive the higher priesthood with its added blessings and responsibilities, and no reason existed for holding these men back. Aaronic males therefore readily accepted invitations for advancement to the higher priesthood, sometimes after just a few months of lesser priesthood service. This left the lesser quorums with continual vacancies, and their meetings through the Nauvoo period were characterized by frequent disruptions of labor, replacements of officers, and revised visiting assignments.

After removal to the Great Basin, Church leaders continued to believe that lesser priesthood offices ought to be filled by capable non-Melchizedek Priesthood adults.[6] But the number of such eligible men proved inadequate for the usual reasons, which were further compounded by the temple endowments newly introduced at Nauvoo: To marry for eternity or to serve full-time Church missions men now had to receive the endowments, which required Melchizedek Priesthood ordination. Faced with shortages, Church leaders turned to two alternative methods of filling the lesser quorums. The most popular and practical was to call Melchizedek Priesthood bearers to serve as *acting* deacons, *acting* teachers, and *acting* priests. In a secondary solution, younger boys were ordained and served as apprentices to the adult teachers.

LOCAL PRIESTHOOD OPERATIONS DURING THE BISHOP HUNTER ERA

Initially, lesser priesthood quorums operated as *stake* rather than *ward* entities. During the first three decades in Utah, each stake was expected to have at least one quorum each of deacons, teachers, and priests, with additional units as needed. When Sanpete Stake organized its lesser priesthood work in 1874, for example, it called forty-eight priests, twenty-four teachers, and twelve deacons—the quorum maximums outlined in the Doctrine and Covenants—with half of each quorum coming from each of the stake's two large settlements, Manti and Ephraim.[7] In time, more populous stakes created ward quorums, particularly for the deacons and teachers, to coexist with the general stake quorums. In Salt Lake Stake, for example, a stake deacons quorum presidency conducted monthly meetings for two decades to which ward deacons quorums presidencies and all other deacons were invited.[8]

Until Brigham Young placed all Church stakes on an equal basis in 1876, many leaders and members accepted Salt Lake Stake as the center stake for the Church, authorized to supervise and direct work in the other stakes.[9] For years, therefore, the presidencies of the Salt Lake Stake's deacons quorum, teachers quorum, and priests quorum were sustained at general conference as general, lesser priesthood officers—they were sometimes termed "General Authorities"—for the entire Church. The stake's monthly deacons, teachers, and priests meetings and a combined stake monthly Aaronic Priesthood meeting frequently attracted lesser priesthood leaders from non–Salt Lake settlements whenever such men were in town. The Presiding Bishopric and local bishops also attended. Initially important, these general meetings faded in significance by the late 1870s, although in individual Salt Lake wards deacons and teachers quorums flourished. Priests quorums, requiring a minimum of twenty-five members back then, rarely if ever existed at the ward level, although some stake quorums were formed.

At the ward level, the bishops, who often served for life, were temporal and spiritual leaders. They filled roles resembling those of pastor, constable, judge, arbitrator, foreman, and mayor. For assistants, they had counselors and local Aaronic Priesthood bearers. Bishops normally developed some type of simple lesser priesthood operations to help oversee their wards, usually calling a few deacons and a body of teachers. Deacons generally took no part in the sacrament ordinance, but served mainly as meetinghouse custodians and ushers, collected fast offerings and meetinghouse funds, and assisted as block teachers. In theory, priests were the primary visiting watchmen, assisted by the teachers. But in practice, priests operated as regular teachers and usually met with the teachers quorums.[10]

Deacons, teachers, and priests were official ward officers and as such were voted on by the membership each year at ward conferences. "It is then expected," taught Apostle John Taylor in 1877, "that Priests, Teachers, and Deacons will hearken to and obey the counsel of their Bishop; and it will be expected that the people will listen to the voice of their Priests and Teachers and those whose business it is to look after their interest and welfare."[11]

Bishops relied heavily upon the lesser priesthood partly because Melchizedek Priesthood quorums and auxiliaries were not well organized during the Hunter era. High priests, if not serving in bishoprics or as stake leaders, did little Church work other than hold meetings and await specific ward assignments. Seventies quorums, being general Church quorums and not stake or ward units, served the broader purpose of recruiting missionaries more than of assisting local bishops. Few elders quorums were organized

before 1877. Also, until the 1870s there were few Sunday Schools, no Primaries, and not many Relief Societies. Young ladies' and young men's programs
developed only after 1869. Therefore, activities of a typical ward during most
of this earlier period generally consisted of a late Sunday preaching service,
perhaps a week night prayer meeting, a biweekly or monthly ward council
or teachers' report meeting, and a fast meeting on one Thursday morning
a month.

Each ward tailored its lesser priesthood operations to its particular
circumstances. Rural wards assigned teachers to districts and urban wards
to blocks—hence the term "block teacher." In the 1850s, some wards had
but one pair of teachers do all the visiting, but as ward populations grew, a
minimum of one teacher per block became the rule, then two. A survey of
Salt Lake bishops in 1870 showed that the wards then had between eighteen and twenty-four teachers each, which meant teaching beats of eight to
twenty families per team. Busy summer months produced little visiting by
teachers, particularly in the farming communities. But during the rest of the
year, visits occurred weekly in some wards, bimonthly or monthly in others.
Teachers were expected to give reports of their visits to the regular biweekly
or monthly ward council meeting or at teachers quorum meeting—which
in many wards were the same meeting.[12]

LOFTY CONCEPTS OF THE
AARONIC PRIESTHOOD'S PURPOSES

Edward Hunter was the General Authority directly in charge of lesser priesthood work. Formerly a Nauvoo bishop and close friend of Joseph Smith,
the energetic and kindly Pennsylvanian taught by letter and sermon a noble
conception of the Aaronic Priesthood, one shared by his contemporary
stake and general authorities. To them, the lesser priesthood bearers had
not only general service duties but also unique and special responsibilities,
without which the local wards and branches could not succeed.

Temporal Assistants to the Bishops

For a multitude of local temporal tasks bishops depended upon their lesser
priesthood teachers, whose monthly or fortnightly meetings they frequently
attended and advised. Sometimes bishops appointed presiding teachers to

take charge of collecting and disbursing fast offerings and other funds, making visiting assignments, keeping ward records, supervising the deacons, and administering the sacrament. Bishops also employed their teachers in such day-to-day work as cleaning canals, grading roads, controlling stray cattle, rounding up goods and funds for various Church projects, acting as neighborhood guards, and caring for the physical needs of the poor.[13]

Watchmen against Iniquity

But teachers' primary priesthood role was to act "as Watchmen to guard against all manner of iniquity," a duty strongly stressed by Bishop Hunter and the other General Authorities. Teachers during this period were regarded as spiritual policemen for the church. "Every move should be understood through every block, and the whereabouts of every man," explained Hunter's counselor Jesse C. Little, "and if there's stealing going forward or whoring, the Teachers should find them out."[14] Erastus Snow was even more specific:

> It is the duty of the Teachers to report to their Bishop the relative standing of those under their supervision—whether their houses are houses of order—whether the wife is good to the husband, and the husband is good to his wife—whether the children are obedient to their parents, and whether the parents are training their children in the way they should walk,—if there is strife where there should be peace, if there are jealousy and discord where love and unity should exist,—whether the mother poisons the mind of her daughter instead of teaching her correct principles; in short— whether the house is what it should be—a house of God ... nothing that may have a bearing on the union and fellowship of the Saints, should escape the notice of the teachers.[15]

Such guardian work entailed visiting and asking questions of family members regarding their loyalty to Church leaders and principles. During most of this period—and not just during the Reformation of 1856—lists of questions were a meaningless routine. Aware of such ineffectiveness, Hunter taught that when a teacher visits "that House is subject to him and the Teacher has the privilege to ask such questions as the Spirit of God may direct him to and no person should go as a Teacher without that spirit."[16]

Teachers were expected to combat a wide assortment of specific troublesome evils such as "drinking saloons & hurdy gurdies," intoxication, Sabbath breaking, "the growth of wickedness among our young people," nonattendance at meetings, criticizing polygamy and Church leaders, not paying tithes and offerings, unpaid debts, and parental neglect. Teachers brought charges against adulterers and handled cases of disrespect for neighbors and property. At quorum meetings or ward councils, teachers occasionally served as a ward court, trying sinners for their memberships. When required by Church leaders, teachers encouraged members to enter into United Orders, to enter into plural marriage, and to cease associating with or buying from enemies of the Church. In light of such responsibilities, it is not without significance that just before Brigham Young's death in 1877, the dying prophet's last conversation with his counselor George Q. Cannon was about teachers. "His great anxiety," said President Cannon, "seemed to rest on the necessity of a more thorough Visitation of every member of the Church by the Priests and Teachers."[17]

Priesthood watchcare was then considered a responsibility of the lesser priesthood. "It was not the calling of the Twelve Apostles to do this," taught President Cannon, "the Lord had placed proper officers, teachers, to do this work."[18] To help them police the Church, teachers repeatedly were told that their particular priesthood office entitled them to special divine aid. "God will honor and give strength to the Teacher who will do his duty," said Bishop Hunter, "and he will have the administration of Angels."[19]

Teachers as Peacemakers: "The Proper Channel of the Priesthood"

Lesser priesthood men were also expected to be the primary peace officers of the Church. Members were told that teachers possessed not only the *right* but also the unique *power* to end disputes and pacify disputants. "There was a power to settle difficulties vouchsafed to the Lesser Priesthood," said Hunter, such that "a Teacher when he would act in the Spirit of his calling and in the order of the Priesthood, could settle difficulties that no other officer or member of the Kingdom of God can accomplish unless under the Priesthood." He explained further that "when cases are settled by aid of the lesser priesthood, the agency of the parties themselves is brought to bear in the matter, but where brought before a Bishops court or High Council the case is decided but not settled, and the parties themselves give up their agency." He warned that if teachers cannot reconcile the parties "it cannot be done," but, conversely, when teachers settled disputes, "they generally remain settled, because they [are] accomplished on the principle of mutual reconciliation."[20]

Enlisting teachers as peacemakers was not simply an option that members might employ, it was the rule of the Church. If members refused to abide "this order of the kingdom," warned Bishop Little, then "the Bishop had a perfect right to deal with them and cut them off from the Church." When high council trials increased during 1862, Bishop Hunter pointed out the remedy: "The Bishops should employ the best Teachers they can get, and have all wrong matters adjusted through the proper channel of the Priesthood." Alert teachers made a difference, according to Salt Lake bishop Nathan Davis: "The success the teachers had in the 17th Ward of adjusting differences that occurred amongst the Saints [was such] that since he had presided [two years] he had not had one Bishops Court." Hunter said that he knew of "many instances where they [teachers] had done a mighty work in the settlement of difficultys."[21]

Teachers' Unique Right to Preside in Homes

Priesthood leaders taught that teachers possessed a special right to preside over each family during official visits in the home, and that members therefore ought to receive their teachers deferentially. As Hunter explained it, teachers had privileges "such that no other officer in the Kingdom of God enjoyed, not even the Prophet Joseph Smith, or President Young; no man can take the presidency in any family, except a Teacher while exercising his duties in visiting amongst the people." Concerning his own block teachers, the Presiding Bishop said: "My feeling is to honor them. No man has a right in entering my house to assume the prerogative of dictating there, but when the Lesser Priesthood call, I yield up to them the control of my family for the time being." John Taylor similarly respected his teachers' priesthood authority: "When they do come, I acquaint my family with it, call them together, and then tell our visitors that we are all under their jurisdiction.... Shall I assume to dictate to those who are above me? No, never." To justify such behavior, Hunter and others often cited a story then popular. When a Brother Oakley visited the Prophet Joseph as a teacher, so one version went, the Prophet called his family together and gave his own chair to

Oakley, telling his family that Brother Oakley presided while acting in that capacity.[22]

The Aaronic Priesthood and the Temple

During Joseph Smith's lifetime, Church leaders, aware of the Aaronic Priesthood's temple connection in the Old Testament, had discussed possible Nauvoo temple roles for the Aaronic Priesthood.[23] During most of the Hunter era, however, no temple existed, although some temple ordinances were performed in the Salt Lake Endowment House and perhaps elsewhere. The Saints eagerly anticipated the day when a temple would be built in Utah, at which time Brigham Young expected to see Aaronic Priesthood involved in part of the temple endowment:

> Most of you, my brethren, are Elders, Seventies, or High Priests: perhaps there is not a Priest or Teacher present. The reason of this is that when we give the brethren their endowments, we are obliged to confer upon them the Melchisedec Priesthood; but I expect to see the day when we shall be so situated that we can say to a company of brethren you can go and receive the ordinances pertaining to the Aaronic order of the Priesthood, and then you can go into the world and preach the Gospel, or do something that will prove whether you will honor that Priesthood before you receive more. Now we pass them though the ordinances [endowment] of both Priesthoods in one day, but this is not as it should be and would be if we had a temple wherein to administer these ordinances.[24]

Evidently this idea that men might receive only the Aaronic portion of the endowment never was implemented. But as late as 1894, President Young's former counselor George Q. Cannon still preached the positive effect that plan could have:

> I have felt for years that something should be done to change this [obtaining endowments too easily] so that instead of it being necessary for a man to receive the Melchizedek Priesthood, he will first manifest his efficiency in the Aaronic Priesthood and show his capabilities and good desires before receiving the higher Priesthood. I firmly believe that this will be so some time and that men

will not get the fullness of the endowment with the ease that they have done but will receive that part which belongs to the Aaronic Priesthood.[25]

Special features designed for the Aaronic Priesthood were provided in the first Utah temple opened in 1877. Following a precedent established at the Kirtland Temple,[26] the St. George edifice included a

> platform with the several pulpits in the western end for the use of the Aaronic Priesthood, namely the Bishopric, or Presidency of the Aaronic Priesthood, the presidency of the Priests' quorum, the presidency of the Teachers Quorum and the presidency of the Deacons quorum ... with the side seats arranged for visiting bishops and for the Priests, Teachers, and Deacons.[27]

The Most Important Laborers in Gathered Zion

Because of their vital temporal and spiritual duties, teachers symbolically were considered the legs and feet of the Church, without which the institution would be crippled. Priesthood minute books contain repeated statements to the effect that "No more important labor rests on any portion of the priesthood than does that of a Teacher." Comparisons between the higher and lesser priesthoods' contributions to the Church often favored the latter. Many believed that "there was more depending upon the lesser Priesthood than the High Priests or Seventies or Elders." One lesser priesthood worker asked, rhetorically, "Where is the influence & responsibility of a Seventy by the side of that of a teacher?" then continued: "It is far easier to convince people of the necessity of being baptized than it is to keep them in the church to instruct them in the principles of life." Another asserted crisply, "They gather, we teach them how to live."[28] In 1877, Hunter made this assessment of the local work of the two priesthoods:

> We meet together as labourers in the kingdom of God. The Kingdom of God could not exist without us, or others like us. It is well for the Elders etc. to meet & keep up their various organizations, they are as a band of Volunteers in a time of peace, but we are the "Regulars." ... We are the people that are called to act. The others meet together, truly, & preach around the Territory. The Seventies

in the nations. The High Priests when they are wanted, but we are "The Labourers." We are called to act. The others are only lay members till they are called to act.[29]

Perhaps Bishop Hunter and other leaders overstated the case somewhat in order to boost the morale of those workers—those jobs bore the designation "lesser." But even discounting some degree of exaggeration, their numerous statements clearly define a large degree of importance and usefulness for the Aaronic Priesthood.

THE AARONIC PRIESTHOOD IN PRACTICE

Temporal laborers. Watchmen with special powers to combat iniquity. The Church's only authorized peacemakers. Specified recipients of the ministering of angels. The only officers allowed to preside in homes in place of fathers. Officers with admitted temple roles. Given these lofty conceptions of lesser priesthood work, it is not surprising that Church leaders a century ago sought to staff teachers quorums with stalwart men.

Ideal: The Best Men as Teachers

"Select the best men for Teachers" was a recurring theme in the Hunter decades. During the 1856 Reformation, when teachers were expected to instigate deep Churchwide repentance, Hunter stressed "the importance of … having wise men as Teachers, which was a high and holy calling." A decade later he counseled: "Bishops should arm themselves with the best teachers they possibly can." One bishop in 1869 "desired to select the best men for Teachers in the 8th Ward, and he considered that though a man without a wife can honor his calling as a teacher, a man that is married has a greater experience & is more fully qualified."[30] Careful recruitment also concerned John Taylor:

> The bishops should be very choice in the selection of teachers, taking the greatest pains to get the best men they could find in their wards, men that sought after God themselves and who were filled with his Spirit; at the same time they should be possessed of good judgment, and capable of giving good advice.[31]

Some exceptions to this ideal were made in the cases of youthful junior companions and of semi-active adults who, needing preparatory priesthood training, served as apprentices accompanying the more qualified teachers.[32]

Alternative: Boys and Young Men as Teachers

During most of the Hunter era, it was desired but not practiced that all older boys receive some preparatory priesthood experience before receiving the Melchizedek Priesthood. Manpower shortages encouraged the use of older boys, and during periodic pushes to revitalize the work and to fill up quo- rums the number of youthful ordinations increased. "It is a difficult task," lamented one bishop, "to find a sufficient quantity of sufficient teachers. I have thought of calling upon some of the boys." Another bishop found his boys receptive to that idea: "It is very hard to get out the older men to act as Teachers but the young men come forward and are willing to take their parts and therefore we have to appoint young men where older ones should be."[33]

The reader must be cautious, however when interpreting terms like "young men" and "boys." What is implied, for example, when Samuel Andrews says about his Seventh Ward deacons: "The *boys* as well as myself belong to the Elders' Quorum"? (italics added). The suggestion here, as elsewhere, is that perhaps males in their early twenties sometimes were classed as "boys." What we do know is that it was common practice for *some* young men and boys, ranging in age from ten to their twenties, in *some* of the wards to serve as ordained deacons, teachers, and priests.[34]

As early as 1849, local leaders were instructed to call "young men" to help with the visiting. Four years later, Bishop Seth Taft suggested that Salt Lake bishops "fill up our quorum, ordain boys to the lesser priesthood, that they may commence in the harness." Another bishop "found it [ordain- ing boys] working well, kept the boys from mischief and recommended the bishops to follow his example." Salt Lake Stake Teachers President McGee Harris counseled: "Take the teachers who are young & learn them their duties." Two years later, Salt Lake lesser priesthood leaders discussed "installing our young brethren in the offices of teachers & Deacons." One Salt Lake bishop "called on the young men of the ward to labor as teachers," and another ordained about twenty young men to act as teachers. Similar ordinations occurred in Provo, St. George, and other settlements.[35]

All too often, however, boys became deacons and remained such until adulthood. "It had been the custom," noted a Salt Lake Stake officer in 1876, "to ordain boys to the office of deacon and allow them to retain this office till they get their endowments when they were ordained Elders."[36] Illustrative, too, is the Kanab Ward, where the bishop at an 1874 priesthood meeting "spoke at length on the duties of deacons, was in favor of ordaining those, who had been called to the office of deacons, to be Elders," whereupon three deacons—ages twenty, eighteen, and twenty-two—were ordained as elders.[37]

Some leaders, recognizing the problem involved in asking boys to do men's work, adamantly opposed ordaining the youth. Well known is Brigham Young's warning in 1854 not to let boys be deacons:

> When you have got your Bishop, he needs assistants, and he ordains Counsellors, Priests, Teachers, and Deacons, and calls them to help him; and he wishes men of his own heart and hand to do this. Says he, "I dare not even call a man to be a Deacon, to assist me in my calling, unless he has a family." It is not the business of an ignorant young man, of no experience in family matters to inquire into the circumstances of families, and know the wants of every person. Some may want medicine and nourishment, and be looked after, and it is not the business of boys to do this."[38]

Bishop Canute Petersen gave similar blunt counsel to his ward priesthood in 1874:

> We might think that these quorums should be filled with young men, but the kingdom of God had increased and there was evils and iniquities in the church, and it is the duty of the lesser priesthood to look after these things, and for this reason men of experience was called for that purpose.[39]

Such sentiments also caused Salt Lake stake priests quorum president Samuel G. Ladd, frustrated in his efforts to raise a full priests quorum, to plead with bishops for help, adding the specific request that they "send good responsible men and not boys." He had always felt that this quorum, the special teachers in the Church, "should be composed of experienced men and he had not seen anything to change his mind."[40]

Despite such feelings, the First Presidency in an 1877 circular letter declared that policy henceforth was that youth should serve as apprentice teachers: "the experienced priest or teacher should have as a companion a young man, so that the latter may have the opportunity of learning the duties of his calling, and becoming thoroughly wise and efficient in the discharge thereof."[41] The practice immediately took hold in many wards but was unevenly followed throughout the Church until 1908, when formal age groupings for young deacons, teachers, and priests, and systematic advancement patterns through each office became policy.[42]

Alternative: Melchizedek Priesthood Men as "Acting" Teachers

While youth were useful apprentices, the Church found that its commitment to ordaining the best brethren as senior teachers was impossible to meet. Men with necessary qualifications were at the same time eligible for and received the greater Melchizedek Priesthood, leaving few, if any, of their type available for the lesser priesthood quorums.

Two solutions, although drastic, could have solved the problem. One, discussed by Brigham Young and George Q. Cannon as noted earlier,[43] was to make the Melchizedek Priesthood harder to receive, reserving it for those men who proved themselves worthy of it during a lengthy period of lesser priesthood service. A second way would have been to assign historical relativity to early revelations, such as D&C 20. By assuming that those instructions had definite validity in the formative years of the Church, before wards were created and ward bishops called and prior to the introduction of the temple endowment, the Church could have announced that the new circumstances in the Rocky Mountain Zion necessitated a different use of its priesthood quorums. This could have involved a de-emphasis of the lesser priesthood's more pastoral duties coupled with a simultaneous emphasis upon the Melchizedek Priesthood's duty to "watch over the Church" given in D&C 20—the solution the Church finally implemented during the twentieth century.

Neither solution, however, was adopted by President Brigham Young and his contemporary Church leaders. Instead, they decided to call Melchizedek Priesthood men to the lesser priesthood work in an "acting" capacity, much like high priests act in the Aaronic Priesthood when called to

be bishops. Calling "acting" teachers became the main method of providing the Church with its Aaronic Priesthood teachers during the Hunter era.

In 1849, immediately after dividing Salt Lake City into wards and calling the bishops, President Young formally requested that leading brethren,
including "the best high priests, the most substantial men," act in the lesser
priesthood. Instructions to bishops two years later were similar: "If there be
no members of the Lesser Priesthood in the Wards to act as Teachers take
High Priests or seventies or any other wise man." The Salt Lake Seventh
Ward reported in 1855 that they had high priests appointed as acting teachers over each block in the ward. George Goddard, secretary to the Presiding Bishopric, calculated in 1872 that "between 3[oo] and 400 teachers are
employed in this city, most of whom hold the Melchisedec Priesthood, and
yet act in the lesser priesthood." The priests in Salt Lake that decade likewise
were mostly acting priests—"men having higher ordinations."[44] In 1873 the
Presiding Bishop counseled:

> We cannot be satisfied, neither can you be safe, without the order
> of the Kingdom being observed.... The Lord says, How can the
> body stand without the feet, etc. We hope therefore, that High
> Priests, Seventies and Elders, if required to fill up these Quorums,
> will be pleased to act in each, and magnify their callings, as Priests,
> Teachers and Deacons.[45]

Double duty—serving in both priesthoods at once—produced some
strange work loads. One deacons quorum president in 1877, Samuel W.
Andrew, had been a deacon for four years, was also a teacher, and belonged
to an elders quorum. George Whittaker, a priests quorum counselor, had
been in Zion over thirty years and "never laboured in any but the lesser
priesthood," even though he had been ordained a seventy before migrating
from England. "I was an Elder before I was a deacon," Matthias Cowley told
a Salt Lake Stake deacons' meeting in the 1870s, and then emphasized how
important it was that acting deacons like himself attend deacons quorum
meetings: "If we were all to stay away because we are Elders or Seventies,
where would the Teachers and deacons' quorums be? Why! Here your
president is a high priest, & his counsellors, Seventies." John H. Picknell,
counselor in the Salt Lake Stake deacons quorum, once outlined to the
deacons his busy schedule: "I've Seventies, Priests', Teachers' & Deacons'
meetings to attend, Teacher in two wards, a Priest in one ... I'm out almost

every night in the month." In cases of loyalty conflicts, said Brigham Young, "It is not the duty of a Seventy or High Priest, who is appointed a Teacher or a Bishop, to neglect the duties of those callings to attend a Seventies' or High Priests' meeting. Attend to the wishes of your Bishop."[46]

The question arose as to whether such "acting" lesser priesthood men needed to be set apart. Generally it was recognized that "Those holding the Melchizedek Priesthood can act in all the offices of the Aaronic Priesthood," but that they must first be "called and set apart for that [lesser] office."[47]

The Problem of Prestige

While General Authorities held lofty concepts of the lesser priesthood's role in the Church, too many rank-and-file members did not share that viewpoint. Many felt that *lesser* priesthood service was in fact a *lesser* honor, and if a choice could be made they would prefer a Melchizedek Priesthood ordination with its added blessings and privileges. And choice was possible because higher quorums continued to actively recruit available men and young men to keep their own ranks filled.

Unordained youths recognized the status differences, and many desired that their first priesthood ordination be to the Melchizedek Priesthood, not the Aaronic. Such attitudes caused Bishop Alonzo Raleigh to warn young men who were "aspiring to become seventy's in their first ordination," that "it would be much better for them to go through the duties of the lessor priesthood and magnify those first."[48]

The already ordained Aaronic males had similar ambitions for higher ordinations, causing Bishop Hunter to warn at various times that he "objected to the brethren striving and hurrying to be ordained into the High Priests or Seventies Quorums, when they are needed to act in the lesser priesthood." One bishop noted there were social pressures involved: "Let an individual be ordained as a Teacher, some kind friend or other tells him he is not in his right place as it was high time he should be ordained High Priest or Seventy, by this means the Kingdom of God is deprived of its legs and feet." Hunter observed, "Everybody wanted to be a High Priest nobody wanted to be a Deacon, people tried to get offices they could not magnify." He forthrightly confessed that the main reason he was unable to properly fill up lesser priesthood quorums during his first two decades as Presiding Bishop was because of "so many seeking to become high priests and seventies."[49] Perhaps the clearest contemporary expression of the Aaronic Priesthood problem is contained in one of Bishop Hunter's letters to Apostle Orson Hyde in 1873: "We have many times tried to fill up these quorums by those who have not received the Melchizedek Priesthood, but have been almost immediately called out to receive their endowments, leaving vacancies that had to be filled with High Priests, Seventies or Elders."[50]

Similarly, some Melchizedek Priesthood men were reluctant to act as lesser priesthood members. Recognizing that "some men because they are Elders or Seventies consider it beneath them to operate as Teachers," Hunter waged a continual struggle for three decades "to make honourable the lessor priesthood." The status problem generated one extreme proposal, not implemented, that if Melchizedek men refused to serve in the lesser callings, they should "be cut off from the quorum they belong to, and remain as private members until they are willing to be useful in the lesser priesthood."[51]

REVITALIZING LESSER PRIESTHOOD WORK

Despite prestige problems, teachers' work *was* performed during these years, but with varying degrees of quantity and quality depending upon the given month, ward, block, teacher or bishop. Since the overall teaching effort did not satisfy the Presiding Bishop, he engineered periodic recruitment and organizing campaigns. The first big push came in the mid-1850s, culminating in the Reformation of 1856–57. Another commenced in 1873, when President Young pointedly challenged Hunter to have at least one full quorum of deacons, teachers, and priests "properly organized" in every *stake*—not mentioning anything about *ward* quorums. It took three years, but in 1876 Bishop Hunter pronounced the effort successful.[52] During Bishop Hunter's last few years, the Aaronic Priesthood quorums, as a result of the 1877 reorganization, generally operated in more wards than before and at an improved level of efficiency.[53]

Leaders found that using Melchizedek Priesthood men as senior teachers, aided by ordained youths, was a fairly workable way of keeping Aaronic Priesthood units operational. But their solution was considered only temporary. As the First Presidency explained in 1877, bishops would use Melchizedek Priesthood men in the lesser offices only "until priests, teachers, and deacons of the necessary experience are found." Similarly, John Taylor stated that year that acting teachers "would remain for the present, but would be changed as soon as arrangements could be made, and exclusive teachers would fill the Quorum." To later generations was left the task of finding a permanent solution.[54]

ORDAINED TEACHERS: A CENTURY'S POSTSCRIPT

Concepts of priesthood ward teaching developed during the Hunter era remained basically unchanged until well after the turn of the twentieth century. Latter-day Saints were reminded in 1902, for example, that "there are in every ward a number of brethren selected to be acting teachers, under the direction of the Bishopric. These are usually men holding the Melchizedek Priesthood, but called to act in the lesser or Aaronic Priesthood for visiting and teaching purposes."[55]

Utilizing "permanent substitutes," rather than properly ordained officers, disturbed some leaders, particularly a General Priesthood Committee established in 1908 to reevaluate, reorganize, and reinvigorate priesthood operations.[56] Including a score of leading Church officials at its peak, the Committee, in the course of its fourteen-year investigation of priesthood matters, found it necessary to directly confront the problem of having two kinds of teachers—acting (adults) and ordained (youth)—functioning in the Church.

On May 5, 1909, these brethren openly debated how the two kinds of teachers related to each other and whether the two should have separate meetings and courses of study. Brigham H. Roberts, defending the traditional concept that both kinds of teachers essentially operated in the same office, opposed separate treatment. Training to do the ward teacher's work, he felt, should be provided only by quorums. Joseph B. Keeler, another noted priesthood expert, disagreed, asserting that "until teachers and priests are qualified to do this work, it will be necessary to call in the elders, seventies and high priests to do the teaching, and that two meetings were not too many." Roberts, cutting to the heart of the old paradox, countered: "When will the quorums ever do the work required of them if they are put aside [and] others appointed to do their work?" Thereupon Keeler pointed out the impracticality of Roberts' view, given the Church practice of filling the lesser quorums with youths: "Even the brightest young men lack experience and it would always be necessary to have older men go with them to assist them in this work."[57]

B. H. Roberts (left) *and Joseph B. Keeler. These men espoused opposing viewpoints as to whether Melchizedek Priesthood holders should do the work of the Aaronic Priesthood. Courtesy Perry Special Collections.*

With majority sentiment favoring the Keeler position, the Committee took two important steps during the next few years to effectively establish two separate and distinct types of teachers in the Church. First, it redefined Aaronic Priesthood work as something for boys to perform, and established for the first time in the Church definite ordination ages for deacons, teachers, and priests as twelve, fifteen, and eighteen respectively. New lists of suggested duties geared to the youthful capabilities of the Aaronic boys were drawn up. Teenage ordained teachers, for example, were asked to:

assist in ward teaching
assist with the sacrament
be instructors for boy scouts
collect ward funds
speak and sing at meetings
notify quorums of meetings

help renovate meetinghouses
care for meetinghouse grounds
cut wood for the poor
be auxiliary officers
be clerks of branches
be choir members[58]

Lists for deacons and priests were also circulated. Since that time similar duties have regularly been given to youthful Aaronic Priesthood bearers. These assignments have provided excellent development and training for the young men, preparing them for greater priesthood service following their Aaronic apprenticeships. But, except for the priests' duty to baptize and bless the sacrament, and the priests' and teachers' duties to visit, teach, and to ordain, most assignments given to Aaronic boys in this century require no actual priesthood authority to perform. During World War II, for example, girls collected fast offerings. Women have also prepared the sacrament tables. President Heber J. Grant once authorized boys with no priesthood to pass the sacrament when ordained boys were unavailable. Serving as officers in auxiliaries and participating in meetings as speakers and singers are opportunities open to all Church members regardless of priesthood ordination or lack of it.[59]

Besides clearly defining lesser priesthood work in youthful terms, the Committee also campaigned to eliminate the traditional concept of the *acting teacher*. Could not Melchizedek Priesthood men visit by virtue of their higher ordinations and therefore cease to act in a lesser priesthood capacity? Such thinking led the committee to create a new kind of teacher, the *ward teacher*, which was a ward position, not a priesthood office: "[Ward teachers] should not consider that they are called away from their own responsibilities to take up the work of a lesser office in the Aaronic Priesthood. Ward teaching is a calling, just as missionary work abroad is a calling, and no quorum is solely responsible for the performance of this duty."[60]

But the traditional acting teachers concept continued to have wide acceptance among leaders and members. President Joseph F. Smith, for example, taught it in the April 1914 general conference while chiding prominent men for refusing to serve as block teachers:

When their presidents or their bishops of the wards in which they live call upon them to visit the Saints, teach the principles of the Gospel and perform the duties of teacher, they coolly inform their bishops that they have graduated from that calling and refuse to act as teachers. Brother Charles W. Penrose is eighty-two years of age. I am going on seventy-six, and I believe that I am older than several of these good men who have graduated from the *duties in the Lesser Priesthood*, and I want to tell them and you that we are not too old to act as teachers, if you will call us to do it.[61]

Similarly, the 1933 Melchizedek Priesthood handbook reported: "At present in many wards there were not enough men to fill up the quorums of the Lesser Priesthood and members of the Higher Priesthood are frequently found officiating as teachers."[62] Three years later, Apostle Joseph Fielding Smith also expressed the traditional view:

> I know of no work more important than that which has been assigned to the Ward Teacher and the Ward Priest. We have throughout the Church quite generally combined these two offices and placed the responsibilities of the Teachers and Priests upon the brethren whom we call [Ward] Teachers.[63]

The old (acting teacher) and new (ward teacher) concepts coexisted and were interchanged with each other for at least three decades. Resulting ambiguity produced a surprising reversion in the late 1920s and 1930s to the original basic ideal of using *ordained* teachers instead of either *acting* or *ward* teachers! Many wards sent increasing numbers of ordained teachers— boys—out as ward teachers, frequently paired together, to the homes of the more active families. Such youth work was justified, urged the *Improvement Era*, because ward teaching "is specifically assigned to the Priests and Teachers of the Church by revelation." It noted with pride in 1934 that "in several stakes the greater part of the teaching is being done by young men of the Lesser Priesthood quorums. Results are reported to be gratifying."[64] For a good example of Aaronic Ward Teaching, *Era* readers were referred to the Cache Stake program where

> Teachers and Priests are given first call when new members of the acting teachers force are needed. Members of the Melchizedek priesthood quorums are called to assist only when there are no available teachers or priests. In some wards nearly all the members of the acting teachers force are members of the Aaronic Priesthood quorums.[65]

But employing boys as the Church's watchmen brought the old paradox again to the surface. How far can the Church move in placing the teaching work upon young men, an important 1937 study of ward teaching asked, and still achieve the primary purpose of teaching as outlined in the revelations?[66] A partial answer came from the Presiding Bishopric in 1940 when they instructed bishops to "discontinue the practice of sending members of the Aaronic Priesthood in pairs, or alone, to do ward teaching," admitting that "people will feel better about it if an older and more experienced brother takes the lead in discussions and inquiries."[67]

Finally in the 1940s the *ward teaching* idea completely replaced the *acting teacher* concept. Then, during the past three decades the ward teaching concept itself has been modified, particularly by the *home teaching* program instituted in the 1960s, which produced two further notable changes in the old traditional concepts about teachers. First, instead of the principle of "selecting" the most qualified men for teaching assignments, the new instruction is that *every* Melchizedek Priesthood bearer by virtue of his higher ordination automatically is a watchman, a home teacher. Second, Melchizedek Priesthood quorum presidencies are responsible for directing the teaching of the families of their own quorum members.[68]

Basic to the home teaching program is a change in scriptural emphasis. Where a century ago the emphasis was on D&C 20:46–55, which places visiting responsibilities upon the priests and teachers, today D&C 20:42— which requires elders to "watch over the Church"—provides the basis for home teaching and makes it primarily a Melchizedek Priesthood function. In 1962, President Marion G. Romney explained the current interpretations of that revelation: "By some it has been thought that some of the directions given in the revelation referred only to ordained teachers. It would seem, however, that the responsibility has been placed upon every bearer of the Melchizedek Priesthood, and the priests as well as upon the teachers."[69]

Leaders of the Church, mindful of revelations given to Joseph Smith and receptive to continuing divine guidance, periodically have redeployed priesthood and auxiliary forces and redefined institutional growth, and the shifting needs of its members. During the past century, the Aaronic Priesthood has received major alterations of theory and practice. By reinterpreting the adult aspects of the work, particularly the teaching obligation, to be Melchizedek Priesthood work, the traditional objective that more qualified men do the teaching generally is achieved. And giving deacons, teachers, and priests more youthful and less demanding responsibilities, Aaronic quorums now are kept filled and Church youth receive important priesthood training.

But Bishop Hunter's generation of leaders would remind us that to achieve this present state of priesthood work, the Church has modified their lofty nineteenth-century concepts of the Aaronic Priesthood. Today's fourteen- and fifteen-year-old teachers, it would appear, while providing useful Church service, nevertheless are not meaningfully credited like teachers were in previous times with special rights and powers to ferret out iniquity, receive the ministerings of angels, reconcile disputants as the Church's exclusive peacemakers, preside as Church officers in homes during official priesthood visits, or possibly participate in any part of the temple endowment. Nevertheless, the Aaronic Priesthood paradox, which Church leaders had to deal with for many decades, finally has been resolved despite some differences with priesthood concepts and practices of the past. The resolution seems pragmatically workable for this present generation.

This article was originally published in BYU Studies *16, no. 3 (1976): 375–98.*

NOTES

1. D&C 20, 68, 84, and 107 are of particular importance regarding Aaronic Priesthood work in general. For discussions of Aaronic Priesthood operations in the Church, see Lee A. Palmer, *Aaronic Priesthood through the Centuries* (Salt Lake City: Deseret Book, 1964); John A. Widtsoe, *Priesthood and Church Government,* rev. ed. (Salt Lake City: Deseret Book, 1965); Joseph B. Keeler, *The Lesser Priesthood and Notes on Church Government* (Salt Lake City: Deseret News, 1904); and Gary L. Phelps, "Home Teaching: Attempts by the Latter-day Saints to Establish an Effective Program during the Nineteenth Century" (master's thesis, Brigham Young University, 1975).

   Essential to understanding priesthood matters during the Bishop Hunter years are three primary sources in particular, from which this study draws most of its information and interpretations: Bishops Meetings with Presiding Bishopric, Minutes, 4 vols., 1849–84 (cited hereafter as Bishops Minutes); Salt Lake Stake, Deacons Quorum Minutes, 1873–77 (cited hereafter as Salt Lake Deacons Minutes); and Presiding Bishops Office, Aaronic Priesthood Minutes, 1857–77 (hereafter cited as General Aaronic Priesthood Minutes). These and all other manuscript sources cited in this paper are found in the Church History Library, The Church of Jesus Christ of Latter-day Saints, Salt Lake City.

2. Joseph Smith Jr., *History of the Church of Jesus Christ of Latter-day Saints,* ed. B. H. Roberts, 2d ed., rev., 7 vols. (Salt Lake City: Deseret Book, 1949), 4:207. See also Doctrine and Covenants 84:33.

3. See Doctrine and Covenants 76:50–65; 84:6–42.

4. See also Doctrine and Covenants 20:51, 53.

5. The Conference Minutes and Record Book of Christ's Church of Latter-day Saints, Belonging to the High Council of Said Church, or Their Successors in Office, Caldwell County, Missouri: Far West: April 6, 1838. This manuscript is referred to, and is cited hereafter, as the Far West Record. Also, Teachers Quorum Minutes at Kirtland, Ohio, Far West, Missouri, and Nauvoo, Illinois, 1841–46; Aaronic Priesthood Minutes and Biographical Sketches, January 13, 1844 to June 15, 1845; and Manchester, England,

Historical Record, 1844–46. Also see Robert L. Marrott, "History and Functions of the Aaronic Priesthood and the Offices of Priest, Teacher, and Deacon in The Church of Jesus Christ of Latter-day Saints, 1829–1844" (master's thesis, Brigham Young University, 1975).

It is noteworthy that an 1838 conference in Missouri resolved that no high priest, seventy, elder, or priest "has any right or authority to preside over or take charge of any branch, society, or neighborhood within the bounds of this Stake; but that the teachers, assisted by the deacons, be considered the standing ministry to preside each over his respective branch." Far West Record, March 10, 1838.

6. Bishops Minutes, June 24, 1851.

7. Sanpete Stake, Aaronic Priesthood Minute Book, 1873–77.

8. Sanpete Stake, Aaronic Priesthood Minute Book, 1873–77; Bishops Minutes, 1849–84; Salt Lake Deacons Minutes, 1873–77; Southern Utah Mission, St. George Stake, 1869–86, Lesser Priesthood Record Book A (hereafter cited as St. George Lesser Priesthood Minutes); General Aaronic Priesthood Minutes, 1857–77.

9. General Aaronic Priesthood Minutes, August 1, 1874. In 1876 President Young squelched the lingering idea that Salt Lake Stake was a center stake for the Church with other stakes subject to its officers. See Bishops Minutes, October 19, 1876.

10. General Aaronic Priesthood Minutes, 1857–77.

11. John Taylor, in *Journal of Discourses*, 26 vols. (Liverpool: Latter-day Saints' Book Depot, 1855–86), 19:56, June 17, 1877.

12. Bishops Minutes; Payson Ward, Utah Stake, Priests Quorum Minute Book, 1876–85, April 26, 1876. General Aaronic Priesthood Minutes, August 5, 1865; Bishops Minutes, February 28, 1854; June 19 and July 31, 1855; June 23, 1870; August 23, 1877; November 26, December 8 and 22, 1881; January 5 and 19 and February 2, 1882; and November 22, 1860.

13. Bishops Minutes, 1849–84.

14. Bishop's Minutes, October 21, 1856; General Aaronic Priesthood Minutes, February 5, 1856.

15. Erastus Snow, in *Journal of Discourses*, 19:131 , October 13, 1877.

16. General Aaronic Priesthood Minutes, November 6, 1875.

17. Bishops Minutes, September 6, 1877, and 1851–84.

18. Sixth Ward, Salt Lake, Record book, October 1869–April 1880; June 12, 1877.

19. General Aaronic Priesthood Minutes, November 7, 1874.

20. Bishops Minutes, January 9, 1879; May 28, 1868; General Aaronic Priesthood Minutes, April 6 and November 2, 1867; February 1, 1873; June 2, 1877; November 7, 1874.

21. Bishops Minutes, July 23, 1868; and April 24, 1862; General Aaronic Priesthood Minutes, December 2, 1863.

22. Bishops Minutes, October 26, 1851; General Aaronic Priesthood Minutes, July 6, 1872; and January 2, 1875; John Taylor, in *Journal of Discourses*, 18:285, November 5, 1876.

23. In 1846, for example, Brigham Young said: "When we see a temple built right, there will be a place for the priests to enter and put on their robes, and offer up sacrifices, first for themselves, and then for the people." Heber C. Kimball, Journal, January 2, 1846, Church History Library.

24. Brigham Young, in *Journal of Discourses*, 10:309, June 11, 1864.

25. George Q. Cannon, *Gospel Truth: Discourses and Writings of President George Q. Cannon,* ed. Jerrald L. Newquist, 2 vols. (Salt Lake City: Deseret Book, 1974), 1:227–28.

26. Lauritz G. Petersen, "The Kirtland Temple," *BYU Studies* 12, no. 4 (1972): 400–409.

27. Account of dedicatory proceedings on January 1, 1877, as reported in *Deseret Evening News,* January 13, 1877.

28. Bishops Minutes, February 3, 1881; General Aaronic Priesthood Minutes, November 3, 1877; March 6, 1875; January 7, 1860; and April 6, 1867.

29. Salt Lake Deacons Minutes, July 29, 1877.

30. General Aaronic Priesthood Minutes, August 1, 1868; March 6, 1869; also Bishops Minutes, April 20, 1880; December 13, 1866; and September 1, 1870.

31. John Taylor, Sermon at Ogden, May 24, 1877, in *Deseret News,* June 6, 1877.

32. Bishops Minutes, October 8, 1855; and January 31, 1854.

33. Salt Lake Deacons Minutes, January 27, 1877; General Aaronic Priesthood Minutes, November 6, 1875.

34. Salt Lake Deacons Minutes, August 5, 1873; and February 4, 1877.

35. Brigham Young Journal, February 16, 1849; Bishops Minutes, February 15, 1853; January 17, 1854; and March 31, 1857; General Aaronic Priesthood Minutes, March 2, 1861; January 3, 1863; March 1, 1873; and January 2, 1875.

36. General Aaronic Priesthood Minutes, May 6, 1876.

37. Kanab Teachers Minutes, January 14, 1874.

38. Brigham Young, in *Journal of Discourses,* 2:89, October 6, 1854.

39. Sanpete Aaronic Priesthood Minutes, February 2, 1874.

40. General Aaronic Priesthood Minutes, January 1, 1876; and January 2, 1875.

41. Circular of the First Presidency, July 11, 1877, in *Messages of the First Presidency of The Church of Jesus Christ of Latter-day Saints, 1833–1964,* comp. James R. Clark, 6 vols. (Salt Lake City: Bookcraft, 1965–75), 2:286.

42. William Hartley, "The Priesthood Reform Movement, 1908–1922," *BYU Studies* 13, no. 2 (1973): 137–56.

43. See text of this article, pages 96–97.

44. Brigham Young Journal, February 16, 1849; Bishops Minutes, November 30, 1851; January 16, 1855; Salt Lake Stake, School of the Prophets, Minutes, December 23, 1872; General Aaronic Priesthood Minutes, July 1, 1876.

45. Edward Hunter to Joseph A. Young, September 18, 1873, General Tithing Store, Letterbooks, 1872–75.

46. Salt Lake Deacons Minutes, January 27, May 26, February 4, 1877; and December 14, 1875; Brigham Young, in *Journal of Discourses,* 9:92, May 7, 1861.

47. Sixth Ward Record Book, June 1, 1877; Bishops Minutes, December 7, 1882; General Aaronic Priesthood Minutes, August 5, 1876.

48. Bishops Minutes, January 19, 1860.

49. Bishops Minutes, January 17, 1854; September 25, 1856; and May 18, 1876; General Aaronic Priesthood Minutes, February 3, 1877.

50. Edward Hunter to Orson Hyde, General Tithing Store, Letterbooks, October 17, 1873.

51. General Aaronic Priesthood Minutes, September 4, 1875; and June 5, 1869; Bishops Minutes, August 13, 1874; and September 25, 1856.

52. Bishops Minutes, 1856–57, particularly September 11, 1873; and May 18, 1876.

53. Circular of the First Presidency, July 11, 1877; also Bishops Minutes, 1877–84.

54. Circular of the First Presidency, July 11, 1877; also Sixth Ward Record Book, June 1, 1877.

55. *Deseret News*, November 20, 1902.

56. Hartley, "Priesthood Reform Movement"; General Priesthood Committee on Outlines, Minutes, 1908–22, inclusive.

57. General Priesthood Committee Minutes, May 5, 1909.

58. General Priesthood Committee Minutes, June 1, 1916.

59. *Church News*, published by *Deseret News*, April 21, 1945, 5; Heber J. Grant, Letter to Henry H. Rolapp, June 28, 1928, Heber J. Grant Letterbook, April 14, 1928, to August 30, 1928, microfilm.

60. "Ward Teaching," *Improvement Era* 16 (November 1912): 79–80.

61. Joseph F. Smth, "Opening Address," in *Eighty-fourth Annual Conference of The Church of Jesus Christ of Latter-day Saints* (Salt Lake City: Church of Jesus Christ of Latter-day Saints, 1914), 7. Italics added.

62. *Priesthood Manual: A Handbook for the Quorums of the Melchizedek Priesthood* (Salt Lake City: Deseret Book, 1933), 16–17.

63. Joseph Fielding Smith to Vernon L. Israelsen, July 14, 1935, reproduced in Vernon L. Israelsen, "Changes in the Numbers and the Priesthood Affiliation of the Men Used as Ward Teachers in The Church of Jesus Christ of Latter-day Saints, 1920–1935" (master's thesis, Brigham Young University, 1937), 22–23.

64. "Melchizedek Priesthood Ward Teaching," *Improvement Era* 37 (April 1934): 229.

65. "Cache Stake Reports Success in Aaronic Priesthood Ward Teaching," *Improvement Era* 37 (June 1934): 364.

66. Israelsen, "Changes in Numbers," 224.

67. "Ward Teaching," *Improvement Era* 43 (December 1940): 748.

68. For a scrapbook-type description of priesthood teaching which overlooks nineteenth century teaching practices, the issues raised by the Aaronic Priesthood paradox, and the priesthood research of Israelsen, Hartley, and Richard Cowan, but which presents some selected important documents about ward and home teaching, see Rex A. Andersen, "A Documentary History of the Lord's Way of Watching Over the Church by the Priesthood through the Ages" (master's thesis, Brigham Young University, 1974).

69. Marion G. Romney, "Opening Address," in *One Hundred Thirty-second Semi-annual Conference of The Church of Jesus Christ of Latter-day Saints* (Salt Lake City: Church of Jesus Christ of Latter-day Saints, 1962), 78.

| | Bishop, |
| 5 | History of the Office |

THE WORK OF THE OFFICE OF BISHOP in The Church of Jesus Christ of Latter-day Saints has evolved over 160 years to accommodate changing Church needs. When the Church was small, bishops were concerned primarily with the temporal needs of the Church, and spiritual needs were left to the Prophet. At the 1846 exodus from Nauvoo, three kinds of bishops functioned: general bishops, ward bishops, and traveling or regional bishops. In 1847 the first Presiding Bishop was called, and was assigned Church-wide temporal and administrative duties. Ward bishops worked under the supervision of the Presiding Bishop, traveling or regional bishops, and stake presidents. In the late 1800s ward bishops were assigned greater responsibility for ward members, seeing to their spiritual as well as temporal needs. Thus the need for traveling or regional bishops gradually diminished and the office soon ceased altogether. Contemporary Church organization includes ward bishops and a Presiding Bishop who is a General Authority.

BEFORE NAUVOO, 1830–1839

Revelation to Joseph Smith restored the office of bishop in February 1831 (D&C 41:9; cf. 1 Tim. 3:1–7). Edward Partridge was called as the

Church's first bishop and was made responsible for operating a storehouse to help the poor (D&C 42:30–39) and for administering property transactions connected with the law of consecration (D&C 42; 58:17). In December 1831, Newel K. Whitney was also called as a bishop (D&C 72). The two served as regional or traveling bishops (D&C 20:66), Whitney for Ohio and the eastern states and Partridge for Missouri.[1] The First Presidency ordained them and called two counselors to assist each one. In November 1831, the Lord had revealed the Aaronic Priesthood organization, designating bishops as the presidents of the Aaronic Priesthood to preside over quorums of up to forty-eight priests (D&C 107:87–88). Bishops Partridge and Whitney helped organize these priesthood quorums and selected and set apart quorum presidents. After the organization of the first stakes in 1834, bishops functioned much like stake officers.

Edward Partridge was called as Presiding Bishop in the Church in 1831. He established a storehouse to care for the poor and administer property transactions under the newly established law of consecration. Courtesy Church Archives.

In response to additional revelations (D&C 42:30–39; 51:1–20; 84:103–104), bishops Partridge and Whitney managed such Church temporal matters as paying bills, buying and selling lands and goods, helping with construction projects, printing, and assisting the poor. In Missouri, where members consecrated and pooled belongings, Bishop Partridge signed the consecration deeds, received donations into a bishop's storehouse, and deeded back donated and purchased properties based on members' needs. He was remunerated for his full-time service.

NAUVOO PERIOD, 1839–1846

In 1841, when the law of tithing replaced deeding all of one's property to the Church, bishops helped receive and disburse tithes. However, the Prophet Joseph Smith as Church President and trustee-in-trust held title to Church properties and established Church financial policies.

The office of ward bishops began with the establishment of the first wards in Nauvoo. There, bishops Newel K. Whitney and George Miller, who replaced Bishop Partridge (who had died in 1840), had general jurisdictions and also served in an assigned municipal ward. By 1842, Nauvoo's thirteen wards each had a bishop with two counselors. Their main tasks were to process tithes and to assist newcomers and aid the poor, which they accomplished with donated fast offerings. Bishops also carried a major responsibility for dealing with ward members in cases of wrongdoing. However, bishops rarely conducted Sunday worship meetings; such services were held outdoors on a citywide or stake basis or in individual homes. Nauvoo bishops collectively organized and directed the work of deacons, teachers, and priests quorums in the city.

By the time of the exodus from Nauvoo, the Church had three types of bishops: general bishops, who in 1845 became trustees for the Church; ward bishops; and traveling bishops sent beyond Nauvoo to receive Church funds.

EXODUS AND EARLY UTAH, 1846–1900

During the exodus, ordained and acting bishops cared for the needy through tithes, offerings, and labor. Winter Quarters was divided into twenty-two wards, each with a bishop. By 1848 bishops in Kanesville, Iowa, exercised civil as well as ecclesiastical authority. On April 6, 1847, Bishop Newel K. Whitney became the first Presiding Bishop for the entire Church.

When Latter-day Saints first settled in Utah, the norm was for each settlement to have a president and at least one bishop (the nucleus of an embryonic stake). Salt Lake City, the largest settlement, was divided into nineteen wards in 1849, each with a bishop and two counselors. When Presiding Bishop Whitney died in 1850, he was replaced by Bishop Edward Hunter, who was given two counselors, thereby creating the first Presiding Bishopric. They were responsible for Church temporal affairs, for local bishops, and for stake Aaronic Priesthood quorums. Bishop Hunter met every two weeks with northern Utah bishops to coordinate efforts regarding public works, tithes, resources, immigration and immigrants, and the needy. However, the First Presidency, not the Presiding Bishopric, made finance and resource policy, and called and released bishops.

In each stake, bishops called men, and later, boys, to fill stake-level deacons quorums, teachers quorums, and priests quorums, and gave them responsibilities in their wards. The basic ward officers for the pioneer Utah period were the bishopric and the teachers quorum, then called block teachers or ward teachers. Under direction of the bishop, teachers visited members in their homes, settled disputes, and helped the needy. Teachers and bishoprics heard charges of wrongdoing and decided guilt or innocence. Bishops, as Church judges, conducted inquiries regarding sin and held bishops' courts, if necessary, to excommunicate, disfellowship, or exonerate. During the reformation (LDS) of 1856–57, bishops and teachers saw to the catechizations interviews and rebaptism of members.

Bishops spent much of their time managing tithing. Most tithes were "in kind," necessitating the creation of bishop's storehouses, which included corrals for animals and bins for farm products. Tithing houses sometimes became commerce centers, serving as trading posts, banks issuing and receiving tithing scrip, wayside inns, and transportation and mail hubs. The Presiding Bishopric issued price valuations for donated and traded products, creating uniform prices for the territory. In the largely cashless pioneer economy, bishops used two-thirds of the local tithes to help the poor and to pay for public improvements. They forwarded one-third of the tithing commodities to Salt Lake City to pay laborers on the Salt Lake Temple and various public works projects. Bishops received a small percentage of the tithes to cover personal expenses incurred while managing the donations. By the mid-1850s, ward bishops had taken over the Presiding Bishopric's task of conducting annual tithing settlements with members.

During the consecration movement in the 1850s and the united order efforts in the 1870s, bishops received, recorded, and dispersed donated properties. Ward bishops recruited resources for use elsewhere, such as products in short supply, special funds, supplies for the militia, and teamsters and wagons to take immigrants west from staging points and supply depots in Nebraska, Iowa, and, later, Wyoming.

Emigrants traveling through Echo Canyon, 1865. Presiding Bishop Edward Hunter oversaw the Church's efforts to help all Saints gather to Utah. Once they arrived, Hunter also directed people to settlements that could support more families and helped them find work. Courtesy Church Archives.

The First Presidency and the Presiding Bishopric supervised local bishops through visits to wards, two annual general conferences requiring the attendance of bishops, distribution of circular letters, and the reports of traveling and regional bishops. Stake presidents served as the bishops' ecclesiastical superior line officers. In the Salt Lake, Cache, and Utah valleys, stake presidents held regular bishops quorum meetings.

During this period, bishops had both temporal and spiritual responsibility for their wards and communities. They called ward officers, conducted meetings and presided over funerals, supervised ordinances, and gave blessings. They assisted the needy through the use of tithes, fast offerings, and volunteer labor. During the 1856 famine, bishops requisitioned foodstuffs to distribute within a ward and to share with other wards. In the mid-1850s some wards created Relief Societies to aid needy Indians. Ward Relief Societies became widespread in the 1870s, and the bishops relied on them to seek out and help the needy.

Elders, seventies, and high priests met in stake quorums and were not directly subject to the bishops. In the 1860s and 1870s, bishops helped organize and supervise Relief Societies for women and other ward auxiliary organizations, such as Mutual Improvement Associations for youth and adults, Sunday Schools, and Primaries for children.

In 1877 bishops presided over wards varying in size from 171 members in Morgan Stake wards (northern Utah) to 808 members in Utah Stake wards (central Utah). Each stake contained an average of twelve wards. An average ward had 432 members, 81 families, 13 high priests, 19 seventies, 38 elders, 6 priests, 6 teachers, and 10 deacons. During a thorough reorganization of the priesthood in 1877, President Brigham Young added 140 wards to the existing 101, retaining 56 bishops and ordaining 185 new ones. Most bishopric counselors were newly called, too, and were required to be high priests. Thus, in 1877 new personnel comprised about 80 percent of the Church's bishoprics.

New instructions directed bishops to account for their ward members; keep Aaronic Priesthood units staffed; attend weekly Aaronic Priesthood meetings and monthly stake priesthood meetings; operate an effective ward teaching program; conduct the sacrament during Sunday School; turn in monthly and quarterly reports of membership, finances, and ward activities; keep accurate records of disciplinary proceedings; support temple laborers; and hold proper Sabbath meetings, thus setting basic patterns for ward organization and procedures in the twenty-first century. Bishops' agents replaced regional presiding bishops. In response to instructions to involve boys eleven to nineteen years old in an Aaronic Priesthood office, bishops called them to be deacons in their wards, beginning the shift of Aaronic Priesthood work to the youth. Bishops continued to call elders and high priests as acting priests and acting teachers to do the ward teaching.

Nineteenth-century Utah bishops were the civic leaders in their communities. They encouraged immigrants to become citizens and to vote. They discussed political matters at Church meetings; backed the development of the telegraph, railroad, mines, canals, and cooperative stores; and established and superintended local schools. The average length of service for all nineteenth-century Utah bishops was eleven years, but 15 percent served for more than twenty years. Bishops had above-average incomes. They entered into plural marriage more than other male members; at least 60 percent of bishops had one or more plural wives.

Because of federal antipolygamy efforts during the 1880s, many bishops were prosecuted or were forced into hiding, thus virtually halting their political involvement. Their wards were incorporated so that they, rather than the general Church, owned meetinghouses, saving them from confiscation by the federal government. The tithing system was disrupted, and tithe paying declined. In 1889 stake tithing clerks replaced the bishops' agents.

1900–1930

Beginning about 1900, after Utah had gained statehood (1896), the economic practices of the Church were modified. By the early 1900s tithing had changed from donations of commodities primarily to cash; tithing houses gradually disappeared, and the collection task became simpler. Fast offerings also were most often donated in cash rather than food.

A priesthood reform movement from 1908 to 1922 designated the Aaronic Priesthood for boys, with ordination ages of twelve for deacons, fifteen for teachers, and seventeen for priests. Each age group received new duties and standardized lesson manuals. Bishops supervised the ward-level quorums and became presidents of the wards' Aaronic Priesthood.

Another change in 1908 required that all ward priesthood quorums cease meeting at separate times and instead meet together weekly in a ward priesthood meeting on Monday nights. For the first time, bishops regularly met with and presided over all ward priesthood groups at once. In the 1930s, ward priesthood meetings shifted from Monday nights to Sunday mornings.

1930–1960

Stakes and wards continued to spread beyond the Rocky Mountain region. Bishops in outlying areas with LDS minorities faced new problems not found in the predominantly LDS state of Utah. Away from the Intermountain West, Church meetinghouses were few in number, and members often lived long distances from one another.

Changes during this period include the creation by the Presiding Bishopric of a central membership file so bishops could receive or send membership records more efficiently, a uniform ward budget system, achievement award programs for the youth, the regular publication of a bulletin from the Presiding Bishopric to be disseminated to all bishops, arrangement of funds for bishops to attend general conferences, and the improvement of the handbook for bishops. Since ward teachers were ward

122 ~ MY FELLOW SERVANTS

officers and personal representatives of the bishop, the bishopric personally selected and interviewed the ward teachers and conducted monthly report meetings with them.

With the introduction of the welfare services program in the late 1930s, bishops established and operated ward welfare projects and mobilized ward support for stake projects. They introduced more efficient methods of collecting and utilizing fast offerings and allocated food and clothing from the new bishop's storehouses to the needy.

DEVELOPMENTS SINCE 1960

The postwar "baby boom" and rapid increases in convert baptisms produced sudden and steep growth in Church membership during the 1960s, which required more wards, bishops, and meetinghouses. The Church established stakes and wards internationally, producing a growing number of non-English-speaking bishops.

To help new bishops, the Church published a wide array of instruction manuals for the various organizations and activities of the Church. By the 1980s, new bishops in the United States received several such manuals, a general handbook of instructions, and various priesthood guidebooks. Because the bishop's tasks became so numerous that many bishops in the 1950s and 1960s were spending most weeknights as well as all day Sunday attending to Church duties, the Church moved to ease and simplify the nature of the bishop's assignment.

In 1964, as part of a new Church emphasis on correlation, "ward teaching," now known as home teaching, became a responsibility of Melchizedek Priesthood quorum leaders, thus removing a major supervisory assignment from the bishops, though bishops continued to visit members in their homes and conduct funerals, visit the sick, and bestow blessings. In the 1970s and 1980s, the bishop's service tenure was generally shortened, although length of service was not set, and ward sizes were reduced. Computerization of membership and financial records simplified bishops' record-keeping tasks. LDS social services became a counseling resource to which bishops could refer members with difficult problems. Monday nights were reserved for family home evenings, when no ward activities were to be held, thus giving both bishops and members more time for their families. By the 1980s, the Church had consolidated all ward meetings, previously spread throughout the week, into one three-hour block on Sunday, saving bishops and members much travel and meeting time, particularly in wards that covered large areas. In 1990, Church headquarters began a quarterly allotment from the general tithing fund to cover ward expenses for wards in North America. This eliminated the bishop's need to solicit ward budget money through donations and fund-raising activities. The Church also simplified its disciplinary procedures.

This article was originally published in Encyclopedia of Mormonism, *ed. Daniel H. Ludlow, 4 vols. (New York: Macmillan, 1992), 1:119–22.*

NOTE

1. Andrew Jenson, *Latter-day Saint Biographical Encyclopedia: A Compilation of Biographical Sketches of Prominent Men and Women in The Church of Jesus Christ of Latter-day Saints,* 4 vols. (Salt Lake City: Andrew Jenson History, 1901–36), 1:219–20, 224. See also Leonard J. Arrington, *Great Basin Kingdom: An Economic History of the Latter-day Saints, 1830–1900* (1958; reprinted Lincoln: University of Nebraska Press, 1966); Dale F. Beecher, "The Office of Bishop," *Dialogue: A Journal of Mormon Thought* 15 (Winter 1982): 103–15; William G. Hartley, "The Priesthood Reform Movement, 1908–1922," *BYU Studies* 13, no. 2 (1973): 137–56; Donald G. Pace, "Community Leadership on the Mormon Frontier: Mormon Bishops and the Political, Economic, and Social Development of Utah before Statehood" (PhD diss., Ohio State University, 1983); John A. Widtsoe, *Priesthood and Church Government in The Church of Jesus Christ of Latter-day Saints* (Salt Lake City: Deseret Book, 1939).

6   Edward Hunter, Pioneer Presiding Bishop

WHEN HEBER J. GRANT WAS YOUNG, his mother once crossed the street diagonally. Presiding Bishop Edward Hunter met her and said with the usual twinkle in his eye and double phrase on his lips: "Rachel, Rachel, go straight, go straight. Be careful. Cut a corner and miss heaven, cut a corner and miss heaven. Keep in the straight path."[1] Young Heber and other youths of his day grew up mimicking the double phrases of the bewhiskered Pennsylvanian, and they repeated many proverbs and aphorisms they knew were his. Although forgotten today, Edward Hunter was a well-known and well-liked General Authority in his day because he was colorful and a bit eccentric, and because his fair but kindly ways of performing as Presiding Bishop pleased so many Saints.

He was a pioneer Presiding Bishop in two ways. First, he presided during most of the Mormon pioneering years and longer, from 1851 to 1883. His firm hand on the Church's temporal reins helped steer it through dramatic transformations in size and procedures. During his thirty-three-year term, the Rocky Mountain Saints' population grew from 11,000 to over 120,000, and the number of wards increased from forty to about three hundred.[2] Because he had direct responsibility for people and resources, such explosive growth in the basically cashless, desert oasis taxed his executive talents.

He also pioneered in terms of the office and calling of Presiding Bishop. The office had barely developed beyond an embryonic stage when Hunter's predecessor, Bishop Newel K. Whitney, died in 1850. During the next decades, Bishop Hunter firmly carved the Presiding Bishopric's niche into the Church's General Authority hierarchy. Of concern here are Bishop Hunter's two most demanding responsibilities: tithing supervisor, with the corollary task of caring for the worthy poor, and president of the Aaronic Priesthood.

THE CALL

When Elder Heber C. Kimball announced to the April 1851 general conference that Bishop Edward Hunter would succeed Bishop Whitney, he warned: "I wish Bro. Hunter to understand that he has now got into a place, where he will be thumped and pulled about. Can you go it?" The large, fifty-eight-year-old bishop—he weighed over 250 pounds—replied, "I will do the best I can." Elder Kimball continued: "I can recommend him to fill that office, as a man of God, and a man of business."[3]

After Edward's conversion to Mormonism in 1839–40, his commitment to the gospel never wavered. Once socially and financially prominent in Pennsylvania, he surrendered the good life of country squire to emigrate to Nauvoo and there consecrated great wealth to the Lord. His loyalty and generosity to Joseph Smith were unbounded, causing Joseph to tell him in the name of the Lord to cease donating. "In all of early Church history," writes a Hunter biographer, "we find no other convert past middle age who had comparable wealth that consecrated his material wealth and mortal life to a similar extent."[4] On another occasion, Joseph Smith told Edward: "I have enquired of the Lord concerning you, and you are favourable in His sight."[5] When Joseph was martyred, Edward passed his loyalty from Joseph to Brigham Young, in part because he witnessed the mystical moment when the mantle of Joseph descended upon Brigham and transformed his appearance. During the trek west, Edward Hunter, who had been Nauvoo Fifth Ward bishop, served as a Winter Quarters bishop and then in 1848 captained a company of a hundred into the Valley.[6]

In 1849, when Salt Lake City was divided into wards, he became the Thirteenth Ward's bishop. When called as Presiding Bishop in 1851, he was judged to be a careful and thorough businessman, a person with "great

Bishop Edward Hunter, second Presiding Bishop for the Church (1851–83), was known for his unique expressions, kind nature, and business acumen. He created the framework under which the functions of the Presiding Bishop were established. Courtesy Church Archives.

knowledge in temporal things." By background he was a farmer, leather curer, a cattle expert in terms of breeding, handling, and judging, and a businessman.[7]

In 1851, the time of Edward Hunter's call, the office of Presiding Bishop was not well defined. The Bishop's role when the law of consecration was being practiced in Missouri was fairly clear, but its role in Nauvoo's temporal affairs was less so. When Newel Whitney, "a most upright and thorough business man," became Presiding Bishop in 1848, President Young directed him to manage tithing, establish home industry, and care for the poor; but the confusion caused by the Utah migration seems to have precluded firm procedures by the time Bishop Whitney died.[8] President Young said that bishops in Nauvoo "never seemed to understand the duty and office of a bishop." Regarding Bishop Whitney, he confessed: "I did often chastise him severely, to try to get him to understand his office." He added that Bishop Whitney, near the end of his life, seemed "to have waked up out of a deep sleep, and began to understand something of his office and duty." By contrast, Brigham once said, Brother Hunter never was chastised like Bishop Whitney. Why?

> Because I knew ... he came into this Church, and had transacted business on a large scale, was a good and competent judge of Horses, Cattle, Cows, Grain Etc; and therefore did not need those severe chastisements that some of you bishops are obliged to take from time to time.[9]

Edward served as Presiding Bishop for one year on a trial basis and then was ordained. Brigham Young and Heber C. Kimball were his counselors. In 1854, Edward was released as Thirteenth Ward bishop. In 1856, Leonard W. Hardy and Jesse C. Little became his counselors, and at that point the three-man Presiding Bishopric as we know it today emerged. Hardy also continued as Twelfth Ward bishop until 1877. Little was replaced in the Presiding Bishopric in 1874 by Robert T. Burton, bishop of the Fifteenth Ward.[10]

We look in vain for indications of formal meetings between the Presiding Bishopric and the First Presidency. Available daybooks for the Historian's Office and the Presidency's Office keep good track of Brigham Young's activities, but mentions of Brigham's meeting formally with Bishop Hunter are rare. Informal consultations seem to have been the rule. During

Edward's first years as Presiding Bishop he met regularly on Sunday afternoons with the First Presidency and members of the Twelve in a prayer
circle, where leaders discussed Church problems and where Edward evidently obtained occasional instructions. After receiving formal counselors
in 1856, Edward was told by the First Presidency "to come into the councils
of the first presidency, and feel that there was his place and prerogative and
not for one moment to think he was intruding."[11]

Bishop Hunter continued a tradition, started by Bishop Whitney, of
meeting regularly with the Salt Lake Valley bishops and others from more
distant wards who could attend. These "town meetings" of bishops, or
bishops quorum meetings, provided Bishop Hunter and the First Presidency a regular forum for instructing and for receiving feedback. The First
Presidency attended, but not regularly. At times they gave Hunter instructions before the meetings, as in 1857 when he "informed the meeting that
he had an interview with the first presidency a short time prior to the meeting and they expressed themselves satisfied with the labors of the Bishops."
Bishop Hunter frequently took policy-type questions raised at the meetings
to the First Presidency for clarification.[12]

During most of this period, the First Presidency's headquarters were in
Brigham Young's office on Brigham's block. Bishop Hunter had an office a
block west in the General Tithing Office. Both offices had their own clerks

*The General Tithing Office served as a receiving and distribution center for all
of Utah Territory. Under Bishop Hunter's direction, several cities built local
bishop's storehouses to serve their specific communities. Courtesy Perry Special
Collections.*

and record books. As near as the system can be pieced together now, the main finance books for the Church were the trustee-in-trust ledger books in the President's office. These master records included records received from daybooks and account books kept by the Church public works clerks and the General Tithing Office clerks. But Hunter's office daybooks, which recorded tithes on hand at the General Tithing Office, evidently were turned in periodically and made permanent records in the trustee-in-trust master books.[13]

Bishop Hunter knew his role was subordinate, second level, a carry-it-out type job rather than a policy-making job. While some members and bishops believed that temporal matters should shift from the First Presidency to the Presiding Bishopric, and that temporal matters ought not to be the concern of the Melchizedek Priesthood, the First Presidency thought otherwise.[14] Said Heber C. Kimball in 1854:

> Many wish for the time when President Brigham Young and his brethren would be relieved from attending to temporal matters and to attend to spiritual matters altogether. You will have to wait for this until we get into the spiritual world.... All things pertaining to this world, both spiritual and temporal, will be dictated by the Prophet.[15]

Brigham Young made his position clear, too. He told a Parowan group in 1855 that Bishop Hunter was called "to help the 1st Presidency in temporal matters." But if the First Presidency could be in two places at once, he added, "they would attend to the Bishop's business." But even God could not be in two places at once, he said, "hence the necessity of helps and governments in the priesthood to aid the presiding authorities."[16] In 1860, Brigham Young said the Presiding Bishopric had charge of temporal matters "and were under the immediate dictation of the 1st Presidency."[17] Willard Richards said that if Bishop Hunter should counsel wrong "it is the business of the First Presidency ... to correct him, from whom he receives his instruction."[18]

One temporal activity the First Presidency did not turn over to the Presiding Bishop was the public works projects. Through the trustee-in-trust office, the Presidency supervised the temple, tabernacle, and other construction projects and workers, paying the workers in tithing goods and scrip issued from Hunter's office.[19]

TITHING MANAGER

Tithing was the portly Bishop's number one responsibility—encouraging, receiving, storing, allocating, and accounting for animal and produce tithes, properties, labor tithes, and some cash.

From Bishop Whitney he inherited no smoothly working tithing operation. So, with the First Presidency, he had to develop, refine, and manage a complicated noncash tithing system that pumped economic life into the basically poor Church. His first summer in the saddle, 1851, he saw tithes barely trickle into the new tithing storehouse's cellars and apartments. Skimpy donations meant Church projects suffered for want of lumber, materials, and laborers. Even a tithe of the tithing due, said the First Presidency's epistle that fall, "would have enabled us to enclose the Temple Block as we had anticipated."[20]

A new tithing push soon came. That September, Bishop Hunter and the First Presidency announced a new program that required not just tithing on increase and labor, but once again, as in preexodus days, on *all* that a Saint possessed, even if he had tithed on all upon conversion—as was then expected. Fall 1851 general conference attenders voted to comply. To launch the stepped-up tithing program, three special traveling presiding bishops were sent to help gather in and forward tithes to the general office.[21] A November circular said that Bishop Hunter "has charge of all receipts and expenditures relating to tithing," and the appraising of properties and recording of donations.[22]

So Hunter's first year proved to be a busy one that left him overwhelmed. "Many times I am so crowded with business," he lamented in October 1851, "that I have not time to treat my brethren with that civility and kindness that they are entitled to and which would be congenial to my feelings."[23] Besides receiving goods and recording them, he had to handle a wave of questions from bishops. How much were cows worth this year? Oxen per yoke? Could wheat be taken in place of property tithing? How should perishables like butter and eggs be stored? Could there be regional storehouses built? The results of the push, announced in April 1852 conference, earned Brigham Young's praise: "There has been more done by the Bishops in the last 7 months than in the previous 7 years, and I feel to bless you." "Never before," the First Presidency broadcast, "has the Lord's storehouse been so well supplied."[24]

The Seventh Epistle by the First Presidency in April 1852 provides one rare disclosure of Church tithes. From 1847 to 1851, the letter noted, $390,261 had come in as tithes. Expenditures, amounting to $354,000, went for public-works shops (blacksmith, carpenter, paint), for a barn and storehouse for tithes, for a bowery and a tabernacle, for factories and lands, for clerks and superintendents, and for provisions for emigration. "Little had been received in cash," the report concluded.[25]

The tithing success earned Bishop Hunter a permanent job. "I am going to present the case of Bishop Hunter," President Heber C. Kimball, First Counselor in the First Presidency, told the April 1852 conference. "He has never been ordained to that calling. We thought we would prove him before we ordain him." They then ordained him on April 11 "to preside over the temporal affairs of our God on the earth," and blessed him with powers to discern, to judge righteously, and "to lift the hearts of the Saints." More traveling bishops were called that conference to assist the Bishop.[26]

Not wanting another year-end inundation at the General Tithing Office, Bishop Hunter changed tithing procedures so that henceforth local bishops settled with tithepayers and made up annual ward tithing ledgers. Tithepaying thus was localized. But local record keeping posed a serious problem. "There never has been a bishop yet who has made a report that would give me any knowledge of the condition of his ward," Brigham Young complained in 1855.[27] He wanted records good enough "that Bishop Hunter can read it right; and know how [much] Oxen, Horses, Cows, Sheep, Lambs, Pigs, Fowls ... Eggs, Butter, and Cheese, Produce of every kind, and money" was given. Bishop Hunter therefore issued a circular letter that explained record keeping, the disbursements of tithing, and answered typical tithepayer questions. From 1852 to 1854, wards received record books and built local tithing storehouses. By 1854 storehouses stood or were being built in Provo, Lehi, Springville, Palmyra, American Fork, and elsewhere.[28]

In 1854 the tithing requirement was turned up another notch when President Young announced in April conference that Saints could move beyond tithing to voluntarily consecrate all their property to the Church. The Saints voted to comply with this law "first given to Brother Joseph." But much interest and sermonizing produced little consecrating, mainly because of legal snags in the deed form. Scripture and tradition place the Presiding Bishop in the role of manager of consecrated properties, as Bishop Edward Partridge was in Missouri. Many Utahns wondered if Edward Hunter would assume the role Bishop Partridge had held. But the deeds were conveyed to Brigham Young as trustee-in-trust and not to the Presiding Bishop. What Bishop Hunter's reactions were to his backseat role in the renewed consecration effort is not known.[29]

However, that Bishop Hunter thought he should play a bigger role in Church temporal management is shown by his proposal in the late 1850s that the Twelve cease earning their own livelihoods and be sustained from general Church funds. Two liked the idea, others were neutral, but some adamantly insisted on earning their own livings. One warned that "if we could do as Bishop Hunter spoke of, we might become dry and dull" and unable to advise Saints on temporal matters. The proposal died.[30]

Today's cash tithing operation seems rather simple when compared to Bishop Hunter's system. Table 1 shows the basics of the complex system.

Labor tithing, which originated in Nauvoo, meant laboring one day in ten for the Church. "When [a man] has worked nine days for himself," said one explanation, "then let him take his team and work a day for public works.... If he idles 150 days of his time in riding and pleasure, he owes 15 days work for the Lord." Labor tithing could be used to pay off tithes in kind. It could be commuted and paid by goods or cash. A tithepayer might even hire someone to perform the labor tithing for him. The labor tithe required not just a man with his work clothes and bare hands but also the labor of his work animals and equipment—wagons, teams, shovels, hammers, and drills. The most frequently mentioned type of labor tithing was hauling, either hauling tithing produce from ward storehouses to the General Tithing Office or hauling building materials to or from public work sites.[31]

Underdeveloped regions needed labor, and labor tithing let able-bodied men make projects happen even when there was no cash. Frequently, Bishop Hunter issued urgent calls for labor tithing, and notices were read from the stand each Sunday telling what days Salt Lake wards were assigned to provide labor tithing for Church projects. Often men waited until after spring, summer, and fall to do labor tithing, but sometimes President Young told Bishop Hunter "to receive no labour tithing in winter when it was not wanted, when labor was needed, then was the time for it to come, or not at all."[32] Labor tithing contributed greatly to the building of temples, tabernacles, meetinghouses, fences, bridges, canals, roads, and storehouses. Labor tithing hauled thousands of wagon loads of tithing goods to regional

TABLE 1.

Tithing System during the Era of Presiding Bishop Edward Hunter, 1851–1883

LOCAL

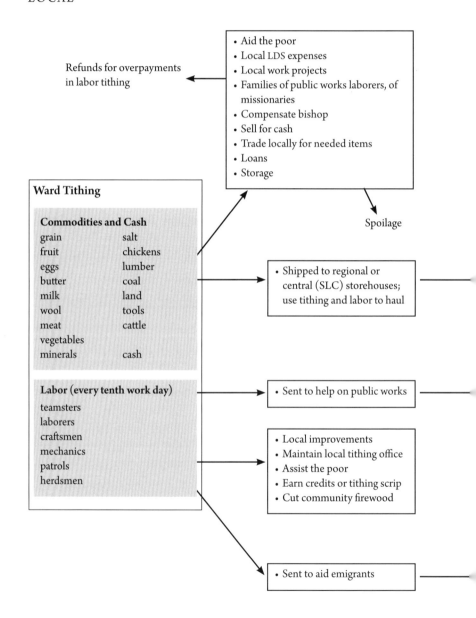

Refunds for overpayments in labor tithing

- Aid the poor
- Local LDS expenses
- Local work projects
- Families of public works laborers, of missionaries
- Compensate bishop
- Sell for cash
- Trade locally for needed items
- Loans
- Storage

Ward Tithing

Commodities and Cash

grain   salt
fruit   chickens
eggs   lumber
butter   coal
milk   land
wool   tools
meat   cattle
vegetables
minerals   cash

Spoilage

- Shipped to regional or central (SLC) storehouses; use tithing and labor to haul

Labor (every tenth work day)

teamsters
laborers
craftsmen
mechanics
patrols
herdsmen

- Sent to help on public works

- Local improvements
- Maintain local tithing office
- Assist the poor
- Earn credits or tithing scrip
- Cut community firewood

- Sent to aid emigrants

REGIONAL OR GENERAL

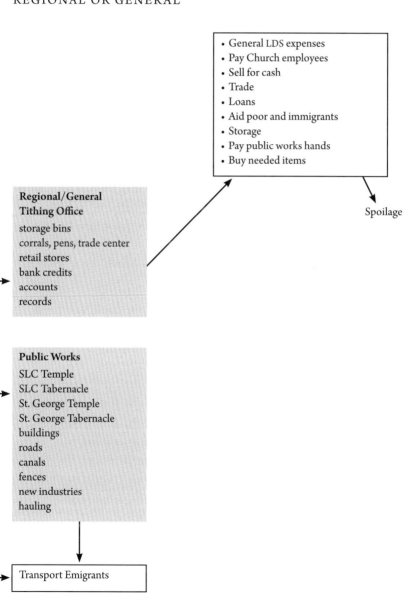

- General LDS expenses
- Pay Church employees
- Sell for cash
- Trade
- Loans
- Aid poor and immigrants
- Storage
- Pay public works hands
- Buy needed items

Spoilage

Regional/General Tithing Office

storage bins
corrals, pens, trade center
retail stores
bank credits
accounts
records

Public Works

SLC Temple
SLC Tabernacle
St. George Temple
St. George Tabernacle
buildings
roads
canals
fences
new industries
hauling

Transport Emigrants

and central tithing stores. It took goods east, across the plains, and brought immigrants west. It carried supplies to needy Indians, to Mormon militiamen during the Indian encounters and the Utah War, to stranded immigrants, and to local poor. During the move south, it helped many Saints.[33]

As manager of tithing products of all kinds, Bishop Hunter constantly faced four main problems: (1) making proper valuation of goods, (2) storing perishable goods, (3) transferring goods around to meet the overall needs of the kingdom, and (4) record keeping.

Fixing prices for specific items was no easy task. How much was a bushel of wheat worth? a five-year-old cow? a chicken? Periodically, the Tithing Office published a price list by weight or measure, prices Bishop Hunter tried to keep in line with gentile merchant prices and with employers' pay rates. Even with prices set, Bishop Hunter often had to judge the value of items, particularly cattle.[34] His humor came out sometimes when he examined the scrawny items submitted to the Lord. Once he asked his clerk, George Goddard: "Is there a law, is there a law, against cruelty to animals?" Goddard said yes. "All good laws ought to be enforced," Hunter muttered; "tithing office chickens, bones sticking through, cruelty to animals, cruelty to animals, ought to be punished."[35]

Tithing's main purpose was to provide for the Church's financial needs. As the First Presidency explained in 1855:

> The tithing furnishes our resources for all of our public improvements, and this is generally paid in grain, vegetables, stock, wagons, labour, and other property, and but very little in money, and with the exception of what is needed for the use of the men employed, has to be turned into cash to procure such other articles as are necessary for properly prosecuting business. The constant investment of the funds of the Church in permanent improvements, trouble of changing, and delay in converting into cash, sometimes unavoidably involve us in debt; but if the brethren will be faithful and punctual in paying their tithing in kind, it will relieve us of all embarrassment, and furnish sufficient for the needful purposes.[36]

"While it required much wisdom and labor to collect [tithing]," one bishop said in 1875, "it required much more wisdom to righteously disburse it, so as to bring about the greatest possible good to the greatest number."[37] Bishop Hunter monitored needs and surpluses, weather and insect reports,

The Deseret News and General Tithing Office, c. late nineteenth century. From this building, tithes were collected and distributed, prices were set for payment in kind, labor was recorded, and certificates for full compliance with the laws of tithing were issued. Courtesy Perry Special Collections.

immigration and crop projections. Balancing supply and demand throughout hundreds of Mormon settlements was tricky. His first priority was supplying the needs of Church headquarters, and the General Tithing Office had standing orders for tithes to come in if not specifically approved by Bishop Hunter for local use and if no more than one hundred miles distant. Conferences provided ideal opportunities for wheeling the goods into the General Tithing Office.[38] Beyond reminders for regular tithes, Bishop Hunter issued emergency appeals whenever the General Tithing Office ran short. Particular bishops often were picked on to provide products he knew their people produced. In 1874, for example, facing a fuel shortage in public buildings and among the poor, he urged the Coalville bishop to send several train carloads of coal.[39]

The quantity of tithing goods flowing into the General Tithing Office cannot be tallied (tithing account books are not available to the public). But an 1852 report of a fifteen-week period of tithes totaled them this way: 5,000 pounds of butter; 2,200 pounds of cheese; 1,150 dozen eggs. At one time, Pleasant Grove shipped fifteen wagon loads of hay and Springville six hundred bushels of wheat. A wagon train from Fort Ephraim brought six wagon loads of wheat, pork, and eggs.[40]

Public works projects proved to be an expensive drain on the treasury. Although historian Leonard Arrington says that public works employees provided bread for themselves, records make clear that many of them depended in whole or large part upon tithing foodstuffs. In 1853, for example, President Young called for tithes because a public works push meant the need for more "provisions to feed the laborers." An appeal in 1854 asked Saints to "allow the men upon the public works the blessing of comfortable meals." In 1857 the Tithing Office was dealing out seven tons of flour weekly to workers. In 1874, Bishop Hunter asked Bountiful leaders to send vegetables quickly, "having many families to supply who labor on the temple."[41]

For most of his term as Presiding Bishop, Hunter employed agents to help funnel the tithes, including traveling bishops, regional presiding bishops who managed regional tithing stores, and various traveling agents. Bishop Hunter and his counselors traveled too. Bishop Hunter had direct contact with regional bishops in Utah and Cache counties, and his traveling bishops and agents supervised outlying counties. Historian Gene Pace has identified twenty-seven regional presiding bishops who served before 1877.[42]

From the early days of temple ordinances, members needed to tithe in order to receive recommends. "Not another soul (will) get an endowment until he has paid his tithing to the utermost and has got his receipt to put in the records," President Heber C. Kimball warned in 1851. Similar statements punctuate the records during the Brigham Young era.[43]

Beyond his duty to receive, store, transfer, and record tithes, Bishop Hunter served as the leading "drummer" for tithing, particularly during lean agricultural years. For example, when the surplus of 1857 was depleted by late 1859, and the General Tithing Office had no bread, he put a get-tough policy into effect. Also, during the United Order push in the 1870s the tithing program continued, and Bishop Hunter still functioned as chief tithing officer.[44]

Bishop Hunter devoutly believed in tithing. No hypocrisy tinged his appeals for people to pay. People Churchwide knew and repeated his slogan, spoken over and over again: "Pay your tithing and be blessed, pay your tithing and be blessed." Teach the people that the payment of their tithing is doing themselves good, he told the bishops.[45]

As chief caretaker of Church tithes, Bishop Hunter had scriptural duty to aid the Lord's poor. He spent much time helping two types of needy: needy emigrants coming to Zion and the needy already there.

Starting in 1850, when Bishop Hunter brought the very first Perpetual Emigrating Fund train of emigrants to Utah, he actively worked to aid the annual immigration effort. He supervised the welcoming of immigrant trains to the Valley, sometimes escorting them in. With the help of local bishops and Saints, he tried to offer places to lodge the first night or two and to provide vegetables and other edibles to gladden the weary travelers.[46] An 1866 account depicts Hunter's role when a wagon train arrived:

> Most of the passengers went with the wagons, having friends northward. Some remained with friends in this city and a few were cared for by Bishop Hunter and his counselors, who attended to their wants in a fatherly manner. The bishop and his council were indefatigable in their exertions for the welfare of the passengers.[47]

When word came that wagon companies were having difficulty in Wyoming, Bishop Hunter called on his bishops to send out relief wagons and cattle. Taking orders from the First Presidency, Bishop Hunter, during the 1860s, orchestrated a vast operation of "down and back" Church team trains, calling on wards to provide wagons and teams to go east to pick up immigrants and bring them to Utah. In 1861 he sent out two hundred wagons, a total that grew to five hundred wagons and teams by 1866.[48]

The First Presidency expected Bishop Hunter, with other bishops' help, to be a population traffic manager, steering new immigrants away from Salt Lake and into valleys where they were needed or where they could find decent livings. In 1852, for example, Bishop Hunter told bishops that some immigrant mechanics could stay in Salt Lake City but that other newcomers had a duty "to move out of the city to those localities where strength is needed, and their labors can be useful."[49] In 1854, Brigham Young requested bishops to inform Bishop Hunter how many new settlers their wards could take. Some of the reports were Pleasant Grove, 40 to 50 Saints; Provo Third, 22; Nephi, 20; Palmyra, 25 or 30 families; Mill Creek Ward, 13 families; Payson, 75 to 80 persons; an Ogden ward, 4 to 5 families.[50] In late 1855, Bishop Hunter told the bishops' meeting that "we are distributing the migration companies very well" and added: "Some are very destitute and ignorant as to the methods of getting a living; they should go into the country. They must be taught, for they are full of faith, but not many works."[51] In September 1861 he reported that he "had been busy for two weeks past in making a distribution of the Emigration through the Territory." Bishop Hunter had to solve problems like that created in the Salt Lake Second Ward when more poor Danes settled there than Bishop Hill could handle; Bishop Hunter arranged for several to move to Sanpete County. In 1869, when the railroad first brought in immigrants all the way to Zion, Bishop Hunter arranged for local Ogden leaders to host and distribute the newcomers. In 1870 he sent twenty Swiss-Germans to Cache Valley to start cheese production there.[52]

The poor already in Utah were also a big concern for the big Bishop. Pioneer poverty is an underrated factor in pioneer history. Life stories of pioneers, if read by the bushel, give the feeling of precariousness for common folk. Accidents ruined workers, including fathers; crickets in 1848, 1849, 1850, and grasshoppers in 1855 and later; famine in 1856; regional shortages; crop diseases; too-hot summers and too-long winters knocked pioneers on their backs financially. Even Provo, an area as developed as any outside of Salt Lake Valley by 1870, had difficulty at that late date raising funds needed by its bishop—the people honestly pleaded poverty.[53] A case might be made that most pioneers lived at or below a poverty level. Most of them suffered silently, aided at times by local bishops, Relief Society sisters, or relatives and friends.

Bishop Hunter's approach to the general poor was constantly to encourage bishops to be sensitive. "Do not make beggars of the poor," he warned. "It has always been my chief object to find employment for the poor," he said by way of advice. He urged bishops to seek out the "modest unassuming people" who silently suffer hunger. "We must watch over the poor." Devise employment or place them in families who have employment for them, he counseled. Every summer he reminded bishops to stockpile wood for winter fuel for the poor.[54]

Only the desperate cases reached the Presiding Bishop's attention, including the handicapped, retarded, and orphaned. Still, the cries of the poor reached the General Tithing Store constantly, some in letter, others in person. One sampling of Hunter's letterbooks from 1872 to 1875 shows him giving attention to hardship cases involving a woman with children needing a home, two boys ages four and six needing a home, a blind sister wanting to reach St. George, a blind and poor man needing clothing, an "idiot or foolish boy," a blind seventy-year-old immigrant, a poor widow who was not paid back a loan, a feeble woman without family, a begging woman with three children, and a blind man from Denmark.[55] In 1873, Bishop Hunter chided a bishop for stinginess in caring for an addled lady and then editorialized:

"She like some other unfortunates who need a little aid have no more claim on one ward than another, but wherever they happen to be, there we expect the Bishop to look after them and not allow them to suffer."[56] Referring to a wife who was mistreated and poor, he said, "such cases absorb nearly half of our time."[57] Incoming letters told of more situations of abuse, neglect, handicaps, misfortune, and even a drug addict who pleaded with Bishop Hunter, "Don't let me die for a few ounces of opium" and then requested that the Bishop or "some other good brother will supply me."[58]

Until asylums and hospitals were built in Utah, the basic method for caring for the handicapped, the retarded and insane, the feeble elderly, and the long-term ill was the cottage system—finding households that would take these cases in return for tithing credits, Church payments, or blessings in heaven.[59]

By the 1860s the problem of housing and feeding the desperately poor had become too burdensome for some bishops. In 1867, President Daniel H. Wells read seventy names of those receiving weekly allowances at the Tithing Office at a total cost of $200 per week—these were in addition to hundreds aided by local bishops. Traveling Bishop Milton Musser surveyed the Church in 1869 and found 1,054 of 109,000 were acutely poor and two-thirds of those, or about 700, were entirely dependent. An idea was discussed that a central poorhouse be set up in wards or in the Valley or that a poor farm be built. The cost of keeping the increasing number of Gentile and LDS needy in single rooms was too great. Why not put them in one house? Brigham Young opposed the poor farm idea, but bishops did not drop the matter. At one point, the bishops tried to turn a ten-acre city lot into a poor farm and home where the able could work, but the plan fizzled.[60]

Bishop Hunter's constant commitment was that none should suffer, and whenever bishops ran out of fast offerings to aid the poor, he approved the use of tithing for that purpose. Although basically kindhearted, he had little patience for lazy and shiftless Saints who loafed around. One time he wearied of seeing women hanging around the tithing storehouse steps "showing their dirty legs" and asked bishops either to pick up the food and deliver it to the women or else have men pick it up "and let the women stay at home."[61] Another time he complained of "chronic beggars, chronic beggars. No good. No good. We have the Lord's poor, the devil's poor, and the poor devils."[62] Of vagrants hanging around the Tithing Office, he remarked humorously: "Hunting work, hunting work; yes, yes, but they don't want to find it very bad." But then he instructed his staff. "Feed them, brethren, feed them—mustn't let them starve."[63]

PRESIDENT OF THE AARONIC PRIESTHOOD

Priesthood theory, in Hunter's day, held that the Presiding Bishop was "President of the Aaronic Priesthood in all the World" and therefore presided over all bishops, priests, teachers, and deacons. But in practice how did that presiding occur? In Bishop Hunter's case, he and the First Presidency agreed on some Aaronic Priesthood matter, and the Presidency then directed him to see that the work was carried out in the stakes. Bishop Hunter, assuming the cooperation of stake officers, in turn instructed bishops and sometimes stake leaders to implement the Aaronic Priesthood work. Bishop Hunter's task as president divides into three activities: (1) presiding over bishops, (2) presiding over Aaronic Priesthood quorums, and (3) participating in ceremonial activities.[64]

"It is the duty of the Presiding Bishop to preside over all Bishops," the First Presidency instructed as early as 1851. However, as president of the bishops, Hunter had no regular voice in selecting them. "There are several Wards without Bishops," he said in 1856 but admitted that he did not know when they would have them. The First Presidency chose the new bishops and then let Bishop Hunter know who they were, sometimes instructing him to ordain the newly chosen men, often instructing him to teach them their duties. Hunter's office kept an up-to-date list of Mormon settlements with their presiding officers, for reference and for correspondence purposes.[65] Newly appointed bishops received instructions from Bishop Hunter and his counselors. An 1877 instruction letter, for example, advises about tithing, meetings ("let them be short and spiritual"), fast offerings and testimony meetings ("have no preaching sermons"), calling block teachers ("select the best and wisest men"), solving disputes ("have all their grievances and disputes settled by the lesser priesthood"), and organizing the lesser priesthood properly ("in your stake . . . a full quorum of 48 priests, 24 teachers and 12 deacons").[66]

If one thing made Bishop Hunter feel like a president, it was when he presided at the twice-monthly bishops' meetings in the city. Because a large percentage of the Church's bishops lived in the Salt Lake Valley and came to these meetings, he had an effective forum. Normally twenty to thirty wards were represented, but during general conference or when the territorial legislature sat, the bishops' meetings' ranks swelled with many "outside" bishops. Although the majority of Church bishops could not attend these meetings, those attending served as a representative body. Their decisions became policy Churchwide. Proceedings and decisions were published in the *Deseret News* or capsuled in circular letters for all bishops to read. The main topics treated in these meetings were tithing, emigration fund donations, public works assignments, specific cases of poor and needy persons, Aaronic Priesthood labors (specifically ward teaching), and domestic manufactures. Also, a wide range of other matters received attention less often: sacrament, baptizing, wheat storage, inoculations, marital and family advice, stealing, voting, land-owning, naturalization, and water problems. These "town meetings" of bishops produced vigorous questioning, challenging, criticizing, disagreeing, and open expressing of opinions.[67]

In addition to the bishops' meetings, Bishop Hunter communicated with bishops by mail. He received and answered many personal letters. He issued circular letters over his signature, which sometimes were cosigned by the First Presidency. After 1861 the Deseret Telegraph sped up communication and reduced the senior bishop's mail pile. Bishop Hunter and his counselors also paid personal visits to stakes and wards. In addition, he had a good, personal, one-to-one contact with bishops who visited his General Tithing Office. Now and then he requested written reports from all bishops, reports containing tithing totals, census figures, or immigration assignment lists. In the bishops' meetings he sometimes called for oral reports from bishops about the numbers in the ward who sustained the Word of Wisdom, numbers rebaptized, numbers of poor, block teaching patterns, and the spirit in ward meetings.[68]

Bishop Hunter often became the man in the uncomfortable middle. That is, he would try to defend bishops against First Presidency criticisms, and then he would have to criticize the bishops. Empathetic and appreciative of bishops generally, and aware of their heavy burdens, he remembered that his ordination called him to lift the drooping spirits. Nevertheless, he disliked foot-dragging by bishops. Home manufacturing, for example, was not a popular topic in the bishops' meetings, causing Counselor Little to admonish that "he did not want to hear any cold water remarks thrown upon it" and that whenever a call came from Brigham Young through the Presiding Bishopric he wanted "a hearty and immediate" support from the bishops.

Hunter blamed some of the 1856 Reformation's chastisements on "the heed-lessness of the Bishops." In 1862 he issued them "a sharp but sensible reproof" for neglecting Aaronic Priesthood matters.[69] Knowing bishops sometimes ignored Bishop Hunter, John Taylor once reminded them: "You bishops are subject to your head, Bishop Hunter, and you cannot shake off the responsibilities that he lays upon you."[70]

Regarding Hunter's role as president of the Aaronic Priesthood quorums, Brigham Young reminded him that "it was the duty of the Presiding Bishop to have a full quorum of Priests, Teachers and Deacons, properly organized in every stake of Zion, and hold there regular meetings."[71] (Notice he said *stake*, not ward.) In Salt Lake Stake, where Hunter served somewhat like a stake bishop, he influenced the calling of its Aaronic Priesthood presidencies. During his term, Salt Lake Stake held stake Aaronic Priesthood meetings, stake deacons quorum meetings, stake teachers quorum meetings, and stake priests quorum meetings. At general conference, when Salt Lake Stake officers were sustained, voters sustained presidencies for a deacons, a teachers, and a priests quorum—one quorum of each in a stake of about twenty thousand Saints.[72]

In some stakes quorums existed; in others they did not. Bishop Hunter said he labored many years to make the lesser priesthood function, to make it "honorable," and in 1873 he won Brigham Young's backing for a pointed epistle instructing him as Presiding Bishop to order stakes to organize quorums.[73] One person Bishop Hunter *gently* ordered was Apostle Orson Hyde in Sanpete Stake, the acting stake president. "This is not done to gratify a personal ambition to dictate [to] President Hyde who is above me," his letter respectfully began, "but simply to discharge a duty imposed upon me.... You will therefore please to have 3 quorums filled."[74] President-Apostle Hyde responded, and soon his stake had one priests quorum—twenty-four priests from Manti and twenty-four from Ephraim (the stake's two leading towns); one teachers quorum—twelve teachers from Manti and twelve from Ephraim; and one deacons quorum—six from each town.[75]

Aaronic Priesthood work was considered adult work. Frequently, high priests, seventies, and elders served as acting deacons, acting teachers, acting priests, much as high priests served as bishops; and a common phrase heard among acting Aaronic Priesthood men was "We are called to act in both priesthoods."[76]

After the Priesthood Reorganizing of 1877, stakes became better organized and expanded the number of quorums, especially deacons units, so
that practically every ward had a quorum.[77]

Bishop Hunter propounded a lofty concept of lesser priesthood work.
In Zion, Melchizedek Priesthood bearers had little to do in wards unless
they performed "acting" lesser priesthood work, such as block teaching.
Hunter's generation believed that only ordained teachers had priesthood
power to reconcile differences between two parties; bishop's courts could
make decisions, but decisions often did not produce reconciliations. The
Aaronic Priesthood had power to discern iniquity and help people repent.
It had the obligation to watch over the members. It could have the ministerings of angels. While many Saints considered the lesser priesthood to
be lesser and lower, Bishop Hunter considered it vital to the Church, and
particularly helpful to overloaded bishops.[78]

Bishop Hunter supervised bishops and encouraged Aaronic Priesthood
work, and he also performed ceremonial functions as Aaronic Priesthood
President. He made official appearances on public occasions. He accepted
speaking invitations. He helped dedicate chapels and buildings. He participated in funeral programs. At general conference and at the Sunday Tabernacle sacrament meetings, he and his counselors sometimes took charge
of the sacrament. Occasionally he spoke at general conferences and priesthood gatherings. When the Salt Lake Temple cornerstones were laid, he
orated and then dedicated a stone on behalf of the Aaronic Priesthood. At
the St. George Temple dedication he represented the Aaronic Priesthood.[79]

Somehow a hosting role developed for him, too, perhaps because his
management of the General Tithing Storehouse made him a food czar.
Starting in 1864, he hosted a series of annual reunions for the Zion's Camp
survivors. He also hosted reunions for the Mormon Battalion survivors.
Sometimes he was chairman of the Twenty-fourth of July program for the
Salt Lake Valley. During the 1870s, he helped launch an annual Old Folks'
Day that became a fine Utah tradition. In 1876, to cite one outing, Bishop
Hunter and his committee arranged for about six hundred excursionists,
half over sixty-five years old, to go by train to Provo. Half the company went
free; the others paid $1. At Provo spring-seated wagons and a band met them,
and off they went to a big picnic. The program included a speech by Bishop
Hunter, band numbers, and songs. Dancing, swings, and reminiscing under

shady trees occupied the afternoon, and then the group returned to Salt Lake, enjoying cake and lemonade, and singing on the way back. Bishop Hunter became well known as the annual producer of the Old Folks' Days.[80]

Because of his position and his wisdom, Bishop Hunter received requests to arbitrate, not in the formal court setting, but by way of opinion. Such requests usually involved money or property disputes beyond the jurisdiction of local bishops, such as problems between the bishops, or those involving General Authorities or people outside of Utah.[81]

LEADER AND FOLLOWER

President Brigham Young and Presiding Bishop Hunter worked basically smoothly together as a temporal team, but not without some differences. On occasion, Brigham asked for more than the Bishop was doing. In 1855 the President severely chastised the bishops, including Bishop Hunter, giving them a "few reproofs." In 1857, Brigham became impatient for 1856 tithing to be settled, and Bishop Hunter responded that he would "take measures to ascertain [it] as soon as possible." Bishop Hunter evidently told bishops to put cellars in the tithing houses, something Brigham Young contradicted. In 1863, Hunter admitted that "he himself had been severely reproved 'by his superiors' and could only account for it on the principle, that Whom the Lord loveth, he chasteneth." In 1872, President Young ordered Bishop Hunter to send a circular to country bishops because the President disliked the waste and spoilage of tithing hay and fodder he saw during a recent trip.[82] When he was chastised for neglect of duty, the Bishop was heard to say: "Thank the Lord, thank the Lord, true son, true son, no bastard, no bastard, whom the Lord loveth he chasteneth."[83]

The yoking of the younger ex-Vermont glazier with the older Pennsylvania squire seemed both compatible and successful. Both men seemed to understand the subordinate position of the Presiding Bishopric relative to the First Presidency. If Bishop Hunter ever disagreed strongly with the President, he and Brigham must have worked it out, or else Bishop Hunter suffered in silence. Possibly on occasion Hunter failed to enforce or emphasize some policies that the President favored, a form of passive resistance. But there is no evidence that Bishop Hunter ever took a strong opposition stance or that he recruited bishops to go against President Young's policies.

Bishop Hunter played his team part well. He was an able man, who consci-entiously sought to perform well and "delighted to labor in the Kingdom," although many times he felt "weary" from it all.[84]

When Brigham Young once praised him while scoring others, Bishop Hunter while walking away was heard to say: "Bishop Hunter, Bishop Hunter, look out, devil's after you, don't get the big head, been praised, been praised, flattery, flattery, stubby toe, fall down, break your neck, look out praise, be humble, Bishop Hunter, be humble, devil catch you sure." Another time he said, "Don't get the big head, Kill you sure, Kill you sure, Killed more men than anything else in the Church."[85] The universally high opinion held of him at his death in 1883 indicates that Edward Hunter's selection as Presid-ing Bishop thirty-two years earlier was an excellent decision by President Young. Edward Hunter was a well-liked leader who by 1875 was regarded as "fatherly" and "kindhearted." Liberal responses by bishops to his calls, he said, "melt my feelings." During his bishopric career, he had tried to do what his setting-apart blessing instructed: "There is nothing so pleasing to me," he said, "as to cheer up the drooping spirit—it was in my blessing by Prest. Young, and I felt it at the time in a remarkable degree."[86]

Edward's personal life, his industries, farms, cattle raising, his plural marriage and family life, his involvement with city government and territo-rial affairs, and his personal involvement in the Deseret Agricultural and Manufacturing Association are explored well in a published biography,[87] so are not part of this assessment.

One day Clio, the Greek goddess of history, interviewed many second-level leaders in world history. She tabulated her findings and concluded that one of the world's toughest jobs is being a number two leader—vice presi-dent, executive secretary, counselor, junior partner—anyone who must administer and execute while lacking independence to frame policy. Many number two men have failed. Clio filed her survey and then whispered to historians to be sure to give credit to number two men who do good jobs. Clio or no Clio, Edward Hunter earned a reputation during his lifetime for being a great man because he learned how to be a good number two man to the strong-willed Brigham Young. In the process, Edward Hunter's time, energy, and ideas contributed greatly to moving Utah through the pioneer-ing stage, and he pioneered in the office of Presiding Bishop, shaping that position into one of the vital executive offices in the restored Church.

This article was originally published in Supporting Saints: Life Stories of Nineteenth-Century Mormons, *Donald Q. Cannon and David J. Whittaker, eds., Specialized Monograph Series, vol. 1, Religious Studies Center (Provo, UT: Religious Studies Center, BYU, 1985), 275–304.*

NOTES

1. Heber J. Grant, Letter to Edward H. Anderson, July 9, 1901, notes in author's possession.
2. William G. Hartley, "The Priesthood Reorganization of 1877: Brigham Young's Last Achievement," *BYU Studies* 20, no. 1 (1979): 3, 6, 27.
3. LDS General Conference Minutes Collection, April 7, 1851, Church History Library, The Church of Jesus Christ of Latter-day Saints, Salt Lake City.
4. William E. Hunter, *Edward Hunter, Faithful Steward* (Salt Lake City: Publishers Press by the Hunter Family, 1970), 70, 268.
5. Hunter, *Edward Hunter,* 73.
6. Hunter, *Edward Hunter,* 78, 80, 89, 91.
7. Hunter, *Edward Hunter,* 133; Presiding Bishopric's Meetings with Bishops, Minutes, April 24 and July 13, 1851; April 11, 1852; and April 7, 1855, Church History Library (hereafter cited as Bishops Minutes).
8. D. Michael Quinn, "The Evolution of the Presiding Quorums of the LDS Church," *Journal of Mormon History* 1 (1974): 31–38; First Presidency, Fourth General Epistle, September 27, 1850, in *Messages of the First Presidency of The Church of Jesus Christ of Latter-day Saints, 1833–1964,* comp. James R. Clark, 6 vols. (Salt Lake City: Bookcraft, 1965–75), 2:60; Bishops Minutes, April 7, 1855.
9. Bishops Minutes, April 7, 1855.
10. Andrew Jenson, *Latter-day Saint Biographical Encyclopedia: A Compilation of Biographical Sketches of Prominent Men and Women in The Church of Jesus Christ of Latter-day Saints,* 4 vols. (Salt Lake City: Andrew Jenson History, 1901–36), 1:236–43.
11. Journal History of the Church, Sunday entries during 1852, Church History Library, microfilm copy in Harold B. Lee Library, Brigham Young University, Provo, Utah; Bishops Minutes, October 7, 1856.
12. The Bishops Minutes covering the period 1849–84; Bishops Minutes, October 27, 1856.
13. Willard Richards, "Circular on Tithing," November 5, 1851, in Journal History of that date; Ronald G. Watt, "The Presiding Bishopric," typescript, in author's possession.
14. Bishops Minutes, February 11 and March 15, 1875.
15. Bishops Minutes, July 16, 1854.
16. LDS General Minutes, taken during conference held in Parowan, May 21, 1855.
17. Bishops Minutes, October 6, 1860.
18. Richards, "Circular on Tithing," November 15, 1851.
19. Watt, "Presiding Bishopric."
20. First Presidency, Sixth General Epistle, September 22 1851, in Clark, *Messages of the First Presidency,* 2:78.

21. First Presidency, Sixth General Epistle, September 22 1851, in Clark, *Messages of the First Presidency*, 2:90.

22. Richards, "Circular on Tithing," November 15, 1851.

23. Bishops Minutes, October 12, 1851.

24. LDS General Minutes, April 9, 1852; First Presidency, Seventh General Epistle, April 18, 1852, in Clark, *Messages of the First Presidency*, 2:92.

25. Clark, *Messages of the First Presidency*, 2:96.

26. Bishops Minutes, April 11, 1852, and July 6, 1857; First Presidency, Seventh General Epistle, April 18, 1852, in Clark, *Messages of the First Presidency*, 2:97; a full discussion of traveling and regional bishops is in Donald Gene Pace, "The LDS Presiding Bishopric, 1851–1888: An Administrative Study" (master's thesis, Brigham Young University, 1978), 62–63.

27. Bishops Minutes, April 7, 1855.

28. Philip K. Smith to Edward Hunter, January 12, 1853, Hunter Incoming Correspondence, Church History Library; First Presidency, Ninth General Epistle, April 13, 1853, in Clark, *Messages of the First Presidency*, 2:113; various Journal History entries during 1854.

29. First Presidency, Eleventh General Epistle, April 10, 1854, in Clark, *Messages of the First Presidency*, 2:139–40; First Presidency, Twelfth General Epistle, April 25, 1855, in Clark, *Messages of the First Presidency*, 2:169–70; Leonard J. Arrington, Feramorz Y. Fox, and Dean L. May, *Building the City of God: Community and Cooperation among the Mormons* (Salt Lake City: Deseret Book, 1976), 69–76.

30. Journal History, February 22, 1859.

31. Journal History, September 8, 1850; Thomas Bullock Minutes Collection, November 5, 1854, Church History Library; General Tithing Store Letterbook, 1872–75; Bishops Minutes, June 18, 1873.

32. Bishops Minutes, October 25, 1853, and October 8, 1863.

33. Bishops Minutes, December 8 and 22, 1857.

34. Bishops Minutes, January 6, 1870, and November 6, 1873; A. M. Musser, "Tithing Data in 1880," holograph; "List of Tithing Offices Prices, Weights, and Measures, 1863," printed announcement, all in Church History Library.

35. H. J. Grant, Letter to E. H. Anderson, July 9, 1901, copy in author's possession.

36. First Presidency, Twelfth General Epistle, April 25, 1855, in Clark, *Messages of the First Presidency*, 2:168.

37. Bishops Minutes, February 11, 1875.

38. Circular to Bishops, July 20, 1854, in Journal History for that date; Journal History, March 19, 1853.

39. Edward Hunter to Bishop William W. Cluff, September 19, 1874, General Tithing Store Letterbook.

40. Leonard J. Arrington, "Paying the Tenth in Pioneer Days," *Instructor* 98 (November 1963): 387; Journal History, December 16, 1854, and November 26, 1860.

41. Arrington, "Paying the Tenth," 386; Clark, *Messages of the First Presidency*, 2:153; Journal History, June 7, 1857; Edward Hunter to Bishop Anson Call, September 10, 1874, General Tithing Store Letterbook.

42. Bishops Minutes; Pace, "LDS Presiding Bishopric"; Provo Bishops' Meetings, 1868–72, Church History Library; Cache Stake, Bishopric Meetings Minutes, 1872–76, Church History Library.

43. LDS General Minutes, September 7, 1851; Bishops Minutes, June 24, 1851.

44. Bishops Minutes, October 8, 1859; General Tithing Store Letterbook, 1872–75.

45. Thomas C. Romney, *The Gospel in Action* (Salt Lake City: Deseret Sunday School Union Board, 1949), 75; Bishops Minutes, April 7, 1855.

46. Hunter, *Edward Hunter*, 119–25.

47. Journal History, October 13, 1850, and March 18, 1868; Bishops Minutes, August 27, 1860, and November 6, 1855; Manuscript History of Brigham Young, 710, August 29, 1866, Church History Library.

48. Bishops Minutes, April 25, 1860; August 13, 1863; and January 25, 1866; Journal History, December 31, 1861, Supplement.

49. Bishops Minutes, September 12, 1852.

50. Hunter Incoming Correspondence for 1854; Bishops Minutes for 1854.

51. Bishops Minutes, November 6, 1855.

52. Bishops Minutes, September 26, 1861; November 6, 1861; and June 24, 1869; Hunter, *Edward Hunter*, 301.

53. Provo Bishops Minutes for 1870.

54. Bishops Minutes, February 12, 1856; September 1, 1870; January 29, 1856; June 3, 1856; June 7, 1853; and July 27, 1865.

55. General Tithing Store Letterbooks, 1872–75.

56. General Tithing Store Letterbooks, 1872–75, October 27, 1873.

57. General Tithing Store Letterbooks, 1872–75, September 16, 1874.

58. Hunter Incoming Correspondence, February 19, 1856.

59. General Tithing Store Letterbooks, 1872–75.

60. General Tithing Store Letterbooks, 1872–75; Bishops Minutes, December 5, 1867; April 15, 1869; January 25 and February 8, 1866; December 5, 1867; September 24 and November 5 and December 3, 1874.

61. H. J. Grant, Letter to E. H. Anderson, July 9, 1901.

62. Bishops Minutes, October 27, 1857.

63. Romney, *Gospel in Action*, 75.

64. Bishops Minutes, October 6, 1860, and January 11, 1877.

65. Willard Richards, Circular on Tithing, November 15, 1851, in Journal History of that date; Bishops Minutes, April 22, 1856. When Jordan Ward needed a bishop, Hunter said he would "inquire of the President" about "appointing a bishop there" (Bishops Minutes, January 7, 1852). On March 14, 1857, Brigham Young wrote to Hunter that "we have nominated and appointed Richard Cook a Bishop to succeed Bp. Thomas Kington of W. Weber, and wish you to give such instruction and counsel as you may deem necessary and attend to his ordination." Hunter Incoming Correspondence. In 1877 Brigham Young stated that Bishop Hunter presided over all bishops, not just those attending the bishops' meetings. See Bishops Minutes, August 23, 1877; Bishops Minutes, April 22, 1856.

66. Bishops Minutes, July 10, 1877.

67. Bishops Minutes, 1849–84.

68. General Tithing Store Letterbook, 1872–75; Hunter Incoming Correspondence; Presiding Bishopric, Circular Letter File, 1851–83, Church History Library; and Bishops

Minutes, 1851–83. Hunter left Salt Lake City to visit outlying wards in 1851, 1853, 1854, 1856, 1861, 1864, 1867, and probably many other times.

69. Bishops Minutes, July 30, 1863; February 13, 1862; and September 30, 1856.

70. Bishops Minutes, January 11, 1877.

71. Bishops Minutes, September 11, 1873, and July 10, 1877.

72. Bishops Minutes, November 25, 1852; see also Presiding Bishop's Office, Aaronic Priesthood Minutes, 1857–77 (which are Salt Lake Stake Minutes) and Salt Lake Stake Deacons Quorum Meeting Minutes, both in Church History Library.

73. Bishops Minutes, August 13, 1874.

74. Edward Hunter to Apostle Orson Hyde, October 17, 1873, General Tithing Store Letterbook.

75. Sanpete Stake Aaronic Priesthood Minutes, 1873–77, Church History Library.

76. William G. Hartley, "Ordained and Acting Teachers in the Lesser Priesthood, 1851–1883," *BYU Studies* 16, no. 3 (1976): 375–98.

77. William G. Hartley, "The Priesthood Reorganization of 1877: Brigham Young's Last Achievement," *BYU Studies* 20, no. 1 (1979): 3–36.

78. Hartley, "Ordained and Acting Teachers," 381–86.

79. Journal History, July 15 and August 19, 1860; and April 4, 1877; *Deseret News*, April 16, 1853.

80. Journal History, October 19, 1864, and October 10, 1870; Hunter, *Edward Hunter*, 137; George Goddard Journal, June 8, 1876, Church History Library.

81. Hunter Incoming Correspondence.

82. Bishops Minutes, May 15, 1855; April 7, 1857; December 17, 1862; June 18, 1863; and October 10, 1872; Jane Rollins to Edward Hunter, December 17, 1862, Hunter Incoming Correspondence.

83. H. J. Grant, Letter to E. H. Anderson, July 9, 1901.

84. Bishops Minutes, September 23, 1856, and May 12, 1857.

85. Heber J. Grant remarks at funeral of Oscar F. Hunter, August 28, 1931, notes in author's possession.

86. *Millennial Star* 45 (November 19, 1883): 737–46; Journal History, June 3, 1875; Bishops Minutes, October 26, 1851, and July 31, 1855.

87. Hunter, *Edward Hunter*.

7   Ward Bishops and the Localizing of LDS Tithing, 1847–1856

TITHING, THE LIFEBLOOD OF The Church of Jesus Christ of Latter-day Saints' financial system, has a history of its own. Although official tithing records are closed to research, Leonard Arrington and other scholars have written several chapters of tithing's history.[1] Chapter one, the Nauvoo beginnings, and chapter two, the exodus, are sketchy. The fourth and fifth chapters about tithing's connections with consecration and United Orders are well written. A later chapter about turn-of-the-century shifts to cash tithes awaits telling.

What follows is a chapter three, dealing with tithing between 1847 and 1856. During this period, new Presiding Bishop Edward Hunter revolutionized the tithing system by making ward bishops, instead of the Presiding Bishop, responsible to receive tithes from, keep accounts for, and make annual tithing settlements with individual Saints.

A previously ignored, undated "Circular" from Hunter to ward bishops, which we can now date to late 1852, initiated the new program.[2] The new system took three years to implement fully and required printed instructions and forms, new record-keeping systems, trainers, and monitors, standardizing valuation lists, building local storehouses, and intermittent scoldings to help bishops and members turn tithepaying into a ward matter.

Daniel H. Wells directed the public-works projects that were completed using labor tithing, which was required for members to be considered full tithepayers. Courtesy Perry Special Collections.

Once they had become established in their Great Basin communities, LDS pioneers were expected to pay three types of tithes: property, increase, and labor. Apostle Parley P. Pratt, on October 7, 1849, gave perhaps the first Utah discourse that details the triple tithe. First, he said, "To fulfill the law of tithing a man should make out and lay before the [Presiding] Bishop [then Newel K. Whitney] a schedule of all his property, and pay him the tenth of it." That is, he should pay a one-time initiatory tithe on all *property* he possessed. "When he has tithed his principal once," Pratt continued, "he has no occasion to tithe again" on that property. But the next year he must pay one-tenth of his *increase* of "cattle, money, goods and trade." A member also owed "the tenth of his time"—a *labor* tithe of each tenth day of man, young man, and work animals and wagons for the days not devoted to producing income or increase.[3]

The first Mormon pioneers had no large-scale "increase" to tithe until their first harvest in 1848. Albert Carrington's personal tithing book pinpoints October 5, 1848, as "the beginning of tithing in this valley"—months before any Utah wards were created.[4]

The exodus from Nauvoo had disrupted stake, ward, and quorum organizations. "Until now," First Presidency Counselor Heber C. Kimball said on February 16, 1849, our organizations "have all been kicked to pieces." To solve the problem, the First Presidency then called a stake presidency and high council, and divided Great Salt Lake City into nineteen wards, each with a bishop. Several country wards also were created.[5]

Newly appointed bishops met together as a quorum, beginning on March 25, 1849. Their meetings became bimonthly. At the initial meeting, Daniel H. Wells, director of the Church's public works projects, said he had "arranged the City into tithing wards and wish the Bishops with their men to be on hand when called upon." His term "tithing ward" referred to labor tithing only, and he soon assigned city wards one by one or in clusters to provide workmen for community projects.[6]

Presiding Bishop Whitney continued to receive, record, and disburse cash and commodity tithes from Salt Lake Valley Saints. When LDS settlements rooted beyond the Salt Lake Valley, bishops in distant wards acted as his agents, funneling tithes and keeping simple records of receipts and disbursements. Bishop Whitney conducted no tithing settlements in 1849 or 1850. He lacked a good storehouse for the commodities/tithes. During 1850 he handled tithing business in a room in the

John Banks was called in 1851 to assist Edward Hunter in his duties as Presiding Bishop. Bishop Banks traveled to outlying settlements to work with the local bishops on the payment and disbursement of tithes. Courtesy Church Archives.

State of Deseret statehouse, in the mint, and in a joiner's shop. Meanwhile, he eagerly watched the rise of walls for the new tithing storehouse. But he died in September 1850 before the place was finished.[7]

In 1851 a series of actions worked together to systematize tithe-handling. First, during April general conference, Bishop Edward Hunter, a skilled businessman, became the new Presiding Bishop six months after Whitney's death. Second, that spring a central tithing storehouse finally opened, with one apartment to store grain, others for a store and a mechanic's shop, and cellars for vegetables.[8] Third, in April leaders announced plans to build the Salt Lake Temple, a project requiring tithing food to feed workmen and tithing materials with which to build.[9] Fourth, during fall general conference, Bishop Hunter received as helpers two traveling presiding bishops, Nathaniel H. Felt and John Banks, whom he assigned to visit outlying wards and "settle with the several Bishops from time to time and report the same to the Presiding Bishop."[10]

Finally, with the tithing office open and capable men called to manage the tithes, Brigham Young shocked conference attenders on September 10, 1851. He required them to covenant by raised hand and voice vote to tithe faithfully and to again pay their initiatory tithe on "all they have got." He asked Saints to "commence anew the tithings and consecrations, and that within thirty days, each Saint should make a consecration of one-tenth of his property, and one-tenth of his interest or income ever after."[11] After the covenanting conference, Bishop Hunter and his staff opened for tithing settlement "business," which lasted until the next March.

A *Deseret News* editorial on November 29, 1851, invited all Saints to settle their tithing accounts. The General Tithing Office, it said, wanted to close up accounts not settled since fall 1848. Many had tithed, the paper said, but had never made settlement since reaching the valley. Only those who settled their tithing could have their names entered in the Church's sacred financial record, The Book of the Law of the Lord, and could receive certificates proving they were full tithepayers. They received one of four tithing certificates: for initiatory property tithes paid prior to September 10, 1851; for labor tithes; for increase tithes; and for property tithes paid in accordance with the September 10, 1851, covenant. "Each person ought to be able to show these four separate certificates to his Bishop this present season." After 1852, the editorial added, only the produce and labor tithing certificates would be required.

Saints, after covenanting, sent a stream of tithing that brought Hunter and his staff new problems. The increase tithe and the labor tithe posed no challenge, but the property tithes on such things as a horse or a house did. "We have got to take one kind of property to pay tithing of another," a bishop pointed out. Hunter said that "when a man is industrious, and has only a span of horses and a cow, we don't want to cripple him. In such cases we will take hewed timber, Poles, wood, lumber, or labor."[12]

But how many feet of lumber was a horse worth? How much tithing labor was an adobe house worth? How many peaches was a cast-iron stove worth? In bishops meetings and by correspondence, the portly Bishop Hunter set standardized valuation and exchange rates. "Cows should be estimated from twenty to thirty dollars," Hunter advised, and oxen at sixty to eighty dollars per yoke. He warned bishops not to appraise low. "When you find a first rate piece of property, put on a first rate price, and a poor piece of property in a decreasing rating." Tithing office clerks could not appraise properties, he announced; only he could.[13] By posting valuation and exchange rates, Hunter opened the door for all ward bishops to soon become tithing appraisers and receivers.

To aid the 1851 tithing settlement at Church headquarters, Church Recorder Willard Richards issued a "Tithing Circular" on November 15 to tithing handlers in Utah and abroad. It called for full and accurate tithing records that listed when payments were received, by whom, and where, and also how, when, and to whom disposed. By October general conference each year, it instructed, all tithing accounts should be submitted to the tithing office. Saints wishing to make tithing settlements must bring receipts from bishops to whom they paid tithes. Utah bishops should make semi-annual reports of their tithing books at conferences. Bishop Hunter and his staff were "to see that all Bishops and agents do their duty, and report according to this circular." A year later, however, the historic 1852 circular cancelled these instructions.[14]

Hunter's office, lacking ward rosters and master lists of Church members, had no way to know how well Saints were paying tithes. So, on January 20, 1852, he asked bishops to help him find out if their people paid tithing. This reversed roles. Previously, bishops wanting to know which ward members paid tithes would ask the General Tithing Office. But now Hunter asked bishops for that information. How could a ward bishop know who paid tithes at the central office? Only by asking each member. Hunter also pressed bishops to give him lists naming people unwilling to pay tithing. This act involved virtually every ward bishop for the first time in the tithing settlement process.[15]

In February 1852 ward bishops learned they soon would receive tithing ledgers, and that Bishop Hunter planned to build regional tithing storehouses, "with a cellar and upper Story." Hunter's assistant, Bishop Felt, advised bishops to obtain tubs for storing tithing butter, pork, eggs, and other perishables.[16]

Hunter finished settling the 1851 tithes on March 25, 1852. The First Presidency judged the year successful. "The brethren generally have been prompt in paying in one-tenth of their property according to their vote of last September Conference," they said, "and never before has the Lord's storehouse been so well supplied with wheat, meat, butter, eggs, vegetables, and other useful articles, and His pasture with cattle, as at the present time." However, Church needs exceeded tithes received, forcing the Church leaders to pay one-fourth of annual expenses from nontithing sources.[17]

After April 1852 general conference, the First Presidency published a rare disclosure of tithes. It shows that between November 1848, the last tithing settlement, and March 27, 1852, tithepayers paid property tithing in accord with the September 10 covenant of one-quarter million dollars.[18]

Capping the tithing push, the First Presidency made Edward Hunter's trial appointment permanent by ordaining him as Presiding Bishop at April general conference in 1852. They also appointed five men as assistant presiding bishops: Seth Taft, David Pettigrew, Abraham Hoagland—three city bishops who retained their offices—and David Fullmer and Daniel Spencer of the Salt Lake Stake's presidency.[19]

Tithing merely trickled during summer 1852, stopping public works for want of materials and food. By fall the plan to make tithing a ward matter was finalized. No October general conference talks of which we have record discuss the change, but during conference week Brigham Young told high priests of a "future plan" of bishops keeping their own books and of members settling their tithes with their bishops. At general conference, Bishops Nathaniel Felt, John Banks, and Alfred Cordon became traveling presiding bishops to assist Hunter.[20]

In November or December 1852, Bishop Hunter issued the historic circular instructing ward bishops to handle, record, process, and forward tithes at the ward level and hold annual tithing settlements with members—tasks his office had handled until then. The two-page, printed, undated circular is addressed "to bishop _____," is signed by Hunter, and includes a "postscript" by Brigham Young. "Hereafter, all the settlements of Tithing with those living in your branch or ward, will be made at your office" is the key phrase of the letter to the bishops.[21]

This major policy statement has been overlooked by historians because, somehow, a library cataloger mistakenly labeled it as an 1860s document. Not only does the context of tithing history date this document to 1852, but we also find a tithing instruction in 1859 that refers to a time when people settled tithing with the General Tithing Office "previous to the Bishops being authorized to do so in 1852."[22]

Tithepaying was being localized, the circular said, because a "rapid increase" in population meant that "our settlements have extended themselves for hundreds of miles on every side." Because of such growth, tithing management required that "some new arrangements" be created to produce "uniformity in all the branches."

The circular next discussed four tithing matters: bookkeeping, appraising, annual settlements, and disbursements.

Bookkeeping: Bishops were warned to "keep an accurate account of all tithing deposited with you" by using a daybook and a ledger. In the daybook "every item of tithing paid, should be plainly and distinctly entered to the credit of the individual." The daybook should be preserved until deposited in Hunter's office. The daybook accounts should be posted in the ledger book. "The necessary forms of Bookkeeping, settlements, reports, etc." accompanied the circular. Bishops should spell names properly and fully and should preserve and file away "all your receipts, orders, and due bills, with the names and dates endorsed on the back, as these will all be required in the settlement of your accounts."

Appraising: The circular gave bishops skimpy advice on how to assign values to donated tithing items. Regarding labor tithing, bishops should be governed "by your own judgment, taking the circumstances of the several cases into consideration." As a general rule, bishops "will allow at the rate of a month for tilling 2 acres of land, and charge four dollars labor tithing per month for the residue of the year; eight dollars a year for tithing on team work for a yoke of oxen, span of horses, or mules, when the owner is not engaged in teaming for wages."

From cows either labor, butter, or a fee was expected: "When a tenth of butter is not paid, you will charge two dollars per annum for each cow." Bishops were told to state on their tithing settlement reports any reasons "why a man's labor tithing is less or more than the usual or general amount," and "if there are any reasons why any man's produce tithing is not as large as would ordinarily be expected."

Hunter inserted a reminder, humorous today but serious then, about quality tithing: "And we wish the Bishops in no wise to countenance nor receive old worn out oxen, kicking cows, scabby sheep." Young's postscript to the circular asked for good materials but insisted that tithes should be paid in the product produced, not with substitutes:

> The individual who neglects to pay a tenth of his butter, eggs, wool, stockings, cloth, &c, but pays the value thereof in wheat, potatoes, squashes, &c.; (while those who employ all their time and means,

in rearing the Temple, and building up the Kingdom, are living with their families upon bread and water, and are destitute of the necessaries of life, or clothing to shield them from the inclemency of the weather,) has not fulfilled the law of tithing. Neither has that person who turns out the old broken-down horse, ox, or cow, while he retains the young and healthy stock, available property, or money in his own possession.

Annual tithing settlements: The circular gave most attention to settlements matters. At least once each year, or oftener, "a full settlement should be made, the books balanced, and the report made to this office, where the General Records are kept" so that "the same may be put upon the record in their proper places, and the individuals may receive a certificate from this office." Bishops and any clerks they employed should sign the reports because "you will be held accountable for all property put into your hand, as also for the correctness and safety of your books."

The circular listed sample questions for bishops to use during settlement interviews:

> Had you any property when you came into the valley, on which you
>   had not paid tithing?
> Had you any money on hand?
> In what were you engaged during the year after you arrived?
> How much land did you till?
> How many teams had you?
> Did you pay a tenth of your Produce?
> Did you pay a tenth of your Hay?
> Did you pay a tenth of your Butter?
> Did you pay a tenth of your Eggs and Chickens?
> Did you make any thing by trading?
> How much did your property increase in your hands?
> Had you any increase of stock?

Disbursement: Regarding the distribution of collected tithes, the letter asked that "All the heavy articles of tithing" be forwarded "as heretofore" to the "General Tithing Store House," where receipts would be issued "which you will enter to their several accounts." Lighter items and "smaller articles of domestic production, such as butter, cheese, eggs, &c, you will receive and credit, and forward as circumstances will admit."

Bishops must not take lightly these new tithing duties, the letter warned: "We shall charge you here as Bishop, with the total amount of tithing received by you, from each person, and it will stand against you until you account for the manner in which the produce and other property have been disposed of." To supervise and train local bishops, "Traveling bishops" would visit the wards, inspect the tithing books, "audit all the accounts of your Ward, and assist in continuing a uniformity of system, and valuation of property."

Should nontithepayers be disciplined? No, Hunter advised, "It is your duty to see that your wards fulfill the Law of Tithing, or let it alone, and in accordance to their works, let their accounts be rendered to the General Office. As this is a matter between them and their God, to us, it matters little whether they pay, or do not." Young's postscript underscored the point: "There is no compulsory or arbitrary power to be exercised over this brethren, in order to coerce the payment of tithing."

Closing the epistle, Bishop Hunter expressed his hopes for the new ward tithing plan: "A strict adherance to the instructions herein contained, will render the business throughout the Territory easy, safe, and uniform."

Although bishops quorum minutes record no mention of the circular, several entries show that bishops knew of the ward tithing plan by the end of 1852. Hunter probably had the circular's instructions in mind at the December 7 meeting when he "remarked upon the multiplicity of business which was increasing upon the hands of the bishops and which before long will call for their whole time to be devoted to it." Also, the bishops gave tithing reports at the December 21 meeting, showing they were busily engaged by then in gathering tithes. In the Tenth Ward, for example, men "were fast settling up their labor tithing." Another bishop said that "none in his ward had refused to pay their tithing." Traveling Bishop Felt advised reluctant bishops that "twas not oppressive in a bishop in demanding the tithing."[23]

Trying out new tithing roles, some bishops encountered problems. In January 1853, Bishop Philip Klingonsmith of Cedar City sent Hunter a report but said he knew it was inadequate because he lacked account books and had never seen a correct form before. He also said he needed a storehouse, tithing office, and larger record books. Some people there claimed they had paid part of their tithes at Hunter's office, which Klingonsmith complained he had no way to verify.[24]

Bishop Abraham Hoagland of Salt Lake's Fourteenth Ward, responding to Hunter's circular, began a "Day Book for Tithing" on December 11, 1852.[25] The book has three hand-ruled columns in which Hoagland recorded daily tithing transactions during 1852 and 1853 by name, credits, and debits. A handful of women and thirty-five of the ward's one hundred males are listed as donors. His busiest tithing month was March 1853, the last month for settling 1852 tithes. By categories, his March tithing transactions were:

Received	Sent to Tithing Office
Eggs 22.5 dozen	19 dozen eggs
Butter 5.5 lbs	4 lbs pork
Soft soap 20.5 lbs	2.75 lbs butter
pork, 4 lbs	basket
cloth, 5.5 yds.	garden seeds
coffee, .5 lb.	5.5 yds. cloth
garden seeds, 7 donations	
socks, 2 pr.	
wood, 2 load	
basket	
blanket, potatoes	
sugar, 2 donations	

Given to Ward Members

Sister Clement:	5 lbs soap,
	1.25 lbs sugar
Mother Taylor:	5 lbs butter
Mother Snyder:	Wood
Bro Voorhees:	Wood

Bishop Hoagland's daybook lists only one tithing settlement—the others no doubt were entered in his missing ledger book, not now extant.

Utah tithepayers, including the 1851 covenanters, made 1852 a good tithing year despite the slack summer—whether or not ward bishops grasped their new tithing tasks. Late in 1852 the general storehouse contained fifteen thousand bushels of grain—a quantity so great that many felt Utah could never have a grain shortage (it did three years later). Bishop Elias Blackburn of Provo reported in November 1852 that: "The produce tithing is coming in well except the Wheat which has not yet been thrashed but I expect it ere long. There has been but few cattle paid in yet upon Property Tithing by the new comers Yet I believe they all manifest good disposition to pay up."[26] By mid-February 1853, Hunter observed that there was never a better spirit of tithepaying.[27]

Just before the April 1853 settlement deadline, Bishop Hunter reminded bishops to handle tithing settlements themselves rather than expecting his staff to do it. Ward bishops, he said, "know better how

As a traveling bishop, Nathaniel H. Felt taught local bishops that asking members for tithes was one of their expected duties. Courtesy Church Archives.

the brethren stood ... than the clerks in the general office." Bishop Felt, liking the new ward tithing system, said he believed that the "time was just at hand when the whole temporal business of the church would devolve upon the bishops." The *Deseret News* reminded bishops that tithing returns were due at general conference. On April 5, Traveling Bishop Cordon said that along his way to Provo he gave bishops forms to fill out and bring to conference.[28]

Tooele Bishop John Rowberry's postconference letter to Hunter shows some complications that distant bishops faced.[29] Rowberry, while settling tithing accounts at Richville and E T City, found some brethren who, because they maintained accounts with the General Tithing Office, refused to settle with him. His books, therefore, showed more unpaid tithing than was so. Produce tithing, he said, was lower than seemed right for their acreage, but their farms were new and lacked adequate water.

During April general conference in 1853, Hunter's staff labored long hours to close the 1852 tithing books. Meanwhile, the Church's need for tithes became visible on April 6 when Saints witnessed the laying of cornerstones for the Salt Lake Temple. Capitalizing on the occasion, several leaders called for tithes and consecrations to flow into the tithing house to "untie" leaders hands, overcome Church indebtedness, and support the workmen. President Young wanted tithepayers to "be as prompt in paying, as you are in feeding your family," so the temple could rise quickly.[30]

The 1852 tithing season ended quietly in April 1853. Conference sermons, bishops quorum minutes, and the First Presidency's April 13 general epistle neither laud nor berate the new ward tithing method. The epistle does note that "storehouses generally are in the various settlements."[31]

Hunter found it remarkable that during the weeks and months after the conference, surprisingly little was said from pulpits regarding tithing.[32]

New Church programs, even then, required more time to implement than leaders expected. It took the ward tithing system three years to root firmly. Bishops quorum minutes for 1854–55 show that some bishops adapted well, while others seemed confused and hesitant. Some Saints disliked paying and settling tithes with their own bishop. Current events, such as the 1854 consecration movement, the 1855 drought, changes in bishoprics, and moves by ward members hampered tithing operations.

The biggest problem plaguing the ward tithing system was bad bookkeeping. During the new system's first year, many bishops discovered their accounting inadequacies. To help them, General Tithing Office clerk Howard Coray gave the bishops quorum bookkeeping instructions on August 30.[33]

The bishops' second tithing settlement season lasted from fall 1853 to April general conference in 1854. That winter Bishop Hunter and staff devoted "constant attention" to "heavy business" at the General Tithing Office. Early in 1854, Bishop Edwin Woolley predicted that recent "smooth doings" regarding tithing matters would soon change into a "storm." Look well to your wards, he advised bishops, "and have the tithing as straight up as possible."[34]

On the eve of the April conference, some tithepayers seemed confused about how to settle their accounts. Bishop Cordon, who was both a traveling bishop and General Tithing Office clerk, reported that "a question arised with many, where shall we settle our tithing? Some said settle with your bishop, but some said at the general office."[35]

That April conference brought no tithing "storm," but, instead, the First Presidency reintroduced the law of consecration. Consecration, however, was a second option for members, and the tithing system continued in place. In fact, some members "over Jordan" chose not to consecrate but salved their consciences by "overpaying their tithing."[36]

Tithing storm clouds billowed in July 1854 when the First Presidency urgently called for tithes to keep public works crews working. Bishops should immediately send to Bishop Hunter all tithing products within a hundred-mile radius of Salt Lake City. The First Presidency asked bishops to compile and send in names of all who should pay tithing, and opposite each name, bishops should note "the amount of wheat and all other grain, and of potatoes, and all other vegetables he raises this season as fast as it can be ascertained; also the amount of stock owned by each person, specifying the yearly increases; and in short, state all the items upon which a saint should rightfully pay tithing, keeping each item in a separate column." Bishop Hunter advised that ward teachers help bishops compile the lists.[37]

Neither tithes nor lists funneled properly into Church headquarters, finally unleashing the storms Woolley had predicted in the form of heated reprimands. One struck that fall, another the next spring, and a final one the next fall during the fiery Mormon Reformation. Together the storms produced a fully functioning ward tithing system from a potentially functioning one.

The first storm struck during Sunday tabernacle services on November 5, 1854, when President Brigham Young preached both morning and afternoon about tithing. He knew not one bishop who understood tithing, he said, criticizing specifically those who thought consecration was an extension of tithing, not tithing's predecessor. People needed picks and wedges, he said, to open their eyes to tithing. "It is the Tithing Office that has built up this city and territory," he asserted, and warned that "if the people do not observe the law of tithing, they will dwindle & be cursed. You cannot play with it. It will make you bleed."[38]

His fiery sermon brought almost instant results, as Heber C. Kimball, his counselor, reported on November 26: "Since President Young and others have dwelt upon tithing, it is coming in first rate." Kimball then poked fun at Bishop Hunter: "Bishop Hunter has become frightened; 'Good heavens' says he, 'what shall we do with the tithing. We have not got room to put it.' 'Why,' says I, 'stretch out, Bishop.'"[39]

Brigham Young issued a second blast during the April 1855 general conference.[40] He told forty bishops assembled in quorum meeting to "wake up and learn to do their duty." "The bishops must be corrected," he continued, "must be striped." He then chided them about poor records. "You do not seem to understand your office," he accused, "there never has been a bishop yet who has made a report that would give me any knowledge of the condition of his ward." "It is the bishops' duty to prepare an account book, and in the beginning of the year to know every man, woman, and child in his ward, and should know their occupation, and how they employ their time." He ordered bishops to "make a schedule of your wards, make a return sheet so that Bishop Hunter can read it right; and know how many Oxen, Horses, Cows, Sheep, Lambs, Pigs, Fowls of all Kinds, Eggs, Butter, and Cheese, Produce of every kind, and money; also the profit on their goods." Only with such information could bishops know that tithing was properly paid.

Some bishops, he said, complained that such a job required their full time, something they could not give. "Well let it take up all your time," he said, "and trust in the Lord for a living." Bishops unwilling to do their duty should resign. "The Bishops should be business men," he warned. "Go to now and make a book; it is as simple as A.B.C." Bookkeeping could be learned "in five minutes." "Make a schedule of every man's property, and see that the tithing is paid" and "that it is put to proper use." Bishops should visit those who refused to tithe and work with them. "The tithing belongs to the Lord," he concluded, "and there wants to be a concentration of faith, and a uniformity in business transactions."

Bishop Hunter, as chief trainer of bishops, pledged that "we will try until we get a report that will be accepted by our President." Keeping his word, Hunter told bishops on May 15, 1855, "We got a few reproofs at Conference," and then he called for reform: "I would like the bishops to feel this storm, and arouse themselves, for they have been lukewarm. I want the Bishops to make out faithful reports—we will have a form printed and distributed among the bishops."[41]

To bishops who had not accepted the new ward tithing system he bluntly said: "It is intended that the Bishops settle with their own wards." A big discussion followed about how "to settle properly with ward members," including the need to visit members in their homes. One bishop rejoiced at the instructions given, "even though we do get a lashing now and then."[42]

Bookkeeping reform was in the wind that summer—along with deadly grasshoppers and a withering drought. Bishop Hunter sent out a new trainer, a Brother Hutchinson, to teach bishops bookkeeping. In June, Hunter informed bishops that instructions about how to settle tithes, as well as printed forms, were being mailed to them. On July 31 he "had an interview with Br. Hutchinson, who is instructing the Bishops on the method of settling with their wards, and how to keep their books. I was much pleased with his ideas on the subject of tithing. I am pleased he is with us." Hutchinson visited the city bishops and planned to revisit. He urged bishops to obtain competent clerks, "which would be a great help to them, and prevent much confusion."[43]

The Church's tithing bookkeeping system changed dramatically in 1855. Ledgers in the Church History Library show that "in 1855 the General Tithing Storehouse began a system of ledgers for each ward."[44] In these books "the ward clerk or bishop would enter the donations received from the member of the ward. Then when the bishop brought the goods to the General Tithing Storehouse, the clerk in the Tithing Office entered them into the Bishops' Ledgers." Brother Hutchinson apparently designed the new record system. One researcher noted:

Probably he (Hutchinson) took the economic census form and adapted it to fit the Church's need. The columns listed almost everything possible the person could own (excluding household items) or produce. In the early schedules the bishop listed not only the tithing paid, but also everything the person owned, but very quickly the bishop listed only the tithing paid.[45]

Starting in 1855, records show, ward tithing schedules first were sent into the General Tithing Office. At that office, the schedules were later bound into three volumes: one for Salt Lake City, one for wards south of the city, and one for wards north.[46]

Drought and insects dried up the 1855 tithing flows. At October 1855 general conference, Brigham Young, sensing guilt among those who had nothing to tithe, told bishops that "it [tithing] is not required if a man has labored faithfully to produce, and his crops have failed." Hunter, eager for bishops to adopt the new bookkeeping system, added that "he wished the bishops clerks to be diligent, and to practice writing and accounts so as to make themselves proficient for their duty."[47]

Bishop Joseph Harker's experience in Butterfield Ward in southwest Salt Lake Valley illustrates how those first ward tithing settlements were conducted. His diary notes that on December 9, 1855, he "gave some instruction on tithing settlement" at a ward meeting. Several days later he "took two horses on tithing." Christmas Eve day he went to Salt Lake City "to get some council on tithing matters." On Christmas Day he "made some tithing settlements." The next day he "went to Harriman to make tithing settlements, 3 days." On December 29 he "came home via Mill Branch and made some tithing settlements." Two days later, he settled more tithing. On January 4 he wrote that some members disliked having him press them for their tithes: "I was making tithing settlements, some of the members said they should settle tithing when they pleased." He spent a week until January 12 at Mill Creek settling tithing. He next mentioned tithing on February 13 when he "was settling my tithing books." Two weeks later, he was "settling my tithing books" with a Brother Bennion. Bishop Harker then turned in his tithing records at Hunter's office and "took Bishop Hunter's council in relation to deficits in the ward."[48]

Public works director Wells lamented that 1855 and early 1856 had been "financially disastrous" for the Church because of drought. Compassionately, leaders did not chastise members for the small tithing totals for 1855.[49]

The 1856 tithing year began in famine but ended with a good harvest. That fall the purifying Mormon Reformation produced the third storm that scorched bishops about tithing, including Bishop Hunter. "There has been too much mere talking" about tithing, First Presidency Counselor Jedediah M. Grant warned him. "Talking so much and not doing is one of the grand evils; it is not for the Bishop to merely talk about people's paying their tithing, and say that they are good fellows, &c, but we want him to *know* that the people pay their tithing, and that they are right." He challenged Hunter to bring those facts to Brigham Young, "reporting faithfully the situation of all the Bishops in the Church, and how they stand in their accounts with the General Tithing Office." Grant told Hunter to call in the tithes in outlying settlements and not wait until April general conference, by which time cats, goats, ducks, rats, mice, geese, and rot would reduce the stored grain.[50]

By late 1856, Latter-day Saints and bishops knew that paying and settling tithing was a ward matter. During subsequent years, Bishop Hunter, through sermons, circular letters, and personal contacts, reminded and updated bishops about how to collect, record, store, and disburse tithes.

The success of annual ward tithing settlements varied year by year due to current events and bishops' talents. In 1857, for example, men on winter military duty in the Utah War could not settle their tithing accounts properly. In 1858 the "move south" disrupted tithing storehouses, payments, and bookkeeping. The year 1859 was the first full tithing year that might be termed "normal" for the ward tithing system—not disrupted by consecration movements, famine, reformation, or war.

The ward tithing system started in 1852 and was fully implemented in 1855. Since then, Church leaders have adopted many procedural changes to upgrade accounting methods, improve storage, guide disbursements and uses of tithes, and switch from tithing in kind to a cash system. Despite such changes, the plan established in 1852, requiring ward bishops to be the primary tithing agents of the Church, continues to be the basic administrative system for managing "the Lord's Tenth."

This article was originally published in New Views of Mormon History, Essays in Honor of Leonard J. Arrington, *ed. Davis Bitton and Maureen Ursenbach Beecher (Salt Lake City: University of Utah Press, 1987), 96–114.*

NOTES

1. Leonard J. Arrington, *Great Basin Kingdom: An Economic History of the Latter-day Saints, 1830–1900* (1958; reprinted Lincoln: University of Nebraska Press, 1966); Leonard J. Arrington, "The Mormon Tithing House: A Frontier Business Institution," *Business History Review* 28 (March 1954): 24–58; Leonard J. Arrington, Feramorz Y. Fox, and Dean L. May, *Building the City of God: Community and Cooperation among the Mormons* (Salt Lake City: Deseret Book, 1976); D. Gene Pace, "Changing Patterns of Mormon Financial Administration: Traveling Bishops, Regional Bishops, and Bishop's Agents, 1851–88," *BYU Studies* 23, no. 2 (1983): 183–95; Dale Beecher, "The Office of Bishop," *Dialogue: A Journal of Mormon Thought* 15 (Winter 1982): 103–15; Richard O. Cowan, *The Church in the Twentieth Century* (Salt Lake City: Bookcraft, 1985), 16–18, 294–97.

2. Edward Hunter, "Circular," (186–?), Church History Library, The Church of Jesus Christ of Latter-day Saints, Salt Lake City. Date should read 1852.

3. Journal History of the Church, October 7, 1849, Church History Library, microfilm copy in Harold B. Lee Library, Brigham Young University, Provo, Utah.

4. Albert Carrington Journals, Tithing Accounts, 1848–54, microfilm of holograph, Church History Library.

5. Council Meeting, Minutes, Brigham Young Collection, February 13, 14, and 16, 1849, Church History Library; Journal History, February 14 and 16, 1849.

6. Presiding Bishop's Meetings with Bishops, March 25, 1849, Church History Library (cited hereafter as Bishops Minutes).

7. Journal History, September 27 and December 14, 1850.

8. First Presidency Fifth General Epistle, April 7, 1851, in *Messages of the First Presidency of The Church of Jesus Christ of Latter-day Saints, 1833–1964*, comp. James R. Clark, 6 vols. (Salt Lake City: Bookcraft, 1965–75), 2:65.

9. Journal History, April 7, 1851.

10. First Presidency Sixth General Epistle, September 22, 1851, in Clark, *Messages of the First Presidency*, 2:90.

11. Journal History, September 10, 1851.

12. Bishops Minutes, September 28, 1851.

13. Bishops Minutes, September 28, 1851; Journal History, November 29, 1851.

14. "Tithing Circular," *Millennial Star* 14 (April 1, 1852): 100.

15. Bishops Minutes, January 28 and February 11, 1852.

16. Bishops Minutes, February 25, 1852.

17. First Presidency's Seventh General Epistle, April 18, 1852, in Clark, *Messages of the First Presidency*, 2:92; Brigham Young, in *Journal of Discourses*, 26 vols. (Liverpool: Latter-day Saints' Book Depot, 1855–86), 1:51–52, April 9, 1852.

18. First Presidency Seventh General Epistle, April 18, 1852, in Clark, *Messages of the First Presidency*, 2:95–97.

19. First Presidency Seventh General Epistle, April 18, 1852, in Clark, *Messages of the First Presidency*, 2:97.

20. Journal History, October 7 and 8, 1852.

21. Hunter, "Circular," (186–?) [1852].

22. Presiding Bishopric, "Instructions to the Bishops," 6, booklet, November 23, 1859, Church History Library.

23. Bishops Minutes, December 21, 1852.

24. Bishop Philip Klingonsmith, Letter to Edward Hunter, January 12, 1853, Hunter Incoming Correspondence folder 4, Church History Library.

25. Abraham Hoagland, Daybook, entries for December 1852 to April 1853, holograph, Church History Library.

26. Elias H. Blackburn, Letter to Edward Hunter, November 19, 1852, Hunter Incoming Correspondence folder 4, Church History Library.

27. Bishops Minutes, February 15, 1853.

28. Bishops Minutes, March 15, 1853; Journal History, March 19, 1853; Alfred Cordon, Letter to Edward Hunter, April 5, 1853, Hunter Incoming Correspondence folder 4, Church History Library.

29. John Rowberry, Letter to Edward Hunter, April 25, 1853, Hunter Incoming Correspondence folder 4, Church History Library.

30. Journal History, April 6, 1853.

31. Bishops Minutes, April 9, 1853; First Presidency's Ninth General Epistle, April 13, 1853, in Clark, *Messages of the First Presidency*, 2:113.

32. Bishops Minutes, June 7 and July 19, 1853.

33. Bishops Minutes, August 30, 1853.

34. Bishops Minutes, October 8 and December 20, 1853; and February 14, 1854.

35. Bishops Minutes, March 28, 1854.

36. Bishops Minutes, April 25, 1854.

37. Journal History, July 20, 1854.

38. Thomas Bullock Minutes, Tabernacle Meeting, November 5, 1854, in Brigham Young Papers, Church History Library.

39. Heber C. Kimball, in *Journal of Discourses,* 2:157–58, November 26, 1854.

40. Bishops Minutes, April 7, 1855.

41. Bishops Minutes, April 7 and May 15, 1855.

42. Bishops Minutes, May 15, 1855.

43. Bishops Minutes, June 19 and July 31, 1855.

44. Ronald G. Watt, "Church Financial Records in the Nineteenth Century," research paper in Watt's personal files.

45. Watt, "Church Financial Records."

46. Watt, "Church Financial Records."

47. Bishops Minutes, October 8, 1855.

48. Joseph Harker, Journal, film of holograph, Church History Library.

49. Journal History, March 11, 1856.

50. Bishops Minutes, October 8, 1856.

Melchizedek Priesthood

8   Brigham Young and Priesthood Work at the General and Local Levels

LIKE AN ADMIRAL COMMANDING a fleet of ships sailing on heavy seas, Brigham Young, during his years as President of the Church, stood at the helm and directed the various offices and officers in the priesthood for the general good of the kingdom of God on earth. And yet, oddly, although biographies of Brigham Young devote much attention to the move west—the gathering, colonization, missionary outreach, Indian relations, economics, politics, and theology—they rarely assess him carefully as a leader of the priesthood or explore in detail how stakes, wards, and quorums—the Church's fundamental organizational units—operated during his administration.[1]

For President Young, the holy priesthood was "a perfect system of laws and government," one that "rules and reigns in eternity."[2] With total certitude he believed that "we have the only true authority, upon the face of the whole earth, to administer in the ordinances of the Gospel."[3]

"The Holy Priesthood is not on the earth, unless the Latter-day Saints have it,"[4] he proclaimed. "There is no act of a Latter-day Saint—no duty required—no time given, exclusive and independent of the Priesthood," he explained in 1858; "Everything is subject to it, whether preaching, business, or any other act pertaining to the proper conduct of this life."[5]

"No man can lawfully officiate in any office in the Kingdom of God," President Young believed, "[that] he has not been called to, and the authority of which has not been bestowed upon him."[6]

"Have we reason to rejoice?" he asked in 1857, and then he answered his own question:

> We have. There is no other people on this earth under such deep obligation to their Creator, as are the Latter-day Saints. The Gospel has brought to us the holy Priesthood, which is again restored to the children of men. The keys of that Priesthood are here; we have them in our possession; we can unlock, and we can shut up. We can obtain salvation, and we can administer it. We have the power within our own hands, and this has been my deep mortification, one that I have frequently spoken of, to think that a people, having in their possession all the principles, keys, and powers of eternal life, should neglect so great a salvation. We have these blessings, they are with us.[7]

Wanting Church members to be able to receive all the priesthood blessings to which they were entitled, he labored constantly to help priesthood bearers at all levels understand and then carry out their duties. At times he redeployed priesthood assignments to best utilize the quorums and officers while advancing the entire fleet through changing and unpredictable currents, winds, and weather.

To be assessed in proper context, Brigham Young's handling of priesthood operations needs to be compared both with prevailing Church practices at the time he succeeded Joseph Smith and with current priesthood functions. President Young presided over the Church for thirty-three years, more than twice as long as Joseph Smith (fourteen years). He presided over a church whose membership grew to more than five times that of Joseph Smith's time, more than 104,000 compared to about 20,000. The Church had a dozen bishops and wards in Nauvoo, but at Brigham's death it had 241—a twenty-fold increase. Joseph's ordained followers numbered perhaps 4,000 maximum, but a priesthood census taken among stakes within a year of Brigham's death found 22,000. During the same period, the number of seventies quorums increased from three to about seventy-five. Joseph Smith died before all ordinances for the dead could be implemented, particularly the sealing of deceased couples together—something Brigham Young later authorized. Joseph never presided over a church filled with believing adults who had received temple endowments; Brigham Young did. During President Young's watch, explosive growth in Church membership produced situations demanding expansion and adaptation by priesthood quorums and governing units.

As we might expect when comparing Brigham Young's era with today's Church, a number of priesthood practices implemented then are different from our day. During the early 1870s, for example, middle-aged LDS stalwart John H. Picknell, an ordained seventy, was a counselor in the Salt Lake Stake deacons quorum presidency. "I've Seventies', Priests', Teachers' & Deacons' meetings to attend, Teacher in two wards, a Priest in one," he once itemized; "I'm out almost every night in the month." At another stake deacons quorum meeting, acting deacon Matthias Cowley explained that "I was an Elder before I was a deacon" and added that "if we were all to stay away because we are Elders or Seventies, where would the Teachers and deacons' quorums be? Why! Here your [deacons] president is a high priest, & his counsellors, Seventies."[8]

During his years as Church President, Brigham Young was instrumental in clarifying and solidifying the function of the priesthood. Not only did he define how succession in the First Presidency should take place, he also set up the structure of wards and stakes through the framework of priesthood callings. Courtesy Perry Special Collections.

While Brigham Young was President, half of the Apostles served at times concurrently as stake presidents. For many years, the seventies quorums, not subject to stake presidents but administered by the First Council of the Seventy, were more numerous than elders quorums. At times, the Salt Lake Stake was the "center stake of Zion," exercising authority over other Utah stakes. Both a ward bishop and a ward president presided in several settlements, a double leadership structure Brigham Young favored. Other priorities sometimes meant that ward bishops served for years without being ordained, and a few bishops had counselors who were not high priests. Although most young men were not ordained to the Aaronic Priesthood, youths as young as fourteen were encouraged to receive their temple endowments, thus receiving the Melchizedek Priesthood without prior ordination to the Aaronic Priesthood.

It is not surprising that priesthood operations in the past differ from those of today, when the dynamic and adaptive sweep of LDS priesthood history from 1829 to the present is examined. Since the 1830s, change has touched most priesthood offices and quorums. For example, at times the First Presidency has included more than two counselors; members of the First and Second Quorums of the Seventy are now General Authorities; the two quorums of the Seventy have shouldered some of the responsibilities once carried by the Quorum of the Twelve Apostles; Assistants to the Twelve once served a vital function and then were phased out; the Presiding Bishopric no longer is responsible for Aaronic Priesthood operations; the Presiding Patriarch's authority over stake patriarchs has been redefined; administrative positions between the general and the stake levels, such as area presidents and area authorities, have been created; the position of regional representative was created and later phased out; terms of service for bishops and stake presidents have shortened over time; stake high councils receive a myriad of assignments beyond their scripturally assigned disciplinary function; stake presidents, rather than General Authorities, now set apart missionaries; the majority of men serving full-time missions once were seventies but now are primarily elders; and home teaching has replaced ward teaching, to cite some of the better-known changes.[9]

All LDS Church Presidents have tried diligently to tailor priesthood instructions, as recorded in the Doctrine and Covenants, to fit the pressing needs of their day.[10] No prophet presided during a period when the seas of changing circumstances churned more than they did during President Young's administration. His biographical record should show that among numerous contributions he made to the shape and development of priesthood operations in the Church, the following twelve are the most important historically:

1. Reconstituting the First Presidency and establishing how succession in the Presidency should take place.
2. Clarifying and institutionalizing the Apostles' roles at home and abroad.
3. Transforming the seventies' office into a major non-General Authority level of priesthood.
4. Institutionalizing and clarifying the role of the Presiding Bishopric.
5. Establishing wards as the Church's primary units of governance and ward bishops as the key local ecclesiastical officer.
6. Institutionalizing stakes to be meaningful intermediate units of administration.
7. Requiring endowments prior to missions or marriage, which caused men to receive the Melchizedek Priesthood, thereby depleting the Aaronic Priesthood of mature males.
8. Requiring boys to serve in at least one Aaronic Priesthood office before reaching adulthood.
9. Establishing patriarchal priesthood ordinances and practices, including the law of adoption, family organizations, and plurality of wives.
10. Preserving, promoting, and refining temple ordinances and rituals for the living and for the dead while making temple blessings available in the Nauvoo Temple, the Salt Lake Endowment House, and the St. George Temple.
11. Directing civic and secular affairs semi-theocratically through priesthood officers.
12. Conducting a thorough priesthood reorganization in 1877, including the issuing of the first "handbook" regarding Church administration.

I deal with these developments below at appropriate places, weaving them into a tapestry designed to showcase individually how each of the Church's priesthood offices and units functioned during Brigham Young's presidency. Each of the presiding quorums is discussed, followed by stake, ward, and local quorum operations.

THE APOSTOLIC PRESIDENCY, 1844–1847

Brigham Young's leadership of the Church began while he was President of the Quorum of the Twelve, a body that collectively succeeded Joseph Smith from August 1844 to December 1847. During that period, he and the Twelve promoted four major priesthood-related ventures.

The first occurred during the October 1844 conference (where he was sustained as President of the Twelve) when the Twelve declared every United States congressional district to be a missionary district and then assigned to each a high priest to reside there and "have entire charge" under the Twelve "of all spiritual matters, superintending the labors of the elders, and the calling of conferences."[11] Seven dozen high priests were set apart to permanent assignments and instructed to take their families with them to those districts. However, unexpected pressures for the Church to leave Nauvoo canceled the assignments.

The second venture, apparently linked to the Twelve's districting of the United States, was President Young's orchestration of a mass-ordination of seventies, expanding the number of seventies quorums from three to thirty (see "The Seventies," below). Apparently Young and the Twelve anticipated a vast missionary push, designed to convert individuals in the United States districts that had just been announced. But, again, the uprooting from Nauvoo and the tremendous work needed to build settlements in Utah allowed Church leaders to send out only a fairly limited missionary force year by year.

As a third priesthood-related measure, President Young implemented the bestowal of the temple endowment upon all Nauvoo adults who were "faithful and worthy" Saints and who wanted to receive that blessing.[12] To be endowed, he taught, is to "possess the keys of the eternal priesthood."[13] Day and night, the Nauvoo Temple stayed open in late 1845 and early 1846, during which time 5,615 adults received the endowment.[14] The availability of the endowment led to the priesthood practice of expecting an LDS male to hold the Melchizedek Priesthood and be temple-endowed before going on a full-time proselyting mission or being sealed in eternal marriage. A byproduct of this expectation was that almost all active, practicing LDS adult males received Melchizedek Priesthood ordinations, thus removing them from the pool of manpower eligible to receive Aaronic Priesthood offices (see "Aaronic Priesthood Quorums and Labors," below).

Fourth, with Brigham Young's guidance, the principle of succession in the Presidency was clarified and implemented. An absolutely critical test for a new organization is whether or not it can survive the passing or loss of its founder. The failure rate is substantial. The Church faced that test when Joseph Smith was killed. It wobbled slightly and dealt with a crucial succession question not fully articulated by revelations, handbooks, or Joseph Smith's teachings. The Prophet's successor was the Twelve as a body, and they directed the Church in lieu of a First Presidency for three-and-a-half years. Not until December 27, 1847, did the Twelve organize a new First Presidency and obtain ratification from the Church's membership. The precedent established then is still followed: the Twelve as a body succeeds a deceased prophet and then selects the senior Apostle, with divine sanction, as the new President of the Church.

THE FIRST PRESIDENCY

During the Brigham Young years, the First Presidency became a powerful quorum with well-defined purposes and procedures.

Personnel

Only six men served as first and second counselors to President Young during his twenty-nine years as President. His first counselors were Heber C. Kimball until 1868, then George A. Smith until 1875, followed by John W. Young until 1877. The president's second counselors were Willard Richards to 1854, Jedediah M. Grant to 1857, and Daniel H. Wells until Brigham's death in 1877. In 1873, Young called five extra counselors, who, a year later, were designated "assistant counselors": John W. Young, George Q. Cannon, Lorenzo Snow, Brigham Young Jr., and Albert Carrington. Joseph Smith had set the precedent for having more than two counselors by having Oliver Cowdery, Hyrum Smith, Joseph Smith Sr., and John Smith simultaneously serve as counselors.

Responsibilities

The First Presidency was responsible for all spiritual and temporal Church matters. They wanted all people to receive the gospel ordinances and temple blessings at the hands of the priesthood and to be set to work building the kingdom of God. They ensured that the basic ordinances of blessing babies, baptizing, confirming, administering the sacrament, and ordaining to the priesthood were performed properly.

One of the First Presidency's priorities was temple building and the performance of temple ordinances. Brigham Young believed that only in a temple could people "receive the ordinances of the holy Priesthood."[15] Fulfilling the Twelve's mandate from Joseph Smith, Brigham Young energetically rushed the Nauvoo Temple to basic completion and arranged for washings, anointings, endowments, and marriage sealings to be administered there. After the exodus from Nauvoo, lacking a Utah temple, he arranged for the temporary Endowment House to be built and placed his counselor Heber C. Kimball in charge of it. Some baptisms for the dead took place. President Young, eager to have a fully-functioning temple operational before he died, dedicated the St. George Temple and installed Apostle Wilford Woodruff as its president.

The First Presidency performed many marriage sealings, including plural marriages. President Young exercised the sealing powers he held by virtue of being President of the Church and holding all the keys of the priesthood. He sealed couples together in celestial marriage and delegated that authority to a few others. Whereas Joseph Smith introduced plural marriage quietly among selected associates, to Brigham Young fell the responsibility of publicly announcing the doctrine and of convincing Latter-day Saints to believe in and participate in polygamy. Through example, public discourse, and private counsel, he championed plural marriage. As a result of his leadership, aided by that of other General Authorities, up to 25 percent of LDS households participated in plural marriage at a given point in time.[16] About two out of five men in good Church standing took plural wives.[17] President Young successfully promoted the principle.

Another sealing ordinance involved sealing family units for eternity. In the context of this ordinance, President Young promoted the law of adoption. Through the law of adoption, Church members whose own parents were not priesthood bearers could become sealed in life and for eternity to General Authorities, thereby joining that authority's family by priesthood adoption. This practice continued until the 1890s.[18]

In terms of manpower and resources, missionary work sometimes took a back seat to settlement and colonizing labors. Nevertheless, President

Young promoted missionary work by involving the Twelve deeply in its management and by sending missionaries throughout the world.

Of necessity, President Young's primary labors were devoted to establishing a home base for the Church, securing a Mormon homeland in the Great Basin. His concern was to help LDS converts reach Zion, to develop agricultural and mineral-production settlements, and to see that the Saints received the gospel ordinances and had ecclesiastical leaders and organizations to belong to. Up to 1877, when President Young reorganized Church units, the Church in gathered Zion had 13 stakes and 101 wards, albeit in varying states of health and functionality. Young's 1877 restructurings (see below) were monumental in the course of the historical development of priesthood work.

Council Meetings with Church Leaders

After the First Presidency was reconstituted in December 1847, they met almost daily with the Twelve at Winter Quarters. In Utah, the two presiding quorums met together often, although a majority of the Twelve rarely was present because of assignments away from Salt Lake City. These meetings were small council meetings that some additional persons attended—usually the senior president of the First Council of the Seventy, the Presiding Bishop, and the president of the Salt Lake Stake (regarded as a "center stake" for the Church—see below). When four men were added to the Quorum of the Twelve in 1849, those attending the historic meeting were the First Presidency; three of the Twelve; Presiding Bishop Newel K. Whitney; high priests president John Young and his counselor George B. Wallace; and Jedediah M. Grant of the First Council of the Seventy.[19]

It appears that President Young regarded the First Presidency not so much as a quorum apart from the Quorum of the Twelve but "as a kind of executive committee of the Twelve."[20] Minutes exist for sixteen meetings of the First Presidency and Twelve in the 1850s, fifteen in the 1860s, and five in the 1870s.[21] Wilford Woodruff's journal itemizes 217 meetings of the First Presidency and the Twelve between 1847 and 1853. Those of the Twelve who were "home" did consult regularly with the First Presidency. Woodruff's annual summaries in his diary show that by the mid-1850s and continuing to 1876, their conjoint meetings became prayer circle gatherings, from seventeen to sixty-six times a year, that served at times as "spiritually oriented council meetings" in which members discussed scriptures, doctrine, history, and occasionally organizational and temporal matters.[22] A review of the minutes of Brigham's meetings with the Twelve "show Brigham Young not always telling them what to do, not often chastising them, but usually sincerely seeking their judgment—seeking to establish and maintain harmony and unity. Most of the meetings took the form of relaxed discussions among peers."[23]

Throughout Brigham Young's presidency, most decisions came from "the President-in-council"—the President, his counselors, available members of the Twelve, one or more of the Seventies' presidency, one or more of the Presiding Bishopric, and one or more from the Salt Lake Stake presidency and the Salt Lake high priests quorum.[24]

General Epistles

Important to Church policy, practice, and belief were the First Presidency's general epistles to the Saints throughout the world. In Nauvoo, President Young and the Twelve utilized this method of communication with the Church worldwide. Then, when the First Presidency was reconstituted, it issued many general instructions during Brigham Young's tenure as President.

The first known document of the apostolic presidency was written by Brigham Young to the Church membership from Boston on July 16, 1844. The Twelve issued a general epistle on December 23, 1847, followed soon after by the First General Epistle of the First Presidency, dated August 1, 1849. A Fourteenth General Epistle is dated December 10, 1856, ending the practice of numbering the general letters. Others followed, however, including two in 1869 and the vital Circular of the First Presidency of July 11, 1877, which ordered the reorganization of stakes and quorums. In addition, the First Presidency sent numerous letters addressed to the bishops.[25]

General Conferences

During Brigham Young's presidency, the Church's annual and semiannual conferences became major forums for the First Presidency and the Twelve to address the Saints, and, unlike at Nauvoo, the conferences took place in suitable conference auditoriums—the original Salt Lake Tabernacle and then the "new" (and now famous) Tabernacle. President Young arranged for clerks to record conference discourses in shorthand so they could be published in the *Deseret News* and in LDS periodicals abroad. A sixteen-page semimonthly publication called *Journal of Discourses* was published in England, which became a monumental reference collection packed with leaders' counsel, including discussions of priesthood theory and practice. It contains 390 sermons by Brigham Young.[26]

Tours to Distant Settlements

The First Presidency adopted a role that was not practiced and probably not needed before the Utah gathering: making visits into the Mormon communities to consult firsthand with local priesthood officers.[27]

Secular Leadership

Before, during, and after his terms as governor of Utah Territory, Young acted forcefully to ensure that priesthood leaders, not unbelieving outsiders or apostates, were the political and economic leaders of the Mormon people. As a result, General Authorities and local Church leaders served prominently in territorial executive, legislative, and judicial positions and as county and city officials.

GENERAL CONFERENCE SUSTAININGS

A look at general conference sustainings between 1849 and 1877, specifically the order in which officers were presented, reveals several variations in priesthood sustaining practices during the Brigham Young period:

1. In 1873, the Church sustained seven counselors in the First Presidency; from 1874 through 1877, the Presidency was readjusted to include two counselors plus five assistant counselors.
2. Up through 1859 and again between 1872 and 1877, President Young was sustained as President and Prophet, Seer, and Revelator, but from fall 1859 to spring 1872, the terms *prophet, seer,* and *revelator* were not used.
3. A Presiding Patriarch or "Patriarch to the Whole Church" was sustained at every conference, although the title varied slightly.

4. Members of the First Council of the Seventy, who were the seven senior presidents of all the seventies quorums, were sustained variously as "President of the Presidency of Seventies and Six Associates," "President of the Presiding Council of Seventies," "President of the First Seven Presidents of the Seventies," "Members of the First Seven Presidents of the Seventies," "President of all the Seventies and Six Counselors," and "Presidents of all the Quorums of Seventies."

5. Until 1860, the Presiding Bishop was sustained without counselors, except on one occasion. At four conferences, the Church sustained Assistant Presiding Bishops and Traveling Bishops.

6. The president and counselors in the Salt Lake Stake presidency were sustained at nearly every general conference, as were the stakes high council, the president and counselors of the high priests quorum, and president and counselors for the stake's priests, teachers, and deacons quorums.

The sustaining order sometimes changed slightly. In 1849 and 1850, the high priests quorum presidency, which was the only such quorum in existence and served as the general quorum (see below) for all high priests in Utah no matter where they lived, was sustained before the Senior Presidents of the Seventies, and at other times before the Salt Lake Stake presidency. The stake presidency was sustained ahead of the Presiding Bishop in 1849, 1850, and 1851, probably reflecting its earlier role as the presidency of the Church in Utah during the first year. The Presiding Patriarch was sustained after the First Presidency and before the Twelve; it was later positioned after the Twelve.

THE TWELVE APOSTLES

Before Joseph Smith died, he placed upon the Twelve the responsibilities for gathered Zion in addition to the foreign ministry. They had crossed the threshold, comparatively speaking, but suddenly had to step forthrightly into the room after the martyrdom. Under Brigham Young, the Twelve learned from hard experience where they fit in the Church's administrative structure.

Although the Apostles were subordinate to the First Presidency "in cases of doctrinal and other pronouncements made as revelation from the Lord," the First Presidency sought and considered their opinions and insights. Once decisions were made, after differences of opinion were aired during discussion stages, the Twelve gave public support "despite any private reservations." President Young felt strongly about securing unity among the General Authorities.[28]

Personnel

While Brigham Young was Church President, there were few changes in personnel among the Twelve, who were relatively young men when called. Only twelve new members were called. And, during that time, four were dropped from the quorum: William Smith (1845), John E. Page (1846), Lyman Wight (1848), and Amasa Lyman (1867).

When the First Presidency was reconstituted late in 1847, it drew three members from the quorum: Brigham Young, Heber C. Kimball, and Willard Richards. Near that same time, Elder Wight was excommunicated. With President Young's approval, the four vacancies were filled on February 12, 1849, by Charles C. Rich, Lorenzo Snow, Erastus Snow, and Franklin D. Richards. The First Presidency ordained these men and continued to ordain all new Apostles.[29]

When the First Presidency and Twelve met together in October 1859 to choose a replacement for Parley P. Pratt, who had died in 1857, President Young asked members of the Twelve to nominate one or two men in writing rather than having the First Presidency nominate someone. Several names were discussed, as were the merits of proven experience versus inexperienced potential. Finally the Twelve deferred to President Young, who selected George Q. Cannon; the Twelve sustained him without dissent.

In 1866, President Young received a revelation to ordain Joseph F. Smith to the apostleship even though there was no vacancy in the quorum. The Twelve approved and helped President Young ordain the new Apostle. Thereafter, though the Twelve did not select new Apostles on their own, their suggestions and opinions were solicited before the calls were issued.[30]

Of four men called into the First Presidency as counselors to Brigham Young after Elders Kimball and Richards, only George A. Smith was from the Quorum of the Twelve.

As noted earlier, rarely was a majority of the Twelve together at one time in Salt Lake City. In fact, the first time the entire Quorum of Twelve was able to meet together in Utah was on October 6, 1868.[31]

Assignments

From 1848 to 1877, President Young constantly gave assignments to members of the Twelve, the two main ones being to preside over missions outside Utah and to establish and direct remote settlements of the Church. A summary of the Apostles' activities shows the following:

> Orson Hyde spent nineteen years presiding over Great Basin settlements between 1854 and 1877. Orson Pratt spent eleven years on missions. John Taylor spent six years on missions. Ezra T. Benson spent three years on missions and nine years presiding over settlements. Charles C. Rich spent twenty-three years presiding over settlements. Lorenzo Snow spent three years on a mission and twenty-four presiding over the Brigham City settlement. Erastus Snow spent eight years on missions and sixteen years presiding over settlements. Franklin D. Richards spent seven years on missions and eight presiding over Weber Valley.[32]

Inherent in the work of presiding over missions was the labor of organizing, scheduling, and arranging finances for each year's emigration. In addition, whenever Apostles returned home from such missions, they helped supervise the LDS emigrants traveling with them, such as happened in 1856 when Elders John Taylor, Erastus Snow, and Franklin D. Richards directed much of the movement. In 1860, Elders Erastus Snow and Orson Pratt went to the eastern United States to supervise LDS emigration.

Another assignment given to various Apostles related to publications and public relations. In the late 1840s, Elder Orson Hyde was sent east to obtain a printing press and then to publish a newspaper at Kanesville, which was named the *Frontier Guardian*. After the Church publicly announced its belief in polygamy, the First Presidency sent Orson Pratt to Washington, D.C., on a public relations crusade. There he published a periodical called *The Seer* for eighteen months in which he defended in print LDS doctrines. Similarly, John Taylor published *The Mormon* in New York, and Erastus Snow published the *St. Louis Luminary*.

First Presidency and Quorum of the Twelve Apostles, 1869. Center front, left to right: George A. Smith, President Brigham Young, Daniel H. Wells. Back row, left to right: Orson Hyde, Orson Pratt, John Taylor, Wilford Woodruff, Ezra T. Benson, Charles C. Rich, Lorenzo Snow, Erastus Snow, Franklin D. Richards, George Q. Cannon, Brigham Young Jr., and Joseph F. Smith. Courtesy Church Archives.

In the mid-1850s, the First Presidency appointed several Apostles to divide Utah settlements into districts and then do "home missionary" work among them, mainly by holding conferences and meetings. They helped promote the Mormon Reformation of 1856. Upon the Twelve's shoulders fell the major work of instituting the Priesthood Reorganization of 1877 (see below).

Seniority

Brigham Young made a major seniority adjustment among the Twelve that proved to be crucial in determining who became his successor. At the time the First Presidency was reconstituted on December 27, 1847, the Twelve, in order of seniority, were: Brigham Young, Heber C. Kimball, Orson Hyde, Parley P. Pratt, Orson Pratt, Lyman Wight, Willard Richards, Wilford Woodruff, John Taylor, George A. Smith, Amasa Lyman, and Ezra T. Benson. But during a meeting with the Twelve in 1875, Brigham ruled that because Elders Hyde and Orson Pratt had separated themselves briefly from the quorum in 1838 and 1842 respectively, they had lost their seniority standings to Elders Taylor, Woodruff, and George A. Smith. And because John Taylor had helped ordain Wilford Woodruff to be an Apostle,

Woodruff's seniority over Taylor in the quorum was not proper, so the two exchanged seniority positions.

When Brigham Young selected five extra counselors in 1874, four of them were members of the Twelve. However, those four served in both capacities and were not replaced within the Quorum of the Twelve.

THE PRESIDING PATRIARCH

On May 24, 1845, soon after Brigham Young assumed Church leadership, Apostle William Smith, the Prophet's brother, was ordained patriarch by virtue of his lineage. Immediately he claimed to have independent presiding authority in the Church and even primacy over the Twelve. (D&C 124:124 placed the patriarch position hierarchically before the First Presidency.) He was excommunicated that fall for apostasy. After that, the hereditary office of Patriarch to the Church was vacant for two years.

John Smith, uncle to Joseph Smith Jr., served as Church Patriarch from 1849 to 1854. Courtesy Church Archives.

John Smith, popularly known as Uncle John Smith (Joseph Smith's uncle), succeeded William on January 1, 1849. In theory, John presided over a "quorum" containing all other Church patriarchs. He died on May 23, 1854.

Brigham Young determined that the position was subordinate to the First Presidency and Twelve and defined the office as being patriarch *to* the Church, not *over* the Church. During Uncle John Smith's tenure, the Presiding Patriarch was sustained *after* the First Presidency and before the Twelve. But when young John Smith (son of Hyrum Smith) succeeded Uncle John, the position was sustained

after the Twelve, showing to the Church its relative position in the hierarchy. The younger John Smith was ordained at age twenty-two under the
hands of Brigham Young and seven of the Apostles on February 18, 1855. In
that position, he bestowed thousands of blessings upon the heads of the
Saints. Patriarchs were called at the local level, but, apparently, no "quorum" of patriarchs was actually organized wherein the Presiding Patriarch
directed or instructed the other patriarchs.[33]

THE SEVENTIES

At the time of the martyrdom, the Church had three seventies quorums.[34]
But under the direction of Brigham Young and the Twelve, new seventies
units were created on such a scale that by the time of the exodus some
thirty were in operation. In August 1844, the First Quorum of Seventies
was divided to provide ten sets of seven presidents, who became the presidents of seventies quorums number two through eleven, effectively disbanding the first quorum. The seven presidents of the first quorum became
the senior presidency over all seventies units, serving as the First Council
of Seventy—the Church's third quorum of General Authorities. That October the Twelve instructed that elders under age thirty-five be ordained as
seventies. Over four hundred were ordained, so that eleven quorums were
filled. By January 1846, the number of quorums increased to thirty, and in
1861, senior president Joseph Young reported that the quorums in Utah then
numbered sixty-two.[35]

Why the number of seventies was so dramatically expanded is not
understood. Apparently Brigham Young and the Twelve wanted these seventies to become a massive missionary force in the near future. "Seventies
were designed to be messengers to every land and kingdom under heaven,"
Apostle Amasa M. Lyman said during dedicatory services of Nauvoo's
impressive Seventies Hall in December 1844.[36] Seventies quorums provided many, perhaps most, of the ordinance workers in the Nauvoo Temple
when washing, anointings, and endowments were administered late in 1845
and early in 1846. During the exodus to the west, seventies were the largest
priesthood body in the Church. At Winter Quarters, seventies helped erect
a Council House, and general conferences of seventies from all quorums
occurred weekly that first winter. Seventies held a five-day jubilee at the
log tabernacle on the Iowa side of the river (present-day Council Bluffs).[37]

Seventies were the largest body of priesthood in Brigham Young's 1847 vanguard party, which included eight Apostles, four bishops, fifteen high priests, eight elders, and seventy-eight seventies.[38] More than one-third of the men serving in the Mormon Battalion (1846–47) were seventies.[39] Drawn from many different quorums, these men expediently formed one "mass" seventies quorum in Los Angeles on April 18, 1847, by electing their own seven presidents under the direction of Levi W. Hancock of the First Council of the Seventy, the only General Authority in the battalion.

During the trek west and then the settlement and colonization of the Great Basin, seventies quorum members became scattered; this was a serious problem, because once a man was enrolled in a particular quorum, he remained a member of it as long as he was a seventy. During the 1850s, the *Deseret News* ran frequent notices of seventies quorums presidents looking for their missing members and occasional inquiries by quorums searching for their presidents.[40] Many dispersed seventies did what the Mormon Battalion had done and regrouped themselves into "mass" quorums (disapprovingly dubbed "muss" quorums by Brigham Young), consisting of all seventies living in a ward or stake, without regard to the particular quorum to which they officially belonged.

Under Brigham Young, the seventies became the backbone of the missionary force. Seventy percent of all missionaries called between 1860 and 1875 were seventies or were ordained such in order to go on missions. New seventies, after returning from missions, were assigned to memberships in existing quorums. Between 1846 and 1856, only six new quorums were organized; but between March and July of 1857, sixteen new quorums were organized, possibly a product of the Mormon Reformation just ending. By the 1860s, the seventies quorums numbered more than sixty.[41]

President Joseph Young, Brigham's brother, being the senior member of the First Council of the Seventy, was the Church's senior president of all seventies. The First Council kept in touch with seventies quorums, which were not under stake jurisdictions. The quorums each met for gospel discussion, held conferences and socials, and advanced various community projects.

During Brigham Young's administration, three confusions developed and lingered for decades concerning the seventies. First, by vastly expanding the number of seventies quorums, he created two levels of seventies: the seven presidents of the first quorum, or First Council, were General Authorities, but the other quorums and their presidents were not. So the

Church had two types of seventies, a practice that continued until October 1986, when local seventies units were phased out and the First and Second Quorums of Seventy were revitalized as General Authority–level quorums.

A second problem involved the authority that First Council members held in comparison to high priests. Seventies could not be high priests, and yet Brigham Young's generation referred to the First Council members as Seventy Apostles.[42] Controversy regarding who had higher authority, seventies or high priests, continued into the twentieth century.

A third problem was that seventies quorums were based on memberships and not on geography; as noted above, they became mixed up, and quorums were depleted when their members moved. Revelations in the 1880s solved this dilemma by putting seventies quorums on geographic footings.[43]

By the time Brigham Young died, the elders in Utah's stakes had come to outnumber seventies by two to one—9,084 compared to 4,477. The elders' number had risen because men were ordained elders in order to receive the endowment.

THE PRESIDING BISHOPRIC

The Presiding Bishop was the last General Authority–level office in the Church's hierarchy to be implemented. That office was authorized by revelation in 1841 (see D&C 124:20–21, 141). However, from then until 1847, Bishop Newel K. Whitney and Bishop George Miller functioned jointly as General Bishops for the entire Church. After the Saints' departure from Nauvoo, Bishop Miller became disaffected from Brigham Young's leadership. So, on April 6, 1847, Bishop Whitney was sustained as Presiding Bishop of the Church.

For a time, his counselors were President Brigham Young and First Presidency counselor Heber C. Kimball. Bishop Whitney's successor, Edward Hunter, served without counselors at first. In 1852, Presidents Young and Kimball were designated as Bishop Hunter's counselors, but then Hunter served again without counselors until 1856. Finally, starting in 1856 and continuing since then, the Presiding Bishop has had counselors who together form the Presiding Bishopric.[44]

From 1849 onward, the Presiding Bishop served President Young and the Church by handling numerous temporal matters, including tithing, and through direct contacts with bishops.[45] Regarding Bishop Hunter's relationship to the First Presidency, Brigham Young stated in 1851 that the Presiding Bishop's duty was to preside over all bishops, and "it is the business of the First Presidency to correct him and from whom he receives his instructions."[46] President Young made it clear that he felt he had upon himself more or less "the responsibility of both priesthoods."[47] The First Presidency framed policy, the Presiding Bishop supervised it, and the local bishops implemented it.[48]

At biweekly meetings with Salt Lake Valley bishops and any others who were in town, the Presiding Bishop dealt with practical and spiritual matters, including the operations of the Aaronic Priesthood and, by association, the Melchizedek Priesthood. Constantly, Bishop Hunter labored to see that the Aaronic Priesthood offices were filled and honored.

To help handle tithing, Bishop Hunter used "assistant presiding traveling bishops" as well as regional presiding bishops from 1851 to 1877. The use of regional bishops became widespread.[49]

STAKES AND STAKE OFFICERS

Early in 1849, to overcome disruptions caused by the exodus from Nauvoo, the First Presidency took several major steps to "regularize church government" in the Salt Lake Valley. They selected John Young, Brigham's oldest brother, to be president of the Church's only high priests quorum; Daniel Spencer to be stake president; a high council with Isaac Morley as president; and John Nebeker as elders quorum president. They appointed Presiding Bishop Newel K. Whitney to organize in Great Salt Lake Valley one quorum each of priests, teachers, and deacons. A committee, chaired by Bishop Whitney but including Brigham Young, divided Salt Lake Valley into nineteen wards and established other wards in nearby areas; each ward soon had its own bishop.[50]

At Brigham Young's death, stakes in the Mountain West numbered twenty, including seven created during the previous five months. During Brigham Young's presidency, the terms *stakes, branches,* and *settlements* were used imprecisely and interchangeably. Always the basic local Church governing unit was a stake. When one place was settled, it was considered a stake in embryo and started with a president. Then a bishop and a high council were added. High councils usually had their own president who was not the stake president. More bishops would be called if more wards were created in that area. Each stake was expected to have one quorum each of high priests, elders, priests, teachers, and deacons. When Sanpete Stake finally established Aaronic Priesthood quorums, Ephraim and Manti each contributed half the needed forty-eight priests, twenty-four teachers, and twelve deacons.

Salt Lake Stake was unusual because of its size and because it was the headquarters location of the Church. Even as late as 1877, one-fifth of Utah Mormons resided in the Salt Lake Stake. Stake sizes then varied from Salt Lake Stake's 19,798 members to tiny Panguitch Stake's 859. The average stake membership, not counting Salt Lake Stake, was 4,421. Stakes averaged twelve wards each, but Salt Lake Stake had thirty-five. For years, Salt Lake Stake served as a type of superior "central stake." Its high council was con-sidered a "general high council" that could be asked to settle problems other high councils could not solve.[51] As noted earlier, Salt Lake Stake officers, including quorum presidents, often were sustained at general conference.

HIGH PRIESTS AND ELDERS

As noted previously, Brigham Young had in mind sending high priests throughout the United States to preside over branches of the Church to be created by a major missionary labor. When Utah was first settled, a high priests quorum was formed in Salt Lake City, which served for several years as a general quorum to which all high priests in Utah belonged. "The High Priests' Quorum is strictly but one quorum," President Young explained in 1861, "though many quorums of High Priests are made to accommodate members of that quorum living in different localities."[52] Kaysville high priests, for example, were enrolled in the general quorum and journeyed to Salt Lake City to attend its meetings.

Brigham Young instructed quorum president David Pettigrew in 1854 to organize high priests in the various settlements into "branch quorums" to make the meetings more accessible and regular.[53] Such branch units, how-ever, did not catch fire very well. Reports at the general quorum during October 1856 general conference revealed that one unit could get only seven out of thirteen members to attend. Other reports from various settlements north and south caused quorum president John Young to call not for a ref-ormation but for a resurrection. In 1862, a general quorum was organized for high priests living outside of Salt Lake County, including among others Davis, Utah, and Weber counties, but no record of its meetings has been found.[54]

"It was a common practice among many of the early bishoprics in Utah to choose counselors who were elders and seventies and who remained as such during their service," one priesthood historian has noted, a practice Brigham Young did not seem concerned about until the 1870s.[55]

Elders' units were formed in some communities and not in others. Meetings, as with high priests and seventies meetings, consisted primarily in the bearing of testimony and admonishings from the quorum leaders to live right, attend meetings, sustain the leaders, and bear their testimonies.[56]

AARONIC PRIESTHOOD QUORUMS AND LABORS

Before the endowment was introduced, which required men to hold the Melchizedek Priesthood before receiving it, adult males served in Aaronic or Melchizedek Priesthood offices as they were needed. Church practice was to have adult deacons, teachers, and priests—men of experience and wisdom—visit the members to help solve their problems, ferret out iniquity, reconcile feuding parties, and teach members to pray and to do their duties.

After the endowment was available, few stalwart men lacking Melchizedek Priesthood could be found for Aaronic Priesthood ordination. As a result, Brigham Young instructed that Melchizedek Priesthood holders be called by bishops or by Aaronic Priesthood quorum officers to act in the lesser offices. During his administration, *acting* deacons, *acting* teachers, and *acting* priests did the Aaronic Priesthood work of caring for meetinghouses, administering the sacrament, assisting the needy, and doing watch-care activity that today is called home teaching. Stake deacons, teachers, and priests quorums, organized in a few stakes, held monthly meetings where presidencies instructed the men in their duties. Although the quorums were stake entities, the work of quorum members always was ward work directed by ward bishops.[57]

As was the case before the exodus to Utah, selected young men received Melchizedek and Aaronic Priesthood ordinations. Their numbers were not large. But in accordance with the philosophy that "the strong take along the weak," sometimes young men served like apprentices with older men in priesthood callings. Most LDS young men, however, first received priesthood when they needed to receive temple endowments.

WARDS, WARD BISHOPS, AND WARD PRESIDENTS

One of Brigham Young's major contributions to priesthood work was making wards an effective local unit of Church administration. Wards with bishops first existed in Nauvoo, created so that the poor could be cared for and funds for Nauvoo needs could be collected.[58] However, no wards held Sunday worship services or had buildings to meet in. By contrast, ward meetings and buildings became a common and central feature in Brigham Young's Utah.

President Young wanted wards (or *branches* or *settlements*) to have both a president and a bishop—a dual leadership. He explained that "as soon as Elders have wisdom sufficient to magnify their calling and Priesthood, we will give to every Branch, no matter how small the Ward, both a Bishop and a President."[59] Several ward presidents were called and served. In 1858, for example, Brigham Young told one settlement leader to "select one of your number for a President, and one for Bishop."[60] Late in 1859, the First Presidency ordained Charles Hancock "to be the President and Bishop in Payson." On June 12, 1872, Brigham Young sent a letter regarding the Perpetual Emigrating Fund "to the Presidents and Bishops of the various Wards throughout the Territory."[61]

At times, President Young selected the bishops. When a Salt Lake City bishop resigned in 1859, Brigham Young informed ward member Andrew Cunningham that "you are hereby requested to fill the vacancy thus created, and commence to act in the office upon receipt of this notification."[62] It was not unusual for President Young to name a bishop for a ward who had to move there to take office. In 1861 he sent advice to Andrew Moffitt, who had been ordained to be the bishop of Manti, replacing Bishop Warren S. Snow, who was leaving on a mission. "Proceed to Manti, at your earliest convenience," Young counseled, "and take charge of all matters and things pertaining to the Bishopric in that place."[63] When Canute Peterson was selected to be Fort Ephraim's bishop, he had to be released as a counselor in the Lehi bishopric.[64] President Young appointed outsider Thomas Callister to move to Fillmore to be the bishop there and to act as "presiding bishop over all the other Wards or settlements in Millard County."[65]

In some cases, President Young allowed people to help select their bishop. In 1855 he counseled North Cottonwood Ward "brethren" to "select some young and vigorous man faithful and capable as your Bishop and I would recommend Bro John Hess as a capable person." But, whomever the ward's brethren selected, Young wanted him to come to the President's office as soon as possible to be ordained.[66]

Late in 1859, the First Presidency sent some of the Twelve to Cache Valley and authorized them to organize the area into a stake. "Upon your selections and elections," the First Presidency instructed the people, "they will set apart and ordain a President to preside over all your settlements, also twelve men to compose a High Council, and a Bishop for each settlement, a settlement, for the present, constituting one ward."[67] Also in 1859, President Young wrote to Apostle Lorenzo Snow in Box Elder County and instructed him to call together the people of Willow Creek Ward and "inform them that they are at liberty and we wish them to select one good man of their number to be their Bishop, and President," whom Elder Snow should then ordain. "If they have no such man, and wish one sent into their Ward to fill those offices," Young added, Elder Snow should attend to it.[68]

Bishops were expected to serve for life, if possible. They were the workhorses of the Church, often managing both religious and secular concerns in their settlements: resource managers, land distributors, public works directors, helpers of the poor and needy, Church court judges, militia advisers, baptizers, blessers of babies and the sick, preachers, funeral conductors, directors of the home teachers of that era, planners and conductors of religious meetings, and enforcers of Church rules. By the mid-1850s, they became involved in annual tithing settlements with their ward members, who previously were expected to settle tithing affairs with the Presiding Bishop.[69]

President Heber C. Kimball, in charge of the Endowment House in Salt Lake City, requested ward bishops to call and interview appropriate candidates and arrange for their presence with letters of recommendation and temple clothing at the Endowment House at the proper times.[70] A form for a bishop's letter of recommendation, created for use in connection with the opening of the St. George Temple early in 1877, states that the person named is recommended as a faithful member, one who has paid tithing and donations, and is worthy to receive what ordinances are written in the blank lines "if endorsed by President Young."[71]

Because of Brigham Young's development of and reliance on bishops, ward bishops have been the Church's workhorse officer in the priesthood, the crucial local leader who brings people and the Church programs, including priesthood operations and ordinances, into a working relationship together.

TEMPLES AND PRIESTHOOD

Construction work on the Salt Lake Temple started in 1853, but progress was slow due to demands in Mormondom's capital for many projects, coupled with the temple's massive construction specifications. President Young alone held the sealing keys for temple work. The responsibility weighed on him, and he felt urgency to share the full range of temple ordinances, particularly the sealing of deceased relatives to each other, in a House of the Lord.

Years before, Joseph Smith had taken Brigham and other Church leaders into a room above his Nauvoo store. There, he divided off the room as best he could and carefully instructed them about the various temple ceremonies. "Brother Brigham," he said when he was finished, "this is not arranged right ... and I want you to take this matter in hand and organize and systematize all these ceremonies."

President Young fulfilled that assignment by personally directing the completion of the Nauvoo Temple and administering ordinances there. In 1871, he dedicated the St. George Temple site and earmarked Church resources to pay for materials and workmen. Labor missionaries were sent from northern Utah settlements to help. "You cannot realize ... how anxious he is to get this temple completed," George Q. Cannon said of Brigham Young in 1876; "he has keys he wants to give in the Temple."

From January to April 1877, President Young presided over dedications of the St. George Temple. In January, endowments for the dead were administered for the first time in this dispensation, some 3,208 by the end of March. He spent time from January to March developing a "perfect form of the endowments," which was read and taught to temple workers in late March. Final dedications took place in April, four months before his death, and Saints immediately engulfed the temple to receive temple ordinances for themselves and others.[72]

The St. George Temple was dedicated in April 1877. Brigham Young knew the proper organization of the priesthood required the use of a fully functioning temple. The St. George Temple was the only temple completed during his tenure as Church President. Courtesy Perry Special Collections.

THE PRIESTHOOD REORGANIZATION OF 1877

After opening the St. George Temple, ailing Brigham Young was suddenly filled with new life. Back in 1842, Joseph Smith had taught that "the Church is not fully organized, in its proper order, and cannot be, until the Temple is completed, where places will be provided for the administration of the ordinances of the Priesthood."[73] With the temple connecting heaven to earth, President Young felt an urgency to refine priesthood operations and make the earthly priesthood better mirror the heavenly one.

Rapid growth and other factors had made stakes, wards, and quorums "somewhat loose," so he felt overwhelming obligations to reform those units' operations. To start the task, he personally presided over a thorough reorganization of the St. George Stake that April. Then, during the middle months of 1877, he engineered sweeping reorganizations of priesthood involving twenty stakes, nine of which he personally conducted.

Only highlights of the extensive reorganization can be mentioned here.[74] Six of the Twelve Apostles were released as stake presidents so they could work in "a larger field than a Stake of Zion." The reorganization created seven new stakes and reorganized the thirteen existing ones. In the twenty stakes, fifty-three of the sixty members of stake presidencies were newly called, including sixteen new stake presidents. Most stakes created new high councils. Elders quorums were created or revitalized. Quarterly stake conferences were instituted, and the Church's first uniform system for keeping statistical records was established. Stakes were asked to build meeting halls for stake priesthood assemblies and quarterly conferences—Temple Square's Assembly Hall was one result. Adding to the existing 101 wards, 140 new ones were created, and 185 of the Church's 241 bishops were newly ordained or set apart. All bishopric counselors had to be high priests. Seventies quorums were severely depleted when many of their members were called into the new bishoprics. Scores of Aaronic Priesthood quorums were created. Probably more than a thousand members received new ward or stake callings. A new policy asking that all young men be given some Aaronic Priesthood office before they reached adulthood produced several hundred youthful ordinations.

The 1877 reordering was the single most important redirecting of priesthood since priesthood authority was restored forty-eight years earlier. The First Presidency's July 11, 1877, letter, which explained what changes were being made and why, was the Church's first priesthood handbook of instructions since publication of the Doctrine and Covenants. The reorganization was a final testament by Brigham Young, who sought all his life to follow accurately Joseph Smith's teachings regarding how priesthood should operate in the Church.

"It is a great joy and comfort to know that he had the privilege of living to complete one Temple and to see it dedicated," Apostle Erastus Snow observed, "and that he superintended the setting in order of the priesthood and the ordinances for the redemption of the dead . . . something he greatly desired to see done before he should pass away."[75]

"The Church is more perfectly organized than ever before, perhaps with the exception of the general assembly at Kirtland," Apostle John Taylor observed that September; "but in some things now we are more stable and complete than we were even then."[76]

In some respects, the Assembly Hall on Temple Square, started in 1877 and completed in 1880, stands as a stately and inspiring memorial to President Young's final priesthood reorganization. It also stands as a tribute to his lengthy stewardship as Church President over the workings of priesthood offices, quorums, and powers from 1844 to 1877.

This article was originally published in The Lion of the Lord: Essays on the Life and Service of Brigham Young, *ed. Susan Easton Black and Larry C. Porter (Salt Lake City: Deseret Book, 1995), 338–70.*

NOTES

1. A recent example, Leonard J. Arrington's monumental *Brigham Young: American Moses* (New York: Alfred A. Knopf, 1985) devotes a chapter to Brigham Young as "President of the Church" (chapter 12), but gives more attention to theology than to priesthood operations. The biography provides only a short, albeit excellent, summary of the priesthood reorganization of 1877, which was one of Young's most important achievements—a culmination of his lifelong labors in behalf of the gathering, of Church organizational refinement, and of temple and priesthood concerns.

2. Brigham Young, in *Journal of Discourses,* 26 vols. (Liverpool: Latter-day Saints' Book Depot, 1855–86), 14:95, April 8, 1871; *Teachings of President Brigham Young,* comp. and ed. Fred C. Collier, 7 vols. (Salt Lake City: Collier Publishing, 1987), 3:230, February 15, 1854.

3. Brigham Young, in *Journal of Discourses,* 2:177, February 18, 1855.

4. Brigham Young, in *Journal of Discourses,* 2:180, February 18, 1855.

5. Brigham Young, in *Journal of Discourses,* 7:66, June 6, 1858.

6. *Teachings of President Brigham Young,* 3:351, October 8, 1854.

7. Brigham Young, in *Journal of Discourses,* 4:299, April 8, 1871.

8. Salt Lake Stake Deacons Quorum Minutes, January 27, February 4, and May 26, 1877; and December 14, 1875, Church History Library, The Church of Jesus Christ of Latter-day Saints, Salt Lake City.

9. Prophets have believed what the Lord said in a revelation on April 14, 1883, to President John Taylor, that Saints should not be troubled "about the management and organization of my Church and Priesthood, and the accomplishment of my work" but should trust the appointed channels. See "Revelation to Pres. John Taylor," in *Messages of the First Presidency of The Church of Jesus Christ of Latter-day Saints, 1833–1964,* comp. James R. Clark, 6 vols. (Salt Lake City: Bookcraft, 1965–75), 2:347–49, 354–55, October 13, 1882, April 14, 1883.

10. John Taylor taught that "it is not wise to have cast iron rules by which to fetter the Priesthood. The Priesthood is a living, intelligent principle, and must necessarily have

freedom to act as circumstances may dictate or require." Meeting, December 15, 1886, First Council of the Seventy Minutes, 1878–94, microfilm, Church History Library.

11. Brigham Young, "An Epistle of the Twelve," *Times and Seasons* 5 (October 1, 1844): 670.

12. "The Prospect," *Times and Seasons* 6 (December 1, 1845): 1050; "January," *Times and Seasons* 6 (January 15, 1846): 1096.

13. Brigham Young, in *Journal of Discourses*, 2:315, July 8, 1855.

14. Russell C. Rich, *Ensign to the Nations: A History of the LDS Church from 1846–1972* (Provo, UT: Brigham Young University Publications, 1972), 3, 24.

15. Sermon, April 25, 1877, reported in *Millennial Star* 39 (June 11, 1877): 371.

16. Danel Bachman and Ronald K. Esplin, "Plural Marriage," in *Encyclopedia of Mormonism*, ed. Daniel H. Ludlow, 4 vols. (New York: Macmillan, 1992), 3:1095.

17. Jessie L. Embry, *Mormon Polygamous Families: Life in the Principle* (Salt Lake City: University of Utah Press, 1987), 38, 51, 63.

18. Gordon Irving, "The Law of Adoption: One Phase of the Development of the Mormon Concept of Salvation, 1830–1900," *BYU Studies* 14, no. 3 (1974): 291–314.

19. Leonard J. Arrington and Ronald K. Esplin, "The Role of the Council of the Twelve during Brigham Young's Presidency of The Church of Jesus Christ of Latter-day Saints," *Task Papers in LDS History, No. 31* (Salt Lake City: History Division of the Historical Department of the LDS Church, 1979), 32.

20. Arrington and Esplin, "Role of the Council of the Twelve," 38.

21. Arrington and Esplin, "Role of the Council of the Twelve," 42.

22. Arrington and Esplin, "Role of the Council of the Twelve," 41.

23. Arrington and Esplin, "Role of the Council of the Twelve," 58.

24. Arrington and Esplin, "Role of the Council of the Twelve," 52.

25. These general epistles are reprinted in Clark, *Messages of the First Presidency*, vols. 1 and 2.

26. Ronald G. Watt, "Journal of Discourses," in Ludlow, *Encyclopedia of Mormonism*, 2:769–70.

27. Gordon Irving, "Encouraging the Saints: Brigham Young's Annual Tours of the Mormon Settlements," *Utah Historical Quarterly* 45 (Summer 1977): 233–51.

28. Arrington and Esplin, "Role of the Council of the Twelve," 37.

29. Minutes of the Twelve, February 12, 1849, Church History Library.

30. Arrington and Esplin, "Role of the Council of the Twelve," 47–48.

31. Andrew Jenson, *Church Chronology*, 2d ed., rev. (Salt Lake City: Deseret News, 1899).

32. Arrington and Esplin, "Role of the Council of the Twelve," 39–40.

33. Irene May Bates, "Transformation of Charisma in the Mormon Church: A History of the Office of Presiding Patriarch, 1833–1979" (PhD diss., University of California at Los Angeles, 1991), 211–24; E. Gary Smith, "The Office of Presiding Patriarch: The Primacy Problem," *Journal of Mormon History* 14 (1988): 35–47. In 1942 the title Presiding Patriarch was replaced by the title Patriarch to the Church.

34. The standard history of seventies' work is James N. Baumgarten, "The Role and Function of the Seventies in L.D.S. Church History" (master's thesis, Brigham Young University, 1960). See also S. Dilworth Young, "The Seventies: A Historical Perspective," *Ensign* (July 1976): 14–21.

35. Account of April 1861 general conference in *Millennial Star* 23 (June 15, 1861): 370.

36. Joseph Smith Jr., *History of The Church of Jesus Christ of Latter-day Saints*, ed. B. H. Roberts, 2d ed., rev., 7 vols. (Salt Lake City: Deseret Book, 1971), 7:339.

37. Journal History of the Church, January 20, 1848, Church History Library, microfilm copy in Harold B. Lee Library, Brigham Young University, Provo, Utah.

38. Journal History, May 29, 1847.

39. Based on the author's comparison of names of seventies listed in the Minutes and Genealogy Book B, and his own compiled roster of the Mormon Battalion.

40. Journal History, December 4, 1851.

41. Orson Pratt said there were sixty quorums of seventies in 1859, in *Journal of Discourses*, 7:186–87, July 10, 1859.

42. During 1877 reorganizations at Logan, Utah, Brigham Young delivered a lengthy discourse in which he explained many priesthood matters, including the seventies–high priests authority issue. See Journal History, May 25, 1877. He said seventies had authority equal to high priests. In practice, however, he insisted that any seventy called into a bishopric be ordained a high priest.

43. William G. Hartley, "The Seventies in the 1880s: Revelations and Reorganizings," *Dialogue: A Journal of Mormon Thought* 16 (Spring 1983): 62–63.

44. D. Michael Quinn, "The Evolution of the Presiding Quorums of the LDS Church," *Journal of Mormon History* 1 (1974): 33–38.

45. William G. Hartley, "Edward Hunter, Pioneer Presiding Bishop," in *Supporting Saints*, ed. Donald Q. Cannon and David Whittaker (Salt Lake City: Bookcraft, 1985), 275–304.

46. Meeting, November 29, 1851, Presiding Bishops Meetings with Bishops, 1849–84, Church History Library.

47. Meeting, February 11, 1875, Presiding Bishops Meetings with Bishops, 1849–84.

48. Donald Gene Pace, "The LDS Presiding Bishopric, 1851–1888: An Administrative Study" (master's thesis, Brigham Young University, 1978), 118.

49. Donald Gene Pace, "Community Leadership on the Mormon Frontier: Mormon Bishops and the Political, Economic, and Social Development of Utah before Statehood" (PhD diss., Ohio State University, 1983), 63. John Banks, Alfred Cordon, and Nathaniel H. Felt were traveling bishops in 1851. Serving in 1852 were David Fullmer, David Hoagland, David Pettigrew, Daniel Spencer, and Seth Taft. Regional presiding bishops included Jacob Bigler (1852–61, Juab County), John Rowberry (1853+, Tooele County), and Chauncey West (Fall 1855+, Weber County).

50. Arrington and Esplin, "Role of the Council of the Twelve," 34–35.

51. For example, in February 1852, President Young instructed Bishop Benjamin Cross of Payson, Utah, to appear with several brethren from his "branch"—who had difficulties with each other at a meeting with the "High Council of Provo"—before the Great Salt Lake City High Council for a hearing to settle the problem. See Thomas Bullock, Letter to Benjamin Cross, Brigham Young Letterbook 1, February 4, 1852, Church History Library. An attempted appeal from South Weber Settlement to the Salt Lake high council is in Brigham Young, Letter to President Daniel Spencer, Brigham Young Letterbook 8, February 26, 1866.

52. During April 1861 general conference, Brigham Young delivered a major address regarding the order of the priesthood quorums, including the order of seniority among the Twelve and the seventies. See *Deseret News*, April 10, 1861.

53. Meeting, January 17, 1856, Cottonwood High Priests Quorum Minutes, 1856–76, Church History Library.

54. Noel R. Barton, "Kaysville: A Study of the Bishoprics and the Organization of the Melchizedek Priesthood Quorums, 1851–1877," typescript, March 1983, 9, Church History Library.

55. Barton, "Kaysville," 5.

56. Barton, "Kaysville," 18.

57. William G. Hartley, "Ordained and Acting Teachers in the Lesser Priesthood, 1851–1883," *BYU Studies* 16, no. 3 (1976): 375–98.

58. William G. Hartley, "Nauvoo Stake, Priesthood Quorums, and the Church's First Wards," *BYU Studies* 32, nos. 1–2 (1991): 57–80.

59. Brigham Young, in *Journal of Discourses*, 10:33, April 8, 1862.

60. Brigham Young, Letter to John Reese and others, September 6, 1858, Brigham Young Letterbook 4.

61. "To the Presidents and Bishops," in Clark, *Messages of the First Presidency*, 2:248–49, June 12, 1872.

62. First Presidency, Letter to Andrew Cunningham, January 10, 1859, Brigham Young Letterbook 5.

63. Brigham Young, Letter to Bishop Andrew Moffitt, April 10, 1861, Brigham Young Letterbook 5.

64. Brigham Young, Letter to Bishop David Evans, February 18, 1867, Brigham Young Letterbook 9.

65. Brigham Young, Letter to Bishop Thomas Callister, April 10, 1861, Brigham Young Letterbook 5.

66. Brigham Young, Letter to the Brethren Residing in North Cottonwood Ward, March 31, 1855, Brigham Young Letterbook 22.

67. First Presidency, Letter to Authorities and Members, Cache Valley, Utah, November 1859, Brigham Young Letterbook 5.

68. Brigham Young, Letter to Lorenzo Snow, July 18, 1859, Brigham Young Letterbook 5.

69. William G. Hartley, "Ward Bishops and the Localizing of LDS Tithing," in *New Views of Mormon History*, ed. Davis Bitton and Maureen Ursenbach Beecher (Salt Lake City: University of Utah Press, 1987), 96–114.

70. Stanley B. Kimball, *Heber C. Kimball: Mormon Patriarch and Pioneer* (Urbana: University of Illinois Press, 1986), 200.

71. Form Letter, Recommendation to Temple, Brigham Young Letterbook 16.

72. William G. Hartley, "St. George Temple: One Hundred Years of Service," *Ensign* (March 1977): 92–94.

73. *History of the Church*, 4:603.

74. William G. Hartley, "The Priesthood Reorganization of 1877: Brigham Young's Last Achievement," *BYU Studies* 20, no. 1 (1979): 3–36.

75. B. H. Roberts, *A Comprehensive History of The Church of Jesus Christ of Latter-day Saints, Century One*, 6 vols. (Provo, UT: Corporation of the President, The Church of Jesus Christ of Latter-day Saints, 1965), 5:516–17.

76. Hartley, "Priesthood Reorganization of 1877," 36.

9	LDS Pastors and Pastorates
	1852–1855

WHEN APOSTLE FRANKLIN D. RICHARDS returned in 1854, after a two-year absence, to serve again as British Mission president, he felt pride in one change he had implemented during his previous term. "It was during that period," he told coworkers, "that the first appointment of Pastors took place, and I find it has been a good arrangement."[1]

Starting in 1852 and continuing into the 1860s, pastors filled a leadership layer between mission presidency and conference presidents in the British Mission. Local initiative gave rise to several Latter-day Saint auxiliary organizations in the nineteenth century, but this creation of an ecclesiastical position, limited to Europe, was unusual for a church with strong centralized authority at its headquarters. Here I define, explain, and illustrate the office and calling of a pastor in Britain during a four-year period, 1852–55. I focus on these years because they were the formative period when the office of pastor was introduced, implemented, and refined, and because there is an unusually rich pool of information about pastors who served then.[2]

MEN OF EXPERIENCE

By mid-1852, Church membership in the British Mission was nearly double that of 1848, although it had declined slightly from an all-time high in 1851.

The mission was experiencing rapid turnover in its membership. President Franklin D. Richards and his one and sometimes two counselors[3] struggled to manage member and missionary work in 700 branches grouped in 50 conferences containing 32,000 Saints in England, Wales, Scotland, Ireland, and nearby islands.[4] In addition, Richards as European Mission president was faced with the task of overseeing Church operations on the Continent.

Many of the mission's conference presidents, branch presidents, and missionaries were British Mormons who were likely to emigrate to Utah in view of newly offered assistance from the Perpetual Emigrating Fund and an increased emphasis on the gathering to Utah. To replace them and to train and supervise their successors would pose a formidable challenge for a mission presidency already straining to maintain the gains of past years. In 1850, when rapid growth had increased the need for local supervision, mission leaders had assigned missionaries to serve as district presidents to help strengthen branches. Now, Franklin Richards needed supervisory help for the conferences.[5] Thus, at a special mission conference in April 1852, Richards called five experienced elders to supervise from two to five conferences and dubbed them "district presidents" at first, then "pastors."[6] Two pastors and pastorates were added during the remainder of 1852.[7]

New Mission President Samuel W. Richards, learning that a small battalion of perhaps eighty elders was arriving from Utah in 1853, picked twelve to be pastors—five to replace departees and seven to fill newly created pastorates.[8] For the next several years, the British Mission operated between twelve and sixteen pastorates at a time.

To effectively represent the mission presidency in supervising the work of local Church leaders and missionaries, pastors needed to be men of experience. It was apparently felt that a period of residence in Utah provided the advantage of more thorough initiation into Church doctrine and practices. A composite profile of the thirty-four pastors who served between 1852 and 1855 shows that thirty-three were elders from Utah, and only John Parry Jr. of Wales had never emigrated.[9] British-born elders from Utah included James G. Willie, William Clayton, Edward Martin, and Charles Smith (England); William C. Dunbar, James P. Park, and Robert Campbell (Scotland); Thomas Jeremy and Daniel Daniels (Wales); and probably John McDonald of Ireland. Most of the thirty-three pastors were married men. Of twenty-nine for whom we have located birthdates, the average age was forty, two were beyond age fifty, and only three were in their twenties.[10]

Samuel W. Richards (standing, back row, right) *was president of the British Mission in the early 1850s. Richards chose missionaries to serve as pastors. Courtesy Church Archives.*

The mission president picked pastors either from the ranks of newly arriving elders from Utah or from among conference presidents. Pastors normally did not have counselors, and they served in an average of two pastorates. Calls and releases came at year's end. After calls were made, the *Millennial Star* announced them. New pastors, armed with a letter of appointment, introduced themselves to conference presidents over whom they would preside. At the next quarterly conference of the conferences involved, pastors were presented for sustaining votes.[11]

Pastors filed reports, not regularly but frequently, with the Liverpool presidency. Fullmer's diary notes his sending pastoral reports by mail or submitting them in person. Records indicate that pastors occasionally visited headquarters, and that presidency members visited and worked in the pastorates. Counselor Daniel Spencer traveled constantly in the pastorates from 1853 to 1855. The most important contact between pastor and mission presidency came during a special London council of elders, May 26–28,

As a counselor in the British Mission presidency, Daniel Spencer traveled throughout the pastorates to work with Church leaders and members. Courtesy Church Archives.

1854, which conference presidents also attended. Here, the presidency clarified mission policies regarding emigration and the calling of local men to be missionaries; discussed doctrinal topics including plural marriage and Adam-God teachings; and directed that branch Sunday schools be started and that branch debts be retired, even if special fast days would be required to do so.[12]

A pastor's primary work was training, assisting, and supervising conference presidents and, through them, the branches. Conference presidents were appointed by the mission president, frequently after nomination by a pastor. Conference presidents were experienced local men or missionaries from America. They depended on Church members for their support and sometimes lived in "conference houses" rented with funds contributed locally. Some conference presidents had their families with them, who also required local support. Except in very large conferences, presidents served without counselors.[13] Each conference had a clerk who handled money, accounts, and reports.

Conference presidents were required to train and oversee branch presidents, among whom there was high turnover; to see that conference and branch records were kept; and to be sure the conference book agent did his job properly. Conference presidents called quarterly conferences, and they visited the branches where they helped the leaders, spoke in meetings, and ate and lodged with members.[14]

Branches varied in size from ten to several hundred members. Some owned meeting halls or chapels, others rented. Branch presidents, usually local men who earned their own livings, served without counselors.[15] They were assisted by a clerk, a book agent, a council of priesthood holders, and priesthood visiting teachers assigned districts within the branch. On Sundays, branch presidents conducted morning, afternoon, and evening services. They held weekly priesthood council meetings and a midweek preaching or prayer meeting. Some conference presidents grouped branches into districts, supervised by district presidents, who were missionaries pulled partially and sometimes fully from proselyting.[16]

Conferences supported from one to ten traveling elders, who were Utah elders or local men serving full time. Traveling elders, when not assigned as district presidents, proselyted by traveling, usually alone, from town to town distributing tracts and trying to hold public preaching meetings. Conference presidents chose specific areas for the traveling elders and notified the mission president of these assignments. A few traveling elders were assigned to cover entire pastorates. One was Elder John McAllister, in Pastor Dorr P. Curtis's pastorate, who described one of his circuits: "[May 20, 1854] I now commenced my travels through the conferences, visiting all the branches of the Church, opening new places, also attending to the several conferences held in the Pastorate."[17]

Typically, pastors followed a circuit, visiting one conference after another and then repeating the process. Pastor John S. Fullmer, for example, started his ministry in late January 1853 by staying with Liverpool Conference President Alexander F. MacDonald for a week while they visited branches. Two weeks later, he moved to the Manchester Conference and lodged at its conference house, where President Perrigrine Sessions lived. Fullmer and Sessions spent a week touring branches. Then Fullmer went to Preston, and with Conference President Robert Menzies he preached to full houses in various branches. Fullmer spent several days among Saints in Preston "teaching privately." After visiting nearby branches, he returned to Liverpool for a quarterly conference there. He then repeated his circuit of the three conferences.[18] Such grass-roots contacts let pastors strengthen and improve local operations and commitment.

Starting in May 1853, Pastor Bunker spent twenty months supervising the Bradford, Sheffield, and Lincolnshire conferences. He lived with Sheffield Branch President John Memmott but traveled constantly. If Bunker had visited a different branch each week, he could not have visited in one year each of the sixty branches in his three conferences. By mid-1853 his pastorate included:

Conference	President	Clerk	Branches	Members
Sheffield	Wm. Glover	J. C. Sanderson	19	888
Bradford	Jn. Albiston	H. J. Jarvis	22	846
Lincolnshire	Chas. Derry	None	19	465[19]

Critical to the pastor's work was his attending each conference's quarterly conference, where he presided. This gathering let him meet with and instruct local priesthood officers, preach to the Saints, review finances, monitor special projects the mission was stressing, hear appeals from local members, mingle with the Saints, and visit them in their homes. Typically, conferences within the same pastorate held quarterly gatherings a week or two apart, to allow pastors to attend.

Pastor Willie penned a good description of a quarterly conference he attended in late March 1854. On Sunday, "the Saints began to flock to Bridport from all the country branches at an early hour," and "many walked 24 miles" to be there. The meetings began with singing at 10:30 AM. Willie gave the opening prayer. This being a business meeting, leaders reviewed branch reports and finances, "after which the Presidents of branches, expressed their views, and desires in spreading the Principles of the Gospel in their immediate neighborhoods." At the 2 PM meeting, Willie talked about sales of books and the *Millennial Star,* emigration and conference funds, and "gave general instruction." At 6:30 PM, Willie spoke to a large gathering of Saints and nonmembers about the resurrection, and a "good spirit was manifested by all present."[20]

PASTORS AND MISSIONARY WORK

Among pastors' major responsibilities was the supervision of proselyting work within their pastorates. Although many of them were effective preachers, they carried strict orders to have others proselyte, not themselves. Some conferences, such as Wales, Preston, Liverpool, South, Derbyshire, and Nottinghamshire, had become pockets of resistance to missionary work, believing that enough preaching had been done already or that their areas were dead to missionary work. By mid-1854 pastors claimed they had reversed these negative feelings.[21]

The mission employed five methods of proselyting. First, traveling elders, when not burdened by responsibilities for congregations, went from house to house and town to town, leaving and retrieving tracts and holding special preaching meetings. Pastors and conference presidents assigned these elders to specific areas to proselyte.

Second, nonmembers were invited to specially called camp meetings, debates, lectures, and discourses. Missionaries publicized the meetings by going door-to-door, distributing flyers, or hiring the town crier to cry it out. Despite strict orders to let other elders do the proselyting, pastors, being good preachers, sometimes contributed their services. For example, on August 14, 1853, Pastor Charles Smith and about fifty Saints and the Leicester Branch choir boarded conveyances to go to a camp meeting they sponsored at Dunton. Smith spoke in the afternoon and Conference President Edward Frost at night. "The meetings were well attended," Smith noted.[22]

Not all outdoor meetings went well. In September 1855 Pastor Dana and Traveling Elder Wolcott sent the town crier through Luton to announce their outdoor preaching. A crowd came, and, when riled up by a minister, started shoving Dana and Wolcott out of town. A nearby townsman shamed the mob until the crisis passed. Being opportunists, the elders called a meeting for the next night, where they and opponents each lectured for one hour. Some nine hundred people paid to witness the event.[23]

Third, branch elders and priests did open-air preaching on Sundays and sometimes on weeknights. In mid-1854, for example, the Glasgow Conference had "open preaching in fifty places." Because of shortages of traveling elders, pastors encouraged local men to do Sunday public preaching.[24]

Fourth, individually and through "tract societies" that some branches organized, local members obtained LDS tracts and loaned them out to nonmembers personally or in letters. Pastors encouraged this sharing of tracts.[25]

Fifth, nonmembers came to branch meetings by invitation or from curiosity. In Manchester, members "placarded the towns, and now many strangers come to hear us."[26] When strangers appeared, leaders usually turned the meeting into a preach-to-proselyte session, especially when pastors were the speakers.

The mission president assigned Utah men who became traveling elders to a pastor's jurisdiction, and the pastor assigned them to one of his conferences. A conference president then assigned the elder to a particular district or region to proselyte or to be a district president. However, a pastor could transfer a traveling elder from one conference to another in his pastorate without the mission president's permission. Likewise, the mission president

214 ~ MY FELLOW SERVANTS

could transfer that elder from one pastorate to another without a pastor's concurrence. A local man called to be a traveling elder by his conference president could be transferred by pastor or mission president. This explains one pastor's complaint that he had had several traveling elders but "they were called to travel in other conferences or retired to their shoemaking, etc."[27]

Traveling Elder William Budge illustrates the jurisdictional realities. Mission Counselor Daniel Spencer assigned him to the Norwich Conference in Pastor Dana's pastorate. Dana told Budge to report to Norwich Conference President Charles Harper. Harper assigned Budge to the Yarmouth District and its six branches. Budge there became part of the "traveling priesthood" consisting of Conference President Harper and six traveling elders, including himself. Later, to Harper's surprise, Pastor Dana transferred Budge away to the Cambridgeshire Conference. A month later, the mission president surprised Dana by moving Budge to the Swiss-Italian Mission.[28]

Baptisms for 1853, 1854, and 1855 averaged close to 4,260 per year—about 85 per conference or 6 per branch.[29] Mission leaders indicated that baptisms would have increased greatly if more proselyting elders were called. In June 1854, when at least sixty-three traveling elders were at work, some conferences called for more; several poor conferences asked for more elders, but only if the men would work "without purse or scrip."[30]

Three causes were cited for the British Mission's shortage of traveling elders in the period of 1852–55. First, Utah could not supply enough. Second, branches could not support British elders if these men had families who had to be supported, too. Pastor Dana admitted he did not call local men to be missionaries. He hesitated because "there was so much opposition by some of the brethren and the Saints generally on account of their poverty, as they said." Later, he called and ordained five "and sent them forth to labor in the pastorate, shifting them as it was deemed wisdom." Third, there was a "practice universally adopted by persons who have sons of suitable age, to send them to the Valley, as pioneers, or to procure means to emigrate the balance of the family."[31]

Some branches relied too heavily on the district presidents for local leadership. Sensing this, Pastor Dana and Conference President Harper in mid-1854 "concluded to cut loose the traveling elders" and "set them to preach among the Gentiles and make Presidents of Branches responsible for the Saints in their charge."[32] Late in 1855, Pastor Fullmer eliminated district presidents from his conferences, and, for the first time apparently, held a conferencewide meeting of all branch presidents:

This was thought advisable because the Districts had been disorganized at the last conference, so these [branch presidents] were called up to receive instruction direct from the President and Pastor and that they might be made to feel the direct responsibility that rested upon them and in short that they might realize there was now no more a middle wall between them and him who presided over the whole conference.[33]

PASTORS AS TEACHERS

Pastors were spokesmen for Church teachings and policies. Utah elders who arrived for early 1853 missionary duty brought with them the Church's first public announcement of plural marriage and were called upon to explain it. During Fullmer's first visits to branches, he preached the new revelation to "full and crowded" meetings. In Liverpool he thought that "the Saints feel first rate about the late revelation," but five months later at Upholland he found the Saints "begin to cavil about the Revelation." At the elders council at London in mid-1854, one conference president observed that "polygamy has got over pretty well, that cloud has vanished away." More troubling, he said, was the last "cat that was let out of the bag"—the teaching "about Adam being our Father and God," a controversial concept then circulating in Utah.[34]

Whether these teachings caused widespread apostasy or severely reduced conversions is yet to be determined, but sources consulted for this study do not indicate dramatic initial impacts. The president of Land's End Conference reported, "Relative to the principles recently revealed, we have not the least difficulty." A late-1854 memorial honoring President Samuel Richards's retirement stated that the shock that leaders expected the two teachings to cause had "to a great extent been prevented."[35] However, longterm effects were yet to be seen.

Pastors explained baptism for the dead, consecration, and proper ways to perform ordinances. Pastor Fullmer corrected one branch for lengthy prayers and for prayers asking for the spirits of Joseph and Hyrum Smith to be with them. He explained that their spirits, unlike the Holy Ghost, were in one place and could not be jumping around the universe. At Oldham Branch, Fullmer ruffled feathers by announcing that men need not advance through each office of the Aaronic Priesthood, as most believed, and then he ordained a man a priest who had not been a deacon or teacher first.[36]

Pastors were responsible for the promotion of all mission and church programs. A major emphasis during this period was emigration, and pastors exhorted Church members to prepare to emigrate and to donate to the Perpetual Emigrating Fund. Pastors supervised each winter's emigration process. During 1853, 1854, and 1855, about two thousand Saints departed annually. All missionaries were expected to help with emigration from January to April, along with devoting themselves to their normal labors. In January 1854, Pastor Bunker met with Sheffield Conference President Matthew Rowan and together they chose six local people to fill that conference's Perpetual Emigrating Fund quota for that season. A year later, in Bradford Branch, Bunker and President Millen Atwood "told old Saints in our Branch to emigrate before the year is out," and then released Branch President Joseph Bean and counseled him to emigrate.[37]

On December 13, 1854, President Franklin D. Richards discovered unfilled space on a ship he had chartered for Danish emigrants. Desperate to fill berths, he asked Pastor Smith to recruit additional emigrants on short notice. Smith contacted Brother West of Barrowash, who agreed to take his family of nine.[38]

Financial concerns claimed much of the attention of mission personnel. Pastors spearheaded a campaign to retire branch debts for Church books and the *Millennial Star*. Saints had been able to maintain subscriptions to the *Star* until they were asked to subscribe to two new Church periodicals, *The Seer* and the *Journal of Discourses*, when English prices were rising and unemployment spreading. As a result, branches fell into debt for the publications sent them.[39]

When Millen Atwood became Bradford Conference president in January 1854, Pastor Bunker told him that the conference owed a formidable debt for mission publications. Bunker and Atwood "laboured diligently" to raise money to retire the debt but had little success. Following the June 1854 elders council in London, however, "new life was given to the [Bradford] Conference" and most branches paid their debts. Atwood was pleased, and credited God, the "wise counsels of Pastor Bunker," and priesthood unity for the success.[40]

Pastors encouraged tithe paying, which, Fullmer learned upon arriving in England, "has hitherto been considered more as a free will offering or donation than a tithing, and is an annual thing, and not limited as to amount." Not until 1856 was tithing more fully explained and expected. Pastors also promoted the Salt Lake Temple fund by preaching and reviewing donation reports. Bunker, for example, talked at a Bradford Conference "particularly about Temple building, and their use, and the great sacrifices that people ought to make to rear these places."[41] Pastors also solicited funds for foreign missions.

Vigilant for signs of backsliding, contention, and iniquity, pastors generally dealt firmly with problems that came to their attention. In late 1853, Pastor Fullmer attended a Manchester quarterly meeting conducted by Conference President Perrigrine Sessions. When an officer "in a bad spirit" criticized a former district president, other members caught his spirit. Sessions failed to calm the situation, and "the Devil

As a missionary in England in the early 1850s, John S. Fullmer recorded some of the trials he and his companions encountered. Courtesy Church Archives.

was about to take the conference." Fullmer took charge and spoke bluntly, and, said he, "My battle axe, and the manner I used it had a most happy effect."[42]

Pastor Fullmer visited the Hyde Branch in April 1853 and found a problem. At the Saturday branch social, Saints used tea instead of other drinks, and on Sunday, few came to meeting and most who did come, slept. To counter the dull spirit, the branch president asked Fullmer to speak. He spent five minutes rebuking the president and members for preferring tea, socials, and sleep to worship. Fullmer told the congregation they were "cold and indifferent, stupid or asleep," depriving the branch of the Lord's Spirit.[43]

In the branches and conferences, whenever pastors found disputing, disagreements, and faultfinding, they tried to straighten out matters. Pastor Fullmer once found Bury Branch rife with contention. He cited branch leaders to a hearing and told them "they very well knew that they had quarreled with every President and Pastor that had been appointed in the conference for years," something he would not tolerate. Pastor Charles Smith learned of a couple who became parents six months after they were married and instructed the Derbyshire Conference president "to deal with them"—i.e., excommunicate the couple. As part of their disciplinary responsibilities, pastors also participated in excommunication proceedings for missionaries.[44]

Once, when Pastor Dana visited Hemel Hempstead Branch, he discerned darkness and iniquity. The branch president said Dana's feelings were wrong. It took two days, but Dana ferreted out two priesthood holders who had taken liberties with female Church members. Before Dana left, the two men were excommunicated and the branch president reproved.[45]

Pastors discovered that excommunicated Saints could become festering sores. For that reason, Pastor Fullmer, for one, taught branch presidents not to be too quick to cut off members, sometimes for trivial transgressions. He urged presidents to "not bury the Saints before they are dead."[46]

Pastor Charles Smith and Nottinghamshire Conference President Henry Savage witnessed an explosion at an Ashfield Branch council meeting. A faction insisted that a couple be excommunicated. When Savage refused, several said they could not sustain him and asked for their own excommunication, which the council granted. Two men threatened Savage, and "many of them went on with disgusting and filthy language, showing they were of the Devil." Pastor Smith interviewed the two people that the dissenters wanted cut off, and was satisfied with President Savage's decision.[47]

More than once pastors had to settle differences between a district president and branch president. For example, Pastor Willie once settled a feud that erupted when District President Ward removed the Southampton Branch president from office for wife beating. Branch members felt aggrieved, claiming Ward lacked authority over their branch. Willie heard their case, then determined that Ward had transcended his calling by assuming the duties of branch president. Willie reinstated the branch president, who declined to serve. So Willie appointed Ward, whom the members now agreed to accept![48]

But most pastoral visits to branches were positive. For example, Fullmer once attended a Wednesday night meeting in the Liverpool Branch where "we had a fine time. Speaking in tongues and interpretations."[49]

At quarterly conferences, pastors watched for practices, attitudes, or ideas that needed correcting. At Preston, Fullmer heard one branch president admit he had not visited all his flock for years, and another say that he deferred to older, more knowledgeable men. Fullmer countered that "a shepherd should look after his flock," and that a branch president, no matter how young, would be upheld by God and given wisdom to govern the branch.[50]

Pastors had occasional differences with conference presidents. As one example, Sheffield President Rowan once disagreed with Pastor Bunker about how to report "scattered" and "lost" members on the half-year report.[51]

Overall, however, pastors and presidents seemed to function smoothly together. President Robert Holt reported in late 1855 a "union of feeling that exists between myself and Pastor [George] Grant, for I can truly say, there has never been the least unkind feeling towards each other. The Saints have seen and felt this." Elder Holt felt pride in carrying out "every measure" that Pastor Grant devised to benefit the work. At the 1854 missionwide council of elders, Pastor Tyler boasted that he "had the united operations of the four Presidents in supporting me in all things." Pastor Dana said that "the Presidents and I have seen eye to eye all the time." Pastor Willie was pleased that he and Conference President George Bramwell "were one in all things."[52]

Church members were expected to provide pastors and conference presidents with lodging, clothes, and other necessities. To enable Pastor Bunker to attend a special London leadership conference in late June 1854, the Sheffield Conference voted to give him £1.10.[53] At a Feast of Oysters held by the Bosham Branch, Pastor Willie noted that "The Saints assisted me with some little means to defray my expenses." Willie kept track of everyone who donated to help him, and when he received an inheritance during his mission, he repaid the donors.[54] In December 1855, the Bristol Branch held a fast day to raise money to buy clothes for Pastor Millen Atwood. Pastor Dana said of his two years: "I have not had to make calls upon any of the Saints, for the small presents I have had have met my demands."[55]

After three years the office of pastor needed refinements. In 1855–56 President Franklin D. Richards made four changes. Henceforth, he said, mission presidency approval was required before pastors could publish any book or pamphlet, transfer missionaries, hold pastoratewide conferences, or attend conferences outside their jurisdictions. Also, in 1855, Church members were urged to recognize the pastors' authority and to "pay the most strict attention to their counsels and instructions."[56]

The individual contributions of pastors to the mission varied. Fullmer's journals indicate that he was a veteran churchman, knowledgeable about doctrine and practices, and an authoritarian leader who spoke his mind and tackled problems head on. Dana's journal reveals him to be an extremely hard worker. "I lost no time when I was traveling either on foot, in the carrs, or omnibuses," he said, to preach "if an opportunity afforded."[57] Willie, an Englishman, spent much time visiting outside his pastorate and seemed less forceful as an administrator. Bunker was a kindly man and a good public speaker.

Although records show no attempts to have a pastor removed or reprimanded, pastors occasionally provoked the ire of at least some with whom they had contact. The local priesthood disliked Fullmer's "sharp reproof" of the Bury Branch. Pastors caused some confusion when they explained practices and procedures differently from the way their predecessors had done. Some pastors disliked aspects of British society or customs, and expressed it. Fullmer, for example, rebuked the Hyde Branch for tea drinking, and walked out of a Royton Branch social, disliking the people's low tastes in amusement and judging the town to be "a dirty stinking place. No Saint ought to live in it."[58] Pastors, like other officers, probably upset people by soliciting new donations and payments on old branch debts from poor Saints.

PASTORS' LONG-TERM EFFECTS

By the time the last of the 1852–53 elders who had served as the first pastors sailed home in 1856, they had given vital leadership to Church operations in the British Isles. Certainly a dozen pastors laboring at a given time eased the mission presidency's burden and provided conferences and branches with closer supervision than the presidency could have given. Pastors had supported, reformed, and enhanced more than four dozen conferences, about a hundred conference presidents, and scores of traveling elders. Several felt they had livened up many units that were dead when they arrived. Pastors helped many conferences reduce their debt loads, tighten up their record systems, and overcome bitternesses caused by elders who had mishandled or misappropriated conference funds.[59]

Despite these contributions, any assessment of the effectiveness of pastors must take into account the fact that their addition failed to reverse the mission's decline in membership, a fact that haunted mission leadership at the time. Seeking an explanation for lack of progress, in mid-1854 Daniel Spencer, counselor in the mission presidency, gave pastors and other leaders partial blame for low missionary and member zeal in some places.

TABLE 1.
British Mission Semiannual Statistics, 1852–55

Period	Confer-ences	Branches	Members	Bapitzed	Excom.	Emi-grated
1852(B)	51	742	32,339			
1853(A)	53	737	30,690	2,601	1,776	1,722
1853(B)	49	726	30,827	1,976	1,413	58
1854(A)	50	698	29,797	2,213	1,330	1,380
1854(B)	51	702	29,441	2,317	1,396	629
1855(A)	48	703	27,771	1,876	1,491	1,589
1855(B)	51	677	26,001	1,835	2,345	482
	−65	−6,338	12,818	9,751	5,860	

Statistics were reported twice yearly in the *Millennial Star* for 1853 and 1854. The 1855 figures are in the British Mission Statistical Reports, LDS European Church Archives. Statistics for the half year ending December 31, 1852, from *Millennial Star* 15 (January 29, 1853): 78, are also cited here to show changes over three full years.

He said he did not think "there is such energy as might be manifested on their part. We are dull and stupid in comparison with those who have gone before us." Leaders, he added, did not "realize our positions sufficiently, or we could create means for building up of the Kingdom." Specifically criticized were those pastors and presidents who harbored beliefs that increased preaching was fruitless, more traveling elders need not be called, finance agents did not need close supervision, elders could not labor without purse or scrip, and members' poverty excused them from Church financial obligations. Yet the overall assessment of Spencer and of conference and branch leaders who worked with the pastors seems to have been positive.[60]

As shown in table 1, the British Mission's membership declined during the 1853–55 period by 6,338, a number almost equal to the emigration total. Baptisms exceeded excommunications; had it not been for emigration there would have been no net loss. Branches declined by 65, although the number of pastorates held steady. Close scrutiny of the figures reveals a loss of nearly 1,500 members unaccounted for by deaths, excommunications, and emigration; why these disappeared from the records is unclear. The lack of

Edward Bunker seved as a pastor over conferences in England and Scotland from 1853 through 1855. Courtesy Bunker family.

mission growth during the pastors' period of service deserves further study; it was probably due largely to factors beyond their control.[61]

Released pastors continued to give leadership to the Church when called. Of those discussed previously, many left for home early in 1856. During the journey, several presided over shiploads of Latter-day Saint emigrants and four became captains of four of the five handcart companies that year—Ellsworth, Bunker, Willie, and Martin.

The British Mission utilized the office of pastor beyond the 1852–55 period studied here. Pastors continued to serve in a similar fashion until Apostles Amasa Lyman, Charles C. Rich, and George Q. Cannon became the new mission presidency in 1860. They ordered pastors to vacate the conference houses (where they were spending too much time in residence), to do more visiting of officers and branches, and to preach more. The trio changed the name of pastor to "district president" and decreed that conferences henceforth send reports and monies direct to mission headquarters, not through the pastors.[62]

A steady and serious decline in Church membership made the pastor layer of leadership unnecessary. Membership, which stood at 30,747 in 1850, slid to 13,853 in 1860, and down to 8,804 in 1870. Conferences decreased from 53 in 1853 to 14 in 1870, or one-fourth the number that existed when the office of pastor was first introduced.[63] The pastoral office of district president was phased out by 1869.[64]

Nearly a century later, in response to renewed membership growth, leaders created the position of Regional Representative to help supervise Church units throughout the world. Similar in many ways to the office of pastor in the 1850s and 1860s, which was limited to Europe, it became a new level of supervision and communication between general authorities and stake or mission presidencies.[65]

This article was originally published in Mormons in Early Victorian Britain, *ed.* Richard L. Jensen and Malcolm R. Thorp *(Salt Lake City: University of Utah Press, 1989), 194–210.*

NOTES

1. *Millennial Star* 16 (August 19, 1854): 513. In its sixth "Article of Faith," The Church of Jesus Christ of Latter-day Saints states belief in biblical church officers, including pastors.

2. Not explored here is pastoral work in Britain after 1855 nor in Denmark, where pastors also served. See Andrew Jenson, *History of the Scandinavian Mission* (Salt Lake City: Deseret News Press, 1927), 124, 129, 153, 170.

3. Daniel Spencer and John Van Cott were mission counselors as of May 14, 1853. Van Cott departed to preside over Scandinavia in August 1854, leaving Samuel Richards and Spencer as the Presidency. In mid-1854 Franklin D. Richards became president and kept Spencer as his sole counselor. Cyrus Wheelock is listed as second counselor on September 8, 1855. British Mission Manuscript History, Church History Library, The Church of Jesus Christ of Latter-day Saints, Salt Lake City.

4. British Mission Manuscript History, December 30, 1853. Each conference contained from four to forty branches. Manchester, the largest conference, had 3,048 members in 33 branches; Carlyle, the smallest, had 142 members in 6 branches.

5. *Millennial Star* 12 (January 15, 1850): 26; *Millennial Star* 12 (February 14, 1850): 58; *Millennial Star* 14 (June 19, 1852): 257–60. Levi Richards had provided similar assistance in 1850, when mission president Orson Pratt sent him to Wales.

6. *Millennial Star* 14 (May 8, 1852): 171; *Millennial Star* 14 (May 15, 1852): 177. As listed by the *Star,* the initial pastors were:

Pastor	Conferences in His Pastorate
Jacob Gates	London, Reading, Kent, Essex
Cyrus H. Wheelock	Manchester, Liverpool, Preston
Robert Campbell	Glasgow, Edinburgh, Dundee
Appleton Harmon	Newcastle-on-Tyne, Carlisle, Hull
Moses Clawson	Lincolnshire, Bradford, Derbyshire, Warwickshire

7. Isaac C. Haight and Dorr P. Curtis. *Millennial Star* 14 (July 10, 1852): 319; *Millennial Star* 14 (December 11, 1852): 666.

8. *Millennial Star* 14 (November 27, 1852): 634. Departees were Wheelock, Gates, Clawson, Haight, and Harmon. Utah elders picked as pastors were John S. Fullmer, John Van Cott, James G. Willie, William Clayton, Chauncey Webb, Richard Cook, Charles Smith, Sylvester Earl, Thomas Jeremy, Daniel Daniels, Benjamin Brown, and John McDonald. See *Millennial Star* 15 (July 30, 1853): 511; and Missionary Record Book A, Church History Library.

9. The thirty-four pastors were Millen Atwood, Israel Barlow, John Barker, Benjamin Brown, Edward Bunker, Robert Campbell, James Carrigan, Moses Clawson, Richard Cook, Dorr P. Curtis, Charles A. Dana, Daniel Daniels, David C. Dille, William C. Dunbar, Sylvester Earl, Edmund Ellsworth, John S. Fullmer, James Ferguson, Jacob Gates, William S. Glover, George D. Grant, Isaac Haight, Appleton Harmon, Thomas Jeremy, Wm. H. Kimball, Edward Martin, John McDonald, John Parry Jr., Charles Smith, Daniel Tyler, John Van Cott, Chauncey G. Webb, Cyrus Wheelock, and James G. Willie.

10. Andrew Jenson, *Latter-day Saint Biographical Encyclopedia: A Compilation of Biographical Sketches of Prominent Men and Women in The Church of Jesus Christ of Latter-day Saints,* 4 vols. (Salt Lake City: Andrew Jenson History, 1901–36; reprint, Salt Lake City: Western Epics, 1971); and Missionary Record Book A.

11. John Van Cott, Journal, January 2, 1853, L. Tom Perry Special Collections, Harold B. Lee Library, Brigham Young University, Provo, Utah.

12. Pastors were responsible to see that conferences submitted reports; see *Millennial Star* 17 (January 13, 1855): 24–27; *Millennial Star* 17 (August 11, 1855): 505. For pastor-presidency contacts, see John S. Fullmer, Diary, April 8 and July 12, 1853; James G. Willie, Diary, April, August, and September 1854, photocopy of holograph, Perry Special Collections; and Daniel Spencer, Diary, 1854–55, Church History Library. The London Conference proceedings were published in *Millennial Star* 16 (July 29, August 5, 12, 19, 26, and September 2, 1854). On Adam-God teachings, see note 34.

13. *Millennial Star* 18 (May 24, 1856): 321–24.

14. *Millennial Star* 12 (August 15, 1850): 246–51; *Millennial Star* 14 (June 19, 1852): 257.

15. *Millennial Star* 18 (May 24, 1856): 321–24.

16. *Millennial Star* 12 (February 14, 1850): 55.

17. *Millennial Star* 14 (June 5, 1852): 227. Richards acknowledged that it was impossible for him to fix the particular fields of labor for traveling elders. John D. T. McAllister, Diary, May 20, 1854, Perry Special Collections.

18. Fullmer, Diary, January through March 1853. *[Editor's note: For more information on Perrigrine Sessions's mission, see Donna Toland Smart, ed., Exemplary Elder: The Life and Missionary Diaries of Perrigrine Sessions, 1814–1893 (Provo, UT: BYU Studies and Joseph Fielding Smith Institute of Latter-day Saint History, 2002.]*

19. *Millennial Star* 15 (July 30, 1853): 511.

20. Willie, Diary, March 26, 1854.

21. *Millennial Star* 16 (July 29, 1854): 465–68; *Millennial Star* 16 (August 12, 1854): 501. Negative views about proselyting were based on (a) millennialistic feelings that the preaching had been done once and that was enough, (b) long-term lack of converts in an area, and (c) a reputed cursing or shaking the dust off the feet by a high Church authority.

22. Charles Smith, Diary, August 14, 1853, Church History Library.

23. Charles R. Dana, Journal and Reminiscences, September 29, 1855, Church History Library.

24. *Millennial Star* 16 (July 29, 1854): 466.

25. British Mission Manuscript History, October 29, 1853. Bristol Branch, Manuscript History, April 3, 1854, Church History Library, mentions a "circulating Tract Society"

in the branch. Also see Dundee Conference report in *Millennial Star* 16 (July 29, 1854): 467.

26. David B. Dille correspondence, *Millennial Star* 16 (July 29, 1854): 467.

27. Dana, Journal, mentioned between his July 22 and October 14, 1854, entries.

28. William Budge, Diary, entries for March, April, July 25, and August 28, 1854, Church History Library.

29. See table 1 in text.

30. *Millennial Star* 16 (July 29, 1854): 467; *Millennial Star* 16 (August 5, 1854): 482; *Millennial Star* 16 (August 12, 1854): 501–2.

31. Dana, Journal, commentary after January 1 and July 22, 1854, entries. *Millennial Star* 17 (May 26, 1855): 324.

32. Dana, Journal, July 14, 1854.

33. Fullmer, Diary, January 13, 1855.

34. *Millennial Star* 16 (August 5, 1854): 482. Regarding the Adam-God teaching, see Leonard J. Arrington, *Brigham Young: American Moses* (New York: Alfred A. Knopf, 1985), 205.

35. Land's End President Joseph Hall, in *Millennial Star* 16 (August 5, 1854): 482–83; and Richards in *Millennial Star* 16 (October 7, 1854): 629.

36. Fullmer, Diary, April 29 and May 1, 1853. After Fullmer ordained Albert Oaks a priest, Oaks related a vision he had had four weeks earlier in which Brigham Young told him he had a great work to do but must await ordination by Fullmer. Oaks had seen Fullmer in the vision and immediately recognized him when he first saw him.

37. Matthew Rowan, Diary, January 23, 1854; Joseph Beecroft, Diary, January 7, 1855, Church History Library.

38. Smith, Diary, December 13 and 14, 1854.

39. *Millennial Star* 16 (August 19, 1854): 514.

40. *Millennial Star* 18 (March 29, 1856): 203.

41. Fullmer, Diary, February 23, 1853; Joseph A. Young's mission report in *Millennial Star* 18 (August 2, 1856): 482; Beecroft, Diary, July 3, 1853.

42. Fullmer, Diary, September 24, 1853.

43. Fullmer, Diary, April 27, 1853.

44. Smith, Diary, September 7, 1853; Willie, Diary, May 4, 1854.

45. Dana, Journal, October 29, 1854.

46. Fullmer, Diary, July 5, 1853.

47. Smith, Diary, October 1, 1854.

48. Willie, Diary, November 8, 1854.

49. Fullmer, Diary, August 3, 1853.

50. Fullmer, Diary, July 1 and 2, 1853.

51. Rowan, Diary, June 24, 1854.

52. *Millennial Star* 18 (February 9, 1856): 92; *Millennial Star* 16 (August 12, 1854): 500, 504.

53. Rowan, Diary, June 24, 1854.

54. Willie, Diary, May 29, 1854, in Marilyn Austin Smith, ed., *Faithful Stewards: The Life of James Gray Willie and Elizabeth Ann Pettit* (Logan, UT: By the author, 1987). Donors are listed on the last page of volume 1.

55. Bristol Branch Manuscript History, Church History Library; Dana's report is in *Millennial Star* 16 (August 12, 1854): 504.

56. *Millennial Star* 17 (July 21, 1855): 457; *Millennial Star* 18 (March 22, 1856): 185–87; Spencer, Diary, November 20 and 25, 1855, Church History Library.

57. Dana, Journal, narration before his May 11, 1854, entry.

58. Fullmer, Diary, April 24 and 27, 1853; January 1, 1855.

59. See pastor reports at the London council in *Millennial Star* 16 (August 12, 1854): 497–505; *Millennial Star* 16 (August 19, 1854): 513–20.

60. *Millennial Star* 16 (August 5, 1854): 490–92. See, for example, Spencer's report of his mission-wide tour in *Millennial Star* 17 (May 26, 1855): 323–26.

61. Essays by Phillips, Jensen, Peterson, and Poll in *Mormons in Early Victorian Britain*, ed. Richard L. Jensen and Malcolm R. Thorp (Salt Lake City: University of Utah Press, 1989), discuss the numerical decline in the British Mission, which accelerated further after the period considered here.

62. Leonard J. Arrington, *Charles C. Rich* (Provo, UT: Brigham Young University Press, 1974), 231; *Millennial Star* 23 (January 12, 1861): 24–25.

63. Richard O. Cowan, "Church Growth in England, 1841–1914," in *Truth Will Prevail*, ed. V. Ben Bloxham and others (Solihull, England: The Church of Jesus Christ of Latter-day Saints, 1987), 216.

64. I have found mention of a district president with jurisdiction over several conferences as late as October 18, 1868. *Millennial Star* 30 (November 14, 1868): 733.

65. Briefly, regional representatives supervised stakes and mission representatives supervised missions. Since the mid-1970s regional representatives have served throughout the Church.

10 The Priesthood Reorganization of 1877
Brigham Young's Last Achievement

DEATH KNOCKING LOUDLY AT HIS DOOR, President Brigham Young labored restlessly in his last five months of life to reorganize the Church's government structures. His priesthood reorganization of 1877, thorough and massive, involved every stake, 241 wards, hundreds of quorums, and more than a thousand leadership positions. But this final achievement has been underrated or ignored by historians, unknown to Church members, and so far is a missing entry on his leadership balance sheet.

The contributions of Young as colonizer, economic director, immigration organizer, preacher-teacher, defender of the faith, and family man are explored in various scholarly probes. But what of his priesthood labors? As head of the fast-growing Church for thirty-three years, he worked through priesthood channels. Thanks to studies by Leonard Arrington, Dale F. Beecher, and Donald G. Pace, we know something about how Young utilized ward bishops. D. Michael Quinn introduces us to some of the inner workings of the then Church hierarchy. James N. Baumgarten's excellent master's thesis at least opened the door on what we need to know about the seventies, then led by Brigham Young's brother Joseph. Gary L. Phelps's and my own research shed light on the work of ward and Aaronic Priesthood teachers. But other priesthood offices and units and their historical developments await researchers' attention, including such fundamental matters as the role and function of the Presiding Bishopric, of stakes and stake presidents and high councils, of high priests, patriarchs, wards, elders, priests and deacons, of basic priesthood ordinances, and of various meetings. Among published histories and biographies about the Brigham Young era, only *The Story of the Latter-day Saints* attributes much importance to Brigham Young's 1877 reorganizings. Other accounts skip the topic entirely or else merely list the stakes affected.[1]

This chapter describes and analyzes the reorganization itself. It provides one more building block historians can use to analyze Brigham Young's use of power and to generalize about how the Church historically has handled the dynamics of change.[2] Offering a deep look at inner Church operations, this study assumes a familiarity on the readers' part with basic Mormon terminology regarding priesthood matters. To understand what happened in 1877, I examine the reform in terms of what changes were needed, how the program was implemented, and what resulted.

The reorganization institutionalized both conservative and innovative elements. As a devoted student and disciple of the Prophet Joseph Smith, President Young knew well the priesthood revelations and also the explanations of those by the revelator himself.[3] After Joseph Smith's death, few, if any, understood priesthood matters better than the Vermont painter-glazier. Part of his 1877 effort, therefore, was to bring priesthood practices into closer harmony with the revelations.

But practical application of those revelations required creativity and innovation. The revelations said *what* but not always *how*. Implementation, therefore, required new approaches at times, as Elder Orson Pratt explained it in 1877:

> To say that there will be a stated time, in the history of this Church, during its imperfections and weaknesses, when the organization will be perfect, and that there will be no further extension or addition to the organization, would be a mistake. Organization is to go on, step after step, from one degree to another, just as the people increase and grow in the knowledge of the principles and laws of the Kingdom of God, and as their borders shall extend.[4]

Brigham Young's failing health by 1877 made needed priesthood reorderings urgent. That April he confessed, "I feel many times that I could not live an hour longer." Knowing the Twelve would succeed him, he became very eager to put the Church in excellent order organizationally for them.

Earlier, in June 1875, he took a major step in this direction by assigning proper seniority to members of the Twelve, making John Taylor quorum president instead of Orson Hyde. Then in 1876, he took another step, clarifying the interrelationship of stakes, by announcing—to the surprise of many leaders—that Salt Lake Stake held no "center stake" authority over other stakes, that all stakes were equal and autonomous relative to each other. By 1877 he wanted the Twelve freed from local assignments—half the quorum served as stake presidents—to assume general leadership again.[5]

Rapid growth in Church membership, another causative factor, was creating serious administrative problems by 1877. A quarter of a century earlier, Brigham Young had presided over but twelve thousand Saints in the Rockies (1852), yet by the 1870s the region had approximately a hundred thousand people, due to immigration and to the number of children born in the territory. To find work and homes, people moved farther and farther away from the main cities.[6] Similar to an adolescent boy going through a quick growth spurt, the Church had outgrown its organizational britches. More "concentrated and localized" units were needed. "The organizations of the stakes of Zion on account of their rapid growth have become somewhat loose," Elder Taylor told Utah Stake that June. "Many things have been left apparently at loose ends," observed Elder Pratt, adding: "The Lord is about to 'right up' the people; and he has inspired him who presides over us, to organize us more fully." Another member of the Twelve, Elder Franklin D. Richards, noted that some priesthood instructions in the revelations had "not been generally observed" in some areas.[7]

What were some of these loose ends? At the stake level, some presidents lacked counselors, some presidencies were not properly ordained and set apart, and in six of the thirteen stakes, Apostles presided as stake presidents: Charles C. Rich (Bear Lake), Brigham Young Jr. (Cache), Erastus Snow (St. George), Orson Hyde (Sanpete), Lorenzo Snow (Box Elder), and Franklin D. Richards (Weber). Some stakes lacked high councils, some had seventies serving on the high council, not all had properly functioning elders quorums, and the holding of quarterly conferences, "a standing revelation which has not been generally observed," had given way to "occasional Conferences in some places." The time had come, Brigham Young decided, for a more substantial and mature organization in the stakes of the Church.[8]

Another unorthodox practice, although not without historical precedent, was having local presiding bishops. Early in 1877, no less than fifteen presiding bishops served various areas. In Bear Lake, for example, William Budge presided over sixteen communities, handling tithing and exercising some ecclesiastical leadership over local leaders. But "things did not move smoothly and pleasantly by a long way," John Taylor admitted. So Brigham Young announced in 1877, "There was no such thing as a presiding bishop" other than the Presiding Bishop, Edward Hunter.[9]

At the ward level, there was widespread need "to introduce the more perfect system of the Aaronic Priesthood," meaning properly ordained bishoprics, because "many irregularities" had developed. In Weber Stake, the fifth largest stake in Utah, "they did not have Bishops to watch over the people, but had Presidents." Some places had acting bishops who needed either proper ordination or replacement. During the reorganizings, one Paysonite noted that "our bishop has never had the privilege of choosing councilors. It is presumed he will now have that privilege." Some bishops had but one counselor. In a few cases, seventies served as bishops' counselors without being ordained as high priests. Some bishops counselors had moved away and had never been replaced. The critical problem posed by these irregularities was that without three high priests, properly ordained and set apart, no bishopric legally could serve as a Church court. As a result "all kinds of little differences" went to high councils for resolution, normal difficulties "which ought to be taken to the Bishops Court." "There is a law regulating these things," Elder Taylor cautioned, "which we hope to comply with."[10]

Critical for the health of a ward was the contact teachers and priests—the home teachers of that generation—had with the families. These officers were responsible for monitoring conduct, dealing with iniquity, and settling disputes among members. While many wards had strong Aaronic Priesthood units, too many did not. Without Aaronic Priesthood workers, wards and stakes were incomplete. Brigham Young's deathbed concern was that bishops see that the teachers be diligent.[11] But staffing Aaronic Priesthood quorums was not easy—they preferred using men rather than boys then—as Elder Richards explained to Bear Lake Stake:

> Stated how the Aaronic Priesthood seemed to be overstepped by members being advanced at once to the higher or Melchizedek Priesthood, and that there did not seem to be enough in the Church who did not possess this higher priesthood to fill up the quorums of the lesser, hence it became necessary to appoint Elders and Seventies

to act as Priests, Teachers, and Deacons.... No stake organization would be complete without them.[12]

Another reason stakes lacked Aaronic units was the hazy concept, erased only in 1876, that officers of Salt Lake Stake's quorums, because they were sustained in general conference, were like General Authorities to their priesthood counterparts in other stakes. Only by April 1877 were all stakes fully informed that each stake, in order to be completely organized, must contain three Aaronic quorums, each with a separate presidency.[13]

Another matter needing attention was the large number of Saints not officially enrolled in any ward. Saints migrating out from settlements in search of work cut themselves off from ward participation. Brigham Young called them "the scattering sheep of Israel in these mountains who acknowledge no particular fold." He wanted all members enrolled in a ward, accounted for, visited, labored with, and their religious conduct monitored.[14]

Why did the reorganization not come before 1877? One possible answer was that population pressures did not reach the breaking point, the unmanageable point, until 1877. Another is that Brigham Young's health had not become precarious until then. A third reason involves the St. George Temple. In my mind, it is no coincidence that the priesthood reorganization began immediately after the first fully functioning temple in Utah Territory was completed at St. George; priesthood and temples are directly interrelated. Leaders in that generation firmly believed that priesthood on earth was but a small extension of heavenly priesthood, a twig on the great heavenly priesthood tree. Because temples are meeting points between earth and heaven, the opening of the St. George Temple made leaders more conscious of the need for earthly priesthood to mirror more fully the heavenly one. Elder Taylor was one who constantly preached that heavenly priesthood patterns, explained in the revelations, must be copied in the earthly Church.[15]

One of Joseph Smith's teachings in 1842, not forgotten by Brigham Young, was that "the Church is not fully organized, in its proper order, and cannot be, until the Temple is completed, where places will be provided for the administration of the ordinances of the Priesthood." Perhaps the connection between temples and stakes went beyond the dedication of two new temple sites during 1877 and the assignment of all the stakes to the Logan, Manti, or Salt Lake temple districts to spur construction. In 1884,

Detail of photo of St. George, with the temple in the background, c. 1890. With the completion of the St. George Temple in April 1877, Brigham Young was ready to implement the reorganization of the priesthood. He began by personally presiding over the reorganization of the St. George Stake on April 4–5. Courtesy Church Archives.

Elder Erastus Snow said, possibly referring to 1877, "Seeing the different stakes of Zion that were being organized we perceived the idea, possibly, of as many temples."[16]

As with the temple connection, the reorganization of 1877 had a connection with the United Order movement. Brigham Young constantly labored to increase temporal and spiritual unity among the Saints. We have no evidence that by 1877 he had changed this conviction voiced in 1862, "I have had visions and revelations instructing me how to organize this people so that they can live like the family of heaven, but I cannot do it while so much selfishness and wickedness reign in the Elders of Israel." In 1874–75, he supervised the implementation of more than 150 United Orders throughout the region. Their serious problems and short lives hurt him deeply, perhaps pointing out to his observant mind many leadership and organizational weaknesses at ward and stake levels. "We are starting in on some things," said John Taylor in November 1876, "to try to get us united on temporal affairs," noting that recently "the spirit of God has been operating upon President Young."[17] Possibly his statement means that plans to reorder the priesthood were then being formulated.

During 1877 the prophet still advocated United Orders. When initially instructing the Twelve about their role in the upcoming reorganizings, he specifically told them to preach temporal and spiritual unity in every stake. He warned those attending April general conference that "we have no business here other than to build up and establish the Zion of God. It must be done according to the will and law of God, after that pattern and order by which Enoch built up and perfected the former-day Zion."[18] Elder Pratt preached that the reorganizings were part of "a plan which the Lord has revealed that will entitle the Latter-day Saints to greater blessings and privileges through which that union will be brought about which we have long desired in our hearts."[19] Those in attendance at October general conference, six weeks after Brigham Young's death, heard Elder Lorenzo Snow emphatically state, "There is no salvation for us only in the United Order. This principle is not going to die out because Pres. Young is gone. We must carry out that principle if we wish salvation."[20] In fact, during the months before his death, Young explained the linkage he saw among United Orders, temple building, and the nearly completed priesthood reorderings:

In consequence of tradition and the weakness of our human nature, we could not bring our feelings to obey this holy requirement [Order of Enoch]. The Spirit had prompted him to see if the brethren would do anything by way of an approach to it, and hence we had commenced to build Temples, which was a very necessary work and which was centering the feelings of the people for a still further union of effort.... He said that after something had been done towards Temple-building, the same Spirit whispered to perfect the organization of the Priesthood.[21]

But temporal and spiritual unity of a group requires individual righteousness. Reduced to its root purpose, the 1877 reorganization was designed to increase righteousness among leaders and members. The Church exists to perfect the Saints, so by improving Church structure the Saints in turn ought to be better influenced to improve themselves. Brigham Young expected the reorderings to produce "a radical change, a reformation, in the midst of this people." If anyone inquired about the reorganizings, he wrote to his son Willard,

We will answer, to more completely carry out the purposes of Jehovah, to give greater compactness to the labors of the priesthood, to unite the Saints, to care for the scattering sheep of Israel in these mountains who acknowledge no particular fold, to be in a position to understand the standing of everyone calling himself a Latter-day Saint, and to consolidate the interests, feelings, and lives of the members of the Church. There are some of the reasons why we are now more fully than heretofore organizing the holy Priesthood after the pattern given us of our Father in Heaven.[22]

Beyond internal causes for the 1877 reorderings, there may have been an external, political one. The 1870s boiled with conflict between Mormons and Gentiles. Skimpy evidence, involving Tooele and Beaver counties, suggests politics did influence the 1877 effort to some degree. The gentile minority in Tooele controlled election machinery, and invalidating Mormon votes would control elective offices. President Young sent in a county outsider, Elder Francis M. Lyman, who as the new stake president worked hard to win back Mormon political control there. In Beaver the General Authorities feared a repeat of the Tooele problem, so they used the 1877 reorganizing conference in Beaver to terminate Mormon political handholding with Gentiles. If other counties faced similar problems, perhaps Brigham Young's goal to create one effective stake per county was some kind of short-term or long-term political defense effort. Assessment of political motives behind the 1877 movement, however, is not possible until we have detailed political studies of the twenty Utah counties and their communities.[23]

Records do not tell us when Brigham Young first contemplated the large-scale reorganization. But as early as January 20, 1877, he had in mind at least a few changes. That day he wrote to Presiding Elder A. K. Thurber in Richfield, responding to Elder Thurber's lament that in all of Sevier County "there is no permanent organization in the Stake except the High Council." Young replied that "in all the settlements" in that county there would be "ordained Bishops as soon as we can get to it." Meanwhile, he said, appoint local leaders temporarily "till we direct otherwise."[24]

By the time of the St. George Temple dedication during April general conference, the reorganization plan was ready and launched. First, on March 30 and again on April 4, Brigham Young explained the plan to the Twelve and instructed them "to travel and organize stakes of Zion in all the vallies of the mountains." To start the movement, he personally presided over the reorganization of St. George Stake on April 4 and 5. Then on April 7 he surprised Fillmorite Francis M. Lyman by privately telling him to "get ready" to move to and preside as stake president over either Davis or Tooele counties—two areas not then stakes. Thus, without fanfare and without announcement that all stakes would be reorganized, the movement had quickly commenced (see table 1).[25]

The schedule for reorganizing the stakes was not worked out all at once but developed as the spring and summer months wore on. During April, three southern stakes were visited and reorganized by General Authorities. But only when Salt Lake Stake was reorganized in mid-May was public announcement made that all stakes would be visited and put in order, includ-

In 1874–75, Brigham Young supervised the organization of more than 150 United Orders throughout the West but found that uniting Church members on temporal affairs was difficult at best and only marginally successful. Courtesy Perry Special Collections.

ing Cache and Weber on the next two weekends. At Logan on May 20, the Twelve met and "decided on appointments for the next 2 months." By the end of May, a nine-conference schedule for June was announced and Brigham Young projected that "there will probably be some twenty-one stakes [twenty were created] in the valleys of Israel." By early June, the work was "engaging the greater portion of the time and attention" of the Twelve, "assisted as far as their duties will permit by the First Presidency." By mid-June, conferences were scheduled for Juab and Sanpete counties, but

TABLE 1
1887 Stake Organizing Conferences Schedule

Date	Stakes	Location	Visiting Authorities														
			BY	BY	AC	JY	GC	LS	DW	OH	OP	JT	WW	CR	ES	FR	JS
April 4–5	St. George	St. George	■			■	■	■	■		■	■		■	■	■	■
April 17–18	Kanab	Kanab						■			■	■			■		
April 22–23	Panguitch	Panguitch				■	■	■	■		■	■		■	■	■	
May 12–13	Salt Lake	Salt Lake	■			■	■	■	■		■	■			■	■	
May 19–21	Cache	Logan	■			■	■	■	■			■		■	■	■	
May 26–27	Weber	Ogden	■			■	■	■	■			■			■	■	
June 2–3	Utah	Provo	■			■	■	■			■	■		■	■	■	
June 16–17	Davis	Farmington					■					■			■		
June 23–25	Tooele	Tooele	■			■	■	■			■	■			■	■	
June 30–July 1	Juab	Nephi	■			■									■		
June 30–July 1	Morgan	Morgan	■							■					■		
July 7–9	Sanpete	Manti	■			■	■	■			■	■			■	■	
July 7–9	Summit	Coalville						■		■					■		
July 14–15	Sevier	Richfield															
July 14–15	Wasatch	Heber								■		■	■				
July 21–22	Millard	Fillmore											■		■		
July 25–26	Beaver	Beaver										■	■		■		
July 28–29	Parowan	Parowan											■		■		
August 18–19	Box Elder	Brigham City	■		■			■				■		■	■	■	
August 25–26	Bear Lake	Paris			■										■	■	
Totals			9	2	2	9	9	11	5	3	6	13	4	4	14	12	1

Sources: Stake Manuscript Histories and Historical Records, MSS, Church History Library.

"further than this we have not decided on," leaving Sevier, Morgan, Summit, Wasatch, Millard, Beaver, Parowan, Box Elder, and Bear Lake conferences yet to be called.[26]

Reorganizings moved too slowly, so by the end of June two or more teams of General Authorities, instead of one, went out to do the work. "We have thus to divide," Brigham Young said, "or we shall not get through with the organization of the stakes in time to commence the quarterly conferences in those that were first organized." In July, three teams organized nine stakes. Then in August, the last two stakes had their turns. No other stake was organized or reorganized until the next January, when the distant Lower Colorado colonies became the Church's first stake in Arizona.[27]

Brigham Young, despite health fluctuations, conducted nine of the twenty reorganizing conferences. "My own health is excellent," he wrote in late April; "the pain which I have so frequently suffered in my stomach after speaking to large congregations, has troubled me but very little of late." But the workload took its toll, and by June 1 he was too feeble to attend part of the Provo conference. Two weeks later, he admitted "in my anxiety to see the house of God set in Order that I have some what overtaxed my strength." His namesake son described the president as "pale," "worn," and "very tired" on June 20. During the summer months, he "seemed to be anxious and restless until he had thoroughly organized the Church," said George Q. Cannon, Young's counselor, and "was so hurried, was so urged in his feelings concerning the organization of the people; pressing matters forward, anxious to get the Priesthood organized and the Stakes everywhere set in order." On August 6, Brigham Young felt "much joy and satisfaction in our labors" and believed that "much good will result."[28]

Overtaxed, he rested in late June in Cache Valley. But in early July he made a hot and dusty circuit into Juab and Sanpete counties. After a six-week break, he reorganized Box Elder Stake on August 18–19. A week later, he learned the twentieth and last stake, Bear Lake Stake, was reorganized. During the following week he died, but had the knowledge that the basic reorganization work was complete and the machinery set in motion to fully reorder wards and quorums at the local levels.

Planning and conducting twenty decision-loaded conferences required much physical and spiritual energy from the Brethren. Once dates were set, local arrangements had to be made. A letter, telegram, or verbal instruction from the First Presidency usually informed local authorities to publicize the conference and notify local Saints to be there. Two weeks before the Tooele meetings, for example, local leaders learned from the First Presidency:

> We will hold meetings in Tooele City, for the organization of a Stake of Zion, on Saturday and Sunday, the 23d and 24th inst. Please notify the various wards and settlements in the County of this fact. We also desire that a statement should be prepared, for that meeting, of the number of Seventies, High Priests, Elders, and members of the Lesser Priesthood in the County.[29]

Two to ten General Authorities attended a stake's conference. Travel was relatively easy between the rail terminals at Franklin, Idaho, and York, a few miles south of Payson. Beyond those railroad lines, however, travel posed problems, as President Young's itinerary in Sanpete County shows:

> After holding meetings in Nephi we shall proceed to Sanpete County. I shall take a carriage with me on the cars to York, but I shall want you to supply me with a good, solid team, (as the carriage carries six passengers), to convey me from the terminus of the railroad to Sanpete and return. If I should conclude to bring my own team I will let you know in good season by telegraph.[30]

John Taylor's party, to reach Bear Lake Stake, left the train at Franklin and traveled in three carriages twenty-two miles to Mink Creek. There, they camped and were met by Bishop William Budge. On the road the next day, they were met in Emigration Canyon by Elder Charles C. Rich—the Bear Lake Stake president—and others. The party arrived at Paris, Idaho, at 3:00 PM the day before the conference opened. Elder Richards, covering a Wasatch Mountain circuit, took trains to Morgan City and to Coalville, but to reach Heber City from there, he traveled by carriage. The return trip lasted from 5:00 AM to 5:40 PM. According to his diary that night, his three weeks of conferences and travels made him "very worn tired weary."[31]

A large, accessible city in each stake hosted its conference. Tabernacles housed the meetings in Salt Lake, Parowan, Logan, Ogden, and St. George stakes. Local meetinghouses served the purpose in Farmington, Panguitch, Tooele, Heber, and elsewhere. At Fillmore they met in the statehouse. Either no meetinghouse was big enough or else summer heat made meetinghouses unbearable, so boweries were used in Utah at Brigham City

John Rowberry was the presiding bishop in Tooele when he received notice of the organization of a stake in his area, just two weeks before the meeting. He created a report detailing the number of seventies, elders, and members of the Aaronic Priesthood for that meeting. Courtesy Church Archives.

(twenty-five hundred capacity but many had to stand outside), Coalville, Manti, Richfield (built for the occasion), Morgan City (one hundred feet square, built the day before), and in Idaho at Paris ("windy and somewhat unpleasant"). Arriving authorities sometimes received colorful greetings, like the "brass band, a concourse of citizens, and a host of Sunday School children" that met Brigham Young at the Brigham City depot.[32]

The conferences had specific purposes. First the extent of the stake was defined by designating which wards, old and new, it included. Apparently, Brigham Young wanted one stake per county, a goal that was all but met: twenty counties and twenty stakes, Iron County having two and sparsely settled Paiute County none. Most of the new stakes had been operating more like independent districts than like parts of old stakes anyway, so their births caused very little confusion.

Tooele illustrates how a new stake was born. Until 1877 all settlements in the county were branches supervised by Presiding Bishop John Rowberry, similar to a district of the Church today. An April 1876 census shows three thousand Saints there. Annual county Church conferences were held in previous years. When the area received stakehood in 1877, the six branches became wards, ranging in size from 27 families and 124 individuals at Vernon to 200 families and 1,195 souls at Tooele. Later, new dependent branches were formed, each with a presiding priest in charge.[33]

Population and geography determined where new stakes should be. (See table 2.) The seven new ones, ranging in membership size from Davis

TABLE 2
Stake Statistics from Early Quarterly Reports following the 1877 Reorganizings (Stakes Ranked according to Size of Membership)

Stake	Date of report	Wards	Families	Members	High Priests	Seventies	Elders	Priests	Teachers	Deacons	Families/ward	Members/ward	High Priests/ward	Seventies/ward	Elders/ward	Priests/ward	Tteachers/ward	Deacons/ward	Average family size
Salt Lake	12/77	35	4021	19798	493	1134	1617	145	166	595	115	566	14	32	46	4	5	17	4.92
Utah	12/77	17	2658	13731	439	631	1149	214	141	280	156	808	26	37	68	13	8	17	5.17
Cache	2/78	24	2155	12022	380	361	1214	257	275	404	90	501	16	15	51	11	12	17	5.57
Sanpete	11/77	18	1623	8760	326	394	791	155	148	153	90	487	18	22	44	9	8	9	5.40
Weber	3/78	16	1494	7904	139	402	691	121	186	155	93	494	9	25	43	8	12	10	5.29
Box Elder	12/77	15[a]	998	5341	192	183	562	113	73	127	67	356	13	12	38	8	5	9	5.35
St. George	12/77	14	816	4592	150	195	453	28	20	75	58	328	11	14	32	2	1	5	5.63
Davis	3/78	8	832	4593	132	174	357	45	53	73	104	574	17	34	45	6	7	9	5.52
Sevier	3/78	11	649	3530	121	85	383	31	90	84	59	321	11	8	35	3	8	8	5.44
Bear Lake	1/78	16	592	3418	82	97	346	14	14	89	37	214	5	6	22	1	1	6	5.77
Tooele	3/78	6	589	3064	97	110	218	23	55	73	98	511	16	18	36	4	9	9	5.20
Millard	3/78	8	489	2501	79	115	215	38	9	71	61	313	10	14	27	5	1	9	5.11
Summit	11/77	10	482	2448	100	65	214	46	46	36	48	245	10	7	21	4	5	4	5.08
Wasatch	2/78	6	392	2296	90	40	162	33	33	34	65	383	15	7	27	5	6	6	5.86
Parowan	3/78	7	373	2122	58	136	153	5	5	16	53	303	8	19	22	12	1	2	5.69
Juab	3/78	4	318	2014	71	121	84	32	32	61	80	506	18	30	21	1	8	8	6.33
Kanab	3/78	6	259	1669	59	52	135	19	19	73	43	278	10	9	23	3	3	12	6.44
Beaver	12/77	5	275	1590	75	25	139	6	6	29	55	318	15	5	28	4	1	6	5.78
Morgan	3/78	9	248	1541	67	35	126	16	16	64	28	171	7	4	14	1	2	7	6.21
Panguitch	3/78	5	170	859	27	22	75	13	13	17	34	172	5	4	15	6	3	3	5.05
Totals		240	19433	103793	3177	4477	9084	1329	1400	2409	81	432	13	19	38	6	6	10	5.34

Sources: Stake Historical Reports 1877–80; Presiding Bishopric, March 1, 1878, Statistical Report of the Stakes, MS, Church History Library.

[a] Box Elder Stake began with sixteen wards but disorganized Corrine Ward by December.

with forty-five hundred to Morgan with fifteen hundred, were about the same population as the seven smallest existing stakes, and the average size of wards was about the same in the seven new stakes (333) as in the comparison stakes (329). Branches became wards where possible. Otherwise, they were attached to an existing ward as dependent branches.[34]

Another vital conference purpose was to select new stake and ward officers or resustain those already in office. President Young usually determined who would be stake president. An exception occurred in Sevier County, where a priesthood council made nominations from which the two visiting Apostles made the final selection. Brigham Young personally appointed Francis M. Lyman as Tooele Stake president. He wanted John Murdock, if he agreed to quit cooperating with Gentiles, retained as Beaver Stake's presiding officer. At Cache Stake, Young asked the outgoing stake president, his Apostle-son Brigham Jr., and others of the Twelve for nominations for stake leaders. They declined, "Make your own appointments, Brother Brigham, and we will vote for them." So he chose Moses Thatcher to be the new stake president. At the Juab conference, prior to the 2:00 PM Sunday meeting, General Authorities in attendance sustained President Young's choice of George Teasdale of Salt Lake City as the new stake president.[35]

What happened to presidencies in the thirteen existing stakes? In the six stakes where Apostles stepped down from being stake presidents, strong local leaders replaced them. In the seven other stakes, four incumbents continued as presidents and three were released: Joel Grover (Juab) became a local bishop, Thomas Callister (Millard) became a stake patriarch, and Albert K. Thurber (Sevier) became a first counselor in the stake presidency. Their places were taken by strong local leaders, except at Juab where Salt Laker George Teasdale was selected.

Seven stakes were new. In them, three of the new presidents had been serving the region as presiding bishops: Willard G. Smith (Morgan), Abraham Hatch (Wasatch), and William W. Cluff (Summit). In three other new stakes, prominent local men received the call. And in one new stake, Tooele, outsider Francis M. Lyman was installed.

Nearly every stake—seventeen of twenty—received new counselors at the conferences. High councils too were created, continued, or reorganized in all stakes. About half the stakes immediately called presidents for the high priests and for the elders quorum; other stakes waited until after the conferences. Only two stakes sustained patriarchs at first, but within a year most had at least one called. Only about one-fourth of the stakes sustained priests, teachers, and deacons quorum presidents at the conferences.

Local priesthood councils participated in nominating other stake and ward officers. The council at Sevier Stake nominated four men for stake president, two dozen for high council, and at least one for each settlement for bishop, including four for Richfield and four for Monroe. Elders Orson Hyde and Erastus Snow and the Sevier council decided on officers all the way down to elders presidency and priests presidents.[36] In Wasatch Stake, Elders Franklin D. Richards and John Taylor did not question that acting Presiding Bishop Abraham Hatch was to be the new stake president. They met with him Friday afternoon and poured over names of Melchizedek Priesthood men, "receiving suggestions as to the fitness of men for various offices." Then, next afternoon, in priesthood council they "determined most of the officers for the Stake."[37]

In Tooele Stake, at a Saturday evening priesthood council, Elder John Taylor "called upon any and all who wished to make nominations of men, who were honest, sober, truthful Latter Day Saints, so they may have plenty of good names to choose from for High Councillors, Bishops and their Counsellors and presidents of Quorums." The next morning, the new stake president met with the Twelve "when names were canvassed to fill the various offices of the Stake." During a lunch break, Lyman met again with the Twelve "when the names of parties to fill the various offices were further discussed and decided upon." At the afternoon session, Elder Taylor presented the selections for sustaining votes.[38]

Nominations and sustainings went smoothly, according to available records. "The Spirit seems to fully approve of our labors and selections," wrote Elder Richards, regarding the Tooele slate. There were several cases of dissent, however. When Brigham Young proposed to Parowan Stake members that William Dame be replaced by Jesse N. Smith as their stake president, "a number of the people objected," and the stake reorganization was postponed from April to July, when William Dame and Jesse N. Smith were sustained as co-presidents. In Salt Lake's Third Ward, members voted down Elder George Q. Cannon's proposal that their long-time bishop be replaced. As a result, President Young appointed a priest that August to preside, and not until December was former Bishop Jacob Weiler put back into his office. Kanab could not unite behind a nominee for bishop until that December.[39]

Sustained, the new officers needed ordinations and settings apart, cere-monies that usually followed the last conference session. Only General Authorities could ordain stake presidents and bishops, but stake presidents handled all other ordinations and settings apart.

Beyond determining boundaries and officers, the conferences had other purposes. One was to instruct. Sermon subjects ranged from the need for temporal and spiritual unity to temple building, children's educations, and duties of priesthood officers. Specific local problems also received comment.

Beaver Stake's unique problems, for example, drew fire from Elders Eras-tus Snow and Wilford Woodruff. They called a special priesthood meeting that excluded anyone not "vouched for" by those present. They first dressed down two Latter-day Saint county judges who threatened Utah's future by issuing questionable divorces to out-of-state parties. Then the Apostles chas-tised the stake president for going "heart and hand with the gentiles," thereby giving Gentiles too much local political power. Brigham Young's instruc-tions were that if John Murdock were not repentant about this, he was to be replaced. He repented and was resustained. Then members themselves were criticized for selling and drinking liquor dispensed at the Mormon co-op

Elders Wilford Woodruff (left) *and Erastus Snow chastized members and leaders of the Beaver Stake for misusing judicial power, accomodating gentile practices and politics, and selling and drinking liquor. Courtesy Perry Special Collections.*

244 ~~ MY FELLOW SERVANTS

store. Elder Snow warned: "I advise you sisters to get together in the capacity of a Relief Society, and gut the store of every drop of liquor in it, and spill the liquor on the ground." Finally, the Apostles cancelled out county central committee nominations for the upcoming election and substituted another man as their handpicked nominee for the legislature. Immediately following the conference, twenty-five of the newly sustained officers were rebaptized, including the stake presidency.[40]

On July 11, after fourteen of twenty stakes were reorganized, the First Presidency issued a lengthy, historic epistle to the Church.[41] It explained the purposes of the reorderings, expounded on priesthood principles to be followed when wards and quorums were organized, and listed a wide range of instructions regarding Church government and duties of officers and members. It served then much like bishops' and stake presidents' handbooks serve today and was carefully and often referred to by local leaders. It represents the constitution of the 1877 movement, the guidebook, the codification of priesthood principles necessary to operating stakes, wards, and quorums. It was the most comprehensive policy statement about priesthood practices since the Doctrine and Covenants was first published. In summary form, the epistle's most important statements included:

Stake presidencies are responsible for all church matters in their stakes.

Bishoprics, to be properly organized, must have three high priests.

There will be no more local presiding bishops.

All members are to be enrolled in a ward or branch, visited regularly, and brought to repentance when necessary. If these conditions are not met, leaders share in their sins.

A priest, teacher, or acting priest presides over branches. Branches and wards should maintain Sunday Schools and Sabbath meetings.

High priests are a stake quorum with unlimited numbers and are not to meet on a ward basis.

Seventies meet only for missionary purposes; otherwise they should meet with high priests or elders quorums.

No more high priests or seventies will be ordained without First Presidency approval.

Quorums must have scriptural minimums in order to organize: no less than ninety-six elders, forty-eight priests, twenty-four teachers, and twelve deacons. Wards should combine if necessary to create quorums with those minimum enrollments.

Melchizedek Priesthood men can serve in lesser priesthood jobs when needed.

Stakes will hold quarterly conferences that General Authorities will visit.

Stakes and wards will compile quarterly reports and submit them to the First Presidency.

Careful transcripts of all bishops courts must be kept.

Members, when moving, must obtain letters of recommendation from previous wards.

Youths should be given some priesthood office; experienced teachers should take along young men during their home visits to train them in priesthood work.

Bishoprics should administer sacrament weekly to Sunday School children.

Parents should instruct their children and send them to Sunday Schools.

Tithing should be paid promptly to aid temple construction.

Every settlement should have YMMIAs and YLMIAs.

Home industry is to be encouraged and developed; grain must be stored.

Stake presidencies should travel through wards frequently and call men as home missionaries to help them preach in the wards.

Local leaders read this epistle publicly and discussed it with local priesthood groups. In August, Brigham Young added two instructions. Raising donations to support temple laborers became the bishops' responsibility rather than the quorums'. Also, stakes were to hold monthly priesthood meetings on the first Saturday of each month. These, like the epistle's instructions, were quickly complied with. Three more additions to the reform plan came right after Young's death: bishops were instructed to hold weekly ward meetings with their Aaronic Priesthood quorums, dates were published for stake conferences for the next six months, and Deseret News Press published forms for ward and stake reports.[42]

The twenty stake reorganizing conferences were but the first phase of the 1877 reorganization movement. The second phase was the post-conference part that reordered priesthood work at the ward and quorum levels. If Brigham Young dominated the first phase, the stake presidencies and ward bishops dominated the second. This second phase involved installing bishops' counselors not already installed; calling and setting apart quorum presidents for elders, priests, teachers, and deacons units; and calling males to fill up the new quorums. Stake presidents made two or three circuits through the wards to complete this phase of the reorganization, sometimes assisted by resident General Authorities.

Salt Lake Stake, with a quarter of all Mormons in Utah Territory, clearly illustrated how the second phase was implemented.[43] Conferences were held in virtually all nineteen city wards and six county wards. Ten new wards were created and staffed. Of thirty-five total wards, fifteen received new bishops; and five acting bishops and twelve acting counselors were ordained and/or set apart. Of 70 total counselors for the 35 wards, 47 were newly called. Of 105 total bishopric personnel in the stakes, 62 (59 percent) were newly ordained because of the reorganization. These changes came during the stake presidency's first circuit in June and July. A second circuit did not begin until November.

During the lull, two major developments occurred. First, in August when the prophet asked stakes to hold monthly priesthood meetings, he specifically instructed Salt Lake Stake to erect a new priesthood hall to house those monthly gatherings. As a result, the Old Tabernacle was razed, and laborers commenced the stately Assembly Hall, which Brigham Young helped design. Second, at October stake conference the stake presidency called thirty-five men as home missionaries to serve as preachers in the wards. Finally, the stake's November 3 priesthood meeting initiated the stake presidency's second circuit of the wards. It was time to create quorums.

The stake also needed new elders quorums. Until 1876, one quorum had served the two dozen wards, its presidency being sustained in conferences. When Brigham Young asked in 1876 for quorums to support laborers for the Salt Lake Temple, quorum president Edward W. Davis set up branch elders units in some of the county population pockets. This loose collection of elders groups, belonging to the one stake quorum, changed radically during the second phase. For the stake's thirty-five wards, fifteen elders quorums were formed. Quorums needed ninety-six members minimum,

The Assembly Hall in Salt Lake City was built specifically as a site for monthly priesthood meetings as directed by President Brigham Young in 1877. Courtesy Perry Special Collections.

an impossibility for most wards, so multiward quorums were formed. The First Ward, for example, with twenty-nine elders, and the Tenth Ward with seventy-nine, combined to become the Second Elders Quorum, joined shortly by elders from the Sugarhouse Ward. Only four quorums were one-ward quorums. For the rest, it took from two to five wards to supply enough elders to create a quorum. By December the *Deseret News* published the new quorum numberings and a list of the fifteen new presidencies.

The stake likewise needed more Aaronic Priesthood quorums. Prior to 1877, there had been stake deacons, teachers, and priests quorums, whose presidencies were sustained at each general conference. Wards often had deacons quorums but none for teachers or priests; they did have groups of ward teachers, but these were not considered Aaronic Priesthood teachers quorums. The ideal continued to be to call mature men into these quorums, but in practice such men received the Melchizedek Priesthood, and the Aaronic quorums were plagued with vacancies. The only solution was to call boys into the work, a solution implemented by the 1877 reorganization.

A September survey showed 170 Aaronic Priesthood bearers in the Salt Lake Stake. Conscious of quorum minimums, stake leaders in early

November doubted the stake had enough ordained teachers to form even two quorums and knew "there were only enough Priests in the whole city to organize one quorum." By December 31, dozens of new teachers were ordained and three quorums formed: one for nine wards with nineteen teachers, one with nineteen teachers from eight wards, and a third with twenty-two teachers from four wards. Thirty-seven priests were ordained so the stake could have one priests quorum. By contrast, deacons units were easy to fill. Most wards could come up with twelve deacons. During November and December, 354 new deacons were ordained in the stake, so that all but two of the thirty-five wards had a quorum, and four wards had more than one. Mill Creek Ward alone set up five. By the year's end, the stake had forty-one deacons quorums.

Other stakes implemented the second phase similarly. Between September and February, Box Elder Stake's Aaronic Priesthood numbers nearly doubled (from 182 to 352). Bear Lake Stake's deacons increased in a few months from thirty-seven to eighty-nine. It took Morgan Stake until February to create one priests quorum. Juab needed until January to start its one elders and two deacons quorums. Beaver Second Ward ordained "a number of young men" as priests and deacons that fall. Sevier Stake created two new elders quorums by its first quarterly conference. A Cache Stake report in December showed one priests quorum had been created ("mostly boys"); one ward said it filled a deacons quorum with "small boys"; one bishop reported his ward had fourteen priests ("mostly young boys"), a full deacons quorum, only one ordained teacher, and a quorum of acting teachers ("older brethren"); and another ward had ordained a number of "young men as teachers to labor with experienced Acting Teachers." Three circuits by the Weber Stake presidency saw them organize or reorganize six elders, six priests, twelve teachers, and eleven deacons quorums by October. By the year's end most stakes had completed their stake, ward, and quorum organizations; and leaders expressed great satisfaction at the changes and improvements made.[44]

Threats to prune the ungodly from the Church were not fulfilled. At least we find no evidence that excommunications escalated in the wake of the reorganizings. This disappointed some, like Isaiah Coombs of Payson who expected a "reformation." Paysonites in August, he wrote, talked much about "the proposed cleansing of the Church by cutting off all dead branches, which it is hoped will soon be inaugurated." Brigham Young, sounding severe in public on the matter, on his deathbed privately told Elder Cannon that "offending members should be carefully looked after and attended to but not dealt rashly with." Erastus Snow's instructions to bishops were similar: they should manifest "that fatherly love, tenderness and anxiety that parents feel for their offspring," a policy that seems to have been followed.[45]

But members were forced to repledge their allegiance or declare their disloyalty when offered the chance to be rebaptized. Many Saints had been rebaptized in 1874–75 during the United Order movements, but many had not. So both types were given a second chance to be rebaptized in 1877, and hundreds of Saints were rebaptized. Elder Richards, installing a new bishopric in Davis Stake, had them "rebaptized, reconfirmed, and ordained and set apart." Leaders in the South Bountiful Ward reported on September 8 that 117 of its 400 members had been rebaptized. On July 5, Bishop Frederick Kesler supervised his ward's rebaptism and then assisted in confirming fifty-nine persons at fast meeting. Part of Wasatch Stake's reorganizing conference included a Sunday morning rebaptismal service. At Fillmore on July 21, two Apostles counseled Saints there "to renew their covenants by baptism" and twenty-two responded. At the Beaver Stake reorganization, twenty-five were rebaptized, including the new stake presidency; then ward rebaptisms followed, totaling over four hundred by November. Parowan members were asked on August 12 "to go and renew their covenants" if they had not done so already. When Tooele Stake organized the Quincy Branch, twenty-one were rebaptized there. Reports dated November 3 from the Sevier Stake listed forty-eight rebaptisms for four wards. Woodruff Ward reported that 80 percent of its 336 souls were rebaptized. Summit Stake in November questioned what course to take regarding "some that had not renewed their covenants," but no answer is noted. The 116 rebaptisms at Nephi that fall made one St. Georgean think a "silent reformation" was under way. The main reason for rebaptisms, counseled Elder Erastus Snow, was "to draw the Saints more closely together and to separate the wheat from the chaff."[46]

As instructed by the July letter, stake presidents began visiting all their wards on a regular basis. During the first stake quarterly conference, most stakes also called home missionaries to visit and speak regularly in ward sacrament meetings. To cite a few examples, Tooele and Millard stakes called twenty, Morgan sixteen, Cache twenty-two, and Utah twenty-four. Some stakes, like Weber, used high councilmen as home missionaries. Others called seventies. A few home missionaries received specific assignments to work with language groups such as the Germans, Swiss, or Native Americans. By December, two-thirds of the stakes had their missionaries called and operating.[47]

Quarterly conferences began in all stakes, replacing the annual, semiannual, and random conferences of the past. With rare exceptions, every quarterly conference, starting that fall, was visited by members of the Twelve or First Presidency. At each stake's first quarterly conference, the officers called in previous weeks to complete the organizations were sustained and set apart. At these quarterly conferences, ward leaders turned in reports so stake leaders could compile quarterly reports to give to the visiting authorities. Table 2 is a Church census for the stakes, based on the fall and winter quarterly conference reports, that show the approximate size and officer range of stakes in late 1877.

By the second quarterly conference, if not the first, nearly every stake reported it was fully organized at the stake, ward, and quorum levels. The reorganization of 1877 was completed, and stakes thereafter settled down to operating with their new machinery, to letting their new officers and units serve, to doing the everyday work of ecclesiastical leadership and followership.

Similar to a train going through a tunnel, the Church entered, passed through, and exited from the 1877 reorganization. What difference did it make? What changes did it produce? Was the Church any better because of the passage? Brigham Young's counselor George Q. Cannon delivered an October assessment that painted Young's reorganization work in heroic proportions:

> He set the Priesthood in order as it has never before been since the first organization of the Church upon the earth. He defined the duties of the Apostles, he defined the duties of the Seventies, he defined the duties of the High Priests, the duties of the Elders and those of the lesser Priesthood, with plainness and distinction and power—the power of God—in a way that it is left on record in such unmistakable language that no one need err who has the spirit of God resting down upon him.[48]

Using Cannon's statement as the frame for judging Brigham Young's last achievement, we will now examine each priesthood office in terms of how the 1877 reorganization affected it.

The Twelve

Six of the Twelve were released as stake presidents because Brigham Young felt they now must work "in a wider and more extended sphere," in "a larger field than a Stake of Zion." He gave them an "increase of responsibility and jurisdiction" for which they would be held to "a stricter accountability" than before.[49]

He expected the movement to give the Twelve a spiritual shot in the arm; in starting the movement he said, "The Twelve must take a different course—that is some of them—or they would lose the crown and others would take what they might have had." Table 1 shows much involvement by the Twelve in the stake reorganizing conferences. They conducted meetings, interviewed, ordained and set apart, preached, met members, and gave private counsel. These were tasks that built them up spiritually, if Elder Franklin D. Richards's diary is representative. He recorded how he felt the Spirit confirm the choices of Tooele Stake's officers. Then in late July, he recorded how John Taylor and he spent time "in searching revelations and sayings of Joseph Smith in Church history on the subject of Priesthood." For part of another day he "read diligently in revelations and history of Joseph Smith." After his Brigham City sermon on priesthood duties, Richards recorded his spiritual feelings: "I thank Thee O lord for the measure of thy Spirit to aid me in my labors in the ministry and for increasing my knowledge in the Gospel of the Holy Priesthood."[50]

A new and major assignment given the Twelve was to visit quarterly stake conferences, something they started doing that fall. Elder Taylor, aware that the Twelve's duties now more than ever made it impossible for them to "pay any attention to their own private affairs," won approval in October conference for the Twelve to receive for the first time "a reasonable recompense for their services" from Church funds.[51]

The Seventies

Unlike the Twelve, the First Council of the Seventy gained no new responsibilities. Rather, they and their six dozen quorums generally lost importance. Seventies needed reorganizing to put their quorums on a strict geographic basis, rather than struggling to retain the no-matter-where-you-live-you-belong-to-your-original-quorum situation. That change came six years later, initiated by a revelation to John Taylor. But, as James N. Baumgarten noted, "It seems strange that more definite steps for organization were not taken" during the Brigham Young era. Perhaps strong positions taken by Brigham and by Joseph Young regarding the authority and status of seventies required both of their deaths before change could come; we need to know much more about the relationship between these Young brothers. But 1877 clearly added to or created situations that made the 1883 changes necessary.[52]

The reorganization set the seventies back in a number of ways. First, if Joseph Young said in 1876 that seventies could ordain high priests and bishops, 1877 realities shattered that theory. The First Council played no meaningful role in the movement, and all seventies called to presiding positions in wards and stakes were first ordained as high priests and then set apart to particular positions—their seventies' authority was not sufficient.

Second, like a reaping machine in a grain field, the movement took seventies by the hundreds—Joseph Young said almost a thousand total—and made them high priests to preside in wards and stakes. Seventies quorums were emptied. Brigham said to Joseph at Logan, "Your quorums are depleted, but no matter, when the Lord has new positions, take them and you will be destined to enjoy all the blessings. It will make no difference whether we are deacons or elders if we are doing our duty."[53]

Third, the depleted ranks were not soon filled. Ending the seventies' practice of freely recruiting new members, Brigham Young ordered that no more seventies would be ordained without First Presidency permission, a position taken specifically to reduce the number of new seventies. Even men called on missions that October were not ordained as seventies as had been customary.[54]

Fourth, seventies were told not to meet as quorums unless they had specific missionary business to conduct; otherwise they should meet with elders or high priests.

Fifth, seventies vigorously responded in 1876 to the call to provide men and to pay them to work on the temples, feeling that assignment gave their quorums needed meaning in Zion; but 1877 instructions took away the fund-raising task and gave it to the bishops. Slight solace came from the fact that, despite losing men and purpose, seventies in a few cases were called upon by stake presidents to serve as home missionaries.

Stakes and Stake Presidents

In early Utah, Salt Lake Stake played a vital role, much like its predecessors in Kirtland, Missouri, and Nauvoo. Salt Lake Stake, in 1877, contained one-fourth of the Church members and a heavy concentration of General Authorities. It served as the main stake, like a center stake of Zion. But as more and more stakes were born, the general role of stakes in ecclesiastical government needed to be clearly identified. The most important product of 1877 was making stakes meaningful governing units between the wards and the General Authorities. This was done by creating new stakes, calling new officers in almost every stake, and giving them more responsibility. Statistically, 1877 did this:

Old stakes reorganized	13
New stakes created	7
New stake presidents	16
New stake counselors	18 sets
New presidency members	53 out of 60

Presidents were made responsible for every person and every program, except seventies' work, within their stake boundaries. Diarist Jens Weibye noted new duties given stake presidents in 1877 that impressed him: "to preside wherever they go in Sanpete Stake, also in High counsils, Relief society, Quorum Meeting, Sabbath School, etc. One of the Presidency of the Stake should be present, in every High Council Meeting, when there is any Busines."[55] Ended in 1877 was a practice, at times common, to have a high council president who was not the stake president. Stake presidents participating in the second phase of the reorganizings benefited from having to preach, instruct, meet members, and seek spiritual guidance. One counselor, after visiting many wards, "was satisfied that the Lord approved of it, for, while engaged in that labor, he realized the power and Spirit of God to a remarkable degree."[56] Such experiences now could happen to these men regularly because of their new assignments to develop quarterly conferences, to conduct monthly priesthood meetings, to visit and speak regularly in the wards, and to keep all their wards properly organized and staffed.

Most stakes created new high councils, bringing more than a hundred new men into those positions. Stakes also established many new Melchizedek

TABLE 3

New Units and Leaders

Old Stake and founding date	Old Stake President / New Stake President	Counselors	Total Wards	New Wards	Old Wards	Old Bishops	Acting Bishops/ Presiding Elders now Bishops	New Bishops
Bear Lake (1869)	Apostle C. C. Rich / William Budge	none / 2	16	15	1	1	12	3
Beaver (1869)	John Murdock / (same)	none / 2	5	0	5	3	1	1
Cache (1856)	B. Young Jr. / Moses Thatcher	none / 2	24	11	13	10	7	7
Box Elder (1856)	Apostle L. Snow / Oliver G. Snow	1 / 2 new	16	14	2	1	7	8
Juab (1868)	Joel Grover / George Teasdale	2 / 2 new	4	3	1	0	0	4
Millard (1869)	Thomas Callister / Ira Hinckley	none / 2	8	7	1	0	5	3
St. George (1869)	Apostle E. Snow / J. D. T. McAllister	2 / 2 new	14	1	13	3	4	7
Parowan (1855)	William Dame / (same)	1 / 1 same	7	1	6	3	2	2
Sanpete (1860)	Apostle O. Hyde / Canute Peterson	none / 2	18	11	7	4	3	11
Sevier (1874)	A. K. Thurber (acting) / Franklin Spencer	none / 2	11	8	3	0	6	5

Old Stake and founding date	Old Stake President / New Stake President	Counselors	Total Wards	New Wards	Old Wards	Old Bishops	Acting Bishops/ Presiding Elders now Bishops	New Bishops
Utah (1852)	A. O. Smoot (acting) (same, ordained)	none 2	17	2	15	13	2	2
Salt Lake (1847)	Angus Cannon (same)	2 2 (same)	35	10	25	15	5	15
Weber (1851)	Apostle F. Richards David H. Perry	none 2	16	16	0	0	10	6
Totals	9 new 4 continued	3 same 28 new	191	99	92	53	64	74
New Stakes								
Davis	Wm. R. Smith	2 new						
Kanab	L. J. Nuttall	none	8	7	1	0	5	3
Morgan	Willard G. Smith	2						
Summit	Wm. W. Cluff	2	14	1	13	3	4	7
Tooele	Francis M. Lyman	2 new						
Wasatch	Abraham Hatch	1	7	1	6	3	2	2
Panguitch	James Henrie	1 (same)						
Totals		14 new	50	41	9	3	21	26
Grand totals		42 new	241	140	101	56	85	100

Sources: Ward and Stake Historical Records, Manuscript Histories, and Minute Books; Andrew Jenson, *Latter-day Saint Biographical Encyclopedia* and *Encyclopedic History of The Church of Jesus Christ of Latter-day Saints*; and various biographical sketches.

Priesthood quorums. They sent home missionaries to wards to speak in and hopefully improve sacrament meetings. They eliminated the office of local presiding bishops; new bishops agents served instead. The 1877 movement also introduced the Church's "first uniform system for keeping records," involving among other things a ward "Long Book" for members' records and a new "Stake Quarterly Report" book. These were "the first formal instruments used by the Church to measure enrollment and ordinance data," and they continued in use until 1900. The 1877 program called for reliable monthly and quarterly reports and statistics from the wards; it also started quorum records books and other historical records. Researchers using the Church History Library today know that for many Church units, regular records date from 1877, even for many units organized well before then.[57]

Salt Lake Stake's reorganizing included building the Assembly Hall for stake priesthood meetings. Other stakes, evidently, undertook similar building projects too. During the next seven years, tabernacles were begun in each city that in 1877 hosted a stake reorganizing conference in a bowery (Morgan, Coalville, Manti, Richfield, and Paris—Brigham City began its tabernacle probably before the reorganizings) and in Cedar City, Provo, Moroni, Panguitch, Wellsville, and Smithfield.[58]

High Priests

Seventies reaped by the 1877 movement were bundled into the high priests quorum, vastly expanding the high priests population. But, like the seventies, high priests had to swallow a humility pill. If 1877 was their report card, they failed. Their units, theoretically schools for preparing future leaders, produced very few of the leaders called in 1877, a fact that bothered Elder Taylor, who noted

> how little prepared the High Priests were to take upon themselves the duties of their office, in presiding over Stakes, Wards, etc. We have had to take hundreds from the Quorums of Seventies and Elders.... If the High Priests had understood and performed their duties, we should not have been in the position we were and compelled to go outside these quorums to find men suitable for presiding.[59]

High priests were reminded that theirs was a stake quorum, so no ward-level meeting should be held. They would continue to have their own president, someone other than the stake president. They could not freely recruit new members as they had in the past.

Elders

Before 1877, elders units had lacked organization and purpose. But that year, they at least multiplied dramatically and were properly organized and officered. No new duties were identified other than holding regular meetings and answering all calls made by their ward bishop.

Bishops and Wards

Similar to a train exiting a tunnel with more cars than it had entered with, Church leaders in 1877 added three new wards for each two it already had and added four new bishops for each one that continued in office:

Old wards	101
New wards	140
Old bishops retained	56
New bishops called	100
Acting bishops or presiding elders called as new bishops	85
Total newly ordained or set apart	185 out of 241
	(3 out of 4)

Although incomplete, records show that well over half of the 482 counselors were newly ordained or set apart. Those new leaders had to learn to function with their ward members, and the members with them. New wards were either former branches or parts split off from existing wards. Branches that became wards had the advantage in most cases of their branch president becoming their bishop and of keeping their same meeting place and meeting schedule, with the addition of quorum and perhaps auxiliary meetings. Wards taken from other wards had a harder adjustment: new leaders, new meeting location, and new organizations to staff. Often they also had to construct new meetinghouses.

Bishops, old or new, assumed additional duties. They were expected to strictly account for their ward members, keep Aaronic units in their ward or their section of the stake staffed, attend weekly Aaronic Priesthood meetings, attend monthly priesthood meetings, operate an effective ward teaching program, conduct the sacrament in Sunday School, turn in monthly and quarterly reports, keep accurate trial records, take over from the priesthood quorums the task of supporting temple laborers, and hold proper Sabbath meetings. Virtually all new bishoprics were properly ordained as high priests and set apart to their callings, thus qualifying as proper Church tribunals.

Priests, Teachers, and Deacons

The 1877 changes revolutionized Aaronic Priesthood work by stipulating that all young men receive some priesthood office instead of just a few youth having that privilege. Youth were the solution to the long-standing dilemma of how to keep lesser priesthood quorums staffed when capable men were recruited to the higher quorums. The new policy was for experienced teachers to take youths with them while ward teaching. The second phase created scores of new Aaronic Priesthood units, most filled with teenaged boys, some of whom became deacons at age eleven. Weber Stake ordained "all the boys above fourteen years not already ordained." Reactions to this new youth priesthood were strongly favorable. An October report from Ogden noted the "great good that had already resulted from organizing the Lesser Priesthood, the young men responding to the call they received in such a manner as enkindled new life and spirit in the hearts of their parents and older members of the Church generally." A Cache bishop said "a source of strength had been opened up through the organization of the Aaronic Priesthood, the young men acquitting themselves creditably." The Salt Lake Stake presidency "felt especially blessed in ordaining the young to positions in the Priesthood."[60]

The duties of priests and teachers to ward teach, and deacons to care for meetinghouses, were not new. But with more and better-supervised quorums, the work was accomplished more effectively. And it was done by youths, giving them some priesthood training before adulthood so that, presumably, they would make better Melchizedek Priesthood bearers.

Members

The movement did cause a reformation among many Saints. Published epistles and sermons, better stake and ward organizations, closer apostolic supervision, more visiting by acting and ordained Aaronic Priesthood bearers, and clearer instructions and expectations helped members toe the line a little better. Probably more than a thousand members received new ward and stake positions through which to grow and serve. Wards lacking Sunday Schools, Mutuals, and Relief Societies organized them to aid and bless their members. Many men had priesthood meetings to attend now that they did not have before. Members not previously part of any ward or branch were now enrolled and at least noticed by some authorities. Sunday School children started to receive the sacrament weekly. Despite strong talk of "lopping off the dead branches," records show no notable increase in Church trials or excommunications. The reorganization movement "has had the influence of Waking Some up that were way off the line of their duty," noted a bishop's counselor in a tiny ward, who then added: "Nearly all the Branch has been rebaptized." Rebaptisms gave members opportunities to repent and reorder their living patterns.[61]

The 1877 reordering was the single most important priesthood analysis and redirecting since the priesthood restorations of forty-eight years earlier. Church history records but few major retoolings of priesthood operations. Those identified include the calling of the first ward bishops in Nauvoo in 1839, the multiplying of seventies units in 1844, the structuring of wards and quorum work in Salt Lake City in 1849, the systematizing of quorum work in 1908, the correlation effort of 1928, and modern correlation programs commenced in 1961. Only the last one compares with the comprehensiveness and magnitude of the 1877 changes.[62]

The reorganization of 1877 was a final testament by Brigham Young, who sought all his life to follow accurately Joseph Smith's teachings as to how priesthood ought to function in the Church. "The Church is more perfectly organized than ever before, perhaps with the exception of the general assembly at Kirtland, but in some things now we are more stable and complete than we were even then," observed John Taylor that September. The semi-gothic Assembly Hall, built 1877–80, still stands on Temple Square as an impressive granite-and-wood memorial of President Young's 1877 priesthood reorganization, his last major achievement as a prophet on earth.[63]

This article was originally published in BYU Studies 20, no. 1 (1979): 3–36, and *received a Mormon History Association "Best Article Award."*

NOTES

1. See bibliography in James B. Allen and Glen M. Leonard, *The Story of the Latter-day Saints* (Salt Lake City: Deseret Book, 1976), for discussion of the basic books about President Young; see also Dean C. Jessee, ed., *Letters of Brigham Young to His Sons* (Salt Lake City: Deseret Book, 1974); and special issues devoted to Brigham Young of the *Utah Historical Quarterly* 45 (Summer 1977) and of *BYU Studies* 18, no. 3 (1978).

   Priesthood studies include Leonard J. Arrington, *Great Basin Kingdom: An Economic History of the Latter-day Saints, 1830–1900* (1958; reprinted Lincoln: University of Nebraska Press, 1966); Leonard J. Arrington, *From Quaker to Latter-day Saint: Bishop Edwin D. Woolley* (Salt Lake City: Deseret Book, 1976); Dale F. Beecher, "The Office of Bishop: An Example of Organizational Development in the Church," *Task Papers in LDS History, No. 21* (Salt Lake City: Historical Department of The Church of Jesus Christ of Latter-day Saints, 1978); D. Michael Quinn, "The Mormon Hierarchy, 1832–1932: An American Elite" (PhD diss., Yale University, 1976); James N. Baumgarten, "The Role and Function of the Seventies in LDS Church History" (master's thesis, Brigham Young University, 1960); Gary L. Phelps, "Home Teaching: Attempts by the Latter-day Saints to Establish an Effective Program during the Nineteenth Century" (master's thesis, Brigham Young University, 1975); William G. Hartley, "Ordained and Acting Teachers in the Lesser Priesthood, 1851–1883," *BYU Studies* 16, no. 3 (1976): 375–98; William G. Hartley, "The Priesthood Reform Movement, 1908–1922," *BYU Studies* 13, no. 2 (1973): 137–56; and Donald G. Pace, "The LDS Presiding Bishopric, 1851–1888: An Administrative Study" (master's thesis, Brigham Young University, 1978).

   Among standard biographies of 1877 participants that fail to discuss the movement meaningfully are those for Wilford Woodruff, Erastus Snow, Charles C. Rich, Franklin D. Richards, Orson Hyde, Edward Hunter, John Taylor, William Budge, and Joseph F. Smith. Of Brigham Young's biographers, only Susa Young Gates and Leah D. Widtsoe, in *The Life Story of Brigham Young: Mormon Leader, Founder of Salt Lake City, and Builder of an Empire in the Uncharted Wastes of Western America* (London: Jarrolds, [1930]), recognized the Churchwide significance for the 1877 reorderings.

   Among standard Church or Utah histories, those by B. H. Roberts and Orson F. Whitney identify the stakes involved but fail to sense the vastness of the movement; the seminary and institute Church history texts, Russell R. Rich, *Ensign to the Nations: A History of the Church from 1846 to the Present* (Provo, UT: Brigham Young University, 1972), and William E. Berrett, *The Restored Church: A Brief History of the Growth and Doctrines of The Church of Jesus Christ of Latter-day Saints,* 10th ed. (Salt Lake City: Deseret Book, 1961), ignore the matter entirely; Eugene Campbell's chapter on ecclesiastical developments in Joel E. Ricks, ed., *The History of a Valley: Cache Valley, Utah–Idaho* (Logan, UT: Cache Valley Centennial Commission, 1956), and Lynn M. Hilton, ed., *The Story of Salt Lake Stake, 1847–1972* (Salt Lake City: Salt Lake Stake, 1972), two of the best stake studies ever written, fail to explore the local impact of the movement; of all the books written about the period, besides *The Story of the Latter-day Saints,* only James R. Clark, comp., in *Messages of the First Presidency of The Church of Jesus Christ of Latter-day Saints, 1833–1964,* 6 vols. (Salt Lake City: Bookcraft, 1965–75), properly credits the 1877 movement with "turning point" significance, 2:295 (see also pp. 283–95).

2. The Mormon History Association *Newsletter* for December 7, 1978, contains a summary of the critiques this paper received when it was read at the MHA session of the Western History Association meetings at Hot Springs, Arkansas, on October 12, 1978.

3. D. Michael Quinn, "The Mormon Succession Crisis of 1844," *BYU Studies* 16, no. 2 (1976): 187–233; see also Ronald K. Esplin's forthcoming PhD dissertation (Brigham Young University, 1980) will demonstrate strong continuity between Joseph Smith's and Brigham Young's presidencies. *[See Ronald K. Esplin, "The Emergence of Brigham Young and the Twelve to Mormon Leadership" (PhD diss., Brigham Young University, 1981; Provo, UT: BYU Studies, 2006).]*

4. Orson Pratt, sermon, May 20, 1877, in *Deseret News Weekly*, July 18, 1877.

5. Brigham Young, in *Journal of Discourses*, 26 vols. (Liverpool: Latter-day Saints' Book Depot, 1855–86), 18:357, April 6, 1877; Reed C. Durham Jr. and Steven H. Heath, *Succession in the Church* (Salt Lake City: Bookcraft, 1970), 73–77; Minutes of Bishops Meetings with the Presiding Bishopric, 1849–84 (cited hereafter as Bishops Minutes), October 19, 1876, Church History Library, The Church of Jesus Christ of Latter-day Saints, Salt Lake City; Salt Lake Stake to that point had jurisdiction over Salt Lake, Tooele, Davis, Morgan, Summit, and Wasatch counties, or one-third of Utah Church membership. Because as an Apostle Elder Hyde had withdrawn briefly from activity, his seniority basis was changed from his ordination date to his reinstatement date.

6. The 1852 census is found in "Report of Bishops in Utah Territory," October 6, 1852, Church History Library; 1877 data based on table 2 in text; see William G. Hartley, "Coming to Zion: Saga of the Gathering," *Ensign* 5 (July 1975): 14–18; see Arrington, *Great Basin Kingdom*; see Milton R. Hunter, *Brigham Young the Colonizer* (Salt Lake City: Deseret News Press, 1940); Richard Sherlock, "Mormon Migration and Settlement after 1875," *Journal of Mormon History* 2 (1975): 53–68; and *Deseret Evening News*, May 14, 1877.

7. Utah Stake Historical Record, June 2, 1877, Church History Library; Orson Pratt, sermon, May 20, 1877, in *Deseret News Weekly*, July 18, 1877; Franklin D. Richards, sermon, in *Deseret News Weekly*, August 25, 1877.

8. Mention of seventies serving on high councils is found in Bear Lake Stake Historical Record, August 25, 1877, Church History Library; Erastus Snow, in *Journal of Discourses*, 19:130, October 13, 1877; Davis Stake Historical Record, June 20, 1877, Church History Library.

9. For a list of the fifteen presiding bishops, see *Deseret Evening News*, July 3, 1877; a life sketch of William Budge is found in Journal History of the Church, January 5, 1877, Church History Library, microfilm copy in Harold B. Lee Library, Brigham Young University, Provo, Utah; Brigham Young's statement is in Parowan Stake Historical Record, April 18, 1877, Church History Library; John Taylor's is in Bishops Minutes, January 24, 1878; see also Pace, "LDS Presiding Bishopric," 58–66.

10. Orson Pratt, sermon, May 13, 1877, in *Deseret News Weekly*, May 30, 1877; Salt Lake Stake General Aaronic Priesthood Minutes 1857–77, March 6, 1875, Church History Library; Isaiah Moses Coombs, Diaries, June 5, 1877, microfilm, Church History Library; John Taylor, in *Journal of Discourses*, 19:53, June 17, 1877.

11. Bishops Minutes, September 6, 1877; Hartley, "Ordained and Acting Teachers."

12. Bear Lake Stake Historical Record, August 27, 1877.

13. Bishops Minutes, October 19, 1876; Bear Lake Stake Historical Record, August 26, 1877; Salt Lake Stake's high council handled trials for other stakes until the 1877 changes reduced the case load greatly, according to Anders W. Winberg, "Aeldste A. W. Winbergs Autobiografi," *Morgenstjernen* 4 (1885):157–60.

14. Brigham Young, Letter to Willard Young, May 23, 1877, Brigham Young Letterbook 14, typescript, Church History Library (cited hereafter as BY Letterbook).

15. John Taylor, in *Journal of Discourses*, 18:81, August 31, 1875; John Taylor, in *Journal of Discourses*, 19:55–56, June 17, 1877; John Taylor, in *Journal of Discourses*, 19:81, July 29, 1877; John Taylor, in *Journal of Discourses*, 19:124, October 7, 1877.

16. Joseph Smith Jr., *History of The Church of Jesus Christ of Latter-day Saints*, ed. B. H. Roberts, 2d ed. rev., 7 vols. (Salt Lake City: Deseret News, 1932–51), 4:601; Erastus Snow, in *Journal of Discourses*, 25:31, February 2, 1884.

17. Brigham Young, in *Journal of Discourses*, 9:269, April 6, 1862; Leonard J. Arrington, Feramorz Y. Fox, and Dean L. May, *Building the City of God: Community and Cooperation among the Mormons* (Salt Lake City: Deseret Book, 1976); more than half of the presidents or bishops listed in *Building the City of God* as being in charge of United Orders in 1874–75 became or continued as bishops in 1877, indicating no general repudiation of United Order leaders; Brigham Young Jr., Diary, April 7, 1877, Church History Library, in *Journal of Discourses*, 18:283.

18. Brigham Young Jr., Diary, March–April 1877, Church History Library; Brigham Young, in *Journal of Discourses*, 18:356, April 6, 1877.

19. Orson Pratt, sermon, May 13, 1877, in *Deseret News Weekly*, May 30, 1877.

20. Coombs, Diary, October 5, 1877.

21. Salt Lake Stake Historical Record Book, August 11, 1877, Church History Library.

22. Brigham Young, in *Journal of Discourses*, 19:43, June 17, 1877; Brigham Young, Letter to Willard Young, May 23, 1877, BY Letterbook 14.

23. Francis M. Lyman, Diary, book 8, summer and fall 1877, photocopy, Church History Library; Beaver Stake Historical Record, July 25, 1877, Church History Library.

24. Brigham Young to A. K. Thurber, January 20, 1877, BY Letterbook 16.

25. Franklin D. Richards, Diary, March 30 and April 4, 1877, microfilm, Church History Library; Francis M. Lyman, Diary, book 8, April 7, 1877.

26. *Deseret Evening News*, May 14, 1877; Richards, Diary, May 20, 1877; Brigham Young, Letter to Willard Young, May 23, 1877, BY Letterbook 14; Brigham Young, Letter to Joseph F. Smith, June 6, 1877, BY Letterbook 14; Brigham Young, Letter to Wilford Woodruff, June 12, 1877, BY Letterbook 14.

27. Brigham Young, Letter to D. W. Jones, June 28, 1877, BY Letterbook 14.

28. Brigham Young, Letter to William C. Staines, May 11, 1877, BY Letterbook 14; Richards, Diary, June 1, 1877; Brigham Young, Letter to Wilford Woodruff, June 12, 1877, BY Letterbook 14; Young Jr., Diary, June 20, 1877; Brigham Young, Letter to W. E. Pack, August 6, 1877, BY Letterbook 15; *Deseret News Weekly*, September 3, 1877.

29. Brigham Young, Letter to "Dear Brother," June 9, 1877, BY Letterbook 14.

30. Brigham Young, Letter to Joel Grover, June 14, 1877, BY Letterbook 14.

31. *Deseret Evening News*, August 29, 1877; Richards Diary, July 10–16, 1877.

32. Bear Lake Stake Historical Record, August 25, 1877; *Deseret Evening News*, August 20, 1877.

33. Tooele Stake Historical Record and Manuscript History, Church History Library.

34. See table 2; Ogden Ward boundaries, established by President Young, "causd a great deal of dissatisfaction" and were readjusted in December 1878. Weber Stake Manuscript History, December 8, 1878, Church History Library.

35. Sevier Stake Manuscript History, June 14 and July 14, 1877, Church History Library; Brigham Young General Minutes Collection, May 21, 1877, Church History Library; Young Jr., Diary, July 1, 1877.

36. Sevier Stake Manuscript History, June 14, 1877.

37. Richards, Diary, July 13 and 14, 1877.

38. Lyman, Diary, book 8, June 23 and 24, 1877; Richards, Diary, June 25, 1877.

39. Richards, Diary, June 25, 1877; Parowan Stake Manuscript History, April 18, 1877, Church History Library; Salt Lake Stake Historical Record Book, 1877 section on ward reorganizations; Kanab Stake Historical Record, Book A, December 8 and 9, 1877, Church History Library.

40. Beaver Stake Historical Record, July 25–27, 1877.

41. "Circular of the First Presidency, July 11, 1877," in Clark, *Messages of the First Presidency*, 2:283.

42. Bishops Minutes, August 23, 1877; "Epistle of the Twelve Apostles and Counselors, to The Church of Jesus Christ of Latter-day Saints in All the World," September 1877, in Clark, *Messages of the First Presidency*, 2:301–2.

43. Salt Lake Stake Historical Record Book, August through December 1877; Bishops Minutes, August 9, 1877; *Deseret Evening News*, December 28, 1877: Salt Lake Stake General Aaronic Priesthood Minutes, May 6, 1876; Bishops Minutes, August 31, 1877; Salt Lake Stake Manuscript History, November 21, 1877.

44. Box Elder Stake Historical Record, August to December 1877, Church History Library; Bear Lake Stake Historical Record, August to December 1877; Morgan Stake Historical Record, February 17, 1878, Church History Library; Juab Stake Manuscript History, January 19 and 20, 1878, Church History Library; Beaver Stake Historical Record, October 27, 1877; *Deseret Evening News*, December 7, 1877; Cache Stake Historical Record, December 20, 1877, Church History Library; *Deseret News Weekly*, October 24, 1877.

45. Coombs, Diary, August 13–15, 1877; Bishops Minutes, September 6, 1877; Erastus Snow, in *Journal of Discourses*, 19:131, October 13, 1877.

46. Arrington, Fox, and May, *Building the City of God*, 154, 171, 215, 269; Richards, Diary, July 24, 1877; Davis Stake Historical Record, September 8, 1877; Frederick Kesler, Journal, book 4, July 5, 1877, Special Collections, J. Willard Marriott Library, University of Utah, Salt Lake City; Richards, Diary, July 11 and 15, 1877; Millard Stake Historical Record, July 21, 1877, Church History Library; Beaver Stake Historical Record, July 26 and September 29, 1877; Parowan Stake Historical Record, August 12, 1877; Lyman Diary, October 23, 1877; Sevier Stake Historical Report, November 3, 1877; Summit Stake Historical Record, November 11, 1877, Church History Library; St. George Manuscript History, October 14, 1877, Church History Library; Beaver Stake Historical Record, July 26, 1877.

47. A. Glen Humphreys, "Missionaries to the Saints," *BYU Studies* 17, no. 1 (1976): 74–100; Historical Records and Manuscript Histories for the various stakes.

48. *Deseret News Weekly*, September 3, 1877.

49. *Deseret News Weekly,* September 3, 1877; "Epistle of the Twelve Apostles," September 1877, in Clark, *Messages of the First Presidency,* 2:300.

50. Young Jr., Diary, April 1, 1877; an entry for that same date in Charles Walker, Diary, microfilm, Church History Library, says the Twelve would "lose their crown and others be appointed" if they did not embrace the United Order; Richards Diary, June 25, July 28, August 2 and 19, 1877.

51. John Taylor, in *Journal of Discourses,* 19:122, October 13, 1877.

52. "A Revelation given through President John Taylor, April 14, 1883," in Clark, *Messages of the First Presidency,* 2:354. This revelation ratified instructions regarding seventies reorganizations given the day before (352–54); see also Baumgarten, "Role and Function of Seventies," 43.

53. Quoted by Joseph Young, First Council of the Seventy Minutes, November 21, 1877, Church History Library.

54. First Council of the Seventy Minutes, August 31, 1877.

55. Jens C. A. Weibye, Diary, July 9, 1877, Church History Library.

56. Joseph E. Taylor of Salt Lake Stake presidency, Bishops Minutes, November 29, 1877.

57. Dennis H. Smith, "Formal Reporting Systems of The Church of Jesus Christ of Latter-day Saints, 1830–1925" (master's thesis, Brigham Young University, 1976), 38, 40, 120–21. Ward splits did "derange" ward records in Salt Lake Stake. Stake Historical Record Book, August 11, 1877.

58. "Most of these buildings followed the lead of the Assembly Hall by adapting elements of the Gothic Revival and other Victorian styles in their architecture, in contrast to the earlier tabernacles which were more in the tradition of the earlier Georgian, Federal, and Greek Revival styles," Paul L. Anderson, "Mormon Tabernacle Architecture: From Meetinghouse to Cathedral," unpublished lecture, Utah Heritage Foundation Lecture Series, Assembly Hall, April 12, 1979.

59. John Taylor, in *Journal of Discourses,* 19:140–41, October 14, 1877.

60. Weber Stake, Hooper and West wards, Elders Quorum Minutes, 1875–86, September 23, 1877, Church History Library; *Deseret News Weekly,* October 24, 1877; Cache Stake Manuscript History, November 3 and 4, 1877; Salt Lake Stake Manuscript History, November 29, 1877.

61. Utah Stake Historical Record, June 3, 1877; Benjamin H. Tolman Jr., Journal, December 1877, Church History Library. In a number of wards and stakes, only the rebaptized were called to positions. In Beaver, "teachers should not be taken from among those who have not been rebaptized." Beaver Stake Historical Record, October 27, 1877.

62. Baumgarten, "Role and Function of Seventies," 31–33; Beecher, "Office of Bishop," 14; Bishops Minutes, March 25, 1849; Hartley, "Priesthood Reform Movement," 137–56; Richard O. Cowan and Wilson K. Andersen, *The Living Church: The Unfolding of the Programs and Organization of The Church of Jesus Christ of Latter-day Saints during the Twentieth Century* (Provo, UT: BYU Publications, 1974), 214, 541–66; Richard O. Cowan, "The Priesthood-Auxiliary Movement, 1928–1938," *BYU Studies* 19, no. 1 (1978): 106–20.

63. John Taylor, in *Journal of Discourses,* 19:146, October 21, 1877; "Epistle of the Twelve Apostles," September 1877, in Clark, *Messages of the First Presidency,* 2:298.

11

The Seventies in the 1880s
Revelations and Reorganizing

"THESE 76 QUORUMS WERE ALL TORN to pieces." That disturbing report card for seventies quorums came from Joseph Young, senior president of all seventies in The Church of Jesus Christ of Latter-day Saints, in January 1880.[1] Such a disrupted state could not long continue, and two "thus saith the lord" revelations to Church President John Taylor—on October 13, 1882, and April 14, 1883—triggered major reconstructions of the work and the quorums of the seventies.[2]

What circumstances prompted the revelations and what responses did they receive? Why was the then-current seventies quorum system malfunctioning? What did the revelations teach and mean in their 1880s context? How fully were the revelations' instructions implemented? How did the First Council of the Seventy interrelate with the First Presidency and the Quorum of the Twelve Apostles regarding seventies' work? Why was the vacant First Quorum of Seventy *not* recreated? What differences did the revelations and restructurings make to seventies' work? What does this episode teach us about the role continuous revelation plays in priesthood history? What seventies problems were left unresolved?

This study draws heavily on seventies' records—those of the First Council and of individual quorums—and is thus biased toward those sources. The diaries of Apostles Franklin D. Richards and Brigham Young Jr. helped compensate for the First Presidency and Quorum of the Twelve minutes, unavailable for the 1880s.

THE SEVENTIES' BEGINNINGS

On February 28, 1835, Joseph Smith announced an unrecorded revelation about the seventies, established a new Melchizedek Priesthood office, and created a distinctively structured quorum of seventy men. The seventies, he taught, were to be "traveling quorums, to go into all the earth, whithersoever the Twelve Apostles shall call them." A month later, a revelation on priesthood (D&C 107) specified that seventies were to "preach the Gospel," "be especial witnesses unto Gentiles in all the world," be a "quorum equal in authority to that of the Twelve," "act under the direction of the Twelve ... in building up the Church and regulating all the affairs of the same in all nations," and to "have seven presidents" chosen "from their own ranks" who "are to choose other seventy ... until seven times seventy, if the labor in the vineyard of necessity requires it." The Twelve were "to call upon the Seventy when they need assistance, instead of any others." Similar to the Twelve, the seventies had "responsibility to travel among all nations."[3]

Joseph Smith further explained that seventies could be multiplied until "there are one hundred and forty-four thousand," should be taken from elders quorums, and "are not to be High Priests." Seventies who had previously been ordained high priests were in office "not according to the order of heaven" and were replaced. During the 1830s, a second and a third quorum were organized. In October 1844 general conference, Church members voted "that all in the Elders' Quorums under the age of thirty-five" become seventies, so that by the time of the exodus from Nauvoo, thirty-five seventies' quorums had been created.[4]

To provide leadership for quorums two through ten, the First Quorum divided itself into nine, seven-man presidencies, leaving the seven senior presidents of the First Quorum with no rank-and-file quorum members after October 1844. These seven men—the First Council of the Seventy—presided over *all* seventies and were sustained as Church General Authorities.[5]

THE SEVENTIES' SITUATION IN THE 1880s

By 1870 the Nauvoo-instituted policy that a seventy belonged to his original quorum for as long as he was a seventy, no matter where he lived, was creating problems. Utah's settlement process scattered members and presidents of the same quorum. Although some quorums kept track of their scattering sheep, others dwindled to one or two presidents and a handful of findable members. Seventies from different quorums who lived in the same community sometimes grouped themselves into an unofficial, local, "mass" quorum. By late 1880, it had become "impossible to reach all the Seventies and for the President to teach their members in a quorum capacity, or that they can be brought together as quorums."[6]

When the decade of the 1880s opened, not only were quorum members scattered and some units disorganized but the quorums had shrunk. Normally when members died, apostatized, or became high priests, their vacancies were filled. But the priesthood reorganization of 1877 turned hundreds of seventies into high priests to fill bishopric and stake positions, then ordered a moratorium on ordaining new seventies—to the great disappointment of Senior President Joseph Young.[7]

Ideally, seventies quorums were training and recruiting grounds for future missionaries, but in practice a man received a mission call first and then was ordained a seventy. As a result, by 1880 the quorums had very little official missionary work to do. "In the wards," one seventies leader said, "there was nothing for them to do, and they became tarnished." A March 1881 report shows that in at least two stakes the seventies had not met together for "several years."[8]

Another problem plaguing the seventies units by 1880 was gray hair. The First Council itself contained only old men. (See table 1.) Horace S. Eldredge at sixty-three was the youngest and Joseph Young, the oldest, was eighty-two. The others were John Van Cott, sixty-five; Jacob Gates, sixty-eight; Levi W. Hancock, seventy-six; and Henry Harriman, seventy-five. Albert P. Rockwood had died in 1879 at age seventy-five, leaving one vacancy.

In April 1880, eight young men became council "Alternates" by advice of President John Taylor and vote of the general conference. These alternates were expected to carry the load laid down by three aged council members living in southern Utah—Elders Harriman, Gates, and Hancock. In addition, twenty-six-year-old William W. Taylor, son of President John Taylor, filled a council vacancy. These nine new men gave the seventies' work new vigor. Seeking even more helpers, the First Council talked about filling up its own First Quorum, vacant since Nauvoo.[9]

Scripturally, seventies exist to do missionary work. However, the council possessed no policy-making responsibility for proselyting. The Twelve,

TABLE 1.

First Council of the Seventy, 1879–89

Members 1879	Death date	Replacement members	Replacement date
Joseph Young	7/16/1881	William W. Taylor (d. 8/8/1884)	4/07/1880
Levi W. Hancock	6/10/1882	Abraham H. Cannon (ord. Apostle 10/7/1889)	10/09/1882
Henry Harriman	——	Seymour B. Young	10/14/1882
Albert P. Rockwood	11/26/1879	Christian D. Fjeldsted	4/28/1884
Horace S. Eldredge	9/06/1888	John Morgan	10/07/1884
Jacob Gates	——	Brigham H. Roberts	10/08/1888
John Van Cott	2/18/1883		

without asking for input from the council, determined when, where, and how many missionaries should be sent out, and then asked the council to supply the men. First Council minutes show that the Twelve, after Brigham Young's death, stepped up the seventies' missionary responsibilities and "were now throwing the labor of preaching the Gospel upon this body." Council records in May 1879 say President John Taylor was "calling upon us constantly" for missionary names.[10]

The First Council, when soliciting missionary nominations, looked mainly to the Salt Lake Stake, where half of all seventies quorums were located. These quorum presidencies met in a Seventies' Council Meeting with the First Council every other week from 1879 (or earlier) to 1884. The meetings were "for preaching missionary purposes" and included short impromptu talks, sermons, quorum reports, and First Council requests for missionary names.[11] Usually thirty to thirty-five different quorums had at least one presidency member there, so missionary business was easy to parcel out. In places beyond Salt Lake, council visits and letters solicited additional nominees.

TEMPORARY STAKE AND WARD SEVENTIES PRESIDENTS

Because missionary demand exceeded supply, the First Council felt frustrated by the chaotic state of seventies units. In fall 1880, after exploring ways to communicate with scattered seventies, the council adopted a new organizational structure that established ward and stake seventies' presidents. A ward president, they reasoned, could become acquainted with and list all seventies residing in his ward, no matter what their official quorums were. If presidents in all wards did likewise, then practically every seventy could be located by ward and identified by quorum. A stake president of seventies could coordinate the ward presidents' work. After testing in the Salt Lake Stake, the new plan won approval from the Twelve and the First Presidency. Early in 1881, ward and stake seventies presidents were called and instructed. They were considered temporary, not replacements for or competitors with existing quorums and presidents.[12]

During this change, Joseph Young died on July 16, 1881. Eulogies portrayed him as a devout, spiritually minded man whose instructions were "rich in the spirit and power of God," a man of "superior wisdom, talent, and ability." By seniority, ailing Levi Hancock became the new senior president. Joseph's vacant slot in the council was not filled until October 1882 by Abraham H. Cannon, twenty-three-year-old son of George Q. Cannon, first counselor in the First Presidency.[13]

The ward and stake plan's primary purposes were "to expedite the furnishing of missionaries and awaken Seventies." The new plan worked well, although some quorums resisted the ward presidents. Newly appointed presidents were instructed that seventies should meet at least monthly, a census of seventies should be sent to the First Council, and families of missionaries must be cared for. Each ward leader was told to compile a list of potential missionaries in his ward by nationality, have the bishop verify the men's worthiness and ability to go, send the list to be cleared by the stake seventies president and stake president, and then forward it to the First Council, usually preceding the twice-yearly general conferences. Approved nominees received form letters from the council asking if they could accept mission calls, provide for their families during the absence, and pay transportation costs. Nominees answered by letter or in person.[14]

One sampling, the verbal and written responses of April 1 and 2, 1882, illustrates the acceptance rate.[15] Of seventy-eight men responding, the First Council approved thirty-five for missions and rejected forty-three. The average age of nominees was forty-four. In this and other samplings, the main reasons why the council turned down men for missions were age, lack of finances, and personal matters the men themselves raised—debts, farming on shares, unable to support family, feeble health, supporting someone else on a mission, an ill relative, or no one to run the business or farm. Names approved by the council were forwarded to the Twelve, and the Twelve called some, rejected some, and ignored some, according to William Taylor:

> It had been laid upon the First Council of Seventies to furnish missionaries from this body, but had not been able to respond to all the calls made upon them, which had given rise to some degree of censure. That many of the Seventies to whom they had written letters had been excused from taking missions, not being financially prepared, others through sickness and other causes. He thought it would be advisable to address a communication to the Presidency and the Twelve, that this matter might be laid before them.[16]

From 1880 to 1883, while the ward and stake system operated, the First Council tried to negotiate the restructuring and reviving of the official seventy-six quorums. In November 1882, for example, President Horace Eldredge asked the First Presidency if the seventies should be consolidated from seventy-six to fifty quorums, for which they had enough manpower, or if the seventy-six units could be filled up? He also asked about filling up the First Quorum. No answers to his inquiries are recorded.[17] However, the First Council's periodic pleas to reform the quorums caused the First Presidency to wrestle with the matter—preparation for the 1882 and 1883 revelations that brought solutions.

REVELATION OF OCTOBER 13, 1882

The revelation John Taylor received on October 13, 1882, is best known for calling Heber J. Grant and George Teasdale to apostleships and Seymour B. Young, Joseph's son, to replace Levi Hancock, who had died the previous June, leaving a vacant position in the First Council presidency. After Seymour Young became a polygamist, as requested by the revelation, the council had three youthful workhorses with their famous fathers' surnames—Taylor, Cannon, and Young.[18]

Two lesser known parts of the revelation also affected the seventies. One part said the Twelve should "call to your aid any assistance that you may require from among the Seventies to assist you in your labors in

Members of the Quorum of the Twelve Apostles in 1882. Courtesy Church Archives.

introducing and maintaining the Gospel among the Lamanites throughout the land. And then let High Priests be selected, under the direction of the First Presidency, to preside over the various organizations that shall exist among this (Lamanite) people."[19]

Leaders responded quickly to this command. Isaiah Coombs, a seventy in Payson heard about the Lamanite work in a November 1882 stake conference and commented in his diary:

> Bro [George] Reynolds says this last Revelation marks a new epoch in our history. That was my view. It shows that the fulness of the Gentiles long looked for has come in, and that henceforth the burden of our labors will be directed to the House of Israel commencing with the Lamanites by whom we are surrounded and who manifest a great anxiety in the matter. Some of the Twelve are going out immediately among them and a majority of the quorum will move out in the same direction early in the Spring. The key is to be turned to that people by the Twelve, and the Seventies will follow up immediately to continue the work among them.[20]

President of the Twelve Wilford Woodruff told a Kaysville audience on December 10, 1882, that "we have now [after a half century of preaching to Gentiles] been commanded to turn to a branch of the house of Israel. Here are the Lamanites, thousands and thousands of them surrounding us. They look to us for the Gospel of Christ. It is our duty to go to them and organize them, and preach to them." He added that "We (the Twelve Apostles, Seventies and others) are called to go forth to preach the Gospel to the Lamanites and organize them. I am glad of it. I have felt for a long time that we should turn our attention to them."[21]

In his 1883 diary, Apostle Franklin D. Richards traced the Twelve's response to the Lamanite instruction. In a March meeting of the First Presidency and the Twelve, he noted, "conversation turned on missionary labor among Indians." In late April, Apostle Teasdale reached Fort Gibson in the Cherokee Nation. By May plans were formulated to proselyte among the "Northern tribes of Indians." Apostle Francis M. Lyman reached the Uintah Basin Indians by late May. "I feel awakened to get out among the Indians of the North," Elder Richards confessed. By June plans called for Apostle Lorenzo Snow to visit the Shoshoni, Bannock, and Nez Perce Indians at

Fort Hall, Idaho, and for Apostle Moses Thatcher to contact the Shoshonis and Crows in the Wind River Mountains. In July men left for the Crow reservation. On October 31, Apostle Teasdale reported on his Indian Territory mission.[22]

After initial enthusiasm among the Twelve, the missions received less attention, although its Committee on Indian Affairs was functioning five years later, in 1888. Available records do not indicate that the First Council or any sizeable group of seventies became part of the Lamanite missions as stipulated in the 1882 revelation.[23]

The 1882 revelation also commanded priesthood bearers and all members to "purify themselves" and to fully organize every priesthood quorum, and that leaders "inquire into the standing and fellowship of all my Holy Priesthood in their several Stakes." It said for all "to repent of all their sins and shortcomings, of their covetousness and pride and self will, and of all their iniquities wherein they sin against me; and to seek with all humility to fulfill my law." Heads of families were warned "to put their houses in order," to "purify themselves before me," and "to purge out iniquity from their households."[24]

The reformation call received immediate response from the Saints, including seventies. At the biweekly general seventies meetings in Salt Lake City, speakers mentioned that the revelation made them introspective and repentant.[25] William Taylor reported on January 3, 1883, that during his visit to stakes and wards he "found a general desire to improve" and "a feeling that the Seventies expect a chastisement if they do not repent of their pride, self will, and covetousness. Many of the brethren hold the revelations as a great blessing and are endeavoring to take a course that is acceptable to the Lord and feel the necessity of purifying themselves and of setting their families in order."[26]

Leaders announced that purification meant, among other things, living the Word of Wisdom. First Council records show that there was definite need for Word of Wisdom adherence, particularly regarding alcohol. From 1879 to 1882, the First Council cracked down on some seventies who were habitually drunk, and on those who operated liquor stores. The council urged seventies in the wards to help the youth avoid the saloons. Word of Wisdom observance soon became a key part of the seventies' reorganization program.[27]

INSTRUCTION AND REVELATION OF APRIL 14, 1883

The 1882 revelation instructed the Twelve to "assist in organizing the Seventies." Subsequently, the Twelve and First Council talked, at least informally, about reorganization methods. On April 13, 1883, the First Presidency, the Twelve, and the First Council met together in President John Taylor's office and discussed "the best method of filling up the quorums of the Seventies and of making the organization of the Seventies the most effective." President Taylor started the meeting by defining the duties of seventies and of the First Council. Next, his counselor George Q. Cannon

President John Taylor and the Twelve were instructed by revelation to organize the seventies by filling the quorums and making the organizations more effective. Courtesy Perry Special Collections.

and Apostles Woodruff, Richards, and Erastus Snow spoke on "the necessity of the quorums being fully organized and acting" in order. The frail Horace Eldredge was in California, but Presidents Harriman, Gates, Taylor, Cannon, and Young were present. According to Seymour Young, the First Council "suggested plans where there were places to fill up in the quorums and of ordaining new members." Attenders also discussed replacing John Van Cott, who had died two months before. Apostle Richards called the session "a lengthy sitting, interesting, and satisfactory."[28]

John Taylor adjourned the meeting until the next morning, Saturday, so he could take the matter "under advisement." That afternoon, his First Council member-son William W. Taylor wrote out "father's views on the organization of the Seventies. Bro. George Reynolds completed this labor and the document was then presented to and approved by his [John Taylor's] counselors."[29]

The next morning, Saturday, April 14, the three groups met again at John Taylor's office. First, George Reynolds read a set of instructions called "conclusions and directions of the Presidency as to method of reorganizing the Quorums of Seventies." Then came a surprise. The brethren read "a *Revelation* given today [that morning] through Pres. John Taylor approving our consideration and conclusion on this subject." Thus, the seventies and the Church received a two-part document that day: *Instructions,* and a *Revelation* sanctioning the *Instructions.*[30]

The *Instructions* first addressed the critical matter of recreating the First Quorum: "In the organization of these quorums in October, 1844, there were ten quorums, each provided with seven presidents, which presidents constituted the First Quorum of Seventies, and of which the First Seven Presidents of the Seventies were members, and over which they presided." But because seventies had greatly increased, "these regulations will not apply to the present circumstances." Further, although the First Quorum had not functioned since 1844, "it would seem there are duties devolving upon its members, as a quorum, that may require their official action." A new method of filling the First Quorum was then explained: "The First Quorum of Seventies may be composed of the First Seven Presidents of the Seventies, and the senior presidents of the first sixty-four quorums. These may form the Seventy referred to [in] the Book of Doctrine and Covenants, and may act in an official capacity as the First Quorum of the Seventies."

Senior presidents of other quorums beyond the first sixty-four "may meet with the First Quorum in their assemblies in any other than an official capacity." When any First Quorum members are absent, presidents of other quorums "can act in the place of such members with the First Quorum."

The First Council finally had official clearance to refill their own quorum, but such action, of necessity, took a back seat to organizing the other quorums.

The *Instructions,* bearing the First Presidency's signatures, ordered a badly needed reorganization of seventies quorums. It called for a geographical method of relocating and refilling existing seventies' quorums: "The headquarters of the different quorums, and the records thereof, may be distributed throughout the various Wards and Stakes." Such distribution should be based on "the number of the Priesthood residing in such locations." Vacancies in the realigned quorums, either in presidency or membership, "can be filled by the ordination of persons residing in the locality" of each quorum. Men transferring to the realigned quorums must bring certificates of standing from the quorum they were leaving and a certificate "of good standing from the Bishop of the Ward to which they belong." Problems about quorum presidents should be reported to the First Council "who may suspend such presidents, if their conduct seem to justify it, pending the actions of the First Quorum." Seventies dropped from fellowship by quorums "should be reported to the High Council having jurisdiction."

The second part of the document, the revelation, came in response to President John Taylor's prayer, "Show unto us Thy will, O Lord, concerning the organization of the Seventies," after presenting the *Instructions* before the Lord for confirmation or disapproval:

> What ye have written is my will, and is acceptable unto me: and furthermore, Thus saith the Lord unto the First Presidency, unto the Twelve, unto the Seventies and unto all my holy Priesthood, let not your hearts be troubled, neither be ye concerned about the management and organization of my Church and Priesthood and the accomplishment of my work. Fear me and observe my laws and I will reveal unto you, from time to time, through the channels that I have appointed, everything that shall be necessary for the future development and perfection of my Church, for the adjustment and rolling forth of my kingdom, and for the building up and the establishment of my Zion. For ye are my Priesthood and I am your God. Even so. Amen.[31]

"These instructions have met our views," said Seymour Young. "God is determined to have a people pure in heart."[32] George Q. Cannon of the First Presidency felt "great joy and satisfaction," adding that "he had for some years felt dissatisfied with the condition of the Seventies." Apostle Richards observed that "the Lord has signified that he is pleased with their organization," and said the labor now facing the seventies was "to gather up all who belong to these quorums" and to "make a more formidable organization than has ever before been in the Church."[33] Three thousand copies of the *Revelation* and *Instructions* were printed and distributed to seventies and stake leaders.[34]

Other council members were out of town, so the three newest members, Presidents Taylor, Cannon, and Young, hammered out the nuts and bolts of the geographic restructurings and submitted a master plan to the Twelve. The trio developed four objectives: (1) to redistribute the quorums fairly evenly throughout the stakes, (2) to convince seventies to join the nearest quorum and to surrender memberships in quorums farther away, (3) to fill up quorums by transferring or newly ordaining seventies, and (4) to create new quorums in areas needing them. On May 9 and 12, the Twelve approved this plan.[35]

To redistribute quorums, the council calculated that seventies ought to be two-sevenths of any stake's total Melchizedek Priesthood bearers. Using the two-sevenths yardstick, they figured out how many seventies and quorums each stake needed. Then the council identified which quorums were surplus and shuffled those units' record books to stakes needing quorums. When possible, quorum headquarters were not moved. Between May and October 1883, the council visited stakes to move quorums and call presidencies where needed. Elder Gates helped reorganize and ordain in stakes south of Millard Stake, and President Eldredge, back from California, helped the trio reorganize the rest.[36]

Salt Lake Stake with 1,100 seventies (one-fourth of the Church's total) was headquarters for forty quorums (half the Church's total). By ratio the stake deserved only seventeen quorums, so the council transferred out more than twenty quorum record books. Due to gaps in quorum records, we can positively identify only ten of the transferred quorums. (See table 2.) Quorums remaining within the stake received fixed geographic boundaries that encompassed from one to a handful of wards, sometimes matching the boundaries of elders quorums created in 1877.[37]

Late in 1883, the council published an up-to-date list of every quorum, its senior president, and his address. At least fourteen headquarters had been moved.

With seventy-six quorums geographically located, the council next assigned seventies to local quorums. The local quorum presidency was assigned to preside over all seventies in their area, whether they belonged to the local quorum or not, so that "all Seventies will have someone to look after them and they can be conveniently reached."[38] Newly ordained missionaries simply joined their closest quorum. Men belonging to an outside quorum were urged, but not required, to "join the Quorums where they are located." The reorganized Twenty-first Quorum, which moved its

TABLE 2
Location of Seventies Quorums, October 1883

Stake	Total 70s Quorums	Quorum Number	Quorum Pres. Location	Transfer from (1883)*
Bear Lake	4	6	St. Charles	
		11	Paris	
		18	Franklin	Salt Lake
		52	Malad	Provo
Beaver	1		Beaver	
Box Elder	3	5	Honeyville	
		58	Brigham City	
		59	Willard	
Cache	8	7	Weston	
		17	Smithfield	
		28	Wellsville	Salt Lake
		32	Providence	Salt Lake
		39	Richmond	
		40	Logan	
		62	Hyrum	Salt Lake
		64	Logan	
Davis	4	55	Kaysville	
		56	Farmington	
		70	Bountiful	
		74	Farmington	
Juab		49	Nephi	
		71	Nephi	
Millard	2	21	Scipio	Fillmore
		42	Fillmore	
Morgan	1	35	Morgan	
Parowan	2	63	Cedar City	
		69	Parowan	
St. George	3	9	Toquerville	
		25	Pine Valley	
		29	St. George	

Source: FCM list, October 21, 1883.
* Other quorums may have transferred but these are the ones that can be documented.

Stake	Total 70s Quorums	Quorum Number	Quorum Pres. Location	Transfer from (1883)*
Salt Lake	17	1, 2		
		4, 5		
		8, 10		
		13, 14		
		16, 23		
		24, 30		
		33, 57		
		62, 72		
Sanpete	6	26	Fairview	Salt Lake
		37	Wales	Salt Lake
		47	Ephraim	
		48	Manti	
		65	Gunnison	Salt Lake
		66	Mt. Pleasant	
Sevier	2	36	Richfield	
		41	Monroe	Salt Lake
Summit	2	22	Wanship	Salt Lake
		27	Coalville	
Tooele	2	31	Tooele	
		43	Tooele	
Utah	10	15	Santaquin	Salt Lake
		19	Spanish Fork	
		34	Provo	
		44	Pleasant Grove	Utah County
		46	Payson	
		50	Spanish Fork	
		51	Springville	
		67	American Fork	
		68	Lehi	
Wasatch	1	20	Heber	
Weber	6	38	North Ogden	
		53	Ogden	
		54	West Weber	
		60	Ogden	
		75	Huntsville	Ogden
		76	Ogden	

headquarters and records from Fillmore to Scipio, illustrates how badly the geographic system was needed: the new members of the Scipio quorum had previously belonged to fifteen different quorums.[39] Some men found it hard to surrender their standings in their old quorums. Some regretted losing seniority in their former quorums.

Quorum presidents living away from their quorum headquarters were asked to surrender their presidencies and join the local quorums. Absentee presidents were termed "a detriment instead of an advantage" to their units. If such men insisted on keeping their original quorum memberships, the men could "be retained as members of the Quorum only, and others be set apart to act as the presidents." The council, when calling presidents for the revised quorums, tried to choose men who had been presidents in their previous quorums. The council also tried to call presidents from different wards encompassed by the quorum.[40]

FILLING QUORUMS AND CREATING NEW ONES

The reorganized quorums had many vacancies. In September 1883, the First Presidency and the Twelve authorized the council to "adopt any method which in their wisdom they may think proper" to recruit new seventies.[41] One way was to round up unenrolled seventies living near a given quorum and enroll them. Then, elders were hand-picked to become seventies, elders who it was hoped met Apostle Wilford Woodruff's criteria that "every man ordained to the calling of a Seventy should have heart, spirit and desire enough about him to go forth when called and to preach the Gospel among the nations, and without this spirit he should not be ordained."[42]

Soon, "many young men were being ordained." At Scipio, for example, twenty-seven elders joined the Twenty-first Quorum in 1883–84. Their average age was thirty-five. Presidents Cannon, Taylor, and Young traveled almost every Sunday in early 1884 to meet with seventies units, and they ordained twenty to forty new seventies each weekend. By April 1884, the council reported that the seventy-six quorums and presidencies were "nearly all filled up." Only First Council members could set apart a senior president of a quorum, but other presidents could be set apart and new seventies ordained by the quorum's senior president with the council's permission.[43]

During the 1880s, the cut-off age for missionaries dropped from fifty-five to forty-five. Some quorums, needing more potential missionaries, wanted to prune off elderly members. The First Council, lacking authority to make high priests of older seventies, discussed the problem with the First Presidency and then announced that old seventies "have the consent of the First Presidency ... to be recommended to the High Priests Quorum."[44] How many men were "promoted out" this way is not documented.

Once quorums were filled and officered, the First Council began creating new quorums where stakes needed them. Table 3 shows twenty-five new units created between 1884 and 1888. Elder George Q. Cannon noted in 1883 that seventies "would continue to increase until they would number one hundred and forty-four thousand ... in fact there was no limit." But by April 1888, after the 101st Quorum was formed, the Twelve ordered another moratorium "for the present" on ordinations except to fill vacancies.[45]

Along with staffing and reorganizing work, the First Council also performed its normal supervisory functions, issued circular letters of instructions, visited stakes and, after 1884, communicated with some quorums by telephone. In 1884 the council created three large districts encompassing all the quorums: William Taylor supervised the First District with twenty-six quorums; Seymour B. Young the Second District with twenty-three; and Abraham Cannon the Third District with thirty-three. When Elder Taylor died suddenly in mid-1884, his supervisory role in the First District passed to newly ordained John Morgan. Each supervisor tried to visit the stakes in his district annually to hold seventies conferences. Their reports punctuate the council's minutes after January 1884.[46]

In 1887 the First Council conducted a survey and found that the forty-four units responding averaged sixty-four men per unit, twenty-four in attendance at monthly quorum meetings, two theological classes per month, and three men on missions.[47]

PURIFYING THE SEVENTIES

The 1882 revelation also called for a purification, so the council added a reform campaign to the reorganizing movement. The purification vehicle proved to be the bishop's recommend. Every seventy, even the council members, had to obtain and submit to his quorum president a certificate signed by his bishop verifying his standing in the Church.

A big hurdle for many was the stipulation that they must obey the Word of Wisdom, a law not strictly enforced in the past. At an 1883 Fillmore Stake conference, Apostle Francis M. Lyman and First Council members William Taylor and Abraham Cannon called for men to be ordained as seventies.

TABLE 3

New Seventies Quorums Created, 1884–1888

Year created	Quorum number	Location
1884	77	Ogden, Utah
	78	Oakley, Idaho
	79	Montpelier, Idaho
	80	Spring City, Utah
	81	Emery County, Utah
	82	Grass Valley, Utah
1885	83	East Arizona
	84	Bannock, Idaho
	85	Kanab, Utah
	86	Panguitch, Utah
	87	Plain City, Utah
	88	Oneida, Idaho
1886	89	St. Joseph, Arizona
	90	Maricopa, Arizona
	91	Emery County, Utah
	92	San Luis, Colorado
1887	93	Salt Lake City, Utah
	94	Salt Lake City, Utah
	95	Salt Lake City, Utah
	96	Wasatch County, Utah
	97	Uinta County, Utah
	98	Weber County, Utah
	99	St. George, Utah
1888	100	Davis County, Utah
	101	Emery County, Utah

Compiled from "Stake and Mission Index to Numbered Seventies Quorums, 1857–1972," Register of Collections, typescript, Church History Library.

At age twenty-three, Abraham H. Cannon filled a vacancy in the First Council of the Seventy, and by age thirty he became an Apostle. Courtesy Church Archives.

Each ward submitted names, but "after a rigid examination in regard to keeping the Word of Wisdom and other duties, but few were found qualified." By contrast, an early 1884 report for Kanab noted: "There has been a good reformation with the Seventies in regard to the Word of Wisdom."[48]

William Taylor explained the new "get tough" policy on the Word of Wisdom as nothing really new. He said it came from Joseph Smith as counsel "but through the Prophet Brigham as a command" and that "the Presidency and the Twelve Apostles have agreed strictly to adhere to it. They have called upon the Presidencies of Stakes to keep it and to teach others." A September 1886 circular from the First Council to all seventies reiterated the reform call voiced in the 1882 revelation: "We would meekly exhort you all to purify yourselves, and to labor to remove from your families everything that is contrary to the mind and will of God."[49]

By October 1884, "hundreds" of seventies were dragging their feet about recommends. The council decided to set a final deadline of April 1, 1887, for men to turn in recommends. When deadline day came, the council announced that "justice demands immediate action" and ordered quorum presidents to "strike from your rolls the names of all who have failed to comply." Such delinquents did not lose priesthood or ward fellowship but lost quorum membership and could not be readmitted without permission from the First Council. How many men were dropped from quorums is not known.[50]

By 1886 the question of how to treat Word of Wisdom backsliders arose. Should they be booted out of quorums? Should they make binding promises to conform? The First Council counselled quorum presidencies that it was unwise to be "too rigid in exacting covenants" and not right to "make them covenant to keep the Word of Wisdom." A report late in 1890 about men added to the Fourth Quorum found that none used tobacco, some occasionally used beer, tea, and coffee, but by promising to do their best they became seventies anyway. In 1888 the council was asked if a quorum president should be "dealt with" if he persisted in using tobacco? The answer: "The line cannot be drawn at present."[51]

MISSIONARY ROLE

All this reorganizing, recruiting, and purifying activity had the primary purpose of producing more missionaries. By 1884 it was again Church policy that missionaries be ordained as seventies, so the seventies resumed their interrupted tradition of being *the* missionary force for the kingdom. The number of seventies serving missions after the 1883 reorganizings was almost double the number serving before the 1877 ban on ordaining new seventies.[52] (See table 4.) The restructured quorums began paying transportation costs for their men called on missions, eliminating a $100 hurdle that had stopped some men before 1883. Also, quorums did a better job of helping families of men away on missions, thereby encouraging more men to go. By late 1885, the First Presidency urged stake presidents to set up 40- to 160-acre "missionary farms" in wards to help sustain missionaries' families, an idea the First Council also endorsed.[53]

To make seventies mission-ready, quorums held monthly or bimonthly meetings for gospel study and teaching practice. Also, the council asked quorums to hold noncompulsory theological classes in each ward. These could be special Sunday School classes or weeknight classes—"any course tending to exercise Seventies in their callings i[s] acceptable." By 1886 some quorums sponsored from one to five theology classes each. Other quorums held weekly classes. These classes, which pioneered the priesthood study-class work of the twentieth century, pursued both theology and nonreligious knowledge "in order that they may combat error upon scientific as well as religious grounds." The First Council warned against in-class debates, "devil's advocate" type representation, and doctrinal speculations.[54]

By late 1885, the First Presidency expressed its dissatisfaction about missionary results to the Twelve. Too many seventies were "so embarrassed by debt that they cannot go." The Apostles were asked to "exercise a supervisory

TABLE 4

Missionary Data from the 1870s and 1880s

	1871–76	1877–83	1884–89
Years	6	7	6
Total missionaries sent	838	1,377	1,421
Total of 70s serving as missionaries	571	725	1,012
Percent of total who were 70s	6,996	5,396	7,196
Average number of missionaries per year	139	197	236
Average number of 70s as missionaries per year	95	104	169

Source: "Missionary Record," typescript, Church History Library.

care over these nominations … so that unworthy representatives of our cause shall not go out."[55]

In the mid-1880s the First Council approved hundreds of men for mission calls, and by July 1887 reported to Apostle Richards that "under the blessings of the Lord we have been able to bring into a moderately complete state of organization the various quorums of the Seventies" and

we have succeeded in obtaining quite an extensive list of names of different nationalities who are well recommended by their respective bishops and co-laborers in the quorums…. We therefore respectfully submit the fact to you that we are now prepared, as we have ever tried to be in the past, to furnish you the names of any number of brethren you may require for missionary labor in any field. We have used the utmost care in the selecting of men for this service.[56]

But Apostle Richards disagreed, saying that the Twelve had "selected the most of the missionaries from the Quorum of Elders and quite frequently from the Young Men's Mutual Improvement Association, and I may say with gratifying success." The Missionary Committee, he said, would continue to use seventies' nominations as but one of various pools of names.

He then announced more rigid qualifications for missionaries and harder clearance procedures.[57]

RECORD KEEPING AND FINANCES

The 1883 reorderings gave a new start to quorum record keeping. "Every quorum should have a recordbook," the council ordered, for minutes, for up-to-date rosters, and for genealogical data on each member. In 1886 the council called for a correct and full genealogical report of the quorums, to be transcribed upon the general First Council records.[58]

In addition to bishops' recommends, seventies were told to obtain a license. Applications for new seventies licenses needed the date of ordination of the applicant, the officiator's name, and the signature of the quorum president and bishop. The Church History Library contains stub-book after stub-book of seventies licenses issued from 1884 to 1889 and after.[59]

Council members had no annual appropriation from the Church to pay council or personal expenses. They were self-supporting, and some found it hard going. Just before he died, Joseph Young made a plea to his fellow seventies for help, telling how he had labored for fifty years to provide for himself and now could not. Levi Hancock, in need, received some aid from the Presiding Bishopric. Seymour Young, on a mission in 1886, asked for $500 and the council turned him down—they did not like the precedent. With quorums revitalized after 1883, the council requested each unit to submit $35 a month—50 cents per man—to a Seventies General Fund. The fund paid for the council's clerk, travel, printing, and mailing. The hope was that the fund would grow large enough "to assist those who are suddenly called to take foreign missions."[60]

THE FIRST QUORUM

For a third of a century, the Church had operated without a First Quorum of the Seventy. Why then did the First Council try to resurrect it in the 1880s? Records do not provide clear-cut answers, but they suggest four.

One possible reason, one that historians need to probe, is that President Brigham Young did not want a First Quorum, that during his presidency of the Church he vetoed the First Quorum's resurrection, and that only after his death in 1877 was the First Quorum a discussable topic again.

Another reason, more substantiated, is that reorganizers of the seventies in the 1880s could not do their work without facing the First Quorum question head-on. To organize and fill all quorums but the first one, the one thought to be the most important, could not be done without debating that quorum's theoretical and practical roles past, present, and future.

A third reason could be that the membership at large, knowing the aging First Council had called a handful of alternates to help it, wondered why the council did not revive its own quorum instead to help out.

A fourth reason could be that Joseph Young, aware that a revitalizing of seventies quorums was upcoming, felt inadequate to lead these anticipated, vigorous units. The First Council's February 1880 minutes hint at this: "Br. Joseph Young said in relation to the Seven First Presidents presiding over all the quorums, that he was afraid of standing with his counselors and presiding over them." The statement, made during a discussion of the First Quorum, suggests that Joseph believed the First Council was but a skeleton crew unable to man the seventies ship properly without the First Quorum. (However, this raises a question with an answer beyond the scope of this study—why did Joseph not keep the old First Quorum going after 1844?)[61]

"The Seventy," the Doctrine and Covenants specifies, "form a quorum equal in authority to that of the Twelve" and can preside over the Church if the First Presidency and Twelve do not exist (D&C 107:24–26). Clearly, seventy-six or more quorums could not be "the Seventy" referred to. "The Seventy" apparently need to be an authority above the level of normal seventies quorums, and by general understanding a century ago "the Seventy" were to be the First Quorum. But who joins that quorum and how is it to be filled? During the 1880s, three methods were considered: (1) the 1844 method, by which the seven presidents of quorums two through ten, when called together by the First Council, constituted "the Seventy"; (2) the method proposed by the 1883 *Instruction* by which the senior president of each of the next sixty-three quorums, when called together by the council, were "the Seventy"; and (3) the First Council's preferred method, the method by which the original First Quorum was filled in 1835, of calling sixty-three independent of their seventies quorum affiliation or office. Lack of consensus about which method to use was one of two major reasons why the First Quorum did not resurrect in the 1880s.

The second major reason seems to be that, although priesthood theory requires a First Quorum, priesthood practice during that decade revealed no urgency for the quorum. "It would seem there are duties devolving upon its members, as a quorum," the 1883 *Instruction* said, "that may require their official action." But what kind of duties and action? The decade's records provide few specifics except that "the Seventy" could hold trials for senior quorum presidents, receive reports, and conduct Seventies business—tasks that the council could easily handle anyway through existing apparatus.[62]

Three times the council had opportunities in the 1880s to resurrect the First Quorum, and three times nothing happened. The first chance came in 1879–80. Late in 1879 the council discussed the desirability of filling the First Quorum, but expressed uncertainty how to proceed. Joseph Young, either from historical amnesia or for personal or practical reasons, did not want to use the 1844 method of filling the quorum with presidencies of other quorums. Other leaders agreed. Council member John Van Cott, for example, "could not see any authority for Presidents of other Quorums being any part of the First Quorum." Seymour B. Young "thought a man could not be President in two places at once." "It was not by being in any particular Quorum that we receive any more authority," Joseph Young explained, "but it is in the organization."[63]

Early in 1880, Joseph asked for and received the Twelve's permission to fill the First Quorum by transferring some of the Eighth Quorum into it and then filling vacancies in both quorums with new seventies. But the plan hit a snag. Elder William F. Cahoon, president of the Second Quorum, told Joseph that at the School of the Prophets in Kirtland, Joseph Smith taught the 1844 method. Joseph Young said he had not known that before—evidently meaning he thought the 1844 idea was Brigham Young's. Accepting Elder Cahoon's testimony, Joseph Young decided that "when he called for a representation of the First Quorum he wanted the Presidency of the Second to the Tenth Quorums to rise."[64]

But a month later, the council was balking at the 1844 method. Alternate Enoch Tripp "spoke of the importance of being governed by what is written in the Revelations. Thought there should be a full and sufficient Quorum comprising the First Presidents with the Presidents of nine Quorums. He wished to see this settled." But Joseph Young decided "he would let everything rest as it was" because he wished to discuss the matter with the Twelve. He also consulted with old timers, including Harrison Burgess, who also remembered Joseph Smith teaching the 1844 plan. Further, the council searched Church histories for items pertaining to the early seventies. Then the matter dropped, and the council did not tackle it again before Joseph Young died in 1881. In November 1882, President Eldredge asked the First Presidency about filling the quorum but no approval came.[65]

The second chance to form the First Quorum came when the 1883 *Instructions* and ratifying revelation *permitted* the First Quorum to be filled by calling the next sixty-three quorums' senior presidents. Obviously, the First Quorum could not be filled by this method until the next sixty-three quorums had senior presidents properly installed. So Wilford Woodruff, president of the Twelve, instructed the council to organize and fill the existing quorums first before the First Quorum. The council obeyed. During the reorganizings, however, some senior presidents of quorums talked of sitting soon in the First Quorum. By late 1883, when the first sixty-four quorums had their senior president properly installed, the First Council could have called the First Quorum together but did not. From 1884 to 1888, the First Quorum topic appeared only once or twice in council minutes, and no action resulted. Perhaps the council was too busy filling old quorums and organizing new ones to tackle the First Quorum matter again.[66]

A third opportunity came in 1889–90. Jacob Gates, new senior president of the council, asked his colleagues to organize the First Quorum.[67] In response they drafted a letter to senior Apostle Wilford Woodruff (the First Presidency was not yet organized after John Taylor's death in 1887) explaining what problems the 1883 method would cause if implemented. Using the sixty-three quorums' senior presidents, the council reasoned, would fill the First Quorum with many elderly men and many living far away from Salt Lake City. Instead, why not fill the First Quorum with individually selected men who were vigorous and who lived close to headquarters? The letter added that, whatever method the Twelve approved, the council wanted permission to assemble the First Quorum members at the next general conference.[68]

The council submitted the letter to the Twelve in early 1889. No answer is recorded in council minutes, but a council letter written half a century later records what happened to the proposal: "When attention was called to the fact that the First Quorum would be scattered all over, and many of its members advanced in years, [so] it would be impossible to function as a quorum, the President [Woodruff] stated 'that we will do nothing with it for the present,' and since then nothing has been done."[69]

MILLENNIALISM

Joseph Smith said that if he lived to be eighty-five he would see the Savior come.[70] Based on that teaching, some Mormons, including seventies, thought the Second Coming would occur in 1890. While the seventies' reorganizings, revelations, and purifyings were not explicitly linked to an 1890 second coming, seventies' records contain occasional millennialistic sentiments. In April 1880, for example, President Joseph Young "said the signs of the times were ominous of a great crisis which were at our doors, indicating a great upheaving and the convulsions of nations, which showed the great necessity of the Seventies being prepared for any emergencies that may transpire and to hold themselves in reddiness for coming events."[71] Joseph Young told a confidant, Edward Stevenson, that he expected to see the Second Coming because Joseph Smith had promised him he "would not sleep" before the coming of the Son of Man.[72] "There were quite a few among us who had but a slight conception of the magnitude of the work," a seventy said in 1883; "as the idea is entertained by some that missionary work was drawing to a close."[73]

For the most part, however, such expressions were quiet. The First Council's own minutes during the 1880s, in fact, lack millennialistic fever. The most direct statement on the subject by a council member came in September of the suspected millennial year, 1890, when President Morgan squelched notions that some Seventies entertained:

> John Morgan said there are likely to be many more quorums of 70s organized (there were now over 100), there are many erroneous notions entertained by the 70s in regard to preaching the Gospel, that their missions would necessarily be short; that the end is very near and the Elders about to be called home &c, but in such things they are mistaken, as the Gospel is to be preached to all nations and will necessarily take a long time; the work has hardly commenced.... Not half the counties in the United States (Southern States especially) have ever heard the Gospel preached.[74]

THE FIRST COUNCIL AS SUBORDINATES

Scripture, including the 1882 and 1883 revelations, teaches that the First Council is subordinate to the Twelve and First Presidency. The council accepted that role but at times found it hard to wait for superiors to grant requests or make decisions. Joseph Young, for example, felt in 1880 that part of their difficulties stemmed from underuse by senior Apostle John Taylor and the Twelve: "If he would call upon us to rally our forces, we would try and be ready; and for his part he wished the Twelve to give us a fair trial, and we would call out missionaries, place our hands upon their heads and bless them."[75]

The Twelve and/or First Presidency determined when to ordain more seventies and when to halt. They approved alternates, and they released them. They approved the ward and stake seventies president experiment. They selected, rejected, or ignored men approved by the First Council for missions. They reviewed and approved the First Council's plans in 1883 for reapportioning seventies quorums among the stakes. They chose not to involve the seventies in the Lamanite missionary work. They tabled the First Council's 1889 proposal to recreate the First Quorum. The First Council readily acknowledged that they took "no important steps without applying to them [the Twelve and First Presidency] in all cases where necessary."[76]

The First Council did exercise some nominating powers regarding new council members. When John Van Cott died, the First Presidency and Twelve asked the First Council to nominate a Scandinavian replacement. When President Eldredge died, the Twelve asked the council for nominees to replace him. Of the four they suggested, B. H. Roberts was chosen.[77]

According to seventies' records, the First Council did not meet regularly with the Twelve. However, there was considerable correspondence between the two units and one-to-one contact between individual council members and Apostles. Seventies' business reached the Twelve and First Presidency informally through William W. Taylor talking to his father, John Taylor, and Abraham H. Cannon talking to his father, George Q. Cannon.

SEVENTIES: HOW MUCH PRIESTHOOD AUTHORITY?

Who has higher authority, a seventy or high priest? That was a troubling question before, during, and after the 1880s. Joseph Young strongly asserted that seventies held higher authority. When a high priest asked to become a seventy in the early 1880s, Joseph Young ordained him and placed him in the Eighth Quorum. Joseph Young also said it was wrong for seventies to become high priests when called into bishoprics. Had not Joseph

Smith rebuked Hyrum Smith for ordaining a seventy a high priest? Had not Joseph Smith and Brigham Young both taught that seventies were "Seventy Apostles" with full "keys, powers, and authority" of the apostleship "to order and set in order the Stakes of Zion, Bishops, Bishops councillors and high councils?" To make seventies become high priests "was contrary to the teachings imparted to him by the Prophet Joseph Smith and his successor Brigham Young." John Van Cott said Brigham once taught that a seventy called to a bishopric ought to be "set apart"—not ordained—to act as a high priest, "for they could act in any calling, and could still be special witnesses [Seventy Apostles]." As late as 1888, the council, in a general epistle, said that men chosen for stake and ward presiding positions "are not required to be ordained High Priests against their choice."

Joseph Young also believed that seventies ordained as high priests did not need to sever their membership ties with seventies quorums. John Van Cott agreed: "Brigham had said that we will take the Seventies back again" who became high priests. By late 1882 some men held dual memberships in both high priests and seventies quorums.[78]

During the 1880s, several situations proved the high priests-seventies controversy was still alive. To illustrate, T. B. Lewis, sustained at October 1882 general conference to join the First Council, admitted he was a high priest and was not installed. Normally the First Council members were not allowed to ordain high priests, and in late 1887 when a council member helped an Apostle ordain a high priest at a stake conference, others of the Twelve judged the action improper. On still another occasion, Apostles Moses Thatcher and Heber J. Grant ordained high priests leaving for missions to the office of seventy, and Abraham H. Cannon, a new Apostle and former First Council member, reacted: "While I believe that a Seventy holds the higher office, there are some, even among the Twelve, who think a high priest is higher." One such was new Church President Wilford Woodruff, who late in 1889 "decided it improper to ordain a high priest to a seventy."[79]

The council maintained that seventies were general officers under its leadership and not stake officers like elders and high priests. But some bishops and stake officers disregarded the First Council and exercised local controls over seventies. Sometimes seventies were called into local positions and made high priests without informing seventies quorum presidents or the council. In a July 25, 1888, epistle the First Council criticized the practice: "It is a matter of regret that heretofore, Bishops of Wards and Presidents of

Stakes have taken from the councils and the membership of these Quorums some of the best men to ordain them Bishops, Bishops Counselors, High Counselors, etc. without consulting the officers of the Quorums from which these men are taken."[80] But two weeks later, either through ignorance of the council's epistle or in deliberate confrontation, Apostle Francis M. Lyman ordained a seventies president a high priest without asking the First Council's approval.[81]

The council also disliked reports that bishops ordered seventies to do things that were beyond a bishop's jurisdiction. "A Bishop has no right to dictate Seventies in regard to their Quorum matters," the council warned; the bishop "has no jurisdiction over Seventies to send them out to preach in other wards than where they reside." But the council also recognized that bishops had the right to call on seventies to fill the office of "acting" elders, priests, teachers, deacons, or even doorkeepers.[82]

POLYGAMY AND THE SEVENTIES

Polygamous seventies in the 1880s, like other Mormon polygamists, had to deal with the "Raid" and the "Underground." As noted, Seymour B. Young added a second wife, as ordered by the 1882 revelation, before joining the First Council. All First Council members that decade were polygamists, though only B. H. Roberts went to jail for polygamy (a fine place to preach the gospel, he said). Seymour Young and Daniel Fjelsted "arranged" to go on foreign missions to avoid arrest. Of seventy-five senior presidents of the seventy-five seventies quorums in 1883, nine were imprisoned for polygamy, or one out of eight. Some men wrote to the council, asking for missions to avoid prison. Of the entire seventies' membership, enough men faced arrest to prompt the First Council to ask quorums to aid families of seventies on the underground or in jail.[83]

During Test Oath struggles in Idaho, some Saints, including seventies, agreed to defend the Church by taking the oath, losing Church membership, and then voting in support of Church-favored candidates and issues. In February 1889, for example, the Fifty-second Quorum in Oneida Stake was in "a deplorable condition" because forty-three members had taken the test oath and lost their Church memberships.[84]

Church leaders used the reorganization movement to enforce the Word of Wisdom but *not* to increase plural marriages. Hundreds of men obtained worthiness recommends from their bishops, and scores of men filled new seven-man presidencies, but no instruction came from the First Presidency, and Twelve, or the First Council that these men needed to be polygamists. In fact, polygamists made poor "Minute Men" missionaries because they had too many obligations. "It was not necessary to load ourselves up with large families," Apostle Brigham Young Jr. told seventies in 1883; "but that when through faith and prayer the Lord calls us to take another wife, it is our duty to do so."[85]

However, the year before, the 1882 revelation had read, "It is not meet that men who will not abide my law [plural marriage] shall preside over my priesthood," thus setting a leaders-to-be-polygamists standard that General Authorities tried to enforce. At the priesthood session of April general conference in 1884, criticism was voiced of David H. Peery because he had resigned his stake president's calling rather than add a wife. In the same meeting, stake presidents Lewis W. Shurtliff, William W. Cluff, and Abraham Hatch were warned that they were holding themselves and the Church back by not taking second wives. Accordingly, the First Council, when selecting new seventies quorum presidents after 1883, gave "preference to those who had embraced the law of celestial marriage."[86]

CONTINUOUS REVELATION AND PRIESTHOOD

In the 1883 revelation, the Lord addressed conservative Saints bothered by changes in Church practice. Similar to an "elastic clause" in the priesthood constitution, the verse informed members that the Lord can make changes in his priesthood. Priesthood leaders, it said, are not to be troubled or concerned "about the management and organization of my Church and Priesthood" but instead should trust the appointed channels and expect, through those channels, necessary future adjustments. Similar expression of priesthood elasticity came when the First Council objected to seventies quorum presidents being taken into bishoprics without the First Council's permission. Was not this wrong, the First Council asked the First Presidency. Presidents John Taylor and George Q. Cannon answered that it was *discourteous* but *not wrong*. Then they added: "While upon this subject, we may say that it is not wise to have cast iron rules by which to fetter the Priesthood. The Priesthood is a living, intelligent principle, and must necessarily have freedom to act as circumstances may dictate or require."[87]

CONCLUSION

The 1880s represent a golden age for seventies work. Beginning the decade disorganized, depleted, and scattered, the seventies, responding eagerly to two "thus saith the Lord" revelations in 1882 and 1883, experienced a large-scale restructuring. No less than fourteen quorums were relocated, hundreds of seventies were changed in their quorum membership, twenty-five new quorums were created, and many new quorum presidencies were called. More seventies served missions, perhaps a hundred more per year, than in the 1870s. Because the average age of men called on missions dropped from above age forty to about the mid-thirties during the decade, returned missionaries brought younger blood into the quorums. Younger replacements for First Council vacancies helped it be more vigorous in supervising the work of the quorums. Because seventies and quorums were easily locatable after 1883, communication between First Council and quorums improved greatly. Pride in being a seventy increased because two revelations specifically expressed divine awareness of and approval of the seventies' calling. When bishops' recommends were required, many seventies made successful efforts to change, especially with regard to the newly enforced Word of Wisdom. Ward theology classes were started. Seventies' record books received vital updatings. Had Joseph Young lived until 1890, his discouragement with the state of things in 1880 probably would have changed to rejoicings over what the decade had done for his seventies.

Despite the major work done on reorganizing the seventies in the 1880s, some fundamental priesthood problems outlasted the decade. One was the long-term debate about how much authority a seventy, especially a First Council member, held compared to a high priest. Also, the First Quorum's resurrection was shelved.[88] The goal of the 1883 revelation and *Instructions* was to place the seventies quorums in "perfect working order." But, ironically, the one matter left unperfected was the vacant First Quorum, the capstone quorum of the entire seventies organization. The long-standing expectation that seventies be missionary-producing quorums found only limited fulfillment: the quorums continued to be retirement places for returning missionaries more than productive training camps for future missionaries. The Lamanite missionary campaign involving the seventies, called for by the 1882 revelation, never materialized. Finally, by geographically distributing seventies quorums throughout the stakes, the 1883 reorganization moved the day a notch closer when seventies would become local officers supervised by stake presidents instead of general quorums supervised by the First Council.

This article was originally published in Dialogue: A Journal of Mormon Thought *16 (Spring 1983): 62–88.*

NOTES

1. First Council of the Seventy, Minutes 1878–1897, Janunary 24, 1880, microfilm, Church History Library, The Church of Jesus Christ of Latter-day Saints, Salt Lake City (hereafter cited as FCM).
2. The two revelations are in *Messages of the First Presidency of The Church of Jesus Christ of Latter-day Saints, 1833–1964,* comp. James R. Clark, 6 vols. (Salt Lake City: Bookcraft, 1965–75), 2:347–49, 352–54.
3. For general histories of the seventies, see S. Dilworth Young, "The Seventies: A Historical Perspective," *Ensign* 6 (July 1976): 14–21; and James N. Baumgarten, "The Role and Function of the Seventies in L.D.S. Church History" (master's thesis, Brigham Young University, 1960). The unrecorded revelation is discussed in Joseph Smith Jr., *History of The Church of Jesus Christ of Latter-day Saints,* B. H. Roberts, ed., 2d ed., rev., 7 vols. (Salt Lake City: Deseret Book, 1957), 2:182, 202 (hereafter cited as *History of the Church*); Doctrine and Covenants 107:25, 26, 34, 38, 93–8.
4. *History of the Church,* 2:221, 476; 7:305; Seventies Record Book B, 1844–48, 31, Church History Library.
5. "To the Presidents and Bishops," in Clark, *Messages of the First Presidency,* 2:353, June 12, 1872.
6. FCM, January 1, 1881.
7. William G. Hartley, "The Priesthood Reorganization of 1877: Brigham Young's Last Achievement," *BYU Studies* 20, no. 1 (1979): 34–35. Evidently Brigham Young asked the Twelve to not take seventies into bishoprics midway through the 1877 reorganizings, saying he was "tired of the egress and ingress" (turnover) of seventies, but was ignored. See FCM, January 24, 1880.
8. FCM, December 13, 1879; First Council of the Seventy, Seventies General Meeting Minutes, 1879–84, March 16, 1881, microfilm, Church History Library (hereafter cited as SGMM).
9. FCM, May 10, 1879; April 10, 1880. Alternates were Edward Stevenson, Aurelius Miner, Enoch Tripp, [?] Ferguson, William Hawk, W. G. Phillips, John Pack, and William H. Sharp.
10. FCM, September 7 ,1878; SGMM, May 7, 1879.
11. SGMM, June 2, 1880; SGMM is a record of these meetings.
12. FCM, June 26, December 25, and November 27, 1880; May 28, 1881; September 1, 1880.

13. SGMM, July 20 and August 3, 1881.
14. FCM, December 25, 1880.
15. FCM, April 1 and 2, 1882.
16. FCM, March 11, 1882.
17. FCM, November 25, 1882.
18. "To the Presidents and Bishops," 2:348–49.
19. "To the Presidents and Bishops," 2:348–49. President Taylor submitted the revelation to the Twelve, the First Council, stake presidents, and others for approval: see John Taylor, Letter to Albert Carrington, October 18, 1882, in *Millennial Star* 44 (November 13, 1882): 732–33.
20. Isaiah M. Coombs, Diary, November 23, 1882, microfilm of holograph, Church History Library.
21. Wilford Woodruff, in *Journal of Discourses,* 26 vols. (Liverpool: Latter-day Saints' Book Depot, 1855–86), 23:330–331, December 10, 1882.
22. Franklin D. Richards, Journal, March 21, April 11 and 15, May 6 and 30, June 6, July 18, and October 31, 1883, microfilm of holograph, Church History Library.
23. Brigham Young Jr., Journal, December 20, 1888, microfilm of holograph, Church History Library.
24. "To the Presidents and Bishops," 2:348–49.
25. SGMM, December 20, 1882.
26. SGMM, January 3, 1883.
27. Young Jr., Journal, September 28, 1883; FCM, November 22 and December 6, 1879; October 23, 1880; November 26, December 3 and 31, 1881; January 14 and 21, February 11, and March 25, 1882; SGMM, December 7 and 22, 1881; January 4 and 18, December 31, 1882; and November 7, 1883. One seventy visited several brothers in saloons "and found in one two hundred youths," SGMM, November 3, 1880.
28. FCM, May 6, 1883; William W. Taylor, Journal, April 13, 1883, microfilm of holograph, Church History Library; Richards, Journal, April 13, 1883; SGGM, May 2, 1883.
29. FCM, May 6, 1883; Taylor, Journal, April 13, 1883.
30. Richards, Journal, April 14, 1883; "To the Seventies," in Clark, *Messages of the First Presidency,* 2:352–54.
31. "To the Seventies," 2:352–54.
32. SGMM, May 2, 1883.
33. Journal History of the Church, April 22, 1883, Church History Library, microfilm copy in Harold B. Lee Library, Brigham Young University, Provo, Utah, account originally in the *Ogden Daily Herald.*
34. FCM, May 6, 1883.
35. FCM, May 9 and 12, 1883.
36. FCM, May 27, 1883; *Millennial Star* 45 (July 9, 1883): 443; SGMM, October 3 and 21 and May 22, 1883; FCM, June 8 and May 20, 1883.
37. *Millennial Star* 45 (July 9, 1883): 443; SGMM, May 27, 1883; Hartley, "Priesthood Reorganization of 1877," 23; FCM, August 12, 1882.
38. Fourth Quorum of Seventies, Minutes, June 12, 1883, microfilm, Church History Library; First Council of the Seventy, Circular Letter, October 22, 1884, Church History Library; FCM, June 11, 1883.

39. FCM, May 27 and June 5, 1883; "Record of the 21st Quorum of 70s," in Thomas Memmott, Journal, microfilm of holograph, Church History Library.

40. FCM, December 2, 1884; First Council of the Seventy, Circular Letter, October 22, 1884, Church History Library; SGMM, June 6, 1883; Memmott, Journal, January 24, 1883; Thirty-third Quorum of Seventies, Minutes, January 15, 1884, microfilm, Church History Library.

41. FCM, September 2, 1883.

42. Robert Campbell, Letter to William Hyde, January 18, 1884, First Council of the Seventy, Letterpress Copybooks, 1884–1909, film of holograph, Church History Library (hereafter cited as Council Copybook).

43. FCM, May 16, 1883; SGMM, October 17, 1883; Twenty-first Quorum Records in Memmott, Journal; Council Copybook, April 11, 1884; FCM, September 29, 1885.

44. FCM, January 29, 1884; January 5 1886; December 1, 1889; March 11, 1882; and August 31, 1887.

45. Journal History, April 22, 1883, from the *Ogden Daily Herald*; Robert Campbell, Letter to Christian D. Fjeldsted, April 19, 1888, Council Copybook.

46. FCM, July 23, October 22, and June 24, 1884; and March 9, 1886; FCM for 1883–90.

47. FCM, December 28, 1887.

48. FCM, November 28, 1883; and April 16, 1884.

49. SGMM, November 21, 1883; FCM, November 28, 1883; and September 29, 1886.

50. FCM, October 21, 1884; December 15, 1886; April 1, 1887; and April 17, 1889.

51. FCM, January 7, 1885; and June 2, 1886; Fourth Quorum Minutes, October 13, 1890; FCM, February 1, 1888.

52. FCM, May 27, 1883.

53. After 1883 the reasons cited in FCM for men not being able to accept missions decreasingly included transportation expense. FCM, July 25, 1888.

54. Thirty-third Quorum, Minutes, April 18, 1886; FCM, March 9, January 25, and February 22, 1888.

55. "Letter of the First Presidency to Wilford Woodruff and the Council of the Twelve," in Clark, *Messages of the First Presidency*, 3:42–43, November 12, 1885; FCM, November 12, 1885.

56. FCM, July 20, 1887.

57. FCM, August 31, 1887.

58. FCM, December 2 and November 6, 1884.

59. FCM, December 2, 1884; and May 16, 1883; Seventies Ordination Certificate Stubs, 1839–1900, microfilm, Church History Library.

60. First Council of the Seventy, Circular Letter, March 10, 1886, Church History Library; FCM, July 14, 1886; FCM, May 1 and October 2, 1880; and February 12, 1881.

61. FCM, February 28, 1880.

62. "To the Seventies," 2:353; FCM, May 16, 1883.

63. FCM, March 13, February 28, and March 20, 1880.

64. FCM, December 22, 1879; March 6, 13, and 20, 1880.

65. FCM, April 17, June 5 and 12, 1880; and November 25, 1882.

66. FCM, May 16 and November 7, 1883; and August 25, 1885.

67. FCM, December 5, 1888.
68. FCM, December 12, 1888, contains the full text of the letter. Early in 1889, the letter was sent to the Twelve. FCM, March 20, 1889. The Twelve intimated they would meet with the First Council (FCM, March 27, 1889) to take action on the letter. That summer, Seymour B. Young consulted with the Twelve on the matter, but no results were recorded. FCM, July 24, 1889.
69. Letter, no author, no addressee, no date, typescript, First Council of the Seventy, Outgoing Correspondence, 1939, Church History Library.
70. Alma P. Burton, comp., *Discourses of the Prophet Joseph Smith* (Salt Lake City: Deseret Book, 1977), 236.
71. FCM, April 17, 1880.
72. Edward Stevenson, Diary, 1878–81, microfilm of holograph, Church History Library.
73. SGMM, February 23, 1883.
74. Fourth Quorum, Minutes, September 8, 1890.
75. FCM, April 24, 1880.
76. Robert Campbell, Letter to Henry Herriman, November 27, 1884, Council Copybook.
77. FCM, April 30, 1884; June 30, 1883; and October 3, 1888.
78. FCM, May 29, 1880; May 21, 1881; June 2, 1880; December 13, 1879; May 29, 1880; April 2, 1881; July 25, 1888; and October 1, 1882; SGMM, May 19, 1880.
79. SGMM, October 18, 1882; FCM, November 30, 1887; and October 9, 1889.
80. FCM, July 25, 1888.
81. FCM, August 8, 1888; and December 8, 1886.
82. FCM, December 8, 1886.
83. FCM, September 11, 1889; July 14 and October 20, 1886; statistics based on name matches between list of senior quorum presidents in 1883 and list of Mormons jailed for plural marriage reasons, contained in Andrew Jenson, "Prisoners for Conscience Sake," manuscript, Church History Library. Those jailed and their quorum numbers: Wm. H. Tovey (4), Charles Monk (19), George Reynolds (24), Edward Peay (34), John F. Dorius (47), Walter Wilcox (57), Hans P. Hansen (58), Thomas Barrett (67), and William Yates (68).
84. B. H. Roberts, *A Comprehensive History of The Church of Jesus Christ of Latter-day Saints,* 6 vols. (Salt Lake City: Deseret News Press, 1930), 6:213; FCM, February 13 and March 20, 1889.
85. FCM, May 27, 1883.
86. "Revelation Given through Pres. John Taylor," in Clark, *Messages of the First Presidency,* 2:348, October 13, 1882; Thomas Memmott, Journal, "Quotation Book," 102–4 (in section on plural marriage under heading called "Notes on remarks made in Priesthood meeting, General Conference, April 1884").
87. FCM, December 15, 1886. The First Council did not always like the elastic approach, for the traditional view of Seventies being Seventy-Apostles gave their quorums more importance. B. H. Roberts became a vocal, perhaps strident, traditionalist regarding seventies. In 1926, Apostle Rudger Clawson, on behalf of the Twelve, while criticizing Roberts for favoring previous revelations, wrote to President Heber J. Grant that previous revelations "must be construed with reference to the whole text of our law and the

principles which control our government. In such a construction it will not be difficult to reconcile present practice or such further policies which may be adopted with the letter and spirit of the texts [of the revelations]." He added:

> The doing of the work of the Lord must always be of chief concern. The whole organization of the Church is, in the last analysis, a facility, an agency for that high purpose. So that, while we do not desire to be understood to make an effort to minimize the value and importance of adhering to the general directions given in the revelations for the organization and mainte-nance of the quorums, we do express the firm conviction that these scrip-tural directions are, as herinbefore stated, subject to the interpretation of the inspired servants of the Lord who preside over the Church, whose interpre-tations will always be made with reference to the needs of the Church and the progress of the work.

Rudger Clawson to President Heber J. Grant, Extracts of Council of the Twelve Min-utes and First Council of the Seventy, 1888–1941, December 9, 1926, microfilm, Church History Library.

88. In October 1975 general conference, Church President Spencer W. Kimball announced the reconstitution of the First Quorum of the Seventy. Since then men have been called into the quorum without regard to previous seventies' quorum affiliation or lack of it. In October 1976 general conference, all Assistants to the Twelve—high priests by ordination—were called into the First Quorum.

12   The Priesthood Reform Movement, 1908–1922

MOST LATTER-DAY SAINTS KNOW A GOOD DEAL about the duties and functions of the various priesthood quorums, but few appreciate the great effort required of past Church leaders to produce the well-ordered priesthood programs that characterize the Church in modern times. Since the restoration of the Aaronic and Melchizedek Priesthoods, the various quorums have been alive and functioning to a greater or lesser degree. But organized and systematic priesthood work as we know it today actually dates from the period between 1908 and 1922, when a specially called General Priesthood Committee instituted a Churchwide priesthood reform and reorganization movement under the direction of president Joseph F. Smith.

THE NEED FOR PRIESTHOOD REFORM

To fully appreciate the importance of this movement, we first need to understand the priesthood practices prior to 1908 that made reform necessary. At that time, 90 percent of Church members lived in Utah, Idaho, and Arizona. Their stakes often covered huge geographic areas and contained as many as twenty wards or as few as three. Individual wards showed similar variations in sizes, ranging from a dozen families to fifteen hundred souls. Priesthood holders numbered about seventy thousand out of four hundred thousand total Church members.[1]

In terms of organization, the priesthood quorums generally lacked strong central direction. Presiding Bishop Charles W. Nibley stated that as of June 1908, he had "no way of becoming directly in touch with the work that was being done in the different quorums of the lesser priesthood."[2] He was soon to learn that some wards had no deacons, and many no priests, and that it was common for older men to perform Aaronic Priesthood functions. Some bishops would not ordain their young men to a particular office until there were sufficient numbers to make a quorum. Others complained they were unable to learn of elders, seventies, and high priests ordained or disfellowshipped among their ward members. Functioning quorums held meetings weekly, biweekly, or monthly, depending on local circumstances. Individual quorums in a given area frequently met on different days of the week, and rarely did many wards have regular general priesthood meetings. Most quorum meetings traditionally were adjourned during summer months, such as the lesser priesthood in one Logan ward that concluded its 1908 meetings on March 30 and did not commence again until November 2—a seven months' vacation.[3] Priesthood activity and instruction, therefore, were dependent upon the dedication or carelessness of local bishops and stake presidents. Some stakes, such as Granite and Jordan, provided their quorums with printed, systematic lesson outlines. But more often the lesson materials were selected by the quorums themselves or by local officers, resulting in some unusual priesthood meetings by our modern standards. One lesser priesthood group, for example, divided its class time between religious lessons and such adventure books as *Tom Sawyer*, *The Jungle Book*, *The Call of the Wild*, *Pigs Is Pigs*, and *Frank among the Rancheros*.[4] In another case, a lesson was given on the life of United States President William McKinley—in a Canadian teachers quorum.[5] In December 1908, a deacons quorum in Ogden "went downstairs and Brother ____ gave a lecture on Ben Hur."[6] Other bishops had their lesser priesthood members meet with the ward mutuals to study Mutual Improvement Association lesson materials.

Despite such diverse efforts to make meetings interesting, the activity level of the lesser priesthood boys was often poor. In a Provo ward, for instance, the deacons were assigned to regular fast offering districts, where a typical monthly collection might be "2 lbs bacon, 40c cash, 1 bottle fruit, 1 pk raisins, 1 can oisters and 43 lbs flour." But the 1903 quorum minutes reveal that rarely did even half of these deacons' districts report any monthly collections.[7] One ecclesiastical official wryly observed that it was easy to get deacons to go on missions but very difficult to get them to function in their quorums.[8]

Examples taken from the minutes of a successful lesser priesthood in a Canadian stake delightfully describe priesthood practices on the eve of the reform movement: in 1894 two boys were appointed by the bishop "to visit all the boys in town and find out what [office in the] priesthood they held and ask them to come to meetings." A few days later, the teachers were appointed to dig a well for a sister in the ward. On one occasion the bishop made his boys pledge to refrain from profanity and tobacco. Feeling the need to get a greater commitment from them, he requested that the boys prepare themselves for rebaptism. All were rebaptized a month later. Near the turn of the century, the priests and teachers began meeting together, minus the deacons. In 1901 the bishop ordained six deacons to the office of priest. The next year, the boys voted to drop their current lesson topics and begin a missionary preparation course. That same year their meeting night was changed to Mondays from Wednesdays due to choir practice on Wednesdays. For their classes the next year, the quorums agreed to study the Junior Mutual lessons. As part of the later lesson, "a moral story was read, but it got tiresome and was moved and seconded that it would be stopped." Each summer the priesthood meetings were discontinued, so the last meeting of spring became a special event. In April 1907 all the priesthood quorums joined together in a closing meeting to which everybody else in the ward was invited, including females who provided musical numbers.[9]

Elder J. Golden Kimball, of the First Quorum of the Seventy, bluntly assessed the

Elder J. Golden Kimball recognized the lack of organization and effective accomplishment of the duties of the priesthood around the turn of the twentieth century. Courtesy Church Archives.

unsatisfactory state of priesthood quorums in 1906 by comparing them with the Church auxiliaries:

> The auxiliaries have been urged forward with great enthusiasm, everywhere, from Canada to Mexico, these organizations are to the front. The Priesthood quorums are apparently weary in well doing, and the officers and members seem to think that their organizations can run themselves. They have become lax in their work and let loose their hold. While the auxiliary organizations have taken the right of way, the Priesthood quorums stand by looking on awestruck.... So the auxiliary organizations are going away up the hill and we, the Priesthood quorums, stand down in the valley and look on. Perhaps you don't like that picture, you men of the Priesthood quorums, but I tell you there is a lot of truth in it.... I am in favor of the Priesthood quorums taking their proper places, and if they do not do it, they ought to be ashamed of themselves, for they have the power and intelligence, and they have the authority.[10]

THE SYSTEMATIC PRIESTHOOD PROGRAM

No one was more distressed about this priesthood slackness than President Joseph F. Smith. In April 1906 general conference, he expressed his oft-quoted hope that one day "every council of the Priesthood in the Church ... will understand its duty, will assume its own responsibility, will magnify its calling, and fill its place in the Church." He predicted that when that day came, the quorums would take over the work done by the auxiliary organizations for "the Lord ... made provision whereby every need may be met and satisfied through the regular organization of the Priesthood."[11] Two years later, he formally requested in April conference that the priesthood quorums become better organized and of more usefulness to the Church. Specifically, he asked that the lesser priesthood boys be given "something to do that will make them interested in the work of the Lord."[12]

To spearhead a more ordered priesthood program, the First Presidency established a General Priesthood Committee on Outlines, which served as a "standing committee on Priesthood work" until its release in 1922. Its primary responsibility was to prepare lesson outlines for the quorums, which in turn involved it in almost all aspects of priesthood work. The committee initially included Rudger Clawson and David O. McKay of the Quorum of the Twelve, plus Charles W. Nibley, Orrin P. Miller, and David A. Smith of the Presiding Bishopric. It was soon enlarged to nearly twenty members, half of whom brought with them valuable experience as general board members of the Sunday school, the Young Men's Mutual Improvement Association (YMMIA), and religion classes.

At its first meeting, the committee sensed a great work was commencing. Stephen L. Richards felt that quorum work had been neglected, and that disinterest by priesthood leaders was due to the "lack of having a general plan to follow." Joseph J. Cannon noted "the auxiliary organizations had been actually doing the work that the quorums should do." David O. McKay rejoiced that the plan given in the Doctrine and Covenants was finally being systematized so that each quorum would no longer choose its own course of study. Rudger Clawson reported that the First Presidency expected that the committee's work "would be the means of bringing in a great many young men who are now neglecting this work." But it was fully realized that their work required "the combined efforts of all those in authority" in order to succeed.[13]

Priesthood problems were thoroughly investigated by the committee during the middle months of 1908. They studied the systematic lessons and weekly meeting plan newly developed by the seventies as well as the systematic quorum work already inaugurated in Weber, Granite, and other stakes. Their final recommendations for revitalizing the priesthood, intended to become operative the first week in 1909, had three main parts. First, all quorums—except the seventies—were to meet in Monday night ward priesthood gatherings. Also, thirty-six lessons were designed by the committee for each for these quorums, to be studied in the weekly meetings. Finally, monthly stake priesthood meetings would be held to preview the next month's priesthood work and to develop classroom teaching skills.[14]

But before appropriate lessons could be written for each quorum, the committee found it necessary to establish age groupings for the lesser priesthood. After 1877 it had been customary in the Church for boys at age twelve to be ordained deacons. But standard age practices for ordaining teachers or priests, or for advancing young men through the priesthood, were lacking. The committee, therefore, suggested certain ages at which specific Aaronic Priesthood ordinations should occur. Bishops were then instructed by the Presiding Bishopric to advance boys when worthy, and unless there are special reasons to the contrary they should be advanced in the priesthood from deacon to teacher and from teacher to priest. There can be no set age when persons should be ordained to the various offices in the Aaronic Priesthood, but we suggest that as near as circumstances will permit boys be ordained as follows: Deacons at twelve, Teachers at fifteen and Priests at eighteen years of age.[15]

The committee's proposals were introduced and approved at October general conference, then at special priesthood conventions in November and December in every stake. Acceptance was enthusiastic. Seventies quorums asked to be included in the new movement and were allowed to join the regular weekly meetings, which began in most wards early in 1909. In one stake, elderly high priests traveled seven or eight miles to attend these classes, even though they were officially excused on account of age.[16] Lesson outlines were ordered by the thousands. The *Improvement Era* became the official organ for the priesthood quorums. One year's experience with weekly meetings, reported the Presiding Bishopric, had confirmed the initial high hopes, for "ward authorities have been brought into close and frequent touch with the male members of their wards, by means of which they have acquired accurate personal knowledge as to the status of those under their watchful care. The social aspect of the meetings is altogether valuable."[17]

The *Era* termed the move "not only a step towards the destined prominence of the quorums in the Church—it was a bound."[18] But as with all new institutional changes, it took time for the new programs to become fully implemented, and periodically regional priesthood conventions were called to infuse new "zest" into the movement. During the first few years, a number of problems related to the new priesthood work became evident and received extensive attention from the committee.

Priesthood quorums did not always coincide with ward boundaries, so when weekly ward priesthood classes were commenced, there was confusion about the relationship between quorum and class, particularly among high priests and seventies. When the latter began missing their seventies' meeting, they received this instruction:

> For the convenience of men who belong to quorums that are widely scattered, and who could not come together frequently for

instruction, owing to the distance to be traveled, a system of ward priesthood meetings has been introduced by the presiding authorities of the Church which divides quorums that are located in more than one ward into ward classes, but this arrangement does not contemplate excusing men from coming together in quorums as the Lord has commanded.[19]

By 1913 ecclesiastical leaders felt it necessary to remind members that bishops were to be the presiding high priests over all local priesthood matters, and that all quorum loyalties, therefore, were subordinate to his local needs and directives.[20]

SUMMERS AND SUNDAYS

Holding weekly meetings during the summer months was a revolutionary practice for a majority of wards, and the change was not easily made. Following a thorough study of the problem, the committee reported in 1909 that:

> It is going to be a difficult task to continue the quorum meetings during the summer ... when the strawberries are ripe, how are we to leave them an hour or two earlier to go to meeting? ... So with the hay, the grain, the fruit. Is our meeting going to be important enough to warrant our leaving these labors once a week to attend? It will not do to work as late as usual on Monday evenings. If we do, we will be too tired to go to quorum meetings; will we have faith enough to feel that we will be as blessed in our temporal affairs by going, as by staying in the field at work.[21]

Only five out of the thirty-one stakes reporting to the committee in 1910 had held summer meetings. But four years later, due to continual pressure from Church officials, nearly 80 percent of the wards were continuing priesthood class work the year round. Generally, however, wards that succeeded in holding summer meetings had to shift their meeting times to Sundays, freeing the weekdays for the hard summer farm work.[22]

In fact, Monday nights were not the preference of many wards, summer or winter. Therefore, in late 1909 the committee proposed that priesthood meetings be on Sunday morning, thereby shifting Sunday School meetings to the afternoon. Questionnaires regarding this idea were sent by the First

Presidency to all bishops. Voting showed only 160 in favor and 430 opposed, so President Smith decided that the successful operation of the Sunday Schools should not be disrupted. However, with written permission, individual stakes were allowed to switch their meetings from Monday nights, and many did. Cassia Stake, for example, argued that "most of the men were on their farms which as a rule were so far from meeting place that regular attendance suffered," and were therefore allowed to meet on Sunday nights, alternating with the Mutuals. Other wards, as mentioned, adopted Sunday priesthood meetings during the summer months, sometimes as part of the Sunday Schools or Sunday MIAs. But Sunday morning meetings did not become the uniform rule until the 1930s.[23]

PROVIDING LESSON MANUALS

The committee's primary assignment was to direct the selecting, writing, editing, printing, and distributing of yearly theology lessons appropriate to the various quorums. This was a huge task, particularly during the first two years when ten new lesson manuals had to be written. Due to summer adjournments and other problems, many classes failed to complete their first two manuals, so 1911 was designed a "catch-up" year and no new lessons were distributed. Subsequently, the committee found two means of freeing itself from extensive annual writing assignments. First, among Aaronic Priesthood quorums, previously used manuals were reissued every two years. Then, starting in 1914, all Melchizedek Priesthood quorums were instructed to study the same annual lessons.

Sometimes leading Mormon writers, James E. Talmage and Orson F. Whitney among them, were requested to write manuals on specific themes, receiving a few hundred dollars to defray writing costs. In other cases, books that had been already published were selected. As a result, such outstanding works as Talmage's *Jesus the Christ*, John A. Widstoe's *A Rational Theology*, Joseph Fielding Smith's *Essentials in Church History*, and Joseph F. Smith's *Gospel Doctrine* were popularized among the Saints as priesthood manuals.[24]

All assigned manuals were screened by a reading committee, who referred questionable statements to the Quorum of the Twelve. It was made clear to the quorums, however, that the lesson books represented opinions of the authors and were not to be considered as authoritative statements of Church doctrine. Enough copies of these yearly lessons were ordered for between 20 and 30 percent of a ward's priesthood membership. Each weekly lesson was designed to teach both theory and practice, to "not only ... inculcate the wisdom and necessity of learning all the instructions and principles given in the revelations of God in good books and in nature, but summons the priesthood with persuasive voice to act upon the truths learned and believed."[25]

CORRELATION OF CHURCH TEACHING

To prevent unnecessary duplication of lesson materials of the priesthood quorums and the auxiliaries, the First Presidency in 1914 established a Correlation Committee. And as more and more priesthood classes came to be held during auxiliary class time, the problem of correlation became complex. There was serious disagreement, for example, as to what lessons should be used by boys whose priesthood class work was part of Sunday School or of Sunday evening YMMIA.

David O. McKay, a recognized leader of the General Priesthood Committee, became spokesman in the Correlation Committee for a radical solution to this problem in 1920. His plan, which was given serious consideration by the General Authorities, would have required that all teaching of the auxiliaries—Relief Society, Primary, and the MIA—and of the priesthood be conducted in the same Sabbath meeting, thereby creating a "Church Sunday School Day." After opening exercises in the Sunday morning meeting, priesthood classes would be held for (1) high priests, (2) seventies and elders, (3) priests and teachers, and (4) deacons. There would be one class for mothers; young ladies' senior and junior classes; two Primary classes would be written for each group, and this would mean fewer manuals to be authored and fewer good teachers to be called. Girls and women would pursue the same courses of study prescribed for boys and men of corresponding ages. Regular auxiliary and priesthood meetings would then be devoted to practical duties and activities. This "tight correlation" plan was studied for two years and tested on a trial basis in five wards. But in 1922 the First Presidency decided against it, concluding that the "existing quorums and associations are competent to plan for and execute the activities of each," although for a brief period in the late 1920s the priesthood classes were held Churchwide on an experimental basis as part of the Sunday School.[26]

REDIRECTING THE YMMIA WORK

The early MIAs had devoted much effort to providing theological instruction for Church members because "the quorums of the priesthood were not sufficiently active." But when the committee undertook to provide systematic priesthood manuals, an important YMMIA function was preempted. Although this led Brigham H. Roberts, of the YMMIA general board, to rejoice that "the Priesthood had been awakened and took possession of its proper field of activity," this change generally created a widespread feeling that the YMMIA organizations had "now filled their mission, and are now ready to pass away." Instead, however, the YMMIA officers redirected that auxiliary into such nontheological areas as "musical, dramatic and other like entertainments and festivities," and to scouting, field sports, athletic tournaments, excursions, and dances.[27]

PROBLEMS OF SMALLER WARDS

Separate classes and lessons for all six priesthood offices proved impractical for most smaller wards. Bishop Nibley noted early in 1912 that in many outlying wards "these were so few holding the Priesthood that he thought it would be best to consolidate the classes."[28] A priesthood census revealed that 177 wards had fewer than 4 seventies, including 46 that had none. Nearly 350 wards had fewer than 7 priests, including 71 wards where there were none. In 225 wards there were fewer than 6 teachers, including 67 wards that had none. On the average, only 11 priesthood holders attended weekly meetings in more than half of the wards in the Church. To expect these to separate into six classes for lessons was unrealistic. Consequently, some consolidation was allowed. Teachers and priests met together in some wards. All three Melchizedek Priesthood quorums, starting in 1914, were provided the same lesson manual, thereby making it easy for these men to have joint classes when circumstance warranted it.[29]

TEACHER DEVELOPMENT

In addition to lack of numbers, many priesthood meetings suffered because of the lack of efficient teachers. It was realized that "young men are so accustomed to good teachers in the schools that they will not long retain interest in a class where they have an indifferent or ill-informed man to teach them."[30] In some areas, bishops and other ward officers felt they should be the priesthood instructors. But the committee cautioned that such men were not called to leadership positions on the basis of teaching abilities, and that only capable teachers should direct quorum lessons. Yet trained teachers were scarce. Stake presidents reported in 1910 that in many wards little or nothing was being done to train and prepare priesthood or auxiliary teachers.[31]

In attacking this problem, the committee periodically published teaching advice in the *Improvement Era.* Also, manuals on teaching methods were distributed. Most stakes held monthly priesthood meetings where lessons were previewed and teaching problems were discussed. But despite such efforts, the Saints were informed in 1915

Presiding Bishop Charles W. Nibley was concerned that the priesthood organization had weak central direction. He implemented a plan with the First Presidency to coordinate activities, correlate lessons, and combine meetings so the priesthood could more effectively fulfill its duties. Courtesy Church Archives.

that "great chaos" still existed Churchwide in methods of teacher supervision. A new approach, weekly ward training classes to develop teachers for all Church organizations, was tried five years later.[32]

ENROLLMENT AND PRIESTHOOD FRATERNITY

Weekly meetings, lesson manuals, and teacher development were but the means by which greater priesthood activity was sought. To evaluate the success of these programs, the committee established a new system of record keeping and reporting. Simultaneously, the Presiding Bishopric cooperated by launching a campaign to "purge and correct" all ward membership records.[33]

Accuracy in record keeping was hampered by the practice, still prevalent by 1911, of "insisting on a recommend from the quorum where the person formerly was enrolled" before relocated members could be considered enrolled members of priesthood quorums. Thus, in 1912 there were 13,308 priesthood members not enrolled in any quorums out of 77,114 total priesthood holders, despite special enrollment drives.[34] The discrepancy between the real and roll book count of priesthood holders is demonstrated by the records of some of the Utah stakes that year.[35]

Stake	Priesthood Holders	Priesthood Enrolled
Alpine	2,346	1,579
Box Elder	1,392	498
Liberty	1,707	680
Tooele	762	53

But when the Presiding Bishopric instructed bishops in June 1914 that any priesthood bearer in their wards should be enrolled in proper priesthood classes "regardless of whether he has been received as a member of the quorum which has jurisdiction in your ward," the enrollment confusion gradually subsided. Two years later, quorum recommends were discontinued.[36]

Contributing to enrollment delinquencies and to priesthood inactivity was the lack of comradeship felt by quorum members. In 1911 the *Improvement Era* reported, "the cultivation of the spirit of fraternity has been neglected in most quorums."[37] To counter this, special missionaries were sent to contact all ward and stake members to encourage priesthood participation, and by 1921 stake missionary work among members and nonmembers had become a permanent program in most stakes in the Church. Priesthood support for the MIA recreational and scouting activities also was increased, and local leaders were urged to develop programs to keep youth off the streets, to support saloon closing campaigns, and to work with juvenile courts.[38] During this period, fraternal orders and exclusive clubs had some appeal among the Saints, and their fraternal aspects were commended to the Church as attributes the quorums should develop. But because scores of brethren had disobeyed Church counsel in order to join fraternities where they could obtain inexpensive life insurance, the committee spent much energy in devising a comparable priesthood life insurance program. "Insurance at exact cost is certainly not the United Order," its report advised, "but it is a preparatory step in the right direction." Numerous problems, however, prevented the adoption of this insurance plan.[39]

REVIVING THE LESSER PRIESTHOOD

Neglect by local authorities and indifference by many boys were two factors responsible for what the *Improvement Era* called an "alarming situation" among Aaronic Priesthood youth.[40] Although there were as many boys between the ages of fifteen and eighteen in 1912 as between twelve and fifteen, there were but 9,300 teachers compared to 20,255 deacons. The *Era* reported that year that "neither the priesthood quorums nor the Sunday School, nor any of the other organizations of the Church are taking care of the certain lot of our young people. There are at least forty percent of them [boys and girls] who are not attending any of our organizations, between the ages of fourteen and seventeen."[41]

A primary cause of this situation was a pervasive lack of dignity and importance accorded the callings of teacher and priest. The immaturity of ordained boys was widely criticized. One committee member, for example, urged that the ordination age for deacons be raised to fifteen, for "as a rule boys were too young to have this honor conferred upon them." Presiding Bishop Nibley proposed that boys prove themselves on missions before being given the Melchizedek Priesthood and temple ordinances. In numerous wards, Aaronic Priesthood boys were not allowed to take charge of the sacrament, and instructions regarding passing the sacrament were addressed in a 1910 *Improvement Era* article to elders, not to holders of the lesser priesthood. The custom still continued in some wards not to advance a deacon in the priesthood until there was reason to ordain him an elder. The committee learned that, contrary to scripture, only 108 bishops, out of 713, personally presided over their own priests groups in 1912. Also, it was admitted by Church officials that ordained priests and teachers were too young to be the backbone of ward teaching, so in their places "acting teachers" were called from among the elders, seventies, and high priests.[42]

A vigorous campaign to make the teachers and priests quorums of importance in the wards was launched by the committee. Ordinations at the recommended ages were urged unless there was "good reason" to disregard the rule. In the first year of the campaign, the number of bishops personally presiding over their priests rose from thirty to nearly five hundred. This "great awakening" continued until the proper organization of priests quorums was announced to the Church in 1915, at which time 6,000 out of 8,830 priests were enrolled.[43] A year later, specific Aaronic Priesthood duties, based on actual ward practices, were identified and circulated for the aid of bishops. They included the following:[44]

Deacons

Collect fast offerings	Assist in caring for cemeteries
Messenger for bishops	Keep order in meetinghouse
Pass sacrament	Maintain meetinghouse grounds
Prepare fuel for widows and old people	Assist in Primary work
	Assist in religion class work
Care for the poor	Act as ushers
Pass out notices	Boy Scout work
Pump organ at meetings	Attend the doors
Keep Church property in good condition	Distribute special notices

Teachers

Assist in ward teaching	Take charge of meetings,
Assist with sacrament	furnish speakers, singing, etc.
Instructors for Boy Scouts	Clerk in branch
Collect ward funds	Officers in auxiliary organizations
Assist in renovating meetinghouses	Notify priesthood quorums of meetings
Cutting wood for poor	Choir members

Priests

Administer the sacrament	Supervise the fast offering collecting
Pass the sacrament	Help bishop with care of tithes
Assist in ward teaching	Help bishop with wayward boys
Take part in meetings	Sunday School officers and teachers
Perform baptisms	Haul gravel and make cement walks around meetinghouse
Mutual officers and teachers	
Ward choristers	Help with teams to level public squares
Messengers for bishopric	Active in guiding amusements

Hold cottage meetings   Missionary work in the ward
Assist the elders   Read scriptures at ward meetings

MAINTAINING AND IMPROVING THE NEW PROGRAM

"Let us impress upon you," the committee urged in 1913, "that nearly 18,000 men meeting weekly for study and contemplation must inevitably result in general good for the Church," and evidence of such results was not hard to find.[45] Weekly attendance at priesthood meetings, aided by the recent organization of priests quorums, had risen by that year to the 20 percent level, a sign to the committee that "we are moving upward."[46] Sacrament meeting attendance likewise was improving. Notable too was increased service by Melchizedek Priesthood bearers, 20,495 of whom were then ward officers and instructors.[47] An "unusual interest" in ward teaching also had been aroused. It was found, for example, that as more men were given ward teaching assignments and the size of districts was reduced, a proportional increase in monthly visits was produced. In 1911, two ward teachers typically were assigned to visit twenty families, and Churchwide only 20 percent of all families were visited. Two years later, the typical district size was down to nine families and the visiting rate doubled to 39 percent. Between 1919 and 1914, home teaching visits increased fivefold, and by 1915 over half of Church families, or 54 percent, were receiving monthly visits. Six years later, the Church home teaching average had increased to 70 percent.[48] In addition to this "far reaching increase in Priesthood activity," the reform movement had produced Churchwide an equally significant "realization of the importance of Priesthood quorums as compared with auxiliary organizations."[49]

Subsequently, the committee sought not only to increase the effectiveness of its programs and to extend such to previously "unreformed" wards, but also to prevent backsliding among the "reformed" wards—a herculean task during the World War I years. Church attendance and activity declined, particularly during summer months, as Mormon farmers sought to increase their production in response to growing wartime markets.

Declines were most notable in Aaronic Priesthood work. Priests quorums were depleted by the military so that remaining priests had to meet with teachers quorums. In many wards, by 1917 a "loose and indifferent state" plagued lesser priesthood quorums and there developed again a need for "a suitable and proper method of organizing and supervising the Lesser

Priesthood of each ward and training the boys in their duties and responsibilities."[50] Individually, bishops responded by devising unique activities for their boys. These ranged from taking deacons along on the bishop's annual house-to-house visits, to assigning priests as special teachers to the widows, aged, and poor, to having teachers go along with older men to conduct fuel surveys and Red Cross, War Savings Bond, and Thrift campaigns among the Saints. But despite such efforts, the postwar years brought Church leaders face to face with "a woeful lack of interest on the part of those holding the Lesser Priesthood in their Church activities," as well as with the task of beginning again to organize and ordain priests.[51]

The project of major importance to the committee during the war years was the compilation of President Joseph F. Smith's sermons and writings just prior to his death in 1918. His accidental remark that "he was leaving no literature or book in his memory," prompted six friends to compile the book *Gospel Doctrine,* which was then edited and published by the committee as a three-year course of study for Melchizedek Priesthood quorums, starting in 1919.[52] Other priesthood reform activities during these years included an effort to separate adult Aaronic Priesthood members into groups with their own officers, so as not "to mix up the old men, with bad habits, with young boys," and the new weekly, teacher-training program noted previously. For the second time, the committee investigated in detail and supported the priesthood insurance idea, which was once again rejected by the First Presidency. Finally, the "Church Sunday School Day" correlation plan, mentioned previously, was the committee's last major project before its release by President Heber J. Grant in December 1922.[53]

SIGNIFICANCE OF THE MOVEMENT

Overall, this reform movement was of immeasurable and lasting importance to priesthood work in this dispensation. Specific results, which became foundation stones for many modern priesthood programs, included the following:

Aaronic Priesthood

Definite age groupings established for each office.
Separate adult Aaronic work proposed.
Specific duties identified for deacons, teachers, priests.

Priests quorums' importance recognized.
Bishops finally assumed presidency over lesser priesthood.

Ward and Quorum Functions

Regular weekly, year round, ward priesthood classes made the rule.
Bishops became presiding high priests over all ward priesthood work.
Priesthood enrolled in proper quorums.
Systematic ward and quorum record keeping introduced.
Effective stake relations with local priesthood established.
Increased local priesthood service as ward officers, ward teachers, etc.
Stake missionary work commenced.

Church Headquarters

Systematic record keeping and report procedures developed.
Communication with wards and stakes greatly improved.
Centralized direction of local priesthood work undertaken.
YMMIA redirected into recreational and cultural activities.
Priesthood work better coordinated with auxiliaries.

Lessons

Annual, systematic courses of study provided to all quorums.
Important Church books thereby made known to members.
Teacher training work pioneered.
All Church teaching became better coordinated.

Finally, there is a direct relationship between this reform movement and modern Church correlation work. Elder Harold B. Lee discussed the connection when he announced the new priesthood correlation program in 1961. After noting periodic surveys that the Church has taken of its ever-changing needs, he said:

> Within the memories of many of the present General Authorities, there have been surveys of this kind, or reexaminations about twenty years apart. One of the first comprehensive studies was undertaken under the general chairmanship of President David O. McKay, who was then the chairman of the general priesthood committee of the Church, and this was about forty years ago. To me it is

a significant thing that this problem of proper correlation seems to have been in President McKay's own mind through all of this time and perhaps as long as he has been one of the General Authorities.[54]

Within the past few years, Church members have seen a number of steps taken in the direction first outlined by President Joseph F. Smith and the General Priesthood Committee since the 1910s and 1920s. The teacher-training program, for example, once conducted by the Sunday School, is now under the control and direction of the priesthood. Relief Society budgets have become subject to ward bishops. YMMIA officers are the same men who direct Aaronic Priesthood work in each ward and are priesthood activity arms. Auxiliary contacts with the homes are handled by the priesthood home teachers. Although there is still room for improvement, the priesthood now appears to be doing what President Joseph F. Smith hoped it would when he forcefully entreated the priesthood in 1908 to assume its rightful role in the functionings of the Church.

This article was originally published in BYU Studies *13, no. 2 (1973): 137–56.*

NOTES

1. General Priesthood Committee Minutes, December 5, 1911, Church History Library, The Church of Jesus Christ of Latter-day Saints, Salt Lake City. See also Joseph B. Keeler, *First Steps in Church Government* (Salt Lake City: Deseret News, 1906), 6–7.
2. General Priesthood Committee Minutes, June 5, 1908.
3. General Priesthood Committee Minutes, October 4, 1910, and April 27, 1911; also, Presiding Bishopric, Policy Directives, box 1, Church History Library; and Logan Fourth Ward Priests Quorum Minutes 1906–10, Church History Library.
4. Logan First Ward Aaronic Priesthood Minutes 1905–10, Church History Library.
5. Cardston Ward, Alberta Stake, Lesser Priesthood Minutes 1897–1909, October 14, 1901, Church History Library.
6. Ogden First Ward First and Second Deacons Quorums Minutes 1906–7, December 14, 1908, Church History Library.
7. Provo First Ward, Deacons Quorum Minute Book 1903–4, Church History Library.
8. General Priesthood Committee Minutes, February 6, 1912.
9. Cardston Lesser Priesthood Minutes.
10. J. Golden Kimball, "Address," in *Seventy-sixth Annual Conference of The Church of Jesus Christ of Latter-day Saints* (Salt Lake City: The Church of Jesus Christ of Latter-day Saints, 1906), 19.

11. Joseph F. Smith, "Opening Address," in *Seventy-sixth Annual Conference of The Church of Jesus Christ of Latter-day Saints* (Salt Lake City: The Church of Jesus Christ of Latter-day Saints, 1906), 3.

12. Joseph F. Smith, "Opening Address," in *Seventy-eighth Annual Conference of The Church of Jesus Christ of Latter-day Saints* (Salt Lake City: The Church of Jesus Christ of Latter-day Saints, 1908), 6.

13. General Priesthood Committee Minutes, June 5, 16, and 23, 1908.

14. General Priesthood Committee Minutes, September 15, 1908. High priests, elders, priests, teachers, and deacons met as localized quorums, while the seventies, due to their unique missionary responsibilities, functioned as general quorums directed by their own general authorities, the First Quorum of the Seventy. Their organizational independence caused many seventies to hold feelings of exclusiveness from other quorums and from ward and stake leaders. As a result of this reform movement, the seventies quorums became more fully integrated into ward and stake priesthood programs, with a simultaneous decline in their importance as general quorums in the Church. They became, in fact, standing ministers at home, and their quorum work became subordinate to the needs of the wards and stakes.

15. Presiding Bishopric, Circular Letter File, January 1, 1909, Church History Library.

16. "Priesthood Quorums Table," *Improvement Era* 12 (April 1909): 500. This "Priesthood Quorums Table" appeared as a regular monthly feature of the *Era* and contained valuable priesthood directives and reports from the General Priesthood Committee; all references to the *Era* which follow are taken from this monthly section, unless otherwise designated.

17. Presiding Bishopric, Circular Letter, January 1, 1910.

18. *Improvement Era* 13 (January 1910): 287.

19. *Improvement Era* 14 (July 1911): 841.

20. *Improvement Era* 16 (April 1913): 648.

21. *Improvement Era* 12 (May 1909): 573.

22. General Priesthood Committee Minutes, November 29, 1910; also *Improvement Era* 17 (May 1914): 692.

23. General Priesthood Committee Minutes, February 15, 1910, and December 6, 1912.

24. General Priesthood Committee Minutes, December 8, 1922.

25. *Improvement Era* 12 (April 1909): 499.

26. General Priesthood Committee Minutes, September 2 and December 8, 1922.

27. "Mutual Work," *Improvement Era* 12 (January 1909): 247; Heber J. Grant, "The Place of the Young Men's Mutual Improvement Association in the Church," *Improvement Era* 15 (August 1912): 875; also Brigham H. Roberts, "Sphere of YMMIA Activities," *Improvement Era* 16 (January 1913): 187–88.

28. General Priesthood Committee Minutes, March 5, 1912.

29. General Priesthood Committee Minutes, March 26, 1912; also *Improvement Era* 17 (May 1914): 692–93.

30. *Improvement Era* 12 (April 1909): 498.

31. General Priesthood Committee Minutes, December 13, 1910.

32. Issues of the *Improvement Era* in 1912 contain monthly teaching suggestions; General Priesthood Committee Minutes, March 25, 1915; Presiding Bishopric, Circular Letter, December 28, 1920.

33. Presiding Bishopric, Circular Letter, January 1, 1910.

34. General Priesthood Committee Minutes, December 5, 1911, and August 6, 1912.

35. General Priesthood Committee Minutes, December 5, 1911.

36. Presiding Bishopric, Circular Letter, June 25, 1914, and March 9, 1916.

37. *Improvement Era* 14 (May 1911): 652.

38. General Priesthood Committee Minutes, March 28, 1911.

39. General Priesthood Committee Minutes, March 28, 1911.

40. *Improvement Era* 15 (May 1912): 656–57.

41. *Improvement Era* 15 (May 1912): 656–57; also Grant, "The Place of the Young Men's Mutual . . . ," *Improvement Era* 15 (August 1912): 877.

42. General Priesthood Committee Minutes, May 5 and December 10, 1909; August 6 and September 3, 1912; and April 2, 1912; *Improvement Era* 13 (April 1910): 570; *Improvement Era* 15 (May 1912): 657.

43. *Improvement Era* 16 (May 1913): 736–38; also General Priesthood Committee Minutes, September 2, 1913, and March 25, 1915.

44. General Priesthood Committee Minutes, June 1, 1916.

45. *Improvement Era* 16 (May 1913): 736–37.

46. *Improvement Era* 16 (May 1913): 736–37.

47. *Improvement Era* 16 (May 1913): 738.

48. *Improvement Era* 17 (May 1914): 692; General Priesthood Committee Minutes, September 29, 1914, and March 25, 1915; also Meeting of the First Presidency and the Presiding Bishopric, August 11, 1921. Presiding Bishopric Miscellaneous, box 1, Church History Library.

49. *Improvement Era* 17 (May 1914): 692–93.

50. General Priesthood Committee Minutes, April 5, 1917.

51. General Priesthood Committee Minutes, October 3 and 10, 1918; November 1, 1917; and June 21, 1921; also, Presiding Bishopric, Circular Letter, June 14, 1918.

52. General Priesthood Committee Minutes, October 3, 1918.

53. General Priesthood Committee Minutes, December 12, 1911; November 1, 1917; and November 4, 1920.

54. Harold B. Lee, "Address," in *One Hundred Twenty-ninth Semi-annual Conference of The Church of Jesus Christ of Latter-day Saints* (Salt Lake City: The Church of Jesus Christ of Latter-day Saints, 1961, 78.

Administrative/Organizational History

13   Organization

Church organization and administration since 1830 have been the result of the restoration of ancient priesthood authority and offices, of decisions made by living prophets receptive to divine revelation, and of practical responses to changing world and Church circumstances. From its inception the Church has been hierarchical, with authority flowing from the President of the Church. Most positions are filled by lay members called to serve without remuneration, and members are entitled to sustain or not sustain decisions and officers proposed by their leaders.

The Foundation

Joseph Smith and Oliver Cowdery received priesthood ordination and baptism under the direction of heavenly messengers in 1829. They then baptized others. This cluster of believers gathered on April 6, 1830, for the formal organization of the Church, with Joseph Smith as First Elder and Oliver as Second Elder. Two months later, the Church held its first conference and soon established a tradition of semiannual general conferences. From the beginning, Church officers were sustained by conference vote, and members and officials received certificates of membership or ordination from conferences.

During the first two years of the Church, deacons, teachers, priests, and elders constituted the local ministry. "The Articles and Covenants" served as a handbook explaining the duties of these officers (see D&C 20).

A revelation in 1831 instituted the office of bishop, initially one for Missouri and another for Ohio. Temporal affairs were their primary stewardship at first; they received consecrations of property in the 1830s, tithes afterward, and cared for the poor. Soon, bishops also received responsibility for disciplinary procedures and for the Aaronic Priesthood. Not until 1839, in Nauvoo, Illinois, did the Church have bishops assigned to local geographical subdivisions called wards, under the jurisdiction of the bishop responsible for the larger region.

The office of high priest was instituted in 1831, with Joseph Smith as the presiding high priest over the Church. In 1832 he chose counselors to assist him, initiating what became the First Presidency. Revelation in March 1833 (D&C 90) gave the Presidency supreme authority over all affairs of the Church; their roles at the head of the hierarchy remain essentially unchanged. Late in 1833, a second general officer, the Patriarch to the Church, was called and ordained.

In 1834 two stakes—geographic entities—were formed (one in Ohio and the second in Missouri) to direct the operation of branches (congregations) and local officers. Stakes were led by a three-man stake presidency and a twelve-member high council (D&C 102). High councils arbitrated disputes, investigated and tried charges of misconduct, and generally oversaw local ecclesiastical operations. Outside stake boundaries, members clustered into isolated branches led by elders or priests.

In 1835 the Quorum of the Twelve Apostles and the Quorum of the Seventy were organized. The Twelve, subordinate to the First Presidency, were assigned by revelation to preside outside organized stakes as a traveling high council. This included ordaining and supervising other officers of the Church outside stakes, including patriarchs. They were also to direct proselytizing in all lands, assisted by the Seventy. The Seventy's presidency of seven, called the First Council of the Seventy, were sustained with other General Authorities in August 1835.

By 1835 revelations defined two orders of priesthood: the higher, or Melchizedek Priesthood, including the offices of high priest, seventy, and elder; and the lesser, or Aaronic Priesthood, comprising priests, teachers, and deacons. Priesthood quorums in the stakes consisted of up to ninety-six elders, forty-eight priests, twenty-four teachers, and twelve deacons, each with its own presidency except the priests, whose president is a bishop.

In fall 1835, the Church published the first edition of the Doctrine and Covenants. The three revelations placed first (now sections 20, 107, and 84) described priesthood and its organization.

Visitations by Moses, Elias, and Elijah in 1836 restored the keys of the priesthood and responsibility to gather scattered Israel and the sealing powers by which families could be linked for eternity in temples (see D&C 109–10). These keys are still the basis for LDS missionary, family history/genealogy, and temple work.

The Kirtland Temple was the site for the restoration of the keys of temple work by Moses, Elias, and Elijah in 1836. Historic American Survey Collection, Library of Congress.

After a mission to Great Britain (1839–41), the Twelve received broadened responsibility, under the First Presidency, for Church government within the stakes as well as outside them, a responsibility they have carried since. In Nauvoo they received temple ordinances and the keys necessary to govern the Church if there were no First Presidency.

To complete Church organization and prepare the women, along with the men, for the temple, in 1842 Joseph Smith organized the women's Relief Society in Nauvoo. A counterpart of priesthood organization for men, the Relief Society was seen as a more integral part of Church organization than were later auxiliary organizations.

In 1841, Joseph Smith established the office of Trustee-in-Trust to manage Church properties at the general level. The role of bishops in temporal affairs thus became subordinate to that of the Trustee-in-Trust, generally the President of the Church. In Nauvoo, and for the next decade after, a Council of Fifty assisted as political and temporal administrators.

The last body in the governing hierarchy to emerge was the Presiding Bishopric. Until 1847 the Church had two general bishops, but that year Bishop Newel K. Whitney became Presiding Bishop. When his successor (1851), Bishop Edward Hunter, received two regular counselors in 1856, the three constituted the first full Presiding Bishopric. Initially, the Presiding Bishopric's primary responsibility was the overall management of temporal affairs, including the supervision of ward bishops in their temporal duties. Beginning in the 1850s, the Presiding Bishopric also oversaw Aaronic Priesthood matters.

The First Presidency, Twelve, Seventy, and Presiding Bishopric—all dating from this first generation—continue to be the main administrative officers of the Church. These General Authority offices are generally life-tenured callings, except in cases of calls to a higher position or removal for cause or health problems, though emeritus status has recently been introduced. The Second Quorum of the Seventy is comprised of men called to serve a five-year period. Between 1941 and 1976, additional General Authorities known as Assistants to the Twelve also served. The office of Patriarch to the Church, which earlier had administrative functions, was eventually limited to giving patriarchal blessings to Church members outside stakes, and in 1979 was discontinued.

After Joseph Smith's death in 1844, the Twelve Apostles led the Church under the direction of senior Apostle and Quorum President Brigham Young. In 1847 he was sustained as President in a new First Presidency. Succession in the Presidency continues to adhere to that basic pattern.

The Pioneer Organization

After migration to the West in the late 1840s, Church organization adapted to facilitate colonization of the undeveloped Great Basin. Church officers directed the establishment of hundreds of colonies and helped provide settlements with economic, political, judicial, social, and spiritual programs. Often, one of the Twelve presided in larger settlements. Mormon villages combined private enterprise and economic cooperation, with bishops or stake presidents supervising the dispensing of land, building of roads, digging of ditches and canals, and conducting of business ventures. Although civil government gradually assumed an increasing role, the Church remained a significant influence in local and regional affairs throughout the pioneer period.

In a largely cashless economy with little investment capital, Church leaders promoted colonization and industrial enterprises by calling individuals on special missions and by using Church resources to foster community enterprises. A Church public works program, directed by the First Presidency and managed by the Presiding Bishopric, provided employment and helped build the Salt Lake Temple and Tabernacle and create other community improvements. In the 1870s, Brigham Young directed the organization of United Orders, economic endeavors managed by stake presidents and bishops. Since tithing donations were usually in "kind" rather than cash, local bishops and the Presiding Bishopric directed a gigantic barter and transfer system that paid for needed services, fed public works employees, and assisted the needy.

Much Church effort went toward assisting with immigration to the Great Basin. The Perpetual Emigrating Fund, a revolving loan fund, helped poorer immigrants, including handcart immigrants, make the trek. In the 1860s, Church wagon trains were sent from Utah to convey immigrants from the railroad terminus. After they arrived in Utah, the First Presidency and Presiding Bishopric directed immigrants to settlements where they were needed.

In the 1850s and thereafter, the ward became the primary Church organization in the lives of the Saints. In the pioneer era, bishops selected by the First Presidency and priesthood "block teachers" called by bishops were the main ward officers. General Authorities maintained contact through semiannual general conferences in Salt Lake City, visits to the settlements, *Deseret News* articles, and epistles.

Missionary work, most of it outside the Great Basin, also had to be organized. In 1850 several of the Twelve opened new missions in Europe. Usually an Apostle residing in Britain supervised all European missionary work. Missions were divided into conferences, districts, and branches, each with a president selected by the line officer above him.

During the 1860s and 1870s auxiliary organizations started locally and then became general Church organizations under the supervision or presidency of General Authorities. These included Sunday Schools; the Retrenchment Association, predecessor to the Young Ladies' Mutual

Improvement Association (YLMIA); the Young Men's Mutual Improvement Association (YMMIA); and the Primary for children. Relief Society for women was revived in Utah and established throughout the Church beginning in 1867.

In 1877, President Brigham Young implemented a massive reordering of wards, stakes, and priesthood quorums. This reform removed the Twelve from local leadership assignments, created new quorums for elders and Aaronic Priesthood, expanded the role of bishops as ward leaders, gave stakes increased responsibility, and, for the first time, involved most young men in Aaronic Priesthood offices. These and other changes at that time, such as quarterly stake conferences and reporting procedures, remained standard for nearly a century.

During the changes of 1877, Elder Orson Pratt explained the Church's organizational flexibility in terms that also foreshadowed future developments:

> To say that there will be a stated time, in the history of this church, during its imperfections and weaknesses, when the organization will be perfect, and that there will be no further extension or addition to the organization, would be a mistake. Organization is to go on, step after step, ... just as the people increase and grow in the knowledge of the principles and laws of the kingdom of God.[1]

Led by prophets, seers, and revelators, the Church has exhibited its flexibility in adapting to changing needs and circumstances.

Elaboration and Continuity

The Church faced the 1880s with a well-developed and well-functioning organization; in addition, it was beginning to create auxiliary organizations for children and youth. Over decades these would mature and be fine-tuned to function more effectively in an increasingly complex world.

Church pioneering institutions also remained. During the 1880s and 1890s, the Church continued to direct colonization and economic development. Building on the cooperative movement of the 1860s and the united orders of the 1870s, by the 1880s the First Presidency was coordinating development and regulated economic competition through a central Board of Trade and similar stake boards. During this period as well, revelations to

President John Taylor initiated a revitalization of quorums of seventy and moved these quorums toward becoming stake rather than general Church entities.

Federal prosecutions of polygamists during the 1880s disrupted Church administration as General Authorities, stake presidents, and bishops went into hiding or left Utah. Franklin D. Richards, an Apostle whose plural wife had died, carried on many of the public functions of general Church leadership under the direction of the First Presidency, who were in hiding. With general Church ownership of property severely restricted, stakes, wards, and individuals formed nonprofit associations to hold Church property, including temples, meetinghouses, tithing houses, and livestock. After the manifesto of 1890 and the granting of amnesty, Church leaders resumed their full administrative duties.

During the 1880s, stake boards or committees were created for YMMIA, YLMIA, Relief Society, Primary, and Sunday School to promote and supervise auxiliary work locally. In 1889 the Relief Society began holding conferences in connection with the Church's general conferences, as did the Primary. By 1902 each of the auxiliaries was publishing its own magazine.

Although an extensive bureaucracy was not necessary until rapid international growth began in the 1960s, between 1900 and 1930 Church leaders modernized management and constructed important new facilities. The Church acquired historical sites, supported hospitals, established recreation centers in local meetinghouses, and erected new offices in Salt Lake City, including a Bishop's Building (1910) for the Presiding Bishopric and auxiliary organizations, and the Administration Building (1917), in which the First Presidency and Quorum of the Twelve still have their offices. Zion's Securities Corporation was created to manage taxable Church properties, and the Corporation of the President was established to oversee ecclesiastical properties.

Church leaders also attended to programs for youth. Early correlation efforts saw the autonomy of Church auxiliaries decline as the Church assumed greater control over auxiliary magazines; the YMMIA's *Improvement Era* became a magazine for priesthood and Church readership. In 1911 the Church adopted the Boy Scout program as part of the YMMIA. In response to the secularization of Utah schools during the late nineteenth century, the Church had created stake academies and conducted religion classes after school for elementary-school children. By 1910 a General Board of

Education supervised thirty-four stake academies: Brigham Young College in Logan, Utah; Latter-day Saint University in Salt Lake City; and Brigham Young University in Provo, Utah. By the 1920s the Church had closed most of its academies or transferred them to the state. Starting in 1912, released-time seminaries provided religious instruction for high school students. In 1926 the first institute of religion for college students opened adjacent to the University of Idaho.

Correlation efforts also extended to the work of priesthood, including missionary work, and to auxiliaries. A Priesthood Committee on Outlines began publishing lesson materials for each priesthood quorum during a priesthood revitalization movement (1908–22). Church leaders also grouped deacons, teachers, and priests by age and defined their duties more fully; instituted weekly ward priesthood meetings, conducted by the bishops; and improved ward (formerly "block") teaching. After 1923, members of the Quorum of the Twelve directly supervised Melchizedek Priesthood work while the Presiding Bishopric supervised the Aaronic Priesthood, and in 1928 the Church published its first Melchizedek Priesthood handbook. A Priesthood-Auxiliary Movement, in 1928–37, made Sunday School the instructional arm and YMMIA the activity arm of priesthood. This plan defined auxiliaries as aids to the priesthood and made the adult Gospel Doctrine class in Sunday School an integral part of adults' Sunday activity. Junior Sunday School for children became part of the Sunday School program Churchwide in 1934.

The Presiding Bishopric began providing aggressive leadership to Aaronic Priesthood work and to the YMMIA in 1938, and shortly thereafter they were given supervision of the young women. They provided counsel to bishops and stake presidents on Aaronic Priesthood, buildings, records and reports, and ward teaching through a weekly bulletin, *Progress of the Church.*

Beginning in 1925 a mission home in Salt Lake City provided training for new full-time missionaries. During the 1920s, radio and motion pictures first helped missionaries convey the LDS message. Stake missionary work (part-time proselytizing by local members), started locally by 1915, was supervised by the First Council of Seventy after 1936. In 1937 the first missionary handbook was published, and in 1952 missionaries began using *A Systematic Program for Teaching the Gospel,* the Church's first official proselytizing outline. In 1954 a Missionary Committee, under General Authorities, began overseeing missionary appointments, the mission home in Salt

Lake City, and publicity and literature. A Language Training Mission for full-time missionaries called to foreign lands opened in 1961 at Provo, Utah, and in 1978 it was expanded to become a Missionary Training Center for most new missionaries. Eventually, Mission Training Centers were established in other countries; collectively, these provide intensive training in dozens of languages.

In 1936, to ease hardships caused by the Great Depression, the First Presidency introduced the Church Security Program. Renamed the Welfare Program in 1938, it established through existing priesthood channels a network of farms, canneries, and factories that sent food, clothing, furniture, and household goods to bishop's storehouses to assist the needy and, later, disaster victims. Soon after World War I, the Relief Society developed a Social Services department to help families. This was gradually expanded to provide professional assistance, available through priesthood leaders, in such matters as counseling, therapy, and adoptive services. Eventually, Social Services joined health services, employment bureaus, and other guidance programs as part of Welfare Services.

To meet the needs of LDS servicemen far from home wards and stakes, Church leaders responded with servicemen's groups on military bases, LDS chaplains, servicemen's coordinators, a Military Relations Committee, servicemen's conferences, seminars to prepare young men for the service, and an English-speaking servicemen's stake in West Germany. Native Americans also received renewed administrative attention. An Indian mission was formed in 1936 in the American Southwest, a general-level Indian Committee in the late 1940s, and the Indian Student Placement Services beginning in 1947.

Challenges of Growth and Internationalization

Between 1960 and 1990, Church membership more than quadrupled, with especially rapid growth outside the United States. Many organizational developments during these decades were designed to streamline operations, enhance communication and leadership training, and focus resources on the needs of Church members far from headquarters.

By the 1960s, three kinds of organizations were operating within the Church: (1) an ecclesiastical system under a priesthood chain of command; (2) auxiliaries, each with its own general officers, manuals, conferences, and publication; and (3) professional services and departments for education, social work, legal affairs, building, communications, accounting, and so forth. Early in the 1960s, efforts began to correlate these organizations. A Correlation Committee consolidated and simplified Church curriculum, publications, meetings, and activities. Further elements of the correlation program, implemented in 1964, grouped priesthood responsibilities into four categories: missionary, genealogy, welfare, and home teaching. Ward teaching became home teaching, giving the priesthood quorums new responsibility for carrying Church programs to LDS families. Wards developed priesthood executive committees and ward councils to coordinate functions and reach out to individuals. In 1965 family home evening was established Churchwide and, in 1970, Monday nights were set aside for families; special manuals provided suggestions for gospel-oriented family activities.

Beginning in 1965 all messages from general Church agencies to wards and stakes were tunneled into the *Priesthood Bulletin*. Regional publications merged in 1967 into a unified International Magazine, published in several languages. In 1971, Church magazines in the United States and Great Britain were restructured with the publication of the *Ensign* for adults, the *New Era* for teens, and the *Friend* for children. By 1970, Church leaders had implemented a worldwide translation and distribution organization with publishing and distribution centers in European countries, the Americas, and the Pacific Rim.

Members of the First Council of the Seventy were ordained high priests in 1961 in order to better assist the Twelve in overseeing the growing number of wards and stakes. Regional Representatives and Mission Representatives of the Twelve were called in 1967 and 1972, respectively (and merged in 1974). These officers played a key role in training and advising local leaders, an increasing number of whom were relatively recent converts with little administrative experience.

Spencer W. Kimball's presidency (1973–85) saw important administrative changes, often in the direction of regionalizing responsibilities. Several functions previously reserved for General Authorities were delegated to stake presidents. In 1975 the First Quorum of the Seventy was reinstated as a body of General Authorities; a decade later the office of Seventy became exclusively a General Authority position. Regional Representatives received limited line authority to supervise stake work (1976). In 1978 the Twelve became more directly involved in such ecclesiastical matters as curriculum, activity programs, and Scouting; the Presiding Bishopric retained responsibility for temporal programs but no longer for the youth. To enhance general Church supervision of local operations throughout the world and at the same time facilitate regionalization, in 1984 an Area Presidency (a president and two counselors, all of the Seventy) was organized for each of several major geographic areas. As the Church expands, boundaries are redrawn, and the number and importance of Area Presidencies increase.

Church programs have also been redesigned to meet the needs of an increasingly international membership. During the 1960s, a labor missionary program (modeled

During his tenure as President, Spencer W. Kimball instituted changes in the administration of the Church, including delegating some General Authority functions to stake presidents and reinstituting the First Quorum of the Seventy as General Authorities. Photo by Mark Philbrick, Brigham Young University.

after one that earlier constructed a college and a temple in New Zealand, and numerous chapels, especially in the South Pacific) helped the Church build meetinghouses in all parts of the world. In the mid-1970s the Church divested itself of hospitals that benefited primarily residents of the intermountain West and focused increased attention on the construction of chapels and temples worldwide—this time not by labor missionaries but by professional builders. A consolidated Sunday three-hour meeting schedule for priesthood, sacrament meeting, and auxiliary meetings was introduced in the United States and Canada in 1980 and later worldwide. By the 1980s, a satellite communications network linked headquarters with many local stakes; that, and the widespread use of videos, made general conferences and communications from Church headquarters much more accessible. By 1990 much of the training of local leaders had been assumed by Area Presidencies and Regional Representatives.

In the 1980s, Church financing became increasingly centralized, relieving local units of a major burden. Beginning in 1982, ward and stake buildings were funded fully from general Church funds (from tithes). In 1990 general funds also became the source for financing all local operations in the United States and Canada.

Although the basic administrative officers date from the founding generation, the challenges faced and the way the Church organizes itself to meet those challenges have changed dramatically. Such changes will continue. As President John Taylor said in 1886, the priesthood must not be fettered by "cast iron rules," for it is "a living, intelligent principle, and must necessarily have freedom to act" as circumstances require.[2]

This article was originally published in Encyclopedia of Mormonism, *ed. Daniel H. Ludlow, 4 vols. (New York: Macmillan, 1992), 3:1035–44.*

NOTES

1. Orson Pratt, "Discourse," *Deseret News,* July 18, 1877, 307. See also James B. Allen and Glen M. Leonard, *The Story of the Latter-day Saints* (Salt Lake City: Deseret Book, 1976); Richard O. Cowan, *The Church in the Twentieth Century* (Salt Lake City: Bookcraft, 1985); William G. Hartley, "The Priesthood Reform Movement, 1908–1922," *BYU Studies* 13, no. 2 (1973): 137–56; "The Priesthood Reorganization of 1877: Brigham Young's Last Achievement," *BYU Studies* 20, no. 1 (1979): 3–36; D. Michael Quinn, "The Evolution of the Presiding Quorums of the LDS Church," *Journal of Mormon History* 1 (1974): 21–38; John A. Widtsoe, *Priesthood and Church Government* (Salt Lake City: Deseret Book, 1954).

2. First Council of the Seventy, Minutes, December 15, 1886, Church History Library, The Church of Jesus Christ of Latter-day Saints, Salt Lake City.

Enough Water

14

Baptism: An Ever Changing Quality

FROM JOSEPH SMITH TO HOWARD W. HUNTER, every president of the Church was baptized outdoors and not in a font. Only in recent times have we had convenient baptismal fonts with clean tile, warm and clean water, dressing rooms, and white baptismal clothes. Baptism requires sufficient water to submerge a person completely, and finding suitable places was not always easy or convenient. In hot, arid deserts and polar regions with freezing temperatures, finding enough water in which to immerse someone is difficult. Not until recent generations, however, has the Church used baptismal fonts in our meetinghouses. Before then, most baptisms were held outdoors in natural bodies of water.

Church history has many interesting stories of baptism that, being performed without fonts, seem unusual by our modern standards. On the day the Church was organized, April 6, 1830, several people hiked from Peter Whitmer's log house down to the shores of nearby Seneca Lake. Among those baptized were Martin Harris and Joseph Smith Sr. The Prophet Joseph stood on the shore and watched; why he did not personally perform the ordinances is not known.

When Joseph Sr. came forth out of the water, Joseph Jr. was overjoyed. He took his father's hand and exclaimed with tears of happiness, "Oh, my God! Have I lived to see my own father baptized into the true church of

Jesus Christ!" Joseph was so filled with the Spirit to see his father and Martin Harris baptized that "he burst out with grief and joy and seemed as though the world could not hold him. He went out into the lot and appeared to want to get out of sight of everybody and would sob and cry and seemed to be so full that he could not live." The Prophet's "joy seemed to be full."

At Colesville, New York, soon after the Church was organized, Joseph Smith conducted a baptism. On a Saturday afternoon, he and three others waded into a stream and, probably with rocks, tree limbs, and logs, "erected a dam across a stream of water" to create a pool big enough for baptisms. But a mob later ripped the dam out and ruined the standing pool. Two days later, the Saints rebuilt the dam and thirteen were baptized.

John Smith, the brother of Joseph Smith Sr., had been feeble in health for six years and was unable to even walk to his barn. Neighbors believed that baptism would kill him. His son, George A. Smith, not yet baptized himself, "cut the ice in the creek and broke a road for forty rods through the crust of two feet of snow, and the day was very cold." Neighbors watched the baptism and were astonished that John survived the freezing experience—they expected him to die in the water. After the baptism, his health began to improve.

Within weeks of arriving in Preston, England, American elders had converts ready for baptism. But where could they perform the ordinance? They picked the River Ribble that ran through Preston. On July 30, 1837, a Sunday morning, they met together on the river's shore. Hundreds of curious Sunday strollers gathered to watch. Two of the baptismal candidates ran a foot race to the water's edge to see who would be baptized first. George D. Watt, the younger and the quicker of the two, won, and has become known in Church history as the first convert baptized in England.

Because Nauvoo was bordered on three sides by the curving Mississippi River, many baptisms took place in the river. On March 20, 1842, for example, Joseph Smith preached at the regular Nauvoo outdoor Sunday meeting and then about 2:00 PM he went to the river's edge near his home. A crowd of Saints lined the river bank. Joseph waded out into the river and baptized eighty persons "for the remission of sins."

Many children and converts were baptized in the Nauvoo Temple's baptismal font. The font, being in the basement, was one of the first parts of the temple finished, and it was put to use immediately. Constructed of pine timber, the font stood in the center of the basement room. It was oval shaped—sixteen feet long east and west, twelve feet wide, and four feet deep. The font rested on twelve wooden oxen, carved out of pine plank, glued together, "and copied after the most beautiful five-year-old steer that could be found in the country." A temporary frame building was built around the font. Water came from a well dug in the basement.

Baptisms also occurred in unique and unlikely places such as aboard ocean-going vessels. Many sailing ships, chartered by the Church, carried Mormon converts from England to America. On board the Saints sometimes converted nonmember crewmen or passengers. How were converts baptized aboard a

George D. Watt was the first person to be baptized in England. He won the honor by racing another baptismal candidate to the River Ribble in Preston, England, on July 30, 1837. Courtesy Church Archives.

sailing ship at sea? During the 1851 voyage of the sailing ship *Olympus,* some fifty people were converted and baptized during two shipboard baptisms. In the first, the crew brought a large water barrel on deck, removed the top and put short ladders inside and out. They filled the barrel waist-deep with sea water. Elders baptized twenty-one persons, male and female, in the barrel.

A second baptism service, of twenty males, took place in the ocean itself. The ship's main hatch cover was suspended by ropes on the ocean's bobbing surface to make a floating platform. The man performing the baptism sat on the platform with legs in the water wearing a safety rope around his body. Each convert descended to the platform by rope ladder, with a safety rope around his body and a stout belt around his waist. He sat to the left of the elder officiating, who grasped the belt around the waist by the right hand,

Daniel P. McArthur baptizing a Shivwitz Indian. Dozens of other tribe members were watching and waiting their turns. Sheriff Augustus P. Hardy looks on, possibly as a witness. Photograph by Charles R. Savage. Courtesy Perry Special Collections.

and the clothing at the back of the neck with the left. The candidate's hands grasped the elder's wrists. Then the convert "was placed beneath the briny wave and brought forth therefrom."

An old photograph in the Church History Library depicts a baptism of Shivwitz Indians in southern Utah. Taken by photographer Charles Savage, it shows St. George Stake President Daniel P. McArthur, in knee-deep water, holding the wrist of an Indian who is about to be baptized. President McArthur is wearing nonwhite pants and a white shirt. On a slope behind the pond sit scores of curious Indians. Standing by the pond is Sheriff Augustus P. Hardy, probably acting as witness. Apparently the entire tribe of some 150 Indians were baptized during this service.

The day after he turned eight, young J. Reuben Clark climbed into a wagon with his family and they rode out to the warm springs, a cluster of brackish ponds in the alkali flats northwest of Grantsville, Utah. The water stung an individual's eyes and tasted bitter, but it was warm and clear. His father baptized him on a ledge in one of the larger pools. Beyond the ledge, some folks said, the pool was bottomless. President Clark was baptized September 2, 1879.

A man in Nebo Stake was very ill and could only be baptized with great care. Someone created a special tank, filled it with warm water, and the sick man was gently baptized. But the person officiating did not stand inside the tank. People wondered if the baptism was valid. Church President Joseph F. Smith decided the man should be baptized again "in the proper way."

Cottbus, forty miles south of Berlin, Germany, had no municipal swimming pool in the mid-1920s, so elders there baptized in the River Spree. Elder Robert Richard Burton described a cold November baptism there of thirty converts. "We found a rather isolated spot where there were trees growing," he said. "The leaves were off the trees, snow was on the ground, and ice was on the river." In a cove, the elders took branches and broke the thin sheets of ice so no one would be cut.

That night, after a prayer in an apartment, they walked to the river. "In the dark the ladies went upstream and the men went downstream and chanced their clothes, standing in their bare feet in the snow and putting on white robes," Elder Burton said, "and banged their head[s] against the stove in order to thaw out those lumps on their heads."

Another photograph in the Church History Library captures a 1947 baptismal service at a swimming pool in Utrecht in the Netherlands. It shows three dozen people, dressed in white clothes, who are sitting on chairs or standing along the side of a large, indoor pool.

Records show that all fourteen of the presidents of the Church were baptized out of doors. Exactly where Joseph Fielding Smith's baptism occurred in still unclear, though records show that he was baptized in Salt Lake City on a hot July day in 1884, so undoubtedly he was baptized outdoors, probably in City Creek. Below lists the baptismal sites of the presidents:

Joseph Smith	Susquehanna River
Brigham Young	Millpond near Mendon, New York
John Taylor	Black Creek in Georgetown, Ontario, Canada
Wilford Woodruff	Icy stream by Richland, New York
Lorenzo Snow	Chagrin River in Kirtland, Ohio

Joseph F. Smith	City Creek, Salt Lake City
Heber J. Grant	City Creek, Salt Lake City
George Albert Smith	City Creek, Salt Lake City
David O. McKay	Spring Creek at Huntsville, Utah
Joseph Fielding Smith	Probably City Creek, Salt Lake City
Harold B. Lee	Bybee Pond in a lime kiln in Idaho
Spencer W. Kimball	Scalding tub, then a canal in Arizona
Ezra Taft Benson	Logan River canal near Whitney, Idaho
Howard W. Hunter	A swimming pool in Boise, Idaho

During the nineteenth century, few Latter-day Saint meetinghouses had fonts. In larger Mormon communities, such as Salt Lake City, Provo, and St. George, one or more fonts were built for use in the winter.

In October 1856, the First Presidency dedicated a baptismal font located near the Endowment House in Salt Lake City. A year later, two Apostles dedicated a font in the city's Fourteenth Ward. In 1861, Brigham Young had a wooden font erected a few rods east of his schoolhouse. About ten by twelve feet, the font was an old wagon bed, redesigned to hold water, with two dressing rooms attached. President Young dedicated it and then told local bishops "they were quite welcome to use it for baptizing, instead of the creek."

In 1875, Bishop Frederick Kesler, a millwright, built a font for the Church for a special group of Indians who were visiting Salt Lake City. The font ran east-west so the officiator could stand facing south, letting the candidate rise facing east—copying a cemetery custom for people to be buried so they could rise in the resurrection facing east.

Brother Kesler's font had running, not standing, water because he and many others then believed that baptisms should take place in running water, as Jesus was baptized. In 1881, Bishop Edwin D. Woolley "spoke in favor of a running stream of water for baptizing."

The First Presidency a century ago urged parents to baptize their children as soon as they turned eight years old, even in winter when small children might be "afraid of the cold water," rather than waiting several months. In 1902, Church President Joseph F. Smith said he knew that "there are perhaps not more than three or four months of the year when the temperature of the water in our streams makes the ordinance comfortable." He therefore asked all stake presidents to build fonts in every "fair-sized" city, complete with dressing rooms and heated water.

In 1890 a new font was dedicated in the southwest portion of the Salt Lake Tabernacle. During most of this century, Salt Lake City stakes held monthly baptismal services at the Tabernacle. That font probably holds the Church record for the number of live baptisms performed.

Because fonts are dedicated, some people have wondered if rivers or lakes should be dedicated prior to being used for a baptism. "Water for baptism need not be dedicated," the First Presidency instructed in 1932.

Raised as a Quaker, Edwin D. Woolley joined the LDS Church and later served as a bishop for many years in the Thirteenth Ward in Salt Lake City. He often emphasized the need for Church members to pay tithes. Courtesy Church Archives.

The Honolulu Tabernacle and grounds have been a tourist site in Hawaii for many years. One of its several outdoor courts once contained a popular baptismal font surrounded by a tropical garden and lily ponds that has been filled in and planted over with floral gardens.

By the 1930s some stakes constructed buildings that contained fonts, but outdoor baptisms were still common. Starting in the 1940s, it became standard for all new stake centers to have fonts. Recent building department policy has been that if people have to drive more than thirty minutes to use a font outside their branch or ward boundary, then their building can have its own font.

In the mid-1980s, several older people in Salt Lake City were asked where they were baptized. Locations they listed were: an ice pond in Humphrey, Idaho, in 1934; a creek in Mantua, Utah, in 1934; the Logan Temple in the 1920s; a canal in Cowley, Wyoming, about 1910; a baptistry in the Provo town park in 1939; and a mill pond in Lehi around 1920.

It is unknown when white baptismal clothes became the standard apparel for baptisms. A 1938 instruction regarding baptismal clothes, long after white clothes became standard, stated:

Persons presenting themselves for baptisms should be dressed in white clothing, which will permit the entire body to become wet as a result of the complete immersion. Bathing caps should be worn. Boots, waders, or other articles of clothing worn by persons officiating, for the purpose of keeping parts of the body dry are not in conformity with the spirit of the ordinance and should not be permitted. Today, stake Primary presidencies or mission officers supervise the buying, issuing, and cleaning of white, modest baptismal clothing.

Millions of people have been baptized by priests and elders in the Church. For more than 160 years, Church leaders gained experience and wisdom about baptismal services. They wanted people's thoughts focused on the prayer, the spirit, and the importance of the ordinance, not on mud, ice, mosquitoes, or immodesty. Therefore, except in remote areas, elders baptize in warm, clean water in comfortable, indoor baptismal fonts at convenient locations.

This article was originally published in Mormon Heritage Magazine 1 *(September/ October 1994):* 22, 24, 26–27.

15   Mormon Sundays

How was the Sabbath kept during Joseph Smith's lifetime? Have we borrowed Sabbath ideas from others? What kinds of public worship services took place before we had spacious, temperature-controlled meetinghouses? Why were priesthood meetings shifted from weeknights to Sunday? Why was fast day changed from the first Thursday to the first Sunday of each month? How has administration of the sacrament varied? How have previous generations defined proper and improper Sabbath conduct?

The answers to such questions reveal that today's busy Mormon Sabbath differs in some particulars from Sabbath routines of previous generations. The prophets have repeatedly authorized changes in Sabbath activities to help meet the changing needs of the Saints.

When the Church was organized on April 6, 1830—a Tuesday—no revelations had yet explained how the Lord wished his Saints to observe the Sabbath. One revelation commanded them to "meet together often to partake of bread and wine in the remembrance of the Lord Jesus" (D&C 20:75), but did not specify that Sunday was the day for doing it. Not until sixteen months later was the sacrament linked to Sunday by revelation (see D&C 59).

So what did these very first members do on Sundays? Basically they observed the day much as they had done as Protestants. Most had New

England roots and by tradition felt deep commitments to Sunday worship. Their forefathers in colonial days had made proper Sabbath conduct a matter of law, requiring regular attendance at church meetings, no work or business activities, and no unnecessary travel. By Joseph Smith's time, the commitment to a sacred day of rest was still very prominent in American society, although in some frontier areas like Missouri, Sabbath breaking was rampant.[1]

Some churches in 1830 held two preaching services, one before noon and a second after lunch. Early Saints, familiar with that pattern of meetings, adopted it, and the former two-meetings-a-Sabbath for all members continued that tradition until the late 1970s.[2]

The very first Latter-day Saint Sabbath meeting of which we have details was a conference held on June 9, 1830. Noted Joseph Smith:

> Having opened by singing and prayer, we partook together of the emblems of the body and blood of our Lord Jesus Christ. We then proceeded to confirm several who had lately been baptized, after which we called out and ordained several to the various offices of the Priesthood. Much exhortation and instruction was given.[3]

Here, just two months after the Church was organized, we see the basic elements of our sacrament meetings today: prayers, sacrament, preaching, and singing.

A month after this meeting, the Lord reinforced the importance of singing by instructing Emma Smith to "make a selection of sacred hymns" for use in Church meetings. "My soul delighteth in the song of the heart," the Lord counseled, "yea, the song of the righteous is a prayer unto me" (D&C 25:11–12). Emma's hymnal, lacking music but with words to ninety hymns, was finally printed five years later.

Our most detailed revelation regarding the Sabbath, Doctrine and Covenants 59, came in August 1831. Here, the Lord tells us that to keep ourselves unspotted by worldly things we are to "go to the house of prayer and offer up thy sacraments upon my holy day" (D&C 59:9). The Lord's Day, or Sunday, is a day he designates for Saints "to rest from your labors, and to pay thy devotions unto the Most High" (D&C 59:10), to "offer thine oblations and thy sacraments … confessing thy sins unto thy brethren, and before the Lord" (D&C 59:12), and a day when meals should "be prepared with singleness of heart" (D&C 59:13). This revelation serves as our "constitution" for Sabbath observance.

The "house of prayer" in those early days often was a private home, a small schoolhouse, or, for large groups, an open-air clearing or grove. It was a common adage, said Elder George A. Smith in 1855, that during the Joseph Smith years "'Mormonism' flourished best out of doors." He recalled that "we failed to erect a building big enough to hold the Saints previous to the death of the Prophet." The largest meeting rooms, those in the Kirtland and Nauvoo temples, could hold but five hundred to one thousand people.[4]

Sabbath services in Kirtland in 1835 continued to follow the pattern of prayer, preaching, and the administration of the sacrament. We do not know what sacrament vessels were used during this period, but they probably were goblets or glasses—serving as the common cup—and plates or baskets. While the sacrament was passing from member to member, preaching was common.

Besides the sacrament, the sermon was the next most important part of Sunday worship. Preaching occupied the major part of each public meeting, and members often were deeply affected by it. Noted W. W. Phelps: "President Smith preached last Sabbath.... He preached one of the greatest sermons I ever heard; it was about 3 1/2 hours long—and unfolded more mysteries than I can write at this time."[5]

Sunday evenings involved a variety of activities, including weddings, prayer meetings in private homes, meetings of quorums, patriarchal blessings, banquets, Church trials, or just visiting with family or friends.

Church Sabbaths in Missouri were similar. "We went regularly each Sunday to Far West," recalled John Bush. Few of the Saints had teams, and even beasts were allowed to rest on the Sabbath, so people walked the distances to the large frame schoolhouse. Added Bush, "Sunday after Sunday quite a crowd of men women and children could be seen wending their way" to the school. Those who could not get in stood at a window. Other Missouri meetings were held in homes, or under a large tree with a wagon serving as the pulpit.[6]

At Nauvoo, where Church membership rapidly swelled to beyond ten thousand, the best Sunday meeting places were an outdoor grove near the temple site and the temple site itself. "This morning I preached at the grove to about 8,000 people,"[7] the Prophet Joseph noted July 3, 1842.

Records fail to inform us how often the sacrament was administered at such huge gatherings, although across the river an Iowa conference resolved in late 1844 "to partake of the sacrament every second Sabbath." In England and other mission areas, small clusters of Saints partook weekly.[8]

It was at Nauvoo that the first wards were created, but these were for tithing purposes, not for regular meeting purposes. Records do not show any ward sacrament meetings in Nauvoo, only the community-wide morning and afternoon meetings.

During the Latter-day Saint migration across the Great Plains, the Saints tried to rest man and beast on Sundays. "Each Saturday night we were to pitch what tents we had and prepare our camps for rest on the Sabbath," noted Wilford Woodruff in April 1847. But sometimes travel on Sunday was necessary: "Started before breakfast for the want of wood and water," Eliza R. Snow noted on August 23, 1846.[9]

Heber C. Kimball's journal describes a spiritual Sabbath the pioneers experienced on May 30, 1847: "At 9 o'clock most of the brethren retired a little south of the Camp, and had a prayer meeting, and as many as chose to, expressed their feelings. At a little before 12 they met again at the same place to partake of the Sacrament." At midday a select group left the camp, found a secluded spot among the bluffs, put on temple clothes, and "offered up prayer to God, for our selves, for this Camp, and all things pertaining to it, the brethren in the army [Mormon Battalion], our families, and all the Saints, President Young being mouth. We all felt well and glad for this privilege of assembling ourselves together in a retired spot for prayer." The rest of the day involved rest and reflection—"There is no jesting, nor laughing, nor nonsense," noted Elder Kimball—a simple dinner, conversation, and at 5 PM another prayer meeting by the leaders until dark.[10]

From 1850 to 1900, the Sabbath day in the Church changed a great deal. Meetinghouses for each ward made ward sacrament meetings and Sunday Schools possible for the first time. Holding local meetings in turn meant that more local members participated in Sabbath activities as class teachers and members, officers and sacrament administrators, speakers, prayer givers, and choir members. Special fast Sundays and quarterly stake conference Sundays were introduced.

At first worship services took place outdoors. Two months after the first pioneers reached Salt Lake, a newcomer visited a Sunday meeting and "found them by the side of a haystack." A year later, a Sabbath service was held "on the south side of the north wall of the Old Fort." One Logan clerk could measure attendance by space occupied: "The meetings today were well attended, the congregation covering over half an acre."[11]

To shade outdoor meetings from the hot summer sun, boweries were built of pole frames covered with brush. But nature, particularly wind, still was troublesome: in St. George they once had to "nail wagon covers round the bowery to protect us from the gale."[12]

The first indoor meeting places, other than private homes, were log or adobe schoolhouses. These often were so small (Toquerville, for instance, had a 20' by 16' adobe house—half the main floor space of suburban homes today—for its nineteen families) that youth often stayed

Latter-day Saint missionaries preaching in Hyde Park, London, c. 1935–38. It was a common practice for missionaries in England to begin speaking in public places and let crowds form during the sermon. Courtesy Church Archives.

home and only adults squeezed into the Sunday meetings. As soon as possible, communities built large rock and brick structures, some with a second story. Some of the more populated communities, such as St. George and Salt Lake City, erected large public tabernacles in addition to ward halls.[13]

Whether outdoors or inside, the Saints' basic Sabbath meetings were the forenoon preaching service and the afternoon sacrament meeting, unless weather prevented them. In multiward areas, where the two worship meetings were stake gatherings, evening ward meetings also were held. Noted George Goddard on the Sabbath in the 1860s: "Went with my wife Betsy to the Tabernacle at 10 a.m. and at 2 p.m.... in the evening went to the 13th Ward meetings."[14]

Gradually community (or stake) sacrament meetings were replaced by ward meetings. The general morning and afternoon meetings in the Salt Lake Tabernacle, for example, ceased in 1876 and in the 1890s, respectively.

To lend variety to ward sacrament meetings, outside speakers often were brought in. General Authorities spent much time visiting wards on speaking assignments. Sermons varied in length from a few minutes to nearly two hours.

During the 1870s, stakes sent "home missionaries" on regular preaching assignments into the wards.[15] Home missionaries continued to visit wards monthly until after the turn of the century—a prototype of modern stake high councilors.

"Going to conference" was a notable occasion in early Utah years. Traveling in wagons, buggies, carts, on horseback, by foot, or by train, many used the trip to general or stake conferences to renew friendships. Stake quarterly conferences, held regularly after 1877, often rotated between leading towns in the stake, and planning for conference guests was a highlight for many families.

Some early wards administered the sacrament only once a month, but after the 1850s, weekly sacrament services characterized most settlements. A notable exception came during 1856–57, when the sacrament was withdrawn for a short period to help the Saints consider seriously the meaning of their church membership.

Bishops often personally administered the sacrament, both in their own wards and in the stake sacrament meetings. One bishop noted in 1874: "At 2 pm I administered the sacrament in the New Tabernacle assisted by my 2 council[ors] and [ward] Teachers."[16]

An elaborate set of sacrament vessels was crafted for the Salt Lake Tabernacle sacrament meetings. It consisted of twelve cups "of massive design in solid silver, with beautifully carved double handles," and twelve plates (later baskets) for the bread. When St. George members discussed what kind of sacrament set to buy, one brother reported how Salt Lake got their set: brethren "threw in their silver watches, spoons, etc.," to make it. Wards likewise obtained their own less expensive sacrament sets, often glass instead of metal.[17]

Sunday Schools were a part of the Protestant background of many early Mormon converts, and records show some sort of Latter-day Saint Sunday School at Kirtland, at Nauvoo, and in 1844 in England. Richard Ballantyne, a former Protestant Sunday School worker, started the first Utah Sunday School in 1849, when fifty youth between the ages of eight and fourteen met in a special room added to his home. Others copied him, so that independent Sunday Schools sprang up in most wards. By the 1870s, two hundred Sunday Schools involved nearly fifteen thousand youth and adults. For the first time, women and children participated directly in a Sabbath meeting as teachers and students, and many men became busy officers and teachers. Singing, praying, scripture lessons, catechisms, and recitations were all part of the school, as were examination days like one Bishop Kesler attended: "The house was well fild, the pieces ware well spoken & a Large No. of Presants ware given out as Reward of merit which consisted in some verry choice Books."[18]

Because Sunday School children usually did not attend the afternoon sacrament meetings, the First Presidency asked that the sacrament be administered in the Sunday Schools. Again, Bishop Kesler provides us a picture of the situation: "I visited our Ward Sunday School & spoke a few minets while the Sacrement was passing around It being the 2nd time that it had been administered unto our children in the Sunday Schools. I gave them ... instruction in Relation thare unto."[19]

Another notable Sabbath change was the involvement of youth in the administration of the sacrament. By the 1870s, boys from age eleven to seventeen were being ordained as deacons. Previously, adults filled most of the Aaronic Priesthood offices, serving as "acting" deacons, "acting" teachers, and "acting" priests. Boy deacons received two major Sunday responsibilities: ushering at meetings and otherwise caring for the ward buildings, and passing the sacrament. Salt Lake deacons were told in 1874:

> How nice it is to see a good boy nice and clean, with clean hands, and hair nicely combed, and walking on his tip-toes to save making a noise, while finding people seats. A good deal depends on a deacon in making a meeting comfortable. We should be there at least an hour before meeting begins. Have the house nice and clean, a clean table and cloth, and take care to keep it clean.[20]

In 1896, fast day was changed from the first Thursday of each month to the first Sunday so that working people and students could attend. On occasion, fast Sundays have been dedicated to special matters. When the flu epidemic raged in 1918 and public meetings were banned, the Church set aside December 22 as a special fast Sunday "for the arrest and speedy suppression by Divine power of the desolating Scourge that is passing over the earth." In 1946 we had a special fast day on August 19 in gratitude for the surrender of

Brigham City Second Ward sacrament meeting, 1909. At this time, mature men still officiated at the sacrament table. Courtesy Church Archives.

Japan, and one in December 1947 for the Saints to "contribute the greatest sum they can give to the relief of the sufferers of war-torn Europe."[21]

One simple Sabbath change in our century was the introduction of tiny, single sacrament cups. The idea was suggested in the 1890s but was not implemented until 1911 when a new type of tray to hold small cups was designed. Quickly the traditional, common cups disappeared, replaced by metal, glass, paper, and plastic cups.[22]

Over the years preaching, singing, and musical numbers accompanied the administration of the sacrament. In 1946 the First Presidency abolished all such distractions. The ideal condition, they said, is to have absolute quiet: "We look with disfavor upon vocal solos, duets, group singing, or instrumental music during the administration of this sacred ordinance."[23]

Another recent change involves music. Because nineteenth-century hymnbooks contained songs more suitable for choirs than congregations, congregational singing waned. But since 1909 our hymnbooks have been designed for the congregation so that members participate at least in the opening and closing hymns.

Older members today recall when ward priesthood meetings were on Monday nights, a practice established in 1908. However, some bishops favored a Sunday priesthood meeting, before or after Sunday School, to cut down on travel demands for those who lived far away from chapels. In the 1930s, when wards were permitted to hold priesthood meetings on Sundays or weeknights, most chose Sunday mornings, a practice now standardized throughout the Church.[24]

Since the early days of the Church, leaders have tried to prevent Sabbaths from becoming too occupied with meetings. In 1904 an exasperated Cache Stake officer noted: "Sunday was so closely occupied that it was as hard a day's work as any other." Two decades later, Elder Melvin J. Ballard publicly observed that "there are too many activities on Sunday evenings." Such sentiments have caused periodic efforts to streamline Sabbath schedules.[25]

One attempt was made between 1928 and 1938, when priesthood classes in many wards were merged with Sunday School classes. The Brethren hoped the Saints would wisely use the new spare Sabbath time:

> Sunday Schools and meetings have been so arranged as to meet the convenience of the people and leave a considerable portion of the Sabbath day without Church appointments. We earnestly

appeal to the people to keep their meeting appointments faithfully and to utilize that portion of Sunday not appointed for meetings in promoting family association in the home, with the purpose of stimulating and establishing greater home fealty, a closer companionship among parents and children, and more intimate relations among all kindred.[26]

Modern circumstances sometimes made it necessary for the Church to simplify the normal Sunday schedule in other ways. In the early and mid-twentieth century, some mission areas where travel was difficult, Sunday meetings were held without a time interval in between. The 1970s energy crisis in the United States caused the First Presidency to direct in December 1973 that "local congregations in areas where members live great distances from meetinghouses were authorized if they choose, to establish a consecutive meeting schedule for all Sunday meetings." Recently, the Church issued special handbooks for smaller units—small branches, groups, and families—that permit the combining of Sunday School and sacrament meetings, and let Relief Society sisters meet while the brethren are in priesthood meetings.[27]

While meeting schedules have shifted over the years, little has changed in terms of the basic counsel given the Saints about personal conduct on the Sabbath. One rule in United Order constitutions was: "We will observe the Sabbath day and keep it holy, devote it to worship, to the study of good books, to rest, to imparting instruction, to attending meeting."[28] Throughout the years since 1830, the restructuring and changing of Sabbath services has been done to help the Saints enhance and fulfill those worshipful purposes. The streamlining of meetings is intended to provide time for individuals to achieve a more spiritually beneficial Sabbath as the Saints return to their homes to meet family and personal spiritual needs.

For a century and a half, the Church has provided excellent meetings to help Saints renew their personal covenants, to learn from speakers and teachers, to learn by teaching and speaking, and to sing and pray and meditate. But attendance at Sabbath meetings is not enough: responsibility for making the entire day holy and spiritually beneficial still belongs to the individual Saints.

This article was originally published in Ensign 8 *(January 1978): 19–25.*

NOTES

1. "Blue Laws," in *Colliers Encyclopedia* (New York: Crowell Collier and Macmillan, 1967), 278–79; see also Joseph Smith Jr., *History of The Church of Jesus Christ of Latter-day Saints,* ed. B. H. Roberts, 2d ed., rev., 7 vols. (Salt Lake City: Deseret News, 1971), 4:538 (hereafter cited as *History of the Church*).

2. James Hastings, *Encyclopedia of Religion and Ethics* (New York: Charles Scribners Sons, 1922), 112.

3. *History of the Church,* 1:84.

4. George Albert Smith, in *Journal of Discourses,* 26 vols. (Liverpool: Latter-day Saints' Book Depot, 1855–86), 3:23, August 12, 1855.

5. Journal History of the Church, June 2, 1835, Church History Library, The Church of Jesus Christ of Latter-day Saints, Salt Lake City, microfilm copy in Harold B. Lee Library, Brigham Young University, Provo, Utah.

6. Pearl Wilcox, *The Latter-day Saints on the Missouri Frontier* (n.p.: By the Author, 1972), 168–69, 190, 200.

7. *History of the Church,* 5:56.

8. Alfred Cordon, Journal, 1839–40, L. Tom Perry Special Collection, Harold B. Lee Library, Brigham Young University, Provo, Utah; "Conference Minutes, New Trenton, Franklin Co. Ia., Nov. 18, 1844," *Times and Seasons* 5 (December 1, 1844): 752.

9. Matthias F. Cowley, *Wilford Woodruff: History of His Life and Labors* (Salt Lake City: Bookcraft, 1964), 264–65; Eliza R. Snow, Diary, August 23, 1846, Church History Library; "From Her Diary," in *Our Pioneer Heritage,* comp. Kate B. Carter, 20 vols. (Salt Lake City: Daughters of Utah Pioneers, 1958–77), 17:346–84.

10. Heber C. Kimball, Journal, May 30, 1847, in *Utah Genealogical and Historical Magazine* 31 (1940): 18–19.

11. John Young, in *Journal of Discourses,* 6:232, April 8, 1857; Journal History, March 18, 1849, and June 15, 1873.

12. Charles L. Walker, Diary, May 6, 1866, Church History Library.

13. Andrew Karl Larson, *"I Was Called to Dixie"* (Salt Lake City: Deseret News Press, 1961), 30; Journal History, February 15, 1877.

14. George Goddard, Diary, March 1, 1857, Church History Library; Salt Lake Stake Manuscript History, 1869–77, Church History Library.

15. Journal History, March 29, 1868; Southern Utah Mission, St. George Stake, 1869–86, Lesser Priesthood Record Book A, December 4, 1879, Church History Library.

16. Dee L. Risenmay, "A Brief History of the Administration of the Sacrament in The Church of Jesus Christ of Latter-day Saints," paper for Religion 543, BYU, 1968, Perry Special Collections; Frederick Kesler, Diary, July 5, 1874, J. Willard Marriott Library, University of Utah, Salt Lake City.

17. Journal History, October 2, 1930; St. George Lesser Priesthood Record Book A, September 16, 1878.

18. Hastings, *Encyclopedia of Religion and Ethics,* 112–13; David O. McKay, "Sunday Schools of the Church," *Improvement Era* 33 (May 1930): 480–81; *Jubilee History of the LDS Sunday Schools* (Salt Lake City: Deseret Sunday School Union, 1900), 9–27; "The Sunday School," in Carter, *Our Pioneer Heritage,* 16:49–65; Kesler, Diary, June 21, 1874.

19. Kesler, Diary, May 31, 1877; Presiding Bishops Meeting with Bishops, Minutes, June 14, 1877, Church History Library.

20. First Presidency Letter, July 11, 1877, in *Messages of the First Presidency of The Church of Jesus Christ of Latter-day Saints, 1833–1964,* comp. James R. Clark, 6 vols. (Salt Lake City: Bookcraft, 1965–75), 2:286; St. George Lesser Priesthood Record Book A, February 24, 1877; Salt Lake Fourteenth Ward First Quorum of Deacons, Minute Book, 1880; and Salt Lake Stake Deacons Quorum, Minutes, March 10, 1874.

21. First Presidency Statement, November 5, 1896, in Clark, *Messages of the First Presidency,* 3:282–83; A. Dean Wengreen, "The Origin and History of the Fast Day in The Church of Jesus Christ of Latter-day Saints, 1839–1896" (master's thesis, Brigham Young University, 1955); "Latter-day Saints Asked to Fast, Pray on Sunday," *Church News,* published by *Deseret News,* August 18, 1945, 1; *Church News,* November 8, 1947; First Presidency Announcement, December 29, 1918, in Clark, *Messages of the First Presidency,* 5:115.

22. Risenmay, "Administration of the Sacrament."

23. First Presidency Letter, May 2, 1946, in Clark, *Messages of the First Presidency,* 6:252; Verena Ursenbach Hatch, *Worship and Music in The Church of Jesus Christ of Latter-day Saints* (Provo, UT: M. Ephraim Hatch, 1968).

24. General Priesthood Committee, Minutes, February 15, 1910; James B. Allen and Glen M. Leonard, *The Story of the Latter-day Saints* (Salt Lake City: Deseret Book, 1976), 500–501.

25. Cache Stake, Historical Record, November 27, 1904, Church History Library; *Improvement Era* 31 (June 1928): 794.

26. Richard Cowan, "Priesthood Auxiliary Movement, 1928–1937," unpublished manuscript, Perry Special Collections; First Presidency statement, September 1, 1928, in Clark, *Messages of the First Presidency,* 5:260.

27. "Save Energy, Church Urges Every Member," *Church News,* December 15, 1973, 3; organization guidebooks for "Family," for "Group," and for "Small Branch," published by the Church.

28. George Albert Smith, in *Journal of Discourses,* 17:254, October 11, 1874.

16   Organization of Wards and Stakes
A Historical Approach

Since 1830 the Church has operated on the fundamental, unchanging priesthood principle that inspired prophets direct the work of priesthood units and members. However, application of that principle to the day-to-day operations of the Church has varied according to ever-changing needs and circumstances.

The nineteenth century, for example, offers us some intriguing and perhaps puzzling priesthood practices when measured by present Church practices. We find, for example, a stake being formed within a branch, high priests serving as deacons, four types of bishops, wards with presidents, and branches with bishops. To help make sense of Church government matters of the past century, five keys to understanding ward and stake history are useful.

1. BISHOPS WERE NOT ALWAYS LINKED TO WARDS

The Church had no wards or stakes when the first general bishops were called in 1831. Not until 1834 were stakes created. Wards were created in 1839. Thus, the first bishops supervised temporal matters in branches, not wards or stakes. When the Kirtland and Zion stakes were formed, the two general bishops functioned almost like stake officers, stake bishops. When Commerce/Nauvoo was divided into urban wards, bishops were appointed

355

over each, and we had the first ward bishops in the Church. These, however, did not conduct meetings on a ward basis, as worship and quorum meetings in Nauvoo were communitywide gatherings not limited by ward boundaries.

For some time, the Church had four types of bishops: Presiding Bishop over the entire Church; local presiding bishops over valleys or settlements having more than one ward; traveling bishops who operated as agents of the presiding bishop to help collect tithes; and ward bishops.

Samuel Atwood, for example, served as a local presiding bishop "to repair to, and to take charge of, and preside over the settlement in Kamas Prairie and on the Weber River," to collect tithing, care for public property, counsel and guide local bishops, and transact Church business.

Another practice, unusual by our standards, was to have ward presidents. Winter Quarters' branches from 1848 to 1852 each had both a president and a bishop. So did Nephi and Manti wards in the 1850s. In 1862, Brigham Young said, "As soon as the elders have wisdom sufficient to magnify their calling and Priesthood, we will give to every Branch, no matter how small the Ward, both a Bishop and a President." The idea, however, was never fully implemented.

2. UNIT DESIGNATIONS WERE USED QUITE LOOSELY

During the nineteenth century, just about any local unit could be and was called a branch. Branches, in fact, predated the formation of the first stakes (1834) and wards (1839). But even after the latter date, a ward or stake might be called a branch. We read, for instance, of the Nauvoo Third Ward Branch. The term *ward* sometimes was used just as imprecisely, as for example aboard immigrant ships, where the passengers were divided into wards, each with a presiding elder. In 1849, New Orleans was divided into four wards, and over each were teachers who were responsible to that city's presiding elder. Similarly, the term *stake* had many meanings. A branch might be called a stake. Units similar to present-day missions were designated as stakes. St. George, for example, is termed a stake many years before an official stake was organized. What is the point? Simply that no one should be troubled when reading that a unit was designated a branch, a ward, or a stake when the unit fails to match our current precise definitions of those terms.

3. SALT LAKE STAKE SERVED AS A CENTER STAKE

For most of Brigham Young's era, Salt Lake Stake had a higher status than all other stakes. Perhaps this came naturally from the fact that so many General Authorities resided there. The stake had a president and high council but never held stake conferences like other stakes. Rather, general conference served the purpose: its officers were sustained at the general conferences right after the General Authorities. At the stake's bishops meetings, the Presiding Bishop, not the stake president, presided. When Parowan high priests needed a new president in the 1850s, they petitioned the Salt Lake Stake high priests quorum presidency to name a replacement, which it did. Finally, in 1876 President Young made an announcement that Salt Lake Stake really possessed no higher status than any other stake, that all stakes were on equal footing. That announcement created no small stir among the bishops who heard it.

4. AARONIC PRIESTHOOD RANKS WERE FILLED WITH MELCHIZEDEK PRIESTHOOD BEARERS

Aaronic Priesthood work then consisted of such adult duties as watching over the Church, ferreting out iniquity, settling disputes, and being ward officers second only to the bishop. Therefore, worthy adults were recruited to fill these positions. When qualified men, not ordained to a priesthood, could not be found to put into the quorums, then Melchizedek Priesthood bearers were called by bishops to serve as "acting" deacons, "acting" teachers, and "acting" priests. Records show cases of men serving double duty in the priesthood. As one example, John Picknell was a seventy, a teacher, and a deacon at the same time. While some boys served in Aaronic capacities ever since the earliest days of the Restoration, only after 1877 did it become Church policy that all active boys receive some Aaronic Priesthood ordination before adulthood. In practice, boys became deacons at ages eleven and nineteen, but many did not receive further ordination until they were called on missions or got married and were ordained as elders. In 1908 the Church established definite ages for deacons, teachers, and priests (twelve, fifteen, seventeen) and stipulated that boys should advance through each of the offices sequentially.

5. LOOSE CHURCH GOVERNMENT PRACTICES WERE TIGHTENED IN 1877

Before Brigham Young died in 1877, he directed a major reordering of priesthood work in the Church. A letter from the First Presidency, dated July 11, 1877, directed that a number of current practices be corrected or eliminated: Apostles no longer would preside over settlements or stakes; unordained acting bishops would be ordained; bishops lacking counselors would receive them; bishopric counselors who were not high priests would be ordained such; many bishops and stake presidents would be replaced by new appointees; young men were to receive some Aaronic position; the offices of traveling bishops and local presiding bishops were eliminated; stakes organized Aaronic Priesthood and elders quorums where there had been none; and high priests quorums and seventies quorums, used to recruiting at will to fill their ranks (to the detriment of other quorums), could ordain no more men without First Presidency approval. Stakes would hold regular quarterly conferences that summer as part of this major Church reorganization, wards and stakes were divided and doubled in number, and many settlements became organized into official Church units for the first time.

While modern students might find the nineteenth-century situation of wards, stakes, and quorums confusing by present standards, when understood in context those practices simply support the tenet that the priesthood is led by a prophet. If change in the Church disturbs some, three ideas might be helpful.

First, one reason we need a prophet is to have change. Otherwise we could as a Church lock into whatever was revealed in the 1830s and maintain it.

A second idea is the application of Elder George A. Smith's cornstalk analogy to Church growth and change:

> Suppose a man should go into a corn-field where the corn is six, eight, or ten inches high, who had not been raised in a country where it was cultivated, . . . and he had never seen such a plant before, and let him employ himself a few days in hoeing it and admiring its beauty,—suppose by some means he becomes perfectly blind for two or three months, and then goes into the field after he has received his sight, he now beholds corn seven, eight, and ten feet high, with large ears upon it,—he would exclaim, "What is this? Who has destroyed the beautiful plants that were here two months

President John Taylor (center), *with George Q. Cannon* (left) *and Joseph F. Smith* (right), *c. 1880. President Taylor received a revlation saying that changes in the organization of the Church would be a normal part of its growth and development. This helped the Saints to understand and accept new callings in the reorganized priesthood structure. Courtesy Perry Special Collections.*

ago?" ... He is told it is the same corn. "Oh, it cannot be, for the corn is little stuff."[1]

Third, we may quote the word of the Lord to President John Taylor in 1883, after significant changes had been made in the operations of the Seventies in the Church. This statement is like an "elastic clause" in our Church government "constitution," explaining how and why the Lord can rearrange priesthood operations when Church needs require such changes:

> Thus saith the Lord unto the First Presidency, unto the Twelve, unto the Seventies and unto all my holy Priesthood, let not your hearts be troubled, neither be ye concerned about the management and organization of my Church and Priesthood and the accomplishment of my work. Fear me and observe my laws and I will reveal unto you, from time to time, through the channels that I have appointed, everything that shall be necessary for the future development and perfection of my Church, for the adjustment and rolling forth of my kingdom, and for the building up and the establishment of my Zion. For ye are my Priesthood and I am your God. Even so. Amen.[2]

(Address given at the CES Church History Symposium at Brigham Young University, August 19, 1977.)

This article was originally published in Religious Educators Symposium on LDS Church History *(Salt Lake City: Church Educational System, 1977), 53–55.*

NOTES

1. George A. Smith, in *Journal of Discourses*, 26 vols. (Liverpool: Latter-day Saints' Book Depot, 1855–86), 7:61, October 6, 1854.

2. "Revelation Given through John Taylor," in *Messages of the First Presidency of The Church of Jesus Christ of Latter-day Saints, 1833–1964*, comp. James R. Clark, 6 vols. (Salt Lake City: Bookcraft, 1965–75), 2:354, April 14, 1883.

17 Nauvoo Stake, Priesthood Quorums, and the Church's First Wards

A RESTORED SEVENTIES HALL STANDS on the north side of Parley Street in Nauvoo, a memorial to one office and quorum of the priesthood. Today, Latter-day Saint guides use the building, originally built in 1844, as an appropriate site for telling about the Church's proselyting efforts, a labor assigned by revelation to ordained seventies. But the hall is also a fitting site for explaining stake and local priesthood work in Old Nauvoo: here, the Nauvoo Stake held many presidency and high council meetings; here, men in Nauvoo's thirty-three seventies quorums, the high priests quorum, and other priesthood groups met, prayed, discussed the gospel, and received and reported on priesthood assignments.

No comparable priesthood hall is found in today's Church of Jesus Christ of Latter-day Saints. Likewise, seventies quorums no longer exist as they once did in nearly every Latter-day Saint stake. Therefore, the restored walls of the Nauvoo Seventies Hall bear mute but sturdy witness that priesthood organization in Old Nauvoo differed in practice and policy from what today's Latter-day Saints see. With the hall as a visual symbol, this article presents a history of Nauvoo priesthood groups and how they operated in the days before fully functional wards and even ward meetinghouses existed. To date, there is no history of priesthood work in Nauvoo or of the Nauvoo Stake, a surprising lack given the fact that Nauvoo was a religious capital. The article also evaluates what differences seven years of priesthood work in Nauvoo made in terms of the historical development of latter-day priesthood work, differences that include the introduction into the Church of wards and ward bishops.

To examine Nauvoo's priesthood work is, as the phrase says, to enter a foreign country.[1] Present understandings of stakes, wards, and quorums enlighten but also confuse the study of Nauvoo's priesthood work. Four factors must be understood by all readers of Church history to interpret Nauvoo source materials correctly.

First, the terms *ward, branch, stake,* and *district* had meanings looser than do today's definitions. For example, Nauvoo High Council minutes mention a decision that the Pleasant Vale "stake" outside Nauvoo should be dissolved and "members of that branch" joined to the Church in Nauvoo— the terms *branch* and *stake* being used interchangeably.[2] For that generation, a branch was a stake, albeit a stake in embryo. (Branches were called stakes in early Utah as well.[3]) A branch first received a president and then, when needed, a high council and a bishop, and at that point it was considered an operational stake. As membership numbers or geography made them necessary, a second, a third, and more bishops were added. An elders quorum and at least one Aaronic Priesthood unit completed a stake's organization.

An example of a one-bishop stake sprouted across the river from Nauvoo. In August 1841, the Zarahemla Stake held a conference at which its presidency, high council, and a single bishop were sustained along with an elders quorum presidency. Bishop Elias Smith reported that the stake had in its lesser priesthood nine priests, thirteen teachers, and four deacons. Elder Lewis Zabriskie reported his elders quorum had "20 members generally in good standing."[4]

For the population of Old Nauvoo, the term *ward* had a different meaning from what it has today. In the eastern United States then and now, a ward is a political subdivision of a city. Wards in Nauvoo were civil divisions for police, tax, election, school, and other municipal purposes. When Church leaders needed to collect funds or to aid the poor, for convenience they let the city's political ward boundaries serve as assignment districts. They placed a bishop in charge of each. Those ward units, however, were not Latter-day Saint entities conducting their own sacrament meetings or having their own quorums. Nauvoo quorums for deacons, teachers, priests, and elders were stake entities, not ward ones, as was the case in stakes before and after Nauvoo.[5]

Second, because Nauvoo was the Church's headquarters, Church general conferences were held in Nauvoo. These conferences served as Nauvoo Stake's stake conferences as well; the stake had no stake conferences of its own. Nauvoo Stake's presidency, high council, and quorum presidents were sustained during general conference sustainings. This practice was found in the Rutland Stake earlier and in the Salt Lake Stake in early Utah.

Third, Aaronic Priesthood offices were held by men, although some older boys were ordained. No priesthood office then correlated with an age group: "Men of all ages seem to have been ordained to any of the offices in the priesthood up to and including elder to start their priesthood career."[6] Likewise, there was no set time period for holding any priesthood office.

Fourth, men generally were ordained to fill specific needs, not just to receive an ordination.[7] From 1830 to 1846, most male converts were not ordained until several months after being baptized. Roger Launius studied a sample of 123 men for whom he could pinpoint baptism and ordination information for this period. Only 10 percent were ordained within a week of baptism, and about 53 percent were ordained at least one year after baptism. He also found that "some men never held the priesthood in spite of seemingly apparent abilities and commitments."[8] By the 1840s, most first ordinations were to the office of elder.[9]

PRECEDENTS

Men pouring into Nauvoo in 1839 and 1840 included ordained elders, priests, teachers, and deacons, and a few former stake high councilmen. They brought to Nauvoo relatively little practical priesthood experience, some of it trial and error, from labors in Kirtland, in Missouri, and in mission areas. Nauvoo became a restarting point for priesthood quorums and labors interrupted elsewhere.

The Church's first two stakes, created at Kirtland and in Missouri in 1834, were each headed by a stake presidency (which was the First Presidency in Kirtland), a high council that handled administrative and judicial matters, and a quorum presidency (irregularly organized) for deacons, teachers, priests, and elders. Each stake had one bishop: Newel K. Whitney for Kirtland and Edward Partridge for Missouri. The bishops' tasks were mainly judicial and financial—collecting and expending Church funds and assisting the worthy poor. Both stakes had high priests quorums. Above the stake level but below the Apostles, the Church by 1840 had three quorums of seventies, sometimes termed "Seventy Apostles."[10]

Studies of the earliest Aaronic Priesthood activities indicate that leaders believed in, but quorums rarely reached, the quorum sizes set by scripture—twelve deacons, twenty-four teachers, and forty-eight priests. By 1839 the Church's main local officers were the ordained teachers, who, under the direction of the stake (usually the stake bishop), visited house to house. They also served as local arbitrators and peacemakers among the Saints. Teachers and priests sometimes were the local presiding officers because high priests and elders were expected to forsake the "standing ministry" in order to proselyte and travel.[11] Deacons, when they did anything, held quorum meetings and assisted priests and teachers.[12]

NAUVOO STAKE

Nauvoo was but a few months old when leaders at the October 1839 general conference created the Nauvoo Stake. Its initial organization consisted of Stake President William Marks, a high council, and three bishops—one for each of Nauvoo's municipal wards. To handle tithes and aid the poor, Bishop Partridge was assigned to the Upper Ward, Bishop Whitney the Middle Ward, and Bishop Vinson Knight the Lower Ward. Conference attenders also sustained Don Carlos Smith "as President of the High Priesthood" and created an elders quorum by appointing thirty-five elders "who all accepted of their appointments" except one. Of these, ten needed ordaining and were ordained by four high councilmen. One conference speaker discussed the "duties of Priests, Teachers, etc." Nauvoo now had a stake organization. That same conference approved the creation of a branch or stake across the Mississippi in Iowa, with John Smith as president, a high council, and Alanson Ripley as bishop.[13] Nauvoo Stake exercised jurisdiction over Nauvoo's bishops, Aaronic Priesthood quorums, and elders, but not over seventies or high priests.

When priesthood authorities laid the cornerstones for the Nauvoo Temple during the April 1841 conference, the ceremony involved Nauvoo's quorums. Men sat together by priesthood office so they could vote by office for the Church officers. Bishop Whitney, acting as Aaronic Priesthood president, presented the First Presidency for a sustaining vote to the seated Aaronic Priesthood; Elders President John A. Hicks presented the matter to the elders; Senior Seventies President Joseph Young to the seventies; High President Don Carlos Smith to the high priests; and Elias Higbee to the High Council. Then the presidents of the quorums were presented for sustaining votes.[14]

At the October 1841 conference, a notable priesthood development was George Miller's replacing deceased Don Carlos Smith as high priests president.[15] William Marks served as Nauvoo Stake's president until the October 1844 conference, when he was dropped and replaced by John Smith, who had presided over the Zarahemla Stake.[16]

George Miller was called in 1841 as president of the high priests quorum. Miller replaced the Prophet Joseph Smith's brother Don Carlos Smith, who had died in August of the same year. Courtesy Church Archives.

NAUVOO BISHOPS

The Nauvoo Stake High Council exercised authority over the ward bishops. Limited records provide only a sketchy history of the interaction between stake and bishop. Of Nauvoo's first three ward bishops, Bishops Partridge and Whitney continued to serve as general bishops with churchwide or regional jurisdictions at times, so their integration within the Nauvoo Stake's structure was ambiguous.[17] The bishops' primary task was "to care for the incoming Saints, many of whom were sick or destitute."[18] On August 16, 1841, as part of business at a special Church conference, Bishops Vinson Knight and George Miller presented "the situation of the poor of Nauvoo" and then spearheaded a collection to benefit the needy.[19]

Nauvoo's original three wards rapidly became too crowded, so the High Council regrouped them into four wards in early 1842. The Nauvoo High

Council minutes for August 20, 1842, record that the council divided Nauvoo into ten wards, matching the new divisions made by the Temple Committee for raising donations and labor, and appointed a bishop for each ward. They voted too that other bishops be appointed over "districts" adjoining Nauvoo "as shall be considered necessary." The council resolved that Samuel H. Smith be appointed as bishop in place of deceased Vinson Knight and that Tarleton Lewis be bishop of the Fourth Ward; John Murdock of the Fifth; Daniel Cam, Sixth; Newel K. Whitney, Seventh; Jacob Foutz, Eighth; Jonathan H. Hale, Ninth; and Hezekiah Peck, Tenth. David Evans was called as bishop of the district south of the city, the Eleventh Ward; Israel Calkins of the district east of the city and south of Young Street; and William W. Spencer of the district east of the city and north of Young Street. Samuel Smith could not accept the appointment, but Lewis, Murdock, Foutz, Hale, Peck, Evans, and Calkins were ordained.[20]

Nauvoo High Council minutes for 1842 show that the council called for and received reports from the ward bishops. On October 1, for example, Bishop Lewis of the Fourth Ward reported "according to the instructions of the Council." On October 15, Bishop Murdock of the Fifth Ward reported he had picked high priests Joseph Fielding and John Lowry for his counselors, which actions the council approved. On October 29, John Hammond reported for the Eleventh Ward, announcing that he and Phillip Ballard had been chosen by Bishop Evans as his counselors. Isaac Higbee reported to the council on the First, Second, and Third wards, after which Hammond introduced a petition from a part of his ward who wanted to be a new "branch." On November 19, the High Council authorized the action after consulting with Joseph and Hyrum Smith, who approved the request. On November 26, the council instructed Hosea Stout to ascertain the exact boundaries of the ten city wards "that the Bishopric may be more perfectly set in order." Stout reported a week later. On December 4, the council voted that Bishop Newel K. Whitney be assigned to preside over the Seventh Ward. On December 11, Bishop Hale of the Ninth Ward appeared before the High Council and "made a very large and elegant report of the situation and standing of his ward, which was accepted."

Sacrament meetings were generally Nauvoo-wide meetings held in the open, in groves, or at the temple site. General Authorities conducted these meetings.[21] No evidence exists that any sacrament meetings were held for a particular ward's membership; other ward meetings, although not common, did occur. For example, Bishop John S. Higbee early in 1845 appointed prayer meetings in his ward, or for part of his ward, "at Bro McKinseys on Thursdays at 4 o'clock." He "appointed Bro. Ormon Butler to take the charge of the meetings." These started on May 1, 1845. At the first meeting, Bishop Higbee gave attenders instructions regarding their children and also appealed for donations so he could help the poor. At the next two ward prayer meetings, he presided. The May 15 meeting was a fast meeting.[22] Bishop Higbee's little diary indicates other duties he performed. He settled disputes and performed weddings. On Sunday, May 4, 1845, he helped administer the sacrament at the general Nauvoo Sunday meeting to between six hundred and eight hundred people.[23]

Hosea Stout, c. 1868. Stout was instructed by the Nauvoo High Council to record the exact boundaries of the ten city wards. After Stout's report, the council moved forward with its organization of the Nauvoo wards. Courtesy Church Archives.

But a bishop's main responsibility continued to be caring for the poor. Wealthy convert Edward Hunter, from Pennsylvania, was ordained a bishop soon after the Martyrdom. During his labors as a bishop, he recalled, the "brethren were liberal in their offerings to the poor. Poor were looked after and made comfortable." He also solicited funds, labor, and materials for the Temple.[24] At the October 1845 conference, Stake President "John Smith ... appointed four bishops to stand at the [temple] door, to take a collection for the benefit of the poor."[25]

An example of how that generation used the terms *ward, branch, district,* and *stake* interchangeably is the Twelve's plan, after Joseph Smith's death, for organizing the Church in the eastern United States. On August 15, 1844, the Twelve proposed dividing that area into districts and branches, each presided over by a high priest. They announced that "bishops will also be appointed in the larger branches, to attend to the management of the temporal funds, such as tithings and funds for the poor, according to the revelations of God and to be judges in Israel."[26]

AARONIC PRIESTHOOD

Lesser priesthood quorums in Nauvoo were stake, not ward, units. Their history of activity is documented in several surviving minute books.[27] Doctrine and Covenants 107:87–88 makes it clear that bishops should be presidents of the Aaronic Priesthood and should preside over priests quorums. In practice, the ideal was not followed. During the Joseph Smith period, in between the uprootings and movings of the members, bishops presided over all of the Aaronic Priesthood, including the quorum presidents,[28] but a priest presided over the priests quorum, not a bishop. In Doctrine and Covenants 124, Vinson Knight was called to be a presiding or general bishop, and Samuel Rolfe, who was not a bishop, to be president of the priests.[29] Also, when a resurrected Kirtland Stake was created in 1841, the stake council called Nehemiah Greenhalgh, who was not a bishop, as president of the Aaronic Priesthood but left it to the stake bishop to reorganize the deacons and teachers quorums at a later date.[30]

Various Aaronic Priesthood quorums were organized and reorganized in Nauvoo before the death of Joseph Smith. On March 21, 1841, Bishops Newel Whitney, George Miller, John Higbee, and Vinson Knight organized Nauvoo's Aaronic Priesthood. For a priests quorum presidency, they picked Samuel Rolfe, Stephen Markham, and Hezekiah Peck. Elisha Everett, James W. Huntsman, and James Hendricks became the teachers quorum presidency; Phinehas R. Bird, David Wood, and William W. Lane presided over the deacons.[31] Deacons met together that June.[32] Teachers quorum minutes show that the quorum met weekly in 1841, but by fall, the meetings were sporadic. In May 1841, they discussed the possibility of visiting each member of the Church, but discussion was laid over until more information on the subject became available.

At a January 18, 1842, Nauvoo Stake High Council meeting, Stake President William Marks said the purpose of meeting was to consider the affairs of the Church, to set in order all things relative to their duty,

> to call on the Bishops and see if they call the Lesser Priesthood together if they do their duty if the Priests visit from house to house if there was no malice no hardness no difficulty in the Church that

Hyrum and Joseph Smith taught Church members their duties as priesthood holders and as Saints in the gospel of Jesus Christ. Library of Congress.

he wished to have them make a record of all who do their duty who keep the word of wisdom &c. He recommended that the Bishops adopt such measures as would be most practicable and useful to bring about such an order of things that their reports be brought before the High Council that they may have a knowledge of their proceedings and the situation of the Church.[33]

Hyrum Smith, representing the First Presidency,[34] explained that bishops were subject to the High Council and that the council should call on the Presidents of the Lesser priesthood to attend the Council & receive instruction, and that he would meet with them if they would notify him of their meetings. That it was necessary for them to go from house to house, to his house, and to every house and see that every family done their duty, that he knew that there were more than one hundred families in town who did not attend to family prayer ... that every ordained member was a watchman on the wall.[35]

Hyrum also said "a record should be kept, by the Lesser Priesthood." He called for a record of members moving in and out, of the excommunicated, and of deaths. The High Council then voted that quorum presidents should meet with them and the First Presidency the next Friday. Bishop Knight reported that the lesser priesthood holders in his ward were doing their duty.

Stake President Marks spoke about helping the poor, so Bishop Knight gave an account of the situation of the poor, reporting that means had become exhausted for their relief. Hyrum Smith said that "there was a general want of action in the Church, that he wanted every one to start anew he knew not of a resolution in all the quorums to stop iniquity."[36]

During the Nauvoo years, some priesthood teaching in homes was done, but how much is not known. One study of Nauvoo priesthood home visiting notes that "their home teaching program did not keep pace with their developments."[37] An oft-repeated story about Nauvoo home teaching concerns seventeen-year-old William F. Cahoon, who visited Joseph Smith—but facts indicate this incident happened well before the Nauvoo period.[38] During a February 4, 1844, meeting, the Nauvoo teachers heard "some very appropriate remark[s] on the subjects [of] visiting the brethren and settling difficulties amongst the brethren." Apparently their next meeting was held almost a year later when the teachers met with the bishops to "reorganize the quorum of teachers, it being previously disorganized by a great number of said quorum joining the seventies and high priests quorums."[39] Samuel K. Gifford recorded that in 1844 he was ordained a teacher "and acted as such to the best of my ability."[40] A year later, by February 1845, the quorum again became organized and teachers again visited members, "generally finding them in good standing." At the next meeting a week later, one teacher reported he had visited in several wards and found the members generally in good standing. He exhorted the others to faithfully perform their duties.[41]

Minutes of the Nauvoo Aaronic Priesthood covering the period from January 1844 to June 1845 provide a detailed look at Aaronic Priesthood operations.[42] Stephen Farnsworth was ordained president of the priests quorum on January 13, 1844, and chose two counselors. But the quorum had barely started when nearly all the priests were ordained as seventies at the April conference. Meanwhile, the teachers quorum began meeting as a separate group and undertook visiting assignments. At the October 1844 conference, presidencies were sustained for priests and teachers quorums. The following January 1845, the Nauvoo bishops met to reorganize the quorum of teachers. Minutes for the January 13 meeting list the new presidency, ordained that day, and thirty-one teachers. After that, both the priests and teachers met in a combined Aaronic Priesthood meeting conducted jointly by the two quorums' presidents. The weekly meetings involved testimony bearing, instruction, assignments, and reports concerning "visiting the Church." Joint meetings were held fairly regularly until at least June

1845, when the minute book ends. Stephen M. Farnsworth continued as priests quorum president in fall 1845. During 1845 the priests visited Saints throughout the city, assisted by teachers and deacons.[43]

Church leaders turned to the Aaronic Priesthood quorums when the state dissolved Nauvoo's city government. In early 1845, the state cancelled Nauvoo's city charter, thereby dissolving the city's police system. Policeman Hosea Stout said the police decided to subdivide Nauvoo and the "County into Quorums of twelve deacons and have a Bishop at their head and they could thus administer in the lesser offices of the Church and preserve order."[44] On March 24, 1845, President Smith and the Twelve ordained new bishops and instructed them to call deacons to be watchmen to "insure peace and good order." Newly ordained Bishop John S. Higbee organized his First Ward into five "districts or wards" each with a bishop (apparently not ordained) "for the purpose of guarding the city from marauders and evil doers." Higbee noted that he ordained Elam Ludington and Jesse D. Hunter as his counselors on March 30 of that year.[45]

David Moore said that after the Nauvoo Charter was repealed, authorities organized the cities into districts and appointed officers over every ten men. "They were called Bishops and Deacons," he said, and guarded the city at night. The organization was kept up during summer 1845. Moore was appointed (apparently not ordained) a bishop and assigned to keep watch of his district one night a week. To guard his very large district on the north side of Nauvoo, which included a steamboat landing, he had a company of thirteen men. "Our weapons was a large hickory cane and a toothpick [a huge knife] the object of the knife to whittle Rascals out of town."[46] These priesthood guards have been romanticized and popularized by being called "whistling and whittling brigades."[47]

In 1845 leaders proposed that deacons should take care of the poor.[48] At the October 1845 conference, held inside the temple, the usual officers were sustained for all quorums but the deacons. Brigham Young therefore announced "that there be a quorum of deacons selected, and a president over them, and that the presiding Bishops see to it, as soon as possible, and make report to this conference, before its close."[49]

Leaders periodically wanted "to fill up" the quorums. By that they meant they wanted enough men in the quorums so quorum meetings and assignments happened, not that quorums must have the twelve, twenty-four, and forty-eight members set for the deacons, teachers, and priests quorums.[50] In October 1842, for example, the Nauvoo teachers quorum numbered only fifteen members.[51] In January 1845, Bishop Newel K. Whitney called a meeting "to fill up the quorums in order that saints might be visited by the lesser priesthood." Records note that "four priests and ten teachers were ordained" at the meeting.[52]

BOYS AND THE PRIESTHOOD

Aaronic Priesthood offices at Nauvoo were filled almost entirely by adults. Because of the duties assigned deacons, teachers, and priests in the revelations, leaders felt that maturity, not age, was the prerequisite for ordination. Nevertheless, in the pre-1846 period, many young men served the Church well in official callings.[53] Orson Pratt became a missionary at age nineteen. Lyman Johnson, later a young member of the Twelve, served a mission when he was twenty. George A. Smith, baptized at fifteen, marched in Zion's Camp and later was ordained a member of the First Quorum of Seventy at eighteen. Peter Whitmer Jr. became one of the Eight Witnesses at nineteen. Daniel Tyler, not quite eighteen, filled a mission by himself when his older companion failed to show up. Joseph Smith's younger brother Don Carlos received the priesthood at age fourteen, filled a mission that year, and at nineteen became the Nauvoo high priests quorum president. Erastus Snow, baptized at fourteen, preached extensively in Ohio, New York, and Pennsylvania before he was nineteen. At nineteen he preached with Joseph Smith at a Far West meeting. Harrison Burgess, eighteen, filled a mission to Vermont. William F. Cahoon says he was seventeen when he was a home teacher. Admittedly these cases are few and most involve older boys or young men, but they do show a willingness at that time to call youths to priesthood service. Later in the

As a member of the First Quorum of the Seventy at age eighteen, George A. Smith was an example of Church leaders' willingness to entrust sober-minded youth with responsible priesthood callings. Courtesy Church Archives.

nineteenth century, the Church in Utah increasingly used this precedent for ordaining faithful and capable youths.[54]

ELDERS

An elders quorum formally existed during most of the Nauvoo years. Lack of records means that the quorum's history can be told only in outline, based mainly on newspaper reports. By 1841, John A. Hicks was elders quorum president.[55] The quorum presidency sometimes was sustained at general conferences. The last presidency mentioned in the records was sustained on April 7, 1845, when members "continued and sustained" Samuel Williams as president, with Jesse Baker and Joshua Smith remaining as counselors.[56] While no quorum roll book survives to show enrollments year by year, membership numbers probably varied. They rose when new elders moved in and when large groups of missionaries, sent out as elders, returned. They fell when elders were called to be seventies or high priests.

Men called on missions during Joseph Smith's presidency were sent out as elders or seventies, a practice that required that some men be ordained before leaving. At general conference in April 1840, "the committee on ordination" (apparently not a stake committee) "reported that they had ordained thirty one persons to be elders." Another fifty men, some of whom undoubtedly had been elders, "had been received into the quorum of the seventies."[57] At the October 1840 conference, "the committee on ordinations reported that they had ordained thirty nine to the ministry."[58] During 1842 and 1843, large numbers of men were called into the elders' ranks. Apostle Brigham Young presided at a special conference in August 1841, held to select experienced men to go into the vineyard. The Twelve sent six elders to various cities and received conference approval to call many others.[59]

A special elders conference convened between April 6 and 12, 1843, conducted by the Twelve. The purpose "was to ordain elders, and send them forth into the vineyard to build up churches." Dozens of names of men were enrolled, and twenty-two men were ordained.[60] Then the April conference saw a mass recruitment for missionary service. One conference purpose, Joseph Smith announced, "was to choose young men, and ordain them, and send them out to preach, that they may have an opportunity of proving themselves, and of enduring the tarring and feathering and such things as those of us who have gone before them, have had to endure." Elder

Lyman Wight asked "if there were any present of the rough and weak things, who wished to be ordained, and go and preach, who have not been before ordained." He then spoke to these men "on the subject of their duty and requirements to go to preach." As a result, under the hands of the Twelve, 275 men were ordained as elders during the conference.[61]

A year later, during the April 1843 conference, the same thing happened. Under the direction of the Twelve, dozens of men were called on missions, twenty-two of whom needed to be ordained as elders first.[62] Three months later, at a special conference of elders held July 3 and 5, several dozen elders were sent on missions.[63]

Again, at the April 1844 general conference, an army of elders was called and sent to most states of the Union. Names of 339 men are listed in the *Times and Seasons,* many of them "experienced and able elders." Their assignment was to preach, to hold conferences, and to expound Joseph Smith's "Views of the Power and Policy of the General Government" in order to find electors who would vote for him for president of the United States.[64]

Other than these mass ordinations for missionary purposes, the Nauvoo High Council sometimes approved of elder ordinations. For example, council minutes note on September 10, 1842, that "Lewis Muedze was also ordained an Elder as he desired to return to Germany to preach the Gospel." On September 17 that year, the council record notes that "Truman Gilbert presented a Recommend from the Kirtland Branch Ohio and was ordained an Elder according to his request." Similarly, "Charles Greenwood requested an ordination, he was recommended by L. Soby, he was ordained."

Quorum presidents sometimes posted notices in the newspaper inviting newly arrived men holding a particular office to meet with that quorum. In July 1840, the *Times and Seasons* carried a notice issued by Iowa Elders Quorum President Daniel Avery calling for elders in Iowa to enroll their names in his quorum by early August "or they will not be considered in fellowship with said quorum." His quorum met, the notice said, on the fourth Saturday of each month at Ambrosia, Lee County.[65]

In March 1841, President John A. Hicks of the Nauvoo elders quorum published a notice "to the Elders Scattered Abroad." He requested that all those who held the office of elder should notify the clerk of the quorum of elders of their place of residence "by letter post piad [*sic*], that we may know where to find them." The time had come, he said, "when it is necessary that every one should render an account of his stewardship if he wishes to continue any longer steward." He was reacting to a problem of men out "in the world calling themselves elders" who had neither license nor recommend from the quorum. Some out in the world claiming to be elders were in fact "unclean persons, some of whom have fled from justice" and "keep not the commandments neither the word of wisdom." Then, as a postscript, quorum clerk Samuel Henderson asked men who formerly belonged to the elders but who had "joined the quorum of Seventies since last spring Conference" to notify him.[66]

John S. Higbee was ordained an elder on July 3, 1839, and although his small journal says nothing about his quorum, it does record that in July 1840 he assisted with the baptisms for the dead, performing about one hundred immersions of people "most of them for their dead relatives."[67]

HIGH PRIESTS

High priests had a quorum in Nauvoo, presided over first by Don Carlos Smith and then by Bishop George Miller.[68] They held quorum meetings, but how often or regularly is not known. Quorum records are scarce, so only a thumbnail history is possible. Similar to the elders presidency, the high priests presidency struggled to find out who should be in their quorum. President Miller, late in 1842, announced that all high priests who had not become members of "the Quorum of High Priests" should enroll in the quorum "upon their arrival in this place." It was their duty, he said, "to apply to the Quorum for admission."[69]

During the October 1844 conference, President Brigham Young gave the high priests a major task. First he had the quorum members come up from the congregation and join together on the right of the stand. He then announced that he wanted to select a number of high priests to preside in each congressional district in the United States. He picked eighty-five high priests to do the job. For this mission, or to replace those called, forty-nine elders were ordained as high priests during the conference. The plan, President Young said, was not for the high priests to tarry six months, but to take their families along and to settle down in those districts. They could return when the temple was finished and receive their endowments, but then they were to return to their districts and turn them into stakes as large as the Nauvoo Stake.[70]

Departures apparently waited for good weather to come early in 1845. John S. Higbee's diary notes that on January 12, 1845, he attended his high priests quorum meeting, and while there, he and fifty other high priests were chosen for a special mission by the Twelve and told to hold themselves in readiness to be sent to the various states.[71] Calls were issued, but for some reason the plan to send high priests eastward was not carried out.

At their January 26, 1845, meeting, the high priests quorum discussed a proposal that they build a high priests hall, 120' long, 80' wide, and 33' high. But Brigham Young convinced them to put the labor and money into finishing the upper room of the Temple so "you can get your endowment, and your priesthood."[72] As a result, no high priests hall was started.

At general conference on October 6, 1845, Bishop Miller, William Snow, and Noah Packard were sustained as the quorum's presidency.

SEVENTIES

Nauvoo had a greater influence on the priesthood office of seventy than on any other office, because both the number of men ordained to be seventies and the number of quorums mushroomed. A question that continues to disturb because it is not clearly answered is why President Brigham Young so vastly expanded the seventies' ranks. On February 28, 1835, Joseph Smith, based on an unrecorded revelation "showing the order of the Seventy," commenced to organize the first seventies unit in the Church. Its seven-member presidency presided over one quorum of seventy men and then over other units of seventy as needed—"until ... seven times seventy, if the labor in the vineyard of necessity requires it." Seventies were not local ministers but were considered General Authorities, traveling ministers, witnesses unto the Gentiles and in all the world, and "seventy apostles." Seventies were called from among the experienced elders.[73]

Records indicate that from one-third to one-half of all missionaries set apart between 1837 and 1843 were seventies.[74] By 1839 a second and third quorum of seventies had been organized. Their work was directed by the seven presidents of the first quorum, who together formed what is termed the First Council of the Seventy. Brigham Young's brother Joseph Young served as senior president of the First Quorum and therefore as president of all of the seventies.

In Nauvoo the seventies quorums met for edification, instruction, and worship. The meetings also helped the presidencies keep track of their members. Until fall 1844, only a few new quorums were added. Andrew Moore, for example, was ordained a president in the Fifth Quorum of Seventy in August 1844. He noted in January 1846 that "I continued to meet with my Quorum once every week to tranceact [sic] business and to see that the Quorum was in union … and to give instructions."[75] To keep their seventy-member quorums reasonably filled, quorums recruited new members from among the elders, Aaronic Priesthood bearers, and the unordained. Individually, many seventies received and filled mission calls during the Nauvoo period. Some were already in seventies quorums when called, and others became seventies because of their mission calls.

At the October 1844 conference, President Brigham Young, in addition to calling high priests "to go abroad and preside" in the eastern states, called for a major expansion of seventies quorums.

He wanted at least ten quorums of seventy, so one purpose of the conference was "to ordain the presidents of the seventies and then fill the quorums of seventies from the elders quorum." The next day, October 8, Heber C. Kimball of the First Presidency "recommended all those elders who are under the age of thirty-five, and also all the priests, teachers, deacons and members, who are recommended to be ordained, to withdraw and receive an ordination into the seventies, which was done."[76]

This expansion of seventies quorums was a major priesthood development during the Nauvoo years. Before the conference concluded, the seventies presidents had ordained approximately four hundred men into seventies quorums. They filled eleven quorums and put forty men into a twelfth quorum. After the conference and for the next several months, more quorums were created and more seventies ordained. Thomas Steed recalled that on April 7, 1845, he "was ordained a seventy with about five hundred others … and joined the 21st Quorum."[77] In December 1845, the thirty-second quorum was organized. By early 1846, seventies units numbered thirty-four.[78]

Why the Twelve called for this build-up of seventies is not explained. Apparently the Twelve had in mind a massive missionary labor in the near future, perhaps to implement what President Joseph Smith had wanted done—Norton Jacob recalled that in 1844 President Smith "directed that all the Elders of Israel should go into the vineyard."[79] President Young told the conference "that the elders young men who are capable of preaching, will be ordained" and that "if an elder wants to go preaching let him go into the seventies. You are all apostles to the nations to carry the gospel; and when we send you to build up the kingdom, we will give you the keys, and power and authority."[80]

This seventies recruitment apparently was part of a two-pronged expansion the Twelve wanted for the kingdom: sending out a large missionary force to convert and baptize new members and sending out high priests to preside over areas where these converts lived. Counselor Heber C. Kimball noted that Brigham Young, when challenged about whether a high priest was higher than a seventy, answered that "the Seventies are ordained Apostles and when they go forth into the ministry, they are sent with power to build up the kingdom in all the world and consequently they have power to ordain High Priests, and also to ordain and organize a High Council."[81] The goal seemed to be the creation of stakes throughout the United States, converted and organized by seventies, who would install the selected high priests as stake presidents. However, for reasons not explained, perhaps because of priorities given to finishing the temple, neither prong of the plan was pushed. Nevertheless, Nauvoo quickly had more seventies than any other Melchizedek Priesthood office. By late 1845, most of the men in Nauvoo who held the priesthood were seventies.

To house the meetings for the many quorums, the seventies constructed their own Seventies Hall, which was completed that winter. On December 26, 1844, the Twelve presided over the first of several days of dedicating the new Seventies Hall as a home for fifteen quorums. That day many of the Twelve and the Seven Presidents sat on the stand. Senior presidents of each of the seventies quorums sat on the right, a choir on the left, and a brass band in front. The congregation was comprised of members of the second and third quorums of Seventy with their families. At a rate of two quorums per day, "each day afforded a new congregation, that all the seventies, with their families, might in turn, participate."[82] At the dedication services, prayers and preachings made clear that seventies "were designed to be messengers to every land and kingdom under heaven" and "to administer salvation." Senior President of the Seventies Joseph Young, on the fourth day, prayed that God would "bless them and their families when they shall go to the Islands of the sea."[83]

The seventies' final notable activity in Nauvoo came during winter 1845–46 when "the Twelve delegated to them [the Presidents of the Seventies] the government of the Temple, while the ordinances were being administered to their quorums." The Twelve's action firmly placed the "responsibility for giving the endowment" to the seventies on the shoulders of the First Presidency of the Seventy.[84]

NAUVOO'S PRIESTHOOD LEGACY

An assessment of local priesthood work during the Nauvoo period shows continuity in terms of what priesthood bearers and quorums had done before in Missouri, in Ohio, and in mission areas, and it identifies several adaptations and changes. What was Nauvoo's priesthood legacy? What started or continued at Nauvoo that became part of priesthood practices in the future? What was enduring and what was temporary?

Nauvoo continued a barely established precedent that stakes were the basic local Church unit. Ideally, a new clustering or settlement of Saints would begin with a presiding officer, who might be called a branch, district, stake, or settlement president or presiding elder. Then, the clustering needed a bishop to handle court cases, moneys, and the poor. Finally, a high council was needed to handle discipline cases and disputes and to make decisions for the settlement. If population grew, more bishops would be added, the settlement subdivided into wards—sometimes called districts or branches—and satellite settlements recognized as being part of the stake. This pattern continued to be followed in Utah for decades.

Local priesthood quorums continued to be stake entities as they had been in Missouri and Kirtland. These included deacons, teachers, priests, and elders quorums. This pattern continued in Utah. Salt Lake Stake, for example, had stake deacons, teachers, and priests quorums until the 1870s. Sanpete Stake during the 1870s had a stake quorum of each, and half of each quorums' members came from one city (Manti), half from another (Ephraim).[85]

Visiting priesthood teachers continued to be the most important local priesthood officers in contact with the members. Before, during the Nauvoo years, and after, visits to the homes were standard priesthood work. Visiting was considered lesser priesthood work, a view that continued through that century. Since Nauvoo, the main activity carried out by local priesthood bearers continues to be visiting members in their homes.[86]

Quorum meetings before, during, and after Nauvoo were the most important self-learning sessions that male Latter-day Saint members attended. When ward Sunday Schools first started in the 1860s, they were for children and youths. Not until the late 1800s was Sunday School generally attended by adults.[87]

A concern before, during, or immediately after Nauvoo was that priesthood quorums have enough manpower to be viable, but not that there be multiple quorums for each office so that all men could be priesthood bearers. The assumption was that a stake should have one quorum each of elders, priests, teachers, and deacons. In time, Utah wards came to have their own groups of teachers and deacons and finally of priests. Until well into the twentieth century, stake elders quorums continued to include more than one ward's elders.

However, the Nauvoo years brought three priesthood changes that, as subsequent years proved, were of paramount importance. Of greatest significance was the creation of subunits called wards, each of which had a bishop assigned to it. Like a very fertile seed, wards headed by bishops became within the decade following the exodus from Nauvoo the essential church unit that cared for, trained, provided ordinances and worship services for, and otherwise served Saints at the local level. The practice of having wards and ward bishops that started in Nauvoo has become a fixture of Church government.

A second important change was caused by the general introduction of the temple endowment and celestial marriages late in 1845. After that, the endowment became required of all men going on missions or receiving temple marriages. Henceforth, men going on missions or marrying had to bear the Melchizedek Priesthood. This policy increased the numbers of elders and seventies by siphoning off practically all men who had staffed the deacons, teachers, and priests quorums. By the earliest days in Utah, Church leaders, lacking non–Melchizedek Priesthood men, had to call elders, seventies, and high priests to be acting deacons, acting teachers, and acting priests in order to keep Aaronic Priesthood work going.[88]

A third major change during the Nauvoo era was the unusual and massive expansion of seventies quorums. After the expansion, most Nauvoo men held some priesthood office. Assuming that Nauvoo's peak population was about 12,000 and that the average household was a family of two parents and three children, then it seems that one-fifth of Nauvoo's 12,000 residents, about 2,400, were men. Of those 2,400, there were 1,823 men by late 1845 who were seventies (making up thirty-four quorums).[89] Add to this number about 300 high priests, including bishops and Apostles,[90] and a score or more of Aaronic Priesthood bearers, and the number of priesthood holders exceeds 2,000. A reasonable estimate, then, is that by late 1846 three-fourths or more of Nauvoo's males held some priesthood office. About 80 percent of these were seventies, making seventies the largest priesthood group in the Church, a distinction they held for the next decade.[91] In the 1847 select pioneer party, for example, there were eight Apostles, four bishops, fifteen high priests, eight elders, and seventy-eight seventies.[92] During the nineteenth century, seventies provided two-thirds of all missionaries called.[93]

Nauvoo's main personalities, location, and dramatic happenings are well known and documented. Even Nauvoo's common people have received scholarly attention in recent years. For the women, the Female Relief Society served briefly to help bond many to the Church organization. Less known but equally important, priesthood quorums in Nauvoo similarly connected men to the Church organization. In those days before wards and therefore before ward sacrament, before priesthood and auxiliary meetings, quorums—during their off-and-on existences—gave priesthood bearers a sense of belonging and camaraderie, a place to discuss, learn, and share experiences, and a range of religious assignments to perform. Priesthood office and quorum membership were ingredients in a glue-mix that by 1845 helped bond most of the Latter-day Saint men in Nauvoo to the Church.

This article was originally published in BYU Studies 32, nos. 1–2 (1992): 57–80.

NOTES

1. David Lowenthal, *The Past Is a Foreign Country* (New York: Cambridge University Press, 1985).
2. Nauvoo Stake High Council Minutes, May 8, 1842, Church History Library, The Church of Jesus Christ of Latter-day Saints, Salt Lake City.
3. William G. Hartley, "Organization of Wards and Stakes: A Historical Approach," in *Religious Educators Symposium on LDS Church History* (Salt Lake City: Church Education System, 1977), 53–55.
4. "Minutes of a Conference Held in Zarahemla, Ia, August A.D. 1841," *Times and Seasons* 2 (September 15, 1841): 547.
5. William G. Hartley, "Ordained and Acting Teachers in the Lesser Priesthood, 1851–1883," *BYU Studies* 16, no. 3 (1976): 375–98; William G. Hartley, "The Priesthood

Reorganization of 1877: Brigham Young's Last Achievement," *BYU Studies* 20, no. 1 (1979): 3–36.

6. Robert L. Marrott, "History and Functions of the Aaronic Priesthood and the Offices of Priest, Teacher, and Deacon in The Church of Jesus Christ of Latter-day Saints, 1829–1844" (master's thesis, Brigham Young University, 1976), 36.

7. Marrott, "Aaronic Priesthood," 24.

8. Roger Launius, "A Survey of Priesthood Ordinations, 1830–1844," *Restoration Trail Forum* 9 (May 1983): 3.

9. Launius, "Survey of Priesthood Ordinations," 3.

10. Milton V. Backman Jr., *The Heavens Resound: A History of the Latter-day Saints in Ohio, 1830–1838* (Salt Lake City: Deseret Book, 1983), 244–48; Donald Q. Cannon and Lyndon W. Cook, eds., *Far West Record: Minutes of The Church of Jesus Christ of Latter-day Saints, 1830–1844* (Salt Lake City: Deseret Book, 1983); D. Michael Quinn, "The Evolution of the Presiding Quorums of the LDS Church," *Journal of Mormon History* 1 (1974): 21–38; Dale Beecher, "The Office of Bishop," *Dialogue: A Journal of Mormon Thought* 15 (Winter 1982): 103–15; James N. Baumgarten, "The Role and Function of the Seventies in LDS Church History" (master's thesis, Brigham Young University, 1960).

11. Meeting of High Council and Bishopric, February 24, 1838, Minutes, in Cannon and Cook, *Far West Record*, 142; for teachers' activities see also the Far West, Kirtland, and Nauvoo Teachers Quorum Minutes, December 1834–December 1845, film of manuscript, Church History Library.

12. John Somers Higbee, Reminiscences and Diaries, 1845–66, Church History Library.

13. "Proceedings of the General Conference Held at Hancock Ill, on Saturday the 5th Day of October 1839," *Times and Seasons* 1 (December 1839): 30–31.

14. "Conference Minutes," *Times and Seasons* 2 (April 15,1841): 375–83.

15. "Minutes of a Conference of the Church of Jesus Christ of Latter-day Saints, Held in Nauvoo, Ill., Commencing Oct. 1st, 1841," *Times and Seasons* 2 (October 15, 1841): 577.

16. See Joseph Smith Jr., *The History of The Church of Jesus Christ of Latter-day Saints,* ed. B. H. Roberts, 2d ed. rev., 7 vols. (Salt Lake City: Deseret Book, 1978), 7:296 (hereafter cited as *History of the Church*).

17. Beecher, "Office of Bishop," 103.

18. Beecher, "Office of Bishop," 104.

19. "Conference Minutes," *Times and Seasons* 2 (September 1, 1841): 521.

20. Nauvoo Stake High Council Minutes, August 20 and 21, 1842; *History of the Church*, 5:119–20; a note on page 120 explains the evolution from three wards in 1839 to four wards and then on March 1, 1842, to thirteen wards. Ward boundaries were readjusted on December 4, 1842. See *History of the Church,* 5:199.

21. William G. Hartley, "Mormon Sundays," *Ensign* 8 (January 1978): 19–25; George W. Givens, *In Old Nauvoo: Everyday Life in the City of Joseph* (Salt Lake City: Deseret Book, 1990), 142–49.

22. Higbee, Diaries.

23. Edward Hunter, Autobiography excerpt, in *Our Pioneer Heritage,* comp. Kate B. Carter, 20 vols. (Salt Lake City: Daughters of Utah Pioneers, 1958–77), 6:325.

24. "Conference Minutes," *Times and Seasons* 6 (November 1, 1845): 1013.

25. "Epistle of the 12 to the Church of Jesus Christ of Latter-day Saints in Nauvoo & All the World—Aug 15 1844," in *Messages of the First Presidency of The Church of Jesus Christ of Latter-day Saints, 1833–1964,* comp. James R. Clark, 6 vols. (Salt Lake City: Bookcraft, 1965–75), 1:236, August 15, 1844.

26. Marrott, "Aaronic Priesthood," 29, 36.

27. Marrott, "Aaronic Priesthood"; Teachers Quorum Minutes for Kirtland, Far West, and Nauvoo, 1838–42; and Nauvoo Aaronic Priesthood Minutes and Biographical Sketches, January 13, 1844, to June 15, 1845, Church History Library.

28. Marrott, "Aaronic Priesthood," 26.

29. *History of the Church,* 4:512; Doctrine and Covenants 124:141–42.

30. "Conference Minutes," *Times and Seasons* 2 (July 1, 1841): 459.

31. *History of the Church,* 4:312.

32. Teachers Quorum Minutes for Kirtland, Far West, and Nauvoo, 1838–42, Church History Library.

33. Nauvoo Stake High Council Minutes, January 18, 1842, 34.

34. Doctrine and Covenants 124:91–96.

35. Nauvoo Stake High Council Minutes, January 18, 1842, 43–35.

36. Nauvoo Stake High Council Minutes, January 18, 1842, 35.

37. Gary L. Phelps, "Home Teaching: Attempts by the Latter-day Saints to Establish an Effective Program during the Nineteenth Century" (master's thesis, Brigham Young University, 1975), 29.

38. William Farrington Cahoon, "Recollections of the Prophet Joseph Smith," *Juvenile Instructor* 28 (August 15, 1892): 492–93. It is generally accepted that this story happened at Nauvoo (Phelps, "Home Teaching," 35), but if so, Cahoon could not have been seventeen as he claims: he was born on November 7, 1813, so if he were "about seventeen years of age," that age would put the story near 1830 and before he was baptized.

39. Teachers Quorum Minutes, January 13, 1845.

40. Samuel Kendall Gifford, Reminiscences, typescript, 5, Church History Library.

41. Teachers Quorum Minutes, February 12 and 19, 1845.

42. Nauvoo Aaronic Priesthood Minutes and Biographical Sketches.

43. Nauvoo Aaronic Priesthood Minutes and Biographical Sketches.

44. Juanita Brooks, ed., *On the Mormon Frontier: The Diary of Hosea Stout 1844–1861,* 2 vols. (Salt Lake City: University of Utah Press and Utah State Historical Society, 1982), 1:27, March 14, 1845.

45. *History of the Church,* 7:388; Higbee, Diaries.

46. David Moore, Journal, L. Tom Perry Special Collections, Harold B. Lee Library, Brigham Young University, Provo, Utah, quoted in Thurmon Dean Moody, "Nauvoo's Whistling and Whittling Brigade," *BYU Studies* 15, no. 4 (1975): 484.

47. Brooks, *Diary of Hosea Stout,* 1:36–37n67; Moody, "Nauvoo's Whistling and Whittling Brigade," 480–90.

48. *History of the Church,* 7:381.

49. "Conference Minutes," *Times and Seasons* 6 (November 1, 1845): 1010.

50. Marrott, "Aaronic Priesthood," 19.

51. *History of the Church,* 5:169.

52. *History of the Church,* 7:351.

53. Adapted from a list in William G. Hartley, "Joseph Smith and Nauvoo's Youth," *Ensign* 9 (September 1979): 26–29.

54. Hartley, "Ordained and Acting Teachers," 375–98; Hartley, "Priesthood Reorganization of 1877," 3–36.

55. *History of the Church,* 4:341.

56. *History of the Church,* 7:392.

57. "Conference Minutes," *Times and Seasons* 1 (April 1840): 94–95.

58. "Conference Minutes," *Times and Seasons* 1 (October 1840): 187.

59. "Conference Minutes," *Times and Seasons* 2 (September 1, 1841): 521.

60. "Elders Conference," *Times and Seasons* 4 (April 1, 1843): 157–58.

61. "Conference Minutes," *Times and Seasons* 3 (April 15, 1842): 761–63.

62. "Elders Conference," *Times and Seasons* 4 (April 1, 1843): 157–58.

63. "Special Conference," *Times and Seasons* 4 (June 15, 1843): 240. Although the issue is dated June 15, it carries news of the July 3 and 5 special conference.

64. "Special Conference," *Times and Seasons* 5 (April 15, 1844): 504–6.

65. "Notice," *Times and Seasons* 1 (July 1840): 143.

66. "To the Elders Scattered Abroad," *Times and Seasons* 2 (March 1, 1841): 340.

67. Higbee, Diaries.

68. *History of the Church,* 2:370, 4:12, 4:424.

69. "Notice," *Times and Seasons* 3 (August 15, 1842): 894.

70. "Conference Minutes," *Times and Seasons* 5 (November 1, 1844): 695–96.

71. Higbee, Diaries.

72. Nauvoo High Priests Quorum Minutes, Miscellaneous Minutes File , January 26, 1845, Church History Library. See also *History of the Church,* 7:54.

73. *History of the Church,* 2:201–4, 221, 346; 7:307; Doctrine and Covenants 107:25. The standard history of seventies work is Baumgarten's thesis, "The Role and Function of the Seventies in LDS Church History" (see n. 9 in this article).

74. First Council of Seventy, Minutes and Genealogy Book B, microfilm, Church History Library; statistics compiled by the author.

75. Andrew Moore, Reminiscences, Church History Library.

76. *History of the Church,* 7:305.

77. *The Life of Thomas Steed from His Own Diary, 1826–1910,* typescript (n.p., n.d.), 11, copy in Church History Library.

78. *History of the Church,* 7:549; Seventies Record Book B, December 21, 1845, Church History Library; Baumgarten, "Role and Function of the Seventies," 32; 34th Quorum of Seventies, Seventies and Quorums, Records, 1844–1975, December 21, 1845, Church History Library.

79. C. Edward Jacob and Ruth S. Jacob, *The Record of Norton Jacob,* typescript (Norton Family Association, 1949), 5.

80. *History of the Church,* 7:307–8.

81. Heber C. Kimball, Journal, Book 93 (November 21, 1845–January 7, 1846), entry dated December 14, 1845, Church History Library. This entry is not in *The Journal of Heber C. Kimball* published by Kraut's Pioneer Press.

82. "Dedication of the Seventies Hall," *Times and Seasons* 6 (February 1, 1845): 794.

83. "Dedication of the Seventies Hall," 797–98.

84. *History of the Church*, 7:566; Seventies Record Book B, January 7 and 8, 1846.

85. Hartley, "Ordained and Acting Teachers"; William G. Hartley, "Priesthood Reform Movement, 1908–1922," *BYU Studies* 13, no. 2 (1973): 137–56.

86. Hartley, "Ordained and Acting Teachers," 378–79; Hartley, "Priesthood Reform Movement," 137–56; see also Phelps, "Home Teaching."

87. Hartley, "Mormon Sundays," 23.

88. Hartley, "Ordained and Acting Teachers," 375–98.

89. Author's tally is based on individual quorum records in Seventies Record Book B.

90. There were 286 high priests who received temple endowments late in 1845. See *History of the Church*, 7:552.

91. Baumgarten, "Role and Function of the Seventies," 32–33.

92. Journal History of the Church, April 18, 1847, 2, Church History Library, microfilm copy in Harold B. Lee Library, Brigham Young University, Provo, Utah.

93. Baumgarten, "Role and Function of the Seventies," 48, 106.

18

Brigham Young's Overland Trails Revolution

The Creation of the "Down-and-Back" Wagon-Train System, 1860–1861

IN LATE APRIL 1861, FOUR LDS CHURCH team trains consisting of some 200 wagons and 1,600 oxen, hauling 136,000 pounds of flour, rolled out of the Salt Lake Valley and headed east for Florence, Nebraska. These were wagons and teams on loan, to be returned when they came back to Utah that fall bringing Mormon immigrants. Manning the trains were about 210 volunteer teamsters and guards. These trains traveled a thousand miles through spring mud and rains and normal trail circumstances, deposited one-fourth of their flour at each of four stations along the way, and reached the Missouri River Valley by late June. There, they loaded up immigrants too poor to buy outfits and conveyed them back to Utah. These "down-and-back" wagon trains—down to Florence and back to Utah—operated at practically no actual cash costs to the Church. The next year, the number of wagons sent from Utah nearly doubled. During the 1860s, Church team trains became the primary wagon trains carrying Saints to Zion, all but eliminating independent wagon trains. About twenty thousand LDS immigrants traveled to Utah during the 1860s, most coming by Church team trains.[1]

The 1861 down-and-back Church trains signaled a revolution in how immigrants, Mormons or not, crossed the plains. The history of the overland trails from 1843 to 1868—the California Trail, Santa Fe Trail, Oregon Trail, and Mormon Trail—has very few turning points in terms of *how* people traveled the routes. Trail routes shifted, true, and trails, year by year, saw improvements and increasing services along the way. But little changed in terms of how people transported themselves west. An estimated three hundred thousand people went west on the Oregon and California trails, while some sixty to seventy thousand Mormons took the Mormon trails to Utah between 1847 and 1868.[2] Almost all of these nearly four hundred thousand people journeyed west in wagons and teams that they already owned or had purchased themselves or as partners, or paid to ride with those who had such wagons.

By the late 1850s, stagecoaches offered a literal change of pace but provided passage to a paltry percentage of all who went west. Certainly, the Mormon handcart system was revolutionary and even was employed in 1859 by at least one company of Pike's Peak gold seekers.[3] But even bolder than the handcart system, Brigham Young's system of down-and-back wagon trains was a remarkable innovation in the history of overland trail travel and of Mormon migration during the 1860s.

UNDERSTANDING THE CONTEXT

To show the magnitude of this new operation and to appreciate its complexities and brilliance, I focus on the origins of the down-and-back idea, when it was first formulated, how it was introduced and tested, and how the system of using wagons and oxen from Utah, on loan, was fully implemented. Put simply, this paper presents the history of the creation and launching of the down-and-back wagon-train system that came to characterize LDS emigration during the 1860s. The title of this paper contains three carefully chosen elements—"Brigham Young," "Overland Trails," and "Revolution," each of which needs introductory comments before we examine the creation of the down-and-back system.

Brigham Young: America's Leading Emigration Promoter

Scholars and media people credit Brigham Young for numerous achievements and involvements, good or ill, that occurred during his watch at the helm of The Church of Jesus Christ of Latter-day Saints (1844–77). Linked tightly to his name are such designations as Church president and prophet, leader of the 1847 pioneers, colonizer, territorial governor, Indian agent, enterprise promoter and developer, husband, and father. One title, however, is conspicuously missing. Despite his identification as "Brigham Young the Colonizer," American and even Mormon historians fail to give him credit as American's premier immigration promoter.[4] Katherine Copman, in her 1921 economic history of the American West, judged Mormon immigration to be "the most successful example of regulated immigration in United States history,"[5] yet the section on "Immigration and Minorities" in the New York Public Library's American History Desk Reference (89–128) says not a word about Mormon immigration. The record speaks for itself: In the annals of American history, no person presided over the mass movement of more people than did Brigham Young.[6] In addition to the sixty thousand or more who reached Utah by sail, train, wagon, and handcart during his administration, thousands more came in organized companies by steamships and the transcontinental railroad during the eight years prior to his death. For more than thirty years, he oversaw a pragmatic and successful system that hired agents, chartered at least 127 sailing ships, engaged riverboats and trains, purchased wagons and livestock wholesale, and organized 329 wagon trains. During the 1860s alone, forty-eight Church down-and-back trains made the two-thousand-mile round trip.[7]

Although the overall contribution of LDS migration to the U.S. emigration story goes mostly unheralded, most specific aspects of the Mormon migrations have received scholarly attention. We know a good deal about the mass relocation of Saints from the Nauvoo area to Utah, the Perpetual Emigrating Fund, and the handcart system, and have a few studies of aspects of the down-and-back wagon-train system.[8] This literature, written mostly by Mormons, acknowledges that Young played a role in mass migration but not straightforward recognition of just how unique a role he played. For example, the *Encyclopedia of Latter-day Saint History* comments with a vague passive verb: "A viable program of immigration was instituted for the tens of thousands of converts who were transplanted to the Great Basin in response to the doctrine of the gathering."[9]

The Overland Trails

Most leading studies of Overland Trail migration end with 1860, thus ignoring nine years prior to the transcontinental railroad. George Stewart's *The California Trail* (Lincoln: University of Nebraska Press, 1962), the best one-volume history of that subject, devotes one chapter to each year of trail travel during the 1840s, a concluding chapter for the entire 1850s, and nothing on the 1860s. John Unruh's prize-winning book, *The Plains Across* (Urbana: University of Illinois Press, 1979), chides Stewart and others for slighting the 1850s and 1860s, then concentrates his own study on the 1850s, likewise stopping at 1860. LDS Assistant Church Historian Andrew Jenson published a twenty-three-part series called "Church Emigration" in the *Contributor* (September 1891–September 1893), which included an essay about every year's travel—identifying and recording details about every LDS chartered ship's company and Atlantic voyages, and every wagon train that ran every year. But, inexplicably, Jenson, too, terminated his study with the year 1860.[10]

Three factors perhaps explain the neglect of 1860s trail travel. First, by 1860 wagon-train travel seemed to be just more of the same over well-traveled routes. Stewart claimed that, by 1860, the trails had achieved the status of "roads."[11] America's Civil War became the significant story of the 1860s, shifting historians' interest to the East. Also, the 1860s volume of travelers going to California and Oregon apparently fell to a trickle, making that decade more like a postscript than a solid story. Merrill Mattes's monumental bibliography of trail diaries lists 339 accounts for the 1860s, compared to 1,040 for the 1850s. Nevertheless, when Mattes factors in the Colorado and Montana gold rushes between 1861 and 1866, he estimates that some 135,000 travelers (averaging 22,000 a year) used the western trails in that half-decade.[12] In contrast, the 1860s were a vital and dramatic decade for Mormon Trail activity, accounting for approximately one-third of total emigration to Zion. The trek was slightly easier then because the roads were better and more settlements had been founded along the way. But it was still a monumental journey for men, women, children, oxen, and wagons, a journey comparable in cost, time, labor, and endurance to travel in the 1850s.

Revolution

History seems to capitalize on important beginnings, key turning points, and highlighted events. In the history of the overland trails, standard histories identify 1843, when the "Great Migration" to Oregon took place, as such a key moment, followed by 1846, which, among other events, included the Donner Party tragedy; the California gold rush of 1849; and 1852, which saw the largest overland traffic ever. Historians give due attention to the beginnings of the overland stagecoach lines and the dramatic Pony Express saga. They note new routes, new posts and supply stations, and peak years for Native American attacks. But until the railroad in 1869, there were few innovations in wagon design or draft animals.

Historians of overland trails do not ignore the innovation represented by Mormon handcarts, although they relish the Martin and Willie disasters and evidence scant understanding of handcart advantages. To my knowledge, however, only one scholar, John Hulmston, has focused on the down-and-back trains, a truly innovative system that the Church experimented with in 1860, implemented in 1861, and used from then until the railroad reached Promontory Summit in 1869. Hulmston calls it "an unprecedented occurrence in the field of nineteenth century transportation," and "an extremely important breakthrough."[13] I call it revolutionary.

MOTIVATIONS FOR CREATING THE DOWN-AND-BACK SYSTEM

The confluence of several elements produced the well-run down-and-back system. Most important were three decades of the Church's commitment to its poor members.[14] The Doctrine and Covenants is peppered with commands and warnings: "Look to the poor and needy, and administer to their relief that they shall not suffer" (D&C 38:35). "Thou wilt remember the poor, and consecrate of thy properties for their support" (D&C 42:30–31, 34, 39). "Ye must visit the poor and needy and administer to their relief" (D&C 44:6). "Remember in all things the poor and needy, the sick and the afflicted, for he that doeth not these things, the same is not my disciple" (D&C 52:40). God is displeased with those who "do not impart of their substance, as becometh saints, to the poor and afflicted" (D&C 105:3). "The widows and orphans shall be provided for, as also the poor" (D&C 83:6). "The bishop … also should travel round about and among all the churches; searching after the poor to administer to their wants by humbling the rich and the proud" (D&C 84:112). "Therefore, if any man shall take of the abundance which I have made, and impart not his portion, according to the law of my gospel, unto the poor and the needy, he shall, with the wicked, lift up his eyes in hell, being in torment" (D&C 104:18).

Second, the Church had already provided or sent wagons to help those in need. Joseph Young, Brigham's brother, had directed the first mass movement of the needy as president of the Seventies; this was the Kirtland Camp, which moved to Missouri in 1838.[15] Next, during winter 1838–39, when the Saints were expelled from Missouri, several hundred members at Far West covenanted to help all Saints leave the state. Working with Brigham Young, the presiding authority while Joseph Smith was in Liberty Jail, a Committee of Removal enlisted members' wagons to aid the needy. A number of the covenanters reached the Mississippi River near Quincy, Illinois, left their families there, and drove two hundred miles back to Far West to rescue others who lacked transportation.[16] A third application of this mutual-aid principle came six years later. When Illinois vigilantes burned more than a hundred buildings owned by Mormons in Morley's Settlement, twenty-seven miles south of Nauvoo, the Saints sent empty wagons down to move the victims into Nauvoo.

Thus, it is not surprising that the Saints attending the October 1845 conference covenanted in the temple to help everyone who needed assistance to move west. This "Nauvoo pledge" drove efforts for the next six years to transport those without adequate outfits. During the fall 1846 exodus from Nauvoo, three rescue teams went from Council Bluffs and Garden Grove to the poor camps, picked up the needy, and moved them to Mormon encampments farther west in Iowa.[17]

According to P. A. M. Taylor, Brigham Young planned for teams to intercept 1848 immigrants at Fort Laramie and take them over the Wyoming leg while the "original teams returned to the Missouri before winter." Taylor continues: "This was not put fully into practice; but aid was sent over shorter distances." During many immigrating seasons, teams went from the Salt Lake Valley to help trail-weary companies during the last hundred or two hundred miles of their journey.[18]

Another effort was the Perpetual Emigrating Fund (PEF), created in 1849, to loan money and extend credits to Zion-bound Saints. Donations allowed the Church to organize its first PEF wagon company in 1850. As planned, Bishop Edward Hunter carried five thousand dollars to Kanesville, Iowa, where he bought teams of oxen and cattle, and, where necessary, wagons, then captained the train back to Utah where the PEF livestock was sold for cash. By that fall, after a single trip, the PEF had nearly twenty thousand dollars to work with.[19] By late 1852, "all the exiles from Nauvoo who wished

Wagon train at Hanging Rock, c. late nineteenth century. During the mid-1800s, sixty to seventy thousand Saints came to Utah in wagon trains like this one. Courtesy Church Archives.

to come had been removed to Zion," which meant that "the obligations of the Nauvoo pledge had been faithfully discharged."[20] Closing the Nauvoo door, however, opened the European portals. Between 1852 and 1856, the PEF expended £125,000 in emigrating the "poor saints" from Europe to Salt Lake Valley.[21]

"Gathering" the poor, however, was the Church's most costly program during the early 1850s. The PEF could not work unless the Saints repaid their loans; but scratching out a living proved to be such a challenge, especially exacerbated by drought and famine during 1855, that the PEF "realized very little from repayments."[22] By early 1855, the fund was depleted.[23]

Faced with the Church's inability to provide expensive wagons pulled by expensive oxen, Brigham Young proposed the creation of handcart brigades.[24] During 1856, five separate handcart companies reached Utah. The first three made the trip without undue hardship. The last two, the Martin and Willie companies, suffered many deaths—about two hundred out of twelve hundred—because they started too late, were caught by a series of blizzards in Wyoming, and took almost double the number as the earlier companies. The Utah Saints again sent rescuing wagon trains into Wyoming.[25]

Despite the costly miscalculation, the First Presidency still reported that "the enterprise, having proved so eminently successful, will in the future enter largely into all our emigrating operations," but with several adjustments and improvements.[26] Between 1857 and 1860, LDS agents sent another five handcart companies west. The ten handcart brigades brought some three thousand Saints to Utah.[27]

As part of modifying the handcart system, Young launched the Brigham Young Express and Carrying Company, or BYX Company. When Utahn Hiram Kimball won a lucrative government mail contract for the route between Independence, Missouri, and Salt Lake City—essentially for the Church—Young arranged heavy investments in wagons and teams, and planned to establish new settlements in key locations along the Mormon Trail. To implement the plan, in 1856 Kimball selected five sites of 640 acres each for five new mail stations along a 250-mile segment of the trail in mountainous central Wyoming that was difficult for wagon trains.[28] By early 1857, square-mile villages, with farms, shops, storehouses, and corrals were under construction, and teamsters and settlers were assigned. In addition to providing services for the express companies, they would also service the handcart travelers.

It was an ambitious but not over-optimistic project—until word leaked out that Johnston's army was coming west to repress the Mormons and that Kimball's mail contract was being voided. By then nearly every Mormon village had sent men to assist in the enterprise, and Utahns had contributed $100,000 (nearly $2 million in contemporary terms). On August 12, 1857, Young issued the order to "break up" (dismantle) all Mormon stations between Laramie and Missouri and close those between Salt Lake City and Fort Laramie. Swiftly, the Mormons abandoned forts and farms, packed, and withdrew to Utah with all movable property and livestock. The net result was that an enormous outlay of labor and materials "was almost a complete loss."[29]

One of the casualties of the Utah War was LDS emigration. British Saints read Brigham Young's order in October: "In view of the difficulties which are now threatening the Saints, we deem it wisdom to stop all emigration to the States and Utah for the present."[30] Even after the Saints accepted the occupying army without bloodshed in spring 1858, emigration was slow to resume; and it was not until late 1858 that Brigham Young could again take up the matter of helping the poor gather to Zion; and even then, he was expressing his hope and guiding principle—not a plan:

> We realize there are many worthy, faithful Saints who are poor and have not the means to emigrate to this place, and that they are exceedingly anxious to do so. Our desire and prayer is that the way may open before them, that the Lord will so order and direct affairs that they may be delivered from bondage and brought to an inheritance with his people. But the Lord's will be done—This we consider the duty of every Saint—to help the poor Saints to gather home to Zion.[31]

The same issue of the *Millennial Star* that carried Young's prayer also carried the lifting of the emigration ban for those who "have means at their hand to gather to Zion." The editor repeated, "No one will receive any help whatever from the P.E. Fund. The deliverance of the Saints depends entirely upon themselves."[32]

Costs remained high, pushing an urgent search for a new system. For the 1859 emigrating season, George Q. Cannon reported that railroad fare from New York City to Florence, Nebraska, was $14.50, plus $22.30 for handcart travel to Salt Lake City (at least $1,300 for a family of four in contemporary dollars). Handcart materials, tents, and wagons had to be purchased with cash. In 1860 a Mormon elder told world traveler Sir Richard Burton that estimated trail costs were approximately $500 for animals, equipment, and supplies—$10,000 in contemporary dollars.[33]

This costly sum, however, did not include travel expenses from Liverpool to Florence. In June 1860 the First Presidency estimated the following costs for one person: $20 from Liverpool to New York and $15 from New York to Florence.[34] Thus, a family of four would pay somewhere around $2,100 in modern dollars to reach Florence and roughly $12,000 to reach Salt Lake City.

The system was under pressure. The number of European converts continued to grow, but the poor fund was exhausted and the handcart system, although it continued until 1860, was not only unpopular but still too costly for mass movement. Faced with this crisis and under covenant to help the worthy poor, Brigham Young and his colleagues thought of the rescue wagon trains and originated the down-and-back system.

A group of Saints traveling to Utah Territory, c. 1866. During the nineteenth century, tens of thousands of Mormon emigrants moved west in wagon trains like the one pictured here. Courtesy Church Archives.

1859–60 TESTS OF THE SYSTEM

With the Utah War settled, Brigham Young planned to send a sizeable wagon train from Utah to Florence to haul freight during summer 1859. In early April, Young announced that some empty teams would start for Florence as soon as weather permitted. Stalled by snow on Big Mountain plus high water in Weber Canyon, the train could not leave until early May, although it was so small, Young lamented, that it would "not be able to do any but its own hauling."[35]

This train belonged to Feramorz Little,[36] a thirty-nine-year-old partner in a freighting business with Charlie Decker, Brigham Young's brother-in-law. Little believed it was possible to travel to the Missouri River and back in one season, cutting out the expense of buying cattle, wagons, and provisions on the eastern end. On May 6, he and Decker departed at the head of a string of wagons pulled by sturdy mule teams.[37] With them Young sent the surveys of Hiram Kimball's abandoned mail station sites and instructions for Horace Eldredge, Church agent in St. Louis, to keep them until some Church representative could file for title in Washington, D.C., or with the Department of Interior. (The effort to file was not successful.) Thirty-five days later, Little and Decker reached Florence, their mules in excellent condition. With a full load of merchandise, they returned on September 1. Little arrived with the small mule train.[38]

Coincidentally that summer, a wagon train belonging to Horton Haight and Frederick Kesler, also hauling Church freight, tried out some new wagons produced by the Peter Schuttler company of Chicago. In August, Eldredge informed Young that the Schuttler firm's St. Louis branch had about five hundred wagons on hand. Young inspected the wagons when Haight and Kesler reached Salt Lake City on September 1 and apparently liked what he saw, since two years later he was encouraging Utah bishops to buy these wagons and import them to Utah for daily use.[39]

Three related problems, each caused by Utah's cash-poor situation, made Little's and Decker's experiment very interesting to Young: the high cost in cash of immigration, the high cash cost of buying imported freight, and a surplus of Utah cattle that could not be turned into cash locally. The PEF Company, even though it was not functioning, had inherited most of the BYX Company's animals. Also, when the U.S. Army pulled out of Utah in 1860–61 because of the Civil War, it sold an unknown number of oxen, horses, mules, and wagons to private citizens and the Church. The army's supplier, Russell, Majors, and Waddell, sold off thirty-five hundred large freight wagons and large numbers of oxen and mules at bargain prices.[40] Simultaneously, the Colorado gold rush was forcing prices of wagons and animals up in the Mississippi River Valley, which meant that Utahns could command good prices for their oxen.[41]

The down-and-back wagon trains, therefore, could fill three purposes simultaneously: (1) bring poor immigrants west cheaply, (2) haul in freight that was not marked up by a middleman, and (3) sell or trade surplus Utah oxen and flour in the Midwest.[42]

During winter 1859–60, Brigham Young considered two options. In January 1860, he sent word to Utah territorial delegate William H. Hooper (1859–61) to persuade a steamboat captain to take a riverboat up a tributary of the Missouri River—the Yellowstone, if possible—into Wyoming.[43] If boats could haul freight that far, Utah teams could meet them and return to Utah the same season. Although Young was still encouraging this plan as late as March, Hooper was unable to find a captain willing to risk his boat on this scheme.

Young's second plan was to send an ox-drawn wagon train of flour to Florence to bring back machinery and goods. It would be a test to see if the oxen held up as well as the mules.[44] It coincided with a plan that George Q. Cannon had suggested in January. If the Church wagon train deposited flour at intervals along the trail, the immigrants would not need to haul an entire trip's worth from the outfitting grounds.[45]

On March 29, 1860, Young informed Hooper that his nephew, Joseph W. Young, would be leaving soon with the flour.[46] In fact, it was not until April 27 that Joseph Young left with thirty wagons, pulled by oxen and a few mules.[47] But even as he was plodding across the plains, the First Presidency was writing enthusiastically to Utah's bishops that the down-and-back plan "promises to be very beneficial."[48] After reminding the bishops of the high costs of immigration and freight, the First Presidency pointed out the advantages of hauling "with teams already in our possession without an outlay of money, which is so scarce." Obviously, the Church leaders assumed that Joseph Young's experiment would be successful, for they alerted the bishops that in 1861 a "much larger ox train" would be needed. The bishops should start planning to send 100 to 150 wagons with three or four yoke of oxen per wagon as soon as spring grass was available. The bishops could also send surplus cattle back East in a herd to be sold, while Church emigration agents would buy the best quality of Chicago wagons—as Young was calling the Schuttler design—for those who deposited purchase money with the Church Trustee in Trust.[49]

It is not clear if Brigham Young received periodic progress reports about his nephew, who reached Florence on July 1 and waited twenty-three frustrating days for freight. Brigham Young's enthusiasm remained high. In August, he wrote to John Van Cott, then president of the Scandinavian Mission, calling the arrangement a "good policy" for 1861 emigration. Optimistically, he predicted that the trip back by the ox teams would "doubtless demonstrate the practicability and good policy of sending ox trains from here in the spring to deposit flour at suitable points on the way down, and freight back with the poor, and such articles as it may be advisable to import."[50] The next month, he again wrote: "We now propose sending an ox train from here again next spring, this season's operations in that line having proved so successful, as far as we have heard."[51]

Joseph Young reached Salt Lake City on October 3, 1860, with 50 wagons, 340 oxen, and 234 horses and mules. His pleased uncle publicly announced that "sending teams to the States proved entirely successful." In fact, "the teams were in far better condition than teams are generally that have only crossed the plains once."[52] This trip was, in Hulmston's terms, the "foundation for the most successful period of immigration in [Mormon] history."[53]

Based on Joseph Young's success, Brigham Young moved firmly forward, getting word to LDS immigration agents in the States and in Europe, and recruiting through Utah ward bishops the requisite wagons and teams and teamsters needed by the next April. Greatly speeding up communication between Young and Hooper was the completion of telegraph lines to Fort Kearney, Nebraska, by November 1860 with Pony Express riders carrying letters between Utah and the telegraph station.[54]

In previous seasons, Mormon wagon trains outfitted whenever enough passengers arrived to create one; but obviously for maximum efficiency, waiting time at the staging point needed to be reduced to the minimum. Young envisioned the entire process of moving people from Europe to Utah as one consecutive, unbroken journey, uninterrupted by layovers. On December 20, 1860, Young wrote Cannon, then serving as European Mission president: "I have thought it might be well to so time the sailing of companies, or at least a good portion of them, from Liverpool that they will reach Florence about the middle and last of June, in readiness to at once start over the plains, without tarrying at any one place for any length of time."[55]

THINKING THROUGH THE PLAN, EARLY 1861

By early January, Brigham Young had worked out a detailed plan that was, according to Hulmston, "a model of ingenuity and practicality," especially in solving the enormous logistical problem of supplying thousands of immigrants with food at the right time and place."[56] The Church would give tithing credit to those who loaned wagons, donated provisions, volunteered to be teamsters or wagon-train personnel, or contributed flour for the periodic trail caches.

On January 14, 1861, Young met with bishops from Salt Lake City and those from outlying settlements who were in the city for the territorial legislative session. He described Joseph W. Young's 1860 round trip, described the problems that this new plan would solve, and explained: "Next season we wish to start a large train, or three or four of them, to go back to the Missouri River and bring home the poor of our people, and to bring also, goods, machinery, and anything that should be brought. Thirty teams and wagons went back last season, but we design the ensuing season to send back two hundred."[57]

For example, Sanpete County needed to provide five wagons, each capable of hauling thirty-five hundred pounds, with at least four yoke of oxen per wagon. Wards could send as many additional wagons as they wanted to haul back goods and freight for ward members, but the quota wagons would haul only passengers. Settlements without wagons could send extra oxen, whose purchase price in the Mississippi Valley would pay for "new waggons brought from Chicago, which will cost only you ninety dollars or a hundred, and it will cost you nothing to bring them here. If you want cheaper wagons you can get one for fifty dollars." (Fifty dollars would be roughly $1,000 in today's figures.) Utah oxen that did not sell at the outfitting camp could be pastured on the prairie until agents Jacob Gates and Nathaniel V. Jones could sell them in St. Louis as draft animals or for meat. Thanks to the Pony Express, Young would be able to advise the agents exactly how many oxen would be coming with the various trains. By the same means, he could inform Church units throughout the East "that our teams are on hand to bear them to the gathering place, invite them to come up to Florence and we will bring them home as far as we have strength." (The Saints in Europe did not know about the plan.)

Those who provided teams, wagons, and supplies would receive labor tithing credited to the PEF, a genuine opportunity for those who owed the PEF to pay back their loans. "I do not suppose we have gathered one cent to a thousand dollars in money that we have paid out," acknowledged Young. He professed himself indifferent to how the trip was credited—regular tithing, labor tithing, PEF donation, property tithing. "Our object is to gather the people together and establish the Kingdom of God, we do not care how it works, but we want to keep the business portion of it straight so as to know where we are."

Young then assigned Presiding Bishop Edward Hunter to organize the quotas of oxen, wagons, and teamsters so that the first train could leave Salt Lake City by mid-April. Young stressed that teamsters should be responsible and careful, since they, not the Church, would be responsible for teams and wagons. Hunter was also responsible for determining the credit for hauling, although Young, not surprisingly, volunteered an opinion: six to ten cents per pound for hauling flour toward Florence and fifteen to twenty cents for hauling freight back toward Utah. Young also insisted that the trains be large enough so that if they "meet twenty or thirty cut throats, they can use them up and feed them to the wolves."

The depth of Young's relief at breaking the log-jam in the gathering must have been audible as he reminded the bishops of the Nauvoo pledge "that we would not cease our operations until we gathered the Saints. I have not ceased one day in trying to fill that vow." He ended by querying the assembly jovially, "Does [the plan] feel soft to their gizzards or does it grind on them and give them pain?"[58]

Two weeks later, when Salt Lake City bishops met for their biweekly meeting on January 31 with the Presiding Bishop, Hunter read the First Presidency's letter of instructions. Young announced that he would send ten teams himself. Heber C. Kimball pledged four outfits and would send more if needed because "he had made a covenant while in Nauvoo never to slacken his efforts until all were gathered, which he intended to carry out."[59]

The next weekend, Young preached in the tabernacle what was now his favorite topic. He wanted the city wards to raise fifty wagons with four yoke of oxen to each wagon. "But the bishops say we be very poor, and it will be hard to turn out so many wagons," he chided sarcastically. Then he appealed to their civic pride. The outlying wards looked to the city "to take the lead in everything." He hoped the Church could send 250 outfits, so Salt Lake City's share would be fifty or sixty. He again promised to send ten personally, and got a vote of support for the city's quota.[60]

Even though Young had assigned Hunter to organize the project, it would have been unlike him to stay out of an effort where his heart and mind were so deeply engaged. The next day, he instructed Apostle Ezra T. Benson, then president of Cache Stake, to send only "good iron-axle Chicago wagon[s]" or, failing that, at least "a wooden axle of Chicago make." The departing "cattle, wagons, and teamsters" would have to "pass the inspection of a competent person" to assure "that all may start in proper condition." Cache Valley, he estimated, could furnish twenty to thirty wagons with their associated teams. He had already rethought the dollar sums he had suggested to Hunter and now told Benson: "The teams will be allowed on labor tithing, $10 a hundred for such freight as they take from here to Florence, or in that proportion for intermediate distances; and $15 a hundred for freight from Florence to this City, also on labor tithing."[61]

A First Presidency letter apparently produced later that month added new details to the plan.[62] The letter reiterated many points covered in the bishops' meeting and added several, including Young's estimate that this plan could save the Church up to $30,000 annually. Wagons from outlying wards should haul tithing wheat to Salt Lake City, where it would be ground into flour. Ward members who donated provisions and bedding to teamsters would receive tithing credit. Each wagon should carry eight, light, thick ox shoes and nails so the oxen could be shod en route as needed. The wagons would be organized into companies of fifty, each with a captain, and all the companies would be under one superintendent or agent. Each company should have four horsemen to herd and guard the livestock when they were unyoked.

Young had apparently fixed on the sums he had included in his letter to Benson: Each Florence-bound wagon would haul flour, for which the team's owner would be credited $10 per hundred pounds, while loads hauled back from Florence would be credited at $15 per hundredweight. Immigrants, especially those unable to provide their own teams and wagons, had first claim on the wagons in Florence.

Included in these instructions was Hunter's meticulously detailed list of required equipment. Each wagon should include one can or keg of tar, a gallon of wagon grease, two water kegs of five-to-ten gallons capacity, and two replacement lashes for the whip, with additional buckskin thongs for splicing and to make "crackers" (to create a popping sound when flipped). Each teamster should bring 250 pounds of flour, forty pounds of bacon, forty pounds of dried beef ("if to be had"), as much butter as the teamster "chooses or can take safely," ten pounds of sugar, four pounds of coffee, a pound of tea, four quarts of beans, a bar of soap, four pounds of yeast in cake form or its equivalent "in soda, acid, or yeast powder," salt for both the teamster and his animals, one "good" buffalo robe, two "good" blankets ("or their equivalent"), a gallon of vinegar in "a stone jug," "some" pickles "if can be had," "two good pairs" of boots or shoes "with grease enough" to keep them waterproofed, three "good" pairs of pants, six shirts, three overshirts, five pairs of socks, enough coats "for comfort," needles, thread, and a "good" gun—double-barrelled shot gun preferable, with plenty of powder, balls, and shot.

The detailed instructions continued. Six teamsters would form a mess, or cooking group. These six should consult before leaving and agree on how to furnish cooking utensils plus such medical supplies as No. 6 Cayenne pepper, purgative pills or castor oil, pain killer composition, liniment, and so forth. Furthermore, each teamster should be provided with ten dollars in cash to give to the wagon master for groceries and other necessaries on the return trip and to pay his ferriage down and back. If money was not available, Hunter recommended that the teamster take an extra thousand pounds of flour to sell for supplying himself with food on the way back.

COLLECTING TEAMS AND SUPPLIES

Actually carrying out these ideal instructions encountered many local realities. The Logan high priests, meeting on February 9, offered several yoke of oxen; wagons with covers, one with only bows; a yoke of oxen with chains, a span of mules, a yoke of old cattle, a single ox, and cooking utensils. In the spirit of the occasion, one brother who had no oxen volunteered to sell his carriage if needed, while another who donated a yoke of oxen said he would donate two if he had them. The quorum leader concluded they could outfit three teams and wagons, the town's quota. Likewise, members donated flour, beans, butter, pork, mittens, coats, guns, lead, cash, quilts, molasses, vinegar, and potatoes to teamsters.[63]

Seven weeks later, on March 29, Bishop Thomas McCullough of Alpine, confessed that his ward could supply only three yoke of oxen and eight teamsters, with outfits for each; the fourth team and wagon must come from richer Provo to the south.[640]

Brigham Young optimistically wrote in mid-February that "the Bishops and people are quite spirited in the matter of raising teams to send to Florence for the poor brethren" and confidently foresaw a large party of "at least 200 teams of 4 yoke each and a larger number of loose cattle."[65] When the Salt Lake City bishops met in the monthly meeting with the Presiding Bishopric on February 28, a disagreement broke out about how much to pay teamsters. Some wards were allegedly overpaying them, creating internal dissatisfaction. The Presiding Bishopric left the amount up to the bishops, who finally worked out uniform compensation. Captains would receive one dollar per day plus rations. Each ward's tithing credit total would be $450 per outfit.[66]

When some Salt Lake City bishops expressed doubt that they could supply labor for two tithing projects simultaneously—the down-and-back train and work on the temple walls—they got a typical carrot-and-stick response from Brigham Young:

When we concluded that we would call upon this city for help, we got all we asked for and more. I say, credit is due to them.... I am satisfied; the Spirit that is within me is satisfied.... [But] if you grudgingly put forth your means to help gather the Saints, it will be a curse to you; it will mildew, and every effort you make will wither in your possession. If you do not wish to help, let it alone.... Will the way be hedged up by the wars and distress of nations? I neither know nor care.... The time will come when men and women will be glad to catch what they can roll up in a small bundle, and start for the mountains, without team or wagon.[67]

ORGANIZING FOUR WAGON COMPANIES

On April 16, four outfits arrived in Salt Lake City from Parowan and Toc- querville. Two days later, the First Presidency reported pleasure at the "cheerfulness, liberality, and alacrity with which so many teams are fur- nished and so many men sent forth."[68] On April 20, wagons from Ogden and Grantsville started for the rendezvous point at the mouth of Parley's Canyon. On Sunday, April 21, news reached Utah that South Carolina had shelled the federally held Fort Sumter, signalling the outbreak of the Civil War. Brigham Young did not revise his down-and-back plan but ordered crews into Parley's Canyon to repair the road. On April 22, an unspecified number of teams from the city's wards joined the camp at the mouth of Parley's Canyon.[69]

On April 23, the First Presidency visited the encampment, organized four wagon trains, and installed Joseph W. Young, Joseph Horne, Ira Eldredge, and John R. Murdock as captains. These seasoned men were "lead- ers of the right stripe ... men who had crossed the Plains, understand camp life and the Indians, and are not afraid of the devils."[70] Joseph W. Young, age thirty-two, had led the previous year's experimental ox train. Horne, forty- nine, was an 1847 pioneer and experienced colonizer; Eldredge, forty-one, had been an 1847 pioneer; Murdock, thirty-four, was a Mormon Battalion veteran who had carried mail for the Brigham Young Express Company to Missouri in the 1850s and had helped with the handcart rescues in 1856.

The First Presidency gave the four captains letters of instructions con- taining the rules. No swearing, drunkenness, gambling, contention, or unreasonable whipping or abuse of cattle were allowed. Troublemakers

A wagon train making its way up a trail, c. mid-nineteenth century. Emigrants were instructed to keep guns and ammunition ready for protection. Courtesy Church Archives.

should be "turned out of the company." Guards should sleep in wagons during the day, and their horses should not be ridden during daytime except for "necessity." The four companies should stay within a few hours' distance for mutual security. At Florence the companies should camp on high ground three or four miles above the Missouri River and near good running water. Teamsters must turn in receipts to their captains detailing kind and weight of freight loaded into their wagons at Florence. All men in the companies should keep their guns and ammunition "in good condition for use at a moment's notice."[71] The trains rolled into Parley's Canyon that same afternoon.

Two weeks later, Brigham Young reported statistics on the train to George Q. Cannon in England: "183 public wagons and 20 private ones, 194 public teamsters and 23 private one, 1,575 public oxen and 124 private, 16–18 guards, 136,000 pounds of flour to be deposited at four sites along the trail for the immigrants, and 34,348 pounds to meet expenses or be sold in Florence."[72]

However, the 1861 PEF tithing credit ledgers give a different total—185 teams, rather than 183—and is probably correct since it names each teamster and his ward. Seventy-five wards sent at least one team—nearly every ward in Utah.[73] As historian Richard Jensen observed, the down-and-back system "effectively involved" the whole Mormon community "in promoting immigration from Europe."[74]

THE 1861 DOWN-AND-BACK TRIP

The four wagon trains rolled into the Florence campgrounds on schedule during the two weeks between June 16 and 30. The journey "down" took fifty-four to sixty-eight days—roughly eight to ten weeks. Meanwhile, in Florence at about the same time the four wagon trains left Salt Lake City, Jacob Gates was developing the outfitting campground. Without knowing how many immigrants to expect, especially given the eruption of the Civil War, he opened a warehouse, created campsites and corrals, set up a weighing machine, and stockpiled tons of foodstuffs and trail equipment. Word did not reach him until May 5 about how many down-and-back wagons were coming. During May and June, when the waves of LDS immigrants arrived from points east, he helped organize those who owned their own wagons into companies consisting of independently owned wagons and saw them off toward the West. When the Utah companies arrived in late June, they became part of Gates's bustling operation.

Nearly four thousand Saints showed up at Florence, including nineteen hundred European converts, most of whom needed Church transportation. Gates made assignments to those who needed to join the down-and-back trains, based on six to twelve people per wagon. Fares were $41 for adults, with half-fares for children under eight, payable after reaching Utah and settling down.[75] More poor Saints showed up than leaders expected, forcing Jacob Gates and Joseph Young, who helped with the organization after his train arrived, to search for additional wagons. To the four down-and-back trains, they added more than seventy-five wagons, some no doubt part of Gates's earlier purchase of 111 prefabricated wagons from the Schuttler firm in Chicago.[76] Young's wagon train, which had numbered about fifty wagons to begin with, became unwieldy at about ninety, so he divided it into two companies captained by Ansel Harmon and Heber P. Kimball, with himself as senior captain.[77] After two to four weeks at Florence, the four Church trains, now totaling about three hundred wagons, started back to Utah, leaving during the first two weeks in July. They transported an estimated 1,719 immigrants (44 percent of the year's immigration, with an average of

8.5 people per wagon) and averaged return journeys of 68 days, thus rolling along at about 15 miles a day.[78]

The down-and-back companies traveled close to each other, as Brigham Young instructed, picking up the flour deposited on their way down. Despite the normal small problems and irritations of overland travel, their trek was essentially safe and routine. "There was a sameness in every day's travel," said James H. Lindford, and "all in all it was a nice trip for the healthy and strong." He noted that "all of the able bodied emigrants walked from Florence to Utah."[79] Including the waiting time in Florence, the four companies spent an average of 147 days—just under five months—to go down and back, arriving with their oxen in good condition, well before snowfall.

On October 2, 1861, the *Deseret News* estimated that between four and five thousand immigrants had reached Utah that summer, and Erastus Snow gave George A. Smith a precise figure of 3,924, including about 1,900 from Europe.[80] In Utah, Church leaders welcomed the newcomers, the immigrants found lodging and work relatively easily, and the down-and-back trains disbanded.

ASSESSMENT

By any measure—not least Brigham Young's critical eye—the down-and-back experiment in 1861 was a success. Brigham Young reported that oxen sent from Utah

> suffered far less loss by deaths and looked much better, as a general thing than those purchased in the states.... The companies have been pleased with their captains and the captains with their companies; and this season's emigration has been signally blessed all the time from their departure from their former homes to their new homes in our peaceful valley.[81]

The primary goal for the down-and-back trains—to assist poor Saints to reach Utah from Florence—was successfully met. "Every Saint who reached Florence and desired to go home this season has had the privilege," John D. T. McAllister wrote to George Q. Cannon. "The sending down of wagons from Utah to Florence is a grand scheme."[82] Of Scandinavians who reached Florence, "not one soul of Danes was left there."[83] Church officials also saw some promise of rejuvenating the PEF's financial health. Those

assisted by Church team trains owed the PEF for that aid, typically $40 to
$60 per person. Agents met the four trains near Salt Lake City so that the
immigrants could sign promissory notes, ranging from 76 cents to $390,
plus 10 percent interest. The notes in the Church History Library—the
record is very incomplete—show that 337 borrowers agreed to repay a total
of $38,285.39, an average of $113.62 each note, to cover their wagon and food
expenses at Florence and across the plains.[84]

Despite this business-like procedure, the separate 1877 tally of the 1861
borrowers shows that 597 had still not paid off their promissory notes fifteen
years later.[85] Although the down-and-back account showed a large deficit,
it was a paper loss more than a cash loss; and most Mormons recognized
that the down-and-back program was, at heart, a "voluntary, cooperative,
community investment in people, that is, in immigrants."[86] One goal of the
down-and-back project was to work around the Church's cash shortage, and
it achieved that purpose.

Besides bringing immigrants at minimal cost to the Church, the enterprise had two other purposes. One was to freight eastern goods in Utah wagons. Except for Church leaders, however, few Utahns in 1861 sent extra wagons
down to Florence to haul back commodities purchased there. The third purpose—to sell surplus Utah cattle at Florence—likewise fell short. Utahns in
1861 sent only 124 surplus oxen to Florence with the down-and-back trains. As
a result, Jacob Gates had to purchase forty-one oxen for $2,522 cash—cash
that could have gone into the hands of Utah cattle owners had they sent down
more oxen.[87]

While the Utah outfits, labor, and flour did not require any significant
cash outlay, nevertheless, the labor tithing credits "paid" by the Church
were sizable. Utah teamsters were expected to donate one working day in
ten for the Church; thus, if they donated their labor, teams, and wagons for
the down-and-back trip, they could receive labor tithing credits, thus reduc-
ing how much tithing labor local bishops received. PEF ledgers show that
nearly two hundred Utah teamsters received more than $80,000 in tithing
credit, an average of about $450 each, as payment for hauling freight and
passengers and as reimbursement for rations, ferriage fees, wagon grease,
and tobacco. In addition, the Church credited wards and ward members for
136,095 pounds of flour at six cents per pound, or about $8,000 in credits.
About sixteen Utahns served as herdsmen/guards, receiving about $100
tithing credit each.[88]

Because of the 1861 success, down-and-back trains became the established system for helping needy immigrants reach Utah from 1862 until 1868, the year before the transcontinental railroad opened. During this period, at least 17,000 more LDS immigrants traversed the Mormon Trail in down-and-back teams. (No trains went in 1865 or 1867.) At least 1,956 Utah teams—an average of 326 wagons per year—participated.[89]

What Brigham Young envisioned in 1859, experimented with in 1860, and directed full-scale until 1868, produced a new chapter in the story of America's western migration. Eastbound wagon trains helped thousands move west, costing sponsor and recipients very little cash. In terms of practicality, workability, and results, Young's immigration leadership in the 1860s served as the crowning achievement of one of the most remarkable entrepreneurs in the history of world migration.

This article was originally published in Journal of Mormon History *28, no. 1 (2002): 1–30.*

NOTES

1. Leonard J. Arrington, *Brigham Young: American Moses* (Urbana: University of Illinois Press, 1985), 283.

2. Stanley B. Kimball, *Historic Resource Study; Mormon Pioneer National Historic Trail* (Washington, D.C.: U.S. Department of Interior/National Park Service, 1991), 4.

3. "A Handcart Train," *Omaha Times,* February 6, 1859, 2.

4. Preston Nibley, *Brigham Young: The Man and His Work* (Salt Lake City: Deseret News Press, 1937); Francis M. Gibbons, *Brigham Young: Modern Moses, Prophet of God* (Salt Lake City: Deseret Book, 1981); Arrington, *American Moses.*

5. Katherine Copman, *Economic Beginnings of the Far West: How We Won the Land beyond the Mississippi,* 2 vols. (New York: Macmillan, 1921), 2:184.

6. The term *emigrant* was used throughout the nineteenth century for anyone who was moving to a different country to become its resident. However, *immigrant* had been coined in 1789 to differentiate one entering a country in contrast to an *emigrant* who was leaving a country. This paper observes that distinction except in quotations.

7. For a list of individual wagon companies and their numbers of people and wagons, see *Deseret News 1977 Church Almanac* (Salt Lake City: Deseret News, 1996), 278–92; and *Deseret News 1997–98 Church Almanac* (Salt Lake City: Deseret News, 1996), 278–92. The ship list is in this second source, 159–67.

8. "Perpetual Emigrating Fund" and "handcart" form individual subject headings in James B. Allen, Ronald W. Walker, and David J. Whittaker, *Studies in Mormon History,*

1830–1997: An Indexed Bibliography with a Topical Guide to Published Social Science Literature on the Mormons (Urbana: University of Illinois Press, 2000), 839, 674. On down-and-back trains, see John K. Hulmston, "Transplant Migration: The Church Trains in Mormon Immigration, 1861–1868" (master's thesis, Utah State University, 1985), 985, and my articles: "The Great Florence Fitout of 1861," *BYU Studies* 24, no. 4 (1984): 341–71; "Diary of a Teenage Driver: Zeb Jacobs on the Mormon Trail," *New Era* 14 (July 1984): 8–11; "'Down and Back' Wagon Trains: Bringing the Saints to Utah in 1861," *Ensign* 15 (September 1985): 26–31; "Down-and-Back Wagon Trains: Travelers on the Mormon Trail in 1861," *Overland Journal* 11, no. 4 (1993): 23–34.

9. Leonard J. Arrington and Larry C. Porter, "Brigham Young," in *Encyclopedia of Latter-day Saint History,* ed. Arnold K. Garr, Donald Q. Cannon, and Richard O. Cowan (Salt Lake City: Deseret Book, 2000), 1378.

10. Slight trail travel, mainly to Oregon or Montana, continued after the transcontinental railroad opened in 1869. Kenneth L. Holmes, ed., *Covered Wagon Women, Vol. 10: Diaries and Letters from the Western Trails, 1875–1883* (Lincoln: University of Nebraska Press, 1991).

11. George Stewart, *The California Trail* (Lincoln: University of Nebraska Press, 1962), 318.

12. Merrill J. Mattes, *The Great Platte River Road* (Lincoln: University of Nebraska Press, 1969), 23.

13. Hulmston, "Transplant Migration," iv–v. John D. Unruh Jr., "Against the Grain: West to East on the Overland Trail," *Kansas Quarterly* 5 (Spring 1973): 72–84, focuses on "turnarounds": (1) either companies or individuals who called it quits partway west and (2) back-traffic from the California goldfields. He found reports that about twelve hundred were planning to return in 1853 and six hundred to a thousand in 1855. He cites Brigham Young as his authority for approximately three to four hundred eastbound overlanders on the trails in 1857; however, he does not mention the Mormon down-and-back trains of the 1860s.

14. William G. Hartley, "'How Shall I Gather?'" *Ensign* 27 (October 1997): 5–17.

15. Church Education System, *Church History in the Fullness of Times* (Salt Lake City: Church of Jesus Christ of Latter-day Saints, 1989), 178–79.

16. William G. Hartley, "'Almost Too Intolerable a Burthen': The Winter Exodus from Missouri, 1838–1839," *Journal of Mormon History* 18 (Fall 1992): 640.

17. Richard E. Bennett, *Mormons at the Missouri, 1846–1852: "And Should We Die"* (Norman: University of Oklahoma Press, 1987), 82–84. Bennett identifies two rescue companies, both from the Council Bluffs area, but a third rescue company also left from Garden Grove. *Journal of Luman Andros Shurtliff, 1807–1884* (n.p., n.d.), 69.

18. P. A. M. Taylor, *Expectations Westward: The Mormons and the Emigration of Their British Converts in the Nineteenth Century* (Ithaca, NY: Cornell University Press, 1966), 138.

19. Fourth General Epistle of the First Presidency, September 17, 1850, in *Messages of the First Presidency of The Church of Jesus Christ of Latter-day Saints, 1833–1964,* comp. James R. Clark, 6 vols. (Salt Lake City: Bookcraft, 1965–75), 2:61. Leonard J. Arrington, *Great Basin Kingdom: An Economic History of the Latter-day Saints, 1830–1900* (1958; reprinted Lincoln: University of Nebraska Press, 1966), 100, provides an illuminating vignette of PEF fund-raising in one northern Utah community. Block teachers solicited contributions from each family in the ward, with the following results: $66 in cash, $58 in produce, $50 in "store pay," $2.50 in corn, 26 bushels of wheat, 10 dozen eggs, and

3 ¾ pounds of butter. Four families gave nothing, two because they were "too poor," and two because they were "too mean."

20. Gustive O. Larson, *Prelude to the Kingdom* (Francestown, NH: Marshall Jones, 1947), 113.

21. Larson, *Prelude to the Kingdom*, 99.

22. Arrington, *Great Basin Kingdom*, 101.

23. Twelfth General Epistle of the Presidency, April 25, 1855, in Clark, *Messages of the First Presidency*, 2:168.

24. Twelfth General Epistle of the Presidency, April 25, 1855, in Clark, *Messages of the First Presidency*, 2:185–86.

25. Rebecca Foster Cornwall and Leonard J. Arrington, *Rescue of the 1856 Handcart Companies* (Provo, UT: Brigham Young University Press, 1981); LeRoy R. and Ann W. Hafen, *Handcarts to Zion* (Glendale, CA.: Arthur H. Clark, 1960), 119–42.

26. Fourteenth General Epistle of the Presidency, December 10, 1856, in Clark, *Messages of the First Presidency*, 2:198.

27. In addition another 5,200 immigrants paid for their own way with wagon trains. (Even those traveling in wagon trains generally walked most of the way to Utah.)

28. Fort Laramie, eighty-five miles northeast of present-day Laramie, Wyoming, was considered the halfway mark on the Mormon Trail, being 522 miles from Winter Quarters (Florence, Nebraska), and 509 miles from Salt Lake City. The five locations were Horse Shoe Creek (43 miles from Laramie), La Bonte River (another 18 miles), Deer Creek (another 37 miles), and Rocky Ridge (152 miles from Deer Creek). See locations and mileages in William Clayton, *The Latter-day Saints' Emigrants' Guide*, ed. Stanley B. Kimball (St. Louis: Republican Steam Power Press, 1848; reprinted St. Louis: Patrice Press, 1983), 12–16.

29. Arrington, *Great Basin Kingdom*, 159–70; quotation is on 170.

30. "Emigration to the States Stopped for the Present," *Millennial Star* 19 (October 17, 1857): 668.

31. "Correspondence: Brigham Young to Asa Calkin," *Millennial Star* 21 (January 1, 1859): 10.

32. "Emigration," *Millennial Star* 25 (January 1, 1859): 8–9. Only 842 sailed that year; *1997–98 Church Almanac*, 162.

33. Sir Richard Burton, *City of the Saints and Across the Rocky Mountains to California* (Niwot, CO: University Press of Colorado, 1950), 139, 85, 87. The specific costs were $180–200 for two yoke of oxen, $25 for a cow, $87.30 for a wagon, $8.50 for a doubled cover, $8 for two ox yokes, $1.50 for an ox chain, $1 for a tar bucket, $9–15 for two large tents, $10 for camp equipment ("axes, spades, shovels, triangles for fires"), $28 for a stove, $25.50 for 600 pounds flour, $14 for 100 pounds of ham and bacon, $13.13 for 150 pounds of crackers (sea biscuits), $9.50 for 100 pounds of sugar, $3 for 25 pounds of crystallized sugar, $4 for 24 pounds of raisins, $3 for 20 pounds of currants, $2.25 for 25 pounds of rice, $6 for 1 bushel of dried apples, $4.30 for a bushel of dried peaches, and $2 for a bushel of beans.

34. Brigham Young, Heber C. Kimball, and Daniel H. Wells, Letter to Bishop Hunter and Counselors and Utah Bishops, June 1860, Brigham Young Letterbook 5, original at Church History Library, The Church of Jesus Christ of Latter-day Saints, Salt Lake City; typescript at Joseph Fielding Smith Institute for Latter-day Saint History, Provo,

Utah (hereafter Smith Institute). Additional Brigham Young correspondence is cited by letterbook number from this typescript edition.

35. Brigham Young, Letters to B. F. Johnson, Santaquin, April 8, 1859, to Asa Calkin, April 28, 1859, to J. W. Cloward, St. Louis, April 28, 1859, and to Joseph E. Johnson, Deer Creek Station or en route, May 4, 1859, all in Letterbook 5.

36. Taylor, *Expectations Westward,* 138.

37. Brigham Young, Letter to Horace S. Eldredge, St. Louis, May 5, 1859, Letterbook 5. No personnel roster has survived, but another Brigham Young letter mentions Daniel Davis, Allen Kelton, "and others." Brigham Young, Letter to Horace S. Eldredge, May 6, 1859.

38. Brigham Young, Letter to Asa Calkin, September 1, 1859, Letterbook 5; Andrew Jenson, "Church Emigration," *Contributor* 14 (July 1843): 438.

39. Brigham Young, Letter to Peter Schuttler, Chicago, September 1, 1859, Letterbook 5.

40. Arrington, *Great Basin Kingdom,* 196.

41. Arrington, *Great Basin Kingdom,* 206.

42. Arrington, *Great Basin Kingdom,* 205–11.

43. Brigham Young, Letters to William H. Hooper, January 30, 1860, March 1, 1860, Letterbook 5.

44. Brigham Young, Letter to William H. Hooper, March 1, 1860, Letterbook 5.

45. George Q. Cannon, Letter to Brigham Young, January 18, 1860, cited and discussed in Davis Bitton, *George Q. Cannon: A Biography* (Salt Lake City: Deseret Book, 1999), 100.

46. Young, Letter to William H. Hooper, March 29, 1860, Letterbook 5.

47. Brigham Young, Talk, January 14, 1861, Brigham Young Sermons, Typescript vol. 1861, Smith Institute; original in Church History Library.

48. Brigham Young, Letter to Edward Hunter and Utah Bishops, June 1860, Letterbook 5.

49. Brigham Young, Heber C. Kimball, and Daniel H. Wells, Letter to Bishop Hunter and Counselors and Utah Bishops, June 1860, Letterbook 5.

50. Brigham Young, Letter to John Van Cott, August 9, 1860, Letterbook 5.

51. Brigham Young, Letter to Joseph E. Johnson, Wood River Center, Nebraska Territory, September 27, 1860, Letterbook 5.

52. Brigham Young, Talk, January 14, 1861, Brigham Young Sermons, Typescript vol. 1861.

53. John K. Hulmston, "Mormon Immigration in the 1860s: The Story of the Church Trains," *Utah Historical Quarterly* 58 (Winter 1990): 28.

54. Young, Letter to Hooper, December 20, 1860, Letterbook 5. The Pony Express opened in April 1860. From Fort Kearney, riders could reach Salt Lake City in less than four days. Anthony Godfrey, *Historic Resource Study: Pony Express National Historic Trail* (Washington, D.C: Department of the Interior/National Park Service, 1994), 56, 64, 77–78, 92. The first coast-to-coast telegraph message was sent October 26, 1861.

55. Brigham Young, Letter to George Q. Cannon, December 20, 1860.

56. Hulmston, "Mormon Immigration in the 1860s," 43.

57. Brigham Young, Sermon, January 14, 1861, Brigham Young Sermons, Typescript vol. 1861.

58. Brigham Young, Sermon, January 14, 1861, Brigham Young Sermons, Typescript vol. 1861.

59. Presiding Bishopric, Minutes of Meeting with Bishops, January 31, 1861, Presiding Bishop Papers, Church History Library.

60. Brigham Young, Sermon, February 3, 1861, Salt Lake Tabernacle, Brigham Young Sermons, Typescript vol. 1861.

61. Brigham Young, Letter to E. T. Benson, February 4, 1861, Letterbook 5.

62. First Presidency, Circular Letter to Bishop Hunter and Utah Bishops, February 1861, Letterbook 5.

63. Arrington, *Great Basin Kingdom,* 210–11.

64. Thomas McCullough, Letter to Leonard W. Hardy and Jesse C. Little, March 29, 1861, Perpetual Emigrating Fund Company Papers, Reports, 1854–68, microfilm reel 20, fd. 81 (Church Teams' Accounts), Church History Library.

65. Brigham Young, Letter to William H. Hooper, February 14, 1861, Letterbook 5.

66. Presiding Bishop, Minutes of Meeting with Bishops, February 28, 1861, Presiding Bishop Papers; Hulmston, "Transplant Migration," 35–36.

67. Brigham Young, in *Journal of Discourses,* 26 vols. (Liverpool: Latter-day Saints' Book Depot, 1855–86), 8:355–56, March 3, 1861.

68. First Presidency, Letter to William H. Hooper, April 18, 1861, Letterbook 5.

69. Journal History of the Church, April 20, 21, 22, 1861, Church History Library, microfilm copy in Harold B. Lee Library, Brigham Young University, Provo, Utah. George A. Smith wrote: "The town has been alive for a few days with wagons and teams neatly and substantially fitted up." George A. Smith, Letter to John Smith, April 23, 1861, Historian's Office Letterbook, Church History Library.

70. John Daniel Thomas McAllister, Statement, Journal History, July 30, 1861. Brigham Young apparently sent five wagons, not ten, as he had initially planned, since he apparently employed only five teamsters: Samuel L. Sprague Jr., Oscar B. Young, Erastus McIntire, Isaac Eades, and Zebulon Jacobs.

71. First Presidency, Letter to Joseph W. Young, April 15, 1861, Brigham Young Letterbook 5.

72. Brigham Young, Letter to George Q. Cannon, May 9, 1861, Letterbook 5.

73. PEF Company, Church Team Accounts, 1861–82, reel 19, fd. 76. Hartley, "Great Florence Fitout of 1861," 351. The total of 185 wagons came from the following wards: one each from Cedar City, Harmony, Springtown, Alpine, Battle Creek, Cedar Fort, Pleasant Grove, Pondtown, Santaquin, Salt Lake Second, Third, Fourth, Six, Seventh, Tenth, Eleventh, and Eighteenth, Big Cottonwood, Herriman, South Cottonwood, Union, East Weber, North Ogden, North Willowcreek, South Willowcreek, Weber Valley, Franklin (Idaho), Hyde Park, Hyrum, Mendon, and Paradise; two each from Parowan, Goshen, Provo Valley, Salt Lake First, Eighth, Ninth, Twelfth, Sixteenth, Seventeenth, and Twentieth, Sugarhouse, West Jordan, Kaysville, Providence, Smithfield, and Willard; three each from Mount Pleasant, Salt Lake Nineteenth, Richmond, and Wellsville; four each from Beaver, Ephraim, Mann, Moroni, American Fork, Payson, Springville, Salt Lake Fourteenth, Millcreek, Grantsville, Tooele, Centerville, Farmington, North Kanyon, and Box Elder; five each from Fillmore, Lehi, Salt Lake Thirteenth, and Logan; six from Nephi; eight from Provo, and eleven from Ogden.

74. Richard L. Jensen, "The Financing of Mormon Emigration in the Nineteenth Century," typescript, 15, Smith Institute.

75. William Jefferies, Journal, summary before entry for September 23, 1861, microfilm of holograph, Church History Library. Jefferies was a passenger in the Joseph W. Young Church team train.

76. Jefferies, Journal, summary before entry for September 23, 1861.

77. However, according to William Jefferies, Journal, typescript, summary entry before entry of July 26, 1861, L. Tom Perry Special Collections, Harold B. Lee Library, Brigham Young University, Provo, Utah, Harmon started as captain of the large train but, after leaving Wood River, took charge of the first division while Joseph W. Young captained the second division. Young later rode back and forth, supervising all four Church trains. He does not mention Kimball's role.

78. John R. Murdock's train left Florence on July 8 with 63 wagons and an estimated 460 immigrants, arriving in Salt Lake City on September 12 after a journey of 66 days. Ira Eldredge's company left the next day with 70 wagons and an estimated 514 immigrants, arriving in Salt Lake City on September 15 after a journey of 68 days. Joseph Horne's company also left on July 9 with 62 wagons and an estimated 453 immigrants, arriving on September 13 after a journey of 65 days. Joseph W. Young waited three days before his double company pulled out—80 wagons and an estimated 292 immigrants, arriving September 23 after a journey lasting 73 days. Hartley, "Great Florence Fitout of 1861," 367; Jefferies, Journal, summary before entry of July 26, 1861.

79. *An Autobiography of James Henry Lindford Sr.* (N.p.: Lindford Family Organization, 1947), 24–25.

80. Erastus Snow, Letter to George A. Smith, June 26, 1861, Journal History.

81. Brigham Young, "Church Emigration of 1861," report to LDS Church leaders in England, copied into Journal History, December 31, 1861, Supplement, 7. He had made a similar statement earlier: "This season's immigration has been signally blest all the time from their departure from their former homes to their new homes in our peaceful vallies." Brigham Young, Letter to George Q. Cannon, September 18, 1861, Letterbook 5. The Eldredge Company experienced six births and ten deaths on the Mormon Trail. Journal of the First Company of Church Train Emigrants, 1861, Ira Eldredge, Captain (journal kept by John Reed), photocopy of holograph, note after entry on September 15, 1861, Church History Library; John Reed, Journal, September 3, 1861, microfilm of holograph, Church History Library.

82. John D. T. McAllister, Letter to George Q. Cannon, July 30, 1861, Journal History.

83. Niels Wilhelmsen, Letter to John Van Cott, August 19, 1861, *Skandinaviens Stjerne* 11 (October 1861): 9–10.

84. PEF Company, reel 9, fd. 30, Promissory Notes, 1861, Church History Library.

85. *Names of Persons and Sureties Indebted to the Perpetual Emigrating Fund Company from 1850 to 1877* (Salt Lake City: Star Book and Job Printing Office, 1877).

86. Arrington, *Great Basin Kingdom*, 211.

87. Perpetual Emigrating Fund Company, Frontier Account Book, reel 1, fd. 14, General Accounts, 1861, microfilm, Church History Library.

88. PEF, Church Team Accounts, 1861; Hulmston, "Mormon Immigration in the 1860s," 30–31.

89. Arrington, *Great Basin Kingdom*, 208.

19 Common People
Church Activity during the Brigham Young Era

"THE PEOPLE CONSTITUTE THE POWER and reality of the Kingdom of God." That fundamental truth, voiced by LDS pioneer bishop Leonard W. Hardy in 1861, is often ignored in Mormon history, which tends to concentrate on Church leaders and programs.[1] Of 150,000 Latter-day Saints over whom Brigham Young presided during his three decades in Utah, barely 1,000 served as leaders from bishopric level up to General Authorities—a ratio of 149 to 1.[2] How did the 149,000 Saints who were not leaders practice their religion?

In 1860 a Salt Lake City bishop reported that most in his ward were "just as faithful as they knew how to be, others as much the reverse, neglecting almost every duty."[3] What did being "faithful" mean back then? What did the bishop have in mind when he said every duty? Or, applying today's terminology, what did it mean in Brigham Young's day to be "active in the Church"?

To be "active in the Church" today is to attend Sunday meetings somewhat regularly, to fulfill a calling, and, if fully committed, to hold and use a temple recommend. By contrast, during Utah's first two decades, the Saints did not go regularly to any church meetings, and ward buildings were too small to allow most members to attend sacrament meeting. For most of that early period, men, women, and children had no Sunday School, Relief

Society, Mutual, Primary, or ward priesthood meetings to attend nor auxiliary callings to fill. Saints had no temples needing their attendance or proxy ordinance work. Therefore, what constituted "being a good Mormon" back then? What follows is an attempt to answer this question.

SIZE OF STAKES AND WARDS

Stake and ward sizes varied dramatically. Brigham Young had no more than 13 stakes to oversee at one time until he expanded the total to 20 stakes just before he died in 1877. Those 20 stakes averaged 12 wards apiece, but 8 stakes had more than 14 wards, and the dominant Salt Lake Stake, where one-fourth of the Church membership lived, had 35 wards.

When Brigham Young died, gathered Zion included 104,000 Saints living in 240 wards. Wards averaged 81 families and 432 members per unit. But Salt Lake Stake's wards were larger than most, averaging 566 members. And wards in the Utah (Utah County) Stake were even larger, averaging 808 members each.[4]

CHURCH ATTENDANCE

Believers who gathered to Zion lived in villages and towns for educational, social, cultural, and religious purposes. There, they belonged to specific wards and stakes and could attend church meetings. The types of meetings, their frequency, and their procedures varied according to local circumstances and habit. "Going to meeting" was more optional then than it is in the early twentieth-first century.

Sunday Meetings

From the first pioneers' first week in Great Salt Lake Valley, leaders provided each Sunday a general (not ward) church meeting or two. When settlements formed outside the valley, the same pattern continued. The norm by the mid-1850s was two public meetings on Sunday conducted for the entire settlement, not just for a ward. Both meetings, usually at 10 AM and 2 PM, were held so that speakers could address the Saints. The afternoon meeting became the people's sacrament meeting.

In Salt Lake Stake, the main Sunday meeting took place on Temple Square. On Sunday afternoons, some of the valley's Saints gathered for the stakewide sacrament meeting and to hear the General Authorities preach. At first the attendees met only during good weather, under a brush-covered bowery. Then the Church built the "Old" Tabernacle, seating capacity 2,500 (less than half of the city's population). It was replaced in 1867 by the "New" Tabernacle, seating capacity of 8,000 (still not quite half of the city's population), which still stands on Temple Square.[5] Other multiward settlements that did not have tabernacles continued the tradition of settlement-wide outdoor Sunday meetings.

During winter months, however, outdoor meetings could not be held, so the Salt Lake Valley and outlying wards conducted their own services in homes or in ward meetinghouses, after such were erected. Even the Old Tabernacle, when it was in use, proved to be too cold during the winter to host the Sunday general meetings. It appears that cold weather caused settlement-wide sacrament meetings to become ward meetings, a major development in the worship history of the Saints. In 1867, because wards by then were conducting Sunday Schools on Sunday mornings, leaders ceased holding the downtown Tabernacle Sunday morning general meeting.[6]

For the Saints who attended, the Sunday services provided varying calibers of speakers, a chance to partake of the sacrament, and sometimes impressive inspiration. An eighteen-year-old diarist in Smithfield, Cache County, commented about her Sunday activities on April 21, 1867: "I have been to two meetings to day. Have listened to the pleasing word of God spoken by His servants and have been much instructed and comforted thereby. Oh! That the honest in heart everywhere might listen to such teaching! Could they do otherwise than to understand and believe."[7]

Martha Spence Heywood, who had no children to care for during most of these years, attended religious services regularly in Salt Lake and then in Nephi when she moved there as an early settler. She noted on Thursday, May 4, 1854, the monthly fast day, that she "attended forenoon and afternoon meetings and felt much benefited thereby." She added that "there was quite a good attendance of females," which implies that such was unusual and worth noting.[8] Among reactions to meetings she recorded in her diary are these: "Today we had a good meeting," "Had a good meeting this forenoon," "Had some good speaking," and "Had a good meeting."[9] Of two Sunday meetings in Salt Lake's bowery, years apart, she noted, "Enjoyed the remarks of Joseph Young in reference to keeping the Sabbath holy," and "Truly comforted and instructed by the preaching" that provided "a variety of good instruction."[10]

Sunday meetings in most settlements were well attended—but only if judged by how full the meeting facility was. If measured by the percentages who "went to church," those meetings were poorly attended. One Salt Lake City ward reported that of its 181 families, only 31 were regularly represented at Sunday meetings, and 97 of the families, or 50 percent, were "perfectly indifferent."[11] Historian Ronald W. Walker points out that "'going to meeting' clearly was not a popular nineteenth-century pastime."[12]

Several factors account for the early Utah Saints' light attendance at Sunday services. The primary cause was inadequate meeting halls. In most areas, the first meetinghouses were too small for everyone in the ward to be seated for Sunday meetings. The Toquerville chapel, for example, was a 20' x 16' adobe house, the size of some family rooms in today's suburban homes, too small to serve the settlement's nineteen families.[13] Although small buildings might be full on a Sunday, the majority of ward members were not in attendance. In 1856, Elder Wilford Woodruff mentioned "wards where they are so crowded." Many meetings, he said, are "as full as people can be" so that "many of the ward have to go home."[14]

In 1861, Brigham Young recommended the building of "substantial Halls in the different wards."[15] In the following sixteen years, many wards built new meetinghouses, but often the new structures were still too small. In 1877, for example, Salt Lake City's Twenty-first Ward designed a new meetinghouse that was about 28' x 43'[16]—enough space to seat only about 180 people. Some communities did build large churches, such as the 85' x 40' edifice Kaysville Ward built by the early 1860s, which could seat 900 Saints. Curtains divided its basement into four classrooms.[17] Ogden built a tabernacle, in use by the late 1850s, that could seat 1,200.[18] Nevertheless, as late as 1877, the *Juvenile Instructor* reported that many children had never partaken of the sacrament because "in many places the meeting houses are too small for them to meet with the grown people, and therefore they have to stop at home while their parents attend meeting."[19]

Often, the first meeting places were either members' homes or simple one-room, log assembly halls.[20] Not only were they small, but often they were crudely finished and uncomfortable. Gunnison Ward's first meetinghouse was 20' x 40', built of logs, with a roof of willows, straw, and earth. The walls were chinked and plastered with mud and whitewashed on the inside. Floorboards did not fit very closely together. Benches were "formidable slabs" with four legs attached. A crude pine table stood in one corner.[21]

Orderville, c. late nineteenth century. A large assembly hall sits in the background. Courtesy Church Archives.

In Tooele "the first public house was built in 1854," John Alexander Bevan recalled. He also described its lack of amenities:

> It was 28 ft. long by 18 feet wide, a log-house with a dirt roof. A fire-place in each end stood lengthwise, north and south, facing the east. There was one small door, and two small windows in front. The chimneys were built of adobe. The fireplaces were large, so that the wood could be stood up in them endways, and make a big fire to give both heat and light. The head of each family made a bench for his family to sit on. These benches were usually made of slabs, with four legs put in on the round side of the slab. . . . Besides the fire for light, they had tallow candles, home-made, and each family was supposed to furnish a candle. The house was used for all purposes, both religious and otherwise. It was the schoolhouse, the meeting house, and the amusement hall. It had a pulpit on the west side near the center. This pulpit, or stand, was about large enough to hold three men.[22]

Local meetinghouses, no matter the size, discouraged attendance by being too hot, too cold, or too smoky. Boweries and other buildings became unbearably hot during summer months. In St. George the first bowery proved to be "too small" for general gatherings. "On every side the assemblies were exposed to the rude blasts of the hot summer, and the deep chilling atmosphere of the winter season."[23] But the new bowery, 85' x 45', while large and neat, suffered from frequent windstorms that blew dust through the willows into the faces of the assembled faithful. Charles L. Walker attended a conference on May 4, 1866, at which "I heard little of what they said, for the wind roared through the willows that covered the bowery, with such violence that it was almost an impossibility to hear the speaker." Two days later, men nailed "wagon covers round the bowery to protect [attendees] from the gale." St. George had a meeting hall, but "it would seat only about a hundred people." Finally, in 1869, a spacious tabernacle opened for Sunday meetings, although it was unfinished. Meetings were held in the basement, for the building exterior was not finished until 1871, the interior, not until 1875.[24]

In 1869, Provo's tabernacle had a new stove that smoked up the room. "I do the best I can when the Stove is red hot," the custodian said. "I put the Coal in quick, but cannot prevent the smoke and flame coming out when the door is opened."[25] Two years later, during a cold December, "several members of the Choir were complaining because of the coldness of the Meeting House." "Unless the room is warmed," a bishop warned, "the people will stay at home."[26]

Other life realities hindered men, women, and children from going to meetings. In that premicrophone era, attendees at the outdoor meetings and in the Old Tabernacle and other larger meetinghouses had trouble hearing and understanding the speakers. On some Sundays, travel to meetings over dirt roads in uncovered wagons was unpleasant and even impossible because of mud, ice, rain, wind, dust, snow, or scorching sun. Sickness and small children kept many Saints home from meetings, especially the mothers. Martha Spence Heywood's excuse for missing her Salt Lake City ward's sacrament meeting one Sunday in January was because of "the bad walking," meaning mud or snow or water, and "the close atmosphere of the house."[27] Farm chores and irrigation turns had to be done, even on the Sabbath. Saints in farming regions developed a pattern of not attending meetings during busy summer months, a practice that lingered into the twentieth century. Also, foreign-speaking immigrants sometimes stayed home from English-speaking sacrament meetings.

Poor quality meetings, too, contributed to nonattendance patterns. Smaller communities lacked enough speakers to give variety to the meetings year after year. Women, it appears, rarely spoke in sacrament meetings. Available speakers often were not good speakers. Therefore, within a few years, a ward's meetings became repetitious and often boring. Illustrating the "dull meeting" problem is Provoan Sidney Alexander Pace's recollection that

> we were in the habit of going into meeting on Sunday and if the speaker was not lively enough, fifteen or twenty of us young boys would get up and walk out of meeting and go down by Bishop Loveless's home.... They used to have large straw stacks and here we went to have our fun....
>
> The Bishop ... gave me a good fatherly talk and gave me a mission to work with the young boys of the ward and get them into meeting and keep them there. He said he didn't care how I did it but he wanted me to do that for him.... By the end of a month's time all the boys would stay in meeting until it was out.[28]

To improve sacrament meetings, the Church called men to be home missionaries to travel in assigned regions and speak in ward meetings and at special conferences.[29]

A lack of fervor among work-distracted Saints likewise lowered the attendance. Lackluster attendance at Provo Tabernacle afternoon meetings in 1872 caused stake president Abraham O. Smoot to ask block teachers "to report why the people do not come to meeting, the turn-out is unwarrantable.... Provo ought to fill this house to overflowing but they do not[,] only when the President [Brigham Young] comes; then they turn out for curiosity. I feel that the people do not enjoy the spirit of their religion." Smoot continued, "There has not been too much preaching, or to[o] lengthy meetings," he said, adding that "a healthy man who complains of two meetings, is weak in the faith." Three years later, the problem persisted, so President Smoot decided to "call the regular meetings wether the people attended or not and thus free himself from all blame."[30]

At the end of 1860, bishops for Great Salt Lake City's twenty wards gave verbal reports at the biweekly bishops meeting, telling of the wards' number of families, attitudes, and participation. The comments dealing with meeting attendance are summarized here (what is notable is that the bishops' perspective seems to have been not what percentage of members attended but how full the meetinghouse was):

> Meetings well attended on Sunday, some few "on the background."
> Meeting well attended.
> Weekly meeting pretty well attended, fast meeting but few attend.
> Sunday meeting well attended, fast meetings not so.
> Sunday night meetings and on fast day well attended.
> Fast meeting well attended.
> Monthly fast meeting well attended, at which they bless their children.
> Good spirit toward attending meetings.
> Good spirit prevails, meeting well attended.
> Meeting tolerably well attended; "some who have lived in the ward six years have never been seen at a meeting, and yet call themselves saints."
> People generally very slack in going to meeting.
> No place for holding meetings.[31]

In some LDS meeting halls, men sat on one side and women on the other, a strange practice not yet well researched. The Old Tabernacle, for a period of time, had a partition running through the center, separating the sexes—women on the north, men on the south. The practice continued in the New Tabernacle, according to an 1867 visitor there—women sat in the middle seats, men in the side seats along the walls. The Parowan Ward meetinghouse was similarly segregated, women on the east side, men on the west.[32] How extensive this practice was is not known.

LDS religious life was centered in the ward and its religious meetings. To outsiders ward sacrament meetings often seemed irreverent, informal, and lacking in good speeches and admirable music. But for many Saints, these ward meetings provided inspiration and appreciated instruction.[33]

Ward Sunday Evening and Midweek Prayer Meetings

In many wards, small numbers of Saints gathered in someone's home for a Sunday-night and a midweek-night prayer meeting. These meetings, which continued throughout Brigham Young's era, primarily featured testimony sharing, singing, and praying rather than preaching.[34] Women as well as men spoke. In Nephi's early days, Martha Spence Heywood sometimes attended the ward's prayer meetings. On Sunday evening, October 12, 1851, she noted that "we met together for worship and had a good meeting" at which two men spoke and then "Sister Gifford spoke a few words and I followed her."[35]

"It stormed so fast Wednesday evening that we had no prayer meeting," she recorded on February 16, 1851, in Salt Lake. "Our prayer meeting last Sunday evening to Brother Leonard's was full and very good." Regarding a Sunday evening prayer meeting in Nephi, Martha Spence Heywood noted, "Our prayer meeting did not amount to much." But on another occasion, she wrote "we had a very good prayer meeting."[36]

Ward Fast Meetings

Continuing a practice started in Nauvoo, wards held fast meetings on the first Thursday of every month. Workers had to leave their jobs for two hours or more to attend. To facilitate their attendance, Church leaders at times sternly reminded Mormon employers to close their doors during fast meeting. In 1874 a gathering of bishops discussed the "very imperfect way" members treated fast meetings. Presiding Bishop Edward Hunter regretted that "so many failed to appreciate the blessings of our fast meetings." One local bishop responded that "our man servants and maid servants should be allowed to go, and our stores and workshops closed, to give all a chance."[37] Two years later, Bishop Hunter reported that for the first time the Salt Lake Stake's public works closed on fast-day morning and would continue to do so in the future so public workers could attend fast meetings. One of Bishop Hunter's counselors, Leonard W. Hardy, added that he believed those who failed to attend fast meetings should pay a double fast offering. "All the Merchants in the Church ought to close their stores on that day and give the clerks a chance to go to meeting," he urged.[38] One month later, the bishops agreed that a petition be drawn up that requested city merchants to close for three hours on fast days. What resulted from this plan is not known.[39]

Priesthood-Related Meetings

In early Utah, high priests groups and elders quorums were few and served little more purpose than for the men to come together for testimony bearing or talks about the gospel. Most ordained men held the office of seventy and belonged to one of the general quorums of seventy. Because nearly all the men sent out as missionaries were ordained as seventies prior to leaving, they needed to join a seventies quorum when they returned. Seventies quorums were numbered quorums so if a man belonged to the Sixteenth Quorum, for example, when he moved, he still belonged officially to that quorum. By the 1860s, Utah had more than sixty such quorums. These were not stake entities, nor were they necessarily linked to a locality. Gradually, seventies belonging to various quorums who lived in the same locality started to meet together in a "mass" quorum for testimony bearing or instruction but not for assignments to do local Church work. During this period, seventies quorum meetings generally saw low attendance.

Where they existed at all, priesthood quorums were stake entities. Stake-level priesthood gatherings included separate monthly meetings for high priests and seventies. Priesthood holders met with their stake quorum officers, who gave instruction and gospel explanation, but the meetings consisted primarily of the men in attendance bearing testimonies. As recorded in the quorum minute books for several of the stakes and settlements, quorum leaders' admonitions indicate that attendance at these meetings generally was less than leaders wanted.[40]

The functions of deacons, teachers, and priests were performed primarily by Melchizedek Priesthood holders. Revelation affirms that "those holding the Melchizedek Priesthood can act in all the offices of the Aaronic Priesthood" if called upon and set apart for that office,[41] so the bishops and stake Aaronic Priesthood quorum presidencies "called and set apart" such men to be *acting* priests, *acting* teachers—the home teachers of that day— and *acting* deacons.[42] Hence, these men were termed the "acting priesthood"—meaning those called into active service. The rest were reserves.[43]

Wards held acting teachers meetings once or twice a month, at which the teachers reported to the bishop about their visits to ward members. These meetings were that generation's equivalent to our modern ward priesthood meetings. Sometimes the group was referred to as a teachers quorum.

To prepare the ward meetinghouse for meetings and, under the direction of the bishop, aid the poor, wards had a few acting deacons. Deacons meetings in larger population areas were monthly stake meetings. In more isolated settlements, deacons, if they met at all, generally attended the acting teachers meetings.

General Conferences and Stake Conferences

Saints' meeting schedules included "going to conference." Thousands flocked to Great Salt Lake City twice a year to attend general conference. (Again, the percentage of total LDS members in Utah who attended general conference was very low.) Traveling in wagons, buggies, and carts, on horseback, on foot, and later by train, many used the trip for spiritual renewal as well as for shopping and renewing friendships. That general conferences sometimes were crowded is shown by Martha Spence Heywood's comments on April 6, 1856. She went to conference at the bowery but found there a "dense crowd," so she went back home.[44]

Quarterly conferences, which were not then termed stake conferences, were held in several different settlements, including American Fork, Bountiful, Farmington, Kaysville, Provo, Tooele City, Fillmore, and Spanish Fork. But they were held between November and January and from June to August, Church leaders apparently letting general conference serve as the other two conferences per year. By the mid-1860s, St. George held stake conferences each May and November. Many special conferences were held whenever General Authorities passed through a settlement.[45]

Dixie's premier diarist, Charles L. Walker, regularly attended local church meetings. He particularly enjoyed a stake conference held in St. George on May 4, 1872. Resident Apostle Erastus Snow, who was serving as the stake president, "spoke in a powerful and very interesting manner on the Power and Authority of the Holy Priesthood. It was rich and very edifying. I could have listened to him all day; it was meat and drink to my soul, and I felt as tho I had a rich feast of spiritual food."[46]

Saints had opportunities in most stakes to attend stake conferences. By the mid-1850s, the Davis Stake was holding twice-yearly conferences, no two in a row in the same community. On March 14 and 15, for example, the conference took place at Kaysville. Nine men spoke during the two days.[47] In some other stakes, the conferences were held less regularly.[48]

SLOW INCREASE IN WARD MEETINGS AND CALLINGS

During the first two decades of the pioneer period, LDS men, women, and children had no church meetings to attend other than the Sunday general worship meetings, prayer and fast meetings, stake conferences, or acting teachers meetings. For most wards during this period, the only ward priesthood officers were the bishopric, the acting teachers quorum, and a few acting deacons. Well into the 1860s, the vast majority of "active" Latter-day Saint adults never held a ward job. Without Relief Societies, Sunday Schools, Mutuals, and Primaries, wards had few positions available for anyone to fill. As a result, most ward members held no ward jobs. The turning point was the third decade, when ward meetings and activities increased as the four auxiliary organizations were introduced, one by one. Thus, only gradually, with the advent of Church auxiliaries, did service in ward positions become a regular part of the committed Mormon's life.

The following beginning dates for Lehi's ward organizations reveal the lack of opportunity for ward jobs that existed for two-thirds of the Brigham Young era:[49]

Bishopric	1851
Elders quorum	1858
Seventies quorum	1862
Sunday School (tried in 1851, died out)	1866
Relief Society	1868
Teachers quorum	1869
High priests quorum	1869
Deacons quorum	1871
Young Ladies' Retrenchment Association	1875
Young Men's Mutual Improvement Association	1875
Primary Association	1878

Males with Priesthood Offices, No Duties

In 1852, 2,200 of Utah's 12,000 total number of residents (men, women, and children) held a priesthood office—or one-fifth of all the people. By 1877, a quarter of a century later, the ratio stood about the same, 22,000 out of 104,000 total. Assuming that about half the total population was above age fifteen and that half of these were males, then the 22,000 who held priesthood offices comprised almost all the males over age fifteen.

However, even though most male adults held a priesthood office, most did not have specific duties to perform. The men were expected only to be ready to accept calls to be acting teachers or to fill proselyting missions if and when such calls came.

In 1852 some 40 percent of priesthood bearers were seventies, and 20 percent were elders. (Seventies then were Melchizedek Priesthood officers, seventy to a quorum, in dozens of quorums that functioned like stake quorums; they were not comparable to today's First and Second Quorums of Seventy, whose members are General Authorities.[50]) By 1877, however, the elder-to-seventy ratio had reversed, and 41 percent of priesthood bearers were elders and 20 percent seventies. The percentages of high priests (14 percent) and Aaronic Priesthood (24 percent) remained unchanged throughout the period.[51] On average, a ward in 1877 had 13 high priests, 19 seventies, and 38 elders, or 70 Melchizedek Priesthood bearers out of 432 members. It had 6 priests, 6 teachers, and 10 deacons, for 22 Aaronic Priesthood bearers total.[52]

Most lesser priesthood bearers were adults, not boys.[53] Church leaders had no expectation that a boy should advance through the ranks—deacon to teacher to priest—or that a boy needed to hold a priesthood office at all. Most young males were ordained first to the Melchizedek Priesthood in their late teens or early twenties to be an elder or seventy.[54]

Acting Teachers

The first ward callings were the bishoprics, including clerks, and then the acting teachers, but only a select dozen or score of men served as acting teachers in a ward. Bishoprics and this corps of teachers "shouldered the ward's leadership and performed its labor."[55]

During Brigham Young's presidency, Melchizedek Priesthood men handled almost all Aaronic Priesthood work in Utah, doing "double duty" by acting in both priesthoods.[56] One older man who was a seventy served as an acting priest in one ward and an acting teacher in two wards and was in the stake's deacons quorum presidency.[57] Another man, an elder, was also both an acting deacon and an acting teacher.[58] Bishop Hunter often exhorted priesthood men to "magnify both priesthoods."[59] The statement "I was an Elder before I was a deacon" was easily understood during the pioneer period.[60]

A man called to be a teacher was expected to visit a big set of families living in the ward. As ward populations grew, he was assigned a companion so that teachers could visit in pairs. Some teams were assigned to visit all the families in a given block, giving rise to the "block teacher" designation. They visited monthly in many wards but only quarterly or randomly elsewhere. A survey in 1870 shows that LDS wards had between eighteen and twenty-four block teachers each, and each team visited between eight and twenty families. Bishops met monthly, or sometimes biweekly, with their acting teachers to receive reports and give assignments.[61]

Then, as now, end-of-the-month visits were common. In 1864, Bishop Leonard Hardy complained about teachers who "put off their visits through the wards to the very last evening before they have to give in their report, this hurrying way of visiting, failed to accomplish the design of a Teachers duty."[62]

By assignment from the bishops, teachers did more than pay visits to members' homes. They settled some disputes, helped the needy, collected fast offerings, obtained needed resources, and administered the sacrament.[63]

Relief Societies

After being shelved in Nauvoo, Relief Societies were organized for a brief period in the 1850s by women in some wards primarily to assist needy Native Americans in their neighborhoods. But no more than three or four societies survived the "Move South," the northern Saints' 1858 evacuation to more southerly settlements, a response to the threat of Johnston's army.[64] For most Mormon women, the Relief Society program was not reorganized until 1867, fully twenty years after the first Saints entered Utah. Therefore, for a full generation, women, most of whom did not attend sacrament meetings regularly, at best attended weeknight prayer meetings. For them, religion was concentrated on interactions at home and with neighbors rather than centered around formal, weekly church attendance.[65]

By the late 1860s, Relief Societies were started in most wards, giving women "church work." Provo's Third Ward Relief Society commenced on December 2, 1868, by voting in twenty-two members. Mary Jane Tanner, the bishop's wife, was the first president. Each week the sisters met in a different house. They debated whether to have two separate society meetings, one a prayer meeting and the other a quilting meeting. At first they tried one meeting at which they had prayer and a hymn and then quilted and sewed. But the atmosphere became too relaxed and gossipy, the minutes note, so they began holding both types of meetings weekly. For a long time, attendance was good at quilting meetings but "very low" at prayer meetings.[66]

Relief Societies copied the priesthood organization in several respects. They called women to be teachers, like the block teachers, to visit the sisters in the ward. They called a few sisters to be deaconesses, doing the work ward deacons did—making the meeting place ready and comfortable for each week's meeting.[67] Because of the existence of ward Relief Societies, a dozen or more women in each ward received "church callings" to serve in positions in the wards.

Sunday Schools for Children

In the early 1850s, Sunday Schools began sporadically in wards here and there, founded by concerned local individuals rather than Church leaders. Richard Ballantyne started the first one in 1849 when fifty youth, ages eight to fourteen, met in a special room added to his home. Other individuals copied him, so independent Sunday Schools sprang up in most wards. Provo started a Sunday School in 1852, which operated off and on. In 1860, the school started meeting in the Third Ward meetinghouse—one Sunday School for four Provo wards. Finally, in 1876 each ward organized its own Sunday School.[68] A Sunday School started in Lehi in 1851 but "was not permanently organized until 1866."[69] In fall 1856, Bishop John Rowberry in Tooele decided his ward needed a Sunday School "for the benefit of the Rising Generation." He appointed Eli Lee to run it, so "Bro. Lee immediately commenced operations by collecting a few of the children together on Sunday mornings, and instructing them, assisted by his wife. For some time, but little progress was made." By 1857 the school had eight classes—five taught by men and three by women.[70]

In 1866, Elder George Q. Cannon launched the *Juvenile Instructor* to help the Sunday Schools, and in 1872 he became the Church's first general superintendent of all the Sunday Schools. By the 1870s, two hundred Sunday Schools involved nearly fifteen thousand youth and adults. Sunday Schools created ward positions that Saints could be called to fill. For the first time, women and children participated directly in a Sabbath meeting as teachers and students, and many men became officers and teachers. Songs, prayers, scripture lessons, catechisms, and recitations were all part of the school. So, too, were examination days, like one Salt Lake bishop Frederick Kesler attended when he found "the house was well fild, the pieces ware well spoken & a Large No. of presants ware given out as Reward of merit which consisted in some verry choice Books."[71]

A revealing picture of Sunday School activity appears in the first statistical report the Deseret Sunday School Union compiled.[72] Their data are for the quarter ending September 15, 1872. In twenty Utah counties and one Idaho stake, the Church had 190 Sunday Schools, of which 149 had reported. These 149 enrolled 13,373 pupils—5,964 boys and 7,409 girls—and had 1,408 teachers—687 men and 721 women. The following table shows the courses of study and the number of classes taught in each:

New Testament	330	Bible	118
Alphabet	206	Miscellaneous	72
First Reader	202	Doctrine & Covenants	54
Second Reader	202	*Juvenile Instructor*	52
Book of Mormon	129	Theology	28

Adults were not the only ones to stay home from Sunday School; so did older youths and young adults. William Dunbar of the Salt Lake City Twentieth Ward became concerned for the ward's young people ages sixteen through twenty-two because

> as a general thing the class I am referring to do not attend Sunday school. They consider that they are too old, that they know too much, or that it is rather humiliating to associate with children; and, with a few exceptions, those I mean are not of the kind who have read the Bible.... They must not expect to study "Mormonism" by reading novels, but they must read the Bible, Book of Mormon, Doctrine and Covenants, Millennial Star, Orson Pratt's Works, the Voice of Warning and many others. These are the works our children must study if they ever find out for themselves the truth of the principles of "Mormonism."[73]

Efforts to Help the "Unchurched" Youth

For two decades, most LDS parents in Utah raised their children without the help of Church programs. This generation of parents believed their children would grow up to be righteous by virtue of living in Zion and away from Babylon. "No thought was bestowed upon their spiritual culture," Eliza R. Snow confessed, with the result that "we had Infidels among them; children of good parents."[74] Children born in the faith, another leader said, "did not seem to value it like those who had left everything for its sake."[75]

Records show that adult Saints complained about a variety of misbehaviors by adolescent boys: rowdyism, vile language, reckless horseback riding, throwing rocks through windows, vandalism, fighting, intoxication, smoking, spitting tobacco juice on church floors, gang behavior, and Sabbath breaking.[76] Adults complained about girls "retailing scandal," drinking tea, being lazy, desiring inappropriate fashions, dancing improperly, dating Gentiles, and relishing novels.[77]

Most teens did not attend Sunday School, believing it was for little children. But in the 1870s, recruitment pushes increased teenage Sunday School enrollments. One teacher said twenty young men in his class "were exceeding rough" at first "but now they attended regularly and their minds were awakened." Another remarked that his class grew from 2 to 110 in two years and that "rowdyism was being dispensed with." Another report said "the Sabbath School had a great effect to restrain boys from whiskey, tobacco and bad habits" and the boys "were more polite and amenable to good advice."[78]

Some of the teenage girls began to receive indirect training and to be further involved in the Church when they started receiving calls to teach the children in Primary following its creation two years after Brigham Young's death.

Leaders, being parents themselves, created additional programs to prevent the young folks from growing up unindoctrinated, untrained, and unappreciative of their religion.[79] Valuing their young people, they launched mutual improvement programs for young women in 1869 and for young men in 1875. The weekly meetings of the YWMIAs and YMMIAs featured "intellectual exercises," "suitable amusements," and programs intended to build testimonies, improve manners, and overcome deficiencies in members' educations.[80]

Illustrating the start-up of youth movements is the Salt Lake City Seventeenth Ward. Its Young Ladies Cooperative Retrenchment Society began in 1870 with nineteen young women as members and a married woman as president. This group resolved to reform in many specific areas: to read Church books, to obey the Word of Wisdom, to remove right-hand gloves when partaking of the sacrament, and to not "retail scandal." Leaders stressed proper dress standards for the girls, some of whom had received their endowment: dressing neatly and plainly, avoiding tight lacing, eschewing long trains or "dresses so short that the tops of our high shoes could be seen," not mutilating temple garments by cutting off the sleeves and collars, not turning garments down "from their shoulders" to go to parties, and not wearing shawls gentile style or bonnets made after gentile patterns.[81]

The ward's retrenchment attendance sagged. One reason was that some girls said "they do not have any thing to retrench in they do not wear ruffles and frills," so why come? The organization folded, then resurrected in 1873. But by 1875 the girls had wearied of meetings where the woman president called on them to stand up and say something. "It seems that we can not say any thing where we are in our meetings," one honest girl said, "but we can talk freely when out of doors." "I think I could speak better if there was no older Sisters present," confessed another. Miss Addie Clayton put the problem in a nutshell: she "hated to refuse to speak yet hated to speak." One effort to boost attendance seemed guaranteed to create guilt in the girls: "If we do not come to meeting," an officer said, "our guardian angel[s] cannot come, and they love to come and converse together."[82]

President Brigham Young's 1875 ban on round dancing stirred up the girls. Some approved a resolution to quit round dancing, some abstained from voting, and some voted in favor of the resolution but with reluctance. Clarissa Smith "presumed there was no girl that like[d] round-dancing as well as she did yet she had said she would quit so she would. The temptation was great." Another pledged "to try by the help of the Lord to quit round dancing, although it was hard." Addie Clayton did not vote because she feared she might break the promise. There was no harm in round dancing, she reasoned, "if harm was not made of it." Jennie Russell pledged, "by the help of the Lord," to quit round dancing and also tea and coffee. Lizzi Smith "liked tea & coffee but was going to stop that & round dancing." One girl liked the dancing ban because she never could get the step right and appreciated an excuse to quit trying.[83]

The Seventeenth Ward's YMMIA held its first meeting on November 2, 1875. Their purpose for organizing was "to learn all they could in regard to the principles of our religion" and to practice public speaking and explaining "our views and ideas." Members participated in discussions, talks, lectures, readings, declamations, and the sharing of personal essays. Discussion topics included the "first principles," Word of Wisdom, and signs of the times. For new participants, it was "the first time that most of them had ever stood before a congregation."[84]

By 1877 a main feature of the YMMIA meetings was questions and answers. An assigned person brought in a question on any religious, scientific, or historical subject. The executive committee assigned a member, someone other than the question raiser, to be the answerer. If no one could answer a particular question, the committee, which included the bishop, would consult with Church authorities "except on Scientific or Historical subjects." Among questions raised were "How high was the tower of Babel?" "Was Moroni a spirit or resurrected being?" "What is the difference between a Republican and a Democrat?" and "When was the first locomotive made?"[85] About twenty young men normally attended the ward's YMMIA meetings.[86] Late in 1877, the Seventeenth Ward's YMMIA and YLMIA agreed to hold joint meetings once a month, an innovation that enlivened both organizations.

Priesthood for Young Men

As part of the multipronged effort to strengthen the youth, priesthood leaders labored on a modest scale to place boys into priesthood harness during the mid-1870s. Salt Lake Stake President Angus M. Cannon wanted bishops "to draw the young men into positions in the Priesthood and thus an excellent experience, and, at the same time, preserve them from evil associations." He personally had noticed a "marked improvement" in his own sons after they were ordained.[87] Priesthood service, proponents argued, like involvement in the auxiliaries, would help keep boys from evil practices while inculcating skills to qualify them for adult church service. To care for meetinghouses, deacons were specifically advised to clean the building; keep dust off the seats; polish the stove; carry in coal; light the fires; have the sacrament trays, table, and clothes clean and neat; usher people to their seats; help keep order during church services; and even clean the "backhouses"—apparently the outhouses.

More Meetings, More Ward Jobs

In his handwritten history of Gunnison Ward, Bishop Christian Madsen explained the evolution in meetings, which provided the opportunity for more people to hold positions in their wards: "In regard to the Ecclesiastical

Cottonwood Ward deacons, 1936. Young men were regularly being ordained to positions in the priesthood by this era. Courtesy Church Archives.

arrangements, there was of course separate meetings both forenoon and afternoon, untill Sunday Schools were introduced, which afterwards occupied the Sunday forenoon. All the year round. In winter time there was Sunday and Thursday night meetings, besides the meetings of Acting Priesthood and Quorums." By November 1877, Gunnison Ward had the following schedule of meetings:[88]

Saturday afternoon:	Priesthood and associations
evening:	Aaronic Priesthood
Sunday 10–12 AM:	Sunday School
2–4 PM:	Sacrament meeting
4–6 PM:	Bishop and acting teachers meeting
Wednesday evening:	Scandinavian meeting
Thursday evening:	Two prayer meetings
One evening a week:	Amusements
One day a week:	Juvenile choir
	Adult choir

SAINTS AND ORDINANCES

The Sacrament

The day after the arrival of Brigham Young in Salt Lake Valley, a Sunday, the advance company partook of the sacrament; in the next few years, the sacrament was sometimes administered only once a month.[89] By the mid-1850s, however, the Saints had the opportunity to partake of the sacrament weekly in the areawide sacrament meetings.

Twice during Brigham Young's years, the sacrament was withheld for short periods. Once was for several months during the Mormon Reformation when the Saints were given time to repent and make restitution prior to renewing their covenants. The other interval came during the Utah War period, 1857–58, when the sacrament was withdrawn while the federal army established itself in Utah. Some of the leaders' concerns about holding Sunday meetings are indicated by instructions given October 1858; bishops were told that "if there are any meetings, let them be prayer meetings" and not preaching services where speakers might say something offensive to the occupation army. "Be careful to controul all that may be said," Presiding Bishop Edward Hunter cautioned, "for an enthusiastic Mormon is more dangerous than an Apostate." Finally, early in August 1859, Brigham Young recommended that local leaders start holding public Sunday meetings again "in all the wards once a week at least." That November, Presiding Bishop Hunter expressed gratitude "for the privilege of again having the sacrament administered in the Tabernacle."[90]

During sacrament meetings, the sacramental water was passed down the rows in a "common cup." These containers were goblets or glasses—tiny individual cups were not introduced until 1911. In 1852 the General Authorities wanted to obtain a special set of sacrament glasses and plates for use in the Sunday afternoon downtown services. They asked members to contribute silver from which to make sacrament vessels. Very quickly they collected silver coin worth $149 and several pounds of silver watch cases, spoons, rings, and other "ornaments." The silver was melted down and then cast by silversmith Israel Barlow to form twelve silver cups. Then in 1855, leaders obtained "six new silver bread baskets." In 1873, Salt Lake City's Ninth Ward dedicated its "silver service for the communion table," purchased with members' donations. Provo wards spent more than four years trying to raise enough through donations to buy a nice sacrament serving set for use in the Provo Tabernacle.[91]

For many years, the methods for blessing and passing the sacrament varied from ward to ward. Often, bishops personally administered the sacrament, both in their own wards and in the settlement-wide sacrament meetings. One bishop noted in 1874 that "at 2 PM I administered the sacrament in the New Tabernacle assisted by my 2 council[ors] and [Acting] Teachers." Some wards blessed bread and water first, then passed both at the same time. In other wards, bishops decided "to bless the bread and water at the Sacrament according to the universal custom" instead of "blessing both before distributing either." While bread and water passed through the congregation, speakers continued their talks. In a valleywide 1854 sacrament meeting in Salt Lake City, for example, after the opening song and prayer, the bread was blessed, and while it passed around, Brigham Young preached a sermon. Then he stopped in midsermon, "blest the contents of the cup," and resumed his talk while the water goblets passed around.[92] An opinion on whether the congregation should kneel was issued in 1868, when Presiding Bishop Hunter told bishops he preferred the "kneeling posture," which "was much more seemly to his mind, than standing as at present."[93]

A few small cases of "misconduct" during the sacrament needed correcting. "Instead of the saints taking a sip of water, at the sacrament and then passing it," one leader complained, "they indulged in the habit of drinking too freely, with the view of quenching their thirst."[94] Some men and women kept their hats on in church, especially in cool weather, and women wore gloves. Bishops were told in 1867 that because "the gentlemen were required to uncover their heads while partaking of it [the sacrament]" as a sign of respect "the ladies should be required to take off their gloves."[95]

Local leaders wondered if children should receive the sacrament during Sunday School time. "In settlements where there are Meeting Houses sufficiently spacious to admit of children attending the public meetings on Sunday afternoon, we suggest that they be encouraged to go there," the First Presidency advised local leaders. But where meetinghouses were too small, bishoprics should serve the sacrament weekly to the Sunday School children.[96] As children usually did not attend the afternoon sacrament meetings, leaders introduced the sacrament into Sunday School. Bishop Kesler's diary noted the innovation: "I visited our Ward Sunday School & spoke a few minets while the Sacrement was passing around, it being the 2nd time that it had been administered unto our children in the Sunday Schools."[97]

Baptisms

Almost all baptisms in early Utah took place outdoors in streams or lakes. Records identify but few baptismal fonts anywhere in Utah. In October 1856, the First Presidency dedicated a baptismal font located near the Endowment House in Salt Lake City. A year later, two Apostles helped dedicate a baptismal font in the city's fourteenth ward.[98] In 1861, Brigham Young had a large wagon boarded up to make a font a few rods east of his schoolhouse. About 10' x 12', it had two dressing rooms attached. The President dedicated it on September 4, 1861, then told the ward bishops "they were quite welcome to use it for Baptizing, instead of the creek."[99]

In 1875 the Presiding Bishop asked Frederick Kesler, a millwright, to build a new baptismal font for a group baptism of Native Americans then visiting Salt Lake City. With boards and pipes, he built the font to run east to west so the officiator would stand facing south, letting the candidate rise facing east, as in the Resurrection.[100] Kesler installed his font to have running, not standing, water, for he believed that baptisms should be, like Jesus' was, in running water.[101]

In 1877 leaders urged parents to baptize children when they turned eight, even in winter, rather than waiting several months. Although children might be "afraid of the cold water," the ordinance should not be postponed.

Rebaptisms

Newcomers to Zion learned upon arrival that they should be rebaptized as an initiatory rite wherein they covenanted and committed to the new religious setting and society they were joining. It was "a kind of standing ordinance for all Latter-day Saints who emigrate here,"[102] following the example set by Brigham Young's 1847 pioneer company.[103] In October 1854, a bishop with thirty-two Danish families in his ward reported that on a prior Sunday, 107 Danes, some of whom were from other wards, were rebaptized.[104] "When Brethren first come in here," Presiding Bishop Hunter instructed in 1856, "they should be rebaptized and set to work."[105]

During Brigham Young's presidency, leaders provided Utah Saints with three opportunities to be rebaptized: during the consecration movement in 1854, the Mormon Reformation in 1856–57, and the united order movement in the mid-1870s. On these occasions, Saints were asked to search their souls and repent sufficiently to be worthy of being baptized once again. During the reformation, almost all adult Saints were rebaptized. For example, some five hundred Saints in the Kaysville Ward—nearly every member of the ward—accepted rebaptism.[106] During the united order campaign, leaders judged that the members seemed to be in a "stupor" and needed to be awakened through renewing their covenants. The Twelve set the example by being rebaptized and preached the necessity of the "elders renewing their covenants with the Almighty by rebaptism"; women were to do the same.[107]

Rebaptisms also took place for other reasons. Ill people were rebaptized to renew their health. People found guilty of serious sin were not cut off from Church membership if they were contrite but were instead instructed to be rebaptized.[108]

Temple Endowments and Marriages

Prior to 1877, Church activity did not involve participation in temple ordinances other than receiving one's own endowments, being married, witnessing marriages, and doing some baptisms for the dead. Endowments were given in the upper floor of the Council House in Salt Lake City from 1851 to 1855, at the Endowment House in Salt Lake City from 1855 until 1877 and even later (until 1889), and in the St. George Temple starting in 1877. Men and women rarely went to these sacred places after receiving their own endowments and being married.[109]

Most of the adult Saints in Brigham Young's time obtained their temple endowments. A total of about seventy thousand adults lived during the three decades studied here. From 1851 to 1876, 43,952 Saints received their endowments—about 70 percent of the total number of adults.[110] Another sizable percentage of adults had been endowed in Nauvoo.

In May 1855, when the Endowment House first opened, the First Presidency strongly encouraged Saints to keep the house busy.[111] Wards received quotas to fill on assigned days, so bishops sent unendowed men and women there to receive the ordinances. Even youths were sent. "We would like to see many of the young and sprightly young persons, who are strict to obey their parents," said Endowment House director and First Presidency Counselor Heber C. Kimball.[112] Records of the Kaysville elders quorum for 1865 show that thirty-six of its first members became elders while in their teens, most being ordained at the Endowment House prior to receiving the endowment.[113]

A bishop asked Brigham Young in 1877 at what age girls might receive endowments, and the prophet replied that "if naturally ripe and early development of mind and body" a girl at twelve could, but "as a general rule 15 is old enough."[114] One age study involves the Endowment House records for 1870, 1872, 1877, and 1878 and the St. George Temple endowment records for 1877 and 1878.[115] These records show that teenagers, particularly girls, commonly received their endowments at young ages. For all recipients under age 30, the average age for receiving endowments was 22 for men and 19.5 for women. However, the most popular age for receiving endowments was 17 for women, followed by 18, 16, and 19. For men, the most popular age for receiving endowments was 23, followed by 24, 20, and 22. Of 1,085 endowments checked in the samples, one in three, or 373, were teenage recipients. A few youths received endowments at 9, 12, and 13, but the youngest age when *significant* numbers of endowments were given was 14 for both boys and girls.

A sampling of Endowment House marriage records for the year 1870 shows that endowment age corresponded with marriage age for girls. That year, the most common age for girls to marry was 17, and the average was 18. A few girls as young as 12 received temple marriage sealings. For women under age 24, the average marriage age was 18, but the average age of the men they married was 25, a difference of seven years. This age gap is smaller than that found by Dean May for Kanab during the 1870s, where women married at the average age of 19 and men at 29. The gap is larger by three years than the age difference Larry Logue found for marriages in St. George, where women and men married at age 19 and 23 respectively.[116]

Scholars continue to refine our estimates of the incidence of plural marriage. Findings vary in terms of total percent of families involved, depending upon time period and what communities were studied. Larry Logue's research shows that in St. George nearly 30 percent of households were involved in polygamy in 1870, and 33 percent were in 1880. All recent evidence conclusively shows that most LDS adult men and women in Utah between 1847 and 1877 were monogamists, not polygamists.[117]

PATRIARCHAL BLESSINGS

It was common practice for Saints to obtain patriarchal blessings. Patriarchs often traveled in circuits so people could receive their blessings. Recipients paid a small fee to reimburse the patriarch for his traveling expenses.

Sometimes Saints received two or more patriarchal blessings in their life-times. Within three weeks of arriving in the Salt Lake Valley in 1850, for example, Martha Spence Heywood sought for and received her blessing from Patriarch John Smith. Three years later, she received a second bless-ing from a Brother Cazier. Many, like Sarah Dugard Crowther, received a patriarchal blessing in Nauvoo and a second one in Utah.[118]

PROSELYTING MISSIONS

Church missionary records show that during the entire 1847–77 period, only 2,657 men entered the mission field—less than one thousand per decade. In 1877, by comparison, Utah had perhaps twenty thousand adult males (a few thousand who lived in the time under discussion had died by 1877). Thus, in terms of missionary service, at best only one man in ten—but probably no more than one in twenty—filled a proselyting mission. Salt Lake City's Sixteenth Ward had 113 families in 1857, or at least one hundred adult males. But during the 1860 to 1877 period, only twelve men left from that ward on proselyting missions—suggesting a rate lower than 10 percent.[119] This small percentage counters an image we have popularized that says because the men were so often called away on missions, significant numbers of women ran farms and families, developing their independence and abilities in new ways.[120]

PERSONAL RELIGION AND WORTHINESS STANDARDS

Saints knew what constituted being a "good Mormon," even if they lived below their own expectations. They understood they should practice the basics of Christian behavior: be honest; do not kill, steal, lie, or commit adul-tery; read scriptures; pray; have family prayer; help the poor; attend church meetings; and teach the gospel in the home. To "teach the principles of the Gospel of Christ to their children at least 10 minutes every day" was one cov-enant parents in Gunnison made in recommitting to live the united order.[121]

Building up Zion

All who "crossed the plains," "gathered to Zion," and then built up Zion were considered good Latter-day Saints until they proved otherwise. "Abide among his saints," the First Presidency urged.[122] The faithful were those who stayed in Zion and obeyed admonitions against going to California or backtracking on the Mormon Trail. They built up Zion by erecting homes, developing farms, caring for their cattle, digging irrigation systems, maintaining village roads, constructing meetinghouses, and helping neighbors. Those willing to physically strengthen the Mormon settlements were considered such stalwarts that problems they might have with smoking, drinking, profaning, Sabbath breaking, and even immoral living did not normally cost them their standing in the community and the Church.[123] Citing Brigham Young, Daniel H. Wells taught,

> "Go to with your mights and build up the kingdom of God, by quarrying the rock, by bringing the timber from the kanyons and making it into lumber, by making adobies, mixing the mortar, burning the lime, and drawing from the elements around us the material necessary to beautify, and build up, and to exalt in every way those principles that essay to establish righteousness over the whole earth." If the word is to build forts, build them; if to raise grain, raise grain.

He added that in his opinion a "woman that makes a yard of cloth accomplishes a good work towards building up the independence of the kingdom of God, and by her works her faith is made manifest."[124]

Catechisms

Members had no annual temple worthiness interviews through which Church leaders could monitor, encourage, and even enforce behavior. So what leverage did the Church have to help members behave righteously? Two Church programs seem to have filled that function: the general rebaptism campaigns noted previously and catechisms,[125] which ward teachers or local leaders used to interrogate the members in a manner somewhat like that of the modern temple recommend interview.

John Jaques published a catechism for children in 1854 that became widely used throughout the Church up through the 1890s, even in Europe, Hawaii, and Samoa. It was primarily doctrinal but included two chapters on commandments—the Ten Commandments and the Word of Wisdom.[126]

During the Mormon Reformation, members were asked a series of questions about their righteousness. The questions dealt with both negative and positive behaviors, the negative ones being murder, adultery, betraying fellow Saints, bearing false witness against a neighbor, becoming drunk, stealing, lying, incurring debts with no intention to pay, underpaying hired help, coveting, profaning, and speaking against Church leaders and teachings. On the positive side, members were asked if they labored faithfully for their wages, paid tithes, kept the Sabbath, and attended ward meetings. Men were expected to preside in their families.[127]

In addition, various reformation leaders spoke out against specific activities they believed offended the Spirit. Novel reading was one. Another was having more enthusiasm for socials than for worship meetings: David Ivins of Utah County, speaking to a meeting of bishops in Salt Lake City, said that "one class of the people fill the Ball Room and, and another class attend prayer meeting."[128]

Worthiness Requirements

The Church had general requirements or expectations regarding worthiness for individuals seeking to obtain their endowments. One year after the Endowment House opened, its director, President Heber C. Kimball, advised the bishops regarding who they should recommend by letter to come for endowments. His requirements for both men and women follow:[129]

> Pay tithing from year to year.
> Pray in your families.
> Do not speak against the authorities of the Church and kingdom of God.
> Do not steal.
> Do not lie.
> Do not swear.
> Do not interfere with the neighbors' things or spouses.
> Respect presiding officers and bishops.

When the St. George Temple opened early in 1877, Saints wishing to go there needed to obtain a recommend from their bishops, who had received blank recommend forms for that purpose. The printed recommend form read, "I hereby recommend _____ as a faithful member of the Church, having paid full Tithings and donations, and as being worthy of receiving (here state the ordinances desired in the Temple), if endorsed by Prest. B. Young."[130]

Another set of worthiness requirements was framed during the united order enlistments in the mid-1870s. One set of united order rules said the member should refrain from swearing, "adultery, whoredom, and lust," vulgar and obscene language and conduct, being contentious or quarrelsome, speaking evil of others, being selfish, wearing a "foolish and extravagant fashion," and buying items from abroad that were being made in Utah. On the positive side, they should pray with their families morning and evening, pray privately, keep the Word of Wisdom "according to the Spirit and meaning thereof," treat family members with kindness and affection, seek the salvation of all mankind and good for all, observe personal cleanliness, keep the Sabbath day holy, return what is borrowed, patronize members of the order, foster and encourage the production and manufacturing of all consumer goods, be simple in dress and manners, labor for mutual benefit, perform labor honestly and diligently, and sustain with faith, works, and prayers those in charge of the united orders.[131]

Tithing

Leaders firmly believed the best way of judging people was by the spirit they showed in the settling of their tithing. As leaders taught regularly in sermons and publications, tithing involved three parts: (1) an initiatory tithe of all one possessed when he or she started paying tithing, usually at the time of conversion; (2) a tithe of increase and income; and (3) a labor tithe.[132] Labor tithing originated in Nauvoo. For every ten days a man and his team did not work for income, such as days spent in riding and leisure, he was expected to work one day for the Church as labor tithing. Or, he could use labor tithing to substitute for paying tithing in kind.[133]

Leaders constantly counseled members to be punctual and strict in paying tithing and offerings to the poor.[134] By the mid-1850s, the Saints paid tithes to their bishops and settled with the bishop at year's end. Late in 1860, when Salt Lake City's bishops gave verbal reports about their wards, most of them commented about the spirit of tithe paying.[135] They made summary statements like these:

Good desire to settle tithing in season.
Good spirit toward tithing.
Most of ward felt well especially toward tithing.
Hard to get donations.

Good spirit to pay tithing.
Good feeling regarding tithing.

Bishop Alonzo Raleigh, and no doubt other leaders, "believed it would come in the course of events that Tithing would be a matter of fellowship, just as much as stealing or drunkenness is now."[136] However, in 1852, President Young explained that nontithe payers were not to be subjected to Church discipline. "There is no compulsory or arbitrary power to be exercised over the brethren, in order to coerce the payment of tithing," he instructed.[137] But he sometimes wished nontithe payers could be disciplined. In 1868 he told bishops that he "really wished they would cut off from the church those members who did not pay their tithing." In September 1876, he stressed how strongly he believed every "good Mormon" must be a tithe payer: "What is a fact, we have become so dull and indifferent, that men are permitted to remain in the church who gave way to habits of intoxication and never pay a cent of tithing, although Jehovah told Joseph that Tithing was a standing law for ever."[138]

We do not know how many Saints did or did not tithe. But the percentage of tithe payers exceeded at least 40 percent of the adults.[139] Tithing records for Spring City show that between 82 and 94 percent paid some tithing during the 1860–68 period.[140]

Fasting and Fast Offerings

Because of the Lord's stern admonition that the Church take care of the poor and needy, fast offerings became almost as basic an obligation for practicing Mormons as their tithes. On occasion, members were warned that "those who failed to pay their offerings were not entitled to the sacrament."[141]

At first, LDS members brought their fast offerings to the meetinghouse. Offerings were food items rather than cash, and bishops distributed the donated food to the needy in the ward, sometimes assisted by the acting priesthood. Later, the bishops assigned deacons or teachers to pick up food donations from the members' homes. In 1871 a Salt Lake City bishop told of "his method to send the teachers round on a fast day morning from house to house, and by these means he obtains sufficient to sustain the poor."[142] In 1876 the Aaronic Priesthood young men in Payson, Utah, collected "about 150 lbs of flour, 2 sacks of potatoes, 2 quarts of Dried fruit 15 or 20 lbs of

Meat and 5¢ in money." The Payson Aaronic Priesthood members gave considerable help in the 1870s to one needy lady in the ward, Sister B. Some boys were sent to purchase a cow for her, others to gather wood for her stove. They regularly brought her flour. They gathered fast offerings for her benefit. They plowed land for her and planted some lucerne for her cow.[143]

At times, members participated in special fasts. "Today all the inhabitants of Cache Valley are required to hold a solemn Fast," a young Cache Valley woman wrote in 1868, "and pray to Him who heareth righteous prayers, that the grasshoppers may not destroy the crops."[144]

Word of Wisdom

John Jaques's catechism posited that good members were expected to obey the Word of Wisdom. However, the Word of Wisdom never became a binding law on Brigham's Saints.[145] For example, moderate drinking was allowed, although drunkenness was not tolerated.

In October 1851, Salt Lake Valley bishops discussed the Word of Wisdom. One bishop noted tithing was a test of fellowship (although not a matter for Church discipline), but the Word of Wisdom was not. Bishop Edward Hunter's counsel on the Word of Wisdom was "as much as possible observe it" and teach the upcoming generation to do it.[146] His counsel to bishops eight years later regarding liquor was that men should "either take it moderately or let it alone entirely."[147] Regarding tobacco, President Young said it was injurious, "but since it is so extensively used, and many seem to place upon it as high a value as bread, why not raise it here, and stop its immense importations."[148]

At the April 1867 conference, President Young instructed bishops that "every Elder in Israel must know that whiskey, tobacko, tea and coffee are not good for them to take" and that "he sometimes felt like making the observance of the Word of Wisdom a matter of fellowship, but it would be thought severe."[149] So, he assigned the bishops to ask members to obey the Word of Wisdom. They did, with good results, at least temporarily. Two weeks later, Salt Lake Valley bishops reported that the majority of Saints had been obeying the Word of Wisdom since conference. "Others were gradually leaving off their use," they said, except "some whose advanced years and long usage, deemed it unwise to abstain."[150] Less than a year later, Bishop Hunter "rejoyced at the general observance of the word of wisdom," at least in Great Salt Lake Valley.[151] The late-1860s campaign brought a slight improvement that was short-lived. (Obedience to the Word of Wisdom did not become a binding worthiness behavior until the twentieth century.)

Morality

Married adults guilty of adultery were dealt with harshly, usually by excommunication. Personal and Church records for Brigham Young's era do not mention youthful sexual immorality, so its extent cannot be known or guessed. At the dawn of the 1870s, one leader boasted that "our young live virtuously until they marry," a standard youths knew they should not violate.[152] Occasionally, teenage girls were victimized by older men, such as stepfathers or masters in the houses where the girls lived as servants. Youths guilty of having consensual sex before marriage received reprimands and loss of religious reputations rather than excommunications. However, they were expected to marry to "make things right." When premarital sex sins were confessed only after the couple had married, forgiveness often came with confession and rebaptism and without excommunication. One young man, for example, "committed himself previous to his endowments" and then married the young woman. The authority hearing the case noted that the Church had been "lenient" with such cases in the past, so the apology of the man was accepted and he was forgiven by being rebaptized.[153]

MISCELLANEOUS CHURCH ASSIGNMENTS AND EXPECTATIONS

To be a member was to deal with appeals to help with a number of Church projects. Perhaps the assignment families accepted that had the most far-reaching impact was to fill calls from Church leaders to uproot and move out to colonies the Church was establishing.

But Church members also frequently filled short-term assignments. Well known is the late 1856 appeal that drew heroic responses from volunteers who rescued the handcart people trapped by Wyoming snows. When a gathering of Spanish Fork Saints heard the call for help, thirteen "young and able bodied men" volunteered and rushed five wagons and teams toward Wyoming.[154] Between 1861 and 1868, hundreds of men and youths from all over Utah went east as volunteers, manning scores of "down and back" wagon trains that brought thousands of immigrants to Zion. Kaysville Ward members, for example, drove nine teams in 1868. A year earlier, that same ward provided thirteen teamsters and teams that hauled thirty-nine loads of cut rock to the Salt Lake Temple site. When Church leaders asked for men to help fill labor contracts for transcontinental railroad construction jobs, men from dozens of wards responded.[155] Appropriately, life sketches by or about men who filled such assignments describe the pride the men felt for giving such assistance to the Church and its members.

Members heard many requests and instructions. Devout members obeyed, and the less faithful disregarded them. Saints were asked in the mid-1850s to consecrate their properties to the Church and, in the 1870s, to pool their properties into united orders. Members offered much resistance to the latter effort, causing President Young to admit a year before his death that "he had been inspired by the Gift and power of God to call upon the saints to enter into the united order, or order of Enoch, and that now was the time, but he could not get the people to enter into it. He had cleared his skirts if he never said another word about it."[156]

In the late 1850s, Saints were told not to exchange their products with the United States Army stationed at Camp Floyd. Early in 1861, President Young "asked the Question, whether there was any harm in taking Wheat, Butter, Eggs, &c to Camp Floyd to sell to our enemies. He answered Yes, for such persons would weep and lament as long as Eternity lasts, if ever they are saved in the Kingdom of God, and the blight inflicted on their Character in the sight of Heaven and all Holy Beings, will never be obliterated."[157]

At times, profanity became a problem. Perhaps the worst outbreak was in 1868–69 among Mormon men in railroad construction crews. Their language bothered President Young so much that he asked bishops "to cut off from the Church any man, who has been working on the railroad, and indulged in cursing, swearing or drunkeness." He was determined "that no man shall have the fellowship of the saints who takes the name of God in vain, and indulges in wickedness."[158]

When Church leaders developed, published, and taught the Deseret Alphabet, members felt obligated to try to learn how to read it. By late 1869, "most of the wards" in Salt Lake City "were using [Deseret Alphabet] books either in their day or Sunday schools."[159] Another expectation outside the usual was for Saints to accept diverse nationalities. In 1864, for instance, Brigham Young remarked on the oneness, and unity that should exist among the saints of God, to cast under our feet every feeling of national prejudice, that inasmuch as the saints have been gathered from different nations, baptized into one faith, and received of the same spirit, we should learn to cherish towards them the kindest of feelings, as saints of God, regardless of the nation that gave them birth.[160]

LEADERSHIP AND FOLLOWERSHIP

Any claim that the early LDS priesthood leaders were dictators who cracked whips, making the Saints jump, is doubly mythical—about the nature of both the leaders and the followers. Utah's early Mormon settlers were not docile sheep easily led anywhere. Southerners, New England Yankees, Scots, Welsh, British, and Scandinavians had inbred streaks of independence that let them balance personal and family needs with Church needs, the scale tipping one way some times and the other way at other times.

Illustrative is Provo's situation between 1868 and 1872, as revealed in minutes of the bishops' meetings in that city.[161] With a charge to "build up Provo" and "make Provo one of the centres of attraction," Brigham Young sent Abraham O. Smoot to Provo in 1868 to be a mayor and what we would now call a stake president. But Smoot found he could not budge the bishops much and that they, likewise, had trouble making the Saints respond to their requests.[162] Smoot met twice monthly with the bishops of the five Provo wards to consult, monitor, and admonish. He instructed that the minutes of those meetings "record all that we do and who does" and "whether we respond to the calls made upon us or not"; the record shows plodding progress at best.[163]

After one year in office, Bishop Smoot felt frustrated by Provoans' unresponsiveness. "When has there been a job completed in this place[?]" he charged. "What is the reason we are not united enough and confidence is lacking[?]" Month by month, year by year, apathy smothered many of his calls for progress, causing him to complain in 1872, "Turn any way you will and ask what you will and you get nothing in any of our public calls."[164] Among public calls not well responded to were those to construct the Provo Canyon road, build a new tithing house, erect adequate meetinghouses and schools, finish off the tabernacle grounds with a well and outhouses, build and operate the woolen mill in Provo, erect adequate schools, and carry out cooperation-type projects. Even a rather simple community effort like obtaining sacrament vessels for the Provo-wide sacrament meetings floundered for over four years.[165]

When Brigham Young and the School of the Prophets pushed cooperative merchandising, Smoot tried to gain Provo's support for the idea. "As we have a head that must dictate," Smoot said of Brigham Young, and "as Bishops and Teachers, we must instruct the people on these things, give the Co-operative System your influence and support." But after laboring for a year to convert the people, one bishop reported, "There is quite an opposition to Co-operation and the [woolen] Factory."[166] Smoot added, "We have not more than 10% of the people who are in favor of or believe and act in Cooperation."[167] As if testifying to disprove charges of priesthood dictatorship, Smoot lamented:

> I would not of myself keep calling on the people to cooperate, build factory, &c. only that the burden is laid upon me by the Priesthood and I want to carry it out. There is a few of clear brain that can see the good of this, but the masses do not see the point, and I think they are getting tired of hearing me talk about it. I would not say another word only as I am required. If the Bishops of Provo and the County do not help me I am left alone. I do not know that there is anything said in the meetings of the people in favor of Cooperation, Factory, &c. I can occasionally hear of it being preached down. I want the Bishops to help me.[168]

The bishops' meeting minutes reveal four causes for Provo's slowness to make projects happen. First, Provo had a good share of "hard people" who possessed traditional English independence. A favorite Mormon motto was "mind your own business," and common people applied that to strangers, neighbors, and Church leaders alike.[169] Second, bishops lacked respect among the Saints. Smoot arrived at a time when leaders' influence had waned for some reason. "Heads here have not the proper influence," Smoot noticed. "I think I can see a feeling of distrust in the people to any measure proposed by authority, and while this lasts with the people we are dead ducks." Provo had good people "disposed to be good Mormons, but they are filled and troubled with doubts and fears." Although bishops "are rising in the esteem of true men in the kingdom," he said, still they lacked "the necessary persuasive powers" to motivate their people.[170] Third, and perhaps more important than the other factors, Provoans had limited resources. Leaders constantly assessed and taxed the people and called for donations for Church projects, apparently beyond the people's ability to pay. "We are poor" was a complaint bishops heard when soliciting funds or goods.[171] The fourth hindrance was leadership style. Bishops rarely minded Smoot's "snubbing our ears and stirring us up to our duties." But rather than dictate, Smoot functioned democratically, feeling that "the bishops as a body are really legislators for Zion." He encouraged, but did not demand, results from bishops holding lifetime tenure. Bishops, in turn, lacked bargaining power with members, unlike today's leaders who can deny temple recommends to unsupportive Saints.[172]

EBBS AND FLOWS OF COMMITMENT

Historian Richard Bushman observed that often published Mormon histories describe well the conflict between the Church and the world but pay little attention to the tensions between God and the Church.[173] In past dispensations, the faith of God's chosen people ebbed and flowed, and the Saints' commitments during Brigham Young's years traced similar ups and downs.

One decade, the 1870s, provides a case study. It was a decade when the Church experienced much "progress"—gaining railroad connections, opening a temple, founding united orders, creating new auxiliary programs, welcoming a continuous stream of immigrants, and restructuring stakes, wards, and quorums. But of spiritual health and progress during that decade, leaders became unusually critical as indicated by their sermons and comments during meetings.

Early in 1871, Presiding Bishop Hunter warned that the people's indifference toward their duties "almost deprived them of their fellowship." He observed that "many were getting sleepy and falling away from the faith."[174] Bishop William Thorne of Salt Lake was "satisfied with his brethren that the people were asleep and did not feel that interist in the work that they should."[175] Minute books are sprinkled with such judgmental phrases as "there needs to be a wakening up and a shaking of the dry bones," time to wake up from "our lethargy," "Mormonism is at low ebb," "the great necessity of a reformation," "things have been at loose ends," "people were all drifting," and "the darkest time since the Church was organized."[176] In May 1874, one officer reported that "Bro. Brigham told us if we drifted further we should be over the precipice."[177]

To counter slackness and to bring greater faith and dedication, Church leaders introduced new programs and projects. But apathy blunted these reform efforts. Regarding the united orders, one Salt Lake bishop confided in his diary, "I am sorry to see so mutch opposition manifested towards the united order as thare is in this city it betokens no good & in consequence of which we maybe made to se[e] mutch sorrow and affliction."[178] Reacting to poor support for temple projects, Brigham Young bluntly chastised the Saints; he "spoke sharply of the tardiness of the people in living our religion and he said we were nigh ready to be spewed out of the mouth of the Lord."[179]

Another reform tool in mid-decade was rebaptism. Members were requested to repent and reorder their lives preparatory to renewing their commitments to the Church by being rebaptized. Presiding Bishop Hunter had high hopes for the plan: "We have been in a lukewarm state for a long time, and he did not know of anything more suited to our present condition than rebaptism."[180] A high priests quorum officer put it plainly: he "compared the Church to day like unto a ship after a long voyage, in a Dry Dock for repairs and needing it."[181] A year after the rebaptism push, however, the general feeling was that it had not done much to improve the people.[182]

Not all leaders felt so judgmental. Bishop Alonzo Raleigh, for example, said in 1875 that "he did not think a greater proportion were apostatizing, and giving way to Drunkenness and Debauchery, than they did do at Nauvoo, or since the first organization of the church."[183]

Records for the 1870s identify many who did right when too many around them were careless. One is John Picknell, an older man. Noting the critical spirit some members manifested toward Brigham Young, he counseled, "Don't find fault, especially with the president, he may do wrong, as well as we, it matters not what those over us may do, its none of our business. If they give us the priesthood, & they apostatize the next day it dont matter to us, we are right if we do right!"[184]

When some priesthood bearers complained they were too busy to attend quorum meetings, Brother Picknell chided them: "You say you have not much time to come to meeting, how much time do you suppose I've to do? I've Seventies', Priests' Teachers' & Deacons' meetings to attend. Teacher in two wards, a Priest in one, [prayer] circle meetings to attend &c I'm out almost every night in the month. I'm after the pay! I can't afford to lose it."[185]

Reacting to unfaithfulness around him, he warned that "one half [of the Church] will turn away, let it not be you nor me" and then added the folksy but straightforward truth: "Every tub must stand on its own bottom."[186]

Stalwarts also are seen in Salt Lake City's Seventeenth Ward Relief Society minute book, which records the sisters' responses to a terrible epidemic in the 1870s that took the lives of many of their children. Determined to unite their faith by praying privately in their homes, they proposed that "at ten o'clock of each day, we retire to a quiet place and pray, that our faith may be concentrated, that we may have wisdom and faith sufficient by our united prayers to stay the diptheria which is now raging among our children, and that on Thursday we abstain from food until after prayers."[187]

Salt Lake City's Eighth Ward assigned Samuel D. Chambers, a former Mississippi slave, to serve as an assistant to the deacons, who took care of the ward meetinghouse and did ushering. A regular guest at the stake deacons meetings, more than once he was the *only* person there other than the stake officers. His testimonies, which quorum clerk Thomas C. Jones recorded, impressed his fellow deacons, most of whom were adults. Samuel joined the Church at age thirteen while a slave in Mississippi. Although lacking contact with the Church for a quarter century, he maintained his testimony. Becoming a free man in 1865, he earned enough money to gather to Zion in 1870 at age forty. His fervor is felt in his recorded testimonies given between 1873 and 1877: "I'm glad that I ever took upon me the name of Christ." "The knowledge I received is from my God. It is a high and holy calling, without the testimony of God we are nothing." He enjoyed serving the Church because he "did not come here [to Utah] to sit down and be still." His desire was to "be active in doing what he can for the building up of the kingdom of God." He attended meetings, ushered at the tabernacle, tithed fully, and endured as a stalwart until his death in 1929 at age ninety-eight.[188]

Just before President Brigham Young died in August 1877, he expressed his wish that the Saints gathered in Zion lived their religion better. "It is a marvel that the Lord did not scatter this people to the four winds," he observed. "It would have been done but for the prayers and faith and works of the humble saints"—the John Picknells, the Seventeenth Ward sisters, and the Samuel Chamberses of the Church.

This article was originally published in Nearly Everthing Imaginable: The Everyday Life of Utah's Mormon Pioneers, *ed. Ronald W. Walker and Doris R. Dant (Provo, UT: BYU Press, 1999), 244–95.*

NOTES

1. Presiding Bishopric Minutes of Bishops Meetings, 1851–84 (hereafter cited as Bishops Minutes), February 28, 1861, Church History Library, The Church of Jesus Christ of Latter-day Saints, Salt Lake City.

2. The 1,000 figure is conservative. Only about 1,250 bishops served in Utah wards during the entire nineteenth century, so for the Brigham Young period, there might have been half that many. Stakes never numbered more than seven, and wards more than about 100 until 1877—just weeks before Brigham Young died. Thus, counting General Authorities (First Presidency, the Twelve, the first Council of Seventy, and Patriarchs), stake presidencies, and bishops, the total is probably under 1,000. For the tally of nineteenth-century bishops, see Donald Gene Pace, "Community Leadership on the Mormon Frontier: Mormon Bishops and the Political, Economic, and Social Development of Utah before Statehood" (PhD diss., Ohio State University, 1983), 80.

3. Bishops Minutes, November 22, 1860.

4. For a detailed population census of Utah Saints in 1877, see chart in William G. Hartley, "The Priesthood Reorganization of 1877: Brigham Young's Last Achievement," *BYU Studies* 20, no. 1 (1979): 27.

5. In late 1853, the city had 5,979 residents; see a bishops' census report in B. H. Roberts, *A Comprehensive History of The Church of Jesus Christ of Latter-day Saints, Century One,* 6 vols. (Provo, UT: Corporation of the President, The Church of Jesus Christ of Latter-day Saints, 1965), 4:18n39; Salt Lake Valley's population in 1870 was 18,337, according to Allen Kent Powell, "Population," in *Utah History Encyclopedia,* ed. Allen Kent Powell (Salt Lake City: University of Utah Press, 1994), 432; also see "Tabernacle" and "Tabernacles," in Andrew Jenson, *Encyclopedic History of The Church of Jesus Christ of Latter-day Saints* (Salt Lake City: Deseret News Publishing, 1941), 858, 860.

6. William G. Hartley, "Mormon Sundays," *Ensign* 8 (January 1978): 23.

7. Louisa Lula Greene, Journal, holograph, April 8, 1867, microfilm, Church History Library.

8. Juanita Brooks, ed., *Not by Bread Alone: The Journal of Martha Spence Heywood, 1850–56* (Salt Lake City: Utah State Historical Society, 1978), 100, entry for May 4, 1854.

9. Brooks, *Not by Bread Alone,* 51, February 2; 56, April 12; 61, June 22; and 70, October 12, 1851.

10. Brooks, *Not by Bread Alone,* 59, June 8, 1851; 127, June 8, 1856.

11. Bishops Minutes, September 1, 1870.

12. Ronald W. Walker, "'Going to Meeting' in Salt Lake City's Thirteenth Ward, 1849–1881: A Microanalysis," in Davis Bitton and Maureen Ursenbach Beecher, eds., *New Views of*

Mormon History: A Collection of Essays in Honor of Leonard J. Arrington (Salt Lake City: University of Utah Press, 1987), 154.

13. Hartley, "Mormon Sundays," 19–25.

14. Miscellaneous Minutes File, January 27, 1856, Brigham Young Papers, Church History Library. See also Joseph Heinerman, "The Mormon Meetinghouse: Reflections on Pioneer Religious and Social Life in Salt Lake City," *Utah Historical Quarterly* 50 (Fall 1982): 340–53.

15. Bishops Minutes, February 14, 1861.

16. "Utah News," *Millennial Star* 39 (August 13, 1877): 527.

17. G. D. Watt, "Dedication of the Kay's Ward Meeting House," *Deseret News Weekly,* September 30, 1863, 81; William Blood, Diary, September 27, 1863, Church History Library.

18. Milton R. Hunter, comp. and ed. (for Daughters of Utah Pioneers, Weber County Chapter), *Beneath Ben Lomond's Peak: A History of Weber County, 1824–1900* (Salt Lake City: Deseret News Press, 1944), 448–49.

19. "Editorial Thoughts," *Juvenile Instructor* 12 (June 15, 1877): 138.

20. Members in Mendon, a town settled in 1859, met first in private homes, then in a log meetinghouse built in 1860, and next in a rock meetinghouse opened in 1866; see Doran J. Baker, Charles S. Peterson, and Gene A. Ware, eds., *Isaac Sorensen's History of Mendon: A Pioneer Chronicle of a Mormon Settlement* (Salt Lake City: Cache County Historical Preservation Commission and Utah State Historical Society, 1988), 29, 30, 50. For another key source regarding LDS meetinghouses, see "Meetinghouses," chapter 5 of C. Mark Hamilton, *Nineteenth-Century Mormon Architecture and City Planning* (New York and Oxford: Oxford University Press, 1995), 77–91.

21. Christian A. Madsen, "Holiness to the Lord: A History of Gunnison, Utah," typescript by Edith J. Romney, 3, included with Gunnison Ward Historical Record, Church History Library.

22. John Alexander Bevan, "The Early History of Tooele," typescript, 11, Church History Library.

23. *The Veprecula,* September 15, 1864, quoted in Andrew Karl Larson, *"I Was Called to Dixie": The Virgin River Basin; Unique Experiences in Mormon Pioneering* (Salt Lake City: Deseret News Press, 1961), 565–66.

24. Larson, *"I Was Called to Dixie,"* 566, 569.

25. "Record of Business Meetings of the Bishop's and Lesser Priesthood of Provo City" (1868–75), January 19, 1869, Church History Library (hereafter cited as Provo Bishops Minutes).

26. Provo Bishops Minutes, December 6, 1870.

27. Brooks, *Not by Bread Alone,* 49, January 19, 1851.

28. "Biography of Sidney Alexander Pace, as Told by Himself," typescript, Church History Library.

29. A. Glen Humphreys, "Missionaries to the Saints," *BYU Studies* 17, no. 1 (1976): 74–100.

30. Provo Bishops Minutes, June 29, 1869; April 23, 1872.

31. Bishops Minutes, November 22, December 6, 1860.

32. Wilford Woodruff, *Wilford Woodruff's Journal, 1833–1898, Typescript,* ed. Scott G. Kenney, 9 vols. (Midvale, UT: Signature Books, 1983–84), 5:269–70, January 2, 1859; Daniel Sylvester Tuttle, *Reminiscences of a Missionary Bishop* (New York: Thomas Whittaker,

ca. 1906), 346; "Parowan Restores Old Church Hall," *Deseret News*, December 4, 1939, 5; A. Barnett, "'We Must Do Right and Be Guided by the Priesthood': A Study of the Parowan Meeting House and Its Role in the Mormon Community, 1860–1890," typescript, 51–52.

33. Heinerman, "Mormon Meetinghouse," 350–53; Davis Bitton, "Early Mormon Lifestyles; or the Saints as Human Beings," in *The Restoration Movement: Essays in Mormon History*, ed. F. Mark McKiernan, Alma R. Blair, and Paul M. Edwards (Lawrence, KS: Coronado Press, 1973), 298–302.

34. Walker, "'Going to Meeting,'" 142.

35. Brooks, *Not by Bread Alone*, 70, October 12, 1851.

36. Brooks, *Not by Bread Alone*, 53, February 16, 1851; 71, October 19, 1851; 103, June 22, 1853.

37. Bishops Minutes, September 24, 1874.

38. Bishops Minutes, June 1, 1876.

39. Bishops Minutes, June 29, 1876.

40. Author's observation based on reading dozens of quorum minute books of that time period, available in the Church History Library.

41. Bishops Minutes, December 7, 1882.

42. Bishop Adam Spiers labeled it a "provision made" to allow the higher priesthood to officiate in the lesser. Tenth Ward, Salt Lake Stake, General Minutes, Teachers Report Meetings, 1874–80, November 6, 1874, Church History Library.

43. William G. Hartley, "Brigham Young and Priesthood Work at the General and Local Levels," in *Lion of the Lord: Essays on the Life and Service of Brigham Young*, ed. Susan Easton Black and Larry C. Porter (Salt Lake City: Deseret Book, 1995), 338–70.

44. Brooks, *Not by Bread Alone*, 120.

45. Journal History Index listings for "conferences" and "special conferences" for the 1849–77 period; A. Karl Larson and Katharine Miles Larson, *Diary of Charles Lowell Walker*, 2 vols. (Logan: Utah State University Press, 1980), entries in vol. 1 for May and November 1866–72.

46. Larson and Larson, *Diary of Charles Lowell Walker*, 1:343.

47. Journal History of the Church, March 14, 1857, Church History Library, microfilm copy in Harold B. Lee Library, Brigham Young University, Provo, Utah.

48. Hartley, "Mormon Sundays," 23.

49. *Lehi Centennial History, 1850–1950, Part 1* (Lehi, UT: Free Press Publishing, 1950), 155–60.

50. Seventies quorums were general quorums directed by the seven-man First Council of the Seventy. Some thirty-three quorums were organized before the Saints left Nauvoo. Most men called as missionaries during the nineteenth century were ordained to the office of seventy and belonged to seventies quorums after they returned. In time the Church had hundreds of seventies quorums, which became stake entities during most of the twentieth century. The First Quorum of Seventy, reconstituted in 1976, became a General-Authority-level quorum whose members replaced the Assistants to the Twelve. Stake seventies quorums were phased out in October 1986, leaving the First Quorum, and later a Second Quorum, also General Authorities, as the only bodies of seventies in the Church. An in-depth history of the seventies, written while they were stake quorums, is James N. Baumgarten's "The Role and Function of the

Seventies in LDS Church History" (master's thesis, Brigham Young University, 1960). Also see S. Dilworth Young, "The Seventies: A Historical Perspective," *Ensign* 6 (July 1976): 14–21.

51. Compare priesthood totals in the 1852 Church census with priesthood totals in the 1878 census figures I charted in my study "Priesthood Reorganization of 1877," 27.

52. William G. Hartley, "Ordained and Acting Teachers in the Lesser Priesthood, 1851–1883," *BYU Studies* 16, no. 3 (1976): 375–78.

53. Hartley, "Ordained and Acting Teachers," 378.

54. William G. Hartley, "From Men to Boys: LDS Aaronic Priesthood Offices, 1829–1996," *Journal of Mormon History* 22 (Spring 1996): 100, 105.

55. Walker, "'Going to Meeting,'" 150.

56. Bishops Minutes, May 26, 1861. Presiding Bishop Hunter called on those present "holding the Aaronic Priesthood to magnify both Priesthoods."

57. Salt Lake Stake, Deacons Quorum Minutes, 1873–77, December 14, 1875, Church History Library (hereafter cited as Salt Lake Deacons Minutes). The man was John Picknell.

58. Salt Lake Deacons Minutes, January 27, 1877.

59. Presiding Bishopric, Lesser Priesthood Meeting Minutes, 1855–78, January 5, 1861, Church History Library (hereafter cited as General Aaronic Priesthood Minutes).

60. Matthias Cowley, Salt Lake Deacons Minutes, May 26, 1877.

61. Bishops Minutes, June 23, 1870.

62. Bishops Minutes, December 1, 1864.

63. Eighth Ward, Salt Lake Stake, General Minutes, 1856–75, January 7, 1857, Church History Library.

64. Jill Mulvay Derr, Janath Russell Cannon, and Maureen Ursenbach Beecher, *Women of Covenant: The Story of Relief Society* (Salt Lake City: Deseret Book, 1992), 63, 75–82.

65. Derr, Cannon, and Beecher, *Women of Covenant,* 71, 82.

66. Provo Third Ward, Utah Stake, Relief Society Minutes, Church History Library.

67. Regarding deaconesses, see the following Salt Lake City wards' Relief Society minutes in the Church History Library: Eleventh Ward Relief Society Minutes, 1869–79 (Eliza R. Snow reorganized the society on March 3, 1869, and said the presidency should set apart deacons and other officers); Eighth Ward Relief Society Minutes, 1874–82 (entries during 1872 show nine women served as deacons, and in 1878 the deaconesses were reorganized and a new deacons' president installed); and the Fifteenth Ward Relief Society Minutes, 1855–73 (on January 1, 1873, four ladies filled the office of deacon).

68. *Jubilee History of Latter-day Saints Sunday Schools, 1849–1899* (Salt Lake City: Deseret Sunday School Union, 1900), 431–32, 452–56.

69. *Lehi Centennial History,* 158.

70. Tooele Branch, Sunday School Records, Church History Library.

71. Frederick Kesler, Diary, typescript, June 21, 1874, Frederick Kesler Papers, Special Collections, Manuscripts Division, Marriott Library, University of Utah, Salt Lake City.

72. *Jubilee History,* 44–45.

73. William C. Dunbar, in *Journal of Discourses,* 26 vols. (Liverpool: Latter-day Saints' Book Depot, 1855–86), 17:16, 18–19, 21, January 4, 1874.

74. Mrs. L. D. Alder, "R. S. Reports," *Woman's Exponent* 6 (February 15, 1878): 138.

75. Salt Lake Deacons Minutes, February 8, 1876.
76. Davis Bitton, "Zion's Rowdies: Growing Up on the Mormon Frontier," *Utah Historical Quarterly* 50 (Spring 1982): 182–95; Bishops Minutes, June 28, 1877; "Sunday School Meeting at Logan City," *Juvenile Instructor* 7 (September 28, 1872): 155; Salt Lake Deacons Minutes, April 14, 1874; Bishops Minutes, December 20, 1860; January 15, 1874; Southern Utah Mission, St. George Stake, Lesser Priesthood Record Book A, January 27, 1877, Church History Library; Salt Lake Deacons Minutes, March 7, April 13, and September 14, 1875; Kanab Ward, Kanab Stake, General Minutes, Ward Teachers Report Minutes, 1872–81, February 16, 1873, Church History Library; Provo Bishops Minutes, August 17, 1869; June 7, 1870; and February 28, 1871; General Aaronic Priesthood Minutes, February 5, 1876; November 2, 1867.
77. For examples, see Salt Lake's Seventeenth Ward Young Ladies Cooperative Retrenchment Society minutes for the 1870s, Church History Library.
78. School General Board Minutes, February 4, 1873, Church History Library.
79. See "Primary," "Sunday School," "Young Men," and "Young Women" entries in *Encyclopedia of Mormonism,* ed. Daniel H. Ludlow, 4 vols. (New York: Macmillan, 1992); *Jubilee History*; Susa Young Gates, *History of the Young Ladies' Mutual Improvement Association of The Church of Jesus Christ of Latter-day Saints, from November 1869 to June 1910* (Salt Lake City: Deseret News, 1911); Clarissa A. Beesley, "The Young Women's Mutual Improvement Association," *Improvement Era* 38 (April 1935): 243, 264–65, 271; and Carol Cornwall Madsen and Susan Staker Oman, *Sisters and Little Saints: One Hundred Years of Primary* (Salt Lake City: Deseret Book, 1979).
80. "'Helps' to the Priesthood," *Contributor* 1 (November 1879): 36–37.
81. "Seventeenth Ward, Salt Lake Stake, Y.L.M.I.A. Minute Book, 1870–92," October 28, November 10, December 22, 1870.
82. Salt Lake Seventeenth Ward, Young Ladies Retrenchment, June 8, 1871; November 17, 1875; January 17, 1877; December 15, 1875; September 13, 1876.
83. Salt Lake Seventeenth Ward, Young Ladies Retrenchment, February 7, 1877.
84. "Seventeenth Ward, Salt Lake Stake, Y.M.M.I.A. Minute Book, 1875–87," microfilm of manuscript, November 16, 1875, and minutes for the 1875–80 period, Church History Library.
85. "Seventeenth Ward, Y.M.M.I.A. Minute Book," March 5, 1877; April 17, 1877; April 10, 1877.
86. "Seventeenth Ward, Y.M.M.I.A. Minute Book."
87. Salt Lake Stake Historical Record Book, 1876–80, November 3, 1877, Church History Library.
88. Report filed for stake conference, November 28, 1877, in Madsen, "History of Gunnison," 195–97.
89. Bishops Minutes, February 25, 1852, comments concerning Salt Lake's Thirteenth Ward.
90. Bishops Minutes, October 28, 1858; December 9, 1858; August 4, 1859; November 24, 1859; Brigham Young to George A. Smith, January 26, 1857, in Journal History, January 26, 1857.
91. Journal History, April 18, 1852; Thomas Bullock Minutes, March 25, 1855, Church History Library; Salt Lake City Ninth Ward Record of Members, January 26, 1873, Church History Library; Provo Bishops Minutes, September 10, 1868; March 12, 1872.

92. Kesler, Diary, July 4, 1874; Bishops Minutes, January 18, 1852, and June 30, 1856; George Goddard, Journal, microfilm of holograph, vol. 18, March 17, 1876, 47, Church History Library; Salt Lake Stake, Minutes, Church History Library, September 17, 1854.

93. Bishops Minutes, April 2, 1868.

94. Bishops Minutes, June 15, 1865.

95. Bishops Minutes, February 21, 1867.

96. Circular of the First Presidency, July 11, 1877, in *Messages of the First Presidency of The Church of Jesus Christ of Latter-day Saints, 1833–1964,* comp. James R. Clark, 6 vols. (Salt Lake City: Bookcraft, 1965–75), 2:289.

97. Kesler, Diary, August 12, 1877. On July 10, 1877, the *Deseret Evening News* published a notice from the Presiding Bishopric requesting bishoprics to "administer the Sacrament of the Lord's supper to Sunday School children in their respective wards, or deputize the authorities of the schools to attend to it." "Local and Other Matters," *Deseret Evening News,* July 10, 1877, 7.

98. Journal History, March 23, 1857.

99. Bishops Minutes, August 1, 1861.

100. Kesler, Diary, March 27, 1875.

101. In 1881, Bishop Edwin D. Woolley "spoke in favor of a running stream of water for baptising." Bishops Minutes, February 17, 1881.

102. Orson Pratt, in *Journal of Discourses,* 18:160–61, July 18, 1875.

103. Woodruff, Diary, August 6, 1847; C. Edward Jacob and Ruth S. Jacob, eds., *The Record of Norton Jacob* (Salt Lake City: Norton Jacob Family Association, 1949), entry for August 8, 1847.

104. Bishops Minutes, October 24, 1854.

105. Bishops Minutes, August 12, 1856.

106. Journal History, September 15, 1856.

107. Bishops Minutes, July 1 and 15, November 4, 1875.

108. Orson Pratt, in *Journal of Discourses,* 18:160–61, July 18, 1875; D. Michael Quinn, "The Practice of Rebaptism at Nauvoo," *BYU Studies* 18, no. 2 (1978): 226–32; H. Dean Garrett, "Rebaptize," in *Encyclopedia of Mormonism,* ed. Daniel H. Ludlow, 4 vols. (New York: Macmillan, 1992), 3:1194.

109. Martha Spence Heywood received her endowment in the Council House on April 16, 1851. See Brooks, *Not by Bread Alone,* 57, April 20, 1851.

110. Endowment House Record, Endowments, 1851–76, microfilm, Special Collections, Family History Library, Salt Lake City.

111. Andrew Jenson, "Endowment House," in *Encyclopedic History of The Church of Jesus Christ of Latter-day Saints* (Salt Lake City: Deseret News, 1941), 230.

112. One such assignment was for Dry Creek, American Fork, Pleasant Grove, and Provo to send twenty people each to receive endowments and Springville to send forty. See Heber C. Kimball to the Bishops of Utah, May 19, 1856, in Journal History, May 19, 1856.

113. Kaysville Ward, Davis Stake, Elders Quorum Minute Book, 1865–77, 1865, Church History Library. To cite one example, Ephraim P. Ellison was endowed on March 24, 1865, when he was fourteen; see Ephraim P. Ellison, Daybook, May 5, 1929, copy in author's possession.

114. Bishop Christian A. Madsen, "Holiness to the Lord: A History of Gunnison, Utah," holograph, 124, microfilm, included with Gunnison Ward Historical Record, Church History Library.

115. Endowment House Record, Endowments, 1870–72, 1876–79, and Sealings of Couples, January to March 1870; St. George Temple, Endowments, 1877–78, microfilm, LDS Genealogical Department.

116. Endowment House Record, Sealings of Couples, January to March 1870; Dean L. May, "People on the Mormon Frontier: Kanab's Families of 1874," *Journal of Family History* 1 (Winter 1976): 182; Larry Logue, *A Sermon in the Desert: Belief and Behavior in Early St. George, Utah* (Urbana: University of Illinois Press, 1988), 56. Logue's statistics are for 1861–80 marriages.

117. Logue, *Sermon in the Desert,* 49.

118. Brooks, *Not by Bread Alone,* 34, October 27, 1850; 100, May 4, 1853; William G. Hartley, *Kindred Saints: The Mormon Immigrant Heritage of Alvin and Kathryne Christenson* (Salt Lake City: Eden Hill, 1982), 58, 64.

119. *Book of Remembrance of the Sixteenth Ward, Riverside Stake* (Salt Lake City: Sixteenth Ward Book of Remembrance Committee, 1945), 16, 83.

120. Missionary Record, I and II, manuscript, Church History Library. My figures support Dean L. May's estimate that half of 1 percent of Church members filled missions, in his "A Demographic Portrait of the Mormons, 1830–1980," in *After 150 Years: The Latter-day Saints in Sesquicentennial Perspective,* ed. Thomas G. Alexander and Jessie L. Embry (Provo, UT: Charles Redd Center for Western Studies, 1983), 56.

121. Madsen, "History of Gunnison," 156 (February 1, 1877).

122. First Presidency, "A Word to the Saints," in Clark, *Messages of the First Presidency,* 2:110 (February 19, 1853).

123. Historian Jessie Embry has noted that "people in early Utah saw little reason to separate church and state. Taking care of the community cattle herd, completing the irrigation project, and trading at the Church's cooperative store were considered religious duties." Jessie L. Embry, "'All Things unto Me Are Spiritual': Contrasting Religious and Temporal Leadership Styles in Heber City, Utah," in *Community Development in the American West: Past and Present Nineteenth and Twentieth Century Frontiers,* ed. Jessie L. Embry and Howard A. Christy, Charles Redd Monographs in Western History, no. 15 (Provo, UT: Charles Redd Center for Western Studies, 1985), 165.

124. Daniel H. Wells, sermon, September 10, 1861, in Journal History, September 10, 1861.

125. Davis Bitton, "Mormon Catechisms," *Task Papers in LDS History, No. 15* (Salt Lake City: History Division, Historical Department, The Church of Jesus Christ of Latter-day Saints, 1976). In the General Bishops Meetings, sentiment favored tolerating adults not obeying Word of Wisdom but expecting youths to live it.

126. See John Jaques, *Catechism for Children: Exhibiting the Prominent Doctrines of The Church of Jesus Christ of Latter-day Saints* (Salt Lake City: George Q. Cannon, 1870). For its many editions, see entries under Jaques in Chad L. Flake, ed., *A Mormon Bibliography, 1830–1930: Books, Pamphlets, Periodicals, and Broadsides Relating to the First Century of Mormonism* (Salt Lake City: University of Utah Press, 1978).

127. Gustive O. Larson, "The Mormon Reformation," *Utah Historical Quarterly* 26, no. 1 (1958): 53–55.

128. Bishops Minutes, February 25, 1852.

129. Journal History, May 19, 1856; Edward Kimball, "Temple Recommend Questions as Indicators of Changing Value Emphasis," typescript, in possession of Edward Kimball.

130. Included in letter from A. K. Thurber to Bishop C. A. Madsen, March 9, 1877, in Madsen, "History of Gunnison," 165.

131. Madsen, "History of Gunnison," 62–64.

132. William G. Hartley, "Ward Bishops and the Localizing of LDS Tithing, 1847–1856," in *New Views of Mormon History: A Collection of Essays in Honor of Leonard J. Arrington,* ed. Davis Bitton and Maureen Ursenbach Beecher (Salt Lake City: University of Utah Press, 1987), 96–114. When Brigham Young was asked how much labor tithing was due from a man with three sons between the ages of fifteen and twenty, he replied, "One tenth of their time." Bishops Minutes, October 8, 1855.

133. William G. Hartley, "Edward Hunter: Pioneer Presiding Bishop," in *Supporting Saints: Life Stories of Nineteenth-Century Mormons,* ed. Donald Q. Cannon and David J. Whittaker (Provo, UT: BYU Religious Studies Center, 1985), 283.

134. Circular of the First Presidency, in Clark, *Messages of the First Presidency,* 2:288.

135. Bishops Minutes, November 22, December 6, 1860.

136. Bishops Minutes, January 19, 1860.

137. Brigham Young, postscript to Edward Hunter, "Circular," [1852], copy in Library Division, Historical Department, The Church of Jesus Christ of Latter-day Saints, Salt Lake City.

138. Bishops Minutes, November 12, 1868; September 21, 1876.

139. Hartley, "Localizing of LDS Tithing," 96–114.

140. Michael S. Raber, "Family Life and Rural Society in Spring City, Utah: The Basis of Order in a Changing Agrarian Landscape," in Embry and Christy, *Community Development in the American West,* 144.

141. Bishops Minutes, October 28, 1869.

142. Bishops Minutes, December 7, 1871.

143. Payson Ward, Utah Stake, Priests [and Aaronic Priesthood] Minutes, December 26, 1876, Church History Library. Regarding care for the needy lady, see minutes for April 12, June 7, 1876; February 28, March 28, June 6, 1877.

144. Louisa Lula Greene, Journal, July 6, 1868, Church History Library.

145. Paul H. Peterson, "An Historical Analysis of the Word of Wisdom" (master's thesis, Brigham Young University, 1972); Leonard J. Arrington, "I Have a Question," *Ensign* 7 (April 1977): 32–33; Robert J. McCue, "Did the Word of Wisdom Become a Commandment in 1851?" *Dialogue: A Journal of Mormon Thought* 14 (Fall 1981): 66–77; Thomas G. Alexander, "The Word of Wisdom: From Principle to Requirement," *Dialogue* 14 (Fall 1981): 78–88.

146. Bishops Minutes, October 13, 1851.

147. Bishops Minutes, May 26, 1859.

148. Bishops Minutes, April 1863.

149. Bishops Minutes, April 4, 1867.

150. Bishops Minutes, April 18, 1867.

151. Bishops Minutes, March 26, 1868.

152. George Q. Cannon, in *Journal of Discourses,* 13:208, October 9, 1869.

153. St. George Stake, Lesser Priesthood Minutes, August 25, 1877, Church History Library.

154. George Hicks, "A History of Spanish Fork," typescript, Special Collections and Manuscripts, Harold B. Lee Library, Brigham Young University, Provo, Utah, 10. See also Rebecca Bartholomew and Leonard J. Arrington, *Rescue of the 1856 Handcart Companies,* Charles Redd Monographs in Western History, no. 11 (Provo, UT: Charles Redd Center for Western Studies, 1992), 8.

155. William G. Hartley, *To Build, to Create, to Produce: Ephraim P. Ellison's Life and Enterprises, 1850–1939* (Layton, UT: Ellison Family Organization, 1997), 69–77.

156. Bishops Minutes, September 21, 1876.

157. Bishops Minutes, April 6, 1861.

158. Bishops Minutes, March 4, 1869.

159. Bishops Minutes, December 9, 1869.

160. Bishops Minutes, October 7, 1864.

161. Provo Bishops Minutes, 1868–1872.

162. Provo Bishops Minutes, November 10, 1868; November 23, 1869.

163. Provo Bishops Minutes, April 2, 1868.

164. Provo Bishops Minutes, July 14, 1872.

165. Provo Bishops Minutes, November 23, 1869; July 14, 1872; and minutes from 1868 to 1872.

166. Provo Bishops Minutes, November 23, 1869.

167. Provo Bishops Minutes, October 15, 1869 [1868]; November 23, 1869.

168. Provo Bishops Minutes, November 23, 1869.

169. Provo Bishops Minutes, November 23, 1869.

170. Provo Bishops Minutes, October 15, 1869 [1868]; November 10, 1868: March 29, 1870.

171. Provo Bishops Minutes, May 21, 1872.

172. Provo Bishops Minutes, March 1, 1870; September 10, 1868; July 20, 1869; August 17, 1869; November 21, 1871.

173. Richard Bushman, "Faithful History," *Dialogue* 4 (Winter 1969): 17–18.

174. General Aaronic Priesthood Minutes, 1857–77, June 1871.

175. General Aaronic Priesthood Minutes, November 3, 1870.

176. Salt Lake Deacons Minutes, December 23, 1876; General Aaronic Priesthood Minutes, September 7, 1870; Salt Lake Stake, High Priests Quorum Minute Book, 1865–1904, Church History Library, May 29, 1875 (hereafter cited as Salt Lake High Priests Minutes); General Aaronic Priesthood Minutes, July 3, 1875; Salt Lake High Priests Minutes, May 30, 1874; Salt Lake Deacons Minutes, June 9, 1874.

177. Salt Lake Deacons Minutes, May 12, 1874.

178. Kesler, Diary, June 28, 1874.

179. Kesler, Diary, June 3, 1875. Kesler is responding to President Young's statement, recorded as, "Unless we lay aside our covetousness and wickedness God will spew us out of his mouth." See Bishops Minutes, June 3, 1875.

180. Bishops Minutes, November 8, 1875.

181. Salt Lake High Priests Minutes, October 30, 1875.

182. Salt Lake Deacons Minutes, April 11, 1876.

183. Bishops Minutes, December 30, 1875.

184. Salt Lake Deacons Minutes, September 11, 1876.

185. Salt Lake Deacons Minutes, December 14, 1875.

186. Salt Lake Deacons Minutes, June 9, 1874.

187. Salt Lake City Seventeenth Ward, Relief Society Minutes (1871–84), manuscript, May 22, 1879, Church History Library.

188. [William G. Hartley], "Saint without Priesthood: The Collected Testimonies of Ex-Slave Samuel D. Chambers," *Dialogue* 12 (Summer 1979): 16–18; William G. Hartley, "Samuel D. Chambers," *New Era* 4 (June 1974): 46–50.

War and Peace and Dutch Potatoes

PRESIDENT CORNELIUS ZAPPEY'S FIRST WEEKS among the war-scarred Dutch Saints made him do much praying—and some weeping. In February 1946, just nine months after the end of a shattering world war, he and Sister Zappey had arrived from the United States to reorganize and rejuvenate the Netherlands Mission.

Acting mission president Jacob Schipanboord had done excellent work. The war had done its work, too. Many of the thirty-two hundred members needed food and clothes. Branches needed to be fully staffed, administered, and adequately housed. The bomb-damaged mission home in The Hague needed windows, doors, repairs, and furniture. Full-time proselyting was to be instituted. And the hatred and bitterness many members felt toward their former enemies somehow had to be dissolved.

The horrors of World War II had begun for tiny Holland in late 1940, when German tanks and troops overran the country in five days. To break Dutch resistance, the German Luftwaffe had wiped out the center of Rotterdam—including the LDS chapel there—in the first major air blitz aimed at a city; forty thousand civilians perished.

For five bitter years, Nazi troops occupied Holland. Many Dutch, to protect family and friends, cooperated. Others resisted. Some did both.

Many Dutch soldiers, resisters, and Jews were executed or taken to prison camps. (Anne Frank was one.)

Both at the beginning of the war, when Germany attacked, and at the end when Allied forces counterattacked, Holland suffered much physical damage. About four hundred thousand homes were damaged or destroyed; eight thousand farms ruined, seven hundred square miles of land inundated when Nazis wrecked dikes holding back the sea, half of the forests destroyed, and 40 percent of the livestock wiped out. Railroad equipment, bicycles, motor vehicles, and in some cases entire factories were confiscated. More than two hundred thousand Dutch people died because of the war. Such destruction and casualties were not as great as those in some countries; still, bitterness ran deep, and the Saints were not immune.

The last months of the Nazi occupation had been the worst. Germany, reeling under the Allies' military impact and running out of supplies, systematically robbed Holland's foodstuffs, fuel, and clothing. This left the Dutch civilians destitute during the biting winter of 1944–45. Some froze. Some starved. One survivor recalls how schoolchildren at one point were lucky to get a carrot for breakfast and potato peel soup for lunch. Another survivor who had several children made the family walk 150 miles from Rotterdam to Groningen, where there was more food, in severe weather. In Amsterdam the daily ration was reduced to one-tenth of normal requirements. This period of hunger hardened feelings even more toward the Nazis and their Dutch collaborators.[1]

Even when the Zappeys arrived, almost a year after the war had ended, hunger still stalked Holland, even though relief goods from America and elsewhere were pouring in, including tons of LDS welfare supplies. From a Church welfare storehouse in The Hague, mission leaders, volunteers, and dilapidated trucks distributed needed items to two dozen branches.

Welfare goods clothed and nourished the body. But what would help the scarred souls? What could dissolve the bitter feelings toward Germans and collaborators about the loss of loved ones?

"Mama, all we can do here is pray for the people to overcome their hate," President Zappey told his wife. But then he went to work to answer his own prayers. A salesman by profession, he set out to convince the Saints of the importance of love and forgiveness. He chose as a mission theme "Love One Another," which he preached in the branches and at mission meetings.[2]

Elder Ezra Taft Benson (second from right), *of the Quorum of the Twelve Apostles, directed Church relief effort in Europe and helped inspire Dutch Mission President Cornelius Zappey to implement the potato-growing program. Courtesy Church Archives.*

Elder Ezra Taft Benson, in Europe directing the Church's relief effort, instructed President Zappey to have the Dutch members be welfare *producers* as well as recipients. President Zappey saw how it could help the Saints learn to work together again and forget their differences. He moved on the instructions at once. Since potatoes were one of Holland's best crops, President Zappey proposed to local priesthood leaders that they start branch or quorum potato projects where they had land. Where they didn't, they were to start sewing projects.

During 1947, Mormon potato patches sprang up in backyards, road medians, vacant lots, and former flower gardens. Planting days became special branch occasions with singing, speaking, and praying, after which the Saints planted seed potatoes obtained from the Dutch government. And it was cooperative. Typically, one member punched a hole in the ground with a stick, a second person dropped the potato in, and a third covered it.[3]

During summer months, many Saints, before going to work, visited their branch's potato patch to water or weed. By autumn the prospects for a good harvest looked bright. Members expected that potatoes produced by their hard work would be used to aid local members.

But President Zappey was thinking farther ahead. In a March 12, 1947, report, President Alma Sonne of the European Mission had painted a harsh picture of conditions in neighboring Germany:

President Alma Sonne of the European Mission reported in 1947 that conditions in Germany were critical. An unplanned meeting with Dr. P. Vincent Cardon, chairman of the United Nations advisory committee on food and agriculture in Geneva, Switzerland, opened the way for the Dutch Mormons' potatoes to be shipped to Germany. Courtesy Perry Special Collections.

What few reserves the people had a year ago are now completely exhausted. This exceptionally severe winter has greatly aggravated their tragic condition. Germany is still not productive. Scarcity of available supplies and lack of distribution facilities have not been conducive to improving the situation. Clothing is almost wholly unobtainable; food continues to be rationed on a sub-subsistence basis.[4]

By summer the crisis still was severe, despite massive relief efforts by Western democracies. Church welfare helped the German Saints, but more was needed. "My people are so hungry," East German Mission President Walter Stover repeatedly told President Zappey during their meetings in Holland.[5]

The closer harvest time drew, the more President Zappey knew the Lord wanted those welfare potatoes sent to the German Saints to supplement the welfare goods coming from the United States. But he wondered how Dutch members would react "if we should ask them for the food for which they had worked so hard to give to the people who had caused them such suffering and depredation—the people who had ruthlessly confiscated the last bit of their food and exposed their little children to starvation."[6]

Facing this hard test of the spirit of the gospel, President Zappey decided to call a mission conference in Rotterdam to propose that the potatoes be shipped to Germany. He worried about how the leaders might react, particularly when the Dutch still were on rationing themselves. He asked mission secretary Johanna Riet to take careful notes during the expected debate. Then, calling on the spirit of the Lord, he preached in behalf of the proposal:

> Some of the most bitter enemies you people have encountered as a result of this war are the German people. We know what intense feelings of dislike you have for them. But those people are now much worse off than you, and we are asking you to send your entire potato harvest to the German saints. Will you do it? Do you want our own saints to die of hunger there?[7]

The leaders, touched by the Spirit, voted for the project.[8]

One hurdle cleared, another large one appeared: laws forbade the export of food grown in Holland. President Zappey, however, trusting the Lord to make the way possible, wrote to the Minister of Agriculture and Food Supply for special permission to ship the welfare potatoes. The blunt reply was: "The exporting of food is absolutely not permitted, and under no circumstances can or will there be an exception made." Refusing to give up, President Zappey filled out more forms. He met with one government official after another. The mission staff fasted and prayed earnestly.

The answer to their prayers came during the fateful meeting at the Amsterdam airport. President Zappey was there to put Elder Sonne on a plane for London. To Elder Sonne's pleasant surprise, he met a close friend, Dr. P. Vincent Cardon from Utah, in the ticket line. Dr. Cardon, chairman of the United Nations advisory committee on food and agriculture in Geneva, Switzerland, had just finished meeting with Dutch food officials. President Zappey requested and received from Dr. Cardon a personal letter of introduction to the Dutch food ministry.[9]

President Zappey did not think that meeting was an accident:

Why should President Sonne return to London on that particular day? Why was it just at the time when passage on the plane from Amsterdam to New York was unavailable, making it necessary for Dr. Cardon to fly to London? Why was it that President Sonne should take the same flight to London when there are five flights daily between Amsterdam and London? For days and days and time and time again, this matter had been made a matter of prayer— that the Lord would open the way so that the Dutch Saints would be able to send these potatoes to the suffering German Saints. The Lord is continually guiding His children and answering their prayers when they ask Him in righteousness for help if they have exerted their own efforts to the utmost.[10]

Dr. Cardon's letter enabled President Zappey to personally explain the Church's welfare program to high government officials. He received permission to ship fifteen tons.

At harvest time, Groningen, Dordrecht, Utrecht, and a dozen other Dutch branches shipped loose potatoes in various size truckloads to The Hague warehouse. The shipments represented many hours of hard work and sacrifice by hundreds of dedicated Saints. The potatoes were sorted, but sacks were in short supply. One day missionary Symen Stam saw some bundles of patched sacks being unloaded from an ocean liner and felt inspired to ask about them. To his surprise, the ship's personnel, once they learned why he needed the sacks, sold him more than five hundred at a reduced price, enough for the welfare project.[11]

As The Hague warehouse filled with the new potatoes, President Zappey discovered that the Lord had blessed their project beyond expectation. Instead of the projected fifteen tons, the warehouse soon held seventy tons—five times what the export permit would allow!

President Zappy went back to the food ministry. Another miracle—an amended permit! But, warned the government, this was "a great exception. Every other church and relief organization which had presented similar proposals had been refused." When the Bureau of Potatoes Directory tried to interfere, President Zappey astonished them by warning that the potatoes belonged to the Lord, and if He willed it, He would see that they reached Germany. President Zappey's doggedness paid off, and full clearance was granted.[12]

Missionary and member muscles moved the mountain of potatoes into ten rented trucks. Then, shortly after midnight on November 6–7, the convoy rolled east, toward the German border. President Sonne observed, "This will go down in the history of the welfare program as an outstanding example of the true love which characterizes the work of the Lord."[13]

Meanwhile, Presidents Stover and Jean Wunderlich of the East and West German missions made arrangements for the potatoes to enter their areas. German Saints, when told to come and pick up fresh potatoes, were astonished— and deeply touched. The West German Mission history noted the arrival on November 16, 1947: "Each member of the Hamburg Branch received 25 pounds. This is a wonderful gesture by the Dutch Saints and the members in Hamburg are grateful."[14]

Cornelius Zappey, President of the Dutch Mission in post–World War II Holland. He was inspired to help heal the animosity of the Dutch people toward the German people by implementing a potato-growing project for the starving German Saints. Courtesy Church Archives.

At Celle, in north-central Germany, Brother Philipp Bauer arranged with city officials to store two truckloads of potatoes in the basement of the municipal finance building. Prisoners helped unload the sacks. Members then came from surrounding branches to load up small trucks with their allotments. Celle Saints, mostly refugee women and children from eastern Germany, as well as nonmember relatives and investigators, received a hundred pounds per person.[15]

Members in Berlin gladly picked up potatoes for eating, and President Stover wisely saved a good supply to use as spring seed potatoes. Then early in 1948, Latter-day Saint military officials in Berlin obtained permission from United States' authorities for the Saints to farm a four-acre section of a

Dutch members filling trucks with potatoes for German Saints. These potatoes were sent to members in both the East and West German mission areas. Courtesy Church Archives.

Dutch Saints loading potatoes onto a boxcar bound for Germany. Courtesy Church Archives.

city park. Members laboriously prepared the ground and on May 6 planted nearly four thousand pounds of Dutch potatoes.

In late June, the Russians imposed the Berlin Blockade, cutting off overland shipments to Berlin (which was located nearly a hundred miles inside East Germany). Western democracies responded with the famous Berlin Airlift, which kept Berliners alive for nearly a year. City residents, fearful that Russia might try to stop the airlift, guarded their foodstuffs carefully. During summer and fall, Church members guarded their potato field against thieves and livestock, counting heavily on their potato harvest to be a bountiful one in case the airlift failed.[16]

During three September days, about sixty-five Berliners—mostly women and older men since the younger men had perished in the war—harvested potatoes by hand. Even the tiniest potatoes were saved. "Every pound of food counts in Germany today," wrote Elder Calvin Clyde, a missionary there. Members dug up sixteen tons of potatoes, an eight-fold return. "It is easy to understand the happiness of all the members of the Church in Berlin and the friends who worked on the project," Elder Clyde reported, "when each of them received 40 lbs. of new potatoes." Again, some potatoes were reserved as seed for the next spring.[17]

Back in Holland, the 1947 potato project had produced a new spirit of unity and love among the Saints. And if President Zappey needed further proof, he saw it in 1948. That year the members, on their own initiative, requested that they again be allowed to aid the German Saints. "The hate was simply out of the branches for the Germans," observed Elder Stam, "on account of doing that great [1947] project."[18] Potato patches were replanted, and the project repeated.

Barely had this decision been made when "fishes" joined the "loaves." Brethren attending a Rotterdam priesthood meeting on February 23, 1948, decided to buy herring to send with the potatoes. Other branches, learning of the idea, raised money, too. The mission home received a telegram on March 9 saying: "You may expect six barrels of herring from the branch and four barrels from the missionaries laboring in Amsterdam."[19]

The fishing town of Vlaardingen was selected as the site to purchase newly salted herring, in the first herring harvest since the waters were finally cleared of mines. When the town learned of the Mormons' 1947 potato project and the plans for 1948, its newspaper praised the Church's welfare program in a feature article on March 5:

These [1947] potatoes were not bought; they were raised by the givers themselves in their free time. All summer long they had worked on it, and lack of experience along this line was made up [for] by unlimited enthusiasm. Evidence was to be given that the Dutch members of the Church were not only willing to receive but also to give. They had received plenty: after the war, the good gifts from the members of the church in America had flowed into their homes, and shipments of food, clothing and covering up to 2 1/2 million guilders' worth were distributed to members and non-members of the Church....

The 'Welfare Plan' is not ended; it is still in full swing.... In the framework of this plan, the Dutch members began in 1947 to raise vegetables, fruit, and particularly potatoes.

Now they have their eyes on another product of Dutch labor: herring! These, too, will be sent to the German members and the large percentage of albumen and fats that is found in the herring will be a valuable addition to their poor food rations. A few weeks ago, this herring project was announced in the branches of the Church in the Netherlands, and already the financial contributions of the members are flowing in.[20]

When the herring were caught, salted, and put into barrels, the Saints purchased eighty barrels—nine tons—and shipped them along with ninety tons of newly dug potatoes to Germany by train in late October 1948.[21]

The shipment filled six railroad boxcars. But the overloaded sixth car broke down and had to be replaced by two others. In Germany the cargo was reloaded into trucks, which then headed for eastern Germany, where the need was greatest.

Welfare supplies other than the Dutch donations were also flowing into the East German Mission. President Stover, using his own funds, purchased in Schleswig-Holstein even more potatoes, so that the German Saints could have a plentiful supply. Other welfare food and clothing arrived from Geneva by way of Vienna, Prague, and Dresden.

Distribution was President Stover's problem. At one point, East Berlin officials decided to confiscate a stockpile in the cellar of Brother Emil Fischer, but President Stover backed them off by using his American citizenship to threaten a diplomatic scene. The Stover family car made many trips into eastern Germany and West Berlin to deliver welfare supplies, including trunkload after trunkload of rather smelly herring. By December, in Berlin alone, every member of the Church received 155 pounds of potatoes and 40 large herring.[22]

That Saints in one country aided Saints in other countries was not unique to the Dutch. Swedes helped Finns. Swiss sent clothes and chocolate to Austrians. Belgian Mormons also sent much of their American welfare supply to German Saints. And in 1948 alone, Church headquarters shipped 25,876 cases of food, including 542 tons of wheat, to aid European Saints.[23]

What was unique about the Dutch project, however, was the magnitude of the effort by so few Saints—of a people who had suffered so much from the Germans. Members of fewer than two dozen branches willingly worked countless hours as volunteer farmers to produce two hundred tons of fresh vegetables badly needed by German Saints and volunteered to donate enough money to purchase eighty barrels of herring—all within eighteen months.

The food was important; but more important were the blessings. It's one thing to talk about brotherhood. It's another thing to actually act like brothers. When President David O. McKay learned what the Dutch Saints were doing, he called it "one of the greatest acts of true Christian conduct ever brought to my attention."[24] The healing of souls was as important as the nourishing of bodies.

When President Zappey returned to his Salt Lake furniture business in 1949, he perhaps did not fully realize that his leadership had helped the Dutch Saints to write one of the finest chapters in the Church's history.

This article was originally published in Ensign 8 *(July 1978): 18–23.*

NOTES

1. Keith C. Warner, "History of the Netherlands Mission of The Church of Jesus Christ of Latter-day Saints, 1861–1966" (master's thesis, Brigham Young University, 1967); see also Gordon Wright, *The Ordeal of Total War, 1939–1945* (New York: Harper and Row, 1968).
2. Interview with Adriana Zappey, February 1973, tape in author's possession.
3. Interview with Johanna Riet Chase, February 1973, notes in author's possession.

4. European Mission Historical Record, March 12, 1947, Church History Library, The Church of Jesus Christ of Latter-day Saints, Salt Lake City.

5. Sister Zappey interview; see also "Dutch Mission Head Tells Story of Welfare Potatoes for Germany," *Church News,* published by *Deseret News,* December 6, 1947, 1.

6. "Dutch Mission Head Tells Story," 6.

7. Frederick W. Babbel, *On Wings of Faith* (Salt Lake City: Bookcraft, 1972), 76.

8. Sister Zappey and Sister Chase interviews.

9. "Dutch Mission Head Tells Story," 6; "They Couldn't Stop the Lord's Potatoes," *Instructor* 94 (May 1959): 152–53; Netherlands Mission Historical Report, entries for October and November 1947, Church History Library.

10. "Dutch Mission Head Tells Story," 6.

11. Symen Stam Oral History, interview by author, June 19, 1974, typescript, Oral History Program, Church History Library.

12. "Dutch Mission Head Tells Story," 7.

13. "Dutch Mission Head Tells Story," 7.

14. Interview with Walter Stover, March 1976, tape in author's possession; interview with Jean Wunderlich, March 1977, notes in author's possession; Jean Wunderlich, Diaries, 1947, Church History Library; West German Mission Manuscript History, November 16, 1947, Church History Library.

15. Interview with Philipp Bauer, March 11, 1976, notes in author's possession.

16. Stover interview; see also "Dutch Potatoes Planted by German Saints," *Church News,* July 25, 1948, 3; and "Saints in Blockaded Berlin Harvest Potatoes," *Church News,* November 3, 1948, 5C.

17. European Mission Historical Report, 1948.

18. Stam Oral History.

19. Netherlands Mission Historical Report, February–March 1948.

20. Netherlands Mission Historical Report, March 5, 1948.

21. Netherlands Mission Historical Report, March 1948.

22. Walter Stover Oral History, August 11, 1976, and Walter Stover and Emil Fischer Oral History, August 31, 1976, interviews by Richard L. Jensen, typescripts, LDS Historical Department Oral History Program, Church History Library; author's interviews with Stover and Wunderlich; "German Saints Strive to be Self-Sustaining," *Church News,* January 19, 1949, 12.

23. Welfare summary, European Mission Historical Report, December 31, 1948.

24. "Dutch Mission Head Tells Story," 1.

Index

Page numbers in *italics* refer to graphics.

Eldredge, Ira, 404
Elias, 18
Elijah, 17, 18, 20
Ellison, Ephraim P., 46
Ellsworth, Edmund, 224
emigrants, *119*, *396*
emigration, 216. *See also* immigrants
Emigration Stake, 70
endowment, 17, 18, 20, 46–47, 96–97, 180,
    199, 380, 438–39
Endowment House, 182, 438, 442
Ensign, 332
epistles and circulars
    on down-and-back wagon trains, 401–2
    practice of issuing, 184
    on priesthood, 54, 101, 201, 244–45
    on purification, 283
    on reorganization of stakes, 244–45
    on tithing, 132, 153, 157, 158, 164
Europe, 64
Evans, David, 366
Everett, Elisha, 368
excommunications, 218, 248, 446

F

family home evenings, 122, 332
Farnsworth, Stephen M., 370, 371
fast day, 349, 423
fast offerings, 71, 302–3, 444–45
Felt, Nathaniel H., 155, 158, 161, *163*
Ferguson, James, 224
Fielding, Joseph, 366
Fifty, Council of, 326
First Presidency, 181–85, *189*, 359. *See also*
    Presidency
    creation of, 324
    interaction of, with Presiding Bishopric,
    129
    interaction of, with Seventies, 290–91
    sustaining of, in conferences, 185
Fischer, Emil, 472
Fjeldsted, Christian D., 268
Fjelsted, Daniel, 293

Foutz, Jacob, 366
fraternity, 312–13
Friend, 332
Frost, Edward, 213
Fullmer, David, 158
Fullmer, John S., 211, 214, 215, 217, *217*, 218,
    219, 220, 223, 224

G

Gates, Jacob, 223, 224, 267, 268, 274, 289,
    400, 406, 408
genealogical data, 286
General Board of Education, 329–30
General Priesthood Committee on Out-
    lines, 59, 105–6, 304, 330
General Tithing Office, *129*, *137*
Germany, 339, 466–67, 472
Gifford, Samuel K., 370
Gilbert, Truman, 374
Glasgow Conference, 213
Glover, William S., 224
Glover, Wm., 212
Goddard, George, 102, 347
Granite Stake, 302
Grant, George D., 219, 224
Grant, Heber J., 70, 107, 125, 270, 271, 292,
    340
Grant, Jedediah M., 48, 168, 181, 183
Grant, Rachel, 125
Grantsville Ward, 56
Greene, John P., 29
Greenhalgh, Nehemiah, 368
Greenwood, Charles, 374
Groningen Branch, 468
Grover, Joel, 241, 254
Gunnison Ward, 418, 433–34

H

Haight, Horton, 397
Haight, Isaac, 224
Hale, Jonathan H., 366
Hamburg Branch, 469

About the Author

UNTIL AUGUST 2009 WHEN HE RETIRED, William G. (Bill) Hartley was an Associate Professor of History at Brigham Young University.

Bill, born in Salt Lake City, spent his boyhood and youth years with his four brothers in Butte, Montana, and the San Francisco Bay Area in Sunnyvale and San Lorenzo, California. His mother was a devout Latter-day Saint with pioneer ancestry; his father, a Southern Pacific executive who grew up in Oregon, was not LDS. Bill graduated from Arroyo High School and attended Brigham Young University. He filled a two-year mission in the Eastern States and Cumorah missions, then resumed his studies and graduated from BYU with bachelors and masters degrees in history. He completed doctoral course work at Washington State University.

In 1972 he joined the staff of research historians assembled by Church Historian Leonard J. Arrington and researched, wrote, and published Mormon history in scholarly journals and Church magazines and media. Bill helped found and then direct for four years the Church's Oral History Program. In 1980, Arrington's team of historians became the Joseph Fielding Smith Institute for Latter-day Saint History at BYU, where Bill also became part of the History Department faculty. During his twenty-nine years at BYU, Bill developed three areas of expertise: the history of the restored priesthood, Mormon Trail emigration, and family histories.

A prolific writer, Bill is the author or coauthor of thirteen books and author of more than a hundred articles dealing with U.S., Mormon, and family history. He is the recipient of four best book awards and five best article awards from the Mormon History Association, John Whitmer Historical Association, Utah State Historical Society, and the Association for Mormon Letters. His award-winning books include *"My Best for the Kingdom": History and Autobiography of John Lowe Butler, a Mormon Frontiersman* (1993), *Stand By My Servant Joseph: The Story of the Joseph Knight Family and the Restoration* (2003), and *Anson Bowen Call: Bishop of Colonia Dublan,* coauthored with Lorna Call Alder (2007). He is coeditor, with Grant Underwood and Robert J. Woodford, of two volumes of the Joseph Smith Papers scheduled for publication in 2012.

Bill served as president of the Mormon History Association and on the editorial boards of the *Journal of Mormon History* and Mormon Historical Studies. As founding president of the Mormon Trails Association and a "trail junkie," Bill has extensively traveled and done on-site research on the Mormon Trail and the Mormon Battalion routes.

Bill married Linda Perry. They have six children and eleven grandchildren.